T0155865

Lecture Notes in Computer Science

Lecture Notes in Artificial Intelligence   **14515**

Founding Editor

Jörg Siekmann

Series Editors

Randy Goebel, *University of Alberta, Edmonton, Canada*
Wolfgang Wahlster, *DFKI, Berlin, Germany*
Zhi-Hua Zhou, *Nanjing University, Nanjing, China*

The series Lecture Notes in Artificial Intelligence (LNAI) was established in 1988 as a topical subseries of LNCS devoted to artificial intelligence.

The series publishes state-of-the-art research results at a high level. As with the LNCS mother series, the mission of the series is to serve the international R & D community by providing an invaluable service, mainly focused on the publication of conference and workshop proceedings and postproceedings.

Minghui Dong · Jia-Fei Hong · Jingxia Lin ·
Peng Jin
Editors

Chinese Lexical Semantics

24th Workshop, CLSW 2023
Singapore, Singapore, May 19–21, 2023
Revised Selected Papers, Part II

 Springer

Editors
Minghui Dong ⓘ
Institute for Infocomm Research
Singapore, Singapore

Jia-Fei Hong ⓘ
National Taiwan Normal University
Taipei, Taiwan

Jingxia Lin ⓘ
Nanyang Technological University
Singapore, Singapore

Peng Jin ⓘ
Leshan Normal University
Leshan, China

ISSN 0302-9743 ISSN 1611-3349 (electronic)
Lecture Notes in Artificial Intelligence
ISBN 978-981-97-0585-6 ISBN 978-981-97-0586-3 (eBook)
https://doi.org/10.1007/978-981-97-0586-3

LNCS Sublibrary: SL7 – Artificial Intelligence

This Springer imprint is published by the registered company Springer Nature Singapore Pte Ltd.
The registered company address is: 152 Beach Road, #21-01/04 Gateway East, Singapore 189721, Singapore

Paper in this product is recyclable.

Preface

The 2023 Chinese Lexical Semantics Workshop (CLSW 2023) was organized by the Chinese Language Information Processing Society (COLIPS) of Singapore, in collaboration with the National University of Singapore (NUS) and Nanyang Technological University (NTU). We were proud to contribute once more to the field of Chinese lexical semantics. COLIPS was established in 1988, dedicated to advancing research in computer processing of Chinese and other Asian languages. In 2004, COLIPS hosted the 5th Chinese Lexical Semantics Workshop (CLSW) in Singapore. In 2008 and 2016, we successfully held the CLSW conference in Singapore again. This year marked the 4th time that CLSW was held in Singapore.

During this conference, we scheduled four keynote presentations that covered various research areas. First, Xu Jie from the Chinese Language and Literature Department of the University of Macau presented on the categorization of negation in Chinese. Next, Dong Minghui from the Agency for Science, Technology, and Research (A*STAR) explored the application of language models in Chinese semantic research. The third presentation was delivered by Su Qi from the School of Foreign Languages at Peking University, sharing research on culture and cultural history conducted under data-driven approaches. Lastly, Du Jingjing from Xiamen University presented the research achievements of the Chinese elementary education standardized version's lexical semantics. These keynote presentations added more academic highlights to the conference.

This conference predominantly showcased in-person presentations, signifying the first significant event since the end of the pandemic. Regrettably, certain authors couldn't join us physically due to various reasons. Nevertheless, we made concerted efforts to keep in touch with remote participants, ensuring their active engagement through online platforms for discussions and interactions. Regardless of the mode of participation, every attendee enriched this conference with their distinctive perspectives and experiences. The enthusiastic involvement in the presentation and discussion sessions fostered a profound exchange of ideas and knowledge, creating a truly inspiring and collaborative academic gathering.

We received a total of 215 paper submissions for this conference. The review work was done using the Microsoft CMT3 system, with a double-blind review process. Each paper was reviewed by 3 reviewers. Scores were given for three major aspects: (1) Impact of the work on society and the research domain. (2) The technical correctness of the work, such as supported by data and other proof. (3) The clarity of the presentation, meaning whether the paper clearly describes the work.

The review scores were further evaluated by 3 program chairs, and decisions were made based on the review scores and the discussions among program chairs when disputes arose among reviewers. After rigorous evaluation and selection, we arranged 113 paper presentations, including 79 oral presentations and 34 poster presentations, covering a wide range of research topics in Chinese lexical semantics. We are grateful for the hard work and contributions of all the authors.

October 2023

Minghui Dong
Jia-Fei Hong
Peng Jin
Jingxia Lin

Organization

Conference Chair

Dong, Minghui   Institute for Infocomm Research, A*STAR, Singapore

Program Committee Chairs

Hong, Jia-Fei   Taiwan Normal University, Taiwan
Jin, Peng   Leshan Normal University, China
Lin, Jingxia   Nanyang Technological University, Singapore

Advisory Committee

Diao, Yanbin   Beijing Normal University, China
Hong, Jia-Fei   Taiwan Normal University, Taiwan
Hsieh, Shu-Kai   Taiwan University, Taiwan
Huang, Chu-Ren   Hong Kong Polytechnic University, China
Ji, Donghong   Wuhan University, China
Jin, Peng   Leshan Normal University, China
Liu, Meichun   City University of Hong Kong, China
Lu, Qin   Hong Kong Polytechnic University, China
Qu, Weiguang   Nanjing Normal University, China
Su, Xinchun   Xiamen University, China
Sui, Zhifang   Peking University, China
Lua, Kim Teng   Chinese and Oriental Languages Information Processing Society, Singapore
Wu, Jiun-Shiung   Taiwan Chung Cheng University, Taiwan
Xu, Jie   University of Macau, China
Zan, Hongying   Zhengzhou University, China
Zhang, Yangsen   Beijing Information Science and Technology University, China
Zhuo, Jing-Schmidt   University of Oregon, USA

Organizing Chairs

Lin, Jingxia   Nanyang Technological University, Singapore
Tan, Xiaowei   National University of Singapore, Singapore
Yuan, Min   National University of Singapore, Singapore

Finance Chairs

Wang, Lei   Huawei and COLIPS, Singapore
Wu, Yan   Institute for Infocomm Research, A*STAR,
                          Singapore

Publication Chairs

Su, Qi   Peking University, China
Tang, Xuri   Huazhong University of Science and Technology,
                          China

Contents – Part II

Computational Linguistics and Natural Language Processing

Corpus Linguistics

General Linguistics

Contents – Part I

Computational Linguistics and Natural Language Processing

Teaching Chinese Pattern Extraction and Its Knowledge Base Construction for Specific Domain Texts

Zuntian Wei[1], Weiming Peng[2,3]([✉]), Jihua Song[1], Shaodong Wang[1], and Mengyu Zhao[1]

[1] School of Artificial Intelligence, Beijing Normal University, Beijing, China
`202121081054@mail.bnu.edu.cn`

[2] Chinese Character Research and Application Laboratory, Beijing Normal University, Beijing, China
`pengweiming@bnu.edu.cn`

[3] Linguistic Data Consortium, University of Pennsylvania, Philadelphia, USA

Abstract. Certain specialized component collocations and high-frequency expressions, known as Sentence Pattern Forms, can be used in textbook compilation and in-person teaching. The selection of Sentence Pattern Forms and the organization of knowledge points depend on the expert's subjective opinion and lack the support of objective evidence. Manual extraction also limits the compilation's effectiveness and thoroughness. This study creates a corpus of vocational textbooks on various majors. At the same time, we develop a knowledge base of extraction principles and provide corresponding algorithms for different Sentence Pattern Forms. Candidate expressions are automatically extracted and filtered by necessary manual screening. This method is more effective and scientific than pure manual extraction since it can cover more Sentence Pattern Forms that expert opinion cannot exhaust.

Keywords: Chinese teaching · Sentence Pattern Forms · Sentence Pattern Structure · Chinese textbook corpus · Automatic extraction algorithm

1 Introduction

Sentence Pattern Form is a frequently utilized concept in Chinese education because it is a typical high-frequency and universal syntactic mode in corpora of diverse subjects. Also, it is a valuable tool for teaching grammar. It is crucial for the development of language sense in learners. The following are some examples of Sentence Pattern Forms taken from Chinese textbooks:

- 从(From)…以后(on)
- 不是(not)…, 而是(but)…
- X不X(or not), 关键(the key is)…
- 要是(if)…一定/肯定(definitely)…

M. Dong et al. (Eds.): CLSW 2023, LNAI 14515, pp. 3–14, 2024.
https://doi.org/10.1007/978-981-97-0586-3_1

- S+要/快要/就要(will)+V+(O)+了(finish)

Nowadays, most Sentence Pattern Form identification and extraction in Chinese education relies on linguist induction. Sentence Pattern Form still needs more conventional definitions, and different studies frequently interpret them differently. Feng Shengli and Shi Chunhong's Trinitarian Grammar [1] summarizes several Sentence Pattern Forms that can teach Chinese from three perspectives. The theory of Construction Grammar was applied to computer information processing by Zhan Weidong [2] from the viewpoint of computational linguistics, and he created a construction knowledge database where many constructions adhere to the features of Chinese teaching Sentence Pattern Form. Sheng Qiaoyi [3] extracted different structural components and generated a pattern knowledge base for international Chinese textbooks. Zhu Shuqin et al. [4] expanded the small-scale treebank to a large-scale knowledge base by splitting and deriving complex instances. He Jing et al. [5] proposed an algorithm based on a "word or POS" match to construct an ancient Chinese treebank quickly.

From relevant research, most existing work involves manual intervention based on computer information processing algorithms. Moreover, the extraction and induction of Sentence Pattern Forms in current textbooks and tutorial books primarily focus on teaching Chinese as a second language. The requirement for Chinese learning combined with specific vocational fields and work activities is becoming increasingly prominent as more and more foreign learners focus on working in services, manufacturing, and trade in Chinese language environments.

Section 2 of this paper defines the formal structure of Sentence Pattern Forms and divides them into three groups depending on their characteristics. The Sentence Pattern Structure (abbreviated as SPS) is a structural framework for syntactical annotation, as described in Sect. 3. The SPS expressions formed after text annotation serve as the input for the Sentence Pattern Form extraction method. Section 4 provides the extraction method's primary flow. Sections 5 and 6 present extraction strategies based on the rule knowledge base and the statistical method.

2 Formal Definition and Feature Analysis of the Sentence Pattern Form

When employing computer processing, it is required to design a formal structure and symbol system because Chinese Sentence Pattern Forms are represented in various ways. Trinitarian Grammar uses the "symbol format+marked words" description method in its sentence pattern [1]. It contains placeholder "…" as well as word forms, POS, sentence components (subject S, object O), and phrase functions (NP, VP). The construction grammar knowledge base comprises constants and variables as the fundamental building blocks of description. The construction's elements can be thought of as mashups of linear sequences [2].

Given that several words can be substituted for the placeholder "…" in sentence components like NP, VP, subject, and predicate, we formally describe the Sentence Pattern Form to create a unified processing framework as follows: A Sentence Pattern Form is a representation of words, POS tagging, or placeholders in a sequence where the terms and POS tagging can be combined using the logical "OR" operator. Placeholders are consistently employed in place of sentence components and phrase function tags because the structural features of placeholders may be derived from sentence content and context.

Typically, Sentence Pattern Forms are generalized from the original corpus material. Placeholders can be considered the abstract component of the Sentence Pattern Form, whereas word forms and POS can be regarded as their characteristic items. Word forms represent words deterministically and have the most vital qualities from the characteristics standpoint. POS specifies the kind and quantity of words. Placeholders restrain neither the amount nor the POS of words. They are maintaining the words and POS that follow a specific rule when referring to the syntactic components of the phrase while extracting patterns is critical.

The hierarchy of Sentence Pattern Form needs to be established from the standpoint of Phrase Structure Grammar. The characteristic items of many sentences only sometimes have dependency relations from the perspective of Dependency Grammar. In contrast to these two structures, the SPS is a formal schema based on Sentence-based Grammar [6]. This approach to sentence analysis is incredibly well suited for Sentence Pattern Form extraction because the Sentence-based Grammar we'll cover in Sect. 3 originates from Chinese teaching. As a result, we decided to build the textbook syntactic treebank using the concept of SPS.

We can broadly categorize common Sentence Pattern Forms used in vocational Chinese teaching that experts assembled into three groups:

Sentence Pattern Forms Formed by Relative Conjunctions. Between two clauses with semantic ties like conformity, transition, and causality, close conjunction is frequently used in complex Chinese sentences. We can use regular expressions to build a knowledge base and realize the automatic extraction of such Sentence Pattern Forms by summarizing the rules of relative conjunctions.

Sentence Pattern Forms Formed by Component Collocations. Certain specific grammatical elements in sentences have relatively constant collocations, such as the collocation of sibling adverbs, prepositions and particles, prepositions and nouns of locality, etc. These elements are typically on the same hierarchy when sentence component analysis using Sentence-based Grammar. The compositional qualities of such forms can be used to write regular expression rules for them. The mutual information between the components gathered by the grouping can then be calculated, and its adoption or rejection can be decided.

Other Sentence Pattern Forms with Undetermined Features. Together with the two types mentioned above, other Sentence Pattern Forms can be utilized in teaching that lack common elements like relative conjunctions and component collocations. Algorithms based on structural coverage and content specificity must be used for extraction for this portion of the Sentence Pattern Form. This type of algorithm, which performs the function of "bottoming", will split and extend certain SPS expressions in the corpus and, to the greatest extent feasible, catch important Sentence Pattern Forms that the first two approaches missed.

3   An Overview of Sentence Pattern Structure

Peng et al. [7] created and developed the Sentence Pattern Structure (abbreviated as SPS), a formal Chinese syntactic structure system based on Li Jinxi's Sentence-based Grammar [8]. It primarily consists of the data storage structure for the outcomes of sentence component analysis and the diagrammatic schema on a two-dimensional plane. Beijing Normal University and Beijing Han-sky Education Technology Co., Ltd have created a digital platform based on this system. The website allows users to annotate Chinese sentences in XML format, which can then be condensed into an "SPS expression" representation.

[9] interprets the structural symbols correlating to the various syntactic components and inserts special symbols between characters to represent different syntactic component information. There are two categories of SPS expressions: primary forms and POS forms. The latter's POS information is concatenated after the word form using a backslash, while the former has no POS information. The essential SPS expression is the input for the algorithm used to extract the Sentence Pattern Forms formed by relative conjunctions. The algorithm input for the other two types of Sentence Pattern Forms is an SPS expression with POS information. [10] presents a persuasive case for the sentence structure hierarchy. The following are the primary principles:

- The sentence structure has a strict hierarchy;
- The vertical distance between horizontal lines in the graphic figure measures the depth of the sentence hierarchy;
- A single-layer SPS expression includes a modified component immediately adjacent to the layer after pruning.

The feature portion of the sentence representation is constrained to a single level of analysis in this hierarchical view. This study uses the engineering technique of Sentence Pattern Form extraction to demonstrate further the efficacy and applicability of sentence structure hierarchical analysis.

4   The Primary Flow of the Extraction Method

4.1   Steps of the Extraction Algorithm

An SPS expression is provided as input to the Sentence Pattern Form extraction algorithm. Preprocessing, pattern creation, and post-processing are the general divisions of the processing phases. Clause segmentation and single-layer expression generation are two processes that are part of the preprocessing stage. For various sentence kinds, the algorithm follows a different processing path. From the standpoint of structural type, Sentence Pattern Forms created by the combination of conjunctions and the variety of sentence components at the same level are closed and constrained. Its properties are located in relatively fixed syntactic elements. We employ an extraction method from a rule-based knowledge base for these Sentence Pattern Forms. Since it is impossible to exhaust all rules, we use statistical methods based on structural coverage and content specificity to extract Sentence Pattern Forms with undetermined features. Word processing, SPS identifier processing, and other procedures are included in post-processing. The resulting database can only contain Sentence Pattern Forms that have been post-processed and meet the formal definition (Table 1).

Table 1. Overview of corpus

Textbook	Word count	Sentence count
Introduction to Automotive Chinese	419	6438
Mechatronics Integration	266	4736
Computer Network	514	8888
Introduction to E-commerce	427	6562
Introduction to Logistics	153	1242
Hotel Management	242	4013

4.2 Single-Layer SPS Expression Generation

Learners should focus more on the sentence's structural elements when learning. They are highly likely to experience interference from complicated and multi-layered modification components. The conjunction "但(but)" in the example sentence below is the form students must memorize. Yet, the original statement's nested modifiers are overly complicated, potentially making it more difficult for learners to understand.

      Example 1. "但(but)' ⟨⟨左后轮(left rear wheel)⟩制动(brake)⟩摩擦片(friction plate)

‖磨损(wear)<⟨较(fairly)⟩严重(severely)。>
Remove nested modifiers to get a single-layer SPS expression.

      Example 2. "但(but)' ⟨制动(brake)⟩摩擦片(friction plate)‖磨损(wear)<严重(se-

verely)。>
The approach may remove nested modifier components one layer at a time during the preprocessing to create a single-layer SPS expression. Such expressions must be free of independent structures, scaffolded structures, and nested modifiers like attributes, adverbs, and complements. The only parts left are the single-layer parenthesis and the trunk components. Contents in nesting brackets are processed one at a time in a queue.

4.3 Word Processing

An SPS expression with POS information is used for Sentence Pattern Form extraction. Slashes and lettered POS tagging follow the word form. Although this format is helpful for computer algorithms to process data, the structure could be more varied for teaching. The word processing process involves combining POS tagging with the grammatical structure of the word to decide the usage. Preserve word forms, preserve POS, replace word forms and POS as placeholders, and neither form nor POS is maintained are the available modes of operation. In addition to ensuring that the original sentence structure is preserved, the POS or placeholders for some words are kept to provide the extracted

Sentence Pattern Form a good generalization capacity. We can get a more universal teaching Sentence Pattern Form in this approach.

Neither Form Nor POS is Preserved. Interjections (/e) and onomatopoeia (/o) in sentences are substituted by placeholders because the word form does not accurately convey the actual content, and the POS only contributes minimally to the completeness of the SPS. At the SPS identifiers processing stage, modifiers in the processed sentence will be erased if they contain no valid word form or POS information.

Replace Word Forms and POS as Placeholders. It is important to note that syntactic elements must be considered while judging verb and noun treatment. The algorithm treats isolated verbs and nouns that appear elsewhere by preserving word forms, while placeholders are adopted if they appear in modifiers. In terms of implementation, the algorithm keeps track of the number of nested bracket layers. The depths of the nested component are stored in an array. The algorithm uses the element values to identify whether the current word is a part of the sentence's backbone.

Preserve POS. We preserve the number of words, measure words, personal pronouns, and time words to maximize the generalization capacity of teaching Sentence Pattern Forms. These words are typically closely tied to their context, and the syntactic collocations and structural information are unaffected when words are replaced with POS identifiers. Only personal pronouns are required to preserve POS.

Preserve Word Forms. Some specific words in the Sentence Pattern Form are significant in terms of semantic expression. More is needed to reflect the sentence's collocation by preserving the POS tagging. The word form must be maintained to make the extracted Sentence Pattern Forms more comprehensive. Common words that must keep their form include nouns of locality, adverbs, demonstrative pronouns, interrogative pronouns, prepositions, conjunctions, and particles. Although the verbs and nouns in the non-modifier components cannot be included in addition to the words mentioned above and adverbs, they are crucial for sentence structure and verb-object collocation. Thus, it should still be in word form.

4.4 Handling of SPS Identifiers and Placeholders

It is required to remove the identifiers and empty modifiers that denote various sentence components, combine subsequent placeholders, and then obtain the final teaching Sentence Pattern Form.

Remove Empty Modifiers and Independent Phrases. Attributes, adverbs, complements, and separate phrases may wind up being empty or consisting of punctuation after word processing. They will be removed.

Delete Structural Identifiers. Structural identifiers are used to distinguish and designate various syntactic components. They can help computers recognize and analyze sentences automatically in the SPS system. The majority of students, however, need to become more familiar with SPS. The integrity and coherence of the Sentence Pattern Form can be better reflected from the standpoint of language expression habits by removing the structural identifiers.

Merge Consecutive Placeholders. The placeholder "…" is used in processes including generating single-layer SPS expressions and word processing. We replace consecutive placeholders with a single one.

5   Extraction Algorithm Based on the Rule Knowledge Base

Sentence Pattern Forms formed by relative conjunctions or component collocations are structurally closed and constrained. We employ algorithms based on the knowledge base for these types of Sentence Pattern Forms.

5.1   Algorithm Based on the Knowledge Base of Relative Conjunctions

In a complex sentence, the collocation of relative conjunctions between two clauses creates a teaching Sentence Pattern Form that is mainly extracted using this algorithm. We can extract the relative conjunctions by matching them with regular expressions stored in the knowledge base. The two clauses typically have a specific semantic link.

Syntactic information should also be considered when creating regular expressions for the rule base. Regular expressions and Unicode characters can match and capture SPS expressions, which use inserted characters to mark syntactic details. As a result, we decided to use an SPS expression as the extraction algorithm's input. The steps are explained below.

Table 2. Sentence Pattern Forms formed by relative conjunctions

Textbook	Number of Sentence Pattern Forms
Introduction to Automotive Chinese	45
Mechatronics Integration	59
Computer Network	128
Introduction to E-commerce	48
Introduction to Logistics	40

The regular expression called "preceding regular expression" matches the preceding clause for each rule in the knowledge base, while the regular expression called "following regular expression" matches the following clause. The regular expressions mentioned above consist of regular modifiers, SPS identifiers, and Chinese characters corresponding to particular content. Specific rules allow the preceding or following clause's regular expression to be empty, meaning neither clause contains validly linked terms. If the match of the preceding or following clause is optional, it is indicated by the variables "preceding optional" and "following optional". The value "one" indicates optional. For instance, if the value of the preceding optional is zero, the rule can only be applied if the preceding regular expression successfully matches the preceding clause. The matching result of the following clause is used if the value of the following optional is one and the following regular expression successfully matches the following clause. When the match is unsuccessful, the matching result from the preceding clause is immediately adopted.

This extraction algorithm extracted Sentence Pattern Forms from the five majors' vocational Chinese textbooks. Table 2 shows the results of this method.

5.2   Algorithm Based on the Knowledge Base of Component Collocations

From the standpoint of dependency grammar, analysis of some Sentence Pattern Forms confirmed by experts reveals that there is no dependency between some components. Nonetheless, in the perspective of SPS, these components are located at the same layer according to the diagrammatic syntactic analysis.

Component collocation rules—composed of SPS identifiers, regular modifiers, and regular metacharacters—are written in standard syntax to match SPS expressions in the textbook's corpus. Table 3 illustrates component collocation rules.

Table 3. Example of regular rules for component collocations

Regular rule	Sample
[(.+?)]	又(also)…又(also)…
[(.+?)∧.*?△(.+?)]	对(with)…来说(regard to)
[(.+?)∧.*?□(.+?)]	在(besides)…之外(and)

Regular rules' parenthesis denotes grouped captures. The candidate pattern set includes the outcomes gathered by the grouping following a successful match. Not every potential form discovered utilizing component collocation rules could be used for teaching. We used Pointwise Mutual Information [11] to measure the degree of correlation between components in the collocation. $PMI(c_1, c_2)$ is the Pointwise Mutual Information between c_1 and c_2.

$$PMI(c_1, c_2) = \log_2 \frac{p(c_1, c_2)}{p(c_1) * p(c_2)} \qquad (1)$$

In the above equation, $p(c_1)$ is the probability that the component c_1 appears in the corpus. $p(c_2)$ is the probability that the component c_2 appears in the corpus. $p(c_1, c_2)$ is the probability that both the component c_1 and the component c_2 appear in one of the collocation rules described above. PMI can be determined by counting the number of SPS expressions that adhere to the regular matching rule. The stronger the correlation between the two components and the larger the PMI, the more likely it will be used for teaching. To effectively select the teaching Sentence Pattern Forms from the candidate pattern set, we calculate the PMI for each record in the candidate set and sort them in descending order. We ran tests on a corpus of Chinese vocational textbooks across six majors after manual filtering, and the results are displayed in Table 4.

Table 4. Sentence Pattern Forms formed by component collocations

Textbook	Original amount	Filtered amount
Introduction to Automotive Chinese	103	58
Mechatronics Integration	94	68
Computer Network	196	129
Introduction to E-commerce	140	91
Introduction to Logistics	13	6
Hotel Management	54	37

6 Extraction Algorithm Based on Structural Coverage and Content Specificity

The benefits of utilizing rules to extract Sentence Pattern Forms are high accuracy and excellent usability of the extraction results. Nevertheless, manually established rules cannot cover every possible statement. In light of this, we provide an algorithm for extracting Sentence Pattern Forms based on structural coverage and content specificity. The algorithm extends and derives the components of a single-layer SPS expression to generate a set of potential Sentence Pattern Forms. Typical and universal teaching Sentence Pattern Forms could be selected by assessing the structural coverage and content specificity.

6.1 Extension and Derivation of SPS Expressions

The procedure described in the previous section is handled by changing nested brackets with placeholders to provide a single-layer expression result after the intermediate expression appears in the queue. The first approach is to obtain the outcome immediately after deleting the nested brackets. The second approach uses the same procedure as the first one, substituting the placeholder "…" for the nested brackets. The third approach to expand is to use component names enclosed by '', such as 'att' in place of nested brackets.

SPS expressions comprised of clauses, expressions with multiple predicate kernels, and expressions with sibling modifiers can all be segmented to increase the number of possible sentence patterns. From a pedagogical perspective, the segmented SPS expressions are more compact if the sentence component itself is restricted within a specific predicate kernel or a specific modifier. It enables students to concentrate more on picking up particular Sentence Pattern Forms. The original SPS expressions are kept and added to the candidate set to prevent losing syntactic information between predicate kernels and modifiers.

6.2 Filter SPS Expressions with Structural Coverage and Content Specificity

Using the placeholder in place of the words and punctuation in the SPS expressions, we can calculate structural coverage and determine the basic structure of the Sentence Pattern Form. The framework is now reduced to placeholders and SPS identifiers.

As a floating-point number between zero and one, the ratio is used for describing the filter scale. We then choose the top-ranking Sentence Pattern Forms for each structural framework. The degree of content specificity we explain below is the metric used to score the Sentence Pattern Forms. The number of Sentence Pattern Forms chosen by each type of structural framework is calculated using the following formula.

$$TopK = Round(Coverage * Ratio) \tag{2}$$

Coverage is the frequency of a particular structural framework being counted in a textbook. The number of Sentence Pattern Forms we select for a particular structural framework is *TopK*. The calculated result is rounded by the *Round*() method. The following is the formula for determining content specificity.

$$Specificity = (\lambda_1 * Word + \lambda_2 * POS + \lambda_3 * Placeholder)/Total \tag{3}$$

$$Total = Word + POS + Placeholder \tag{4}$$

Among them, $\lambda_1, \lambda_2, \lambda_3 \in [0, 1]$. *Word*, *POS* and *Placeholder* represent the number of word forms, POS taggings, and placeholders. It can be seen that the contribution weight of word form, POS, and placeholder frequency to the content specificity value decreases in sequence. When teaching a Sentence Pattern Form, we include as many sentences of various structural types as possible. At the same time, Sentence Pattern Form's distinctive content should be as precise and comprehensible as feasible. Consequently, a balance between structural coverage and content specificity must be achieved. Hence, in order of content specificity, we will sort the Sentence Pattern Forms matching to each type of structural framework. Experts provide a supplementary evaluation of the top K's Sentence Pattern Forms based on objective data before sorting. Here, we take $\lambda_1 = 1$, $\lambda_2 = 0.5$, $\lambda_3 = 0.2$. We experimented using a corpus of Chinese vocational textbooks across six majors and a 10% ratio. Some sample results have been chosen to be exhibited below (Table 5).

Table 5. Sample results categorized by the structural framework

Structural framework	Number of Sentence Pattern Forms
··· ‖ ··· │ ···	46
··· ‖ ··· │ (···) ···	43
··· ∧ (···) ···	23
··· ‖ ··· : ··· │ ···	7
··· ‖ ··· │ { ··· }	7

7 Conclusion

Several standardized and often-used Sentence Pattern Forms extracted by the three methods mentioned above will be categorized according to the structural framework. The analysis's findings indicate that specific distinct syntactic structures are located in most Chinese Sentence Pattern Forms with educational value. Besides, the engineering technique of layer-by-layer extracting confirms the efficacy of sentence structure hierarchical theory at the application level. In this study, teaching Sentence Pattern Forms are categorized, several processing approaches are determined for various categories, and a knowledge base of extraction rules is built. After producing the candidate set, the extraction algorithm based on relative conjunctions, component collocations, structural coverage, and content specificity must compute the required weight and supplement it with manual screening to achieve adopted Sentence Pattern Forms. The method can help experts uncover some Sentence Pattern Forms that do not have traditional syntactic properties yet commonly arise in the domain corpus instead of pure manual extraction.

According to the extraction effect, the larger the knowledge base of relative conjunction and component collocation rules, the less valuable Sentence Pattern Forms are missed. The workload required for manual screening will be less onerous if the recommendation weight is calculated more accurately. In the subsequent work, we will outline more collocation principles and improve the calculation method of recommended weight.

Acknowledgments. This work was supported by the National Natural Science Foundation of China (Grants No. 62007004, 61877004) and the Major Program of Key Research Base of Humanities and Social Sciences of the Ministry of Education of China (22JJD740017).

References

1. Feng, S., Shi, C.: Trinitarian Grammar Structure Function Context Teaching Guide for Elementary and Intermediate Chinese Grammar. Peking University Press, Beijing (2015)
2. Zhan, W.: On theoretical issues in building a knowledge database of Chinese constructions. J. Chin. Inf. Process. **31**(1), 230–238 (2017)
3. Sheng, Q.: Automatic Acquisition and Application for Structural Patterns on International Chinese Teaching. Beijing Normal University, Beijing (2017)
4. Zhu, S., Peng, W., Song, J., Guo, D.: The extraction of Chinese sentence pattern instance based on diagrammatic treebank. J. Chin. Inf. Process. **31**(5), 32–39 (2017)
5. He, J., Song, T., Peng, W., Zhu, S., Song, J.: An efficient approach to ancient Chinese treebank construction based on "Word or POS" match. J. Chin. Inf. Process. **31**(4), 114–121 (2017)
6. He, J., Peng, W., Song, J., Liu, H.: Annotation schema for contemporary Chinese based on JinXi Li's grammar system. In: Liu, P., Su, Q. (eds.) CLSW 2013, LNCS, vol. 8229, pp. 668–681. Springer, Heidelberg (2013)
7. Peng, W., Song, J., Sui, Z., Guo, D.: Formal schema of diagrammatic Chinese syntactic analysis. In: Lu, Q., Gao, H. (eds.) CLSW 2015, LNCS, vol. 9332, pp. 701–710. Springer, Cham (2015)
8. Li, J.: A New Chinese Grammar. The Commercial Press, Beijing (2001)
9. Peng, W.: The Theory and Practice of Chinese Information Processing in Sentence-based Grammar. Foreign Language Teaching and Research Press, Beijing (2021)

10. Peng, W., Wei, Z., Song, J., Yu, S., Sui, Z.: Formalized Chinese sentence pattern structure and its hierarchy analysis. In: Dong, M., Gu, Y., Hong, J. (eds.) CLSW 2021, LNAI, vol. 13249, pp. 293–305. Springer, Cham (2022)

11. Chen, Z.: Applied Linguistics Research in China at the Turn of the Century. Sinolingua, Beijing (1999)

Probability Distribution of Dependency Distance of Mongolian Nouns

Dulan[1](✉) and Dabhurbayar[2]

[1] Inner Mongolia Normal University, Zhaowuda Road 81, Hohhot 010022, China
1026634236@qq.com
[2] Inner Mongolia University, College Road 235, Hohhot 010021, China

Abstract. Based on the written and spoken language treebanks, this paper applies quantitative linguistics methods to statistically analyze Mongolian nouns and their dependency distance distributions. The results showed that the proportion of nouns in the Mongolian written language treebank was 35.58%, and the proportion of nouns and pronouns was 39.61%. In the Mongolian spoken language treebank, the proportion of nouns was 22.11%, and the proportion of nouns and pronouns was 33.12%. These findings closely align with results from prior research, further confirming the regularity of the proportion of nouns in human natural language. In terms of dependency distance distributions, the distributions of noun dependency distances in both the written and spoken treebanks fit the right-truncated Waring distribution and right-truncated modified Zipf-Alekseev distribution. This result is consistent with previous research. Moreover, the "long tail effect" can be seen from the fitting results, that is, as the dependency distance increases, its frequency decreases. This implies that there is also a tendency to minimize dependency distances in nouns.

Keywords: Noun · Dependency Distance · Quantitative Study

1 Introduction

Based on previous studies, we can observe that, in Mongolian, although research on nouns has been conducted on various aspects, the majority of it is qualitative, with only a minority of it being quantitative research. Moreover, in the field of quantitative linguistics, most previous studies have been based on the analysis of the entire corpus or text, in order to demonstrate the universal laws and quantitative characteristics of language. In contrast, research on individual word classes is relatively scarce. To date, there has been no study employing quantitative linguistic methods to investigate the distribution of dependency distance in Mongolian nouns.

In terms of the dependency distance distribution, Ferrer-i-Cancho (2004) concluded that the dependency distance distribution follows an exponential function through the principle of maximum entropy. Conversely, Liu (2007) deduced that the distribution of dependency distance is a discrete power law function by assuming an inverse relationship between the frequency of variables and their relative rates of change. For the above

M. Dong et al. (Eds.): CLSW 2023, LNAI 14515, pp. 15–26, 2024.
https://doi.org/10.1007/978-981-97-0586-3_2

different research results, Lu and Liu (2016) found through multiple model fitting and comparison that the distribution of dependency distance in human language falls between exponential and power law distributions, and can be described by a mixed exponential and power law model. Subsequently, the dependency distance has been analyzed among many other studies (Wang and Liu, 2017; Lu and Liu, 2020; Hua et al., 2023). In addition to the distribution of dependency distance, researchers believe that there is a tendency for dependency distance minimization in language, and have confirmed that dependency distance minimization is a universal rule in human language (Liu, 2008; Liu, 2009; Temperley, 2007; Temperley, 2008; Gibson, 2000).

2 Corpus and Methods

The corpus sources for this paper are two types of dependency treebanks for written and spoken language, both of which have been constructed in recent years by the quantitative linguistics research team of Inner Mongolia University. The written and spoken corpora have been compiled separately. The written language corpus is selected from 18 channels of the "China Mongolian News Network" from 2013 to 2014, including "News Center", "New Pastoral Area", "Market", "Education", "Special Topics", "People", "Social Life", "Health", "Culture and Art", "Mongolian Studies", "Mongolian College Students", "Mongolian Speakers", "Literature", "Entertainment", "Mongolian Medicine", "Legal Consultation", "Charity", "Books", etc., with a total of 136 articles, 4,111 sentences, and 99,873 words.

The spoken language corpus is selected from 18 columns on the website of Inner Mongolia TV from 2012 to 2016, including "MERGED-UN CIGVLGAN", "UDESI-YIN J0G0G", "HAVLI-YIN HOTOCI", "M0NGG0L EM EMNELGE", "NEYIGEM AJIGLALTA", "$AGAJAGAI YAGVN-DV AGIBA", "TOROYIN B0D0LG_A-YIN TAYILVMJI", "NADADV YARIHV YAGVM_A BAYIN_A", "HAYIR_A-YIN HELHIY_E", "TV ORTEGE", "ONODUR", "NASVN-V NAMVR", "ULIGER", "VRVSHAL", "0D0D TUGEHU CAG", "M0NGG0LJIN GVW_A", "UNEN MORDEL", "JALAGVS", etc., with a total of 8 h, 7 min, 39 s and 101,856 words. The parenthetical phrase was deleted, and 5,039 sentences and 58,983 words were selected.

Corpus processing is a prerequisite for quantitative research on noun-related issues. In this paper, by performing fixed phrase annotation, part-of-speech tagging, and dependency parsing, a corresponding dependency treebank was obtained. Finally, the treebank was imported into Microsoft Excel to construct the existing corpus. After processing, the final corpus is shown in Table 1. The corpus contains attribute fields such as dependent id, dependent, dependent part of speech, governor id, governor, governor part of speech, and dependency type. We have proofread and revised the existing treebank to further enhance the corpus.

Utilizing the processed dependency treebank, this paper will primarily employ quantitative linguistic methods to investigate the distribution of nouns and noun dependency distances in both written and spoken treebanks. Dependency distance refers to the linear distance between governor and dependent, that is, the difference in word position

Table 1. Format of the Mongolian Dependency Treebank.

ID	Dependent	POS	ID	Governor	POS	Dependency type
0	MAN-V	(Rb;Fc11)	1	GER	(Ne1)	ATT
1	GER	(Ne1)	3	HUCIRDELTEI	(Ax)	SUBJ
2	YOSOTAI	(Ax)	3	HUCIRDELTEI	(Ax)	ATT
3	HUCIRDELTEI	(Ax)				HEAD
4	SIDE	(Sb)	3	HUCIRDELTEI	(Ax)	MP-AUX

between the two words with a dependency relation in a sentence (Liu, 2009:252). A positive dependency distance indicates that the governor comes after the dependent, while a negative dependency distance indicates that the governor comes before the dependent.

The Excel function was used to extract the data. After calculating the dependency distance, we used the Altmann-Fitter 3.1.0 fitting software to fit the dependency distance data from both the written and spoken corpora. In the Altmann-Fitter fitting software, a satisfactory fit is determined when the C value is less than 0.01 and a good fit when the C value is less than 0.02. A value of R^2 greater than 0.90 indicates a very good fit, while values greater than 0.80 indicate a good fit. However, an R^2 value above 0.75 signifies only an acceptable fit and any value below 0.75 should be regarded as unsatisfactory.

3 Results and Discussion

3.1 Distribution of Mongolian Nouns

The distribution of word classes is a crucial invariant in a language, as it not only reveals the universality of a language but also its unique characteristics (Yin, 1986). In previous studies, Hudson (1994) counted nouns based on Brown and LOB corpora and concluded that nouns account for approximately 37% of the English written language. He proposed that there seems to be regularities in language of which most of us have been completely unaware—regularities which involve the statistical probability of any randomly selected word belonging to a particular word-class. To further verify the universality of the proportion of nouns in human natural language, Liu (2009) conducted statistical analysis on a self-constructed treebank and obtained the result that nouns account for about 39.29% of all words in Chinese. Liang and Liu (2013) conducted similar statistical analysis on the corpus of seven languages and found that the proportion of nouns in all seven languages was approximately 37%. Li et al. (2019) investigated three significant German corpora and discovered that the occurrence of nouns in written German is approximately 38%. The results of the study show that the proportion of nouns in all languages is almost 37%. Therefore, is the proportion of nouns in Mongolian also approximately 37%?

To answer this question, we counted the nouns in both written and spoken corpora and calculated their proportions. In Hudson's (1994) study, the proportion of nouns includes the proportion of common nouns, proper nouns, and pronouns. The Mongolian word class tag set distinguishes common nouns (Ne) into two categories: countable nouns (Ne1) and uncountable nouns (Ne2). Proper nouns (Nt) are categorized into personal names (Nt1), place names (Nt2), institutional names (Nt3), and other nouns (Nt4). Pronouns are categorized into personal pronouns (Rb), demonstrative pronouns (Rj), interrogative pronouns (Ra), reflexive pronouns (Ro), range pronouns (Rx), indefinite pronouns (Rt), distinguishing pronouns (Ri) and action pronouns (Rv). According to Li (2019), Hudson excluded punctuation marks from the total word count in his research. Therefore, we did not consider punctuation in this study either. In the written treebank, 13469 punctuation marks were removed, leaving a total of 86404 words. In the spoken treebank, 7148 punctuation marks were removed, leaving a total of 51835 words.

Table 2. Percentage of nouns in written and spoken treebanks.

POS	Written treebank		Spoken treebank	
	Number of words	Percentage	Number of words	Percentage
Ne1	16115	18.65%	7213	13.92%
Ne2	10135	11.73%	3386	6.53%
Nt1	1205	1.39%	237	0.46%
Nt2	1521	1.76%	407	0.79%
Nt3	497	0.58%	26	0.05%
Nt4	1266	1.47%	193	0.37%
Rb	840	0.97%	1655	3.19%
Rj	1646	1.91%	3107	5.99%
Ra	250	0.29%	234	0.45%
Ro	176	0.20%	202	0.39%
Rx	245	0.28%	110	0.21%
Rt	91	0.11%	250	0.48%
Ri	214	0.25%	149	0.29%
Rv	21	0.02%	0	0.00%
Total	34222	39.61%	17169	33.12%

Table 2 shows the proportion of nouns in written and spoken language. Among them, the common nouns in the written language treebank account for 30.38%, the proper nouns account for 5.20%, and the pronouns account for 4.03%. The common nouns in the spoken language treebank account for 20.44%, the proper nouns account for 1.67%, and the pronouns account for 11.00%. In both written and spoken language treebanks, countable nouns account for the largest proportion, while action pronouns account for the smallest proportion. The specific order in written language is as follows: Ne1 > Ne2 > Rj > Nt2 > Nt4 > Nt1 > Rb > Nt3 > Ra > Ri > Rx > Ro > Rt > Rv, the specific order in spoken language is as follows: Ne1 > Ne2 > Rj > Rb > Nt2 > Rt > Ra > Nt1 > Ro > Nt4 > Ri > Rx > Nt3. Comparing the distribution of nouns in written and spoken language, we can see that although the proportion of common nouns and proper nouns in spoken language is lower than that in written language, the proportion of pronouns is higher. The reason is that spoken language corpora contain many conversations, and conversations involve more known content, resulting in the use of more pronouns. This is also consistent with the statistical result of Yin (1986:433) that the frequency of pronouns in spoken language is more than twice as high as that in written language.

Overall, the proportion of nouns in written Mongolian is 39.61%, similar to that of other written languages, which is around 37%. Among them, the statistical result of 39.29% by Liu (2009) is the closest. The reason for such a close result may be attributed to the content of news corpora in the constructed corpus. Given that news corpora call for more nouns to convey information, the distribution of nouns is higher when compared to other genres. Considering the proportion of nouns in Mongolian spoken language, it accounts for 33.12%, which is in close proximity to the range of 30%–32% reported in Hudson's (1994) study, which was based on Biber's (1988) spoken language corpus. In summary, the proportion of nouns in Mongolian further confirms the existence of a universal characteristic in human natural languages.

3.2 The Probability Distribution of Noun Dependency Distances Based on Written Language Treebank

Since we already know the distribution of nouns in the text, we will analyze the distribution of their dependency distances. According to previous research (Ferrer-i-Cancho, 2004; Liu, 2007), the distribution of dependency distances follows a power-law distribution and an exponential distribution. Specifically, Liu (2007) selected six texts from the Chinese dependency treebank and found that the probability distribution of dependency distance follows the right truncated Zeta distribution. Wang and Liu (2017) found that the probability distribution of dependency distance of different genres and sentence lengths is well captured by the right truncated Waring distribution, in addition to the right truncated Zeta distribution. Lu and Liu (2020) explored English noun phrases and found that their dependency distance frequency distribution conforms to the right truncated modified Zipf-Alekseev distribution. However, most of the research has been conducted on the entire corpus rather than individual word classes. Therefore, this paper will investigate the distributional characteristics of the dependency distances of nouns to determine if they also follow the distribution mentioned above.

We investigate the distribution of dependency distances for nouns as both governors and dependents in the written language treebank. We add the dependency distance for the governors and dependents of nouns using Altmann-Fitter 3.1.0 for fitting the data. The results of the fitting are shown in Table 3. Based on the parameters $C < 0.01$ and $R^2 > 0.90$ in the table, it can be determined that the dependency distance distribution of nouns fits well with the right truncated Waring distribution, the right truncated modified Zipf-Alekseev distribution, and the right truncated Zeta distribution. Table 4 and Fig. 1 show the fitting results of the distribution of dependency distance of nouns and the right truncated modified Zipf-Alekseev distribution.

From Table 4, we can observe the dependency distance of nouns. Based on the data, we can see that the MDD of the nouns in the text is 2.16. Among them, there are 39,998 dependencies with a dependency distance of 1, accounting for the largest proportion of all dependency distances, reaching 66.34%. The second is the dependencies with a dependency distance of 2, with 9091, accounting for 15.08% of the total dependency distance. Moreover, there are 3,654 dependencies with a dependency distance of 3, accounting for 6.06% of all dependency distances, and 2,144 dependencies with a dependency distance of 4, accounting for 3.56% of all dependency distances. In summary, the dependencies with DD $\leq$ 4 accounts for 91.04% of all dependencies, while the dependencies with DD > 4 accounts for only 8.96% of all dependencies. The proportion difference and distribution trend of dependency distance can be more clearly seen from the bar chart. Figure 1 illustrates that adjacent dependencies are more prevalent than non-adjacent dependencies. Moreover, as the dependency distance increases, its frequency decreases significantly, indicating the "long-tail effect".

Table 3. Fitting results of dependency distance distribution of nouns in the written language treebank.

Distribution	X^2	$P(X^2)$	C	DF	R^2
Right truncated Waring (b,n)	342.6887	0.0000	0.0057	117	0.9999
Right truncated modified Zipf-Alekseev (a,b;n = x-max, α fixed)	225.2082	0.0000	0.0037	74	0.9997
Right truncated Zeta (a; R = x-max)	515.1045	0.0000	0.0085	140	0.9998

3.3 The Probability Distribution of Noun Dependency Distances Based on Spoken Language Treebank

We investigate the distribution of dependency distances for nouns as both governors and dependents in the spoken language treebank. We add the dependency distance for the governors and dependents of nouns using Altmann-Fitter 3.1.0 for fitting the data.

In the fitted result, the parameters of the dependency distance of nouns fit to the right truncated Zeta distribution are C = 0.0280, R^2 = 0.9988. Although the R^2 value is greater than 0.90, the C value is greater than 0.02. Therefore, the fitting result is poor. The parameters of the noun dependency distance distribution fitted to the right-truncated Waring distribution and right truncated modified Zipf-Alekseev distribution are listed in Table 5. It can be seen that the parameters C < 0.02 and R^2 > 0.90, both distributions are fitted very well. Table 6 and Fig. 2 show the fitting results of the distribution of dependency distance of nouns and right truncated modified Zipf-Alekseev distribution.

From Table 6, we can observe the dependency distance of nouns. Based on the data, we can see that the MDD of the nouns in the text is 2.04. Among them, there are 15,543 dependencies with a dependency distance of 1, accounting for the largest proportion of all dependency distances, reaching 63.20%. The second is the dependencies with a dependency distance of 2, with 3747, accounting for 15.24% of the total dependency distance. Moreover, there are 1,931 dependencies with a dependency distance of 3, accounting for 7.85% of all dependency distances, and 1,127 dependencies with a dependency distance

Table 4. Fitting the right truncated modified Zipf-Alekseev distribution to the dependency distance of nouns in the written language treebank.

X[i]	F[i]	NP[i]
1	39998	39998.00
2	9091	8517.70
3	3654	4056.79
4	2144	2275.18
5	1217	1410.17
6	883	935.74
7	615	652.64
8	553	472.91
9	411	353.20
10	304	270.37
11	208	211.26
12	202	167.96
13	131	135.53
14	118	110.79
15	109	91.59
16	98	76.49
17	76	64.45
18	59	54.74
19	57	46.84
20	50	40.34
21	30	34.95
22	37	30.45
23	31	26.66
24	26	23.46
25	20	20.73
26	13	18.39
27	10	16.38
28	10	14.63
29	8	13.12
30	12	11.80
31	9	10.64
32	12	9.63
33	14	8.73
34	9	7.94
35	8	7.23

(*continued*)

Table 4. (*continued*)

X[i]	F[i]	NP[i]
36	8	6.60
37	1	6.04
38	1	5.54
39	5	5.09
40	3	4.68
41	3	4.32
42	5	3.99
43	5	3.69
44	3	3.42
45	1	3.17
47	3	2.74
48	4	2.55
49	2	2.38
50	2	2.22
51	1	2.07
52	4	1.94
53	3	1.82
56	1	1.50
57	1	1.41
60	1	1.18
61	3	1.12
64	1	0.94
67	1	0.80
68	1	0.76
84	1	0.35
91	1	0.26
95	2	0.22
101	1	0.18
107	1	0.14
160	1	0.03

$a = 1.3617$, $b = 0.2610$, $n = 160.0000$, $a = 0.6633$, $X^2 = 225.2082$, $P(X^2) = 0.0000$, $DF = 74$, $C = 0.0037$, $R^2 = 0.9997$

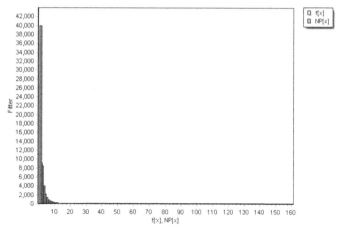

Fig. 1. Fitting the right truncated modified Zipf-Alekseev distribution to the dependency distance of nouns in the written language treebank.

of 4, accounting for 4.58% of all dependency distances. In summary, the dependencies with DD ≤ 4 accounts for 90.87% of all dependencies, while the dependencies with DD > 4 accounts for only 9.13% of all dependencies. The proportion difference and distribution trend of dependency distance can be more clearly seen from the bar chart. Figure 2 illustrates that adjacent dependencies are more prevalent than non-adjacent dependencies. Moreover, as the dependency distance increases, its frequency decreases significantly, indicating the "long-tail effect".

Table 5. Fitting results of dependency distance distribution of nouns in the spoken language treebank.

Distribution	X^2	$P(X^2)$	C	DF	R^2
Right truncated Waring (b,n)	333.8944	0.0000	0.0136	42	0.9966
Right truncated modified Zipf-Alekseev (a,b;n = x-max, α fixed)	46.9965	0.0424	0.0019	32	1.0000

The paper focuses on the distribution of dependency distances for nouns, using both written and spoken treebanks, based on dependency grammars. Before commencing the research, we carried out a study on the distribution of nouns in both written and spoken language. In terms of noun distribution, we have conducted a statistical study on nouns and pronouns in both written and spoken language. The statistical results indicate that in the Mongolian written treebank, the proportion of nouns is 35.58%, and when combined with pronouns, their proportion is 39.61%. In the Mongolian spoken treebank, the proportion of nouns is 22.11%, and when combined with pronouns, their proportion is 33.12%. These findings closely align with results from prior research (Liu,

Table 6. Fitting the right truncated modified Zipf-Alekseev distribution to the dependency distance of nouns in the spoken language treebank.

X[i]	F[i]	NP[i]
1	15543	15543.00
2	3747	3757.32
3	1931	1977.72
4	1127	1123.73
5	730	680.67
6	476	433.85
7	292	288.10
8	188	197.85
9	149	139.73
10	110	101.05
11	70	74.58
12	43	56.03
13	42	42.75
14	25	33.07
15	29	25.90
16	31	20.51
17	15	16.40
18	7	13.24
19	8	10.77
20	9	8.83
21	1	7.29
22	3	6.06
23	5	5.07
24	4	4.26
25	1	3.60
26	1	3.06
27	1	2.61
29	2	1.92
31	1	1.44
36	1	0.74
45	1	0.26

$a = 0.5948, b = 0.5514, n = 45.0000, a = 0.6320, X^2 = 46.9965, P(X^2) = 0.0424, DF = 32, C = 0.0019, R^2 = 1.0000$

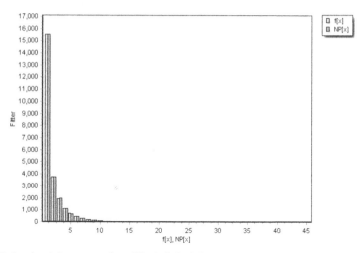

Fig. 2. Fitting the right truncated modified Zipf-Alekseev distribution to the dependency distance of nouns in the spoken language treebank.

2009; Hudson, 1994), further confirming the universal characteristic of the proportion of nouns in human natural languages.

In terms of dependency distance, we conducted a statistical analysis of the distribution of noun dependency distances in both written and spoken language and fitted the data using Altmann-Fitter 3.1.0 software. Through fitting, it was found that in the written language treebank, the distribution of noun dependency distance fits very well with the right truncated Waring distribution, the right truncated modified Zipf-Alekseev distribution, and the right truncated Zeta distribution. In the spoken treebank, the distribution of noun dependency distance fits well with both the right truncated Waring distribution and the right truncated modified Zipf-Alekseev distribution. Based on the above results, the probability distribution of noun dependency distance in both written and spoken languages conforms to the right truncated Waring distribution and the right truncated modified Zipf-Alekseev distribution. This result is consistent with existing research findings (Wang and Liu, 2017; Lu and Liu, 2020). Moreover, we can observe the "long tail effect" in the fitted figures, which implies that as the dependency distance increases, its frequency decreases. This implies that there is a tendency to minimize dependency distance in nouns.

Compared to traditional linguistic research, this paper is not only methodologically novel, advancing the studies of quantitative linguistics in the Mongolian academic community, but also expands the existing research on quantitative linguistics in terms of content. Furthermore, through this paper, we can derive quantitative features of the distribution of noun dependency distances, which can be applied to language teaching and syntactic analysis research and application. Therefore, adopting the methods of quantitative linguistics to study Mongolian nouns, in order to uncover their quantitative features, falls under a new research with significant academic value and practical application.

Acknowledgments. This research is supported by the Fundamental Research Funds for the Inner Mongolia Normal University (2023JBYJ001).

References

Ferrer-i-Cancho, R.: Euclidean distance between syntactically linked words. Phys. Rev. E **70**(5), 1–5 (2004)

Liu, H.: Probability distribution of dependency distance. Glottometrics **15**, 1–12 (2007)

Lu, Q., Liu, H.: Does dependency distance distribute regularly? J. Zhejiang Univ. (Humanities Soc. Sci.) **46**(4), 63–76 (2016)

Wang, Y., Liu, H.: The effects of genre on dependency distance and dependency direction. Lang. Sci. **59**, 135–147 (2017)

Lu, J., Liu, H.: Do English noun phrases tend to minimize dependency distance. Aust. J. Linguist. **40**(2), 1–17 (2020)

Hua, Y., Li, J., Bi, Y.: Research on Korean "Long-Before-Short" preference from the perspective of dependency distance. In: Su, Q., Xu, G., Yang, X. (eds.) Chinese Lexical Semantics. CLSW 2022. LNCS, vol. 13496, pp. 132–142. Springer, Cham (2023). https://doi.org/10.1007/978-3-031-28956-9_11

Liu, H.: Dependency distance as a metric of language comprehension difficulty. J. Cogn. Sci. **9**(02), 159–191 (2008)

Liu, H.: Dependency Grammar from Theory to Practice. Science Press, Beijing (2009)

Temperley, D.: Minimization of dependency length in written English. Cognition **105**(2), 300–333 (2007)

Temperley, D.: Dependency-length minimization in natural and artificial languages. J. Quant. Linguist. **15**(3), 256–282 (2008)

Gibson, E.: The dependency locality theory: a distance-based theory of linguistic complexity. In: Marantz, A., Miyashita, Y., O'Neil, W. (eds.) Image, Language, Brain: Papers from the First Mind Articulation Project Symposium, pp. 94–126. The MIT Press, Cambridge (2000)

Yin, B.: Quantitative research on Chinese parts of speech. Stud. Chin. Lang. **6**, 428–436 (1986)

Hudson, R.: About 37% of word-tokens are nouns. Language **70**(2), 331–339 (1994)

Liang, J., Liu, H.: Noun distribution in natural languages. Poznań Stud. Contemp. Linguist. **49**(4), 509–529 (2013)

Li, Y., Duan, T., Liu, H.: Is the distribution of nouns an invariant in human languages?—an investigation based on written german corpora. J. Zhejiang Univ. (Humanit. Soc. Sci.) **49**(6), 39–48 (2019)

Biber, D.: Variation Across Speech and Writing. Cambridge University Press, Cambridge (1988)

The Use and Evolution of Colors in Written Chinese Since the Late Qing Dynasty

Yiwei Xu[✉] and Gaoqi Rao

Beijing Language and Culture University, Beijing 100083, China
1824649938@qq.com

Abstract. Color words serve as the linguistic embodiment of color usage, forming a subsystem of the human vocabulary that is intimately tied to production, life, and emotions. These words carry rich cultural connotations, national characteristics, and reflect the zeitgeist and cultural tendencies. In this paper, we amalgamate Chinese and foreign color theories to analyze the usage, distribution, coloring domains, and co-occurring words of Chinese color words. This analysis is based on data from Chinese newspapers spanning from the Foreign Affairs Movement of the late Qing Dynasty to the present. We map the distribution of color words in Chinese written language over 1872–2015. Our study reveals that different eras are characterized by different theme colors, and color words evolve in tandem with societal development and the enhancement of people's understanding. The scope, variety, and connotation of color words continue to expand, leading to increasingly rich chromatograms. The coloring domains of color words are becoming more extensive, and their connections with objective entities are becoming more abundant. The usage and evolution of color words are closely linked to policy changes, the social and historical environment, and cultural development. They exhibit a sensitivity to the times, and the national cultural psychology and social customs underlying the color words are also changing. Color words are increasingly dissociating from religion and regime, finding widespread usage in political, economic, and cultural fields, and their importance is steadily increasing.

Keywords: Written language · Color · Chinese color words · Word chronological evolution · Modern Chinese

1 Introduction

Among the three constituents of the language system, vocabulary exhibits the most immediate and dynamic response to societal changes, serving as a mirror that reflects these transformations. Color, in itself, is an abstract concept—a visual effect on light produced by humans through the interplay of eyes, brain, and cognitive experience. Color words are linguistic constructs created by humans to describe colors, and they serve as the primary carriers of colors in language. These words are intimately tied to human production and life, constituting a significant part of the vocabulary system. In all national languages, color words are abundant, highly active, and imbued with rich cultural connotations.

M. Dong et al. (Eds.): CLSW 2023, LNAI 14515, pp. 27–41, 2024.
https://doi.org/10.1007/978-981-97-0586-3_3

Newspapers, as publications conveying information that are regularly distributed to the public, swiftly and directly reflect changes in social development, novel information, and significant historical events. "Shun Pao" and "People's Daily," as representative examples of modern Chinese newspapers, provide a substantial and stable corpus. This corpus serves as a crucial window to observe changes in the modern Chinese language and socio-historical life from a linguistic perspective. This paper utilizes "Shun Pao" (1872–1949) and "People's Daily" (1950–2015) as samples of continuous Chinese language-using media from the Foreign Affairs Movement to the present day to construct a corpus. Based on the corpus of Chinese newspapers spanning from 1872 to 2015, a total of 144 years, we form a lexicon of color words. Building upon previous studies, we conduct an investigation into Chinese color words in terms of their frequency, co-occurrence frequency, and coloring domain, among other aspects.

Building upon previous research, we conduct temporal analyses of Chinese color words, exploring the temporal shifts in the color spectrum of color words in news and public opinion from the late Qing Dynasty to the contemporary era. We scrutinize the fundamental colors of themes across different periods and the temporal connotations they embody.

The study of color words primarily commenced following the period of reform and opening up. Yao Xiaoping (1988) provided an overview and critique of the theory of basic color words, segmenting the evolution of Chinese basic color words into five stages [2]. The research and discourse on modern Chinese color words have been notably vigorous. The primary focus is the discussion of the basic color words in Chinese. According to corpus statistics from a comprehensive dictionary, the eight words "red, yellow, green, blue, purple, black, white, and grey" have the longest generational history, the most potent productivity, and the highest usage frequency. Li Hongyin (2001) proposes that there are nine basic color words in modern Chinese, namely red, yellow, green, blue, purple, brown, black, white, and grey [5]. Harbin Institute of Technology's "TongYiCi CiLin" (Mei Jiaju et al., 1983) includes the following basic color words: white, black, red, green, yellow, blue, brown, ochre, blue, purple, and grey, totaling 11 words [21]. Scholars have also conducted multifaceted and multidisciplinary discussions on the comparative study of Chinese color words with other languages, the cognition of color words, the classroom teaching of color words, the connection between color words and the teaching of Chinese as a foreign language, as well as the characteristics of various emergent color words in terms of vocabulary, syntax, pragmatics, semantics, and so forth. From the perspective of cultural linguistics, Yu Fengchun (1999) discusses the humanistic features of Chinese color words. He posits that the humanistic features of Chinese color words "are determined by the local conditions, religious beliefs, stereotypes of thinking, and conditions of production and life of the ethnic group" [18].

2 Definition and Classification of Basic Color Words

Basic color words are terms that articulate the most fundamental color concepts. They serve as generalizations of various color categories, with the majority of other color words being derived from these basic color words. The topic of basic color words has been the subject of extensive discussions within the field of linguistics. These discussions have varied across different national languages and historical periods. While the outcomes of academic discussions on basic color words in Chinese differ, the majority are based on, or borrow from, the basic color word hypothesis. This hypothesis was proposed by American scholars Berlin Brent and Paul Kay in the 1960s. It serves as a foundational framework for understanding the categorization and usage of color words in various languages.

2.1 Basic Color Word Theory

The seminal theory on basic color terms by Berlin Brent and Paul Kay was articulated in their book "The Universality and Development History of Basic Color Terms," published in 1969. Through the study of the basic color word systems of over ninety human languages worldwide, they boldly proposed the "basic color terms" theory. This theory encompasses several key points [1].

By definition, basic color words should satisfy several fundamental criteria:

a) They must be a single morpheme, i.e., the meaning of the word can be directly inferred from the morpheme.
b) They possess an independent color meaning, that is, the color referred to does not belong to another color gamut.
c) They are not limited to referring to a specific type of object. For instance, the Chinese word "皑" (ái, which describes a white appearance, often used in the context of frost and snow) would need to be excluded.
d) They are psychologically significant and stable. That is, the subjects do not alter their views on the color due to changes in context, and do not have different judgments based on their personal usage.w) "need to be excluded". d) Is psychologically significant and stable. That is, the subjects do not change their views on the color due to the change of context, and do not have different judgments according to their personal usage.

Berlin and Kay propose that the eleven basic color word categories: black, white, red, yellow, green, blue, brown, pink, orange, purple, and gray, are prevalent in most human languages. In essence, these 11 basic color categories should be present in any human language, and the sequence in which these 11 basic color categories are recognized and produced is consistent across different language systems. Subsequently, Kay and McDaniel integrated the mathematical theory of fuzzy sets with the biological theory of visual neural response to establish a novel system of basic color categories and the sequence of their occurrence. This innovative approach provided a more comprehensive understanding of the categorization and usage of color words across various languages (Fig. 1. Corrected universal occurrence order of basic color words).

2.2 Evolution of Basic Chinese Color Words

Yao Xiaoping (1988) presents and critiques Berlin and Kay's theory of basic color words, highlighting the discrepancies between this theory and the actual evolution of basic color words. He then discusses these inconsistencies using examples from the Chinese language. Yao Xiaoping traces the evolution of basic Chinese color words from

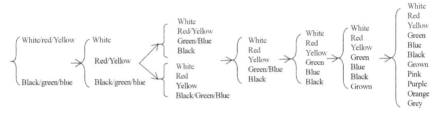

(According to Kay and McDaniel, 1978:639 original figure)

Fig. 1. Corrected universal occurrence order of basic color words

the Yin-Shang period, delineating five stages. The criteria for determining basic color words in the Basic Color Word Theory, as well as the number of basic color words, their word formation ability, frequency of use, and historical development, are all taken into account in Yao Xiaoping's staging. This staging effectively illustrates the evolution of basic color words in Chinese. Drawing on Yao Xiaoping's modern staging, this paper posits that the categories of modern Chinese basic color words are black, white, red, yellow, green, blue, purple, grey, brown, and orange. The study is conducted based on these categories [2].

3   Chinese Color Words in Newspaper Corpus

3.1   Corpus Resources

The corpus database utilized in this paper is derived from the corpora of "Shun Pao" and "People's Daily," spanning from 1872 to 2015, a total duration of 144 years. The "Shun Pao" corpus comprises approximately 900 million words (inclusive of Chinese words, punctuation marks, numbers, alphabetic words, etc.), covering a period of 78 years (1872–1949). The "People's Daily" corpus encompasses about 700 million words, spanning 66 years (from 1950 to 2015). The two newspapers succeed each other in time, fulfilling the need for a large-scale, long time-span corpus for the study of word ephemera.

3.2   Color Words in Shun Pao and People's Daily Overview

Color words constitute a significant component of the Chinese vocabulary system. Chinese color words exhibit diverse usage, rich semantics, and variations, and they carry substantial cultural connotations.

This paper is predicated on the basic color words of modern times mentioned above, namely "black, white, red, yellow, green, blue, cyan, purple, gray, brown, orange," and extends sub-categories. A total of 29 color categories are utilized as the center to compile color words and their related words to form a color word list. The corpus primarily originates from "Shun Pao" and "People's Daily," and is organized according to the semantic connotation of each subcategory. The extraction of color words and their related words in this paper primarily employs a combination of stratified sampling and manual screening. Initially, 144 texts from Shun Pao and People's Daily are grouped by year, with every 5 years forming a group. Each group randomly selects one year's text corpus, and data is extracted from Shun Pao and People's Daily using the aforementioned keywords to form a preliminary color words word list. Subsequently, noises are manually removed, and Python code is run to eliminate deactivated words. Finally, duplicates are removed, and names of named entities and non-Chinese constituents such as human names, place names, official names, etc., are excluded to form a color words and their related words word list. Due to the large size of the corpus, the number of word types used in the corpus is about 6 million words out of approximately 910 million word instances.

Furthermore, the words in the word list encompass not only words that simply denote the meaning of color but also words that are composed of color words. To prevent the inclusion of non-color words that do not express the meaning of color due to semantic generalization, the following provisions are made:

Words in the structure of "color word+noun" should be able to be directly mapped to a thing of color. That is, according to its semantic nature, the color word is retained if it still expresses the meaning of color in the construction; retained if the meaning of color is somewhat deflated, but the meaning of color can still be deduced; eliminated if the meaning of color is highly deflated. It is considered that the color words carried in the names of places, people, officials, and organizations do not belong to the scope of the study and are eliminated. For the color words and their related words in brand names, they are retained or eliminated according to the regulation. Category classification according to the position of the color indicated by each color word in the color gamut, combined with linguistic classification, is divided into 11 categories, namely, black, white, red, yellow, cyan, green, blue, purple, grey, 棕/褐(zōng/hè, Different Word Forms of Brown in Chinese), orange.

Based on this, a total of more than 4,900 color words and color-related words in the Shun Pao and People's Daily were finally assembled and used to explore the issues related to the category of basic color words. For example: 煤黑(méi hēi), 墨黑(mò hēi), 蓝宝石(lán bǎo shí), 蓝皮书(lán pí shū), 紫铜(zǐ tóng), 紫霞(zǐ xiá), 灰哔叽(huī bì jī).

4 Evolution of High-Frequency Theme Colors Over Time Evolution

4.1 Theme Colors in Shun Pao and People's Daily

Regarding the historical staging of modern Chinese, we adopt Diao Yanbin's statement that "the period of the modern Chinese national common language should start from the May Fourth Movement, and the period of 1840–1949 is the transition period from modern Chinese to modern Chinese". The publication of "Shun Pao" spanned from 1872 to 1949, and the publication of "People's Daily" has been ongoing from 1946 to the present. With an overlap of four years, these two newspapers are temporally well-connected, providing a solid foundation for our comparative study of modern Chinese color words.

In this paper, the basic color categories that appear more frequently in each historical period are referred to as "theme colors." By analyzing the changes in high-frequency theme colors across different periods, we can gain insights into the social environment, national culture and psychology, and the development of the characteristics of the times behind them. Table 1 and Table 2 illustrate the differences in the percentage of the total number of each basic color category in the 144-year corpus texts of the Shun Pao and the People's Daily.

Table 1. Differences in the total share of each basic color category in the Shun Pao

White	Red	Yellow	Black	Green	Cyan
35.09%	16.51%	16.40%	11.32%	6.72%	6.07%
Blue	Purple	Grey	Brown	Orange	
3.63%	2.46%	1.05%	0.42%	0.33%	

Table 2. Differences in the total share of each basic color category in the People's Daily

Green	Red	Cyan	White	Yellow	Black
26.18%	18.75%	18.52%	13.24%	10.22%	8.23%
Blue	Grey	Purple	Brown	Orange	
1.89%	1.31%	1.25%	0.31%	0.11%	

As can be inferred from the aforementioned table, our data results seem to contradict the cognitive order theory of basic color words. Although the category of "black" is in the earliest stage of the universal occurrence order of basic color words as per Berlin and Kay's theory, it occupies a significantly smaller proportion of the words in "Shun Pao" and "People's Daily" compared to the category of "white". However, the actual evolution process of basic color words in each language system is quite complex, and the cognitive order and high-frequency usage cannot be directly compared.

From a sociolinguistic perspective, "Shun Pao" and "People's Daily", as typical newspapers in modern and contemporary Chinese, cater to adult language societies whose language acquisition is already mature. The use of color words is a mature social-ization behavior for these societies, and the use of color words and the cognitive order of colors and their acquisition order have been decoupled in actual social life. Therefore, the cognitive order of color words has little impact on actual application.

Furthermore, the cognition of earlier colors follows different development paths. For instance, the "red" color category, due to its early generation, gradually differentiated in meaning. In addition to expressing "red", it can also be used to express "festive", "revolution", and many other meanings. It is also widely used in people's names, place names, and other naming entities. At this point, the meaning of the "red" category is not only limited to expressing the color, and its usage scope naturally broadens. On the other hand, the "black" color category, due to its earlier recognition, solidified into our basic concepts. In many cases, there is no topic, and therefore it does not need to be specifically mentioned. These are two paths in the evolution of the use of color words.

In addition, "Shun Pao" and "People's Daily", as regular newspapers issued earlier in China, needed to gradually explore the characteristics and norms of news writing, and had to bring new information. Therefore, for the earliest color to achieve cognition, if it doesn't carry a large amount of information, and has fewer varieties of words under its jurisdiction, it is naturally understandable that it has a low total frequency.

The chromatograms of the modern succession are obtained based on the frequency of occurrence of color words and their related words in the year-by-year corpus text of the Declaration and People's Daily. The chromatograms change over time (as shown in Fig. 2. Historical changes in the color spectrum of the Shun Pao and People's Daily). The chromatograms are interpreted in such a way that the longer the relative length of the color block represented by each theme color, the higher the frequency of its occurrence in that year.

In order to better explore the thematic color of each historical period and reduce the impact of data fluctuations in individual years on the results, this paper divides the 144 years of corpus texts into seven groups according to the publication time of Shun Pao and People's Daily, based on the major historical events and socio-political changes, which are the period of the Late Qing Dynasty, 1872–1911; the period of the Republic of China, 1912–1927; the period of the National Government, 1928–1937, the Anti-Japanese War period 1938–1945, the Liberation War period 1946–1949, Early Establishment of the People's Republic of China 1950–1978, and the period of reform and opening up 1979–2015.

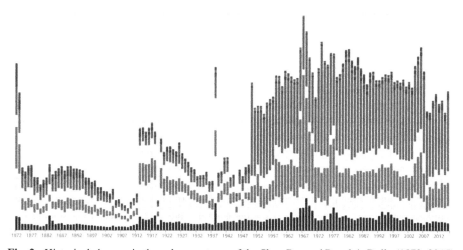

Fig. 2. Historical changes in the color spectrum of the Shun Pao and People's Daily (1872–2015)

4.2 Co-occurrence of Color Words in Shun Pao and People's Daily

Co-occurring words are terms that frequently appear together in a corpus and are often assembled in collocations. These words can be utilized to understand, to a certain extent, the semantic environment in which the color words are situated. The strength of the association between the co-occurring words also reflects, to some degree, the association between the semantics represented by these words. Since sentence-reading symbols only began to appear in the corpus of the Shun Pao in 1906, this paper extracts high-frequency co-occurring words within a span of 10 words before and after the words in the list of color words, according to the length of the article. To ensure that the high-frequency co-occurring words obtained are capable of revealing or expressing valid information, only nouns, verbs, and adjectives are retained as a result.

Simultaneously, items with the same or similar meanings were merged. For instance, "dressed", "wear", "wearing", and "wearing" were consolidated. More ambiguous ones were also eliminated. For example, "中(zhong)" can mean "中国(zhōng guó)", "中间(zhōng jiān)", "里面(lǐ miàn)", "中心(zhōng xīn)", etc., and such terms were excluded due to their ambiguity.

During the late Qing period, the themes of co-occurring words in mid- and high-frequency thematic colors were primarily centered around commerce and trade. This included merchant houses, advertisements, brand names, "sell" verbs, articles (mostly sellable commodities), and more. There were also references to European and American countries, such as foreign banks, Britain, and the U.S. The 1870s was a period of great prosperity for the foreign affairs movement. The foreign affairs faction recognized the importance of developing the national economy, leading them to put forward the slogan of "seeking wealth". As a result, the civil industry founded in the later part of the foreign affairs movement mainly put products on the market as commodities. This period of Chinese society saw not only a more prosperous domestic industry and commerce but also a large influx of foreigners and foreign goods. International trade also developed to a certain extent. The names of British, American, and other European and American countries were not only related to commerce and international trade but also partly related to foreign affairs. During this period, due to the location of "Shun Pao" in Shanghai, the economic development was more advanced and the concentration of the rented area was higher. The "Shun Pao" largely reflects the commercial development and the consumption and entertainment life in Shanghai in the late Qing Dynasty. The co-occurring words of low-frequency theme colors were mainly concentrated in landscapes and Botanical, etc., and were highly literary, which is due to the fact that the Shun Pao has published novels and essays for a long period of time.

The themes of high-frequency co-occurring words of each theme color were decentralized during the Republic of China period and the national government period. The themes of high-frequency co-occurring words of medium-high frequency theme colors mainly revolved around the fields of commerce and trade, agriculture, Medical science, Botanical, landscape, industry, etc., among which commerce and trade were related to the most. After the September 18th Incident in 1931, the advertisers of national goods linked the current situation with the goods, combined the consumption of national goods with the anti-Japanese salvation movement, and called on the national people to unite to defend the country against the enemy [18]. High-frequency theme colors in some parts co-occur with other theme color words in high frequency. The number of things related to color words increases in this period, and the description of the same thing or different things is more colorful. Since the period of the Republic of China, the use of color combinations of clothing and other commodities has become more varied due to the influences of social changes, social movements, and social trends. The co-occurring word of low-frequency theme color, "gray" is mainly concentrated in the textile industry. During this period, "gray beige", "gray cloth Gray cotton jacket" appeared very frequently, and the colors of popular clothing, shoes, and hats were mainly "black" and "white". The colors of popular clothing, shoes, and hats are mainly inclined to "black", "white" and "gray", which is also related to the fact that modern industrial products such as the textile industry are mainly put on the mass market as commodities. "Brown" is mainly centered on cosmetic products and their effects, commerce, and so on; "Orange" is related to the medical field, mostly related to medicinal herbs and diseases; "Purple" was mainly related to the medical field during the Republic of China, in addition to "copper wire" in the industrial field. During the Nationalist government, it was more diversified, not only with commerce and trade, Medical science, but also in the industrial field.

4.3   Evolution of the Coloring Domain of the High-Frequency Theme Colors

Color words, serving as adjectives used to describe colors, are integral to the language. They cannot be separated from the central object they describe, and the distribution and frequency of the use of color words are largely influenced by the coloring object. To better study the relationship between color words and objective things, this paper refers to the classification of the specific coloring object of the color words by Tang (2014). That is, the coloring objects are categorized into broad categories, essentially according to the nature of the semantic field of coloring objects, termed as the "coloring domain" [19].

The "People's Daily" and other sources are divided into 12 coloring domains in total. These include:

a) Fabrics: This category includes textiles, leather garments, flags, etc.
b) Food group: This category is for items that can be consumed by people, including eating, drinking, and smoking.
c) Objects category: This category includes various things and odds and ends in the production, office, and living areas.
d) Industrial: This category includes things in all areas of light and heavy industry, including industrial supplies and products, transportation, etc.
e) Human body category: This category includes things or expressions related to the organs and tissues of the human body.
f) Medical science: This category includes words related to drugs, symptoms, and medical organizations in the fields of Chinese medicine, Western medicine, and nursing.
g) Landscape category: This category includes the scenery presented in a certain area, including natural scenery and landscape architecture.
h) Botanical: This category includes varieties of non-edible plants in nature.
i) Animals: This category includes a variety of animals that actually exist in nature.
j) Political coloration: This category includes words with ideological or class coloration, words with bias in political position, legal, administrative, military, etc.

k) Religion: This category includes words with meanings or characteristics related to religion, including religious terms, religious concepts, religious objects, and divine beings and animals.

l) Other: This category contains cultural, economic, social idioms, social customs, etc.

These categories provide a comprehensive framework for understanding and analyzing the use of color words in various contexts. The categorization of the coloring domains of the Shun Pao and the People's Daily and examples are shown in Table 3.

Table 3. Examples of various coloring fields

Fabrics	青绸裤(qīng chóu kù), 素蓝哔叽(sù lán bì jī)
Food group	黄苞米(huáng bāo mǐ), 赤豆(chì dòu), 绵白糖(mián bái táng)
Objects category	红灯(hóng dēng), 红烛(hóng zhú), 黑玻璃(hēi bō lí), 黑板(hēi bǎn)
Medical science	赤色药丸(chì sè yào wán), 白滞丸(bái zhì wán), 黄芪(huáng qí)
Human body category	鼻赤(bí chì), 黄板牙(huáng bǎn yá), 赤瞳(chì tóng), 腹紫(fù zǐ)
Industrial	红洋漆(hóng yáng qī), 红铜(hóng tóng), 赤铁矿(chì tiě kuàng)
Other	螳螂捕蝉黄雀在后(táng láng bǔ chán huáng què zài hòu)

In the "People's Daily", the color word coloring domains "Landscape category" and "Industrial" have the highest number of word types. Notably, the proportion of the total word types accounted for by "industrial" has seen a significant increase. Following these are the domains "Food", "Botanical", "Medical science", "Animal", and "Other". The domain "Religion" has the least number of word types. This distribution of word types across different domains provides insights into the usage of color words in various contexts. It reflects the societal focus during different periods, as well as the evolution of language use in response to changes in society and culture.

Based on the above word list of coloring domains, the frequency and frequency of occurrence of words in each domain in the corpus text year by year are counted (frequency = frequency/total frequency of each coloring domain * 100%), and then classified and counted. Among them, those with a frequency greater than 10% are regarded as major coloring domains, and the major coloring domains in each period are as follows (Table 4).

In general, the main coloring domains in each period are primarily medical, fabric, landscape, food, animal, and others. In the "Shun Pao", medical advertisements accounted for a large proportion of advertisements and were issued continuously. These advertisements involved many diseases and herbs, such as "pus containing white", "white powder", "white turbid", etc. Therefore, the "medical" domain became one of the main coloring domains.

During the late Qing dynasty, the "fabric" field became one of the main coloring fields. Then, into the late foreign affairs movement, the foreign affairs faction began to build civil industry. Light industry during this period saw significant development.

Since the founding of the People's Republic of China, the highest frequency in the field of "fabric" is "red flag", followed by "three red flags" (a slogan of the Communist Party of China (CPC) put forward in 1958). The term "red flag" is the most frequently used term in the field of "fabric". The original meaning of "red flag" is "red flag", which

Table 4. Main coloring fields in each period

1872–1911	Fabric, Landscape
1912–1927	Medical science, food
1928–1937	Medical science, Food, Landscape
1938–1945	Medical science, Food, Landscape
1946–1949	Fabrics, food, animals, landscapes
1950–1978	Fabric, Landscape, Medical science, Food Group
1979–2015	Landscape, Other, Medical, Fabric

can also be used to denote the national flag of China, the brand name of an automobile, the name of a publication, or as a metaphor for the advanced, such as "Red Flag Units". It covers a wide range of fields including politics, culture, industry, and economy. However, its original meaning is "red flag", so it is also categorized into the field of "fabric".

The field of "landscape" has become the most important coloring field after the founding of the People's Republic of China, especially since the reform and opening up, which focuses on ecological protection. Green development has become the theme of the times, and the field of "landscape" has become the coloring domain with the highest proportion.

In addition, since the reform and opening up, the "other" domain has joined the main coloring domains, which contains mainly cultural, economic, social idioms, social customs, etc. The increase in the proportion of "other" domains reflects that the connection of color words in this period is getting wider and wider, and Chinese society is showing a diversified and solid development.

4.4 High Frequency Theme Color Ephemeral Characteristics

In the preceding discussion, we examined the contextual background of the era, societal trends, and historical events encapsulated within the color terminology. This analysis was conducted by scrutinizing the metrological characteristics, which include the frequency of high-frequency theme colors and recurrent co-occurring words. Based on the aforementioned data, the ensuing features can be encapsulated as follows:

Primarily, it is noteworthy that each era is characterized by a singular high-frequency solid theme color. In the corpus of modern Chinese newspapers exemplified by the Shun Pao, the high-frequency solid theme color is "white". Conversely, in the corpus represented by the People's Daily, the high-frequency theme color is identified as "green".

Secondly, the disparity in the color spectrum between the two distinct periods is considerably pronounced. This disparity is attributable to the social milieu, national cultural psychology, and the unique characteristics of the respective eras. The frequency of color terminology exhibits substantial fluctuations during specific years or periods. The frequency fluctuation of each theme color in the People's Daily is more stable compared to that in the Shun Pao. The data oscillation in individual years is less frequent and more moderate in the People's Daily than in the Shun Pao. This can be attributed to the fact that the usage of color terminology is intimately linked with changes in the social environment, significant historical events, and incidents impacting production and lifestyle. The social situation in modern China has been subject to sharp oscillations, with major historical events, political incidents, and wars occurring with high frequency. This has made it challenging to conduct social production and life in an orderly fashion, thereby leading to more drastic data reactions.

Lastly, it is important to note that different eras are characterized by distinct high-frequency theme colors. In the corpus of modern Chinese newspapers represented by the Shun Pao, the high-frequency theme colors are "white", "red", and "yellow". However, in the corpus represented by the People's Daily, the high-frequency theme colors are "green", "red", and "cyan". The temporal changes in high-frequency theme colors are primarily associated with the following factors:

The Birth of a New Style of Advertising in the Shun Pao. Advertisements were a primary source of revenue for the newspaper, with medical advertisements occupying a significant portion of the newspaper's space and being published continuously. In the modern era, among the words associated with the color "white," two of the top five most frequently occurring words were related to diseases, namely "white turbidity" and "white gonorrhea." This might be attributed to the fact that pharmaceutical advertisements constituted a large proportion of the advertisements in the "Shun Pao," which relied heavily on advertisements for its income. At one point in 1893, pharmaceutical advertisements accounted for more than 30% of the total advertisements, indicating their substantial presence in the newspaper. This prevalence of medical advertisements could have influenced the frequent association of the color "white" with medical terms in the newspaper's content [17].

Historical and Cultural Factors. In the discourse of historical changes in color terms, it is essential to consider historical and cultural factors. In China's traditional culture, "yellow," symbolizing harmony, is considered the foremost among all colors. This color holds significant importance in the cultural psychology of the Chinese nation and was once viewed as the symbolic color of the Chinese nation. "Yellow" has been a symbol of monarchical power since ancient times, and the monarchical dictatorship in the Qing Dynasty reached its zenith. Therefore, in the Shun Pao, a representative of the modern corpus, "yellow" can be considered the primary reflection of the social and cultural psychology of that time. "Red" holds a high status in the national psychology of the Chinese people, with positive connotations such as auspiciousness, festivity, and good luck. It is highly representative of Chinese color culture, hence its widespread use in modern times with a high frequency of appearance. With societal and historical development, "red" in modern times is associated with justice, happiness, progress, and red revolutionary themes. The scope of its use has further expanded, and it occupies a pivotal position in the culture of the Han nationality. The evolution of color terms is a fascinating reflection of the changing times and cultural shifts.

Evolution of the Lexical Meaning of Color Words. In modern times, cyan has rarely combined with black, and Yao Xiaoping (1988) [14] excludes cyan from the category of basic colors in modern Chinese, and thus considers it can be classified as a "green" color.

Social Thinking. In contemporary times, "green" and "cyan" have supplanted "yellow" and "white" as the high-frequency theme colors, primarily due to the prominence of agriculture and environmentalism. The Shun Pao, an urban life newspaper, was primarily targeted towards the middle class, petty bourgeoisie, intellectuals, and other elites of the time, with less focus on rural society. Since the establishment of the People's Republic of China, it has been recognized as a socialist country under the people's democratic dictatorship led by the working class and based on the alliance of workers and peasants. The People's Daily, as an organ of the Central Committee of the Communist Party of China (CPC), has the responsibility to publicize the Party's propositions and social trends. The CPC has traditionally emphasized its roots in the countryside, solidarity with the peasants, and attention to agriculture. Especially after the reform and opening up, with the change of social trends, in the category of "green" belonging to the People's Daily, the most frequent words belonging to the category of "green" in the early days of the founding of the People's Republic of China are "greening, green fertilizer, green, oasis, turquoise". In addition, the co-occurring words in the category of "green" and "green" in the early period of the founding of the People's Republic of China were mainly concentrated in the field of agriculture, such as "fodder, wheat, mu, crops", etc., but also put forward "green water and green mountains is the golden silver mountain" and other familiar slogans, visible "ecological protection" "Green development" "green life" has become an important trend in social development. Therefore, the fact that "green" became a high-frequency theme color during this period is mainly due to the importance that society placed on agricultural development and greening (the activity of planting Botanical to improve the environment) during this period. Green is the most distinctive color of China's development today.

5 Conclusion

This study conducts a comprehensive analysis of color terms and their associated words found in the Chinese newspaper corpus of Shun Pao (1872–1949) and People's Daily (1950–2015), spanning a total of 144 years. The analysis focuses on theme colors, co-occurring words, and coloring domains. It aims to explore the national cultural psychology, social development, and underlying connotations of these color terms, based on the changes in color spectrum over time and the basic theme colors in different periods. The utilization and evolution of color terms are intimately connected with policy shifts, socio-historical context, and cultural development, exhibiting a certain sensitivity to the zeitgeist. Different eras are characterized by distinct high-frequency theme colors. The shifts in these high-frequency theme colors are primarily associated with the emergence of a new advertising style in The Shun Pao, the evolution of color term meanings, historical and cultural factors, as well as societal trends. The co-occurring words of color terms have transitioned from the light industry field to the heavy industry field, and from the political field to a multitude of social fields, in tandem with the changing times. In contemporary times, the principal coloring domains of color terms encompass

Medical science, fabrics, landscapes, food, and animals. Since the establishment of the People's Republic of China, under the influence of a stable social environment, "other" domains have been incorporated into the main coloring domains, reflecting the robust development of social diversity in China during this period. In general, color terms are continually evolving with the progression of social history, production, and life, as well as the enhancement of people's level of understanding. The scope, variety, and connotation of color terms are constantly expanding, and the color spectrum is becoming increasingly rich. The coloring domain of color terms is becoming more extensive, and its connection with objective things is becoming more abundant. Color terms are increasingly detached from religions and regimes, and are widely used in various fields such as politics, economy, and culture. Their status is becoming more prominent, and the national cultural psychology and social customs they reflect are also changing.

Indeed, this study does have certain limitations. It does not include a newspaper corpus from 2016 to the present, which leaves the use and evolution of color terms in the recent period unexamined. The research primarily provides a macro-level analysis and interpretation, with data fluctuations in individual years not thoroughly studied or explained. These areas could be potential avenues for further research to provide a more comprehensive understanding of the topic.

Acknowledgments. Project supported by Youth Program of Humanities and Social Sciences of the Ministry of Education "Measurement of Vocabulary Usage in Chinese Newspapers since the Late Qing Dynasty" (20YJC740050).

References

1. Berlin, B., Kay, P.: Basic Color Terms: Their Universality and Evolution, p. 4. University of California Press, Berkeley (1991)
2. Yao, X.: A Review of the Theory of Basic Color Tones–Annotation of the Evolutionary History of Basic Chinese Color Words, Foreign Language Teaching and Research, vol. 1 (1988). (in Chinese)
3. Dong, Z.: An ephemeral measurement study of the text of the People's Daily. Heilongjiang University (2020). (in Chinese)
4. Huang, Y.: Cultural meanings of Chinese color words. Tianjin Normal University (2006). (in Chinese)
5. Li, H.: Expression of color categories in Chinese. Lang. Teach. Res. **06**, 56–62 (2004). (in Chinese)
6. Liu, J.: Composition of color words. Lang. Teach. Res. **02**, 71–77 (1985). (in Chinese)
7. Xue, Y., Yang, Zh.: Color words and color word theory. Res. Foreign Issues **2013**(01), 75–81 (2013). (in Chinese)
8. Xun, E., Rao, G., Xiao, X., Zang, J.: Development of BCC corpus in the context of big data. Corpus Linguist. **3**(01), 93–109+118 (2016). (in Chinese)
9. Xun, E., Rao, G., Xie, J., Huang, Zh.: Construction and application of an ephemeral retrieval system for modern Chinese vocabulary. J. Chin. Inf. **29**(03), 169–176 (2015). (in Chinese)
10. Yang, J.: A study on the history and current status of red color words. Nanjing Normal University (2020). (in Chinese)
11. Zhang, L.: Overview of color words in Upper Old Chinese. Sichuan University (2007). (in Chinese)

12. Zhang, X.: Study on the popular color vocabulary of clothing in the Republican period. Donghua University (2021). (in Chinese)
13. Zhu, X.: Research on the evolution of layout design of Shanghai Shun Pao. Hangzhou Normal University (2018). (in Chinese)
14. Wang, G., Rao, G., Xun, E.: Construction of verb-object knowledge base from BCC corpus. J. Chin. Inf. Process. (01), 34–42+53 (2021). (in Chinese)
15. Li, Z., Gao, T., Huang, G., Rao, G.: Modern Chinese diachronic corpus construction and the language development based on a 77-year corpus. In: Su, Q., Xu, G., Yang, X. (eds.) Chinese Lexical Semantics. CLSW 2022. LNCS, vol. 13495. Springer, Cham (2023). https://doi.org/10.1007/978-3-031-28953-8_29
16. Li, Q., Rao, G.: Militarization of newspaper language–diachronic study of war metaphor in People's Daily. In: Liu, M., Kit, C., Su, Q. (eds.) Chinese Lexical Semantics. CLSW 2020. LNCS, vol. 12278. Springer, Cham (2021). https://doi.org/10.1007/978-3-030-81197-6_50
17. Ge, Y., et al.: A Study of <Shun Pao> Medical Advertisements and the Concept of Hygiene in Modern Shanghai (1872–1901), Chinese Nationalities Expo, vol. 6 (2009)
18. Yu, F.: On the humanistic characteristics of Chinese color words. Northeast Normal Univ. J. **5** (1999). (in Chinese)
19. Gao, J.: Anti-war mobilization in wartime commercial advertisements - taking <Shun Pao> as an example (1931–1937). In: Studies on the Japanese Invasion of China and the Nanjing Massacre, vol. 1, no. 1 (2019). (in Chinese)
20. Tang, T.: A study on the measurement of color words in <Jinpingmei lexicon>, Ph.D. dissertation, Department of Chinese Language and Literature, Soochow University, p. 9 (2014). (in Chinese)
21. Mei, J., Zhu, Y., Gao, Y., et al.: An attempt to compile a dictionary of Chinese analogous meanings–an introduction to The Synonym Lexical Forest. Dictionary Res. **1983**(01), 133–138+47 (1983). (in Chinese)

A Study of Identification of Chinese VO Idioms with Statistical Measures

Xueyi Wen, Yi Li, Yuanbing Zhao, and Hongzhi Xu[(⊠)]

Institute of Corpus Studies and Applications, Shanghai International Studies
University, Shanghai, China
hxu@shisu.edu.cn

Abstract. This paper describes a study of unsupervised identification
of Chinese VO idioms by examining the Verb-Object (VO) pairs derived
from the dependency structure of sentences. We test several statisti-
cal measures, including Point-wise Mutual Information (PMI), $P(o|v)$,
$P(v|o)$, Salience, and Selectional Association. The experiments show that
PMI performs the best in automatically identifying real VO idioms,
which is consistent with previous studies on other languages. On the
other hand, PMI tends to rank low-frequency items (very often noise)
high. It obtained a 36% F1 score in the successful identification of real
VO idioms among the top 100 of the ranked VO pairs. We thus suggest
that syntactic features are not enough to identify VO idioms in an unsupervised framework, and more sophisticated methods with consideration
of more semantic information are required.

Keywords: Chinese VO Idioms · Multi-Word Expressions · MWEs
Identification

1 Introduction

Multi-Word Expressions (MWEs) are attracting more and more attention in the
NLP field as they pose a big challenge in various tasks including syntactic and
semantic parsing, information retrieval, machine translation, and others [1,2].
Among all kinds of MWEs, Verbal MWE, namely VMWE, is the most important category as it plays a key role in framing the core meaning of sentences. The
PARSEME project [3] is focused on the identification of VMWEs from the text
in many different languages. In the PARSEME annotation guideline, VMWEs
are divided into five coarse categories: verbal idiom (VID), light verb construction (LVC), verb particle construction (VPC), inherently reflexive verbs (IRV),
and Multi-verb construction (MVC). The five categories exhibit a big difference
in terms of both semantics and syntax and thus should be better tackled separately. The PARSEME group also held a series of shared tasks of automatic
identification of VMWEs in supervised framework [4,5].

There are many studies of identifying verb particle constructions with unsupervised methods [6–8]. However, few studies of unsupervised extraction of VO

M. Dong et al. (Eds.): CLSW 2023, LNAI 14515, pp. 42–51, 2024.
https://doi.org/10.1007/978-981-97-0586-3_4

idioms are available except for [9,10]. In this paper, we present a study for automatically identifying Chinese verbal idioms which typically consist of a head verb with an object, e.g. *wa qiangjiao* (lit. dig the bottom of a wall) 'undermine the foundation of something', *chi bimengeng* (lit. eat closed-door soup) 'encounter cold reception', and so on. We adopt an unsupervised framework for the identification of Chinese VO idioms. The method tries to differentiate the objects that form idioms with their head verb (e.g. *cu* 'vinegar' and the verb *chi* form the idiom *chi cu* 'be jealous') from all the other objects of the same verb that do not form idioms (e.g. *fan* 'meal' and *chi* 'eat' form the phrase *chi fan* 'eat a meal').

We try different statistical measures for the VO idiom identification: Pointwise Mutual Information (PMI), conditional probabilities $P(o|v)$ and $P(v|o)$, Salience, and Selectional Association. Experiments show that PMI performs the best in identifying VO idioms. Conditional probability $P(v|o)$ is the second best, implying that if an object strictly selects a particular head verb, they are likely to form a VO idiom. While PMI is very effective in identifying such idioms, there are cases they don't work very well. Particularly, when both the verb and the object are flexible, it cannot identify them very well. Among the top N lists ranked by different measures, the best performance is obtained by PMI at around 36% in the F1 score. This suggests that statistical measures alone cannot solve the task and more sophisticated methods that take more semantic information in consideration are needed.

The remainder of the paper is organized as follows. In Sect. 2, we describe in detail the statistical measures we use for the discovery of Chinese VO idioms. In Sect. 3, we discuss our experiments including the testing data and the performance of each statistical measures in identifying Chinese VO idioms from corpora. Section 4 concludes our study and lists out our future work.

2   Methods for Identification of Chinese VO Idioms

We use several different statistical measures that have been commonly used to identify MWEs in NLP tasks. The first one is Point-wise Mutual Information (PMI) as shown in Eq. 1. PMI has been used in previous studies for extracting MWEs in other languages [11,12].

$$PMI(v, o) = \log \frac{P(v, o)}{P(v)P(o)} \tag{1}$$

Salience is usually used to find salient collocations under certain relations, e.g. the typical objects for a particular verb as in the so-called word sketch [13]. The salience value of a VO pair is the product of the logarithm of their frequency and the PMI value, as shown in Eq. 2. It remedies the drawbacks of PMI tending to rank low-frequency items high.

$$salience(v, o) = \log(1 + count(v, o)) \times PMI(v, o) \tag{2}$$

Selectional Association, proposed by Resnik [14], was originally used to model verbs' selectional preference and has also been used for unsupervised MWEs extractions [10]. Selectional Association is defined in Eq. 3.

$$A(o|v) = \frac{P(o|v) \log \frac{P(o|v)}{P(o)}}{\sum_{o'} P(o'|v) \log \frac{P(o'|v)}{P(o')}}$$ (3)

We can see that the measures above are strongly associated with the conditional probabilities $P(o|v)$ or $P(v|o)$. So, we also include these two measures in our test list to make a more complete comparison.

To calculate the above measures, we first estimate the probability of $P(v,o)$, $P(v)$ and $P(o)$ according to Eqs. 4, 5 and 6, where $count(v,o)$ is calculated by counting all occurrences of a particular VO pair in the corpus. Then, the conditional probabilities $P(o|v)$ or $P(v|o)$ can be calculated through the Bayesian formula. Subsequently, PMI, Salience and Selectional Association can be calculated as well.

$$P(v,o) = \frac{count(v,o)}{\sum_{v'} \sum_{o'} count(v',o')}$$ (4)

$$P(v) = \frac{\sum_{o'} count(v,o')}{\sum_{v''} \sum_{o''} count(v'',o'')}$$ (5)

$$P(o) = \frac{\sum_{v'} count(v',o)}{\sum_{v''} \sum_{o''} count(v'',o'')}$$ (6)

3   Experiments

The goal of this study is to automatically identify VO idioms in an unsupervised way. This is achieved by differentiating the objects among all possible objects taken by a particular verb that can form idioms with the verb. The underlying principle is that idioms are usually featured with the so-called idiosyncrasy [9,12] or non-compositionality [10], which can be captured through statistical measures, typically PMI and others.

Since the syntax parsing accuracy has been very satisfying due to the development of deep learning technologies, rather than using window-based methods for calculating the measures we make use of dependency structures to extract VO pairs. Take the verb *chi* 'eat' for example. Firstly, we extract all its possible objects, i.e. words that form a 'VOB' (verb-object) dependency relation with the verb. Then, the measures are calculated for each object (type) it takes. Finally, all objects are ranked based on different measures. Ideally, the objects, e.g. *bimengeng* (lit. close-door soup) 'cold reception', *bawangcan* (lit. king-dish) 'dine and dash', and so on, which form idioms with the verb, will be at the top of the ranked lists. We can thus evaluate a statistical measure by measuring how many real idioms appear at the top of the ranked lists. For comparison, we calculate precision, recall, and F1 scores on the top-N items of the ranked lists with N varying from 1 to end.

3.1   Corpus Data and Processing

For experiments, we use the Chinese-English part of the OpenSubtitles Corpus of the Open Parallel Corpus (OPUS) [15]. This raw corpus contains over 150 million characters. We randomly chose 20% of the data for our study. We clean the data by removing garbled codes, extra blank lines, and non-Chinese characters from the original text. Moreover, traditional Chinese characters are transformed into simplified ones using the OpenCC toolkit[1]. Then, the sentences are fed into the LTP (Language Technology Platform) package [16] to obtain their dependency structures. Then, we extract all dependency pairs that form verb-object (VOB) dependency relations or front-verb-object (FOB) dependency relations (the object appearing on the left of the verb). All the VO pairs are finally saved for the next step.

3.2   VO Idiom Annotation

Annotating all VO pairs is very time consuming. In this study, we select 15 verbs that bear relatively concrete meaning and are also capable of forming VO idioms with proper objects are selected. Based on corpus we prepared, we count the frequencies of all the VO pairs regarding the selected verbs. The 15 verbs totally form 4,086 VO pairs (types). We find that low-frequency objects are very often noise caused by wrong word segmentation or automatic dependency parsing. To reduce the effect of noise, we exclude the objects whose absolute count is less than 3 or the frequency of the VO pair is 1. After filtering, 1,129 VO pairs remain for annotation. Finally, each of the VO pairs is manually annotated as idiom or non-idiom. Finally, 50 VO pairs are annotated as idioms. The details of the data are shown in Table 1

While for most cases, the judgment of whether a VO pair is an idiom or not is not difficult, there are several cases that are a little problematic. The first is when the object carries the meaning of an idiom and the verb also has a separate sense that can combine with the idiomatic meaning of the object. For example, in *kang zhongdan* (lit. carry a heavy pole) 'take big responsibility', the object *zhongdan* already has the meaning of 'responsibility' and the verb has the meaning of 'bear/take'. For such cases, we still label them as idioms since the literal meaning (i.e. carry a heavy pole) is still available. However, for the VO pair *kang zeren* 'bear the responsibility', the object *zeren* 'responsibility' doesn't have the meaning of a physical object that can be carried. In other words, the meaning of the whole is simply the combination of the verb and the object. So, we don't label such cases as idioms. The second problematic situation is when the VO pairs are ambiguous in terms of literal meaning vs. their idiomatic meaning, e.g. *dai maozi* which can express either the literal meaning 'wear a hat' or an idiomatic meaning 'bear a certain reputation'. For such cases, we also label them as idioms since they have the ability of expressing idiomatic meanings.

---

[1] https://github.com/BYVoid/OpenCC.

Table 1. Selected verbs, their frequencies, the number of objects (type) before and after filtering, and the number of idioms associated with the verbs.

Verb	Freq	#Object	#Obj-Filtered	#Idioms	#Examples
bai 'place'	226	141	25	5	bai wulong make gray cloud 'blunder'
bao 'hug'	710	212	52	1	bao datui hug thigh 'rely on'
ca 'wipe'	311	161	43	2	ca pigu wipe butt 'clear up a mess'
chang 'sing'	783	293	77	7	chang shuanghuang act two-man-comic-show 'echo each other'
chi 'eat'	7,671	1,554	506	12	chi doufu eat toufu 'take advantage of'
dai 'wear'	1,233	351	99	1	dai gaomao wear tall-hat 'flatter'
he 'drink'	4,306	552	143	2	he xibeifeng drink northwest-wind 'go hungry'
kang 'lift'	61	44	6	2	kang zhongdan carry heavy-burden 'take big responsibility
mo 'rub'	63	52	7	1	mo yanggong dawdle work 'pretend to work hard'
sao 'sweep'	111	67	11	3	sao xing sweep mood 'dampen one's spirit'
tiao 'pick'	394	230	51	3	tiao ci pick thorn 'nitpick'
wa 'dig'	405	182	52	3	wa qiangjiao dig the-bottom-of-a-wall 'poach members from others'
yao 'bite'	590	167	43	4	yao yaguang grit one's-teeth 'make unremitting efforts'
zuan 'drill'	57	42	9	3	zuan kongzi squeeze-in a-hole 'exploit an advantage'
Total	16,964	4,086	1,129	50	/

3.3   Experimental Result and Discussion

Based on the dependency parsed corpus as described above, we calculate all five measures for each object of a particular verb and then rank all the VO pairs according to the values. To evaluate and compare the efficacy of the five different measures in identifying VO idioms, we calculate the precision, recall, and F1 scores based on the top N VO pairs of the ranked lists. The result is shown in Table 2. We can see that PMI gives very high precision in the top 10 VO pairs, where 8 of them are idioms. The conditional probability $P(v|o)$ performs the second best. This means that the favor of a head verb given an object is a good indicator of being idioms. Salience does not perform very well in this task, which is not surprising since it is mainly designed to identify salient/typical objects of a given verb, which seems to be the opposite goal of identifying idioms. Selectional Association, although has been used for identifying VO idioms [9], it does not perform as well as PMI and $P(v|o)$ according to the experiment. The best performance in F1 score is around 0.36 obtained by PMI with the value of N between 50 and 100. Figure 1 shows the overall trend of the recall and F1 changes of the top N VO pairs ranked by different measures. Again, PMI performs the best among the five different statistical measures.

Table 2. Performance on the top N of ranked lists by different measures.

Top-N		5	10	50	100	300	500
Prec	PMI	**0.8**	**0.8**	**0.36**	**0.27**	**0.143**	**0.1**
	Sal	0.0	0.0	0.08	0.08	0.09	0.094
	$P(o|v)$	0.0	0.1	0.16	0.15	0.103	0.078
	$P(v|o)$	0.4	0.5	0.32	0.21	0.107	0.074
	SelAssc	0.2	0.2	0.24	0.21	0.123	0.08
Rec	PMI	**0.08**	**0.16**	**0.36**	**0.54**	**0.86**	**1.0**
	Sal	0.0	0.0	0.08	0.16	0.54	0.94
	$P(o|v)$	0.0	0.02	0.16	0.3	0.62	0.78
	$P(v|o)$	0.04	0.1	0.32	0.42	0.64	0.74
	SelAssc	0.02	0.04	0.24	0.42	0.74	0.8
F1	PMI	**0.145**	**0.267**	**0.36**	**0.36**	**0.246**	**0.182**
	Sal	0.0	0.0	0.08	0.107	0.154	0.171
	$P(o|v)$	0.0	0.033	0.16	0.2	0.177	0.142
	$P(v|o)$	0.073	0.167	0.32	0.28	0.183	0.135
	SelAssc	0.036	0.067	0.24	0.28	0.211	0.145

Table 3 shows the top ten VO pairs selected by the five different measures. We can see that in the list of PMI, most of the VO pairs are real idioms. The

Table 3. Top 10 VO pairs ranked by different measures. The '*' symbol indicates idioms. Note that only the verbs and the objects are listed, there may be other constituents appearing between them in real sentences.

	PMI	Salience	P(o|v)	P(o|o)	P(v|o)	SemAssc
1	mo fangzhu grind mill-owner 'mill owner'	he bei drink cup 'drink a cup of'	chang ge sing songs 'sing songs'	mo fangzhu grind mill-owner 'mill owner'	mo fangzhu grind mill-owner 'mill owner'	chang ge sing songs 'sing songs'
2	*zuan kongzi squeeze-in a-hole 'exploit a loophole'	he jiu drink wine 'drink wine'	bao wo hug me 'hug me'	*wa qiangjiao dig the-bottom-of-a-wall 'poach members from others'	*wa qiangjiao dig the-bottom-of-a-wall 'poach members from others'	*sao xing sweep mood 'dampen one's spirit'
3	*sao xing sweep mood 'dampen one's spirit'	he kafei drink coffee 'drink coffee'	he bei drink cup 'drink a cup of'	*yao yaguan grit one's-teeth 'make unremitting efforts'	*yao yaguan grit one's-teeth 'make unremitting efforts'	he bei drink cup 'drink a cup of'
4	*zuan yanli dig into the hole of X 'become indulged in'	chi dongxi eat something 'eat something'	he jiu drink wine 'drink wine'	chang waiwen sing foreign song 'sing a foreign song'	chang waiwen sing foreign song 'sing a foreign song'	he jiu drink wine 'drink wine'
5	*sao luoye sweep the leaves 'remove the rotten stuff'	chi yao have medicine 'have medicine'	yao wo bite me 'bite me'	chang loutaihui sing on balcony scene 'perform on the stage'	chang loutaihui sing on balcony scene 'perform on the stage'	*bai zishi make posture 'strike a pose'
6	sao yinmai sweep gloom 'dispel the gloom'	chang ge sing songs 'sing songs'	*sao xing sweep mood 'dampen one's spirit'	*he menjiu drink sulking alcohol 'drink alone'	*he menjiu drink sulking alcohol 'drink alone'	yao kou bite mouth 'have a bite of'
7	*bai wulong make gray cloud 'make a blunder'	chi wanfan eat dinner 'have dinner'	yao ren bite people 'bite someone'	*he tangshui drink sweet water 'drink sweet soup'	*he tangshui drink sweet water 'drink sweet soup'	mo fangzhu grind mill-owner 'mill owner'
8	*kang zhongdan carry a heavy pole 'take big responsibility'	he shui drink water 'drink water'	kang qiang take a gun 'take a gun'	*chi bawangcan eat king-dish 'dine and dash'	*chi bawangcan eat king-dish 'dine and dash'	bao wo hug me 'hug me'
9	*wa qiangjiao dig the-bottom-of-a-wall 'poach members from others'	chi wufan have lunch 'have lunch'	bao ni hug you 'hug you'	he bailan drink Baijiu 'drink Baijiu'	he bailan drink Baijiu 'drink Baijiu'	wa dong dig a hole 'dig a hole'
10	*bai choulian make smelly face 'make the face'	chi fan have meal 'have meal'	bai zishi make posture 'strike a pose'	chi shengrou eat raw meat 'eat raw meat'	chi shengrou eat raw meat 'eat raw meat'	he kafei drink coffee 'drink coffee'

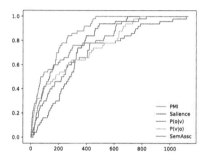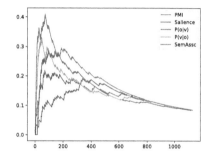

Fig. 1. Recall (left) and F1 (right) scores on Top-N of lists ranked by different measures with the value of N varies from 1 to 1129.

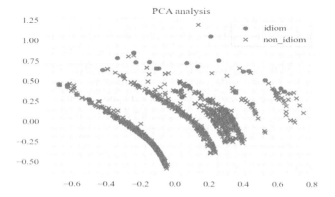

Fig. 2. Visualization of the distribution of VO-idioms and non-VO-idioms.

exceptions are *mo fangzhu* (lit. grind mill-owner) '(supposed) mill owner'[2] and *sao yinmai* (lit. sweep gloom) 'dispel the gloom'. Salience is mainly designed for identifying typical objects that may not necessarily reflect the idiosyncrasy of the VO pair. From its definition as shown in Eq. 2, we can see that it favors frequent items. Thus, there are no idioms ranked in the top 10 of the list. $P(o|v)$ has a similar idea to Salience in the sense that given a verb, it favors high-frequency objects. So, it also identifies typical objects rather than idioms. $P(v|o)$ implies a different principle from $P(o|v)$ in that given an object, it selects the typical verb that takes it. Take *bawangcan* (lit. king-dish) 'dine and dash' for example, whenever it appears, it is easy to predict that the verb that takes it as the object is *chi* 'eat'. However, for objects like *loutaihui* 'balcony scene', they have a similar effect that the head verbs are easy to predict and are thus ranked high by $P(v|o)$. Selectional Association is a combined measure of $P(o|v)$ and PMI in

---

[2] This is an example of parsing error. The correct segmentation should be *mofang zhu* 'mill owner'. The parser wrong recognizes this as a verb *mo* 'grind' plus an object *fangzhu* 'mill owner'.

that it takes both of them into consideration the logarithm part if equivalent to PMI as shown in Eq. 3.

The experiments show that the distribution of verbs and objects in VO idioms are to some extent differentiable from the others. We normalize the statistical data, select the statistical index, and then use PCA to reduce the dimension into 2 for visualization purposes. Figure 2 shows the distribution of VO idioms in a two-dimensional space. We can see that the VO idioms are generally located at the top part compared to others and are quite distinguishable from the others.

Although PMI shows a very high precision in the top-10 list, it fails to identify some VO idioms as well. According to its definition, it basically models the tightness of the VO collocations. Thus, for VO collocations with both a flexible verb and a flexible object, PMI is not good at identifying them. Take *chi cu* (lit. eat vinegar) 'be jealous' for example. The verb *chi* 'eat' can take a large set of objects. At the same time, the object *cu* 'vinegar' can also appear in a number of verbs. For such examples, we suggest that pure statistical measures cannot effectively identify them. Instead, semantics must be taken into account. There are studies of modeling the semantic 'anomaly' by comparing word vectors and contextual vectors. If they differ significantly, then it suggests the presence of idioms. For the example *chi cu* (lit. eat vinegar) 'be jealous', its literal meaning (reflecting the domain of dining) diverges from its context (reflecting a situation of being jealous). We will test this idea in future.

4   Conclusion

In this paper, we present a study of the automatic identification of Chinese VO idioms using different statistical measures. Based on the experiments on fifteen Chinese verbs associated with their objects, it can be concluded that PMI is good at identifying objects of the verbs that form VO idioms. Such discovered VO idioms share a common pattern that the objects strictly select the verb, i.e. with high conditional probability $P(v|o)$. This indicates the idiosyncrasy of Chinese VO idioms in terms of syntactic distribution. When the objects of VO idioms are flexible and can select a large set of possible verbs, i.e. with a relatively flat distribution, PMI cannot identify them effectively. Thus, purely statistical methods on the appearance of the verbs and their objects are not enough. A potential way to solve the issue of ambiguous VO collocations that convey both idiomatic and literal meanings is to consider the context and exploit more semantic features. We will explore this in future.

References

1. Constant, M., et al.: Multiword expression processing: a survey. Comput. Linguist. **43**(4), 837–892 (2017)
2. Sag, I.A., Baldwin, T., Bond, F., Copestake, A., Flickinger, D.: Multiword expressions: a pain in the neck for NLP. In: Gelbukh, A. (ed.) CICLing 2002. LNCS, vol. 2276, pp. 1–15. Springer, Heidelberg (2002). https://doi.org/10.1007/3-540-45715-1_1

3. Savary, A., et al.: PARSEME-PARSing and multiword expressions within a European multilingual network. In: 7th Language & Technology Conference: Human Language Technologies as a Challenge for Computer Science and Linguistics (LTC 2015) (2015)
4. Savary, A., et al.: The PARSEME shared task on automatic identification of verbal multiword expressions. In: The 13th Workshop on Multiword Expression at EACL, pp. 31–47 (2017)
5. Ramisch, C., et al.: Edition 1.2 of the PARSEME shared task on semi-supervised identification of verbal multiword expressions. In: Joint Workshop on Multiword Expressions and Electronic Lexicons (MWE-LEX 2020) (2020)
6. Baldwin, T., Villavicencio, A.: Extracting the unextractable: a case study on verb-particles. In: COLING-2002: The 6th Conference on Natural Language Learning 2002 (CoNLL-2002) (2002)
7. Chen, S., Yang, L., Zhou, J.: A study of nominal verbs in modern Chinese based on Shannon-Wiener index—case studies on "Bianhua" words. In: Su, Q., Xu, G., Yang, X. (eds.) Chinese Lexical Semantics, pp. 52–64. Springer, Cham (2023). https://doi.org/10.1007/978-3-031-28953-8_5
8. Zhou, S., Wang, C., Xun, E.: Recognition of disyllabic intransitive verbs and study on disyllabic intransitive verbs taking objects based on structure retrieval. In: Su, Q., Xu, G., Yang, X. (eds.) Chinese Lexical Semantics, pp. 265–282. Springer, Cham (2023). https://doi.org/10.1007/978-3-031-28953-8_21
9. Fazly, A., Cook, P., Stevenson, S.: Unsupervised type and token identification of idiomatic expressions. Comput. Linguist. **35**(1), 61–103 (2009). https://doi.org/10.1162/coli.08-010-R1-07-048, https://aclanthology.org/J09-1005
10. Van de Cruys, T., Moirón, B.V.: Semantics-based multiword expression extraction. In: Proceedings of the Workshop on A Broader Perspective on Multiword Expressions, pp. 25–32 (2007)
11. Baldwin, T., Bannard, C., Tanaka, T., Widdows, D.: An empirical model of multiword expression decomposability. In: Proceedings of the ACL 2003 Workshop on Multiword Expressions: Analysis, Acquisition and Treatment, pp. 89–96 (2003)
12. Fazly, A., Stevenson, S.: Distinguishing subtypes of multiword expressions using linguistically-motivated statistical measures. In: Proceedings of the Workshop on A Broader Perspective on Multiword Expressions, pp. 9–16 (2007)
13. Kilgarriff, A., Tugwell, D.: Sketching Words. Lexicography and Natural Language Processing: A Festschrift in Honour of BTS Atkins, pp. 125–137 (2002)
14. Resnik, P.: Semantic classes and syntactic ambiguity. In: Human Language Technology: Proceedings of a Workshop Held at Plainsboro, New Jersey, 21–24 March 1993
15. Lison, P., Tiedemann, J.: OpenSubtitles 2016: extracting large parallel corpora from movie and TV subtitles (2016)
16. Che, W., Feng, Y., Qin, L., Liu, T.: N-LTP: an open-source neural language technology platform for Chinese. arXiv preprint arXiv:2009.11616 (2020)

Sensory Features in Affective Analysis: A Study Based on Neural Network Models

Yuhan Xia[1], Qingqing Zhao[2], Yunfei Long[1(✉)], and Ge Xu[3]

[1] School of Computer Science and Electronic Engineering, University of Essex, Wivenhoe Park, Colchester CO4 3SQ, UK
yl20051@essex.ac.uk
[2] Institute of Linguistics, Chinese Academy of Social Sciences, Beijing, China
zhaoqq@cass.org.cn
[3] College of Computer and Control Engineering, Minjiang University, Fuzhou 350108, China

Abstract. This study proposes an ensemble model to incorporate sensory features of lexical items in English from external resources into neural affective analysis frameworks. This allows the models to take the combined effects of bi-directional feeling between the sensory lexicon and the writer to infer human affective knowledge. We evaluate our model on two affective analysis tasks. The ensemble model exhibits the best accuracy and the results with 1% F1-score improvement over the baseline LSTM model in the sentiment analysis task. The performance shows that perceptual information can contribute to the performance of sentiment classification tasks significantly. This study also provides a support for the linguistic finding that correlations exist between sensory features and sentiments in the language.

Keywords: Affective analysis · Sensory feature · Sentiment

1 Introduction

Affective analysis, a broader term for sentiment analysis and emotion recognition, is highly demanded in the social media text analysis. It is also crucial for various applications, such as opinion based product recommendation [1], opinion mining [2], and medical artificial intelligence (AI) [3]. Although affective analysis has been studied extensively using different methods applied on different types of data, text is one of the most important types of data so far [4]. Existing research on affective analysis mainly centers on learning features through the use of neural networks, such as Convolutional Neural Network (CNN) [5], Gated Recurrent Unit (GRU) [6], Long-Short Term Memory Network (LSTM) [7], Memory network [8], and Pre-trained transformer strategies [9]. Those models, though achieving promising results, have also presented drawbacks in terms

This work was supported by Central Leading Local Project "Fujian Mental Health Human-Computer Interaction Technology Research Center", project number 2020L3024.

of explainability, as their grey box approaches are unable to highlight the salient words or phrases that link to the affective information and thus contribute less to reflect human-understandable emotion components [10]. However, the neural networks approach, which learns from large-scale raw data while devaluing a myriad of existing external resources (e.g., linguistic ontology, cognition-grounded data, and affective lexicon), has showed great usefulness in feature engineering approach and could thus complement the automatic learn features for the neural model to human cognition process. Furthermore, with the recent neural cognitive trend in Natural Language Processing (NLP), it has been shown that modern language algorithms partially converge towards brain-like solutions among all NLP tasks, where affective analysis is one of the most cognition driven tasks [11]. Specifically, two phenomena rally behind the cognitive theories of affective analysis [12]. First, people react to the same event with a variety of different emotions, where the reaction is subject to individuals' biases based on their cognitive experiences. Second, different events may trigger the same emotion, as there are only a limited number of emotional reactions cognitively. Thus, cognition grounded data obtained in crowdsourcing should be helpful in building a cognitive driven neural model for the affective analysis.

This study incorporates sensory features of lexical items from external resources into neural affective analysis frameworks. This allows the models to take the joint effects of bi-directional feeling between the external knowledge and the text to infer human affective knowledge. To the best of our knowledge, this study is one of the first to explore the coupled effects of manually annotated affective vectors and neural networks for the affective analysis, which somehow involves the implicit engagement of human readers to help sentiment prediction. In the rest of our paper, Sect. 2 gives a review of sensory features in language resources, and Sect. 3 presents our models based on the sensory features. To obtain empirical evidence, Sect. 4 shows a series of experiments based on five benchmark datasets with comprehensive comparisons on different models. The last section is conclusion.

2   Sensory Features in Affective Analysis

The sensory features employed in this current study are mainly derived from the sensory rating task on lexical items, which has been initiated by Lynott and Connell [13]. In the task, participants were asked to rate the extent to which they can experience something denoted by a lexical item by feeling through touch, by tasting, by seeing, by hearing, and by smelling. Lynott et al. [14] have added one more dimension for the sensory features of English lexicon (i.e., the modality of interoception).

In terms of the correlation between sensory features and sentiments in the language, Winter [15] is one of seminal work. The study has found that sensory features related to taste and smell are more emotion loaded for English lexicon. Similarly, this pattern has also been observed for Mandarin Chinese [16], except that gustatory features are more positive, while olfactory features are more negative. Thus, this study presumes that the correlations between sensory features and sentiments should be incorporated into neural network models for the affective analysis in the text.

3   Our Model

This section elaborates how the affective awareness based on the perceptual features in the English lexicon is employed and incorporated into the neural sentiment classification frameworks for the affective analysis.

3.1   External Sensorimotor Resource

The external resource utilized by this study is The Lancaster Sensorimotor Norms [14], which was collected through the ratings of 3,500 individual participants of English native speakers using Amazon's Mechanical Turk 1 platform. The Lancaster Sensorimotor Norms covers the annotations in six perceptual modalities (touch, hearing, smell, taste, vision, and interoception) and five action effectors (mouth/throat, hand/arm, foot/leg, head excluding mouth/throat, and torso) for 39,707 lexical concepts. The range of the vector is from 0 to 5. As this study focuses on the affective analysis, we only employ the perceptual information in the six modalities, where the value of each dimension is denoted as v_j, $j \in [0, 5]$. For example, the vector of "blue" is $[0.25, 0, 0.15, 0.5, 0, 4.45]$, corresponding to the auditory, gustatory, haptic, interoceptive, olfactory, and visual score.

3.2   Model Structure

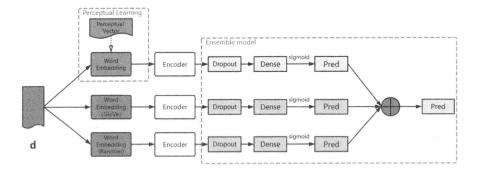

Fig. 1. The architecture of our model

Input and Output. The goal of sentiment analysis is to assign an affective label for a piece of input texts, reflecting the writers' attitude. The label types can either be binary for polarity indication or numerical for both polarity and strength. Let D denote a collection of documents for sentiment classification. Each document $d \in D$ is first tokenized into a word sequence with maximum length n, then the word embeddings W^i of these sequence are jointly employed to represent the document $d = \{w^1, w^2, \ldots w^i, \ldots w^n\}, \quad i \in \{1, 2, \ldots, n\}$.

To inject the sensory features into the neural framework, we apply a word embedding layer. We use perceptual vector to encode the input document d in Fig. 1. For sensory learning, each word embedding is first factorized into 6 embedding factors, each of which will be adapted to capture sensory semantics over each sensory dimension (i.e., auditory, gustatory, haptic, interoceptive, olfactory, and visual domains) through training. In other words, the sensory representation of the word is directly expressed in lexicon-level. For the other two groups, we choose the more traditional embedding models. One is based on the GloVe [17] pre-training model for word embedding, and the other uses random embedding.

LSTM encoder adopts the mode of gated mechanism, including Input Gate, Forget Gate, and Output Gate. Its core is Cell State, which refers to the state of the cell used for information dissemination. Memory Cell accepts two inputs: the output value of the last time h_{t-1} and the input value at this time x_t. Send these two parameters into the Forget Gate first, and get the information with less weight f_t. f_t is the information that we want to forget.

$$f_t = \sigma(W_f \cdot [h_{t-1}, x_t] + b_f) \tag{1}$$

Then we can enter the Input Gate and get the information to be updated i_t, which is the information with larger weight compared with the previous cell. Input Gate also gets the cell state $\tilde{C}_t$ at this time.

$$i_t = \sigma(W_i \cdot [h_{t-1}, x_t] + b_i) \tag{2}$$

$$\tilde{C}_t = \tanh(W_C \cdot [h_{t-1}, x_t] + b_C) \tag{3}$$

With Forget Gate and Input Gate, we can update cell state C_t.

$$C_t = f_t \cdot C_{t-1} + i_t \cdot \tilde{C}_t \tag{4}$$

Finally, the output values of the Forget Gate and Input Gate are combined to calculate the output signal h_t, where at the same time, h_t is also the input signal of the next time.

$$o_t = \sigma(W_o \cdot [h_{t-1}, x_t] + b_o) \tag{5}$$

$$h_t = o_t \cdot \tanh(C_t) \tag{6}$$

Ensemble learning. In the final classification layer, we should fuse the features from both the two regular representations learning branches and perceptual learning branch. To that end, the three branches first handle the sentiment classification tasks separately. The learned document representations from each branch are first fed into the dense layers with sigmoid activation to yield the sentiment prediction. The document vector v is a high level representation of the document and can be used as features for document classification:

$$p = \text{sigmoid}(W_c v + b_c) \tag{7}$$

We use the Binary Cross-Entropy of the correct labels as training loss:

$$L = -\frac{1}{N} \sum_{i=1}^{N} y_i \cdot \log(p(y_i)) + (1 - y_i) \cdot \log(1 - p(y_i)) \tag{8}$$

So far, we have obtained the sentiment prediction of three kinds of word embedding sources. Finally, the three branches are fused to the final prediction result through voting.

4 Experiment Results

Performance evaluations are conducted on two datasets and our model is compared with a series of commonly used baseline methods.

4.1 Datasets

The two benchmarking datasets include movie reviews from IMDB, and a toxic comment dataset [18]. For IMDB dataset, the reviews are collected from IMDB website, where each review is associated with a binary sentiment label indicating positive or negative polarity. The toxic comment dataset which is widely used for toxic detection and Kaggle competition founded by Jigsaw and Google. This dataset is seven classes and the types of toxicity are: toxic, severe toxic, obscene, threat, insult, and identity hate. We merge six types of toxic as positive, no toxic as negative.

Table 1 shows the statistics of the five datasets for experiments including the number of the train set, the number of test set, the ratio of classes, the number of vocabulary and the number of classes. They exhibit different characteristics, allowing the model evaluations in various scenarios.

Table 1. Statistics of the two benchmark datasets

Dataset	N_{train}	N_{test}	$R_{classes}$(pos:neg)	N_{voc}	C
IMDB	25,000	25,000	25,000:25,000	88582	2
Toxic Dataset	119,621	39,874	16,149:143,346	166465	2

4.2 Baseline Methods

To examine the effects of perceptual knowledge in experimental comparisons, three baseline systems are used in the evaluation in Table 2.

Their main settings are described as follows:

Table 2. Evaluation of different methods; best result in accuracy is marked in bold

Models	IMDB			Yelp13		
	ACC	F1	AUC	ACC	F1	AUC
LSTM-Random	0.865	0.856	0.857	0.962	0.803	0.868
LSTM-GloVe	0.880	0.882	0.883	0.964	0.805	0.871
LSTM-Perceptual	0.870	0.869	0.858	0.964	0.803	**0.877**
Ensemble Model	**0.892**	**0.891**	**0.889**	**0.966**	**0.814**	0.875

- **LSTM-Random** takes 128 dimension random embeddings to represent the document vectors and use LSTM as classifier.
- **LSTM-GloVe** takes the word embeddings of GloVe pre-train model to represent the document vectors and uses LSTM as classifier.
- **LSTM-Perceptual** takes the word embeddings of perceptual six-dimension-vector model to represent the document vectors and uses LSTM as classifier.
- **Ensemble Model** gets the final prediction is made by integrating the above three baseline models.

4.3 Performance Evaluation

The performance measures we use include Accuracy (ACC), F1-score (F1) and Area Under Curve (AUC) for our model. Table 2 shows the result of our experiment. In these two groups of sentiment classification tasks, Ensemble Model exhibits the best accuracy, but the accuracy of LSTM-Perceptual is less than LSTM-GloVe. This proves that for some vocabularies in some documents, perceptual information representation is helpful for sentiment classification. But not all vocabularies are applicable. The ensemble Model also achieves the best performance at F1 and AUC in IMDB. But the results are with only a 0.2% accuracy improvement over other models in Toxic Dataset. One possible explanation is that the toxic dataset is extremely unbalanced. As shown in Table 1. The ratio of positive cases to negative cases is only 0.11:1. Therefore the accuracy is usually very high and will not be greatly improved. In this unbalanced data set, the value of F1 is particularly important. F1-score can show the actual ability of the model on the unbalanced data set. Another reason may be that there are limited connections between sensory words and toxic language behaviors. The ensemble Model exhibits the best accuracy and results with a 1% F1-score improvement over other models. The above data shows that sensory information representation can improve the performance of sentiment classification tasks.

4.4 Case Study

To explore how sensory modalities knowledge improves sentiment classification tasks, we explore the specific case study. First, we chose the word "sad," which ultimately represents negative. In the GloVe pre-training word embedding, another word that describes negative "gloomy" only has a similarity of 0.36 with "sad." In contrast, in our perceptual space vector model, "gloomy" and "sad" have a similarity of up to 0.99. This shows that in some cases, the perceptual vector model has a more beneficial effect on sentiment classification than the traditional methods and makes the classification results tend to be correct.

5   Limitation

Despite the promising results achieved by our proposed model, there are still several limitations that should be noted.

Firstly, the external sensory resource used in our study, The Lancaster SensorimotorNorms, is limited to English and may not generalize well to other languages.

Secondly, the annotations collected through crowdsourcing may be subject to individual biases and variations in interpretation. Future studies could utilize more extensive, more diverse sensory lexicons and more standardized annotation methods.

Thirdly, our model mainly considers the lexical-level features, and it does not consider the context and discourse-level information, which might play a crucial role in sentiment analysis. Therefore, further research is needed to explore how to integrate contextual information with sensory features to improve the performance of the affective analysis.

Finally, our proposed ensemble model still relies heavily on the traditional neural network architecture with ensemble learning, which may not be the most optimal or efficient approach for incorporating sensory information. Future research could use alternative machine learning techniques, such as attention mechanisms or graph neural networks, to better utilize the unique features of sensory data and improve the performance of affective analysis tasks.

6   Conclusion

This paper proposes a novel cognition-grounded model to improve the neural sentiment analysis model through sensory features of lexical items from external resources. An ensemble model takes the combined effects of bi-directional feeling between the external knowledge and the writer to infer human affective knowledge. The ensemble model considers both textual and sensory features. Evaluations of benchmark datasets validate the effectiveness of our method in sentiment analysis and related tasks, as our method outperforms other baseline approaches that use local context information to build their neural models. Thus, sensory data containing significant affective meaning can be leveraged into affective analysis tasks. The ensemble mechanism can also be combined with other models to provide room for further improvement. An important finding of our work is that sensory rating data gives a better gain in capturing synonyms and is closely related concepts than original word embedding information. This explains the improved performance of the sentiment-related task. While in the toxic language detection task, our work has a relatively limited improvement.

Our work also indicates that the quality and scale of sensory lexicon greatly influence the ensemble model's effectiveness. We anticipate even more significant improvements with a larger scale of data in more fine-grained sensory information. Another future work is building a more deep-level fusing model by leveraging affective lexicon into both feature and model levels.

References

1. Dong, R., O'Mahony, M.P., Schaal, M., McCarthy, K., Smyth, B.: Sentimental product recommendation. In: Proceedings of the 7th ACM Conference on Recommender Systems, pp. 411–414 (2013)
2. Long, Y., Lu, Q., Xiang, R., Li, M., Huang, C.R.: A cognition based attention model for sentiment analysis. In: Proceedings of the 2017 Conference on Empirical Methods in Natural Language Processing, pp. 462–471 (2017)
3. Malins, S., et al.: Developing an automated assessment of in-session patient activation for psychological therapy: codevelopment approach. JMIR Med. Inform. **10**(11), e38168 (2022)
4. Lin, Z., et al.: Modeling intra-and inter-modal relations: hierarchical graph contrastive learning for multimodal sentiment analysis. In: Proceedings of the 29th International Conference on Computational Linguistics, pp. 7124–7135 (2022)
5. Kim, Y.: Proceedings of the 2014 Conference on Empirical Methods in Natural Language Processing (EMNLP), pp. 1746–1751. Association for Computational Linguistics, Doha, Qatar (2014)
6. Yang, Z., Yang, D., Dyer, C., He, X., Smola, A., Hovy, E.: Hierarchical attention networks for document classification. In: Proceedings of the 2016 Conference of the North American Chapter of the Association for Computational Linguistics: Human Language Technologies, pp. 1480–1489 (2016)
7. Chen, H., Sun, M., Tu, C., Lin, Y., Liu, Z.: Neural sentiment classification with user and product attention. In: Proceedings of the 2016 Conference on Empirical Methods in Natural Language Processing, pp. 1650–1659 (2016)
8. Long, Y., Ma, M., Lu, Q., Xiang, R., Huang, C.R.: Dual memory network model for biased product review classification. In: Proceedings of the 9th Workshop on Computational Approaches to Subjectivity, Sentiment and Social Media Analysis, pp. 140–148 (2018)
9. Fang, H., Xu, G., Long, Y., Tang, W.: An effective ELECTRA-based pipeline for sentiment analysis of tourist attraction reviews. Appl. Sci. **12**(21), 10881 (2022)
10. Nazir, A., Rao, Y., Wu, L., Sun, L.: Issues and challenges of aspect-based sentiment analysis: a comprehensive survey. IEEE Trans. Affect. Comput. **13**(2), 845–863 (2020)
11. Cambria, E., Olsher, D., Rajagopal, D.: SenticNet 3: a common and common-sense knowledge base for cognition-driven sentiment analysis. In: Twenty-Eighth AAAI Conference on Artificial Intelligence (2014)
12. Long, Y., Xiang, R., Lu, Q., Huang, C.R., Li, M.: Improving attention model based on cognition grounded data for sentiment analysis. IEEE Trans. Affect. Comput. **12**(4), 900–912 (2019)
13. Lynott, D., Connell, L.: Modality exclusivity norms for 423 object properties. Behav. Res. Methods **41**(2), 558–564 (2009)

14. Lynott, D., Connell, L., Brysbaert, M., Brand, J., Carney, J.: The Lancaster sensorimotor norms: multidimensional measures of perceptual and action strength for 40,000 English words. Behav. Res. Methods **52**(3), 1271–1291 (2020). https://doi.org/10.3758/s13428-019-01316-z
15. Winter, B.: Taste and smell words form an affectively loaded and emotionally flexible part of the English lexicon. Lang. Cogn. Neurosci. **31**(8), 975–988 (2016)
16. Zhao, Q., Huang, C.-R., Lee, Y.-M.S.: From linguistic synaesthesia to embodiment: asymmetrical representations of taste and smell in Mandarin Chinese. In: Wu, Y., Hong, J.-F., Su, Q. (eds.) The 18th Chinese Lexical Semantics Workshop (CLSW-2017). LNAI, vol. 10709, pp. 406–413. Springer, Cham (2018). https://doi.org/10.1007/978-3-319-73573-3_38
17. Pennington, J., Socher, R., Manning, C.: GloVe: global vectors for word representation. In: Proceedings of the 2014 Conference on Empirical Methods in Natural Language Processing, EMNLP 2014, pp. 1532–1543 (2014)
18. Wulczyn, E., Thain, N., Dixon, L.: Ex Machina: personal attacks seen at scale. In: Proceedings of the 26th International Conference on World Wide Web, pp. 1391–1399 (2017)

Corpus Construction of Critical Illness Entities and Relationships

Kunli Zhang$^{(\boxtimes)}$, Chenghao Zhang, Wenxuan Zhang, and Hongying Zan

School of Computer and Artificial Intelligence, Zhengzhou University,
Zhengzhou, Henan, China
{ieklzhang,iehyzan}@zzu.edu.cn

Abstract. Entity and relational corpus construction is a key part of information extraction and knowledge graph construction. Based on the existing norms of medical entity relationship at home and abroad, we established a disease-centered entity and relationship classification schema according to the characteristics of examination and treatment of cancer-related diseases under the guidance of medical experts. Combined with dictionary, rules, T-Roberta-BiLSTM-CRF entity recognition model and RoBERTa-GSI-PM relation extraction model, we annotate medical texts from multiple sources through multiple rounds of iteration. A Critical Illness entities and relationships Corpus (CIC) was constructed, guided by professional doctors throughout the process, and regular spot checks and consistency checks were taken to ensure the quality of the corpus. Finally, a corpus containing 64,735 entities and 47,222 triplets was constructed, and the consistency of entity and relation annotation reached 0.84 and 0.93, respectively. This corpus provides data basis for medical text information extraction of critical diseases and further research on a series of medical knowledge graph applications.

Keywords: Critical illness · Corpus construction · Entity and relationship annotation schema

1 Introduction

In recent years, the development of smart medical care in China has entered a new stage, and profound changes have taken place in the management mode of hospitals, public medical services and medical teaching and research work. Medical knowledge graphs and deep learning technologies are the core driving forces for its development. In this process, the first step is to transform the massive unstructured medical data into a computer-readable knowledge graph. Knowledge graph is a kind of the semantic web technologies, which is a graph-based data structure composed of nodes (entities) and edges (relationships between entities) [1]. As an efficient data storage method, medical knowledge graphs formally describe medical entities and their relations, such as <spneumonia, clinical symptoms, high fever>.

M. Dong et al. (Eds.): CLSW 2023, LNAI 14515, pp. 61–75, 2024.
https://doi.org/10.1007/978-981-97-0586-3_6

Knowledge extraction techniques, through manual or automated methods, acquire the fundamental elements of knowledge graphs, including entities, relations, and attributes, from medical data. Therefore, the construction of named entity recognition and relational extraction corpus provides data basis for medical information extraction and medical knowledge graph, and is further applied to medical knowledge search engine, clinical decision system, intelligent medical question answering and personalized healthcare service.

With the effective control of severe infectious diseases and the extension of human life expectancy, cancers have become one of the major diseases that seriously endanger human health. According to the cancer report released by the International Agency for Research on Cancer (IARC) of the World Health Organization in 2020 [2], lung cancer, liver cancer and breast cancer are the most common malignant tumors with the highest incidence and mortality. As the basic tool of teaching in colleges and universities, the power and rigor of teaching materials have been recognized by experts in the field. In addition, through the web crawler technology, medical knowledge can be obtained from multiple sources such as Medical Encyclopedia Website [3] and 39 Disease Encyclopedia Website [4], as a supplement to teaching materials.

Therefore, based on multi-source medical knowledge of major diseases, referring to the existing medical named entity relationship annotation schema, we study the characteristics of cancer text in terms of examination, clinical manifestations and treatment, and formulates entity and relationship annotation specifications mainly for lung cancer, liver cancer and breast cancer, which provides data for medical named entity recognition and relation extraction, critical illness knowledge graph construction and clinical data mining.

2 Related Work

Medical texts are usually semi-structured data such as electronic medical records and medical textbooks, and unstructured data such as clinical guidelines and medical journals. Among them, the research work of medical entity and relation extraction originated from electronic medical records. Electronic medical record is a typical form of clinical text, which is a digital medical record stored in the information system of medical institutions in the process of medical informationization. Since 2010, the I2B2 evaluation has proposed the challenge of entity extraction and relation classification for the application of natural language processing in medical text, and released a series of electronic medical record information extraction data sets, which provide corpus and benchmark for researchers, and the work of English medical entity relation extraction is launched. The entity types of I2B2 2010 [5] dataset are divided into three categories: medical problem, examination and treatment. The specific standards refer to UMLS (unified medical language system) established by the National Library of Medicine, and define the relationship between them. It is very difficult to obtain and label electronic medical records because of privacy. Mizuki et al. [6] proposed the TCIR-10 MedNLP task and 50 Japanese EMR annotated corpora. Because the annotated documents were fabricated by the physician, only including the contents of the complaint and diagnosis. These works provide a valuable reference for the research of Chinese electronic medical records.

The research of Chinese medical named entity recognition and relation extraction started late. Yang Jinfeng et al. [7]analyzed the structure and text characteristics of Chinese electronic medical records, divided entities into five categories: disease, disease diagnosis classification, symptom, examination and treatment, and emphasized the importance of modification information to entities. Finally, a large-scale and well-classified named entity and relationship annotation corpus of Chinese electronic medical records is constructed. Its division system, construction process and experience lay the foundation for the follow-up related research. Electronic medical record is closely related to personalized medicine, and electronic medical record in different departments has its own characteristics. Ye Yajuan et al. [8] combined the characteristics of diabetes electronic medical record format, added the modification information of time to disease and symptoms, and constructed the diabetes electronic medical record entity relationship database (DEMRC). On this basis, Chang Hongyang et al. [9] constructed the entity relationship corpus of stroke and cardiovascular electronic medical records.

Except for electronic medical records, there are researches on medical textbooks and multi-source medical knowledge. Zan Hongying et al. [10] developed an annotation schema including 12 types of entities and 45 types of sub-relations for multi-source medical texts. After manual annotation, automatic extraction was carried out by rule-based and machine learning method. The whole process was supervised by medical experts to ensure quality, and a large-scale knowledge graph CMeKG 1.0 including 106 common diseases, more than 200,000 entities and more than 1 million relations was established. Liu Tao et al. [11] constructed a pediatric entity relationship corpus and developed a pediatric medical knowledge question answering system on this basis. Zhang Kunli et al. [12] constructed the obstetrics knowledge graph in a semi-automatic way according to the characteristics of obstetrics data. In addition, Han Yangchao et al. [13] also optimized and annotated symptoms from existing knowledge graphs and mainstream medical websites, classified entities into symptom ontology, attack site and prone groups, and constructed Chinese symptom knowledge base.

After comparison, The characteristics of the existing entity-relationship corpora can be summarized as follows:(1) Only a few electronic medical records contain oncology data, and there is still a lack of multi-source cancer-related major disease corpora;(2) The text format and entity relation type of electronic medical record and medical textbook have different characteristics, and their classification schema is also different.

3   Critical Illness Entity and Relation Annotation Schema

Cancers typically refer to malignant tumors, and their pathogenesis, epidemiological characteristics, diagnostic methods, and treatment approaches differ significantly from those of other diseases. The characteristics of cancer-related texts can be summarized as follows:

(1) Cancer can metastasize to three sites: the site of onset, the site of involvement, and the site of metastasis.
(2) The staging of cancer is an important index for guiding treatment and judging prognosis, and TNM (Tumor Node Metastasis Classification) is the most widely used.
(3) Examinations for cancer are categorized into five types. Radiological examination, cytological examinatio, laboratory examination, tumor marker examination and ancillary examination.
(4) Cancer needs to be differentiated from benign tumors.
(5) Cancer is treated with comprehensive therapy, mainly surgery, chemotherapy and radiotherapy, sometimes interventional therapy, and other adjuvant therapy.
(6) The diagnosis of cancer should be combined with imaging pictures and imaging reports, in which the images are divided into pathological images and normal images.

Referring to the multi-source knowledge graph annotation schema [10] and the Chinese medical knowledge graph named entity and relationship annotation schema and specification [14], combined with the characteristics of cancer text, under the guidance of medical experts, the major disease entity and relationship annotation specification is formulated. The textbook is organized by semi-structured format, introducing different diseases according to a certain classification schema. For specific diseases, it covers most common types of medical named entity relations according to the structure organization of definition, epidemiology, etiology and pathogenesis, classification, clinical manifestation, examination, diagnosis and differential diagnosis, treatment, prevention and prognosis. Therefore, this schema is disease-centered and defines 11 types of entities. Table 1 shows the classification of entity relation annotation schema for critical illnesses. Relations between disease and nine types of entities was defined, which included 10 types and 39 subtypes. Terms and its definitions are interpreted in relation, there are also "Synonymous" relation between disease and disease, term and term, symptom and symptom, respectively.

Medical entities such as diseases, sites and terms, shall belong to one of ICD-10 classification and UMLS semantic types or be defined by Baidu Encyclopedia and Medical Encyclopedia. There are several basic principles for annotating named entities: First, non-overlapping annotation, that is, the strings of different entities can not be crossed; Second, no nested annotations, i.e., a string of an entity cannot appear on a string of another entity's string; Third, entities should contain as few punctuation marks and conjunctions as possible (and, or, and, etc.).

Explanation for Special Cases:

(1) If there is entity nesting, prioritize annotating it as a longer entity while ensuring semantic integrity. For example, in case 1, "Chest CT" (胸部 CT) should be annotated as a medical examination.

Table 1. Critical Illness Entity Relation Annotation Schema.

Subject	Relation		Object
Disease	Disease classification	Complications	Disease
	Differential diagnosis	Synonym	
Disease	Site of onset	Affected site	Site
	Site of metastasis		
Disease	Clinical symptoms	Clinical signs	Symptom
Symptom	Synonym		Symptom
Disease	Radiological examination	Cytological examination	Examination
	Laboratory examination	Tumor marker examination	
	Ancillary examination		
Disease	Pharmacological treatment	Surgical treatment	Treatment
	Radiation therapy	Interventional therapy	
	Adjuvant therapy		
Disease	Pathogenesis	Risk factors	Disease
	Pathophysiology	Genetic factors	
	Medical history		
Disease	High-risk population	Peak season	Epidemiology
	Epidemic region	Incidence rate	
	Mortality rate	Latent period	
Disease	Pathological imaging	Normal imaging	Image
Disease	Medical department	Prevention	Others
	Prognosis		
Term	Explanation		Concept
Term	Synonym		Term

(2) Differentiate between terms and diseases. In cases where it is "disease name + definition of the disease," the disease should be annotated as a term. For example, in case 2, "Acute Bronchiolitis" (急性细支气管炎) should be annotated as a term.

(3) Symptom entities may be separated by commas. When annotating, ensure semantic integrity and allow for the inclusion of punctuation marks. In case 3, "further increase and contraction of platelet aggregation" (血小板黏集堆进一步增大、收缩) should be annotated as a symptom. Symptoms such as "headache" (头痛), "nausea" (恶心), and "vomiting" (呕吐) should be annotated separately as symptoms, as shown in case 4.

Eg:

(1) Chest CT shows bilateral infiltrates in the lungs.

(2) Inflammation is a fundamental pathological process primarily characterized by a defensive response of living tissues with a vascular system to various injurious stimuli.

(3) Platelet aggregation further increases and contracts, forming irreversible platelet fusion clumps.

(4) Brain metastasis can cause symptoms of increased intracranial pressure, such as headache, nausea, and vomiting.

4   Corpus Construction Process

Xia et al. [15] divided the annotation modes into three types: Domain expert annotation, crowdsourcing annotation and group annotation. We adopt the mode of domain expert combined with group annotation. To ensure the reliability and professionalism of the annotated data, We have invited medical experts to supervise construction process, and the consistency is calculated by F score and other criteria. An efficient, user-friendly and full-featured annotation platform can greatly improve the efficiency of annotation and reduce the labor time cost. The annotation work is based on the entity relationship annotation platform [16], which is re-developed and deployed to make it applicable to the annotation of entity relation schema of critical illness.

4.1   Data Preprocessing

Table 2 is the statistics of the data sources of this corpus. The corpus mainly focuses on the critical illness related to lung cancer, liver cancer and breast cancer. Because *Internal Medicine* [17], *Surgery* [18] and *Medical Imaging* [20] are general practice textbooks, only the chapters related to the target diseases are selected, while the corpus from other sources is reserved.

Table 2. Data Source Description.

Source	Content	Structure	Size
Internal Medicine [17]	A book contains comprehensive description of medical diseases, chapters about respiratory and digestive systems are selected	Semi	1,180,000 words
Surgery [18]	Description of the disease from the perspective of surgical diagnosis and treatment, focusing on oncology, thoracic surgery, etc	Semi	1,000,000 words
Pathology [19]	The etiology, pathogenesis and pathophysiology of the disease were introduced in detail	Semi	430,000 words
Medical Imaging [20]	From the perspective of disease examination and diagnosis detailed introduction	Semi	200,000 words
Breast Cancer Breast-Preserving Therapy [21]	A comprehensive introduction to breast-conserving therapy for breast cancer	Non/Semi	380,000 words
Medical Encyclopedia Website [3]	Medical encyclopedia website covering diseases, symptoms, examinations and other medical health knowledge	Semi	180,000 words
39 Disease Encyclopedia Website [4]	Medical Encyclopedia website, including the introduction of the entry	Non	10,000 words

The original text is obtained from the electronic textbook through OCR technology and cannot be directly used for annotation. It needs to be further manually proofread and formatted, including the following processing: (1) Correction of wrong characters and punctuations;(2) Remove unnecessary blank space between texts;(3) Delete irrelevant contents such as headers, footers and references;(4) For picture only its title is reserved, and the table will be deleted completely. The text obtained in this way has consistency in format and content, which is convenient for the training of labeling personnel.

It requires some domain knowledge for annotators, so we train the annotators by selecting some typical texts with comprehensive coverage as pre-annotation texts. Notice that the schema will be updated and improved during the formal annotation process. When formally annotating, the textbook text is annotated manually, and the multi-source medical knowledge is annotated automatically and manually. The construction process of the corpus is shown in Fig. 1.

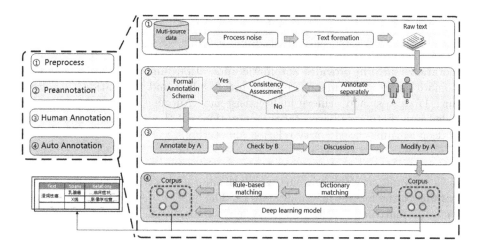

Fig. 1. Construction of Entity Relation Corpus of Critical Illness.

4.2   Human Annotation

We adopt the group annotation mode, supplemented by the supervision of domain experts. The annotation work is done in stages, with each stage annotating a batch of text. In order to improve the quality of labeled text and reduce unnecessary rework, we control the quality of labeling through the following measures:

(1) During the whole annotation cycle, problems where the annotator can not determine and schema that need to be improved, will be recorded in shared documents and discussed regularly.

(2) At each stage, each text file will be annotated three times by two persons. Person A shall annotate the original text for the first time, and person B shall check the inconsistent annotated text for the second time. Two persons shall discuss and confirm the reasonable solution. For the unsettled question, will be discussed by and the correction work shall be finished by person A.

(3) Regularly spot check the text that has been marked, so that timely find out the problems of annotators.

(4) Considering that the quality of entity annotation will affect the quality of relation annotation, annotators shall annotate all entities before their relations.

(5) The group has the guidance of doctors to ensure the rationality of annotation schema.

4.3   Automatic Annotation

Although the accuracy is high, manual labeling is time-consuming and laborious, and the scale of manual annotation data is still very small compared with massive medical texts, while automatic annotation can quickly supplement new corpus with manual annotation data, taking into account both scale and efficiency. The annotation platform provides automatic annotation functions. On the basis of automatic annotation, manual further proofreading and annotation can often reduce labor cost and achieve high consistency. Automatic annotation can be divided into dictionary-based entity annotation, rule-based relation annotation and deep learning-based entity relation annotation.

Dictionary-Based Entity Annotation. Dictionary-based entity annotation has the advantage of high accuracy, which automatically tags entities in text according to the longest matching pattern. The quality of the dictionary greatly affects the matching result. After manually annotating a part of the data, we obtain an initial dictionary. Before application, the dictionary needs to be manually optimized. Untypical entities, such as "hepatitis", can contain prefixes of variable length (viral hepatitis, chronic hepatitis), which are not necessarily in the dictionary and can cause mismatches, so atypical entities should be filtered out. Long entities are rarely matched, such as "thyroid follicular epithelial cell hypertrophy", should be deleted. In addition, the entity type of "hypertension" and "edema" require context to determine (diseases or symptoms), such entities are also deleted. The annotation platform provides the function based on dictionary matching, so in the subsequent annotation process, the entity is automatically annotated by the dictionary first, and then manually proofread and annotated on this basis.

Rule-Based Relation Annotation. Rule-based relational annotation needs to be performed on the basis of entity annotation. There are certain patterns in the text between entity pairs, by summarizing the annotated text, we can construct a specific rule set for each relation. Taking the relation subtype of "clinical symptoms" as an example, the construction process is as follows. First, count all the sentences that contain the relation, and summarize the phrases that indicate the existence of the relation. For example, when the text format between the disease entity and the symptom entity is "clinically manifested as", "clinically present", "major ictal symptoms include", etc., there is usually a clinical symptom relationship between the entities. Then it is formulated as a regular expression according to the pattern of "modification+keyword+entity". For the algorithm, based on the result of entity annotation, the regular expression matching method is used to determine whether the relationship between disease entity and symptom entity exists. 3lists the rule definitions and examples for the Clinical Symptom relationship subtype (Table 3).

Table 3. Rule-based relation annotation example.

Heuristic rule	{modification}+ {keyword}+{entity}	Example: Patients with decompensated liver cirrhosis may exhibit a rapid increase in ascites.
	{modification}+ {keyword}+{entity}+ {modification}+{keyword}	Example: Hepatitis A and hepatitis E are acute in onset and often have symptoms such as fever, chills, abdominal pain and nausea in the early stage.
Modification	Clinical symptoms	may,mainly,usually,will,...
keyword		Clinical symptoms include,Clinical presentation is characterized by,Lead to,Accompanied by,Noted as,Symptoms comprise,Symptoms such as,

Entity Relation Annotation Based on Deep Learning. In order to analyze the performance of the corpus on the deep learning model, we conducted experiments on the current mainstream entity recognition and relation extraction models. These model can be directly applied to the algorithm factory of the annotation platform, and the effect is better than the method based on dictionary and rules. The automatic annotation is carried out in the later stage of the annotation project, thus further reducing the labor cost.

(1) T-Roberta-BiLSTM-CRF

For the entity recognition task, the T-Roberta-BiLSTM-CRF model [22] is used for experiments. As shown in Fig. 2, the model combines the characteristics of medical data from different sources and further trains the corpus as the target data. The model is composed of source module and target module, the source domain is a RoBERTa model, the source task is to use medical data to fine-tune the RoBERTa model, and the learned parameters will be further embedded as the target domain. The target domain consists of an embedding layer, an encoding layer, and a decoding layer, and the target task is to train and test the model using the target data.The RoBERTa model is a pre-trained model, which converts each word in the text into a vector, which is used as the input of the downstream task structure model BiLSTM layer. The BiLSTM layer outputs the vector representation combined with the context, and then completes the entity recognition through the CRF layer. We divide the data into 9928 training set, 1241 validation set and 1242 test set according to the ratio of 8:1:1. The parameters in the experiment are set as follows: Learning rate 3e-4, dropout ratio 0.5, character embedding dimension 200, batch size 12, training rounds 30.

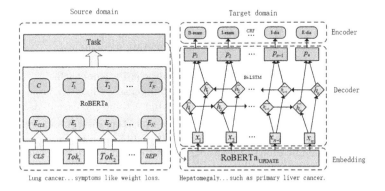

Fig. 2. The framework of T-Roberta-BiLSTM-CRF.

Table 4. Results of T-Roberta-BiLSTM-CRF model.

type	P(%)	R(%)	F1(%)
Disease	89.08	85.19	87.09
Symptom	68.41	73.83	71.02
Examination	85.62	85.62	85.62
Site	85.67	78.91	82.15
Other	70.58	92.30	80.00
Treatment	87.07	87.61	87.34
Image	71.79	70.0	70.88
Term	73.25	91.30	81.29
Epidemiology	69.38	77.27	73.11
Sociology	69.06	69.06	69.06
Definition	64.10	60.97	62.5
All	82.66	81.77	80.21

The results of entity recognition are shown in Table 4, and the overall F1 score is 80.21%, which is close to the level of manual labeling. "Disease", "examination", "site" and "treatment" reap high F1 score because they are shorter strings and have relatively specific boundaries. However, entities such as "epidemiology", "sociology", "concept", etc. are usually longer, and there is less instances for "image" and "other" entities, so the performance of these entity types is low.

(2) RoBERTa-GSI-PM model

For the relation extraction task, we used the RoBERTa-GSI-PM model [23], as shown in Fig. 3. The model integrates graph structure information through GCN, uses triples related to critical illnesses as external knowledge embeddings, fuses with text embeddings to get input representation, then extracts entities through pointer network, and finally completes relation classification through multiple heads. The word embedding part of the model consists of two parts, which are respectively from the outputs of the RoBERTa and GCN models, and the two output vectors are spliced and input into the pointer network for entity recognition, and then pass through a Sigmoid layer, and finally, multi-head selection is carried out for the relationship classification between entity pairs, which can effectively solve the problem of triple overlap. The data was split in a 7:1:2 ratio to yield 13683 training, 1955 validation, and 3910 test sets. The whole network has a learning rate of 5e-5, dropout ratio of 0.5, word vector embedding dimension of 300, batch size of 4, and 70 training epochs.

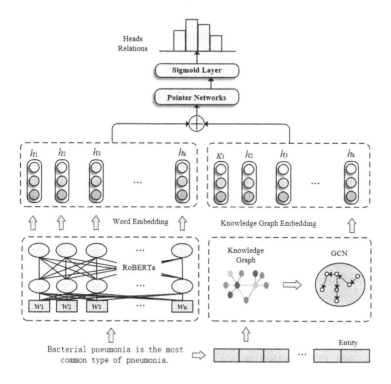

Fig. 3. The framework of RoBERTa-GSI-PM model.

Table 5 shows the experimental results. It can be seen that the precision of relation extraction reaches 80.38%, and the recall rate is lower than the accuracy rate, which is due to the fact that the multi-choice classification method may extract redundant relations. Except the results of disease-image and disease-sociology were lower, the F1 values of other relations reached more than 75%, which was consistent with the situation of manual annotation.

Table 5. Result of Relation Extraction from Roberta-GSI-PM Model.

type	P(%)	R(%)	F1(%)
Disease -Disease	82.65	73.52	77.82
Disease-Symptom	78.26	74.14	76.15
Disease-Site	79.74	73.08	76.26
Disease-Sociology	81.29	65.96	72.83
Disease-Epidemiology	81.22	78.34	79.75
Disease-Examination	78.51	76.77	77.63
Disease-Treatment	79.93	79.66	79.79
Disease-Image	71.42	66.37	68.80
Disease-Other	81.01	83.11	82.05
Term-Definition	88.00	66.66	75.86
Term-Term	86.96	80.80	83.76
All	80.38	75.41	77.81

5 Construction Results and Analysis

Annotation, is also essentially a process of classification, and consistency is generally measured by kappa value [24] or F score [25]. If the unlabeled text is used as the negative example of the named entity annotation, the number of negative examples is too large to be counted. In this case, the F score is close to the kappa value, so the F value is used to measure the consistency of the annotation in our work. Among them, the consistency of named entities and relations reaches 0.8431 and 0.9386, respectively. Both of them reach 0.8, which indicates that the consistency of annotations is reliable [26].

In the whole process, more than 3.56 million words of text are annotated, which are transformed into the common formats of named entity dataset and relation extraction dataset respectively, and some errors caused by manual operation are filtered out. 64,735 entities and 47,222 relation triples are obtained. See Fig. 4 for more detailed statistics. As shown in Figure, disease type entities have the largest number, which shows the rationality of disease-centric schema to some extent. There are also a certain number of other types, such as site, symptoms, treatment, examination, sociology, term and epidemiology, which are more frequently used in practical applications, and similarly, the number of relations between them is relatively large.

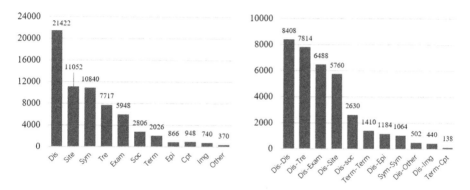

Fig. 4. Entity and relation quantity statistics.

In order to show the results of corpus construction more intuitively, we store the entities and their relations in the form of knowledge graph through the annotation platform. Each disease is visualized in a disease-centric manner and can be quickly searched by disease name. As shown in Fig. 5, circular nodes represent entities, and arrows represent relationships, which can be interpreted as: Bronchial lung cancer needs to be differentiated from chronic bronchitis and obstructive pneumonia. The population over 40 years old is the most frequent population. Chest CT, bronchoscopy and other imaging examinations can be taken during examination. The clinical symptoms are often high-pitched dry cough accompanied by dyspnea.

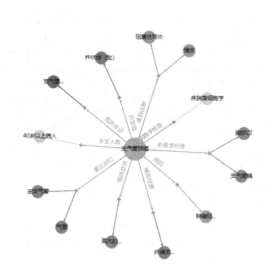

Fig. 5. Example of Visualization of Corpus Construction Results.

6 Conclusion

We studied the construction process of entity and relation corpus of critical ill-nesses. Referring to the existing medical entity and relationship classification systems at home and abroad, the characteristics of diagnosis and treatment of cancer text are analyzed, and the entity and relationship annotation schema of critical illness knowledge graph based on lung cancer, liver cancer and breast cancer is formulated. Then, the multi-source medical texts are annotated by a series of automatic annotation methods based on dictionary, rule and deep learning in the way of domain expert + group annotation, and the corpus of critical illness entities and relations is constructed in a multi-round iterative mode. In the whole process, various methods are combined to control the quality of corpus. Finally, a corpus containing 64,735 entities and 47,222 triples is constructed, and the consistency of entity and relation is 0.8431 and 0.9386 respectively. The corpus can be further used for medical text information extraction and medical knowledge graph construction, which is of great significance to the auxiliary diagnosis of critical illnesses, intelligent question answering and personalized medical service development.

Acknowledgments. We thank the anonymous reviewers for their constructive comments, and gratefully acknowledge the support of Major Science and Technology Project of Yunnan Province (202102AA100021), and Henan Province Science and Technology Department Science and Technology Tackling Project(232102211033).

References

1. Wikipedia. Knowledge graph. https://en.wikipedia.org/wiki/Knowledge_Graph. Accessed 23 Nov 2023
2. Wild, C.P., Weiderpass, E., Stewart, B.W.: World Cancer Report: Cancer Research for Cancer Prevention. International Agency for Research on Cancer, Lyon (2020)
3. Medical Encyclopedia Website. https://www.wiki8.com/. Accessed 23 Nov 2023
4. 39 Disease Encyclopedia Website. https://jbk.39.net/. Accessed 23 Nov 2023
5. Uzuner, Ö., South, B.R., Shen, S., et al.: 2010 i2b2/VA challenge on concepts, assertions, and relations in clinical text. J. Am. Med. Inform. Assoc. **18**(5), 552–556 (2011)
6. Morita, M., Kano, Y., Ohkuma, T., et al.: Overview of the NTCIR-10 MedNLP Task. NTCIR (2013)
7. Yang, J.F., et al.: Corpus construction for named entities and entity relations on Chinese electronic medical records. Ruan Jian Xue Bao/J. Softw. **27**(11), 2725–2746 (2016)
8. Ye, Y., Hu, B., Zhang, K., et al.: Construction of corpus for entity and relation annotation of diabetes electronic medical records. In: Proceedings of the 20th Chinese National Conference on Computational Linguistics, pp. 622–632 (2021)
9. Chang, H., Zan, H., Ma, Y., et al.: Corpus construction for named-entity and entity relations for electronic medical records of stroke disease. In: Proceedings of the 20th Chinese National Conference on Computational Linguistics, pp. 633–642 (2021)

10. Zan, H., Dou, H., Jia, Y., et al.: Construction of chinese medical knowledge graph bsed on multi-source Corpus. J. Zhengzhou Univ. (Nat. Sci. Edn.) **52**(2), 45–51 (2020)
11. Zan, H., Liu, T., Niu, C., Zhao, Y., Zhang, K., Sui, Z.: Construction and application of named entity and entity relations corpus for pediatric diseases. J. Chin. Inf. Process. **34**(5), 19–26 (2020)
12. Zhang, K., Hu, C., Song, Y., Zan, H., Zhao, Y., Chu, W.: Construction of chinese obstetrics knowledge graph based on the multiple sources data. In: Dong, M., Gu, Y., Hong, J.-F. (eds.) Chinese Lexical Semantics: 22nd Workshop, CLSW 2021, Nanjing, 15–16 May 2021, Revised Selected Papers, Part II, pp. 399–410. Springer, Cham (2022). https://doi.org/10.1007/978-3-031-06547-7_31
13. Zan, H., Han, Y., Fan, Y., et al.: Construction and analysis of symptom knowledge base in Chinese. J. Chin. Inf. Process. **34**(4), 30–37 (2020)
14. Yue, D., Zhang, K., Zhuang, L., Zhao, X., Byambasuren, O., Zan, H.: Annotation scheme and specification for named entities and relations on Chinese medical knowledge graph. In: Hong, J.-F., Zhang, Y., Liu, P. (eds.) Chinese Lexical Semantics: 20th Workshop, CLSW 2019, Beijing, China, June 28–30, 2019, Revised Selected Papers, pp. 563–574. Springer, Cham (2020). https://doi.org/10.1007/978-3-030-38189-9_58
15. Xia, F., Yetisgen-Yildiz, M.: Clinical corpus annotation: challenges and strategies. In: Proceedings of the Third Workshop on Building and Evaluating Resources for Biomedical Text Mining (BioTxtM 2012) in Conjunction with the International Conference on Language Resources and Evaluation (LREC), Istanbul, pp. 21–27 (2012)
16. Zhang, K., Zhao, X., Guan, T., et al.: A Platform for entity and entity relationship labeling in medical texts. J. Chin. Inf. Process. **34**(6), 117–125 (2020)
17. Ge Junbo, X., Yongjian, W.C.: Internal Medicine, 9th edn. People's Medical Publishing House, Beijing (2018)
18. Xiaoping, C., Jianping, W., Jizong, Z.: Surgery, 9th edn. People's Medical Publishing House, Beijing (2018)
19. Hong, B., Yilei, L.: Pathology, 9th edn. People's Medical Publishing House, Beijing (2018)
20. Ke, X., Qiyong, G., Ping, H.: Medical Imaging, 9th edn. People's Medical Publishing House, Beijing (2019)
21. Benyao, L.: Breast Cancer Breast-Preserving Therapy. Tsinghua University Publishing House, Beijing (2004)
22. Zhang, K., Zhang, C., Ye, Y., et al.: Named entity recognition in electronic medical records based on transfer learning. In: Proc. Int. Conf. Intell. Med. Health **2022**, 91–98 (2022)
23. Song, Y., Zhang, W., Ye, Y., et al.: Knowledge-enhanced relation extraction in Chinese EMRs. In: 2022 5th International Conference on Machine Learning and Natural Language Processing, pp. 196–201 (2022)
24. Jean, C.: Assessing agreement on classification tasks: the kappa statistic. Comput. Linguist. **22**(2), 249–254 (1996)
25. Hripcsak, G., Rothschild, A.S.: Agreement, the f-measure, and reliability in information retrieval. J. Am. Med. Inform. Assoc. **12**(3), 296–298 (2005)
26. Artstein, R., Poesio, M.: Inter-coder agreement for computational linguistics. Comput. Linguist. **34**(4), 555–596 (2008)

Research on the Structure of Pediatric Epilepsy Electronic Medical Records Based on Transfer Learning

Yu Song[1], Pengcheng Wu[1], Dongming Dai[1], Kunli Zhang[1], Chenghao Zhang[1], Hengxing Zhang[3(✉)], Xiaomei Liu[2], and Jie Li[3]

[1] School of Computer and Artificial Intelligence, Zhengzhou University, Zhengzhou 450001, Henan, China
[2] Kunming Children's Hospital, Kunming 650032, Yunnan, China
[3] Zhengzhou Zhongye Technology Co., Ltd., Zhengzhou 450001, Henan, China
729348611@qq.com

Abstract. Medical institutions commonly utilize electronic medical records (EMRs) to document patients' medical conditions, which contain valuable medical information. However, EMRs often consist of semi-structured or unstructured data, presenting significant challenges in processing and analysis. This paper addresses the needs of subsequent tasks such as assisting diagnosis and information extraction (IE). We present the process of structuring electronic health records based on pediatric epilepsy cases, including EMRs structural analysis, data preprocessing, named entity recognition (NER), and data integration. NER is a critical step in the processing pipeline. Therefore, we propose a pediatric epilepsy EMRs entity recognition model, T-RoBERTa-BiLSTM-CRF, based on transfer learning. After training on the constructed pediatric epilepsy dataset, T-RoBERTa-BiLSTM-CRF is used to perform NER tasks in EMRs structuring, achieving an F1 score of 79.25%. Identified medical entities are integrated at the text level to achieve EMRs structuring aligned with the needs of subsequent tasks.

Keywords: Structured Electronic Medical Records · Pediatric Epilepsy · Transfer Learning · Named Entity Recognition

1 Introduction

Epilepsy is a prevalent brain disorder, and due to the immature development of the brain in children, pediatric epilepsy is more complex and challenging to diagnose compared to epilepsy in adults. With the widespread adoption of hospital information systems, the cost of processing large amounts of data has significantly reduced. Efficiently organizing and utilizing existing pediatric epilepsy-related information and swiftly and accurately extracting valuable information from this massive data to discover new knowledge will greatly propel advancements in medical research and lead to significant breakthroughs.

M. Dong et al. (Eds.): CLSW 2023, LNAI 14515, pp. 76–90, 2024.
https://doi.org/10.1007/978-981-97-0586-3_7

EMR data records detailed diagnostic and treatment processes of patients as well as professional diagnostic outcomes by doctors. It is a primary source of crucial reference in clinical activities, making EMRs a treasure trove for large-scale health data analysis. Among the data, the quantity of semi-structured and unstructured data far exceeds that of structured data. However, these semi-structured or unstructured data contain a wealth of valuable medical knowledge. These types of data pose a significant obstacle to improving diagnostic accuracy and are relatively challenging to process. Therefore, the task of structuring electronic health records is imminent.

In this study, we aimed to address the needs of subsequent tasks such as assisting diagnosis and IE, focusing on the EMR structure of pediatric epilepsy. We analyzed and processed the data, performed NER, and integrated the information accordingly. NER was identified as a critical task in the structuring process of pediatric epilepsy EMRs. Given the limited availability of pediatric epilepsy EMR data, conventional machine learning methods often fell short of expected performance. Inspired by transfer learning, we proposed the T-RoBERTa-BiLSTM-CRF model for NER in pediatric epilepsy EMRs based on transfer learning, recognizing its potential to overcome data scarcity challenges and enhance performance.

2   Related Work

The transition from paper-based medical records to EMRs signifies a significant evolution. Research on structuring EMR text data holds immense value, not only in imparting patients with a comprehensive comprehension of their health status but also in aiding auxiliary diagnosis to support informed medical decision-making by physicians. Consequently, undertaking a sequence of structured processes encompassing NER, medical entity extraction, and data integration for Chinese EMR text data (which predominantly comprises unstructured data) is imperative.

NER task constitutes a pivotal aspect of IE within natural language processing and stands as a cornerstone in structuring EMRs. In the context of EMRs structuring, NER task involves the identification and classification of named entities such as diseases, onset times, allergy history, imaging tests, symptoms, drugs, and more within unstructured EMRs. Deep neural networks currently represent the most effective implementation for NER models in EMRs. Zan et al. [1] used Chinese word segmentation and entity labeling as guidance to construct a standard for pediatric medical texts, providing a data foundation for related research. Chowdhury et al. [2] proposed a novel multitasking bidirectional RNN model aimed at enhancing the performance of NER task in EMRs. Yu et al. [3] leveraged the BioBERT model based on Google BERT to automate the labeling of clinical problems, treatments, and tests within EMRs. An et al. [4] innovatively combined character embedding and character label embedding to enhance the performance of Chinese clinical NER. This was achieved by introducing a multi-head attention mechanism and integrating it with a medical dictionary, effectively capturing weight relationships between Chinese characters and multilevel semantic feature information.

Transfer learning involves leveraging previously acquired knowledge from a source model and applying it to enhance the learning capabilities for a new task [5]. The knowledge already acquired is referred to as the source domain, while the domain where new learning is intended is known as the target domain. Transfer learning aims to establish a mapping relationship from the source domain to the target domain. In cases where data is limited, migration learning can be employed to share knowledge between two data sets, reducing data labeling costs for the task while improving model performance. The learning process of migration learning is illustrated in Fig. 1. In the medical domain, migration learning using large pretrained models applied to publicly available medical texts (e.g., medical textbooks and EMRs) has gained prominence as a preferred approach for medical entity recognition. Zhang et al. [6] combined training on both public domain and medical domain texts to enhance entity recognition, effectively addressing the challenge of small dataset sizes. Wang et al. [7] proposed a dual migration learning model using label-aware Maximum Mean Discrepancy (MMD) to develop an interprofessional NER system in the medical domain. This model substantially reduces the need for labeled data and minimizes the consumption of human and material resources.

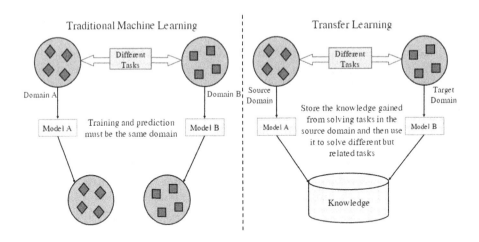

Fig. 1. Transfer learning process diagram.

3   Electronic Medical Record Analysis and Preprocessing

The majority of acquired EMRs exist in a semi-structured format, encompassing partially structured content. This structured aspect of the data significantly contributes to enhancing the accuracy of NER task. It becomes imperative to conduct a comprehensive structural analysis and implement effective structuring procedures for the existing EMRs.

3.1   Structured Process

In preparation for subsequent tasks such as auxiliary diagnosis and IE, a crucial initial step involves comprehensive data preprocessing of the existing pediatric epilepsy EMRs. Following this preprocessing phase, the focus shifts to the extraction of relevant medical entities. The process is shown in Fig. 2.

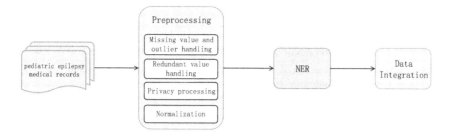

Fig. 2. Flowchart of structured EMR processing for pediatric epilepsy.

3.2   Analysis

Presently, the composition of EMRs in China adheres to the guidelines set forth by the Basic Specifications for EMRs (for Trial Implementation) [8], initially released in 2010. This document serves as a foundational guide, centering on the patient as the primary subject of the record. The records are predominantly structured in a free text format. This section provides a detailed analysis and description of the fundamental structure and characteristics of EMRs, utilizing actual pediatric epilepsy medical records for reference. Table 1 outlines the primary contents of each section within these records.

According to the objective of facilitating diagnostic research, a meticulous review and consultation with expert physicians led to the selection of four key sections from the semi-structured data of EMRs for pediatric epilepsy. These sections encompass medical history, nuclear magnetic description, blood test index, and diagnostic conclusion. Specifically, the attention was directed towards the initial page of the case and the initial episode section within real EMRs. A comprehensive analysis of the available EMR data enabled the elucidation of the primary structure and content description of EMRs pertaining to pediatric epilepsy, as detailed in Table 2.

Table 1. Structure and content of EMRs for pediatric epilepsy.

Structure	Content
Case Home	Patient personal information and brief medical information
Discharge Records	Patient admission, hospitalization, important examinations and results, discharge status and medical advice
Admission Records	The records formed by the physician's analysis and summarization of the information obtained after the patient's admission to the hospital
Course Records	Records of the patient's treatment process written by the treating physician or on-call physician after admission to the hospital
Surgical Records	Records of previous procedures performed by the patient
Anesthesia Records	Records of the anesthesia experienced by the patient
Inspection Report	Patient lab results, such as blood tests
Check Report	Patient test results, such as CT, MRI
Delivery Report	Results of sending patient samples to other institutions for testing
Temporary Medical	Records of medical orders for specific periods (examinations, surgeries, etc.)
Body Temperature List	Records of body temperature measurement
Nursing Information	Nursing care records (drug use, etc.)
Self-contained Report	Patient's own report card

The primary structure and essential components of the EMR for pediatric epilepsy, as outlined in the table above, are succinctly described below.

Chief Complaint. it represents the prominent reason for the patient's visit or the most apparent signs or symptoms experienced, along with the duration of the condition. Typically, it is based on the patient's own account of symptoms and does not employ diagnostic terminology. The chief complaint is typically succinct and concise, usually comprising no more than 20 words. It serves as the fundamental source for the symptom-related segment of the structured medical record.

Presenting History. It meticulously documents the onset and progression of the disease, encompassing changes from the initiation of symptoms to the time of consultation and treatment.

Personal History. past history, family history: This section primarily records the patient's individual birth history, past health status, previous illnesses, surgical records, and relevant familial medical history, including genetic or infectious diseases within the family.

Table 2. Structure and content of EMRs for pediatric epilepsy.

Main structure		Main content description
Medical history	Chief complaint	Describe the patient's key symptoms
	Past history	Patient's previous physical condition, history of trauma and surgery, allergy history, vaccination history, family social history, etc.
	Presenting history	Birth history, feeding history, growth and development history, etc.
	Current medical history	Describe the time of the patient's illness, symptoms at the time of illness, treatment, diagnosis, medications taken, and other information
MRI description	MRI description information	Include text of the patient's CT or MRI findings
	Diagnostic MRI Conclusions	Diagnostic findings from patient CT or MRI examinations
Blood test indicators		Contains the results of more than three hundred blood test indicators, selecting 22 blood test indicators such as thyroid, trace elements, electrolytes, and blood routine
Diagnostic	Diagnosis of disease name	Name of the patient's diagnosed disease
	Diagnostic disease codes	Patient's diagnosis disease code

Nuclear Magnetic Examination. This part entails the documentation of CT and MRI findings, serving as a vital foundation for the diagnosis of epilepsy.

Blood Test Indicators. This section primarily records the outcomes of specific test items obtained from the patient's blood test.

Diagnostic Conclusion. Representing a preliminary diagnostic outcome, this segment encapsulates the initial diagnostic conclusion derived from the admission record.

3.3   Data Preprocessing

Typically, data sourced from hospital databases of EMRs manifests as diverse, incomplete, and redundant. Consequently, efficient medical record structuring necessitates thorough data preprocessing. This procedure encompasses handling missing values, outlier identification, redundant data elimination, privacy preservation, and normalization.

Missing Value and Outlier Processing. Certain data attributes may exhibit missing or anomalous values due to human error or system malfunctions. For instance, when extracting patient information, if the procedure name is missing or abnormal, the respective data entry should be disregarded. However, in scenarios such as blood test data where the absence of upper and lower limits is noted, disregarding the data is not appropriate. In cases where the data attributes are independent and discrete, the mode of the remaining valid values can be employed to substitute the missing or abnormal values. Conversely, for evenly distributed data, the mean of the remaining valid values can be utilized for substitution, as illustrated in Equation (1).

$$\bar{x} = \frac{\sum\limits_{i=1}^{n} x_i}{n} \tag{1}$$

where $\bar{x}$ represents the mean calculation result, x_i denotes a valid data value, and n is the count of valid data. Moreover, when missing data values are present in other data sources, it is imperative to retrieve information from the available data sources to complete this Dataset.

Redundant Data Processing. Redundancy primarily arises from repetitive recording of data values or inconsistent attribute expressions. For instance, a patient is transferred to another hospital for treatment. It can also result from duplicated symptom descriptions in medical records following clinical examinations by different physicians. Within EMR, fields like chief complaint, past medical history, and present illness history often contain redundant data. To address redundancy, punctuation marks such as ' 。 ', ' , ', ' ; ', ' ！ ', and '？ ' can be utilized as delimiters. Then, the fields can be evenly divided based on their length, after which matching and deduplication of the divided fields can be performed. Finally, the processed data can be concatenated and restored in the appropriate order.

Privacy Processing. Patient's personal and parental information contain a significant amount of sensitive data. De-identification becomes a critical step in processing EMR data to ensure privacy. To effectively integrate context information from EMRs and de-identify sensitive information such as age, name, and address, the TS-GRU model is employed [9].

Normalized Processing. In the section concerning blood test indicators, a standardized approach is employed to gauge the numerical data derived from diverse blood test indicators. This standardization involves uniformization of units and magnitudes pertaining to the values of each test indicator. Given the distinct measurement standards associated with various features, normalization of blood test data is imperative. The chosen normalization technique is the max-min normalization method, wherein the upper and lower bounds of each indicator serve as the measuring units, as shown in Eq. (2).

$$x_{normalization} = \frac{x_{real} - x_{min}}{x_{max} - x_{min}} \quad (2)$$

where x_{real} represents the actual value of a patient's blood test indicator, x_{min} represents the lower limit of the normal range for this blood test indicator, x_{max} represents the upper limit of the normal range for this blood test indicator, and $x_{\text{normalization}}$ represents the result after data normalization.

4 Named Entity Recognition Based on Transfer Learning

In the realm of EMRs, methods for NER are crucial for identifying medically significant entities related to diagnosis, including disease names, symptoms, and drug names. Inspired by transfer learning, recognizing a certain similarity among data from different sources within the same field, it is possible to mitigate the challenge of data scarcity and enhance the model's learning capabilities, this paper proposes a transfer learning-based model, T-RoBERTa-BiLSTM-CRF.

4.1 Model Architecture

The T-RoBERTa-BiLSTM-CRF model is structured with distinct modules for the source and target domains. The source domain module's essence lies in the RoBERTa model [10], initially trained using CMeEE [11]. The learned parameters from this training serve as embeddings for the target domain. On the other hand, the target domain module encompasses three key components: an embedding layer, an encoding layer, and a decoding layer. The encoding layer is facilitated by a Bi-directional Long Short-Term Memory (BiLSTM) network, while the decoding layer employs a conditional random field (CRF) model [12]. The primary objective of this model is to be trained and tested using EMRs specific to pediatric epilepsy. For a visual representation of the model's architecture, refer to Fig. 3, with detailed descriptions of each component provided below.

Source Domain. During the process of transfer learning, a requisite degree of similarity between the source domain and the target domain is essential. In this model, the source domain data comprises a multi-source medical dataset, while the target domain specifically employs EMR data pertaining to pediatric epilepsy. The data within these domains, denoted as X, and the expression for the probability distribution $P(x)$ governing the generation of X, are defined as follows:

$$D = \{X, P(x)\}, x \in X \quad (3)$$

The labels Y and the prediction function f(x) involved in the task are defined as follows:

$$T = \{Y, f(x)\} \quad (4)$$

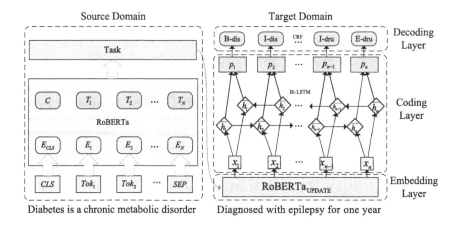

Source Domain   Target Domain

Fig. 3. T-RoBERTa-BiLSTM-CRF model structure diagram.

The function $f(x)$ is denoted as $p(y|x)$, where $y \in Y$. The source domain D_s primarily serves for transfer, while the target domain D_t represents a novel task. The learning tasks associated with D_s and D_t are denoted as T_s and T_t respectively. Formally, given the source domain D_s and T_s, as well as the target domain D_t and T_t, the objective is to learn the prediction function $f(\cdot)$ for the target domain D_t under the condition that $D_s \neq D_t$ or $T_s \neq T_t$.

Embedding Layer. The RoBERTa model, trained on the CMeEE dataset, serves as a crucial tool for extracting semantic feature representations from text sequences. For a given input text $T = \{t_1, t_2, t_3, \dots, t_n\}$, a multi-layer bi-directional encoder network is built utilizing the transformer structure to process the text sequence. Each layer integrates contextual information and generates word vectors $H = \{h_1, h_2, h_3, \dots, h_n\}$ corresponding to T. These word vectors in H encapsulate language information representations acquired during the pre-training phase of the model.

Coding Layer. The BiLSTM model is employed to distill essential features from named entities. Extending the LSTM model, the BiLSTM incorporates an extra LSTM layer with a reversed order relative to the original layers. This design enables the BiLSTM to encompass a more comprehensive understanding of contextual information. The forward and backward LSTM layers focus on capturing semantic and temporal features of the context, respectively. Their outputs are merged to yield a complete semantic representation of the EMRs. The evolution of the output h_t of the BiLSTM at time t can be elucidated as follows:

$$\overrightarrow{h}_t = \overrightarrow{LSTM}(x_t) \tag{5}$$

$$\overleftarrow{h}_t = \overleftarrow{LSTM}(x_t) \tag{6}$$

$$h_t = \left[\overrightarrow{h}_t \oplus \overleftarrow{h}_t \right] \tag{7}$$

where $\overrightarrow{h}_t$ and $\overleftarrow{h}_t$ denote the hidden state of the forward and backward LSTM layers, respectively. $\overrightarrow{h}_t$ captures forward semantic information using the forward LSTM layer, while $\overleftarrow{h}_t$ captures backward semantic information using the backward LSTM layer. $\text{LSTM}^{\rightarrow}(x_t)$ represents the semantic and temporal feature representation from the beginning up to the current time step, while $\text{LSTM}^{\leftarrow}(x_t)$ represents the semantic and temporal feature representation from the end up to the current time step. h_t represents the amalgamated semantic and temporal feature representation, comprehensively capturing contextual information from the EMRs at time t.

Decoding Layer. The decoding layer employs a CRF model to assign labels to the globally optimal sequence. The output sequence from the BiLSTM layer is denoted as $X = \{x_1, x_2, \ldots, x_t\}$, and the corresponding probability matrix is denoted by P. If there are n words in the sentence and s possible labels, then the probability matrix P is an $n \times s$ matrix, where P_{ij} represents the predicted probability of the i-th word being assigned the j-th label. The transition matrix is denoted as A and has a size of $s + 2$. A_{ij} represents the transition probability from label i to label j. For the predicted sequence $Y = \{y_1, y_2, \ldots, y_t\}$, where y_1 and y_t represent the start and end labels of the predicted sentence, the scoring function is defined as follows:

$$S(X, Y) = \sum_{i=0}^{n} A_{y_i, y_{i+1}} + \sum_{i=1}^{n} P_{i, y_i} \tag{8}$$

Therefore, if we denote $\widetilde{Y}$ to represent the true annotated sequence and Y_X to represent all valid label sequences that can be obtained through the likelihood function formula, the probability of all possible label sequences $Y = \{y_1, y_2, \ldots, y_t\}$ for the text sequence $X = \{x_1, x_2, \ldots, x_t\}$ generated after the *Softmax* layer can be calculated as follows:

$$P(Y \mid X) = \frac{\exp^{S(X,Y)}}{\sum_{\widetilde{Y} \in Y_X} exp^{S(X,\widetilde{Y})}} \tag{9}$$

The likelihood function for training the label sequences can be expressed as follows:

$$\log(P(Y \mid X)) = (S(X, Y) - \log \sum_{\widetilde{Y} \in Y_X} exp^{S(X,\widetilde{Y})}) \tag{10}$$

During the prediction phase, the formula for obtaining the output label sequence with the highest overall probability is as follows:

$$Z^* = \underset{\widetilde{Y} \in Y_X}{argmax} S\left(X, \widetilde{Y}\right) \tag{11}$$

In the decoding layer, CRF is used to calculate the relationship between adjacent labels to obtain the globally optimal label sequence. Constraints are added during entity label prediction, and the label sequence with the maximum probability is selected as the output.

4.2 Dataset

CMeEE Dataset. The dataset used in this study is the source dataset obtained from the CBLUE community and released as part of the CHIP2020 evaluation task. This dataset is designed based on the definition of nine types of named entities in the medical domain.

Pediatric Epilepsy Dataset. For the task of structuring pediatric epilepsy dataset, a comprehensive collection of medical knowledge was acquired. This dataset encompasses 18 distinct types of entities.

4.3 Results and Analysis

The target domain model was trained utilizing the pediatric epilepsy dataset, which consisted of 8,362 records. These records were partitioned into training, validation, and testing sets in an 8:1:1 ratio. The training set comprised 6,688 records, the validation set included 836 records, and the testing set encompassed 838 records. The specific experimental results are shown in Table 3.

Table 3. Structure and content of EMRs for pediatric epilepsy.

Entity	P	R	F1	Entity	P	R	F1
Disease	0.83	0.86	0.85	Omen	1.00	0.91	0.95
Symptom	0.81	0.88	0.84	Treatments	0.68	0.52	0.59
Age	0.76	0.71	0.73	MRI	0.66	1.00	0.80
Drug	0.91	0.91	0.91	Step	0.80	0.84	0.82
Examine	0.75	0.81	0.78	Epidemiology	0.75	0.93	0.83
Body	0.80	0.90	0.85	Cause	0.74	0.79	0.76
Surgery	0.81	0.75	0.78	Sociology	0.55	0.59	0.57
EEG	0.85	0.87	0.86	Explanation	0.59	0.66	0.62
Others	0.91	0.81	0.86	Prognosis	0.88	0.88	0.88
Total					**0.78**	**0.80**	**0.79**

we integrated the medical history and MRI examination results sections and used the model to perform NER on pediatric epilepsy EMRs. The dataset comprises a total of 37,539 identified entities. Given the substantial presence of medical history and prevailing illnesses in the dataset, symptom entities constitute the majority, making up approximately 49.9%. Following closely are drug entities and disease entities, accounting for approximately 16.5% each. Additionally, other entity categories make up 15.4% of the dataset. The model evaluation results are shown in Table 4.

Table 4. Evaluation of NER in EMRs.

Entity	P	R	F1	Entity	P	R	F1
Disease	0.88	0.90	0.89	Omen	0.92	0.90	0.91
Symptom	0.85	0.87	0.86	Treatments	0.78	0.72	0.75
Age	0.65	0.61	0.63	MRI	0.74	0.88	0.81
Drug	0.88	0.98	0.93	Step	0.83	0.81	0.82
Examine	0.81	0.87	0.84	Epidemiology	0.76	0.87	0.81
Body	0.85	0.87	0.86	Cause	0.83	0.74	0.78
Surgery	0.92	0.95	0.93	Sociology	0.59	0.61	0.60
EEG	0.61	0.67	0.64	Explanation	0.60	0.62	0.61
Others	0.65	0.77	0.71	Prognosis	0.86	0.88	0.87
Total					**0.82**	**0.86**	**0.84**

Subsequently, the model was compared with multiple entity recognition models through experimental evaluations. The goal was to verify the performance of the proposed model in NER. The models used for comparison included baseline models (BiLSTM-CRF), pretrained model-based entity recognition models (BERT-BiLSTM-CRF, RoBERTa-BiLSTM-CRF). The specific results can be found in Table 5.

Table 5. Overall comparison of NER in pediatric epilepsy EMRs

Dataset	Model	P(%)	R(%)	F1(%)
Pediatric Epilepsy Dataset	BiLSTM-CRF	68.91	70.24	69.57
	BERT-BiLSTM-CRF	75.78	78.13	76.95
	RoBERTa-BiLSTM-CRF	76.62	79.03	77.82
	T-RoBERTa-BiLSTM-CRF	**77.83**	**80.66**	**79.25**

The experimental findings reveal that incorporating pretrained language models enhances the model's ability to accurately comprehend contextual information and identify multi-level language features when compared to the baseline model BiLSTM-CRF. Specifically, the BERT-BiLSTM-CRF model demonstrates a notable 7.38% improvement in F1 score. Even though the pretrained language model RoBERTa was originally trained on non-medical data, its utilization of dynamic masking strategies and training on a larger-scale dataset results in a respectable 0.87% improvement in F1 score for NER task on the pediatric epilepsy EMR dataset. Remarkably, the proposed T-RoBERTa-BiLSTM-CRF model, leveraging medical data for transfer learning, exhibits a substantial 1.43% improvement in F1 score compared to the RoBERTa-BiLSTM-CRF model in NER task on the pediatric epilepsy EMR dataset. This underscores the efficacy of data transfer between diverse sources within the same domain for entity recognition, building upon the foundation of pretrained language models.

5   Data Integration

Following data collection, data preprocessing, and NER task utilizing transfer learning, entity information within the electronic health records of each patient was acquired. Integration was executed to align with the demands of subsequent tasks, including auxiliary diagnosis and IE.

Chief Complaint. The chief complaint describes the primary symptoms experienced by the patient, representing the most prominent disease-related information perceived by the patient. In the data preprocessing stage, we performed deduplication to obtain structured chief complaint data. Subsequently, we conducted entity recognition on this data, resulting in crucial symptom information for each patient.

Past Medical History. The integration of the medical history data involves preserving specific information from different fields: In the "past medical history" field, we retain key symptomatic information related to the patient's medical conditions. In the "trauma and surgical history" field, we retain information about surgeries the patient has undergone. In the "allergy history" field, we keep identified allergic medications. For the "vaccination history" field, we represent administered vaccinations as 1 and denote non-administered ones as 0. Within the "family medical history" field, we preserve information regarding illnesses of family members.

Present Illness. The current medical history data mostly consists of lengthy text. We structured the data based on entity types such as symptoms, diseases, surgeries, medications, and cranial imaging manifestations. Specific details are shown in Table 6

Table 6. Example of structured data on current medical history.

Medical entity	Attributes
Disease	Epilepsy; Intracranial infection; Spasm
Symptom	Cough; fever; convulsions; drooling when swallowing poorly; sudden head tilt; clusters of attacks, drowsiness after attacks; dull eyes; swallowing; swallowing movements with or without hand automatism; inability to function after falling to the ground Walking, no cough, phlegm in throat, fever
Drug	Levetiracetam tablets; bid; Prednisone; Topiramate tablets; Nitrazepam
Body	Frontotemporal and parietal lobes
Treatments	High pressure
MRI	The sulci of each lobe of both cerebral hemispheres are widened and deepened; the lateral ventricles and third ventricle on both sides are slightly enlarged

6   Conclusion

This article focuses on the core process and key techniques of structuring EMRs based on pediatric epilepsy, addressing the needs of subsequent tasks such as assisting diagnosis and IE. In the data preprocessing stage, we utilized mean imputation to handle missing and abnormal data, employed the TS-GRU model to de-identify patient information, and normalized the blood test data. For named entity recognition, given the limited and challenging annotation of the pediatric epilepsy dataset, we adopted a transfer learning approach and proposed the T-RoBERTa-BiLSTM-CRF model for named entity recognition in pediatric epilepsy EMRs.

In this model, we used the RoBERTa model trained on the CMeEE dataset as the source domain and employed the trained model as the embedding layer for the target domain. We used BiLSTM as the encoding layer to extract crucial features and CRF as the decoding layer to label the optimal sequence. The T-RoBERTa-BiLSTM-CRF model was trained using the pediatric epilepsy dataset constructed in this study, and the trained model was then used to perform named entity recognition tasks in structuring pediatric epilepsy EMRs. Finally, identified medical entities were integrated to achieve EMR structuring aligned with the needs of subsequent tasks such as assisting diagnosis.

Acknowledgement. We appreciate the constructive feedback from the anonymous reviewers and the support provided for this research by the following projects: Yunnan Province Science and Technology Major Project (202102AA100021), and Henan Provincial Department of Science and Technology Science and Technology Tackling Project (222102210231).

References

1. Hongying, Z., Wenxin, L., Kunli, Z., Yajuan, Y., Baobao, C., Zhifang, S.: Building a pediatric medical corpus: word segmentation and named entity annotation. In: Chinese Lexical Semantics: 21st Workshop, CLSW 2020, Hong Kong, China, 28–30 May 2020, Revised Selected Papers 21, pp. 652–664. Springer (2021). https://doi. org/10.1007/978-3-030-81197-6-55
2. Chowdhury, S., et al.: A multitask bi-directional RNN model for named entity recognition on Chinese electronic medical records. BMC Bioinformatics **19**, 75–84 (2018). https://doi.org/10.1186/s12859-018-2467-9
3. Yu, X., Hu, W., Lu, S., Sun, X., Yuan, Z.: Biobert based named entity recognition in electronic medical record. In: 2019 10th International Conference on Information Technology in Medicine and Education (ITME), pp. 49–52. IEEE (2019). https:// doi.org/10.1109/ITME.2019.00022
4. An, Y., Xia, X., Chen, X., Wu, F.X., Wang, J.: Chinese clinical named entity recognition via multi-head self-attention based bilstm-CRF. Artif. Intell. Med. **127**, 102282 (2022). https://doi.org/10.1016/j.artmed.2022.102282
5. Weiss, K., Khoshgoftaar, T.M., Wang, D.: A survey of transfer learning. J. Big data **3**(1), 1–40 (2016). https://doi.org/10.1186/s40537-016-0043-6
6. Zhang, K., Yue, D., Zhuang, L.: Improving Chinese clinical named entity recognition based on bilstm-CRF by cross-domain transfer. In: Proceedings of the 2020 4th High Performance Computing and Cluster Technologies Conference & 2020 3rd International Conference on Big Data and Artificial Intelligence, pp. 251–256 (2020). https://doi.org/10.1145/3409501.3409527
7. Wang, Z., et al.: Label-aware double transfer learning for cross-specialty medical named entity recognition. In: Proceedings of the 2018 Conference of the North American Chapter of the Association for Computational Linguistics: Human Language Technologies, Volume 1 (Long Papers), pp. 1–15 (2018). https://doi.org/10. 18653/v1/N18-1001
8. Li, X.: Ministry of health issues basic specifications for electronic medical records. Chin. Commun. Phys. **13**, 1–21 (2010). (in Chinese)
9. Zhao, Y.S., Zhang, K.L., Ma, H.C., Li, K.: Leveraging text skeleton for de-identification of electronic medical records. BMC Med. Inform. Decis. Mak. **18**, 65–72 (2018). https://doi.org/10.1186/s12911-018-0598-6
10. Liu, Y., et al.: Roberta: a robustly optimized bert pretraining approach. arXiv preprint arXiv:1907.11692 (2019).
11. Zhang, N., et al.: Cblue: a chinese biomedical language understanding evaluation benchmark. In: Proceedings of the 60th Annual Meeting of the Association for Computational Linguistics (Volume 1: Long Papers, pp. 7888–7915 (2022). https:// doi.org/10.18653/v1/2022.acl-long.544
12. Lin, B.Y., Lu, W.: Neural adaptation layers for cross-domain named entity recognition. In: Proceedings of the 2018 Conference on Empirical Methods in Natural Language Processing, pp. 2012–2022 (2018). https://doi.org/10.18653/v1/D18-1226

Semantic and Phonological Distances in Free Word Association Tasks

Marc Allassonnière-Tang[1] (iD), I.-Ping Wan[2]([✉]) (iD), and Chainwu Lee[3]

[1] National Museum of Natural History/CNRS/University Paris City, Lab Ecological Anthropology UMR 7206, Paris, France
marc.allassonniere-tang@mnhn.fr
[2] Graduate Institute of Linguistics/Research Center for Mind, Brian, and Learning/Program in Teaching Chinese as a Second Language, Phonetics and Psycholinguistics Laboratory, National Chengchi University, Taipei, Taiwan
ipwan@g.nccu.edu.tw
[3] Phonetics and Psycholinguistics Laboratory, National Chengchi University, Taipei, Taiwan

Abstract. Free word association tasks are used to evaluate different hypotheses proposed by interactive and cascade models of speech processing. The interactive model predicts a small semantic and phonological distance between the target and the response words, whereas the cascade model predicts that the responses are semantically close to the targets but are phonologically far from the targets. One hundred forty-five stimuli tested with 22 participants resulted in 2289 tokens available for testing. The phonological and semantic distances were automatically measured using Levenshtein distance and word embeddings; additional metadata over 10M drawn from the Academia Sinica Corpus in Taiwan was computed. The results show that the stimuli and the responses are closer than random semantically and phonologically, supporting the predictions from the interactive models. However, we also observe that the semantic distance is shorter than the phonological distance. A concomitant increase in chronometry is found with longer semantic distance.

Keywords: Word association · Word-embedding distance · Levenshtein distance · Models of spreading activation · Models of spoken word production

1 Introduction

Several research studies investigated the network structure of the lexicon by analyzing the representation levels of word production. Models of word production generally consist of two elements. The first element is lexical selection, which is the selection of a single word unit from the mental lexicon. The second element is word form retrieval, which has two stages: the semantic stage and the phonological stage. Classical models propose that lexical items are semantically organized in the first stage. Then, they are phonologically organized in the second stage [1, 2]. Within such models, information flows in one direction and is processed independently at each stage. More recent spreading activation models (i.e., connectionist models) propose that information flows and/or

M. Dong et al. (Eds.): CLSW 2023, LNAI 14515, pp. 91–100, 2024.
https://doi.org/10.1007/978-981-97-0586-3_8

connects bidirectionally between nodes of semantic and phonological information [3, 4]. Within this connectionist approach, two types of spreading activation models have been proposed: interactive two-step models and cascade models.

In interactive models [3, 5], activation spreads across semantic nodes by sharing semantic features (e.g., superordinate/subordinate/antonym) at the semantic level. In parallel, at the phonological level, onset/rhyme division is made in terms of syllable structure. Activation can spread between the semantic and the phonological nodes. For example, an activation of a semantic node can also trigger the activation of phonological nodes. In cascade models [6, 7], activation spreads at the semantic level first but not at the phonological level. Various semantic nodes compete at the semantic level, and the output of the competition is then passed on to the phonological level. To summarize, both the interactive models and the cascade models propose that activation spreads through a network of semantic and phonological nodes. However, interactive models suggest that activation can spread across the semantic and phonological nodes, while cascade models propose that the activation is processed first at the semantic level and gets organized only at a later stage at the phonological level. In Mandarin, Wan [8, 9] used a natural spoken corpus of Mandarin speech errors and found that meaningless strings of phonemes occur in errors due to their higher occurring frequency and relevance to phonological structures [8, 9]. Tang and Wan [10], Wan and Allassonnière-Tang [11] further investigated speech processing models to deal with the effect of frequency and position-in-utterance between sequential pairs of words within spoken corpora.

In addition to natural spoken corpora, free-word association tasks are also one of the commonly used methods to assess which type of model (between the interactive and the cascade models) is more likely to reflect the inner structure of human speech processing. In free-word association tasks, a target word is presented, and participants are asked to respond by producing the word that comes to their minds first. The response and the response time can both be recorded and measured. Based on such an experiment, different model types have other predictions with regard to the output of participants. One of the main differences is that the interactive model predicts a small semantic and phonological distance between the targets and the response words, whereas the cascade model predicts that the responses are semantically close to the targets but are phonetically far from the targets. The main aim of this study is to evaluate these two different predictions based on data from Mandarin speakers.

2   Materials

A set of 145 Mandarin target words was selected for the experiment by controlling for word frequency, part-of-speech, syllable structure, tone structure, and imageability. Most of these criteria were based on Taiwan's Academia Sinica Balanced Corpus 3.0 (Chinese Knowledge and Information Processing [12, 13]. For example, words from a similar frequency range were selected based on their occurrence frequency in the Academia Sinica Balanced Corpus. As another example, a similar proportion of imageability was manually classified based on the semantic features in Extended-HowNet 2.0 [14], e.g., the targets were controlled to not over-represent concrete nouns versus abstract nouns.

The experiment was conducted using E-Prime 3.0. in the Phonetics and Psycholinguistics Laboratory at National Chengchi University. First, the ethical measures were explained to the participants. Ethical criteria included information about the anonymization of data, data storage, lack of health-related risks, and formal consent. Upon acceptance, the experiment began with introductory slides explaining the procedure of the experiment. Upon seeing a word presented on the screen, participants were asked to provide one associated word in Mandarin. E-Prime recorded each response of the participant through an AKG headphone/microphone set. The participants were reminded not to repeat the targets during the experiment. The participants could also choose not to respond to the stimulus. Before the experiment started, a series of trials were provided as a warm-up session. If any responses without association were produced during the practice trials, a reminder with examples was provided before the actual experiment. The responses of the trials were not included in the final data. During the experiment, the stimuli were randomized for each participant to avoid a bias of order. The definitive database contains 145 target/cue words for which 22 participants (13 females and 9 males) generated a single response. After removing null or erroneous responses, a total of 2983 responses were collected. The participants did not have diagnosed language impairment. They were reimbursed for their participation.

3   Method

This section describes how the phonological distances and semantic distances are calculated. The following R (R-Core-Team [15]) packages are used during the analysis: ggrepel [16], Rtsne [17], stringdist [18], tidyverse [19].

3.1   Phonological Distance

The stimuli and the responses are first transcribed into IPA (International Phonetic Alphabet). To allow the direct comparison between different tones, we first convert the original multi-digit encoding to single-digit encoding, that is, $55 = 1, 35 = 2, 21 = 3, 51 = 4$. The symbols such as aspiration are also merged with the IPA symbol to identify as a phone in the language. For instance, $[t^h]$ counts as one 'symbol' rather than two. Then, the Levenshtein distance is used to measure the phonological distance between the stimuli and the responses. This metric takes into account how many operations are needed to turn one string of phones into another. As shown in Fig. 1, changing the word 'Shakespeare' into 'Jacques Pierre' requires two substitutions, a deletion, and an insertion, which results in a Levenshtein distance of four. At the same time, we also need to consider the difference in length between the two words. For instance, the distance between a short word and a long word will always be significant (due to the number of deletion/insertion needed). Thus, we normalize the Levenshtein distance along a $0 - 1$ scale by dividing it by the length of the longer word [20]. Taking the example again in Fig. 1, between 'Shakespeare' and 'Jacques Pierre,' the latter is longer with 8 elements. Thus, the normalized Levenshtein distance is 4/8, which is 0.5.

   An example of how this metric is applied to the current data is shown in the following. The stimulus [tʂoŋ1wən2] 'Chinese (language)' results in the response [iŋ1wən2] 'English (language).' The distance between the two words is two since the required changes are one substitution and one deletion. This distance is normalized by dividing two by the

Shakespeare	→	Jacques Pierre
ʃ	Substitution	ʒ
ɛi	Substitution	a
k		k
s	Deletion	
p		p
i		i
	Insertion	e
r		r

Fig. 1. An example of the Levenshtein distance [20]

longest of the two words, 'Chinese (language)' with eight items. Thus, the normalized distance is $2/8 = 0.25$.

The normalized Levenshtein distance provides a measure of the distance between the stimuli and the responses. To assess how big or small the measured distance is, two additional distances are added as random baselines. First, we consider the Levenshtein distance between the stimuli and randomly selected responses. Second, we consider the Levenshtein distance between the stimuli and totally random words from the Academia Sinica corpus, which consists of 11,245,330 words with corresponding IPA and tone markers. We conducted ten random samplings for each baseline to avoid effects from coincidental samples. A visualization of the results is shown in Fig. 2. We can observe that the phonological distances measured between the stimuli and the responses are not very different from the two distances measured with the random datasets. That is to say, the responses of the experiments are only slightly closer phonologically than random words.

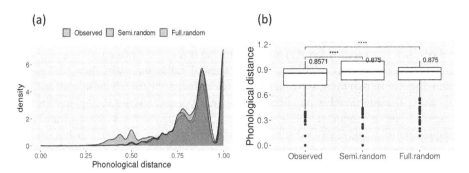

Fig. 2. The density distribution of the phonological distance measured on the responses and the two random baselines.

Additional visualization based on box plots and testing based on Wilcoxon tests with Bonferroni corrections shows that the phonological distance measured between the stimuli and the responses is significantly smaller than the phonological distance measured between the stimuli and the random datasets ($p < 0.001$). However, the effect size is small. For example, the median of all three measurements is 0.8571, while their respective means are 0.8083, 0.8659, and 0.8658. Additional details are available in the supplementary materials.

3.2 Semantic Distance

The semantic distance is extracted with the method of word embedding. This method refers to the process of embedding words into a vector space [21–23]. The association between words and vectors is done in such a way that the similarities between words are reflected through the similarities between vectors. In other words, each word in a corpus is assigned a vector depending on the context in which it is occurring. The vectors of each word can then be used to measure the semantic similarity between different words [24, 25]. In the current analysis, we use the method of fast text embeddings [26, 27]. The embeddings are generated with the entire data of the Academia Sinica Corpus, which consists of 11,245,330 words. The parameters of the word embedding model are set to capture semantic information [25]: bag-of-words with a symmetric context size of five words. These parameters mean that for each occurrence of each word, its five preceding and five following words are considered as occurring contexts. The parameter 'bag-of-words' indicates that the order of the context words is not taken into account. The dimensionality of the word embedding model is set to 300 dimensions. The minimum threshold of frequency is set to ten. That is to say, words that occur less than ten times are not included in the embeddings.

An example of how the semantic similarities are mirrored through word embeddings is shown in Fig. 3. These embeddings are generated from the Academia Sinica corpus. In this simplified visual representation, semantically related words are located close to each other in the semantic space. For instance, fruit-related words such as 'apple' and 'banana' are clustered together in the semantic space. Likewise, for education-related words such as 'school,' 'teacher,' and 'student.'

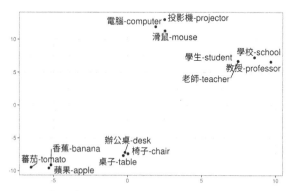

Fig. 3. A visual representation of word embeddings generated from the Academia Sinica Corpus. The axes refer to the reduced dimensions of the word embeddings.

The semantic distance between two words can be measured based on their cosine similarity, which refers to the angle between the two words. Two vectors with the same orientation have a cosine similarity of 1, two vectors oriented at 90 degrees relative to each other have a similarity of 0, and two vectors diametrically opposed have a similarity of -1. The distance between the two words is then calculated by $1 -$ the cosine similarity. As an example from the embeddings generated with the Academia Sinica corpus, the cosine distance between 'apple' and 'orange' is $1 - 0.4317 = 0.5683$, while the cosine distance between 'apple' and 'school' is $1 - 0.1415 = 0.8585$. These numbers mirror the intuitive guess that 'apple' and 'orange' share a smaller semantic distance than 'apple' and 'library.'

The semantic distance between the stimuli and the responses is calculated based on the cosine distance in word embeddings. The two measures of random semantic distance are also calculated in the same way as for phonological distance. The first random distance refers to the distance between each stimulus and a randomly selected response. The second random distance relates to the distance between each stimulus and a word selected at random from the Academia Sinica corpus. An overview of the three distances is shown in Fig. 4.

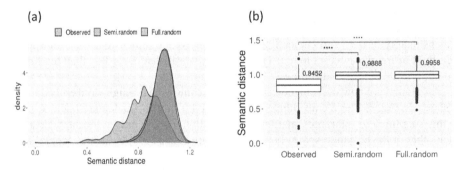

Fig. 4. The density distribution of the semantic distance measured on the responses and the two random baselines.

The semantic distances measured between the stimuli and the two random datasets are quite different. The semantic distance between the stimuli and the responses is generally shorter than the semantic distance between i) the stimuli and the randomized responses (Sem.random) ii) the stimuli and the random words from the Academia Sinica corpus (Full.random). Visualization by boxplots and Wilcoxon tests with Bonferroni corrections indicate that the semantic distance between the stimuli and the responses is significantly smaller than that measured on the random datasets. The effect size is more significant than with phonological distance. For example, the median for the observed distances is 0.8452 while 0.9888 and 0.9958 for the random datasets. Similar observations are made when considering the mean of 0.8299, 0.9801, and 0.9917 for the three measurements.

3.3 Comparing Phonological and Semantic Distances

The distances measured in Sect. 2 have shown that, as expected, the semantic and the phonological distances measured between the stimuli and the responses are significantly smaller than the distances between random words. This comparison allows us to verify that the automatic measurements of phonological and semantic distance reflect reality. Responses generated by participants are semantically and phonologically related to the stimulus. This relation is more robust than what one would get by sampling random words.

As a reminder for the hypothesis we are testing, the interactive model predicts a small semantic and phonological distance between the target and the response words, whereas the cascade model predicts that the responses are semantically close to the targets but are phonetically far from the targets. We calculate the gap between measured and random distances to make such a comparison. Taking phonological distances as an example, we take each pair of stimulus and response and calculate their phonological distances. Then, for each stimulus, we calculate its distance with the random word it is compared within the entirely random dataset. Finally, we consider the difference between the distances for responses and random words. This gap is normalized by being divided by the random distance, which is more extensive. The exact measurements are conducted for semantic distances. Based on this methodology, we obtain two measures: the phonological and semantic gaps between the actual responses and random gaps. If the phonological gap is larger than the semantic gap, it means that responses are semantically closer to the stimuli than phonologically. If the phonological gap is smaller than the semantic gap, it infers that responses are phonologically more immediate to the stimuli. If the gaps are equal, it indicates that the semantic and phonological distances between the stimuli and the responses are similar. The comparison of the semantic gap and the phonological gap is visualized per iteration as well as the phonological distance for each stimulus across participants in Fig. 5.

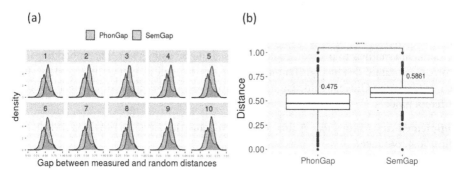

Fig. 5. The density distribution of the gaps between measured distances and random distances. The numbers 1 to 10 indicate the ten random samples.

The results show that, across all iterations, the semantic gap between the responses and the random words is much larger than the phonological gap between the responses and the random words. This indicates that the responses are semantically closer to the stimuli. This gap difference is significant across all iterations based on Wilcoxon tests with Bonferroni corrections (p < 0.001). The effect size is large. For example, the median of the semantic gap stabilizes around 0.6 across all iterations, while the phonological gap is stable at 0.48 across all ten iterations. Testing with mixed models controlling for participant and stimuli as random effects also shows that the semantic gap is significantly smaller than the phonological gap (Estimate = 0.08568, Std error = 0.0009594, t value = 89.305, p value < 0.001). There is no effect of gender and word frequency, while the reaction time is negatively correlated with the semantic and phonological gaps.

4   Conclusion

Interactive and cascade models of speech processing have been evaluated by free word association tasks. We used the Levenshtein edit distance as a representation of the phonological distance, while the method of word embeddings represented semantic distance. Both measured distances were compared with random phonological and semantic distances to allow comparability between the two distances. The analyses show that the responses are phonologically and semantically closer to the stimuli than random words, which supports the interactive models. Furthermore, the responses of the participants are semantically closer to the stimuli than phonologically, showing that free-word association is more likely to result in semantically associated words rather than words that share phonological relatedness. The latter observation requires additional investigations.

In terms of future development, starting with the measurements of phonological distances, each editing operation, such as insertion or deletion, was given the same weight. It could be interesting to give different weights to each operation based on its inferred cost during speech processing. Second, the comparison between the distances could be considered as not straightforward. On the one hand, semantic distance is generated from an embedding distance. On the other hand, phonological distance is measured with edit distance. It could be argued that the two distances are, in fact, measuring different things, and they cannot be compared directly. In the current paper, we consider that such comparison is adequate for the purpose at hand since we consider embedding distance as a distance measured with the change of context for each word. Nevertheless, potential alternatives to overcome such issues could be using phoneme embeddings. In terms of semantic distance, different experiments, as well as embedding models such as word2vec and Glove, could also be tested to assess the variation of the results across different models.

Supplementary Materials. A link to supplementary materials is provided as follows: https://osf.io/du8eh/.

Acknowledgment. We appreciate valuable and constructive comments from the anonymous reviewers and the editor. We would also like to thank the participants for their comments and questions in the 24th Chinese Lexical Semantics Workshop at the National University of Singapore. Thanks also go to Professor Wei-yun Ma for releasing the coding of CKIP parser, and Professor Li-hsin Ning and Professor Jiahong Yuan for the traditional HMM coding on the phonetic forced alignment in Mandarin. Thanks also go to many brilliant research assistants in the Phonetics and Psycholinguistics lab: Yun-shan Hsieh, Pu Yu, and Howard Yan. All remaining errors of analysis or interpretation are our own. This research was supported in part by a three-year grant from National Science and Technology Council to the corresponding author in Taiwan (MOST 98-2410-H-004-103-MY2).

References

1. Fromkin, V.: The non-anomalous nature of anomalous utterances. Language **47**, 27–52 (1971)
2. Garrett, M.F.: The analysis of sentence production. In: Bower, G.H. (ed.) The Psychology of Learning and Motivation, pp. 133–175. Academic Press, San Diego (1975)
3. Dell, G.S.: A spreading-activation theory of retrieval in sentence production. Psychol. Rev. **93**, 283–321 (1986)
4. Butterworth, B.: Lexical access in speech production. In: Marslen-Wilson, W. (ed.) Lexical Representation and Process, pp. 108–135. MIT Press, Cambridge (1989)
5. Warker, J.A., Dell, G.S.: Speech errors reflect newly learned phonotactic constraints. J. Exp. Psychol. Learn. Mem. Cogn. **32**, 387–398 (2006)
6. Levelt, W.J.M., Roelofs, A., Meyer, A.S.: A theory of lexical access in speech production. Behav. Brain Sci. **22**, 1–38 (1999)
7. Roelofs, A.: A spreading-activation theory of lemma retrieval in speaking. Cognition **42**, 107–142 (1992)
8. Wan, I.P.: Mandarin speech errors into phonological patterns. J. Chin. Linguist. **35**, 185–224 (2007)
9. Wan, I.P.: Consonant features in mandarin speech errors. Concent. Stud. Linguist. **42**, 1–39 (2016). https://doi.org/10.6241/concentric.ling.42.2.01
10. Tang, M., Wan, I.P.: Predicting speech errors in Mandarin based on word frequency. In: Su, Q., Zhan, W. (eds.) From Minimal Contrast to Meaning Construct, pp. 289–303. Springer, Cham (2020). https://doi.org/10.1007/978-981-32-9240-6_20
11. Wan, I.P., Allassonnière-Tang, M.: The effect of word frequency and position-in-utterance in Mandarin speech errors: a connectionist model of speech production. In: Liu, M., Kit, C., Su, C. (eds.) Chinese Lexical Semantics, pp. 491–500. Springer, Cham (2021). https://doi.org/10.1007/978-3-030-81197-6_42
12. CKIP (Chinese Knowledge and Information Processing). Part-of-Speech Analysis of Academia Sinica Balanced Corpus of Modern Chinese. Technical Report, No. 93-05, Version 3. Academia Sinica, Taipei (2004)
13. Huang, C.-R., Chen, K.J., Chang, L.P., Hsu, H.L.: The introduction of sinica corpus. In: Proceedings of ROCLING VIII, pp. 81–89 (1995)
14. Ma, W.-Y., Shih, Y.-Y.: Extended HowNet 2.0–an entity-relation common-sense representation model. In: Proceedings of the Eleventh International Conference on Language Resources and Evaluation (LREC 2018) (2018)
15. R-Core-Team: R. A Language and Environment for Statistical Computing. Vienna: R Foundation for Statistical Computing (2022)
16. Kamil, S.: Ggrepel: Automatically Position Non-Overlapping Text Labels with Ggplot2. R Package Version 0.8.1 (2019)
17. Krijthe, J.: Rtsne: T-Distributed Stochastic Neighbor Embedding Using a Barnes-Hut Implementation (2015)
18. Van der Loo, M.P.J.: The Stringdist Package for approximate string matching. The R Journal **6**, 111–122 (2014)
19. Gagolewski, M.: Genieclust: fast and robust hierarchical clustering. SoftwareX **15**, 100722 (2021)
20. Dunn, M.: Language phylogenies. In: Bowern, C., Evans, B. (eds.) The Routledge Handbook of Historical Linguistics, pp. 190–211. Routledge, New York (2015)
21. Levy, O., Goldberg, Y.: Dependency-based word embeddings. In: Proceedings of the 52nd Annual Meeting of the Association for Computational Linguistics, vol. 2, pp. 302–308. Association for Computational Linguistics, Kerrville (2014). https://doi.org/10.3115/v1/P14-2050

22. Mikolov, T., Sutskever, I., Chen, K., Corrado, G.S., Dean, J.: Distributed representations of words and phrases and their compositionality. In: Burges, C.J.C., Bottou, L., Weiling, M., Ghahramani, Z., Weinberger., K.Q. (eds.) Advances in Neural Information Processing Systems, pp. 3111–3119. Curran Associates, New York (2013)

23. Pennington, J., Socher, R., Manning, C.: Glove: global vectors for word representation. In: Proceedings of the 2014 Conference on Empirical Methods in Natural Language Processing (EMNLP), pp. 1532–1543. Association for Computational Linguistics, Kerrville (2014). https://doi.org/10.3115/v1/D14-1162

24. Gaume, B., Tanguy, L., Fabre, C., Ho-Dac, L.-M., Pierrejean, B., Hathout, N., et al.: Automatic analysis of word association data from the Evolex psycholinguistic tasks using computational lexical semantic similarity measures. In: Sharp, B., Lubaszewski, W., Sedes, F. (eds.) Natural Language Processing and Cognitive Science (NLPCS), pp. 19–26. Jagiellonian Library, Kraków (2018)

25. Lebret, R., Collobert, R.: Rehabilitation of Count-Based Models for Word Vector Representations. In: Gelbukh, A. (ed.) Computational Linguistics and Intelligent Text Processing, pp. 417–429. Springer, Cham (2015). https://doi.org/10.1007/978-3-319-18111-0_31

26. Bojanowski, P., Grave, E., Joulin, A., Mikolov, T.: Enriching word vectors with subword information. Trans. Assoc. Comput. Linguist. **5**, 135–146 (2017). https://doi.org/10.1162/tacl_a_00051

27. Mouselimis L.: fastText: Efficient Learning of Word Representations and Sentence Classification using R. R package version 1.0.3 (2022). https://CRAN.R-project.org/package=fastText

Suffix ʔe51 in Zhangzhou: An Interdisciplinary Explorations

Yishan Huang[(⊠)]

Linguistics Department, The University of Sydney, Camperdown, NSW, Australia
yishan.huang@sydney.edu.au

Abstract. This study explores how the single suffix ʔe51 contributes to word formation in Zhangzhou Southern Min. Semantically, this suffix is extraordinarily polysemantic, which can express a wide range of semantic meanings, including smallness, closeness, and affection; tool and equipment; people of a particular characteristic; people of a specific occupation; sense of lightless and slowness, and sense of small quantity among others. Morpho-syntactically, this suffix fulfills multiple roles as a nominalizer, nominal marker, and adverbialier, and the lexical bases that can be suffixed are cross-categorical, involving seven different types. Phonologically, the ʔe51 suffixation can invoke a special tone sandhi pattern on the bases, resulting in their tonal realization to be different from their regular sandhi process. Distributionally, the occurrence of this suffix is subject to several constraints involving semantics, morpho-syntax and phonology. This study strengthens our understanding of the suffixing system in this dialect and contributes important linguistic data to the typology of word formation in world's natural languages, while shedding an important light on how Sinitic languages should be better defined from the interdisciplinary perspective.

Keywords: ʔe51 · Suffixation · Semantics · Morpho-syntax · Phonology · Interface · Constraint · Zhangzhou

1 Introduction

Languages vary considerably concerning what morphological processes are available in their word formation, how frequently the processes are used, and what types of information are encoded in the processes [1–5]. Given this flexibility and diversity, languages are classified into different types, such as analytic and synthetic, depending on their word-building competence and productivity. For example, Sinitic languages, along with Yoruba and Vietnamese, are often cited as exhibiting an extreme degree of analyticity with no affixation, which makes them qualified as isolating [1–4]. In contrast, Latin, along with Russian languages, are classified as synthetic because their exploiting affixation as a primary method to encode multiple grammatical categories, such as person, number, tense, mood, and voice among others [5].

However, in their inventory of affixal elements, inflectional and derivational affixes are increasingly discovered in those so-called isolating languages [1–4, 6–13]. For example, in Mandarin Chinese, nouns are, in general, not inflected for grammatical gender,

M. Dong et al. (Eds.): CLSW 2023, LNAI 14515, pp. 101–115, 2024.
https://doi.org/10.1007/978-981-97-0586-3_9

number, or person but the exception is observed in the plural suffix -men for human nouns and pronouns, as illustrated in (1). Likewise, verbs can be inflected for aspect, with various aspectual suffixes including the Perfective -*le*, Experiential -*guo51*, and Progressive/Durative -*zhe* [1–4], as illustrated in (2). Given an increasingly high ratio of morphemes per word, it is questionable to define the spontaneous Chinese languages as morphologically isolating as conventionally assumed [2–4, 11].

(1) Mandarin Plural Suffix

ren35-men 'person-plural'
lao214.shi55-men 'teacher-plural'
hai35.zi214-men 'kid-plural'
ni214-men 'you-plural'
nan35.ren35-men 'man-plural'
nü214.ren35-men 'woman-plural'

(2) Mandarin Aspectual Suffix

zou214-le 'go-perfective'
zuo51-guo 'do-experiential'
zou214-zhe 'go-progressive'

Driven by the intriguing phenomenon of affixation in those so-called isolating languages, this paper investigates how affixation is encoded and contributes to word formation in Zhangzhou, an under-described Southern Min dialect spoken in Southern Fujian province in Mainland China. It particularly focuses on the behavior of suffix ʔɐ51. Semantically, this suffix is extraordinarily polysemantic, which can extensively expand and modify existing lexical meanings of the bases and derive lexemes covering a wide range of semantic domains that include smallness, closeness, and affection; tool and equipment; people of a particular characteristic or physical appearance; people of a specific occupation; sense of lightless and slowness, and sense of small quantity among others. Morpho-syntactically, this suffix ʔɐ51 can fulfill multiple roles as nominalizer, nominal marker, and adverbializer, whose attachment can substantially alter the part of speech of the bases, resulting in four processes comprising verb-to-noun, adjective-to-noun, verbal phrase-to-noun, and adjective phrase-to-adverbial phrase that can be generalized in spontaneous data. Phonologically, the ʔɐ51 suffixation can invoke a special tone sandhi pattern on the bases, resulting in their tonal realization to be different from their regular sandhi process that is triggered by the right-dominant tone sandhi system in this Southern Min dialect. Distributionally, the occurrence of this suffix in the process of word formation is also subject to several constraints from the linguistic factors of semantics, morpho-syntax, and phonology.

This study provides a comprehensive exploration of this suffix ʔɐ51 as a productive morphological device in Zhangzhou Southern Min. It aims to address three specific research questions: (a) what lexical bases can undergo suffixation with this suffix ʔɐ51? (b) What consequences can be induced in terms of semantics, morpho-syntax, and phonetic-phonology, and (c) what linguistic factors may constrain the encoding of this suffix in the word formation? The exploration fills in the research gap and is supposed to broaden and strengthen our understanding of how this suffixing contributes to word formation in this dialect. It contributes valuable empirical data to the typology of suffixation in word's natural languages, while shedding an important light on how Sinitic languages should be better defined from the interdisciplinary perspective.

2 Zhangzhou and Speech

2.1 Zhangzhou City

Zhangzhou is a prefecture-level city in Southern Fujian of Southern China, covering an area of approximately 12,600 square kilometres and a registered population of about 5.10 million in the 2020 census [14, 15]. This city faces the Taiwan Strait to its east but borders the Fujian cities of Xiamen, Quanzhou, and Longyan on its east, northwest, and west, respectively, while its southwest region borders the Chaozhou city of Guangzhou province. The colloquial language spoken by native Zhangzhou people is Southern Min, known as Hokkien and referred to as Zhangzhou speech in this study.

Regional variation can be perceived in the sound system among its administrative areas [14–16]. The study thus restricts the description to the urban area of Longwen and Xiangcheng districts, which is conventionally considered to be historically-socially-geographically-culturally-and-linguistically representative of Zhangzhou [11] and have received documentation since the 19th century, though the majority are in phonetics and phonology [8, 9, 14–24]. Only Yang [8, 9] has described the suffix ʔɐ51 but she did not explore how different linguistic levels contribute to encode this suffix in the word formation in this dialect. Thus, this study is a breakthrough to advance our knowledge in this regard.

2.2 Zhangzhou Syllables

The synchronic Zhangzhou speech can be generalised as having a C(G)V(X) syllable template in which onset and nucleus are obligatory while glide and coda are optional to occur [21, 22]. Prevocalic glides possess an independent syllable component (G) status, while postvocalic glides belong to one type of syllable coda (X). Oral vowels, nasalised vowels, and syllabic nasals can occur as nuclei, while glides, nasal consonants, and obstruent codas can occur in the coda position. The segmental system of Zhangzhou speech comprises 15 onsets, 2 prevocalic glides, 13 nuclei, and 8 codas in its segmental system, as summarized in Table 1.

2.3 Zhangzhou Tones

Zhangzhou possesses eight lexical tones, as illustrated in Table 2 with their pitch realization and corresponding name in Middle Chinese tonal category. However, to fully appreciate this assertion needs one to recognise multidimensional characteristics of tonal realisations across different linguistic contexts [14, 15]. This is because tones with a similar pitch contour can differ considerably in other phonetic parameters, such as duration, syllable type, and phonation. Similarly, tones that have an identical realisation in citation are found to be different in other linguistics contexts, such as at the non-right dominant position of multisyllabic constructions [14, 15, 24].

Table 1. Phonemic inventory for Zhangzhou syllables

Component		Phoneme
C	onset	p, pʰ, ɓ, t, tʰ, ɗ, k, kʰ, ɟ, ts, tsʰ, s, z, ɦ, ʔ
G	glide	j, w
V	nucleus	i, e, ɛ, ɐ, ɔ, ɵ, u, ĩ, ɛ̃, ɐ̃, ɔ̃, m, ŋ
X	coda	j, w, m, n, ŋ, p, t, k

Table 2. Examples of Zhangzhou citation tones

Tone		Pitch	Example 1	Example 2
1	Yinping	[35]	/tɐŋ35/ 'east'	/kɔ35/ 'mushroom'
2	Yangping	[22]	/tɐŋ22/ 'copper'	/kɔ22/ 'glue'
3	Shang	[51]	/tɐŋ51/ 'to wait'	/kɔ51/ 'drum'
4	Yinqu	[41]	/tɐŋ41/ 'frozen'	/kɔ41/ 'look after'
5	Yangqu	[33]	/tɐŋ33/ 'heavy'	/ɦɔ33/ 'rain'
6	Yinru	[41]	/tɐp41/ 'answer'	/kɔk41/ 'country'
7	Yangru	[221]	/tsɐp221/ 'ten'	/tɔk221/ 'poison'
8	Yangru	[22]	/tsi22/ 'tongue'	/kɔ̃ 22/ 'snore'

2.4 Zhangzhou Tone Sandhi

Zhangzhou presents a typically right-dominant tone sandhi system [14, 15, 24]. The sandhi domain is found to be characteristically sensitive to the boundary of syntactic phrases. Tones at the non-right-most position of syntactic phrases undergo alternation in their relations at both phonological and phonetic levels. In contrast, tones at the right-most position have their realisations categorically similar to their corresponding citation forms but are subject to a certain degree of variation at the phonetic level, because of their sensitivity to the preceding tones and utterance-final effect. Table 3 illustrates the pitch realisation of individual tones in the disyllabic context, with tone 2 serving as the carrier.

Apart from this, special sandhi patterns can be identified in the field, whose occurrences are severely constrained by very specific morphosyntactic factors, and their tonal realization show dramatically different realisations from those identified in the regular tone sandhi process. For example, tones before the suffix ʔɐ51 undergo a different sandhi pattern. The pitch of the eight tones is realised as either a high level [55] or a rising contour [35] in this suffixing context, depending on their pitch contour shape in citation. This will be discussed in detail later in this paper.

Table 3. Examples of Zhangzhou tonal realizations in disyllabic context

T	Non-right most position			Right-most position		
	X+2	pitch	Example	2+X	pitch	Example
1	1+2	[33]	/tsʰɛ̃1.tɛ2/ 'raw tea'	2+1	[34]	/tɛ2.hwɐ1/ 'camellia'
2	2+2	[33]	/ʔɐŋ2.tɛ2/ 'black tea'	2+2	[211]	/tɛ2.ɗɐw2/ 'tea house'
3	3+2	[25]	/tsɐ3.tɛ2/ 'morning tea'	2+3	[52]	/tɛ2.ɓi3/ 'dried tea'
4	4+2	[63]	/swɐ̃4.tɛ2/ 'unpacked tea'	2+4	[41]	/tɛ2.tjɐm4/ 'tea store'
5	5+2	[32]	/ʔjɔŋ5.tɛ2/ 'have tea'	2+5	[33]	/tɛ2.tsʰju5/ 'tea tree'
6	6+2	[65]	/sip6.tɛ2/ 'moisten tea'	2+6	[41]	/tɛ2.sik6/ 'tea colour'
7	7+2	[32]	/sik7.tɛ2/ 'colourful tea'	2+7	[211]	/tɛ2.sit7/ 'tea dessert'
8	8+2	[32]	/pɛ8.tɛ2/ 'Bai tea'	2+8	[211]	/tɛ2.ɦjɵ8/ 'tea leaf'

3   Zhangzhou Suffix ʔɐ*51*

The suffix ʔɐ51, a native normaliser functioning similar to a combination of suffixes *zi214*子 and *er35*儿 in Mandarin, is the most productive affix in the word formation in Zhangzhou. Its attachment can extensively expand and enrich the semantic domain, part of speech, and phonological feature of this dialect. It is diachronically related to the lexeme kjɛ̃51 for 'son, child', corresponding to the word zi214 in Mandarin [8–10], but has been evolved as a dominant diminutive suffix. This suffix further evolves into an important nominal marker and nominalizer that can occur in multiple morpho-syntactic contexts, comprising nouns, verbs, adjectives, verbal phrases, nominal phrases, adjective phrases, and classifiers. In the meanwhile, its occurrence can intrigue a special tone sandhi phenomenon on the bases, showing an integral interface between phonetics, phonology, morphology, and syntax. The following descriptions are to illustrate how the suffixing of ʔɐ51 behaves multifunctionally in this dialect, with a focus on its distribution, semantics, grammatical function, and interface with prosody.

3.1   Attached to Nouns

The suffix ʔɐ51 can be attached to nouns of a wide range of semantic domains, such as kinship term (e.g., tsɐw55-ʔɐ51 'daughter'), person name (e.g., kwɐn35-ʔɐ51 'Juan'), animal name (e.g., ke35-ʔɐ51 'chicken'), food (e.g., kɐm35-ʔɐ51 'orange'), plant (e.g., tsʰju35-ʔɐ51'tree'), vehicle (e.g., tsun35-ʔɐ51 'boat'), building (e.g., tsʰu55-ʔɐ51 'house'), stationary (e.g., tsʰɐ55-ʔɐ51 'eraser'), and clothing (e.g., sɐ̃35-ʔɐ51 'cloth') among others. Morphologically, the derived words maintain the part of speech as their nominal bases. Phonologically, the lexical bases are dominantly monosyllabic.

Functionally, there are two main roles that this suffix ʔɐ51 can perform on the nominal bases. The first one is to serve as a diminutive marker to convey the meaning of smallness and affection. It typically occurs after kinship terms (e.g., tsɐw55-ʔɐ51: daughter), person name (e.g., kwɐn35-ʔɐ51 'Juan') and animal name (e.g., tsjɐw55-ʔɐ51 'bird', as illustrated in (3). For example, with suffix ʔɐ51, the word sun35-ʔɐ51 become a colloquial expression to refer to one's nephew/niece with a sense of affection. In this case, it behaves similar like the suffix er214 儿 in Mandarin as in nü214-er35 'daughter', juan55-er35 'Juan', and niao214-er35 'bird'.

(3) Suffix ʔɐ51 as a diminutive marker

after a kinship term

tsɛw55-ʔɐ51 'daughter-ʔɐ51: daughter'
sun35-ʔɐ51 'nephew/niece-ʔɐ51: nephew/niece'
ʔi35-ʔɐ51 'sister-in-law-ʔɐ51: sister-in-law'

after a person's name

ʔɔŋ33 sjɔk65.kwɛn35 → kwɛn35-ʔɐ51 'Juan'
tɛn33 ti63.ʔwi51 → ʔwi55-ʔɐ51 'Wei'
ɦwĩ33 ʥe32.ʔjɔŋ51 → ʔjɔŋ55-ʔɐ51 'Yong'

after an animal name

ke35-ʔɐ51 'chicken'
ʔɐ55-ʔɐ51 'duck'
tsjɛw55-ʔɐ51 'bird'

However, in each semantic domain, there present strict restrictions on what sort of bases can be attached. For the kinship term category, the suffix ʔɐ51 can only be attached to lexical bases that specifically refer to those people belonging to a younger generation, such as tsɛw55-ʔɐ51 'daughter', or a younger member of the same generation, such as ʔi35-ʔɐ51 '(younger) sister-in-law'. For the person's name category, this diminutive suffix can only occur after the last syllable of the first name to express affection and closeness. For example, given someone is called ʔɔŋ33 sjɔk65.kwɛn35 in which ʔɔŋ33 is her family name, and sjɔk65.kwɛn35 is the first name, it is common for her family members to address her as kwɛn35-ʔɐ51 to show their closeness and affection. For the animal's name category, only those domestic livestock of small physical size can be attached by this suffix to convey smallness, such as chicken (e.g., ke35-ʔɐ51 'chicken') and duck (e.g., ʔɐ55-ʔɐ51 'duck').

Another role is to serve as a nominal marker when it occurs after nouns of other semantic categories. This function is the most productive to cover a wide range of semantic domains, such as food (e.g., kɐm35-ʔɐ51 'orange'), plant (e.g., ɦjə35-ʔɐ51 'leaf'), vehicle (e.g., tsun35-ʔɐ51 'boat'), utensil (e.g., tsʰjɐ35-ʔɐ51 'ladle'), building (e.g., tsʰu55-ʔɐ51 'house'), stationary (e.g., tsʰjə55-ʔɐ51 'ruler'), furniture (e.g., ʔi55-ʔɐ51 'chair'), clothing (e.g., ʔe35-ʔɐ51 'shoe'), and nature (e.g., tʰɐm35.ʔɐ51 'pond') among others. In this situation, this suffix ʔɐ51 behaves similar to the Mandarin suffix zi 子 that functions as a pure nominal marker, such as xie35-zi 'shoe', yi214-zi 'chair', ju35-zi 'orange', and ye51-zi 'leaf'. More examples can be referred to in (4).

(4) ʔɐ51 as a nominal marker

after food name

kɐm35-ʔɐ51 'orange'

dɐj35-ʔɐ51 'pear'

swɐ̃j35-ʔɐ51 'mango'

after a plant name

tsʰju35-ʔɐ51 'tree'

ɦjə35-ʔɐ51 'leaf'

tsʰiŋ35-ʔɐ51 'Banyan tree'

after a vehicle name

tsun35-ʔɐ51 'boat'

dun35-ʔɐ51 'tire'

pɐj35-ʔɐ51 'bamboo raft'

after a utensil name

ʔwe35-ʔɐ51 'pan'

tsʰjɐ35-ʔɐ51 'ladle'

pwɐ̃35-ʔɐ51 'plate'

after a building name

tsʰu55-ʔɐ51 'house'

tʰjɐw35-ʔɐ51 'pillar'

after a furniture name

ʔi55-ʔɐ51 'chair'

tə55-ʔɐ51 'desk'

after a stationary name

tsʰɐ55-ʔɐ51 'eraser'

tsʰjə55-ʔɐ51 'ruler'

pʰɔ35-ʔɐ51 'exercise book'

after clothing name

sɐ̃35-ʔɐ51 'cloth'

kʰɔ55-ʔɐ51 'trousers'

ʔe35-ʔɐ51 'shoe'

after nature name

ɦə35.ʔɐ51 'river'

kɐw35.ʔɐ51 'ditch'

tʰɐm35.ʔɐ51 'pond'

3.2 Attached to Verbs

The suffix ʔɐ51 can be attached to verbal bases and transform their word class to be nominal. The suffixation is to specify a tool, utensil, or equipment that is used to accomplish an action and/or activity as denoted by its corresponding verbal base. For example, the word tʰwi35-ʔɐ51 which means 'hammer' is derived from the verb tʰwi22 meaning 'to hammer' with this suffix ʔɐ51. Likewise, the word tsʰjɐm55-ʔɐ51 'fork' is formulated based on the verb tsʰjɐm55 that means 'to spear'. In this case, this suffix can be seen functioning as a deverbal normalizer that transfers a verb to a noun in this morphological context. More examples of this function can be seen below in (5).

(5) Suffix ʔɐ51 after verbs

ʥɛ̃55-ʔɐ51 'to clamp-ʔɐ51: pliers'
tʰwi35-ʔɐ51 'to hammer-ʔɐ51: hammer'
ɦɐp55-ʔɐ51 'to clip-ʔɐ51: clip; tong'
tsʰjɐm55-ʔɐ51 'to spear-ʔɐ5: fork'
ki63-ʔɐ51 'to saw-ʔɐ51: saw; hacksaw'

3.3 Attached to Adjectives

The suffix ʔɐ51 can occur after adjective bases and transfer their word class to be nominal. In other words, this suffix functions as a de-adjective normalizer in this morphological context. Semantically, the derived words refer to those individual people who possess a particular characteristic as expressed by the related adjective base. For example, the noun pwi35-ʔɐ51 which means 'fat person' is derived from the adjective pwi22 'fat' with the suffix ʔɐ51. More examples can be seen in (6).

(6) Suffix ʔɐ51 after adjectives

pwi35-ʔɐ51 'fat-ʔɐ51: fat person'
ʥɔŋ35-ʔɐ51 'fool-ʔɐ51: fool person'
sin35-ʔɐ51 'new-ʔɐ51: new person'
dɐw55-ʔɐ51 'experienced-ʔɐ51: experienced person'
ɓɔ̃33.sin35-ʔɐ51 'crazy-ʔɐ51: insane person'

3.4 Attached to Noun Phrases

The suffix ʔɐ51 can be attached to certain noun phrases to derive new lexemes that specify individuals who are featured of a particular physical characteristic or have a psychological problem. For example, the word ɖ̃ɵ63.kʰɐ35-ʔɐ51 that means 'a tall person' is constructed by attaching the suffix ʔɐ51 to a noun phrase ɖ̃ɵ63.kʰɐ35 that means 'tall foot'. The derived words are dominantly nominal and used in the colloquial context.

Thus, this suffix also serves as a pure nominal marker, with its semantic function like that in an adjective-ʔɐ51 pattern. More examples can be seen in (7).

(7) after noun phrases

tsʰɛ̃33.ɓɛ̃35-ʔɐ51 'blind eye-ʔɐ51: blindman'
pɐj35.kʰɐ35-ʔɐ51 'lame foot-ʔɐ51: lame person'
dɵ63.kʰɐ35-ʔɐ51 'tall-foot-ʔɐ51: tall person'

3.5 Attached to Verbal Phrases

The suffix ʔɐ51 can occur after certain verbal phrases but transfers the part of speech to be nominal, while shifting the semantics to refer to an individual person who holds an occupation denoted by its corresponding verbal base. For example, the verb phrase tsɵ63.ɦi41 means 'to perform an opera' while the derived lexeme tsɵ63.ɦi55-ʔɐ51 is used to address the person who performs the local opera. Thus, this suffix serves as a deverbal phrase-normalizer in this specific context. However, the addressing through the attachment of ʔɐ51 conveys some sort of unrespectful and informal meaning, which is dominantly used in the colloquial setting, especially in the old society in this Southern Min culture. More examples of this formation can be seen in (8).

(8) Suffix ʔɐ51 after verbal phrases

tsɵ63.ɦi55-ʔɐ51 'to perform opera-ʔɐ51: local opera actor; performer'
tʰɐj33.ti35-ʔɐ51 'to kill pig-ʔɐ51: pork butcher'
ɓe32.ɦi35-ʔɐ51 'to sell fish-ʔɐ51: fish seller'
ɓɔ35.ʔe35-ʔɐ51 'to repair shoe-ʔɐ51: cobbler'
tʰi63.tʰɐw35-ʔɐ51 'to shave head-ʔɐ51: barber'

3.6 Attached to Adjective Phrases

The suffix ʔɐ51 can be attached to adjective phrases and convert their category into adverbial phrases to express a semantics of lightness and slowness. In other words, the suffix ʔɐ51 functions as an adverbializer, which is similar to the suffix -ly in English and -de 地 in Mandarin. The adjective bases have to be in a reduplicated form, show-ing a strict restriction on the selection of lexical bases. For example, the adverbial phrase ɓɐn35.ɓɐn35-ʔɐ51 meaning 'very slowly' is derived by reduplicating the adjec-tive ɓɐn35 'slow' with the suffix ʔɐ51. More examples can be seen in (9). Morpho-syntactically, the derived expressions can be used to modify verbs to form verbal phrases, such as ɓɐn35.ɓɐn35-ʔɐ51-kjɛ̃22 that means 'to walk slowly'.

(9) Suffix ʔɐ51 after adjective phrases

ɓɐn32.ɓɐn35-ʔɐ51 'slow.slow-ʔɐ51: very slowly'
kʰiŋ33.kʰiŋk35-ʔɐ51 'light.light-ʔɐ51: very lightly'
ʔwen35.ʔwen35-ʔɐ51 'steady.steady-ʔɐ51: very steadily'
ɓwi33.ɓwi33.ʔɐ51 'slight-slight-ʔɐ51: very slightly'

3.7 Attached to Classifiers

The suffix ʔɐ51 can be attached to some classifiers either in their single forms or redu-plicated forms to create numeral-classifier-ʔɐ51 or numeral-classifier-classifier-ʔɐ51 patterns. Semantically, the main function of these patterns is to emphasize the limited amount of the nominal entity being counted, such as tsit32.tjɐm55-ʔɐ51 'a tiny dot of', and tsit32.si35.si35-ʔɐ51 'a tiny teaspoon of'. The reduplicated form delivers an extra sense of reduction in quantity. More examples about the suffixing on classifiers can be seen in (10). Morpho-syntactically, the two patterns can be further attached by nouns to form classifier phrases, such as tsit32.tjɐm55-ʔɐ51-ʔju22 'a dot of oil' which modifies the noun ʔju22 that means 'oil'. Similarly, tsit32.si35.si35-ʔɐ51-ʔjɐm22 'a tiny teaspoon of salt' which modifies the noun ʔjɐm22 meaning 'salt'.

(10) Suffix ʔɐ51 after classifiers

Single forms

tsit32.tjɐm55-ʔɐ51 'one dot-ʔɐ51: a tiny dot of'
tsit32.ti55-ʔɐ51 'one drop-ʔɐ51: a tiny drop of'
tsit32.si35-ʔɐ51 'one teaspoon-ʔɐ51: a tiny spoon of'

Reduplicated forms

tsit32.tjɐm35.tjɐm55-ʔɐ51 'one.dot.dot-ʔɐ51: just a little tiny dot of'
tsit32.ti63.ti55-ʔɐ51 'one drop.drop-ʔɐ51: just a tiny drop of'
tsit32.si35.si35-ʔɐ51 'one teaspoon.teaspoon-ʔɐ51: just a tiny teaspoon of'

4 Discussion

As described, the suffix ʔɐ51 is very productive to formulate new lexemes in this dialect, significantly enlarging the inventory of local vocabulary by either altering semantic meanings or changing the part of speech of lexical bases, or both. Table 4 summaries the encoding of this suffix, while the following discussion generalizes some salient features about its suffixing from the perspectives of (1) semantic function (2) morpho-syntactic function (3) interface with prosody, and (4) occurrence constraint.

4.1 Semantic Function

The suffix *ʔɐ51* presents an extra-ordinarily polysemantic characteristics. It can be attached to the bases of several different word classes (noun, verb, adjective, noun

Table 4. Summary of ʔɐ51 suffixation in Zhangzhou

Suffix	Input	Output	Semantics	Morpho-Syntax	Prosody
ʔɐ51	noun	noun	diminution, closeness affection, smallness	nominal marker	special tone sandhi
		noun	pure nominal marker		
	verb	noun	tool and equipment	nominalizer	
	adjective	noun	people of a particular characteristics	nominalizer	
	noun phrase	noun	people of physical disadvantage	nominal marker	
	verbal phrase	noun	people of a particular occupation	nominalizer	
	adjective phrase	noun phrase	sense of lightness and slowness	nominalizer	
	classifier	classifier phrase	sense of small quantity	adverbializer	

phrase, verbal phrase, adjective phrase, and classifier) to create new lexemes across various semantic domains. As shown in Table 4, the semantics that this suffix can encode are cross-categorical, broadly comprising smallness, closeness and affection (e.g., tsɐw55-ʔɐ51 daughter-ʔɐ51:daughter), tool and equipment (e.g., ɦɐp55-ʔɐ51 'to clip-ʔɐ51: clip; tong'), people of a particular characteristics (e.g., pwi35-ʔɐ51 'fat-ʔɐ51: fat person'), people of a physical or psychological disadvantage (e.g., ɓɔ33.sin35-ʔɐ51 'crazy man-ʔɐ51: insane person'), people of a specific occupation (e.g., pʰɐ63.tʰi55-ʔɐ51 'to forge iron-ʔɐ51: blacksmith, ironsmith'), sense of lightless and slowness (e.g., kʰiŋ33.kʰiŋ35-ʔɐ51 'light.light-ʔɐ51: very lightly'), and sense of small quantity (e.g., tsit32.ti63.ti55-ʔɐ51 'one drop.drop-ʔɐ51: just a tiny drop of') among others.

The polysemantic characteristics of this suffixation is also reflected in the aspect that, even within the same grammatical category, the suffix ʔɐ51 can be attached to the bases of a wide range of semantic domains. For example, when attached to a nominal bases to deliver a diminutive function, the bases can cover kinship terms (e.g., tsɐw55-ʔɐ51 'daughter') and person names (e.g., kwɐn35-ʔɐ51 'Juan') to convey a semantics of closeness and affections, and cover animal names (e.g., ke35-ʔɐ51 'chicken') to deliver a semantics of smallness. Similarly, when attaching to a nominal category but serving as a pure nominal marker, the bases that can be attached by this ʔɐ51 are very diverse, covering food (e.g., dʑej35-ʔɐ51 'pear'), plant (e.g., tsʰiŋ35-ʔɐ51 'Banyan tree'), vehicle (e.g., pɐj35-ʔɐ51 'bamboo raft'), utensil (e.g., tsʰjɐ35-ʔɐ51 'ladle'), building (e.g., tsʰu55-ʔɐ51 'house'), nature (e.g., kɐw35.ʔɐ51 'ditch'), stationary (e.g., pʰɔ35-ʔɐ51 'exercise book'), and clothing (e.g., ɓwe35-ʔɐ51 'sock') among others. As seen, the semantic information that the suffix ʔɐ51 can convey are multifarious, so are the bases that can be suffixed by this ʔɐ51.

4.2 Morpho-syntactic Function

The suffixation of ʔɐ51 can encode multiple morphosyntactic roles in the formation of new lexemes or new phrases in this Southern Min variety. As summarised in Table 4, the roles that the suffix ʔɐ51 performs include (a) nominaliser (e.g., tʰwi35-ʔɐ51 'to hammer-ʔɐ51: hammer') that derives lexemes of a nominal category from the bases of a non-nominal part of speech; (b) nominal marker (e.g., kɐw35.ʔɐ51 'ditch-ʔɐ51:ditch') that maintains the nominal category of the bases over the suffixation, and (c) adverbialiser (e.g., tsit32.si35.si35-ʔɐ51 'one teaspoon.teaspoon-ʔɐ51: a tiny teaspoon of') that changes the word class to be an adverbial.

As seen, this suffixing process can extensively change the word class of the bases and derive new lexical items of a different category. Four different derivational processes can be generalised, including verb-to-noun (e.g., ħɐp55-ʔɐ51 'to clip-ʔɐ51: clip; tong'), adjective-to-noun (e.g., ɠɔŋ35-ʔɐ51 'fool-ʔɐ51: fool person'), verb phrase-to-noun (e.g., tʰɐj33.ti35-ʔɐ51 'to kill pig-ʔɐ51: butcher'), and adjective phrase-to-adverbial phrase (e.g., ɓɐn32.ɓɐn35-ʔɐ51 'slow.slow-ʔɐ51: very slowly'). Likewise, the bases that can undergo this derivational suffixation are also cross-categorical, ranging from the noun, verb, adjective, classifier, noun phrase, verb phrase, and adjective phrase among seven different types. Thus, the suffixation can cause dramatic changes in the morpho-syntactic category of the bases, while alternating their semantic meanings.

4.3 Interface with Prosody

The suffix *ʔɐ51*, which itself has a lexical tone of high falling pitch, can trigger a special tone sandhi process on the bases, rendering them to have different tonal realisations from their corresponding forms in citation and the forms occurring at the non-rightmost position of general morpho-syntactic contexts [14, 15, 24]. Specifically, tones of the bases are realised as either a high level [55] or a rising pitch contour [35] in this specific morpho-syntactic context, depending on their pitch contour in citation. In general, the base with a falling pitch contour in citation, regardless of whether it is a high falling or a mid-high falling contour, is realized as a high-level [55] contour before this suffix. On the contrary, the base with a non-falling pitch contour in citation, regardless of whether it is rising or level, is realised as a rising pitch [35]. For example, tone 3 has a high falling [51] contour in citation (e.g., kɐw51 'dog'), while the pitch is changed to a rising [35] contour in the general sandhi (non-right-most) position (e.g., kɐw35.ɓɵ51 'bitch'); but before this suffix ʔɐ51, the pitch is changed to be a high level [55] (e.g., kɐw55-ʔɐ51 'dog'). Examples of this special tone sandhi are illustrated in (5). This special tonal alternation can be considered to be entirely morphologically conditioned by this suffix

ʔɐ51, showing a close interface between semantics, morpho-syntax, and prosody in this morphological process of word formation (Table 5).

Table 5. Special tone sandhi before the suffix *ʔɐ51*

Base	Citation	General Sandhi			Before ʔɐ51 Example	
T1	[35]	[33]		i33.ɓɵ51 'sow'	[35]	ti35-ʔɐ51 'pig'
T2	[22]	[33]		ɦi33.dwĩ33 'fish egg'	[35]	ɦi35-ʔɐ51 'fish'
T3	[51]	[35]		kɐw35.ɓɵ51 'bitch'	[55]	kɐw55-ʔɐ51 'dog'
T4	[41]	[63]		tsʰu63.tsu51 'landlord'	[55]	tsʰu55-ʔɐ51 'house'
T5	[33]	[32]		ɦi32.kʰɐŋ51 'ear piercing'	[35]	ɦi35-ʔɐ51 'ear'
T6	[41]	[65]		tik65.kɵ35 'bamboo pole'	[55]	tik55-ʔɐ51 'bamboo'
T7	[221]	[32]		ʥɔk32.tsu35 'jade beads'	[35]	ʥɔk35-ʔɐ51 'jade'
T8	[22]	[32]		tsi32.tʰɐj35 'tongue fatal'	[35]	tsi35-ʔɐ51 'tongue'

4.4 Occurrence Constraints

Although this suffixing is productive in this dialect, the process is severely constrained to create new lexemes that are grammatically well-formed. The conditioning factors are multifarious, comprising semantics, syntax, and morpho-syntax.

(1) Semantic condition

The occurrence of this suffix can be strictly limited to certain semantic domains. Specifically, it can only suffix those kinship terms that denote a younger generation (e.g., sun35-ʔɐ51 'nephew/niece-ʔɐ51: nephew/niece') or a younger member of the same generation (e.g., ku35-ʔɐ51 'brother-in-law-ʔɐ51: brother-in-law') to express one's affection and closeness, while it is prohibited from occurring in those kinship terms that indicates an elder generation. Similarly, this suffix *ʔɐ51* can refer to a particular group of people but only those who are physically and psychologically reduced, such as have a disadvantaged appearance (e.g., pwi35-ʔɐ51 'fat-ʔɐ51: fat person' or have a mental problem (e.g., ʥɔŋ35-ʔɐ51 'fool-ʔɐ51: fool person').

(2) Morpho-syntactic condition

The suffixation with this ʔɐ51 can be morpho-syntactically constrained, reflected in the selection of lexical bases to form grammatically well-formed expressions. For example, the suffix ʔɐ51 can be attached to adjective phrases and convert their syntactic category into adverbial phrases to express a semantics of lightness and slowness. However, the adjective bases are requested to be in a reduplicated form. Such as, the adverbial phrase ɓɐn35.ɓɐn35-ʔɐ51 that means 'very slowly' is derived by reduplicating the adjective ɓɐn35 'slow' with the suffix ʔɐ51 to indicate an action that is conducted slowly. Similarly, the suffix ʔɐ51, denoting a person with a certain profession, requires the base to be either a noun phrase (e.g., tsʰɛ̃33.ɓɛ̃35-ʔɐ51 'blind eye-ʔɐ51: blindman') or a verb phrase (e.g., tʰɐj33.ti35-ʔɐ51 'pork butcher').

(3) Phonological condition

Some cases exist where only parts of the lexical bases, rather than the entire bases, can be attached by this suffix to express a particular semantic function. This constraint mainly occurs on suffixing ʔɐ51 as a diminutive marker to personal names. In this case, neither the full name, the family name, nor the full first name can be suffixed. Instead, only the last syllable of the first name can be attached by this suffix to denote the feeling of affection and closeness. For example, given a person's full name is ɦwĩ33 ɟe32.ʔjɔŋ51 (ɦwĩ33 is the family name, while ɟe32.ʔjɔŋ51 is the first name), it is only grammatically well-formed to address him as ʔjɔŋ55-ʔɐ51 to show closeness, whereas it is ill-formed to call him as *ɦwĩ35-ʔɐ51 and *ɟe32.ʔjɔŋ55-ʔɐ51 within the social-cultural backwound of the Southern Min community. The condition involves which syllable can be suffixed, and thus can be considered to be phonologically relevant.

5 Conclusion

Although only one suffix is discussed in this study, its suffixing has become an important morphological phenomenon in Zhangzhou Southern Min, which can substantially influence the semantics, morpho-syntax and phonology of this dialect. Semantically, this suffix presents an extraordinarily polysemantic characteristics that can richly expand the local vocabulary. Morpho-syntactically, this suffix fulfills multiple roles as a nominalizer, nominal marker, and adverbialier, which can substantially change the part of speech of lexical bases. Phonologically, the ʔɐ51 suffixation can invoke a special tone sandhi pattern on the morphemes that occur immediately before this suffix, showing a close interface between different linguistic levels. Distributionally, the occurrence of this suffix and also the selection of the bases may subject to several constraints from semantics, morpho-syntax and phonology. This study fills in the research gap of suffixation study in this dialect, while strengthening our understanding of how this single suffix ʔɐ51 contributes to word formation in this Southern Min variety. The comprehensive exploration also contributes vital well-attested linguistic data to the generalization of area characteristics of suffixation within the Sino-Tibetan language family, but also to the typology in world's natural languages. The multiple linguistic functions of this suffix ʔɐ51 and its inducing impacts on the internal structures of this dialect substantially question the conventional impression that defines Sinitic languages as being isolated because of lacking affixation in their morphological system, while shedding an important light on how Sinitic languages should be better defined from the interdisciplinary perspective.

References

1. Liao, W.: Morphology. In: The Handbook of Chinese Linguistics, Huang, C., Audrey, Y., Li, A. (eds.) John Wiley & Sons (2014)
2. Arcodia, G., Basciano, B.: On the productivity of the Chinese affixes −兒 −r, −化 −huà and −頭 −tou. Taiwan J. Linguist. **10**(2), 89–118 (2012)
3. Basciano, B.: Morphology. In: Sybesma, R., Behr, W., Gu, Y., Handel, Z., Huang, J., Myers, J. (eds.) Encyclopedia of Chinese Language and Linguistics. Brill, Leiden (2017)

4. Arcodia, G., Basciano, B.: Chinese Linguistics: An Introduction. Oxford University Press, Oxford (2022)
5. Bybee, J., Pagliuca, W., Perkins, R.: In: Croft, W., Denning, K., Kemmer, S. (eds.) On the Asymmetries in the Affixation of Grammatical Material Studies in Typology and Diachrony, pp. 1–42. John Benjamins, Amsterdam (1990)
6. Banfi, E., Francesco, G.: The 生shēng/Sheng Complex Words in Chinese Between Morphology and Semantics. In Proceedings of the sixth Mediterranean Morphology Meeting, Morphology and Dialectology, pp.190–204 (2007)
7. Cao, F., Liu, X.: Correspondence of form and meaning in the grammaticalization of min diminutives. Lang. Linguist. **9**(3), 629–657 (2008)
8. Yang, X.: On the combination and the evolution of the decorative word 'Zai' in Zhangzhou dialect (Zhangzhou Fangyan Zai zhui yuci de Zuhe yu Yanbian). J. Chuxiong Norm. Univ. **23**(12), 28–32 (2008)
9. Yang, X.: Tone sandhi of the suffix [a] 仔 of Zhangzhou Dialect in Fujian Province (Zhangzhou fangyan 'Zai'zhuici de Liangzizu Liandu Biandiao). Fangyan **1**, 50–55 (2006)
10. Chappell, H.: A sketch of Southern min grammar. In: Vittrant, A., Watkins, J. (eds.) The Mainland Southeast Asia Linguistic Area, pp. 176–233 (2019)
11. Fan, J., Ding, C.: The semantic differences and substitution restrictions of -Zhe(着) and Zhengzai(正在). In: Hong, J.F., Su, Q., Wu, J.S. (eds.) Chinese Lexical Semantics (CLSW 2018). LNCS. Springer, Cham (2018)
12. Chen, Z.: The common origin of diminutives in southern Chinese dialects and Southeast Asian languages. Linguist. Tibeto-Burman Area **22**(2), 21–47 (1999)
13. Li, C.: An analysis of the grammaticalization, coercion mechanisms and formation motivation of the new construction 'XX Zi' from the cognitive perspective. In: Dong, M., Gu, Y., Hong, J.F. (eds.) Chinese Lexical Semantics (CLSW 2021). LNCS. Springer, Cham (2022)
14. Huang, Y.: Tones in Zhangzhou: Pitch and Beyond. Cambridge Scholar Publishing, Cambridge (2020)
15. Huang, Y.: Tones in Zhangzhou: Pitch and Beyond. Doctoral thesis: Australian National University (2018)
16. Ma, C.: Studies of Zhangzhou Dialect (Zhangzhou Fangyan Yanjiu). Zongheng Chubanshe, Hongkong (1994)
17. Lin, B.: Zhangzhou Vocabularies" (Zhangzhou fangyan cihui). Fangyan 1–3 (1992)
18. FJG. Fujian Province Gazette-Dialect Volume (Fujian Shengzhi-Fangyan juan). Fangzhi Chubanshe, Beijing (1998)
19. ZZG. Zhangzhou City Gazette-Dialect Volume (Zhangzhou shizhi -fangyan juan). Zhongguo Shehui Kexue Chubanshe, Beijing (1999)
20. Gao, R.: Introduction to the Sound System of Zhangzhou (Zhangzhou Fangyan Yinxi Lveshuo). In Minnan dialect-studies of Zhangzhou variety (Minnan Zhangzhou Fangyan Yanjiu), p. 109. Zhongguo Wenlian Chubanshe, Beijing (1999)
21. Huang, Y.: Zhangzhou Southern Min: Rhyme Tables, Homonyms, Heteronyms, Vernacular Documentation. Lincom Europa, München (2019)
22. Huang, Y.: Zhangzhou Southern Min: Syllables and Phonotactics. Lincom Europa, München (2021)
23. Huang, Y.: Nasality in Zhangzhou: distribution and constraint. In: Proceedings of the 25th Conference of the Oriental COCOSDA, 24–26 November 2022. Hanoi University of Science – Vietnam National University of Hanoi, Hanoi (2022)
24. Huang, Y.: Right-dominant tones in Zhangzhou: on and through the phonetic surface. In: Proceeding of the 34th annual Conference on Computational Linguistics and Speech Processing in Taiwan, 21–22 November 2022, Taipei Medical University (2022)
25. Tsao, F.-F., Liu, H.-H.: Correspondence of form and meaning in the grammaticalization of min diminutives. Lang. Linguist. **9**(3), 629–657 (2008)

Does Bert Know How 'Virus' Evolved: Tracking Usage Changes in Chinese Textual Data

Jing Chen[⊠], Le Qiu, Bo Peng, and Chu-Ren Huang

Department of Chinese and Bilingual Studies, The Hong Kong Polytechnic University, Yuk Choi Road 11, Hung Hom, Kowloon, Hong Kong, China
{jing95.chen,22068051R}@connect.polyu.hk,
{peng-bo.peng,churen.huang}@polyu.edu.hk

Abstract. Recent studies indicated a trend of quantifying lexical semantic changes with distributional models. In this study, we investigated whether state-of-the-art language models can tell us the story of how a word developed its senses over time. Specifically, we exploited the Bert model to obtain sense representations and quantitatively track usage changes after performing sense classification for each occurrence of targets in a historical newspaper dataset(People's Daily(1954–2003). Our experiment provided a positive answer to the research question, as the model has an overall precision score of 91.82% on classifying senses against human judgments. We also charted usage changes of targets, which demonstrates a possible way to (semi-)automatically observe the development of word meanings.

Keywords: Usage changes · Sense representations · Sense classification · Sense distribution

1 Introduction

Distributional models have recently been integrated into studies of historical semantics, which has demonstrated an advantage on the quantitative side with their probabilistic nature [1,2]. For example, evaluating whether and to what extent a word has changed over time is a flourishing research topic that stands at the intersection of historical semantics and distributional semantics in the past two decades [3,4].

Computational studies on lexical semantic changes predominately adopted static word embeddings to represent word meanings in different time bins and then compare them between time bins [1,3,5]. While this type of embeddings outperformed others in several evaluation tasks, its interpretability in terms what sense(s) has changed is still limited mainly due to the model architecture [4,6,7]. In contrast with using one abstract vector to represent one word in the underlying corpus, more recent contextualized word embeddings could represent word tokens with different embeddings, which further represent different usages of a word type

M. Dong et al. (Eds.): CLSW 2023, LNAI 14515, pp. 116–125, 2024.
https://doi.org/10.1007/978-981-97-0586-3_10

[8,9]. This state-of-the-art computational model has shown its power to capture usage or sense changes in the diachronic corpus or sense divergences between other types of corpora [10,11].

Studies using contextualized word embeddings to track sense changes focus on English data, while Chinese datasets are awaiting further investigation. We know very little about whether contextualized word embeddings, such as Bert, can identify a Chinese word that has usage changes. If yes, whether *Bert* can further tell us how this change happens in a continuous and quantifiable way.

To answer these two questions, we first take *Bert* to obtain sense representations for target words with the help of *Xiandai Hanyu Cidian(7th edition)* [12] and to classify usage distributions of each target word in yearly textual data of a diachronic corpus, *People's Daily* Newspaper dataset. Our method roughly follows [10]. In this study, we focus on lexical usage changes that happened during the period preceding and following the *Reform and Opening Up* in the recent history of China.

Our study further suggested that contextualized word embeddings, such as Bert, could serve as a tool to supplement traditional lexicographic work by providing a continuous track of how the usages evolved in the underlying historical corpus.

2   Related Work

There are mainly two ways to signal usage changes over time using distributional models. The predominant type is 1) to obtain meaning representations that build for each target word in different temporal bins, either relying on the sparse co-occurrence matrix [13–17] or using the prediction-based vectors [18–22], and 2) to compare word representations in the temporal dimension, which further indicated meaning changes over time. Another paradigm takes the topic-based method, such as Latent Dirichlet Allocation (LDA, [23]), to identify the changes of topics that a word appeared, and further to hint usage changes over time [24,25].

Although most studies focus on quantifying whether and to what extent a word has changed as a whole, several studies investigated sense changes by differentiating senses with context vectors or 'graphs'. For example, [13,14] represented each occurrence of target words as context vectors and then calculated changes in the semantic density [13,14]. [26] represented target words and their syntactic features using graphs, where nodes are target words and edge weights are the number of features that two corresponding words share in common, and further identified changes of 'graphs' as sense changes.

With the very recent development in computational science, contextualized word embeddings have shown a remarkable advantage over static word embeddings in polysemy-related tasks, such as machine translation [27,28]. Contextualized word embeddings, such as Bert, have recently been used to detect lexical semantic changes over time. It first 1) retrieved token embeddings for every occurrence of a target word in the underlying corpus and 2) acquires usage representations for each target word by either supervised [10] or unsupervised [11] clustering those token embeddings into different groups.

[11] exploits the Bert model to obtain token embeddings for each word in the list of 100 changed words derived from [29] and then adopts the K-Means clustering to group these representations into different types. Usage changes thus could be identified and quantified. In contrast with this unsupervised clustering, [10] classified each token embedding into different meaning groups by first training sense representations for those that identified in the Oxford Dictionary.

3   Methodology

Considering the time and efficiency, we adopted a method similar to that of [10]. We first take Bert to obtain sense representations for a list of target words extracted from [30], a book covering lexical semantic changes that were identified in the period of *Reform and Opening Up*. And we used a reference dictionary, [12], that defines the number of senses that a target word needs to be differentiated. By doing so, we then discuss when and how each of them has changed in this period of history.

3.1   Corpus

The dataset exploited in this study is derived from *People's Daily*, which is one of the most popular newspapers in China and covers a wide range of topics. Our dataset has almost daily coverage from 1954 to 2003, and the daily news within this time range is sorted based on its release date and stored in a Markdown format. The overall dataset has 31.4 million word tokens.

3.2   Target Words

We manually picked up words that were identified as changed words during the *Reform and Opening Up* in [30]. Besides, we took *Xiandai Hanyu Cidian* [12] to check whether new senses identified in the book are stable and have been absorbed into dictionaries.

Considering the historical dataset that we have, we further checked whether sentences containing target words are used in continuous yearly data and whether it has limited occurrence in our data. After filtering those words, we finally collected 16 target words.

3.3   Sense Representations

The Bert model is initially trained based on a large scale of data with two specific tasks, predicting masked token representations (Masked Language Model, MLM) and the next sentence (Next Sentence Prediction, NSP) [8]. It can be fine-tuned for downstream tasks, which proved to be very efficient. In this study, we used

Chinese-BERT-WWM [31], with 12 layers, 769 hidden dimensions, and 110M parameters, for experiments.

For each word-of-interest, we first manually extracted all senses listed in [12] and collected at most 10 sentences for each sense from the CCL corpus[1] as inputs.

For each word w_i, its usages are defined as $s_a, s_b, ..., s_i$ with reference to the dictionary [12]. For each sense of w_i, we first retrieved token embeddings from relative input sentences and took the average of these token embeddings as sense representations. More specifically, we obtain token embeddings for target words from the last layer of the *BERT* model based on its position in each sentence. For those bisyllabic words and trisyllabic words, we first concatenated token embeddings of each character in the word according to their position in the sentences and then took the average as representations.

By doing so, we got 42 sense representations for 16 target words[2].

3.4   Sense Classification

We first extracted every sentence containing a target word from the historical newspaper dataset with a yearly granularity. We then fed each sentence into the Bert model to retrieve token embeddings for the occurrence of the target word in the sentence.

To classify token embeddings into different sense groups, we calculated cosine similarities between the token embedding and each sense representation, respectively. Token embeddings thus can be classified into different groups based on the highest similarity scores.

4   Evaluation on Sense Classification

To evaluate sense classification, we randomly sampled 100 sentences for each target word from this 50-year dataset, then we got 1600 sentences for annotation in total. We recruited two native speakers holding an MA degree in linguistics to identify the sense of each target word in each sampled sentence.

Table 1 shows a sample of the annotation environment, asking each annotator to indicate their understanding of each occurrence of a target word in the sampled sentences. Annotators can indicate the sense of the target word in each sampled sentence, referencing the senses listed in the dictionary. Besides, he or she can also mark the sentence as 'NA' to indicate the error of word segmentation on target words and as 'P' to refer to the ambiguity of the target word in the underlying context. The inter-rater agreement in general is pretty high, with a *cohen's kappa* score of *0.935*.

---

[1] CCL corpus: http://ccl.pku.edu.cn:8080/ccl_corpus/index.jsp, and the BCC corpus: http://bcc.blcu.edu.cn.

[2] We excluded those senses that have very few sentences found in both the CCL corpus and the BCC corpus.

Table 1. Annotation sample. *Year* and *index* refer to the releasing year of this sentence and its index in all sentences containing this target word 病毒 *bingdu, 'virus'* in this year.

Year	Index	Sentence	Annotator1	Reference
1995	265	计算机"幽灵"病毒有了克星		病毒：1. 比细菌更小的病原体 2. 指计算机病毒
2003	925	对乙肝病毒携带者的歧视和恐惧，都缘于对相关知识的不了解		

Setting sampled sentences with the same sense indicated by both two annotators as golden answers, the overall accuracy of the Bert model reaches *91.82%*. Table 2 shows more overall statistics.

Table 2. Overall statistics of the Bert-WWM model against our golden answers. Valid samples refer to the number of sample sentences that are set as golden answers.

Overall accurracy	Cohen's kappa	Valid samples	Correctly classified	Incorrectly classified
91.82%	0.8739	1455	1336	119

Among all 16 target words, 载体 *zaiti, 'carrier'*、起步 *qibu, 'starting point or initial stage'*、出台 *chutai, 'introduce or put forward'*、滑坡 *huapo, 'landslide'*、联姻 *lianyin, 'marriage or alliance'* have higher precision, with scores above *95.00%*. In contrast, 病毒 *bingdu, 'virus'*、消化 *xiaohua, 'digest'*、下海 *xiahai, 'go into the sea or enter the market'* have lower precision scores descending from *80.68%* to *73.02%*, as illustrated in Fig. 1.

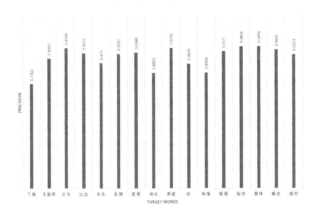

Fig. 1. Target words and their precision scores against human judgments

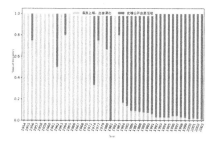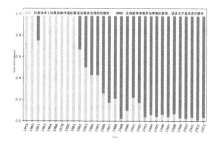

Fig. 2. Normalized stacked bar charts for two target words: *chutai*(left) and *zaiti*(right). Colors represented different senses of target words in the appearing years.

5 Discussion

As reported in Sect. 4, the Bert model has achieved quite a good classification performance on five target words, 载体 *zaiti*, *'carrier'*、起步 *qibu*, *'starting point or initial stage'*、出台 *chutai*, *'introduce or put forward'*、滑坡 *huapo*, *'landslide'* and 联姻 *lianyin*, *'marriage or alliance'*, which are with precision values above *95.00%*. These five words are identified as words with two senses, and one sense of each target shows strong usage dominance in our samples. For example, around *95%* samples for both 载体 and 出台 suggested preferences in their emergent senses over their original meanings, *data or information carrier* and *introduce or launch*, respectively.

We further charted sense distributions of 载体 *zaiti*, *'carrier'* and 出台 *chutai*, *'introduce or put forward'* using our historical data. As demonstrated in Fig. 2, the left one illustrated that the sense *introduce or launch* of the target word 出台 *chutai*, *'introduce or put forward'* took over the absolute dominance in usages around the 1980 s in our newspaper corpus. Similarly, the sense *data or information carrier* of 载体 *zaiti*, *'carrier'* won a particular preference starting from the 1980 s, regardless of its few appearances from the 1950 s to the 1970 s.

As for targets with lower accuracy in classification, we found that these words have more identified senses, especially are more sophisticated. For example, the target 下海 *xiahai*, *'go into the sea or enter the market'* that is with the lowest precision score has 4 identified senses in the reference dictionary [12]. Among them, Sense 1 and Sense 2 are more closely related, with different profiling in terms of the aims of the action, *into the sea*, as generally *entertainment* for sense 1 and *make a living* for sense 2. The sophisticated differentiation between them posed a challenge to our model, as 7 out of 17 incorrectly classified samples were confused by these two senses.

下海 'Xiahai'
- 1. 到海中去: ～游泳 (Go into the sea: Go swimming in the sea.)
- 2. (渔民)到海上(捕鱼): 初次～, 头晕、呕吐是难免的((Fishermen) Go out to sea (fishing): It's inevitable to feel dizzy and nauseous on the first time going out to sea)

- 3. 指业余戏曲演员成为职业演员 (Amateur opera performers becoming professional actors.)
- 4. 旧时指从事某些行业(如娼妓、舞女等)(In the past, it referred to engaging in certain professions (such as courtesans, dancers, etc.).)
- 5. 指放弃原来的工作而经营商业(To give up one's original job and start a business)

Besides the sophistication of senses, the model is also confused by overlying the salient distributions of senses. For example, the Bert model lost its score in classifying the target word in sentences like '著名歌星李玲玉近日已"下海"办公司' *Famous singer Li Lingyu recently "entered the market" by starting a company..* '歌星(singer)' and '办公司(start a company)' are salient features for Sense 3 and Sense 5. Similarly, it also happens in the case of the polysemous word 消化 *xiaohua, 'digest'*, which has three identified senses, as in *digest food, digest knowledge*, and *digest supplies(talents, goods)*. When the typical distribution features of Sense 2 and Sense 3 interplayed within one sentence, the model usually would be misled.

In terms of the case 病毒 *bingdu, 'virus'*, we unexpectedly found the misclassified targets predominantly appeared in the context of '艾滋病毒' (HIV). Although the original similarity scores for classifying these targets showed minor differences between the two senses, it told us to provide more input sentences to obtain more accurate sense representations. The case of '病毒' *bingdu, 'virus'* also suggested that the fluctuations in usage dominance are under the influence of social context. As in Fig. 3, the usage of *computer virus* has had an emergent

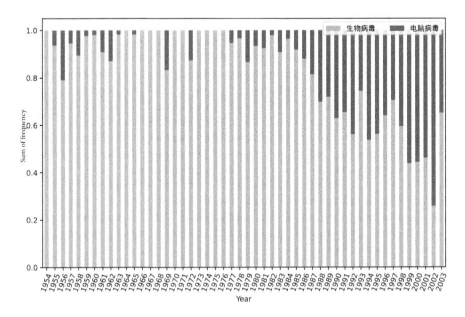

Fig. 3. A normalized stacked bar chart for sense distribution of 病毒 *bingdu, 'virus'* in our data

dominance in usage since 1979. However, this dominance changed suddenly in the year of 2003, as the SARS-CoV disease swept China at that time.

6   Conclusions

To sum up, we investigated the usage changes of Chinese words with a state-of-the-art model, Bert-WWM. Our results indicated a positive answer to our research question: Can the Bert model capture the semantic development of a Chinese word? Our results showed that Bert performs well on classifying usages in the historical dataset against human judgments, with an overall precision of 91.82%. We further discussed three possible reasons, the sophistication, the overlying of distributional features of senses, and the lack of sufficient training sentences, which could lead to misclassification. By charting the usages of 病毒 *bingdu, 'virus'* in our underlying corpus, we suggested that it is possible to quantify sense distribution and observe usage changes dynamically. We also found that the fluctuation of usage is under a strong influence of social context.

In the next step, we plan to boost our model's performance on sense classification with improvements from three identified reasons, which served as a better grounding for charting the sense distribution of words from a diachronic perspective. Besides, we will test our model with more target words.

References

1. Hamilton, W.L., Leskovec, J., Jurafsky, D.: Cultural shift or linguistic drift? Comparing two computational measures of semantic change. In: Proceedings of the 2016 Conference on Empirical Methods in Natural Language Processing, Austin, Texas, November 2016, pp. 2116–2121. Association for Computational Linguistics (2016)
2. Hamilton, W.L., Leskovec, J., Jurafsky, D.: Diachronic word embeddings reveal statistical laws of semantic change. In: Erk, K., mith, N.A. (eds.) Proceedings of the 54th Annual Meeting of the Association for Computational Linguistics (Volume 1: Long Papers), Berlin, Germany, August 2016, pp. 1489–1501. Association for Computational Linguistics (2016)
3. Tahmasebi, N., Borin, L., Jatowt, A.: Survey of computational approaches to lexical semantic change detection, chap. 1. Language Science Press (2021)
4. Schlechtweg, D., McGillivray, B., Hengchen, S., Dubossarsky, H., Tahmasebi, N.: SemEval-2020 task 1: unsupervised lexical semantic change detection. In: Proceedings of the Fourteenth Workshop on Semantic Evaluation, Barcelona (online), December 2020, pp. 1–23. International Committee for Computational Linguistics (2020)
5. Kulkarni, V., Al-Rfou, R., Perozzi, B., Skiena, S.: Statistically significant detection of linguistic change. In: Proceedings of the 24th International Conference on World Wide Web, WWW '15, Republic and Canton of Geneva, CHE, pp. 625–635. International World Wide Web Conferences Steering Committee (2015)
6. F Dubossarsky, H., Hengchen, S., Tahmasebi, N., Schlechtweg, D.: Time-out: temporal referencing for robust modeling of lexical semantic change. In: Proceedings

of the 57th Annual Meeting of the Association for Computational Linguistics, Florence, Italy, July 2019, pp. 457–470. Association for Computational Linguistics (2019)

7. Chen, J., Peng, B., Huang, C.-R.: Tracing lexical semantic change with distributional semantics: change and stability. In: Su, Q., Xu, G., Yang, X. (eds.) Chinese Lexical Semantics: 23rd Workshop, CLSW 2022, Virtual Event, May 14–15, 2022, Revised Selected Papers, Part I, pp. 244–252. Springer Nature Switzerland, Cham (2023). https://doi.org/10.1007/978-3-031-28953-8_19

8. Devlin, J., Chang, M.W., Lee, K., Toutanova, K.: BERT: pre-training of deep bidirectional transformers for language understanding. In: North American Chapter of the Association for Computational Linguistics (2019)

9. Radford, A., Narasimhan, K., Salimans, T., Sutskever, I.: Improving language understanding by generative pre-training (2018)

10. Hu, R., Li, S., Liang, S.: Diachronic sense modeling with deep contextualized word embeddings: an ecological view. In: Proceedings of the 57th Annual Meeting of the Association for Computational Linguistics, Florence, Italy, July 2019, pp. 3899–3908. Association for Computational Linguistics (2019)

11. Giulianelli, M., Del Tredici, M., Fernández, R.: Analysing lexical semantic change with contextualised word representations. In: Proceedings of the 58th Annual Meeting of the Association for Computational Linguistics, Online, July 2020, pp. 3960–3973. Association for Computational Linguistics (2020)

12. Chinese Academy of Social Science Department of Chinese Lexicography, Institute of Linguistics. Contemporary Chinese Dictionary (Xiandai Hanyu Cidian), 7th edn. Commercial Press, Peking (2019)

13. Sagi, E., Kaufmann, S., Clark, B.: Semantic density analysis: comparing word meaning across time and phonetic space. In: Proceedings of the EACL 2009 Workshop on GEMS: Geometrical Models of Natural Language Semantics, March 2009, pp. 104–111 (2009)

14. Sagi, E., Kaufmann, S., Clark, B.: Tracing semantic change with Latent Semantic Analysis, pp. 161–183. De Gruyter Mouton, Berlin, Boston (2012)

15. Tang, X., Qu, W., Chen, X.: Semantic change computation: a successive approach. World Wide Web **19**(3), 375–415 (2015). https://doi.org/10.1007/s11280-014-0316-y

16. Tang, X.: A state-of-the-art of semantic change computation. Natural Lang. Eng. **24**(5), 649–676 (2018)

17. Rodda, M.A., Senaldi, M.S., Lenci, A.: Panta rei: tracking semantic change with distributional semantics in Ancient Greek. Italian J. Comput. Linguist. **3**, 11–24 (2017)

18. Kim, Y., Chiu, Y.I., Hanaki, K., Hegde, D., Petrov, S.: Temporal analysis of language through neural language models. In: Danescu-Niculescu-Mizil, C., Eisenstein, J., McKeown, K., Smith, N.A. (eds.) Proceedings of the ACL 2014 Workshop on Language Technologies and Computational Social Science, Baltimore, MD, USA, June 2014, pp. 61–65. Association for Computational Linguistics (2014)

19. Eger, S., Mehler, A.: On the linearity of semantic change: investigating meaning variation via dynamic graph models. In: Erk, K., Smith, N.A. (eds.) Proceedings of the 54th Annual Meeting of the Association for Computational Linguistics (Volume 2: Short Papers), Berlin, Germany, August 2016, pp. 52–58. Association for Computational Linguistics (2016)

20. Gonen, H., Jawahar, G., Seddah, D., Goldberg, Y.: Simple, interpretable and stable method for detecting words with usage change across corpora. In: Proceedings of

the 58th Annual Meeting of the Association for Computational Linguistics, Online, July 2020, pp. 538–555. Association for Computational Linguistics (2020)

21. Rosenfeld, A., Erk, K.: Deep neural models of semantic shift. In: Proceedings of the 2018 Conference of the North American Chapter of the Association for Computational Linguistics: Human Language Technologies, Volume 1 (Long Papers), New Orleans, Louisiana, June 2018, pp. 474–484. Association for Computational Linguistics (2018)

22. Yao, Z., Sun, Y., Ding, W., Rao, N., Xiong, H.: Dynamic word embeddings for evolving semantic discovery. In: Proceedings of the Eleventh ACM International Conference on Web Search and Data Mining, February 2018. ACM (2018)

23. Blei, D.M., Ng, A.Y., Jordan, M.I.: Latent dirichlet allocation. J. Mach. Learn. Res. **3**, 601–608 (2001)

24. Lau, J.H., Cook, P., McCarthy, D., Newman, D., Baldwin, T.: Word sense induction for novel sense detection. In: Proceedings of the 13th Conference of the European Chapter of the Association for Computational Linguistics, Avignon, France, April 2012, pp. 591–601. Association for Computational Linguistics (2012)

25. Lau, J.H., Cook, P., McCarthy, D., Newman, D., Baldwin, T.: Learning word sense distributions, detecting unattested senses and identifying novel senses using topic models. In: Proceedings of the 52nd Annual Meeting of the Association for Computational Linguistics (Volume 1: Long Papers), Baltimore, Maryland, June 2014, pp. 259–270. Association for Computational Linguistics (2014)

26. Mitra, S., Mitra, R., Riedl, M., Biemann, C., Mukherjee, A., Goyal, P.: That's sick dude!: Automatic identification of word sense change across different timescales. In: Proceedings of the 52nd Annual Meeting of the Association for Computational Linguistics (Volume 1: Long Papers), Baltimore, Maryland, June 2014, pp. 1020–1029. Association for Computational Linguistics (2014)

27. Wiedemann, G., Remus, S., Chawla, A., Biemann, C.: Does BERT make any sense? Interpretable word sense disambiguation with contextualized embeddings. arXiv:1909.10430 (2019)

28. Pilehvar, M.T., Camacho-Collados, J.: WiC: the word-in-context dataset for evaluating context-sensitive meaning representations. In: Proceedings of the 2019 Conference of the North American Chapter of the Association for Computational Linguistics: Human Language Technologies, Volume 1 (Long and Short Papers), Minneapolis, Minnesota, June 2019, pp. 1267–1273. Association for Computational Linguistics (2019)

29. Gulordava, K., Baroni, M.: A distributional similarity approach to the detection of semantic change in the Google Books ngram corpus. In: Proceedings of the GEMS 2011 Workshop on GEometrical Models of Natural Language Semantics, Edinburgh, UK, July 2011, pp. 67–71. Association for Computational Linguistics (2011)

30. Diao, Y.: Xinshiqi Dalu Hanyu de Fazhan yu Biange 新时期大陆汉语的发展与变革. Hung Yeh Publishing, Taibei (1995)

31. Cui, Y., Che, W., Liu, T., Qin, B., Wang, S., Hu, G.: Revisiting pre-trained models for Chinese natural language processing. In: Proceedings of the 2020 Conference on Empirical Methods in Natural Language Processing: Findings, Online, November 2020, pp. 657–668. Association for Computational Linguistics (2020)

The Evolution of "X huà" in the Press Since the Late Qing Dynasty

Xingyu Hu[✉], Zilin Yi, and Gaoqi Rao

Beijing Language and Culture University, Beijing, China
1443389328@qq.com

Abstract. This paper examines the evolution of the "X huà" of the newspaper ShenBao and People's Daily through an econometric approach, and describes the manifestation of the "X huà" over time since the late Qing Dynasty. The paper finds that the proportion of "X huà" basically did not increase at the stage of ShenBao, but steadily increased at the stage of People's Daily. The number of "X huà" words as a whole showed a tendency to rise and then fall, with no growth before the 1920s, fluctuating and rising after the 1920s, and stabilizing after a sudden drop in the 21st century. In the "X huà", not only nouns and adjectives, but also verbs, distinguishing words, and adverbs can enter the "X" component. It is possible that new multi-syllabic words will enter the "X" slot, but it is expected that few new "X huà" words will appear in the future, and the number of word types will tend to stabilize. The proportion of "X huà" words will continue to increase over the years.

Keywords: "X huà" · Chronological evolution · ShenBao · People's Daily

1 Introduction

Among the three elements of language, vocabulary develops and changes at the fastest speed and reflects the society most sensitively. As the only form of media throughout modern history, Newspaper can truly reflect the social landscape and changes of the times. In this paper, we connect the ShenBao and People's Daily, which have not been combined by our predecessors, by measuring the development of "X huà" in the press as a base point to explore the language usage situation in the social changes, with a view to grasping the social development and contemporary connotations embedded in the "X huà". This paper follows the concept of "word mold" proposed by Li [1], which consists of two parts: "mold label" and "mold slot", with "mold label" referring to the unchanged words in the word mold and "mold slot" referring to the empty space in the word mold. The "X huà" concept consists of two parts: "huà" is "mold label" and "X" is "mold slot".

The structure of "X huà" has attracted much attention because of its high frequency of use. Scholars have studied the syntactic and semantic features and evolution of "huà" from the perspectives of modern linguistic theory, generative grammar and cognitive linguistics. In recent years, the research on "X huà" mainly focuses on the following three aspects.

Firstly, research focuses on the meaning of "X huà". With regard to the grammatical nature of the word "huà", it is generally believed that "huà" has the characteristics of an affix or word-final. According to Wang [2] and Guo [3], "huà" is roughly equivalent to the English word-final "-ize", which can transform nouns and adjectives into verbs, in other words, it can be used as a verb marker. Some scholars (Zhang [4]; Hu [5]; Deng [6]) believe that "huà" can participate in word formation as an affix.

Secondly, research focuses on the classification of "X huà". In this area, there are classifications based on the lexical nature of "X" in "X huà" (Zhang [4]; Hu [5]; Deng [6]), as well as classifications based on the number of syllables in "X" (Guo [3]; Zhang [4]; Deng [6]), classifications based on grammatical features (Guo [3]; Hu [5]; Yun [7]), and classifications based on semantic features (Hu [5]; Zhou [8]).

Thirdly, research focuses on the emergence and evolution of "X huà". Regarding the origin of "huà", there are different views in the academic community. Wang [2] and Fei [9] examined that Chinese word endings have gone through the process of indoctrination to change to word endings, and pointed out that "X huà" originated from Japanese. The main view held by the academic community is that "huà" is the result of the Chinese language's own virtualization, and the influence of foreign languages is only its motive. Shi [10] points out that "huà" began to be virtualized in the Ming and Qing Dynasties, and became popular in the May Fourth Movement.

Empirical evidence shows that diachronic measurement research is practical for revealing and explaining linguistic phenomena and evolution. Based on the corpus of the press, such as ShenBao and People's Daily, Li [11], Xia [12], and Li [13] have adopted the method of measurement to observe the course of language development and the social phenomenon it implies.

From a comprehensive point of view, the semantic features, grammatical characteristics, and the process of generation and evolution of "X huà" have been studied from various angles and aspects, but little attention has been paid to the quantitative study of "X huà". In this paper, we would like to explore the temporal changes of "X huà" from a new perspective of measurement.

2 Study Design

2.1 Corpus Resources

In this paper, we select the two most influential mainstream Chinese newspapers since the late Qing Dynasty, ShenBao and People's Daily. ShenBao was founded in 1872 and ceased publication in 1949, and has operated for 78 years, and is known as "the encyclopedia of modern history". People's Daily was founded in 1946, and after the founding of the People's Republic of China, it became the largest circulation newspaper in mainland China. The two newspapers have a good temporal continuity, which can ensure the continuity of the corpus since the late Qing Dynasty. In this paper, 78 years of corpus of ShenBao (1872–1949) and 70 years of corpus of People's Daily (1946–2015) are collected. The two newspapers cover a total of 144 years of corpus, totaling about

2.7 billion words. In addition, this paper also queried the relevant corpus in ShenBao with the help of BCC corpus diachronic search[1] function [14–17].

2.2 Steps of the Study

The dataset is divided into 148 txt texts in terms of years. Firstly, the text was preprocessed, including jieba segmentation and manual intervention of some of the erroneous segmentation. Then, data extraction was carried out to form a preliminary "X huà" word list, and the word list was manually de-noised and de-used words were removed. Finally, the corpus is extracted using the "X huà" word lists. Since not all mold label "huà" is a class of affixes, controversial words need to be screened in the process of de-noising, mainly based on the following four criteria:

(1) If the mode label "huà" can be replaced by the remaining fifteen items in the Great Chinese Dictionary, it will be deactivated. For example, in "政化(zhèng huà)", "huà" has the meaning of "教化(jiào huà)", but not be virtualized; in "移化(yí huà)", "huà" has the meaning of "风气(fēng qì)". They need to be eliminated.

(2) "huà" in chemical substances is retained. Lv [18] classified the "huà" in "氧化铝(alumina)" as a suffix. Zhao [19] also recognizes "huà" in "硫化氢(hydrogen sulfide)" as an emergent suffix. This suggests that in "noun/verb/adjective + huà + noun", "noun/verb/adjective + huà" is more closely linked, and it is first combined to form a word, and then combined with "noun". We adopt the viewpoints of the two scholars and we retain the mold label "huà" in chemical substances.

(3) The name of a place or a person is "X huà" needs to be eliminated. For example, the place name "遵化(zūn huà)" "兴化(xīng huà)" "彰化(zhāng huà)", etc., and the person's name "雷化(léi huà)".

(4) The "X huà" which has a vague and uncertain boundary, needs to return to the corpus to make a judgment. For example, "风化(fēng huà)" is a noun in ShenBao, and "huà" is the meaning of "教化(jiào huà)", so it is not included in the word list for the time being; "风化(fēng huà)" as a verb appears in People's Daily in 1948, in which "huà" has been virtualized "to transform into a certain nature or state", so it was put into People's Daily for statistical purposes.

3   "X huà" in the Press Corpus

This chapter adopts a total-division analysis, first examining the 144 years of diachronic changes in ShenBao and People's Daily as a whole, and then expanding to analyze the changes in the respective phases of ShenBao and People's Daily.

3.1   "X huà" in ShenBao

After removing the stop words, this paper extracts "X huà" year by year, obtains the number of word types and frequency of "X huà" in ShenBao, and plots the total number of words in ShenBao over the years to find out the change of the proportion of "X huà" over the years.

---

[1] BCC corpus retrieved over time at http://bcc.blcu.edu.cn/hc.

Number of word types and total fenquency of "X huà" in ShenBao

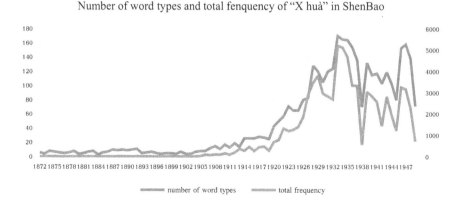

Fig. 1. Number of word types and total frequency of "X huà" in ShenBao.

As shown in Fig. 1, the number of word types of "X huà" in ShenBao on the whole shows a trend of low starting point, low upper limit and small fluctuation; before the 20th century, there were only a few "X huà" word types, basically maintained at less than 10, and this phenomenon was maintained until around 1906; after the 20th century, the number of word types of "X huà" began to climb in two stages: the first one was from 1902 to 1919, the number of word types grew slowly with little increase. After the 20th century, the number of "X huà" words began to climb in two stages: the first stage was from 1902 to 1919, the number of word types grew slowly with a small increase, and the second stage was from 1919 to around 1935, the number of word types continued to climb with a significant increase until it reached its highest point in 1933, when the number of word types was 170. After 1935, the number of word types slipped off a cliff, and then rebounded after 1945, with a slight recovery, and then dropped to a low point in 1949. The development of the total frequency of "X huà" in ShenBao is basically the same as the number of word types: there was basically no increase in the frequency of "X huà" before 1919, and the frequency fluctuated and increased after 1919 until it reached the highest point in 1933. After 1935, the frequency dropped significantly, and then rebounded slightly in the fluctuations.

It is worth noting that the term "欧化 (europeanize)" first appeared in ShenBao in 1904 and has remained in use ever since. This suggests that the use of foreign words was accepted and introduced into China in the twentieth century, although only in a few areas.

Major historical events have had an impact on the increase or decrease in the number of word types. After the May Fourth Movement, the introduction of the trend of Western learning made "X huà" flourish. 1919 was the junction of the two climbs in the 20th century, and in the first two decades of the 20th century, the increase was relatively slow, with the number of word types not exceeding 30, but after the May Fourth Movement, due to the introduction of foreign words, it was necessary to produce more "X huà", thus "X huà" flourished after the May Fourth Movement. Words such as "拉丁化(latinize)", "

教育化(educationalize)", and "艺术化(artisize)" were produced during the May Fourth Movement. During the eight years of the War of Resistance, the number of word types declined significantly. After the outbreak of the war, Shi Liangcai was adamant in his demand for anti-Japanese resistance and democracy, and the news published in ShenBao naturally had a tendency to be "X huà", which was not abundantly used in military news; after the victory of the war in 1945, the number of words types "X huà" rebounded accordingly.

In addition to this, the increase or decrease in the number of word types is also constrained by the size of the corpus. In 1938, the number of articles was the smallest in all the years, and in 1945, only 10 months were included, while in 1949, only the first 5 months were included because of the suspension of the publication of the newspaper. According to Fig. 1, the lower number of words types "X huà" in 1938, 1945, and 1949 has much to do with the size of the corpus.

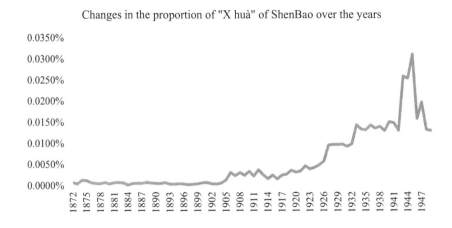

Fig. 2. Changes in the proportion of "X huà" of ShenBao over the years.

Figure 2 shows that the proportion of "X huà" as a whole shows a gradual upward trend. The frequency of "X huà" is almost negligible before the 20th century, and then gradually increases after the 20th century. The proportion of "X huà" gradually increases in the first half of the 20th century, and reaches the maximum in 1945, and then falls back sharply. In 1945, the number of word types of "X huà" was 80, less than half of that of 1934, but the proportion of "X huà" in 1945 was more than twice that of 1934. This is mainly due to the size of the corpus, as the total number of word types in 1945 is about 10.2% of that in 1934, and the large base of the denominator leads to a large difference in the proportion of "X huà". Nonetheless, the overall change in "X huà" can be roughly observed based on the change in the proportion.

The number of "X huà" additions in a year reflects the degree of acceptance of the new "X huà" by the newspaper in that year, and objectively depicts the situation of language life in that year. By counting the first appearance of "X huà" in the newspaper in each of the past years, a chart of the annual number of new "X huà" in the newspaper was compiled.

3.2 "X huà" in People's Daily

After deactivation, this paper extracts "X huà" year by year, and obtains the number of word types and frequency of "X huà" of People's Daily in all years, and plots the total number of words in People's Daily in all years to find out the change of the proportion of "X huà" in all years.

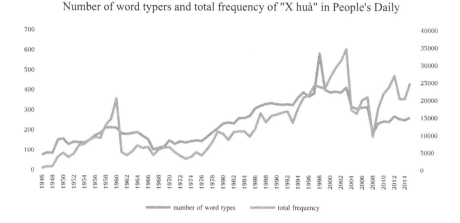

Fig. 3. Number of word types and total frequency of "X huà" in People's Daily.

As can be seen from Fig. 3, the number of word types of "X huà" in People's Daily shows an overall trend of a high starting point, a high upper limit and a large fluctuating range. The number of word types of "X huà" in People's Daily had an obvious upward process in the initial stage, and then dropped slightly after 1965, and then began to climb after 1976 until it reached a peak in 1998, with a total of 584 words, and then the number of word types began to drop sharply, and then warmed up and stabilized a little bit after the 21st century. After that, the number of word types began to drop sharply, and then slightly warmed up and stabilized after the 21st century decade. The development of the total frequency of "X huà" in People's Daily is more or less the same as the number of word types, which increased steadily before 1960, then dropped sharply and stayed low, and then increased significantly after the end of the Cultural Revolution, reaching its highest point in 2003. After that, the frequency dropped sharply and showed signs of recovery after 2008.

Similarly, the occurrence of historical events has an impact on the increase or decrease in the number of word types of "X huà". The Cultural Revolution was a decade of stagnation, during which people's minds were bound and China was virtually cut off from foreign countries, and there was a corresponding decline in the term "X huà", which reflects the diversity of development. After the Cultural Revolution, ideas were liberated, and the number of "X huà" words began to grow. With the advent of Reform and Opening up, China's links with the outside world were put back on track, and "X huà" took off, reaching its peak in 1998.

After 1998, however, the number of word types of "X huà" began to plummet, reaching a low point in 2008, and then showing signs of a slight rebound. This paper suggests that there may be two reasons for this: first, at the turn of the century, there is a gradual demise of old words. Old words are eliminated by society and are no longer used. Secondly, people are pursuing the principle of economy, and more "X huà" will only add to the burden, so many "X huà" words are no longer used.

Changes in the proportion of "X huà" of People's Daily over the years

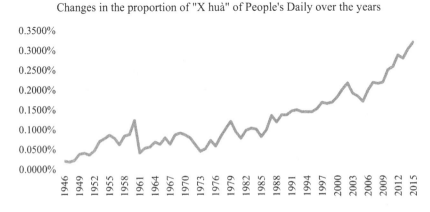

Fig. 4. Changes in the proportion of "X huà" of People's Daily over the years.

As can be seen from Fig. 4, the proportion of "X huà" shows an overall trend of slow growth, with individual periods of decline in the middle. This indicates that the frequency of "X huà" has been increasing over time. Specifically, during the first 15 years of People's Daily, the proportion of "X huà" basically rose steadily, and then began to decline after 1960, a phenomenon that lasted until the end of the Cultural Revolution, and then after 1976, the proportion of "X huà" began to increase at a slower rate, and then faster after 2005. The maximum value of the proportion fell in 2015, and it can be predicted that the proportion of "X huà" will still continue to grow after 2015. After 2005, although the richness of "X huà" words is weakened, the usage rate has increased, coupled with the total number of words in People's Daily has decreased compared to the previous one, resulting in a significant increase in the share of "X huà".

The yearly additions of "X huà" in People's Daily were successive to that of ShenBao in 1945, which is a chronological relationship. By counting the first appearance of "X huà" in People's Daily over the years, a chart of the number of "X huà" additions to People's Daily was created.

4 Evolutionary Analysis of "X huà"

The mold label "huà" has been used for a long time, but less frequently, in which the modal groove "X" is monosyllabic, and thus "X huà" as a whole is basically bisyllabic. Bisyllables have always been the standard phonetic step in Chinese rhythmic structure (Feng [20]). The "X huà" that emerged after the May Fourth Movement was nothing more than "new wine in old bottles". However, there is no doubt that under the influence of the May Fourth Movement, "X huà" has flourished, driven by the influx of foreign words and neologisms.

4.1 Lexicality of the Mold Slot "X" in "X huà"

In order to further explore the grammatical function of "X huà", and to find out what constituents can act as the mold slot "X" in it, this paper organizes the 738 "X-izations" obtained after removing stop words, and obtains the lexical chart of the mold slot "X" in "X huà".

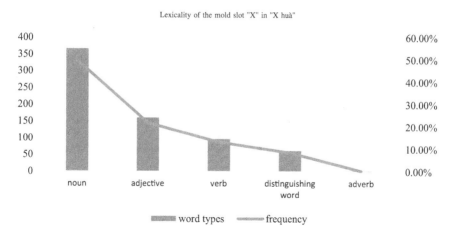

Fig. 5. Lexicality of the mold slot "X" in "X huà".

According to Shen [21], "huà" is added after a noun or adjective to form a verb, indicating the transformation into a certain nature or state. As can be seen from Fig. 5, the constituents entering the mold slot "X" are not only nouns and adjectives, but also other lexical properties such as verbs and distinguishing words. In detail, the proportion of nouns entering the "X" slot is the largest, constituting more than half of the lexical varieties of "X huà". Adjectives have the second highest proportion of "X", accounting for about 20% of the word types, verbs have the third highest proportion of "X", accounting for about 15% of the word types, followed by distinguishing words at about 10%, and a small number of adverbs have been able to get into the "X".

In the division of lexis, the problem of concurrent words will arise, the method adopted in this paper is: according to the dictionary interpretation, to determine whether there is the phenomenon of concurrent words, if the mold slot "X" belongs to concurrent words, placing the words in the original text to determine the meaning of its meaning in the context, and compare with the dictionary interpretation, to see which lexical property it belongs to. Take "自动化(zì dòng huà)" as an example, there are two meanings of "自动(zì dòng)" in the dictionary[2] [22]:

(1) Adverb, of one's own accord; not by human power. Such as automatic help, automatic burning, etc.
(2) Distinguishing word, for that which is operated directly by a mechanical device without the use of human power. Such as automatic control, etc.

According to its example, "自动化(zì dòng huà)" means the normal operation of mechanical equipment without direct human involvement. This coincides with Interpretation 2, which identifies "自动" as the distinguishing term for the mold slot in "自动化(zì dòng huà)".

4.2 Evolution of the Number of "X huà" Syllables

Shen [21] has summarized the number of syllables in the mold slot "X" in "X huà": "X huà" belongs to the single-modal posterior word mode, and the combination pattern of the generated words is mostly the three-syllable "2 + 1" pattern. The combination pattern of the words generated is mostly trisyllabic "2 + 1", part of it is disyllabic "1 + 1" pattern, and a small part of it is "multi + 1" pattern. However, the conclusion is not supported by actual data. Table 1 shows the syllable count based on the 738 "X huà" words after removing the stop words.

Table 1. Statistics on the number of syllables in the mold slot "X" in "X huà".

The "X huà" model	Number of word types	Proportion
X (monosyllabic) + huà	157	21.27%
X (disyllabic) + huà	555	75.20%
X (trisyllabic) + huà	16	2.17%
X (tetrasyllabic) + huà	8	1.08%
X (pentatonic) + huà	2	0.27%

According to Table 1, the mode slot "X" in "X huà" can be monosyllabic, disyllabic, trisyllabic, etc. Among them, the number of disyllabic modes accounts for about three-quarters of the total number. Among them, the number of two-syllable modes accounts for about three-fourths of the total number of modal slots "X", in other words, "2 + 1" three-syllable modes in the "X huà" is absolutely dominant. The proportion of the mold slot "X" being monosyllabic is 21.27%, which also occupies a larger share, and the "1 +

---

[2] Editorial Office of Dictionary, Institute of Languages, Chinese Academy of Social Sciences, Modern Chinese Dictionary, Beijing: Commercial Press, 2005 edition, p. 2089.

1" disyllabic pattern also occupies a certain proportion in the "X huà". The proportion of mold slot "X" is trisyllabic is only 2.17%, and "3 + 1" four-syllable pattern only accounts for a small part of "X huà". When the number of syllables in the mold slot "X" exceeds two, the number and proportion of "X huà" decreases sharply with the increase of the number of "X" syllables. It is still difficult for polysyllables to enter the mold slot "X", and these polysyllables that enter the mold slot "X" are mostly abstract nouns.

Based on the change of the proportion of "X huà" over the years, the number of syllables of mold slot "X" was counted according to the different periods of ShenBao and People's Daily, and Table 2 was obtained in order to show the evolution of the number of syllables of "X huà" over the years.

Table 2. Statistics on the number and proportion of words with different syllables of "X huà" by period.

All periods	X (monosyllabic) + huà		X (disyllabic) + huà		X (polysyllabic) + huà	
1872–1900	31	93.94%	2	6.06%	0	0
1901–1919	36	81.82%	8	18.18%	0	0
1920–1949	61	23.64%	190	73.64%	7	2.71%
1946–1965	31	16.76%	147	79.46%	7	3.78%
1966–1976	0	0	20	95.24%	1	4.76%
1977–2015	2	0.88%	213	94.25%	11	4.87%

As can be seen from Table 2, the proportion of monosyllabic mold slot "X" shows an overall decreasing trend as time progresses, while the proportion of disyllabic mold slot "X" runs in the opposite direction, with a gradual increase overall. There is also a small but negligible increase in the proportion of polysyllabic mold slots "X". Specifically, prior to the 20th century, monosyllabic words had an absolute advantage in entering mold slot "X", with only a small number of disyllabic words able to do so. In the 20th century, the proportion of monosyllabic words entering the mold slot "X" has slightly decreased, but still has a clear advantage, and the proportion of disyllabic words entering "X" has also slightly increased. After the May Fourth Movement, monosyllabic "X" plummeted, replaced by a surge of bisyllabic "X", and at the same time, polysyllabic words could also serve as the mold slot "X".

In the first 20 years of the existence of People's Daily, the proportion of monosyllabic words entering the mold slot "X" declined slightly, while the proportion of disyllabic "X" increased slightly. In the decade of the Cultural Revolution, monosyllabic words were no longer accepted in the mold slot "X", while the proportion of disyllabic words "X" continued to climb, occupying an absolute advantage. After the end of the Cultural Revolution, the new monosyllabic "X" showed signs of re-emergence, but the proportion was negligible, basically still dominated by the disyllabic "X", and the proportion of multi-syllabic words able to enter the mold slot "X" has been increasing slightly.

4.3 Evolving Trends in "X huà"

Diao [23] divides the modern Chinese period into four stages: the "huà" suffixes show a "U"-shaped development, in other words, the "huà" suffixes change from flourishing to declining, and then from declining to flourishing. In this paper, we will not explore its statistical sources for the time being, but only discuss the time period of its classification, which is a bit different. In addition, it is not appropriate to take the total frequency of "X huà" statistics, as "X huà" itself will naturally increase over time. According to the development of its "U" shape, "X-ization" has strong word formation ability, but according to the word list, after entering the 21st century, the word formation ability of "X huà" obviously shows a tendency of decline. Based on the changes in the proportion of "X huà" and the number of word types over the years, this paper makes three speculations on the development trend of "X huà":

(1) The mold slot "X" will always be dominated by two-syllable words, and it is unlikely that single-syllable words will enter the mold slot "X", and in the future, more multi-syllable words may enter the mold slot "X". In the future, more multi-syllabic words may enter the mold slot "X".

(2) The number of annual additions of "X huà" has basically stagnated in the first fifteen years of the 21st century, and it is expected that there will be few new "X huà" in the future, and the number of word types will stabilize.

(3) The proportion of "X huà" has basically been on the rise over the years, and will remain so in the future. Although the number of word types is stabilizing, the frequency of use will increase and the scope of use will expand.

5 Conclusion

This paper chooses two highly influential newspapers, ShenBao and People's Daily, to depict the gradual change of "X huà" through measurement, and obtains some interesting conclusions. First, by studying the changes in the number and proportion of "X huà" words over the years, this paper finds that the proportion of "X huà" in ShenBao shows a gradual upward trend on the whole, and the number of word types of "X huà" shows a trend of low starting point, low upper limit and small fluctuation. The proportion of "X huà" in People's Daily shows a slow growth trend on the whole, with a drop in the middle of some time periods, and the number of word types of "X huà" shows a trend of high starting point, high upper limit and large fluctuation on the whole. The increase or decrease in the number of word types is constrained by major historical events and the size of the corpus. Secondly, through the study of the mold slot "X", this paper explores its grammatical function, and learns that not only nouns and adjectives but also other lexemes such as verbs, distinguishing words and adverbs can enter the mold slot "X". Thirdly, this paper predicts the development trend of "X huà", and it is presumed that the mold slot "X" will always be dominated by two-syllable words, in other words, "X huà" will be dominated by the pattern of "2 + 1", and new polysyllabic words may enter the mold slot "X" in the future. However, it is estimated that there will be few new "X huà" in the future, and the number of word types will be stabilized. The proportion of "X huà" has basically been on the rise over the years, and will remain so in the future.

However, there is still room for improvement in this paper. The study of the mold slot "X" could be more in-depth, and whether it could be analyzed from the perspective of semantic features. In addition, the motivation for the affixation of the mold label "huà" in "X huà" still needs to be further studied.

Acknowledgments. Project supported by Youth Program of Humanities and Social Sciences of the Ministry of Education "Measurement of Vocabulary Usage in Chinese Newspapers since the Late Qing Dynasty" (20YJC740050).

References

1. Li, Y.-M.: Word mold. The characteristics of the Chinese language. In: Fuyi, X. (ed.) Beijing Language and Culture. University Press, Beijing (1999). (in Chinese)
2. Wang, L.: The History of the Chinese Language. Zhonghua Shuju, Beijing (1980). (in Chinese)
3. Guo, C.: Grammatical features of verbs ending in "huà". Chinese Lang. Learn. (03), 32–37 (1982). (in Chinese)
4. Zhang, Y.-Q.: A hierarchical sequence of functional weakening in "huà" final verbs. Chinese Lang. (01), 50–54 (2002). (in Chinese)
5. Hu, S.-B.: Talking about the word-final "huà". J. Shangrao Teachers' Coll. (Soc. Sci. Edn.) (02), 71–77 (1982). (in Chinese)
6. Deng, D.: Distributional morphology of the modern Chinese morpheme "huà" and its commonalities and differences with the English suffix -ize. Foreign Lang. Teach. Res. **52**(06), 830–843+958–959 (2020). (in Chinese)
7. Yun, H., Jun, X.: Reconsideration of words with the suffix "huà". Chinese Lang. Learn. (01), 26–27 (1994). (in Chinese)
8. Zhou, G.: A discussion on words with the suffix "huà". Chinese Lang. Learn. (06), 12–15 (1991)
9. Fei, W.-B.: Comparison and Interpretation of the Chinese Affix "huà" and its English Counterpart. Southwest Jiaotong University (2003). (in Chinese)
10. Shi, H.-G.: The origin and meaning of word-final "huà" and the semantic features of the verb "X huà". J. Beijing Radio Tele. Univ. (02), 41–44 (2009). (in Chinese)
11. Li, Q., Rao, G.: Militarization of newspaper language - diachronic study of war metaphor in people's daily. In: Liu, M., Kit, C., Su, Q. (eds.) Chinese Lexical Semantics, CLSW 2020. LNCS, vol 12278, pp. 593–602. Springer, Cham (2021). https://doi.org/10.1007/978-3-030-81197-6_50
12. Xia, E., Rao, G.: Diachronic changes and multi-dimensional quantitative analysis of sentence complexity in contemporary Chinese Written Language. In: Liu, M., Kit, C., Su, Q. (eds.) Chinese Lexical Semantics. CLSW 2020. LNCS (LNAI), vol. 12278, pp. 618–630. Springer, Cham (2021). https://doi.org/10.1007/978-3-030-81197-6_52
13. Li, Z.-X., Gao, T.-L., Huang, G.-J., Rao, G.-Q.: Modern Chinese diachronic corpus construction and the language development based on a 77-year corpus. In: Su, Q., Xu, G., Yang, X. (eds.) Chinese Lexical Semantics, CLSW 2022. LNCS, vol 13495. Springer, Cham (2023)
14. Rao, G.-Q.: Zeitgeist: Historical buzzword extraction based on newspaper corpus and implicit theme modeling from 1946 to 2015. Res. Lang. Plann. (02), 40–58 (2016). (in Chinese)
15. Rao, G.-Q.: A preliminary study on the detection of linguistic normative validity based on computational methods–an example of the work on the collation of anagrams. Lang. Strategy Res. **1**(06), 55–63 (2016). (in Chinese)

16. Xun, E.-D., Rao, G.-Q., Xiao, X.-Y., Zang, J.-J.: Development of BCC corpus in the context of big data. Corpus Linguist. **3**(01), 93–109+118 (2016). (in Chinese)
17. Xun, E.-D., Rao, G.-Q., Xie, J.-L., Huang, Z.-E.: Construction and application of a diachronic search system for modern Chinese vocabulary. J. Chinese Inform. **29**(03), 169–176 (2015). (in Chinese)
18. Lv, S.-X: Eight Hundred Words of Modern Chinese. Commercial Printing House, Beijing (2017). (in Chinese)
19. Zhao, Y.-R.: Grammar of Spoken Chinese. Commercial Press, Beijing (2012). (in Chinese)
20. Feng, S.-L.: On "rhyming words" in Chinese. Chinese Soc. Sci. (01), 161–176 (1996). (in Chinese)
21. Shen, G.-H.: Study on Chinese derived neologisms. China Social Science Press, Beijing (2015). (in Chinese)
22. Dictionary Editorial Office, Institute of Languages, Chinese Academy of Social Sciences. Modern Chinese Dictionary. Commercial Press, Beijing (2005). (in Chinese)
23. Diao, Y.-B.: History of Modern Chinese. Fujian People's Publishing House, Fuzhou (2006). (in Chinese)

Distribution of Motifs in Mongolian Word Length

Lingxiong Bao[1], Dahubaiyila[1(✉)], and Wuyoutan[2(✉)]

[1] School of Mongolian Studies, Inner Mongolia University, Hohhot 010021, China
blx2023@yeah.net, dabhvrbayar@163.com
[2] College of Liberal Arts, Baotou Teacher's College, Baotou 014030, China
oyvtan1995@163.com

Abstract. Word length is a crucial metric in text quantification. Investigations into Mongolian word length motifs have profound implications for broadening Mongolian lexical studies and quantitative linguistics. The present study adopts a linear sequence perspective, amalgamating the concept of Mongolian word length with motifs. It explores the distribution characteristics of Mongolian word length motifs across five genres—*prose, poetry, news, political,* and *legal.* The findings reveal that the distribution of Mongolian word length motifs aligns with the Zipf-Mandelbrot model, and that the distribution of the lengths of Mongolian word length motifs conforms to the Hyperpascal model. These results indicate a regularity in Mongolian word length motifs. Parametric differences are observed in genre distribution, and the fitting results reveal discrepancies among the parameters of the Zipf-Mandelbrot and Hyperpascal models across various genres. It reveals that word length motifs may be employed as indicators for genre classification.

Keywords: Mongolian word length · Word length motifs · Quantitative research · Language law

1 Introduction

The language system is hierarchical and complex, composed of various language units such as phonics, phonemes, syllables, morphemes, words, phrases, clauses, and sentences. The properties of words have always been a topic of extensive research within both traditional and modern linguistics. Word length, referring to the measurement of a word's length, typically in terms of letters, phonemes, or syllables, has been explored since the 19th century. Scholars like British mathematician Morgan and American physicist Mendenhall have pioneered in this field. Morgan's work revealed promising results by associating word length with authorship identification. Mendenhall, who conducted calculations of average word length based on a text corpus, inferred that individuals unwittingly reveal their personal habits in crafting sentences with words. He proposed that this feature could serve to authenticate authorship. Following his work, scholars across various disciplines have imbued the study of word length with interdisciplinary academic perspectives. This includes applied mathematicians who viewed the concept through lenses such as vector, probability theory, and mathematical statistics. Likewise, experts from biology and physics have analyzed it from a complex network theory perspective.

Numerous studies have been conducted on word length distribution. Scholars, as per statistical data, have probed the distribution of word length in over 70 disparate languages [1], inclusive of minority languages such as Mongolian [2] and Zhuang [3].

Motif is a special language unit that can be applied to words, sentences, paragraphs, chapters, and other units [4]. It is a new unit that refers to a series of continuous values with equal or increasing length [5]. Scholars have conducted a series of studies combining the properties of word, clauses, and sentences with the concept of motif [5–8]. The primary languages involved in these studies are Chinese, English, German, Russian, Italian, and Japanese.

The exploration of word length motif has witnessed considerable advancements in recent years. There exists an extensive body of literature on word length motif research within the Indo-European language family [8]. Chen [9] systematically examined the characteristics of word length motifs in Chinese, employing a corpus encompassing Chinese texts spanning over 2000 years. The results of this study validated established linguistic rules, while simultaneously uncovering previously unidentified laws within language structure. Sanada [10] examined the distribution characteristics of word length motifs in Japanese, offering fresh insights into how predicate-postpositive languages investigate motif structures, a revelation of significant reference value for SOV languages.

In the realm of word length motifs, scholars have achieved certain progress. However, despite numerous studies on word length motifs across various languages, re-search on minority languages within China, such as Mongolian, remains conspicuously scarce. Specifically, the exploration of word length motifs in Mongolian is still in its formative stages.

Hence, the current study aims to fill this research gap by incorporating past studies and using five representative genres of Mongolian texts—*prose, poetry, news, political,* and *legal,* as the corpus. This research primarily seeks to address the following questions:

(1) What is the distribution of word length motifs in Mongolian? Do they adhere to existing linguistic laws?
(2) What is the distribution of the length of word length motif in Mongolian? Do they comply with related linguistic laws?
(3) Do the parameters of language modeling hold statistically significant implications?

By addressing these questions, the present study strives to propel the research on word length motifs in minority languages and widen the field of quantitative linguistics. The employment of quantitative linguistic methods in studying the Mongolian language can expose previously undiscovered attributes and laws, thus enhancing Mongolian linguistic theory.

2   Methods and Data

The selection of an appropriately sized corpus is a subject of debate among scholars. Some advocate for a larger corpus, arguing that it presents a more representative depiction of language characteristics. Conversely, others argue that an overly extensive corpus can obscure the discernment of language patterns. Bearing these contrasting viewpoints in mind, the present study adopts a mixed approach, incorporating both small and large corpora. The focus of this study is solely on written Mongolian language data. Five instances each of prose, poetry, news, and political texts were sourced from the "1-Million-Word Modern Mongolian Corpus" with individual text word counts ranging between 1,000 and 2,000 words. To balance the corpus size, the legal corpus was derived from the Civil Code of the People's Republic of China (Mongolian version). Texts with a word count of approximately 10,000 were selected to ensure corpus size equilibrium. Consequently, the small corpora created include the prose corpus, the poetry corpus, the news corpus, the political corpus, and the legal corpus; the creation of the large corpus is a result of integrating these five small corpora.

2.1   Corpus Preprocessing

Word processing, which is fundamental to Mongolian information processing, has been accomplished. In Mongolian, words are separated by space, which suggests that word segmentation could be straightforward. However, there are still numerous practical challenges. From a natural language processing perspective, Mongolian word segmentation techniques require manual inspection due to their relative immaturity. In this study, non-Mongolian characters, numbers, and punctuation marks are required to be deleted.

2.2   Word Length Measurement Unit

While there are commonalities among human languages, each language also possesses its unique characteristics. The units of measurement for word length vary across different languages. For instance, in spoken Chinese, the pinyin alphabet, phonemes, and syllables are utilized as units of measurement, whereas, in written Chinese, strokes, components, and characters are employed [9: 22]. In the field of quantitative linguistics, syllables are the most common unit of measurement for word length. Previously, Narisong [2] examined the distribution of word length in Mongolian, deploying syllables as the unit of measurement.

Mongolian is a phonemic script. A syllable typically comprises several phonemes, though, in certain instances, a single phoneme (a vowel or specific consonants) is sufficient to form a syllable. Mongolian displays an asymmetry between spoken and written syllables, predominantly manifested in the prevalence of syllables with complex consonants in spoken language. In many languages worldwide, including Mongolian, a vowel serves as the primary constituent of a syllable. Huhe [11] applied experimental phonetic methods to categorize Mongolian spoken syllables into 22 types. Meanwhile, Bai [12] recognized four basic forms of syllable segmentation in Mongolian information processing based on written language, with an additional six forms identified for foreign words.

In this study, the syllable segmentation standards proposed by Bai [12: 233] are employed. Basic forms encompass vowel (EGEQI, "sister"), vowel + consonant (ALBA, "kill"), consonant + vowel (SARA, "moon"), and consonant + vowel + con-sonant (GAL, "fire"). Special forms include consonant + vowel + vowel (ARSLAZ, "lion"), consonant + vowel + vowel + vowel (ALPS, "star"), vowel + consonant + vowel + vowel (BARS, "tiger"), vowel + consonant + vowel + vowel + vowel (MARKS, "Marx"), vowel + vowel + consonant + vowel (HLCR, "nuclear"), and vowel + vowel + consonant + vowel + vowel (SPIRT, "alcohol"). For automatic syllable segmentation, the Latin transcription standards of the Inner Mongolia University Mongolian Language Corpus are utilized, with the count only extended to the number of vowels present in each word. Then, counting the syllables of words, Python programs was first employed for computing syllabic lengths of words and run to analyze each document.

It is, however, pertinent to pay attention to certain details, such as fixed phrases and case category variation. A fixed phrase is comprised of a combination of two or more words that articulates a specific meaning. In this study, a chain of words linked by equal signs (" =") is treated as a single unit during word length calculations. For instance, the phrase "$ALTAR = B0LTAR" (rough) consists of four syllables.

Mongolian is an agglutinative language, and case category variation is a significant characteristic of agglutinative languages. In Mongolian, a case is denoted by appending a specific component to a noun [13: 149]. In Mongolian, cases are used to indicate the relationship between words and their functions in phrases and sentences, mostly separated in writing, such as genitive case (-YIN, -V/-U, -VN/-UN), dative case (-DV/-DU, -TV/-TU), accusative case (-I/-YI), instrumental case (-IYAR/-IYER, -BAR/-BER), ablative case (-ACA/-ECE), and comitative case (-TAI/-TEI). In the Mongolian Latin form corpus, these cases are represented by a hyphen ("-"), rendering the processing relatively straightforward. For example, the phrase "ABV-YIN" (father's) contains two syllables: "A" and "BV-YIN". As cases are additional elements, they are placed after the preceding syllable during syllable segmentation.

In present study, the unit of measurement for word length is the syllable. Treating fixed phrases as a single word and not counting case as syllables aligns with Mongolian grammar and morphological theories.

2.3 Word Length Motif

Quantitative linguistics [14, 15] concentrates on language units, their attributes, and the relationships between them. The interdependence of language units is paramount, as a small change in one unit can have far-reaching consequences. However, the sequential behavior and structure of the objects under investigation have often been neglected [16]. Hence, Köhler proposed the "motif", defined as a sequence of equal or increasing continuous numerical values. The information of the sequential structure is neither dependent on any linguistic unit nor on a specific linguistic method or grammar, and it is also applicable to any linguistic unit. Despite this, studies focusing on the sequential structure of word length are relatively scarce, with more emphasis placed on other aspects while ignoring the sequential characteristics. Interestingly, individuals unwittingly employ word length motifs in speech. For instance, when communicating with an infant learning to speak, simpler structures with shorter word length motifs are naturally used.

Motifs can be classified into the following categories [17: 90]:

L-motif is a continuous series of equal or increasing lengths values.

F-motif is a continuous series of equal or increasing frequencies values.

P-motif is a continuous series of equal or increasing polysemy values.

T-motif is a continuous series of equal or increasing polytextuality values.

The present study, word length and motif are combined, which can be called word length motif. The word length motif serves as a new approach to analyze word length sequences. According to the definition provided above, a length motif is the longest sequence of continuous equality or growth in the word length sequence. The values on the sequence represent the attribute values of the corresponding units in the frame units studied, thereby reflecting the attributes of those language units. The motif can be flexibly degraded or upgraded. Additionally, the L-motif can be further elevated to an LL-motif, and it can also be combined with frequency to create an FL-motif.

The definition of word length motif, consider the following examples: "HOIDEIGE-YIN / BAYIIDAL / $ALITAR = BOLITAR,CAGI-VN/BAYIIDAL/0IR0IG_A = B0SIHAIG_A,EILEISU-TEI/$ANGIDA / BVITA-TAI / CAYIIDAM-I / DAIGAIJV, HAIYA / NIIGE / HAIR _ A / GERI-ECE / VITVIG _ A / SVGVNAGLAN _ A." (" /" participle mark, " –" case mark, " =" compound word mark, " I" syllable mark, meaning: "In a rural setting, where simplicity prevails, and amidst a turbulent situation, one may encounter a smoking dark house while traversing the desert.").

When measured in syllables, the word length motif for this sentence is "3–2–4–1–2–6–3–2–2–2–3–2–2–2–1–3-5" (with "-" separating different word length values). Based on the definition of continuous equal or increasing sequences, the word length motifs can be identified as follows:

(3).

(2–4).

(1–2-6).

(3).

(2-2-2–3).

(2-2-2).

(1–3-5).

The word length motif of a sentence has been derived. Furthermore, the length sequence of motifs can also be obtained, resulting in a length distribution of "1–2–3–1-4–3-3". By applying the definition of length motifs, three second-order length motifs (LL-motifs) can be further identified, namely (1–2-3), (1–4), and (3–3).

These numerical values allow us to simulate characteristics of language units, from which we can further infer features of linguistic styles.

3 Results and Discussion

3.1 The Distribution of Mongolian Word Length Motif

Word length is one of the attributes of words, and word length sequences can reflect the characteristics of a language. Previous research has confirmed a strong correlation between word length and the quantity of information conveyed by words, with longer words often utilized to articulate abstract concepts [18]. Empirical evidence has demonstrated that the usage of nouns significantly surpasses that of verbs and adjectives in academic and legal genres, whereas in prose, the frequency of verbs exceeds that of nouns [19, 20].

The lengths of word length motifs in *prose, poetry, news, political,* and *legal* are arranged in descending order. The results are presented in Table 1, Table 2, Table 3.

Table 1. Distribution of word length motif in *news* and *prose*

News	Rank	Freq	Word length motif	*Prose*	Rank	Freq	Word length motif
	1	3	158		1	2–3	201
	2	2–3	139		2	2	156
	3	2	133		3	3	151
	4	2–4	131		4	2–2–3	139
	5	1–3	118		5	1–3	130
	6	1–2	114		6	2–2	126
	7	1–3-4	113		7	2–4	122
	8	2–2–4	111		8	2–2–4	111
	9	2–3-3	111		9	2–3-3	116

Statistical analysis suggests that a word in Mongolian typically does not exceed 10 syllables, with this consideration focused exclusively on verbs. The rationale behind considering only verbs is their role as the core and most stable component of a sentence. Conversely, nouns represent the most unstable word category. As society advances, new noun terminologies constantly emerge, potentially leading to a continual increase in word length. In Mongolian, the longest word length motif is "2–2-2–2-2–2-2–2-2–2-2–3", yielding a motif length of 12, whereas the shortest word length motifs are "2", "3", and "4", each with a motif length of 1. Across five genres, there are 301 unique word length motifs, totaling 2972 motifs. In different genres, the most frequent word length motifs include: "3" in *news*, "2–3" in *prose*, "2" in *political*, "4" in *legal*, and "2–3" in *poetry*. The word length motif "2" is the most frequent across all five genres, indicating that in Mongolian, words composed of two syllables are most common.

It can be observed that the distribution of word length motifs varies among different genres, although they generally concentrate in the "2," "2–3," and "3". Notably, *legal* genre has a distinct characteristic in terms of word length motifs, with the most common

Table 2. Distribution of word length motif in *political* and *legal*

Political	Rank	Freq	Word length motif	Lagal	Rank	Freq	Word length motif
	1	2	155		1	4	154
	2	2–3	143		2	1–4	146
	3	3	138		3	2–4	143
	4	1–3	126		4	2	142
	5	2–2	124		5	3	142
	6	1–2	123		6	2–2-4	141
	7	1–2-3	122		7	2–5	140
	8	2–2-3	121		8	1–5	139
	9	2–4	119		9	2–2-3	136

Table 3. Distribution of word length motif in *poetry* and overall distribution

Poetry	Rank	Freq	Word length motif	overall	Rank	Freq	Word length motif
	1	2–3	136		1	2	286
	2	2	135		2	3	281
	3	3	134		3	2–3	279
	4	1–3	125		4	1–3	197
	5	2–2-3	121		5	2–4	195
	6	2–2	115		6	2–2-3	188
	7	2–3-3	115		7	2–2	171
	8	2–2-4	115		8	1–4	162
	9	2–4	113		9	2–2-4	158

Table 4. Parameters of Zipf-Mandelbrot model for genre word length motifs

Genre	a	b	R^2
Prose	1.0869	4.2762	0.9689
Poetry	1.2900	3.9007	0.9919
News	1.0826	1.5496	0.9274
Political	1.0568	1.2023	0.9823
Legal	1.4532	5.1476	0.9921

motif being "4", followed by "5". This indicates that legal language often employs longer words, predominantly nouns, reflecting the unique style of the legal genre. Furthermore, the frequency of word length motifs tends to be higher for smaller motifs, which can be attributed to the phenomenon of linguistic economy. When describing things, individuals subconsciously tend to choose the simplest and shortest vocabulary.

Compared with the distribution of word length motifs in Chinese, in modern writ-ten Chinese, the most frequent word length motifs are "1–2", "1-1-2", "1–2-2", "1-1-1-2", "1-1-1-1-2", and "1-2-2-2" [9: 112]. This distribution diverges significantly from that observed in Mongolian. In the Mongolian word length motifs distribution, "1" is exceedingly rare, indicating the scarcity of words with one syllable in the Mongolian lexical system. In Mongolian, the distribution of "1–1 + 2" motifs are virtually non-existent.

As reflected in Table 3, the distribution of word length motifs varies across different subjects, but generally coalesce around "2", "2-3", and "3". The *legal* genre show-cases the most distinctive motif, with "4" emerging as the most common word length motif, followed by "5". This reveals that words in legal language typically comprise 4–5 syllables, signifying a distinct genre with a high preponderance of nouns. This further corroborates that word length motifs can reflect not only the unique word length com-binations of Mongolian but also the idiosyncratic characteristics of different language styles.

3.2 The Probability Distribution of Mongolian Word Length Motif

Quantitative linguistics encompasses three laws, namely, distributional law, functional law, and developmental law. The Zipf-Mandelbrot model is a typical example of a distri-butional law. Köhler and Naumann [21] found that L-motifs and F-motifs can be utilized for text classification.

In Sect. 3.1, the distribution of Mongolian word length motifs was investigated, using syllables as the measure. Subsequently, the Zipf-Mandelbrot model is employed to observe the probability distribution of word length motifs.

Zipf-Mandelbrot [22] model formula:

$$F(r) = \frac{c}{(b+r)^a} \left(c > 0, a > 0, b > -1, r \in R^+ \right)$$

where $F(r)$ is the frequency, a and b are parameters, and c is a normalized constant. The law in the distribution of Mongolian word length motifs was further examined using the Altmann-Fitter software for fitting.

The results confirmed that the Mongolian word length motifs comply with the Zipf-Mandelbrot model. The trend of the graph and the fitting parameters both indicated suc-cessful fitting. Fittings are performed across five genres, all yielding successful results. Due to space constraints, we exemplify the fitting situation of the word length motif in news, as depicted in Fig. 1., where the x-axis represents different word length motifs and the y-axis represents the corresponding frequency. $F(x)$ is the observed value, and $NP(x)$ is the predicted value.

In the previous section, the distribution of word length motifs was examined across *prose, poetry, news, political*, and *legal* genres. Subsequently, the Zipf-Mandelbrot model fitting parameters across these five genres are scrutinized.

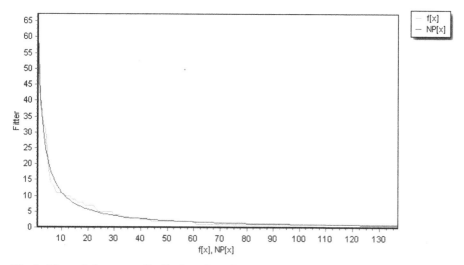

Fig. 1. The rank frequency distribution of word length motifs modeled by the Zipf-Mandelbrot

As shown in Table 4 that the fitting results of five genres are very good, high determination coefficient R^2 values are observed across all genres, with all $R^2 > 0.9$ ($R^2 > 0.80$, good; $R^2 > 0.90$, very good; $R^2 > 0.75$, acceptable; $R^2 < 0.75$, unacceptable). The highest R^2 values are manifested in *political* and *prose*, while the lowest R^2 value is found in *poetry*. The a-value generally is distributed between [1,1.5), and the b-value is distributed between [1,5.2). Notably, certain differences are observed. The *political* genre is found to possess the largest b-value, succeeded by *legal* genre, while the smallest b-value is observed in *poetry* and *news* genres.

These findings demonstrate that word length motifs, on the one hand, reflect the characteristics of different linguistic styles. On the other hand, the study of the distribution of word length motifs holds statistical significance. Most importantly, the length of the Mongolian word length motif exhibits certain regularity, conforming to the Zipf-Mandelbrot model.

3.3   The Distribution of the Length of Mongolian Word Length Motif

Based on the definition of motifs, it is known that they have a heritage characteristic, and the length of the second-order motifs can be calculated based on the length of the first-order motifs. Consequently, the features of second-order length motifs (LL-Motifs) in Mongolian word length are explored. To further verify the distribution characteristics of the length of Mongolian word length motif, the research is conducted based on the above-mentioned five genres. Firstly, the length of word length motif of different genres was examined; subsequently, the data were fitted; and finally, the parameters were analyzed. The distributions of word length motif lengths for *prose, poetry, news, political,* and *legal* are as follows:

As indicated in Table 5, "L" represents the length of the word length motif, and "freq" represents the number of all word length motifs of a certain length in the text. In the

Table 5. Length of word length motif in different genres

Prose	L	Freq	Poetry	L	Freq	News	L	Freq	Political	L	Freq	Legal	L	Freq
	1	161		1	195		1	201		1	197		1	180
	2	183		2	287		2	294		2	262		2	237
	3	173		3	259		3	255		3	230		3	228
	4	192		4	202		4	164		4	166		4	160
	5	220		5	163		5	142		5	141		5	139
	6	116		6	127		6	115		6	120		6	116
	7	115		7	112		7	102		7	109		7	105
	8	112		8	105		8	102		8	103		8	102
	1	161		9	103		9	101		9	101		9	103
	2	183		10	103		10	102		10	102		10	101
				11	103								11	101
				12	105									

genre of *prose, poetry, news, political,* and *legal,* significant similarities and differences can be observed in the lengths of word length motifs."

Firstly, in terms of the lengths of the different word length motif, the legal has the fewest categories of word length motif, while the prose has diverse categories. The longest word length motif is discovered in prose, with a length of "12". This phenomenon is attributed to prose genre which are biased towards remembering events and people with ups and downs, are more readable and use different word sequences to highlight these features, thus resulting in the richest lengths of different word length motif. The length of word length motif in political and news is the same as "10", whereas in poetry, it extends to "11". Poetry genre has the characteristic of rhyme, which is the mark of differentiation from other literary genres. This, in turn, leads to a richer assortment of word length motif lengths, but still fewer than that found in prose.

Secondly, in terms of the frequency of different word length motif lengths, the descending order of occurrences in legal is $4 > 2 > 3 > 1 > 5 > 6 > 7 > 8$; in prose it is $2 > 3 > 4 > 1 > 5 > 6 > 7 > 8 = 12 = 10 = 11 = 9$; in *political* it is $2 > 3 > 1 > 4 > 5 > 6 > 7 > 8 > 10 > 9$; in *news* it is $2 > 3 > 1 > 4 > 5 > 6 > 7 > 8 > 10 > 9$; in *poetry* it is $2 > 3 > 1 > 4 > 5 > 6 > 7 > 9 > 8 > 10 = 11$.

The observations derived from the study suggest that in Mongolian, the motifs of length "2", "3", "4", and "1" are prominently prevailing, with "2" featuring as the most recurrent. A generic phenomenon where the longer the motif length, the less frequently it occurs.

An examination of five distinct genres reveals that word length motifs demonstrate a combination of unique and share characteristics with respect to their lengths and frequencies. It intimates that the length of word length motifs has the potential to capture linguistic nuances. Divergent genres present distinctive distribution patterns of word length motif lengths, implying that these lengths could be instructive in addressing genre classification concerns. Nonetheless, these implications necessitate further empirical validation.

3.4 The Probability Distribution of the Length of Mongolian Word Length Motif

Previous research findings consistently proved that the length of word length motif conforms to the Hyperpascal model [9, 23]. Considering this, an investigation is conducted to determine whether the length of Mongolian word motifs could also be represented by the Hyperpascal model. The Hyperpascal [23] model formula:

$$P(x) = \frac{\binom{k + x - 1}{x}}{\binom{m + x - 1}{x}} q^x p_0, x = 0, 1, 2, \cdots$$

Köhler [23] explained the linguistic significance represented by the fitting variables k, m, and q. He pointed out that there is a tendency to form compact expressions in natural language. For example, a phrase is typically composed of two or more words, and the same meaning can be expressed in a more concise manner, which may lead to an increase in word length. Therefore, a more compact expression at one level is often accompanied by a more complex expression at the next level. Here, the variable k represents this trend. Another tendency is the minimization of word length. During lexical evolution, longer words may be generated, which inevitably leads to an increase in motif lengths. However, a continuous increase in word length does not conform to the rules of lexical evolution or the habits of the human brain, as we tend to unconsciously choose shorter words when speaking. This behavior restricts the use of longer words, and the variable m represents this constraint trend. The variable q indicates the impact of average word length on motif length.

Table 6. Parameters of Hyperpascal model for genre lengths of word length motifs

Genre	k	m	q	c	R^2
Prose	5.9031	1.1600	0.2438	0.0151	0.9836
Poetry	1.8645	0.4287	0.4060	0.0078	0.9946
News	3.5098	0.6948	0.3080	0.0201	0.9823
Political	1.5890	0.4064	0.4013	0.0058	0.9936
Legal	1.8450	0.3451	0.3332	0.0162	0.9872

As seen from Table 6, the fitting results of five genres are very good, high determination coefficient R^2 values are observed across all genres, with all $R^2 > 0.9$ and the C values are generally low, with all $C < 0.01$ ($C < 0.01$, very good; $C < 0.02$, good). The lengths of word length motifs in *prose, poetry, news, political,* and *legal* conform to the Hyperpascal model, validating our hypothesis that Mongolian word length motif lengths comply with this model. Due to space limitations, we only provide an example of the fitting situation of word length motif lengths in *news*, as shown in Fig. 2, where the *x*-axis represents different lengths of word length motifs and the *y*-axis represents corresponding frequencies. $F(x)$ is the observed value, and $NP(x)$ is the predicted value.

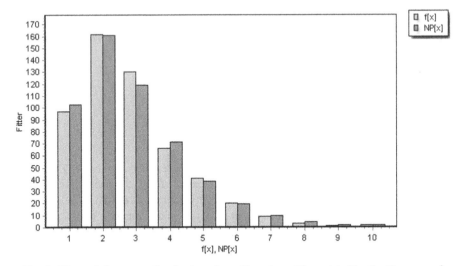

Fig. 2. The rank frequency distribution of word length motifs modeled by the Hyperpascal

In term of the fitting parameters of the genre, the distribution range of k value is [1.5,6), the distribution range of m value is [0.3,1.2), and the distribution range of q value is [0.2,0.5). The k value and m value of *legal* is both larger than those of the other four genres, which shows that the distribution effect of k value and m value in *legal* is the most obvious, which is related to the frequent use of longer proper nouns in legal genres. There is a proportional relationship between the k value and the m value, while an inverse relationship between the q value and the k and m values. This can then be interpreted to mean that k, m, and q values are effective variables for distinguishing between different genre features.

4   Conclusion

This study adopted a new language unit— "motif" to explore the characteristics of word length distribution sequences in Mongolian. The main research directions include: (1) the distribution characteristics of Mongolian word length motif; (2) the distribution characteristics of the length of Mongolian word length motif.

Through this research, it is discovered that: (1) the word length motif designated as "1" is scarcely observed in Mongolian, suggesting a rarity of words with a singular syllable count within the Mongolian lexical system. Moreover, the distribution of word length motif and its fitting parameters vary in different styles, further validating that the distribution of the word length motif can reflect the characteristics of different linguistic styles. The distribution of the Mongolian word length motifs adheres to the Zipf-Mandelbrot model. (2) Regarding the distribution characteristics of the length of the word length motif, it was found that Mongolian word length motifs of "2", "3", "4", and "1" are predominantly common, with "2" registering the highest frequency. The longer the length motif, the lower its frequency of occurrence, which fully reflects the widely existing "principle of least effort" in human languages. The distribution of the length of Mongolian word length motif shows some regularity, conforming to the Hyperpascal model.

Considering these findings, forthcoming studies necessitate more comprehensive and systematic inquiries across diverse domains—for instance, exploring whether there are differences in the word length motif between Mongolian, as agglutinative language, and other language types. Sanada [10] used a non-increasing sequential series to investigate the distribution characteristics of the Japanese word length motif. Whether Mongolian and Japanese, both as SOV languages, share similarities in this aspect is a future research focus. This study offers a preliminary exploration of the characteristics of the Mongolian word length motif, and the findings lay a foundation for subsequent related research.

Acknowledgment. This research is sponsored by the Key Projects of the National Social Science Foundation of China (Nos.19AYY018); Inner Mongolia Autonomous Region Higher Education Applied Linguistics Innovation Team Project; Postgraduate Scientific Research Innovation Project of Inner Mongolia University.

References

1. Popescu, I-I., Naumann, S., Kelih, E., Rovenchak, A., Overbeck, A., Sanada, H. et al.: Word length: aspects and languages. In: Köhler, R., Altmann, G. (eds.) Issues in Quantitative Linguistics 3, Dedicated to Karl-Heinz Best on the Occasion of his 70th birthday, vol.13, pp. 181–224. RAM, Lüdenscheid (2013)
2. Narisong., Jiang, J., Liu, H.: Word length distribution in Mongolian. J. Quant. Linguist. **21**(2), 123–152 (2014)
3. Wei, A., Lu, Q., Liu, H.: Word length distribution in Zhuang language. J. Quant. Linguist. **28**(3), 195–222 (2021)
4. Köhler, R., Naumann, S.: Quantitative Text Analysis Using L-, F- and T-Segments. In: Preisach, C., Burkhardt, H., Schmidt-Thieme, L., Decker, R. (eds.) Machine Learning and Applications, pp. 637–646. Springer, Heidelberg (2008)
5. Köhler, R.: Linguistic Motifs. In: G, Mikros., J, Macutek. (eds.) Sequences in Language and Text, pp. 89–108. De Gruyter Mouton, Berlin (2015)
6. Huang, W.: Length Motifs of Words in Traditional and Simplified Chinese Scripts. In: Liu, H., Liang. (eds.) Motifs in Language and Text, pp.109–132. De Gruyter Mouton, Berlin (2017)
7. Wang, Y.: Quantitative genre analysis using linguistic motifs. In: Liu, H., Liang. (eds.) Motifs in Language and Text, pp.165–180. De Gruyter Mouton, Berlin (2017)
8. Liu, H., Liang, J.: Motifs in Language and Text. De Gruyter Mouton, Berlin (2017)
9. Chen, H.: Quantitative studies of Chinese Word Length. Zhejiang University, Doctor (2016). (in Chinese)
10. Sanada, H.: Distribution of motifs in Japanese texts. In: P, Grzybek., E, Kelih., J, Macutek. (eds.) Text and Language. Structures-Functions-Interrelations-Quantitative Perspectives, pp.183–193. Praesens, Wien (2010)

11. Huhe.: Syllables in Mongolian. Minority of language of China **4**, 73–78 (1998). (in Chinese)

12. Bai, S., Hu, Q., Mu, Ren.: Implementation and application of mongolian syllable segmentation algorithm. In: Proceedings of the 11th National Symposium on Ethnic Language Text Information, pp. 242–246. Xiyuan Publishing House, Beijing (2007). (in Chinese)

13. Qinggertai.: Modern Mongolian grammar. Hohhot: Inner Mongolia People's Publishing House, Hohhot (1991) (in Mongolian)

14. Dulan., Dabhvrbayar.: A Study of the Polysemy Distribution of Mongolian. In: Wu, Y., Hong, J., Su, Q. (eds.) Chinese Lexical Semantics, CLSW2020, LNAI, vol.12278, pp. 341–348. Springer, Berlin (2021). https://doi.org/10.1007/978-3-030-81197-6_40

15. Yan, J., Liu, H.: Quantitative Analysis of Chinese and English Verb Valencies Based on Probabilistic Valency Pattern Theory. In: Minghui, Dong., Yanhui, Gu., Jia-Fei. (eds.) Chinese Lexical Semantics, CLSW2021, LNAI, vol.13250, pp.152–162. Springer, Berlin (2022). https://doi.org/10.1007/978-3-031-06547-7_12

16. Köhler, R.: Sequences of linguistic quantities report on a new unit of investigation. Glottotheory **1**(1), 115–119 (2008)

17. Köhler, R.: Linguistic motifs. Sequences Lang. Text. **69**, 89–108 (2015)

18. Garcia, D., Garas, A., Schweitzer, F.: Positive words carry less information than negative words. EPJ Data Sci. **1**, 1–12 (2012)

19. Liu, Y.: Statistical Linguistics. Tsinghua University Press, Beijing (2014). (in Chinese)

20. Wuyoutan.: Syntax Quantitative Research Based on Mongolian Academic Corpus. Doctor, Inner Mongolia University (2022) (in Chinese)

21. Köhler, R., Naumann, S.: A syntagmatic approach to automatic text classification. Statistical properties of F- and L-motifs as text characteristics. In: P, Grzybek., E, Kelih., J, Mačutek. (eds.) Text and Language. Structures-Functions-Interrelations-Quantitative Perspectives, pp.81–89. Praesens, Wien (2010)

22. Mandelbrot, B.: An informational theory of the statistical structure of language. Commun. Theory **84**, 486–502 (1953)

23. Köhler, R.: The frequency distribution of the lengths of length sequences. In: Genzor, J., Buckova, M. (eds.) Favete linguis: Studies in honour of Viktor Krupa, pp. 145–152. Slovak Academic Press, Bratislava (2006)

Construction of Knowledge Base of Non-Core Argument Based on Serial Verb Construction

Shufan Zhou[(✉)], Guirong Wang, Gaoqi Rao, and Endong Xun

Beijing Language and Culture University, Beijing, China
zhshf9797@163.com

Abstract. Non-core argument, an additional component of a sentence, plays an important role in semantic analysis, which can expand the basic predicate structure and form complex propositions. Non-core arguments usually need to be cited by case markers, including not only prepositions but also verbs. This study focuses on verb-guided non-core arguments, as well as an investigation of the expression of non-core argument role relationships based on serial verb construction, which is different from the previous method that mainly focused on preposition-guided non-core arguments. In this study, a new set of non-core argument role classification systems is proposed. At the same time, newspapers and periodicals corpus containing structural tree information in BCC corpus are chosen for obtaining serial verb collocation data. Through disambiguation and non-core argument role identification, the presented method eventually achieved 25517 examples of triple collocations and constructed a verb-guided non-core argument knowledge base, which provides data support for natural language processing and language theory research.

Keywords: Serial Verb Construction · Non-core Argument Role · Verbal Guide Words · Knowledge Base

1 Introduction

The predicate is the center of the syntactic structure and semantic interpretation of the sentence, and the predicate and its related semantic components together form the basis of semantic understanding. Modern syntactic theory affirms that each verb-related semantic component in a sentence should be assigned a specific semantic role. Whether in linguistic research or in the semantic role labeling of natural language processing, function words are considered as the main means of identifying and guiding arguments, and prepositions such as '在' (zài), '于' (yú), '从' (cóng), '向' (xiàng), '用' (yòng) are regarded as the most typical non-core argument guide words, and most of the research in the academic circles are also focused on this. However, it is undeniable that some substantive words also have the ability to give the semantic role of the argument. At the same time, because Chinese lacks morphological changes, grammatical forms are constrained in collocations, and collocations contain semantic information. Around a specific verb, its non-core argument is guided by another verb, and non-core argument role relationship is reflected in the serial verb collocation whose former direct component is a verb-object phrase. For example, the serial verb construction '到北京开会' (*dào běijīng kāihuì*, 'go to Beijing for a meeting'), '到' (*dào*, 'go') as a verbal guide word guides the location argument '北京' (*běijīng*, 'Beijing') of the central verb '开会' (*kāihuì*, 'attend a meeting'), and the prefixed '到' (*dào*, 'go') and '北京' (*běijīng*, 'Beijing') are used as additional components to modify semantically '开会' (*kāihuì*, 'attend a meeting').

In view of this, this study builds a verb-guided non-core argument knowledge base based on serial verb construction with the support of big data. The triple collocation of "verbal guide word—non-core argument—central verb" constitutes a semantic network. Each node in the semantic network is related to each other due to the relationship of semantic roles. The three components in the triple collocation can be mapped to a general formal semantic representation framework such as knowledge graph, which provides an incision for the identification of non-core arguments in the absence of function word markers in the sentence, and helps computers better understand natural language. For linguistic research, further analyzing the specific conditions for verbs to play the role of marking thematic roles and the categories of non-core argument roles that can be assigned in collocations is not only of great significance to the study of Chinese argument structure, but also enriches the theoretical construction and typological research on the representation of semantic role relations under the serial verb framework.

2 Research Status

Regarding the verb-guided non-core arguments under the serial verb framework, there have been relevant studies in linguistics. Durie [1] pointed out that the serial verb construction in various languages mostly use one verb to introduce the semantic case of another verb, so according to the different functions of the two verbs, the serial verb construction is often divided into semantic sub-categories such as place sequence and tool sequence. Lord [7] pointed out that in some languages, sequence structure can be used to express case role relationship, such as place, receiver, beneficiary, adjunct case, tool, patient, etc. He affirmed that the case-marking function of verbs was developed in the context of sequential verb constructions, and through the process of "blurring" or "de-semanticization", verbs lost their lexical semantic content, and thus lost their morphological and syntactic abilities. Liu [8] analyzed this type of verbs from the perspective of diachronic grammaticalization. He believed that from a diachronic point of view, it is easy to grammatically change content words that mark thematic roles into function words that mark thematic roles, and pointed out that the grammaticalization of verbs that mark thematic roles is mainly based on the verb-object structure and the serial verb construction containing the verb-object phrase as the syntactic environment. The word order of verbs and objects in Chinese is "verb + object", and the verbs that mark thematic roles will cause a series of re-analyses. The serial verb construction re-analyses are prepositional phrases that modify the following verbs, and the verb-object phrases are reanalyzed as prepositional phrases. The thematic category of the object remains unchanged, but the direction in which it is related has changed, from the thematic role of the original verb that marks thematic role is reanalyzed to the thematic role of another main verb, and the verb that marks thematic role has become a syntactic preposition and thematic role marker. In addition, apart from the prepositional verbs that mark thematic roles, Liu also affirmed the role of other content words in assigning semantic roles to arguments. Taking the Chinese spatial role assignment system as an example, he pointed out that there are various means of expression for thematic roles, and the elements of marking thematic roles are both substantive and functional, both verbal and nominal, both prepositional and post positional. Several means of marking thematic roles can work at the same time, or only one means can work.

At present, there have been some theoretical studies on the introduction of semantic cases by verbs in the academic circles, but there is a lack of quantitative analysis and empirical research. However, linguistic research in particular requires reliable methods, and with regard to natural language understanding, the use of statistical methods to research and express research results that can be used by computers. In this study, the serial verb collocation data of the preceding verb as the argument case marker is obtained from a large-scale real corpus, and the semantic role identification of the non-core argument guided by the verb is conducted, and a non-core argument knowledge base based on serial verb construction is constructed. Based on large-scale real corpus, it is more objective and authentic to study verbal argument role markers and the semantic role categories of the non-core arguments they guide.

The research line of this study is roughly as follows: Firstly, based on the results of previous research, the non-core argument role classification system is established, which is used as the basis for the subsequent identification of argument roles in the knowledge base. Secondly, the serial verb collocations are automatically extracted from the newspaper domain data of the BCC corpus containing structural tree information, and the extraction results are disambiguated. Then, with the help of HowNet and supplemented by manual identification, the semantic roles of the non-core arguments guided by verbs are determined, a non-core argument knowledge base based on serial verb construction is constructed. Finally, a statistical analysis is carried out on the knowledge base, and the specific conditions for the preceding verbs to play the role of assigning roles in the serial verb construction and the types of argument roles that can be assigned are summarized.

3   The Non-Core Argument Role System

Knowledge base construction requires not only the support of grammatical framework, but also the analysis of semantic level. Considering the need to identify non-core argument roles under the serial verb framework, this study first establishes a set of non-core argument role classification system, which is used as the basis for the subsequent identification of argument roles in the knowledge base.

There have been many previous studies on the non-core argument roles. The case system established by Lin [9] and the argument role hierarchy system established by Yuan [16] are two representative semantic role systems, in which each semantic role lists the corresponding prepositional case markers. At present, these two systems have been developed in Chinese information processing. Lin et al. [10] used "situation" to indicate the scope of a character's activities, and "situation" is divided into three levels: dependence, environment, and basis-reason. The "dependence" is further divided into "

工具 (instrument)", "材料 (material)", and "方式 (method)". The "environment" is further divided into "范围 (scope)", "时间 (time)", "处所 (place)", and "方向 (direction)". And the "basis-reason" is divided into "依据 (accordance)", "原因 (cause)", "目的 (purpose)". Yuan [17] defined the possible arguments of verbs as "peripheral arguments". The peripheral arguments include dependent arguments and environmental arguments. The dependent arguments are divided into "工具 (instrument)", "材料 (material)", and "方式 (method)", and the environmental arguments are divided into "场所 (location)", "源点 (locative source)", "终点 (target destination)", and "范围 (scope)". Comparing the two classification systems, it is found that Lin and Yuan's "工具 (instrument), 材料 (material), and 方式 (method)" are consistent in terms of nomenclature and definition; Lin's "处所 (place)" and Yuan's "场所 (location)" are different in name but same in fact; Yuan subdivides the "方向 (direction)" into "源点 (locative source)" and "终点 (target destination)"; compared with Lin's "范围 (scope)", which specifically refers to "the field or scope involved in the event and the accompanying conditions", Yuan's "范围 (scope)" includes "the quantity, frequency, amplitude, time and other related matters involved in actions and behaviors", while Lin lists "时间 (time)" and "数量 (quantity)" as two independent semantic roles; in addition, Lin's system also has a semantic role representing basis-reason. Since "数量 (quantity)" has no clear case mark, the role of "数量 (quantity)" is not included in the research scope of this study. Based on this, this study integrates the classification systems of the two scholars and identifies 11 semantic roles as the non-core argument roles examined in this study. The fused non-core argument role classification system is shown in Table 1:

Table 1. Non-core argument role classification system.

non-core argument role	dependence	工具 (instrument)
		材料 (material)
		方式 (method)
	environment	范围 (scope)
		时间 (time)
		场所 (location)
		源点 (locative source)
		终点 (target destination)
	basis-reason	依据 (accordance)
		原因 (cause)
		目的 (purpose)

4   Construction of the Knowledge Base

From the goal of this study, the construction of a knowledge base of non-core arguments based on serial verb construction mainly includes two aspects: obtaining more accurate serial verb collocation data and effectively identifying non-core argument roles. In this section, we will introduce the construction of the knowledge base in four steps: the extraction of serial verb construction, the disambiguation of serial verb construction, chunk center word extraction, and non-core argument role identification.

4.1   The Extraction of Serial Verb Construction

4.1.1   Data Source

The acquisition of serial verb construction in this study is based on BCC (Beijing Language and Culture University Modern Chinese Corpus) [14]. The total word count of BCC is about 15 billion words, and the corpus involves many fields such as newspaper, literature, microblog, science, synthesis, and ancient Chinese, etc. The forms are diverse, including original corpus, sub-word corpus and lexically labeled corpus, and it can also support the corpus search for phrase structure tree. The newspaper corpus is the most standardized and contemporary, and the phrase structure tree can better reflect the structural hierarchy of sentences, the category and function of phrases. In order to more rigorously and accurately examine the use of serial verb construction that express the role relationship of non-core arguments in written language, this study selects the newspaper corpus (about 2 billion words) containing structure tree information in the BCC corpus to obtain the data of serial verb collocation.

The structure tree information in this study is called from the Chinese Syntactic Structure Treebank constructed by Lu et al. [11]. The Treebank is syntactically represented as chunked phrase structure trees (see Fig. 1), including three types of chunks: syntactic constituent chunks that form the basic structure of sentences, cohesive chunks that act as cohesive contexts, and auxiliary chunks that express additional semantics. The Treebank tags mainly include chunk property tags, chunk function and purpose tags, and sentence boundary tags (see Table 2). 1–4 in Table 2 are the chunk property tags. NP, VP, and UNK are mainly used to describe the nominality or predicate of the subject, the object, the whole predicate and the core predicate. NULL is used to uniformly mark the chunking properties of other constituents. 5–9 in Table 2 are the function tags of the chunk, which describes the syntactic roles of the chunk units in terms of syntax. 10–11 in Table 2 are the purpose tags of the chunk, which describes the connection function and the tone function of the chunk units from the discourse function and interpersonal function. 12–15 in Table 2 are the tags of sentence boundaries and levels. At the sentence structure level, the treebank is centered on the predicate in the longest phrase chunk acting as a predicate, labeling the subject-predicate-object structure of the longest subject chunk, object chunk and predicate, and the adverbial-head-complement structure of the longest adverbial chunk, complement chunk and predicate, which can clearly identify the functional chunk boundaries and the relationship between them.

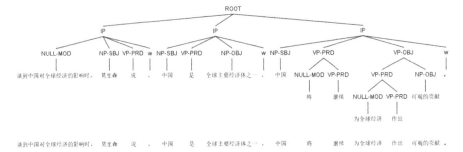

Fig. 1. Example of a chunked phrase structure tree.

Table 2. Treebank tag sets.

Serial number	Symbol	Tag type	Serial number	Symbol	Tag type	Serial number	Symbol	Tag type
1	VP	predicate chunk	6	NPRE	nominal predicate	11	AUX	auxiliary chunk
2	NP	nominal chunk	7	MOD	adverbial, complement	12	ROOT	single sentence or complex sentence
3	UNK	chunk that predicates juxtaposed with nouns	8	SBJ	subject	13	IP	complete clause
4	NULL	other property chunk	9	OBJ	object	14	HLP	one-member sentence or fragment
5	PRD	predicate	10	CON	cohesive chunk	15	W	punctuation

4.1.2 Extraction Method

The two direct constituents that constitute a serial verb construction can be individual verbs or verb structures, and this study examines serial verb constructions where the former direct constituent is a verb-object phrase. In this study, we first extract the chunked combination sequences consisting of the longest predicative declarative chunk (VP-PRD), the somatic object chunk (NP-OBJ), and the predicative declarative chunk (VP-PRD) from the BCC corpus of newspaper corpora containing structural tree information, such as '将到医院看望' (*jiāng dào yīyuàn kànwàng*, 'will go to the hospital to visit') in "[ROOT[IP[NP-SBJ[他 r]][VP-PRD[NULL-MOD[将 d]][VP-PRD[到 v]]][NP-OBJ[医院 n]][VP-PRD[看望 v]][NP-OBJ[同事 n]][w[。x]]]]". The longest declarative chunk may be just a core predicate, or it may include adverbial chunks (NULL-MOD) and complementary chunks (NULL-MOD) that modify or complement a core predicate. In order to extract the data in a comprehensive and complete way, this study summarizes the distribution pattern of the declarative chunk, adverbial chunk and complementary chunk in the longest declarative chunk and expresses them formally into four categories, after which regular expressions are used to retain the sequences of chunked combinations that meet the conditions, and 1309540 data are obtained, which are presented in the form of rows. The categorical extraction is now illustrated in Table 3.

Table 3. Categorical extraction of serial verb chunk sequences.

Serial number	Serial verb chunk sequence	Example
1	[VP-VRD] [NP-OBJ] [VP-PRD]	a. 前往 机场 送行
2	[VP-PRD] [NP-OBJ] [VP-PRD with NULL-MOD]	b. 听 我 慢慢讲 c. 劝 他 休息一下 d. 找来 一根绳子 把老伴和自己捆在一起
3	[VP-PRD with NULL-MOD] [NP-OBJ] [VP-PRD]	e. 自西安抵达 上海 访问 f. 合起来 资本 达到 g. 都合起来 资本 达到
4	[VP-PRD with NULL-MOD] [NP-OBJ] [VP-PRD with NULL-MOD]	h. 分别代表 本国政府 在协定上签字 i. 已经作为 一条重要的方针 包括在党的社会主义建设总路线的要点中 j. 另有 7人 偷躲在地窖里 k. 救起来 她 还是会跳 l. 约一下 时间 凑一起 m. 约一下 时间 尽快凑一起 n. 当即救起来 她 还是会跳 o. 都举起来 棍子 跑过去 p. 立刻盘算起来 价格 向后退了几步

The first type of serial verb construction does not contain adverbials and complements within the two declarative chunks, for example, in example a, the two core predicates '前往' (*qiánwǎng*, 'proceed towards') and '送行' (*sòngxíng*, 'see someone off') are neither modified by adverbials nor complemented by complements. The second type of serial verb construction contains adverbials and complements within the latter part of the declarative chunk, for example, in example b, the latter part of the core predicate '讲' (*jiǎng*, 'speak') is modified by the adverbial '慢慢' (*mànmàn*, 'slowly'); in example c, '休息' (*xiūxī*, 'rest') is supplemented by the complement '一下' (*yíxià*, 'for a moment'); and in example d, '捆' (*kǔn*, 'tie') is modified by both the adverbial '把老伴和自己' (*bǎ lǎobàn hé zìjǐ*, 'take my wife and myself') and the complement '在一起' (*zài yìqǐ*, 'together'). The third type of serial verb construction contains adverbial and complementary chunks within the preceding declarative chunk, such as example e, where the preceding core predicate '抵达' (*dǐdá*, 'arrive') is modified by the adverbial '自西安' (*zì xī'ān*, 'from Xi'an'), example f, where '合' (*hé*, 'combine') is supplemented by the complement '起来' (*qǐlái*), and example g is modified by both the adverbial '都' (*dōu*, 'all') and the complement '起来' (*qǐlái*). The four type of serial verb construction contains adverbials and complements within the two declarative chunks, such as examples h-j, where the first core predicate is modified by a adverbial, example h, where the second core predicate '签字' (*qiānzì*, 'sign') is modified by the adverbial '在协定上' (*zài xiédìng shàng*, 'on the agreement'), example i, where '包括' (*bāokuò*, 'include') is supplemented by the complement '在党的社会主义建设总路线的要点中' (*zài dǎng de shèhuì zhǔyì jiànshè zǒng lùxiàn de yàodiǎn zhōng*, 'in the main points of the CPC's general line of socialist construction'), and example j, where '躲' (*duǒ*, 'hide') is complemented by both the adverbial '偷' (*tōutōu*, 'secretly') and the complement '在地窖 里' (*zài dìjiào lǐ*, 'in the cellar'); in examples k-m, the first core predicate is complemented by the complement, in example k, the last core predicate '跳' (*tiào*, 'jump') is modified by the adverbial '还是会' (*háishì huì*, 'still'), in example l '凑' (*còu*, 'gather') is complemented by the complement '一起' (*yìqǐ*, 'together'), and in example m '凑' (*còu*, 'gather') is modified by both the gerund '尽快' (*jǐnkuài*, 'as soon as possible') and the complement '一起' (*yìqǐ*, 'together'); in examples n-p, the first core predicate is modified by both the adverbial and the complement, in example n, the second core predicate '跳' (*tiào*, 'jump') is modified by the adverbial '还是会' (*háishì huì*, 'still'), example o '跑' (*pǎo*, 'run') is complemented by the complement '过去' (*guòqù*, 'over'), and example p '退' (*tuì*, 'retreat') is modified by both the adverbial '向后' (*xiànghòu*, 'back') and complemented by the complement '几步' (*jǐbù*, 'a few steps'). The above cases cover all the cases of serial verb chunk sequence examined in this study, and are used as the basis for a comprehensive extraction of serial verb data.

4.2 The Disambiguation of Serial Verb Construction

Due to the roughness of the treebank annotation specification in the treatment of issues related to multi-category words, and the existence of errors such as inaccurate identification of sentence boundaries in the actual annotation, and due to the limitation of the chunk tagging in the semantic constraints, there existed some non-serial verb construction types of sentences in the initially extracted serial verb construction data. Therefore, this study summarizes linguistic knowledge through corpus observation and introspective approach to further disambiguate the extraction results.

4.2.1 Disambiguation for Treebank Labeling Specification

Huang and Liao [5] pointed out in < Modern Chinese > that there is no phonological pause between verbs or verb phrases used in linking sentences, and there is no need for any connective words. Corresponding to the description of treebank chunk tagging, connective words belong to the articulated chunk (NULL-CON), however, for engineering considerations, the treebank annotation specification stipulates that some connective words with the same form of conjunction and adverb are treated as adverbs uniformly, and are classified into the adverbial chunk (NULL-MOD). Such as the pair of connective words '要...就...' (*yào...jiù...*) in '要保证 一定的质量 就必须有' (*yào bǎozhèng yídìng de zhìliàng jiù bìxū yǒu*, 'to ensure a certain level of quality, it is necessary to have') and the single connective words '却' (*què*) in '多次向有关部门反映 这个情

况 却无济于事' (*duōcì xiàng yǒuguān bùmén fǎnyìng zhège qíngkuàng què wújìyúshì*, 'report this situation to the relevant departments multiple times but it has been of no avail') are all labeled as a adverbial. In this study, based on the description of Li [12], and supplemented with the connective words mentioned by Huang and Liao [5], a word list of connective words is formulated, based on which the data containing connective words in the adverbial chunks are deleted for the above two types of cases.

4.2.2 Disambiguation for Data Labeling Errors

Regarding punctuation, there were two main types of labeling errors in the data.

(1) Punctuation marks indicating pauses are mislabeled into the middle nominal object chunk (NP-OBJ). E.g.:

    a. 今天过 情人节… 明天加班.

jīntiān guò qíngrénjié… míngtiān jiābān.

'today celebrate Valentine's Day... Work overtime tomorrow'

    b. 与这江河一起激荡 /我 与这霓虹灯一起闪烁.

yǔ zhè jiānghé yìqǐ jīdàng /wǒ yǔ zhè níhóngdēng yìqǐ shǎnshuò.

'shake with this river /I blink with this neon light'

(2) Groups of punctuation marks that do not appear in pairs in the middle of a nominal object chunk (NP-OBJ). E.g.:

    c. 高呼 "毛主席 万岁.

gāohū "máozhǔxí wànsuì.

'chant "Chairman Mao long live'.

    d. 一定要抓好 典型"、"面上的工作 要先抓好.

yídìng yào zhuāhǎo diǎnxíng"、"miànshàng de gōngzuò yào xiān zhuāhǎo.

'must focus on typical examples", "practical work must first focus on'

In example a, the pause "…" is wrongly placed at th e end of the object chunk when it should actually be the end of the preceding complete phrase (IP), and in example b, "/" is wrongly placed at the beginning of the object chunk when in fact '我' (*wǒ*, 'I') after "/" is the subject of the following '与这霓虹灯一起闪烁' (*yǔ zhè níhóngdēng yìqǐ shǎnshuò*, 'blink with this neon light') rather than the object of preceding '与这江河一起激荡' (*yǔ zhè jiānghé yìqǐ jīdàng*, 'shake with this river'); example c is the subject-verb phrase as object structure, '毛主席万岁' (*máozhǔxí wànsuì*, 'long live Chairman Mao') as a whole is the object of '高呼' (*gāohū*, 'chant'), example d '一定要抓好典型' (*yídìng yào zhuāhǎo diǎnxíng*, 'must focus on typical examples') and '面上的工作要先抓好' (*miànshàng de gōngzuò yào xiān zhuāhǎo*, 'must first focus on practical work') is a juxtaposition of the two components, in fact, within the object chunk, only '

典型' (diǎnxíng, 'typical examples') is the object of '一定要抓好' (yídìng yào zhuāhǎo, 'must focus on'), and '面上的工作' (miànshàng de gōngzuò, 'practical work') is the subject of the following '要先抓好' (yào xiān zhuāhǎo, 'must first focus on'). In this study, we counted all the punctuation marks indicating pauses in the data, and deleted the data for the above two major types of labeling errors.

4.3 Extraction of Chunk Center Words

In order to more directly understand non-core argument role relationships expressed in this kind of serial verb construction, and to clarify the verbal guide words guiding the non-core arguments, this study further extracts the center words of the two predicative declarative chunks before and after, and the nominal object chunk in the middle, for example, the words '花' (huā, 'spend'), '人民币' (rénmínbì, 'RMB') and '购买' (gòumǎi, 'purchase') in the phrase '两年前花 8万元人民币 从北京作曲家肖白处购买了' (liǎngnián qián huā 8wànyuán rénmínbì cóng běijīng zuòqǔjiā xiāobáichù gòumǎi le, 'purchased from Beijing composer Xiao Bai for 80,000 RMB two years ago') constitute a triple collocation.

The extraction of the chunk center word includes the extraction of the core verb and the extraction of the core noun.

In the extraction of core verbs, this study first excludes the adverbial and complement part (NULL-MOD) within the predicative declarative chunk (VP-PRD) and locates the core predicative declarative chunk (VP-PRD) among them. When there is no verb within the chunk, no further reservation is made for this part of the data, such as "[VP-PRD[替 p]][NP-OBJ[他 r]][VP-PRD[高兴 a]]"; when there is and is only one verb within the chunk, that verb is the core verb, such as '拿' (ná, 'take') in "[VP-PRD[NULL-MOD[迅速 ad]][VP-PRD[拿 v]]"; in addition, the specification of treebank annotation stipulates that some common verbs that are resultant complements immediately following the verb, such as '见' (jiàn, 'meet'), '完' (wán, 'finish'), '懂' (dǒng, 'understand'), '成' (chéng, 'accomplish'), '住' (zhù, 'stay'), '为' (wéi, 'be') and so on, are labeled with the core verb as a declarative, so the number of verbs in some core predicative declarative chunks is more than one, and for this part of the data, the words labeled with the core verb are eliminated, for example, the core verb in "[VP-PRD[写 v][完 v]]" ends up being '写' (xiě, 'write'). Finally, given that the noun element in the middle of a serial verbal sentence is only the object of the preceding verb, whereas the noun element in the middle of a pivotal sentence is the subject of the following verb in addition to being the object of the preceding verb, a further distinction is made between pivotal sentences and serial verbal sentences. Considering that the previous verb of the pivot in a pivotal sentence has obvious semantic features, we first collect these verbs with specific semantic features, construct a pivot verb lexicon, and then formally delete part of the pivotal sentence based on it. The pivot verb lexicon here is developed based on Huang, Liao [5], Xing [15] and Li [13], and the verbs expanded on this basis by The Thesaurus of Synonyms [6], which are 218 in total.

In the extraction of core nouns, considering that the nominal object chunk (NP-OBJ) is either a single noun, or a phrase of a structural type such as partial positive, union, cognate, and so on, so this study defaults to the right semantic center of the nominal object chunk. According to the segmentation result, the last noun in the NP-OBJ chunk is extracted as the core noun, such as '方针' (*fāngzhēn*, 'policy') in "[NP-OBJ [一条 m][重要 a][的 uj][方针n]]]".

For the sake of terminology, this study notates the studied serial verb triple collocation as "v1*n*v2", where "v1" is the former verb, "n" is its object, and "v2" is the verb in the latter direct component.

4.4 Non-Core Argument Role Identification

The research work in this study has huge data, and it would be difficult to identify the thesis roles purely manually. While HowNet [2] constructed by Mr. Dong Zhendong contains rich semantic role information. HowNet uses 90 semantic roles (including 83 semantic roles filled by the argument) and describes 100,000 items in Chinese and English in conjunction with the sememe. Each word in HowNet consists of a specific semantics that describes its most basic meaning. The sememe includes four categories of events, entities, attributes, and attribute values, and each category of event sememe "strictly specifies the corresponding necessary semantic role framework" [3] (i.e., the semantic roles of the event sememe and the roles' corresponding sememe). When it is known that an event sememe and another entity or attribute sememe have a certain argument role relationship, the argument roles in a serial verb triple collocation can be deduced from the argument role relationship between the event sememe that describes "v" and the entity or attribute sememe that describes "n". Therefore, in this study, with the help of information on event sememe and their argument role frameworks from HowNet, and supplemented by manual labor, we identify the roles of the argument "n" of "v2".

1) In the HowNet, "The concept or denotation and its description of each word form a record" [4]. Taking the verb '放炮' (*fàngpào*, 'set off artillery') as an example, the conceptualization is as follows, "DEF = {firing|射击:instrument = {weapon|武器:domain = {military|军}}}". The basic meaning of '放炮' (*fàngpào*, 'set off artillery') is explained by the first sememe "firing|射击" after "DEF = {". Thus, consider "firing|射击" as event sememe describing verb '放炮' (*fàngpào*, 'set off artillery'). In this study, we first find all the nouns that can be described by the entity and attribute sememe and all the verbs that can be described by the event sememe. Some of the words correspond to the sememe in Table 4.

2) In "DEF = {firing|射击:instrument = {weapon|武器:domain = {military|军}}}", the content following the first colon specifies event sememe "firing|射击"'s essential role "instrument". The role "instrument"'s corresponding value is entity sememe "weapon|武器". That is entity sememe "weapon|武器" can act as event sememe "firing|射击"'s "instrument". This study summarizes the semantic role framing information for all event sememe. The following is an example of event sememe "GoInto|进入" (details are provided in Table 5). In the Table 5, event sememe "GoInto|进入" has eight essential roles, each of which in turn corresponds to specific values under each role, which is various type of sememe.

(3) To summarize, with the help of the correspondences between "v2" and the event sememe, "n" and the entity or attribute sememe, and at the same time linking to the event sememe, the semantic roles of that event sememe and the information of the

Table 4. Some of the words and the sememe describing the words.

Verb	Event sememe	Noun	Entity and attribute sememe
呈(*chéng*, 'assume')	be|是	木版(*mùbǎn*, 'block')	tool|用具
纯属(*chúnshǔ*, 'be purely')	be|是	木棒(*mùbàng*, 'stick')	tool|用具
取自(*qǔzì*, 'derive from')	obtain|得到	木棍(*mùgùn*, 'stick')	tool|用具
荣获(*rónghuò*, 'honorably receive')	obtain|得到	路费(*lùfèi*, 'travelling expenses')	expenditure|费用
受惠(*shòuhuì*, 'favored')	obtain|得到	旅费(*lǚfèi*, 'travelling expenses')	expenditure|费用
受益(*shòuyì*, 'benefited')	obtain|得到	旅资(*lǚzī*, 'travelling expenses')	expenditure|费用

entity or attribute sememe corresponding to the roles, it is then possible to query the semantic roles of the argument "n" of "v2". However, the categorization of some words by HowNet is multi-faceted, and a part of "n" in the triple collocation data has more than one denotation, which may serve different semantic roles. For example, in "花*元*买", "买" is described by the sememe "buy\|买", one of the denotations of "元" is "money\|货币", and the other is "time\|时间", and the argument role "cost" for "buy\|买" corresponds to "money\|货币" and the argument role "time" corresponds to "time\|时间". Therefore, in the absence of contextualization, the semantic role of the argument "元" of "买" could be either "cost" or "time". For this type of data, this study refers to the frequency information of various semantic roles guided by "v1", supplemented by manual analysis to identify all data with multiple semantic roles.

(4) It should be noted that, considering the need to identify semantic roles only for non-core arguments, this study selects only 18 roles (instrument, material, cost, means, method, location, LocationThru, LocationIni, SourceWhole, source, Location-Fin, ResultWhole, time, duration, scope, according to, cause, and purpose) as non-core argument roles against the interpretation of semantic roles in HowNet, and then corresponds the non-core argument roles selected from HowNet to the non-core argument role classification system in Table 1, as shown in Table 6.

Finally, given that the current data contains misanalyzed non-core argument roles and still contains serial verb construction that do not express non-core argument role relationship, this study first preserves semantic roles for each verbal guide words based on the Zipf's Law adhering to the "high frequency" criterion. As stated in the Zipf's law, for the lexical distribution of a language, the number of occurrences of a very few high-frequency words (types) already covers the majority of the total number of words in a corpus, whereas about half of the total number of words (types) occur only once in this corpus. The distribution of semantic roles for verb-guided non-core arguments similarly follows the Zipf's law. Therefore, in this study, for each verbal guide word, the high-frequency 80%

Table 5. Semantic role framework for the event sememe "GoInto|进入".

Require role	The value corresponding to the role
LocationFin	InstitutePlace|场所 LandVehicle|车 aircraft|飞行器 facilities|设施 house|房屋 part|部件 place|地方 room|房间 shape|物形 ship|船 waters|水域
LocationIni	location|位置 part|部件
LocationThru	facilities|设施
agent	human|人
instrument	coupon|票证 document|文书 expenditure|费用 tool|用具
location	location|位置 part|部件
manner	InSequence|有序 covert|隐秘 lonely|孤 unlawful|非法
means	fly|飞

of the semantic roles of the non-core arguments it leads are selected. Based on this, further manual proofreading of semantic roles, while excluding data of serial verb construction that are not expressing the non-core argument role relationship, 25517 instances of triple collocations of verb-guided non-core arguments based on serial verb construction are finally obtained.

Table 6. Correspondence method between non-core argument role system and non-core argument role of HowNet.

Non-core argument role system	Non-core argument role of HowNet
工具 (instrument)	instrument
材料 (material)	material
	cost
方式 (method)	means
	method
场所 (location)	location
	LocationThru
源点 (locative source)	LocationIni
	SourceWhole
	source
终点 (target destination)	LocationFin
	ResultWhole
时间 (time)	time
	duration
范围 (scope)	scope
依据 (accordance)	AccordingTo
原因 (cause)	cause
目的 (purpose)	purpose

5   Knowledge Base Structure and Analysis

5.1   Forms of Knowledge Base

The study finally find a total of 25517 instances of triple collocations of verb-guided non-core arguments based on the serial verb construction. The knowledge base constructed based on this contains information about the central verbs, verbal guide words, non-core argument instances and the semantic role categories they act as, giving all its non-core argument roles for each verb, and the guide words and their corresponding argument role instances for each non-core argument role. The final presentation of the knowledge base is shown in Table 7, ". Non-core Argument Role - Central Verb _ Verbal Guide Words" as a directory, and instances of argument roles under each directory are listed in descending order of frequency.

5.2   Correlation Analysis of Non-core Argument Roles

There are 11 categories of non-core argument roles identified in this study, and each category of non-core argument roles has corresponding verbal guide words. The distribution of each type of non-core argument roles, the number of corresponding verbal

Table 7. Knowledge base presentation.

.场所-访问_来
中国 154
我国 123
上海 47
沪 46
闽 41
大陆 20
福建 10
日本 6
北京 5
福州 3
香港 3

guide words and the average number of instances guided by the verbal guide words of that semantic class are now specified in Table 8:

Table 8. Relevant statistics around various types of non-core argument roles.

Non-core argument role	Number of instances of non-core argument role	Number of verbal guide words	Average number of instances guided by verbal guide words	Example
场所 (location)	14593	1269	11	抵达*上海*访问
工具 (instrument)	5934	1122	5	乘坐*飞机*抵达
时间 (time)	1964	296	7	利用*假期*参加
材料 (material)	1013	337	3	利用*材料*制造
方式 (method)	744	128	6	采用*方法*治疗
源点 (locative source)	556	142	4	离开*上海*回国
终点 (target destination)	490	226	2	瞄准*市场*深入
范围 (scope)	114	66	2	围绕*问题*反映
依据 (accordance)	68	32	2	参照*说明*使用
原因 (cause)	38	31	1	遇*车祸*身亡
目的 (purpose)	3	3	1	奔*目标*学

As shown in Table 8, overall, the distribution trends are roughly the same for the number of instances of some kind of semantic role filled by a verb-guided non-core argument and the number of verbal guide words corresponding to that semantic role. Among the semantic roles played by verb-guided non-core arguments, "场所 (location)" appears most frequently, with its number of instances accounting for 57% of the total number of role instances. This is because, on the one hand, the names of places are diversified, spatially including not only land, but also oceans and the seabed, and even gradually expanding to other celestial bodies in the universe, and on the other hand, semantics in non-physical space are also heavily metaphorized as location, such as the semantics of '家庭' (*jiātíng*, 'home') in "深入*家庭*教授" is embodied as "场所 (location)". Comparing the high-frequency occurrences of "工具 (instrument), 时间 (time), and 材料 (material)", the difference in the number of instances of "场所 (location)" and these three roles is very large, but the difference in the number of their corresponding verbal guide words varies from large to small, with a large difference between "场所 (location)" and "时间 (time) and 材料 (material)", but a difference of only 147 between "场所 (location)" and "工具 (instrument)", which shows that, although the role of "场所 (location)" occurs with a very high frequency, there is only a limited number of verbal guide words that can lead to the arguments acting as the role of "场所 (location)". While "依据 (accordance), 原因 (cause) and 目的 (purpose)" has very few instances and verbal guide words, especially "目的 (purpose)" has only 3 instances and verbal guide words.

In addition, the average number of instances of roles guided by each semantic class of verbal guide words shows that, although all of them can guide arguments that fill a certain class of semantic roles, the ability of different semantic classes of verbal guide words to guide this type of arguments varies. Verbal guide words in the semantic category "场所 (location), 时间 (time), 方式 (method), 工具 (instrument)" has a strong ability to guide its class of arguments, with the average number of role instances guided by the "场所 (location)" category up to 11, which is consistent with the high-frequency characterization of the number of role instances and the corresponding number of verbal guide words for "场所 (location)". The average number of role instances guided by the "时间 (time), 方式 (method) and 工具 (instrument)" category of verbal guide words are also above 5. The "原因 (cause) and 目的 (purpose)" category of verbal guide words are less capable of guiding its class of arguments, with an average number of role instances of only 1 each, which is also related to the fact that the number of role instances and corresponding verbal guide words for "原因 (cause) and 目的 (purpose)" is very small itself.

5.3 Correlation Analysis of Verbal Guide Words

In this study, we have counted a total of 2354 verbs that can guide non-core arguments based on the serial verb construction, some of which can only guide arguments with a single semantic role, while others can guide arguments with multiple semantic roles. The distribution of the number of verbs and the types of roles they guide is now specified in Fig. 2.

As shown in Fig. 2, of these 2354 verbs, 1559 are capable of assigning a specific semantic role to the arguments by themselves, and this class of verbs has a high degree

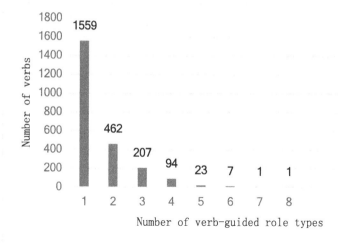

Fig. 2. The distribution of the number of verbs and the types of roles they guide.

of virtualization. For example, the semantic roles of the non-core arguments guided by the verb '去' (*qù*, 'go') are all "场所 (location)", and the semantic roles of the non-core arguments guided by '援引' (*yuányǐn*, 'cite') are all "工具 (instrument)". The other 795 verbs are able to lead to multiple-role arguments that need to be contextualized in order to qualify the semantic roles, and these verbal guide words that are able to lead to multiple-role arguments tend to be more substantive in meaning or to have more than one denotational item. In this study, the context is made explicit with reference to the sememe information, and the combination of verb and context is specifically subdivided into two categories:

1) Some verbal guide words only need to specify the semantics of the arguments, i.e., collocate with a specific entity or attribute sememe, in order to qualify the non-core argument roles based on the serial verb construction. E.g:

A. 到-InstitutePlace|场所 到*银行*办理.
B. 到-time|时间 到*昨天*结束.

When the verbal guide word '到' (*dào*, 'arrive') is paired with the entity sememe "InstitutePlace|场所", the semantic roles of nouns described by "InstitutePlace|场所" are all "场所 (location)". Such as the word '银行' (*yínháng*, 'bank') is described by "InstitutePlace|场所" and '银行' (*yínháng*, 'bank') in "到*银行*办理" acts as the role of "场所 (location)". When the verbal guide word '到' (*dào*, 'arrive') is paired with the entity sememe "time|时间", the semantic roles of nouns described by "time|时间" are all "时间 (time)". For example, the word '昨天' (*zuótiān*, 'yesterday') is described by "time|时间", and '昨天' (*zuótiān*, 'yesterday') in "到*昨天*结束" acts as the role of "时间 (time)". A total of 3326 such "Verbal Guide Word - Entity or Attribute Sememe" frames were counted.

2) Some verbal guide words need to specify both the semantics of the argument as well as the semantics of the subsequent verb, i.e., paired with specific entity or attribute sememe and event sememe, in order to be able to qualify the non-core argument roles based on the serial verb construction. E.g:

    A. 借-facilities|设施-disseminate|传播 借*媒体*传达.
    B. 借-facilities|设施-display|展示 借*舞台*表演.

When the verbal guide word '借' (*jiè*, 'borrow') is paired with the entity sememe "facilities|设施", the argument described by "facilities|设施" is able to fulfill more than one semantic role, which is further determined by the event sememe that describes "v2". When "借-facilities|设施" is paired with the event sememe "disseminate|传播", the semantic role of the argument described by "facilities|设施" is "工具 (instrument)". For example, in the case of "借*媒体*传达", '媒体' (*méitǐ*, 'medium') is described by the entity sememe "facilities|设施" and '传达' (*chuándá*, 'convey') is described by the event sememe "disseminate|传播", and in such a context, the semantic role of '媒体' (*méitǐ*, 'medium') is "工具 (instrument)". When "借-facilities|设施" is paired with the event sememe "display|展示", the semantic role of the argument described by "facilities| 设施" is "场所 (location)", for example, in "借*舞台*表演", '舞台' (*wǔtái*, 'stage') is described by the entity sememe "facilities|设施", and '表演' (*biǎoyǎn*, 'perform') is described by the event sememe "display|展示", and in such a context, the semantic role played by '舞台' (*wǔtái*, 'stage') is "场所 (location)". A total of 3836 such "Verbal Guide Word - Entity or Attribute Sememe - Event Sememe" frameworks have been obtained.

3) Of course, in individual cases, the framework of "Verbal Guide Word - Entity or Attribute Sememe - Event Sememe" still cannot qualify the semantic roles of the arguments, and the determination of the semantic roles of the arguments needs to depend on the specific objects described by the sememe. E.g:

    A. 利用-material|材料-produce|制造 利用*资源*制作.
    B. 利用-material|材料-produce|制造 利用*纸笔*制作.

The semantic role of '资源' (*zīyuán*, 'resource') in "利用*资源*制作" is "材料 (material)", and the semantic role of '纸笔' (*zhǐbǐ*, 'paper and pen') in "利用*纸笔*制作" is "工具 (instrument)". The main reason for this situation is that some of the concepts described in HowNet's sememe are too general, and '资源' (*zīyuán*, 'resource') and '纸笔' (*zhǐbǐ*, 'paper and pen'), which are quite different in meaning, are roughly categorized together as the sememe "material|材料". Therefore, in the collocation "利用-material|材料-produce|制造", different words described by the sememe "material|材料" correspond to different semantic roles for the same event sememe "produce|制造".

6   Conclusion

In this study, we constructed a knowledge base of non-core arguments based on the serial verb construction and performed exhaustive semantic role determination on it, which provides large-scale data support for the analysis of argument structure and the determination of semantic roles under the serial verb framework, and is important for syntactic semantic analysis for natural language processing. At the same time, the verbs for guiding non-core arguments and sememe frames statistically obtained from big data can in turn provide new ideas for the linguistic theory construction of the non-core argument alignment problem.

However, the work in this study has some shortcomings. First, considering the complexity of multi-domain texts and the difficulty of noise reduction, this study only extracted the corpus in the newspaper domain at the initial stage, so domain mobility needs to be further examined. Second, the initial identification of the role of the arguments in this study was made with the help of the HowNet tool, and the size of the knowledge base constructed on the basis of this is limited in view of the fact that the corpus may contain concepts that are not described by the HowNet. Finally, due to the richness of Chinese semantics, on the basis of analyzing the corpus argument roles using the semantic role framing information of the HowNet event sememe, the final determination of the argument roles still requires a great deal of manpower.

In the subsequent work, we extend the data extraction to a multi-domain corpus, and also consider to extend the coverage of the corpus with the HowNet Event Semantic Role Framework using the sememe information, thus expanding the data scale. At the same time, other perspectives and tools are also explored to assist in the identification of semantic roles and reduce the difficulty of manual identification.

References

1. Durie, M.: Grammatical structures in verb serialization. Complex predicates, pp. 289–354 (1997)
2. Dong, Z., Dong, Q.: HowNet and Chinese Studies. Contemp. Linguist. **01**, 33–44+77 (2001) (in Chinese)
3. Dong, Z., Dong, Q., Hao, C.: Theoretical findings from HowNet. J. Chinese Inform. Process. **04**, 3–9 (2007). (in Chinese)
4. Dong, Z.: Representation of semantic relations and construction of knowledge systems. Appl. Linguis. **03**, 79–85 (1998). (in Chinese)
5. Huang, B., Liao, X.: Modern Chinese (Revised sixth Edition) (Volume 2). Higher Education Press, Beijing (2017). (in Chinese)
6. Kang, S.: New Compilation of Synonymous Thesaurus. Shanghai Lexicographical Publishing House, Shanghai (2015). (in Chinese)
7. Lord, C.: Historical change in serial verb constructions. J. Benjamins (1993)
8. Liu, D.: Fugitive Meta-Reals and Grammaticalization. Pan, W.: Oriental Languages and Cultures. Orient Publishing Center, Shanghai (2002) (in Chinese)
9. Lin, X., Wang, L., Sun, D.: A Dictionary of Chinese Verbs. Beijing Language and Culture Institute Press, Beijing (1994). (in Chinese)
10. Lin, X.: Further in-depth study of grammatical relations in modern Chinese. Chinese Language Learning. **05**, 11–15 (1993) (in Chinese) 文章
11. Lu, L., Jiao, H., Li, M., Xun, E.: A discourse-base Chinese chunkbank. Acta Automatica Sinica. 1–12 (2021). http://kns.cnki.net/kcms/detail/11.2109.TP.20200521.1558.007.html. (in Chinese)
12. Li, X.: Lecture Notes on Imaginary Words in Modern Chinese. Peking University Press, Beijing (2005). (in Chinese)

13. Li, L.: Modern Chinese Sentence Patterns (Updated). The Commercial Press, Beijing (2001). (in Chinese)
14. Xun, E., Rao, G., Xiao, X., Zang, J.: The Development of BCC Corpus in the Context of Big Data. Corpus Linguist. **01**, 93–109+118 (2016) (in Chinese)
15. Xing, F.: Three Hundred Questions on Chinese Grammar. The Commercial Press, Beijing (2002). (in Chinese)
16. Yuan, Y.: A study of the valency of Chinese verbs. Jiangxi Education Publishing House, Nanchang (1998). (in Chinese)
17. Yuan, Y.: On the hierarchical relation and semantic features of the thematic roles in Chinese. Chinese Teach World. **03**, 10–22+2 (2002) (in Chinese)

The Application of Chinese Word Segmentation to Less-Resourced Language Processing

Meng-hsien Shih[✉] [iD]

National United University, Miaoli 360302, Taiwan
mhshih@nuu.edu.tw

Abstract. It has been more than half a century since the first million-word Brown Corpus was constructed. However, the lack of resources has posed a challenge to corpus construction and language processing for low-resource languages. Therefore, the corpus construction of most local languages such as Hokkien in Taiwan is still under development. In this paper, a Chinese segmenter based on syntactic analysis is adapted with a Hokkien dictionary (from Taiwan's Ministry of Education) to segment words in Hokkien texts. The proposed approach reports an accuracy rate of 87.50% in correctly separating the lemmas from the example sentences in the dictionary, and an average performance of 92.78% in testing with additional six unseen Hokkien e-paper articles. The source code of the proposed Hokkien segmenter is released with an online corpus of Hokkien word segmentation. This segmenter can be used to construct larger Hokkien corpus with segmented words, and apply to the segmentation of other less-resourced languages in the Chinese language family including Hakka.

Keywords: Chinese word segmentation · Less-resourced language processing · Lexical resource

1 Introduction

It has been more than half a century since the first million-word Brown Corpus [1] was built. The absence of resources, however, makes the language processing and corpus construction difficult for low-resource languages including Taiwanese Hokkien (Minnan). Although recently [2] have skipped the writing system and translated speech from Hokkien to English, word segmentation is still the fundamental step in the pre-processing and corpus construction of syllabic languages including Chinese, Japanese, and Hokkien (languages of alphabetic writing systems such as English and Indo-European languages use spaces to separate words in a sentence). This study exploits example sentences in the Dictionary of Frequently-Used Taiwan Minnan (from Taiwan's Ministry of Education), to build a Hokkien corpus with word segmentation. A corpus query interface is also released for researchers of the Chinese language family.

2 Literature Review

Since the construction of the Brown Corpus [1], we have witnessed significant development of corpora in most languages around the world. In recent years, [3] even introduced the concept of a Monitor Corpus, which continuously expands in size with time, and the Corpus of Contemporary American English (COCA) of this design had reached one billion words in 2020.

Concerning the Chinese language resource, Table 1 presents the corpus size and the sampling year range of current main Chinese corpora in Taiwan. Although most Chinese resources have been segmented in words and even tagged with part-of-speech information, even Chinese texts in different countries (e.g., Singapore, Malaysia, and the Philippines) need to be segmented with different models, in order to achieve a better accuracy rate [4].

Table 1. Comparison of main Chinese corpora in Taiwan [5]

		Academia Sinica Balanced Corpus	Chinese Gigaword (from LDC)	Corpus of Contemporary Taiwanese Mandarin
mode	written	17 million characters	2,800 million characters	3,600 million characters
	spoken	0.38 million characters	n/a	40 million characters
years		1981–2007	2000–2010	1999–2020

On the other hand, corpora of native languages in Taiwan are still under development. Table 2 shows that most Hokkien language corpora do not have balance texts with part-of-speech tagging.

Table 2. Comparison of Hokkien Corpora in Taiwan [6]

		Taiwan Hokkien Spoken Corpus	Taiwan Hokkien Child Corpus	Taiwanese Corpus	NTHU Taiwanese Corpus
mode	written	n/a	n/a	9 million words	1.76 million words
	oral	0.8 million words	0.24 million words	n/a	
sampling era		modern	modern	modern	modern and early modern

As shown in the tables above, corpora for Taiwan's native languages are still under development. While several comprehensive Chinese corpora with word segmentation and part-of-speech tagging are available online for users to query, Hokkien corpora were built with early limited work before 2007, the year when the Taiwanese Hokkien Character Set was officially recommended by Taiwan's Ministry of Education. Therefore, at this point in time it is appropriate to construct a Taiwanese Hokkien corpus based on the newly adopted Taiwanese Hokkien Recommended Character Set.

3 Methodology

With the lexicon and part-of-speech information from the Dictionary of Frequently-Used Taiwan Minnan (released by Taiwan's Ministry of Education, MoE), we adapted the Articut API, originally designed for Chinese word segmentation, for Hokkien word segmentation. Articut segments Chinese words based on syntactic rules [7, 8]. However, the original Chinese part-of-speech tagset in the segmentation system is divided into seven major categories, while the MoE Hokkien dictionary has 17 parts of speech. Therefore, we first mapped the 17-tag Hokkien part-of-speech tagset to the seven major categories used in the Articut Chinese segmentation system to enhance the accuracy of Hokkien word segmentation, as shown below.

Mapping between the part-of-speech tagset in MoE Hokkien Dictionary and that in Articut Chinese segmentation system:

- 名 (Noun) → < ENTITY_noun >
- 代 (Pronoun) → < ENTITY_pronoun >
- 數 (Number) → < ENTITY_num >
- 量 (Classifier) → < ENTITY_classifier >
- 時 (Time) → < TIME >
- 助 (Auxiliary) → < FUNCTION >
- 動 (Verb) → < ACTION_verb >
- 形 (Adjective) → < MODIFIER >
- 副 (Adverb) → < MODIFIER >
- 嘆 (Exclamation) → < CLAUSE_particle >
- 介 (Preposition) → < FUNCTION >
- 連 (Conjunction) → < FUNC_conjunction >
- 位 (Locative) → < RANGE_locality >
- 聲 (Voice) → n/a.
- 態 (Mood) → n/a.
- 疑 (Interrogative) → < CLAUSE >
- 熟 (Idiom) → < IDIOM >

4 Evaluation of Word Segmentation Results

Since there is no manually segmented Hokkien dataset (especially with the newly adopted MoE Recommended Characters) available for reference, this study focuses on the Hokkien word segmentation of the example sentences in the MoE Hokkien Dictionary. The evaluation considers only whether an example (target) word in the example sentence is correctly segmented, disregarding the segmentation of other words in the sentence. The accuracy rate of the segmentation is calculated as Eq. 1.

$$Accuracy = \frac{count\,of\,correctly\,segmented\,example\,words}{count\,of\,example\,sentences} \qquad (1)$$

Table 3 displays the results of word segmentation accuracy for the Hokkien example sentences. The results indicate that word segmentation accuracy for Hokkien is approximately 87.50%. We believe this level of accuracy is sufficient for linguistic research.

Table 3. Accuracy of the proposed Hokkien word segmentation (example sentences only).

	Articut	With Hokkien Lexicon
Count of correctly segmented examples	4,243	9,688
Count of all example sentences	7,036	11,070
Accuracy	60.30%	87.50%

5   Testing Procedure and Analysis

For further evaluation, six additional unseen Hokkien articles from MoE's Reading to Understand Hokkien (閱讀越懂閩客語) were tested with the adapted segmenter. In total, 256 words were incorrectly segmented among the 3548 words in the six articles, as shown in Table 4. In other words, less than 10% of the unseen articles were segmented incorrectly.

Table 4. Performance on six testing Hokkien articles.

No.	words	errors	performance
1	655	50	92.37%
2	601	50	91.68%
3	554	40	92.78%
4	606	40	93.40%
5	611	30	95.09%
6	521	46	91.17%
	3,548	256	92.78%

Although in the test some unknown words not listed in the MoE Hokkien dictionary could be segmented with the help of the correctly segmented context words, in other cases there were still some out-of-vocabulary (OOV) errors. Part of these errors occurred because of the reduplication within adjective words. For example, one OOV error came from the reduplicated adjective 芳貢貢 (*fragrant* in English), which was not listed in the current released MoE dictionary. Such errors can be identified with reduplication rules and be fixed in the later version of Hokkien segmenter.

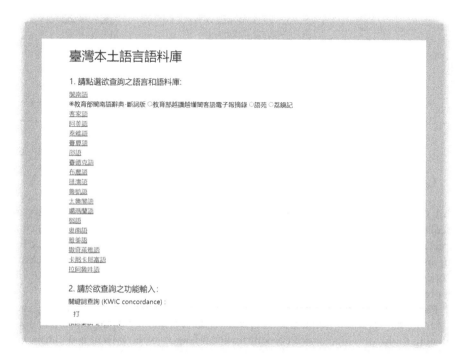

Fig. 1. Online user interface to query the Hokkien corpus with word segmentation

Figure 1 demonstrates the interface for user to query the Hokkien corpus with word segmentation online (https://mhshih.github.io/corpus/index.htm). Figure 2 shows the query results for the concordance of 打 (*hit* in English).

查詢結果共15筆符合：

n_no	詞性	詞目	音讀	異用字	又見音	近義詞	反義詞	left_print	例句斷詞	right_print	中文例句
1660	動	打	tánn		tá			這馬的人嫁粧定定攏	打	現金。	現代人的嫁妝常常都打現金。
1673	動	失人禮	sit-lâng-lé	失儂禮				看場合	打	扮，才袂失人禮。	看場合打扮，才不會失禮。
1688	動	打扎	tánn-tsah	打紮				陣會有一位好命的婦人人	打	扎新娘。	嫁娶的時候會有一位好命的婦人攏扶新娘子。
1688	動	打扎	tánn-tsah	打紮				失敗的時佳哉有伊共我	打	扎。	我做生意失敗時還好有他幫助我。
1719	動	打扮	tánn-pān			妝娗(tsng-thānn)		參加宴會著愛	打	扮較嬌咧。	參加宴會要打扮漂亮一點。
1764	名	打馬膠	tá-má-ka					這條路是用	打	馬膠鋪的。	這條路是用柏油鋪的。
1772	動	打桶	tánn-tháng					阮阿公過身，	打	桶兩禮拜才出山。	我爺爺過世，停柩兩個禮拜才下葬。

Fig. 2. Query results for the concordance of 打 (*hit* in English)

6   Conclusion

This study exploited the lexicon and part-of-speech information in the Dictionary of Frequently-Used Taiwan Minnan (released by Taiwan's Ministry of Education), to construct a Hokkien corpus with word segmentation. The corpus offers a query interface for linguistic research in the Chinese language family. The core code for the corpus website is open-source on GitHub,[1] providing a valuable resource for researchers interested in less-resourced local languages in Taiwan.

Future work includes expanding the corpus to include part-of-speech tagging and extending the approach to process other low-resourced Sinitic languages, further contributing to the development of corpora for local languages in Taiwan and enhancing part-of-speech tagging for these languages.

Acknowledgments. The author would like to thank Professor Yueh-chin Chang in National Tsing Hua University with her discussion on this work. This article is also written with AI assistance.

References

1. Kucera, H., Francis, W.N.: Computational analysis of present-day American English. Brown University Press, Providence (1967)
2. Chen, P.-J., et al.: Speech-to-Speech Translation for A Real-world Unwritten Language. (2022). https://doi.org/10.48550/arxiv.2211.06474
3. Davies, M.: The corpus of contemporary American English as the first reliable monitor corpus of English. Literary Linguist. Comput. **25**, 447–464 (2010)

---

[1] https://github.com/mhshih/Taiwanese-Corpora.github.io.

4. Jiang, S., Fu, Y., Lin, N.: Construction and Evaluation of Chinese Word Segmentation Datasets in Malay Archipelago. In: Dong, M., Gu, Y., Hong, J.-F. (eds.) Chinese Lexical Semantics, pp. 172–183. Springer International Publishing, Cham (2022)
5. Gao, Z.-M.: Preliminary Research on the Construction of National Corpus, Taiwan Ministry of Culture (2020)
6. Su, C.-T.: Corpus-based Hokkien Analysis and Teaching. Unpublished presentation (2022)
7. Wang, W., Chen, C., Lee, C., Lai, C., Lin, H.: Articut: Chinese Word Segmentation and POS Tagging System, https://api.droidtown.co, Accessed 11 Oct 2022
8. Lu, S.-E., Lu, B.-H., Lu, C.-Y., Tzong, R., Tsai, H.: Exploring Methods for Building Dialects-Mandarin Code-Mixing Corpora: A Case Study in Taiwanese Hokkien. In: Findings of the Association for Computational Linguistics: EMNLP 2022, pp. 6316–6334. Association for Computational Linguistics, Abu Dhabi, United Arab Emirates (2022)

Research on Automatic Summary Method for Futures Research Reports Based on TextRank

Yingjie Han[1], Tengfei Chen[1(✉)], Xiaodong Ning[2], and Heguo Yang[2]

[1] School of Computer and Artificial Intelligence, Zhengzhou University, Zhengzhou, Henan, China
ieyjhan@zzu.edu.cn, tengfeichen@gs.zzu.edu.cn
[2] Zhengzhou Commodity Exchange, Zhengzhou, China

Abstract. Futures research reports, authored by futures analysts, delve into various aspects such as futures contracts, the macro-environment, industry trends, and industry chains. These reports provide crucial information for comprehending trends in futures trading. The accurate identification and extraction of key data from extensive futures research reports poses a significant challenge for market regulators. An automatic summarization method for futures research reports is proposed. Firstly, key sentences are extracted from a futures research report using a self-constructed word list integrated lexical chain in the field of futures. Secondly, key sentences are represented as vectors that incorporate term frequency-inverse document frequency. Thirdly, the TextRank algorithm is employed to extract candidate summary. Finally, the maximum marginal relevance algorithm is employed to supplement some crucial but easily missed key sentences, thereby ensuring the informativeness of the summary. ROUGE is used to verify the validity of the method. Experimental results demonstrate that our method is both simple and effective in automatic summarization of futures research reports.

Keywords: Futures Research Report · Text Summary · TextRank · Maximum Marginal Relevance · Lexical Chain

1 Introduction

Futures research reports are comprehensive documents that encompass information about the macroeconomic environment of the futures market and industry-specific data. These reports are the culmination of meticulous research conducted by futures analysts on various aspects such as futures commodities, contracts, industry trends, and industrial chains. The reports can be categorized into daily reviews, weekly reviews, monthly reports, quarterly reports, annual reports. They serve as crucial information that aid regulatory officials in understanding the dynamics of the futures market. There may be the following problems when manually summarizing research reports. This can be a labor-intensive task due to the sheer volume of research reports produced daily. In addition, critical information may be missed which may bias the analysis. Therefore, automated or semi-automated approaches help in processing such large amounts of information.

A company called Dehydration Reports [1] predicts stock prices by manually collecting and analyzing research reports. However, a lot of manual work needs to be done within a limited time. Another study [2] used a rule-based approach. A platform is built to extract key elements from futures research reports. These key elements include author name, institutional affiliation, report title, rating, target price, net profit, and return on equity. At the same time, entities, phrases and titles related to futures are also automatically extracted. However, the evidence and conclusions that reflect current futures market conditions are not well extracted.

An automated summary technology is proposed to be used in futures research reports. First, the key sentences are extracted from the research report using the futures keyword table combined with lexical chains. These key sentences are then constructed into a set of key sentence vectors using the method of fusing word vectors and term frequency-inverse document frequency (TF-IDF) [3]. Subsequently, candidate summaries are extracted with the TextRank algorithm [4] based on these key sentence vectors. Next, each research report sentence is also converted into a sentence vector. Supplementary summaries are extracted through the Maximum Marginal Relevance (MMR) [5] algorithm within the entire research sentence vector. Finally, the effectiveness of the method is verified using ROUGE [6].

2 Problem Description

Automatic summary technology [7] is used to produce a summary from a text using algorithms. The summary encapsulates the essence of the text while being significantly shorter. And the automatic summary of futures research reports is a single document extraction technology. In this technology, several sentences in a single futures research report are extracted as a summary. All key information of interest to futures market regulators including market trends, trading patterns and risk descriptors are included in this summary.

The formal definition of the method is as follows: Let $D = \{w_1, w_2, ..., w_n\}$ be the original text of the futures research report, composed of n sentences. The goal is to obtain a summary $Y = \{y_1, y_2, ..., y_m\}$ where $m << n$ and $y_i (1 \leq i \leq m) \in D$ [8]. The process of the method is illustrated in Fig. 1. The method extracts sentences containing key information (highlighted in red font) from the report and reorganizes them into a report summary.

By reviewing the Futures Research Reports, it was found that the following problems exist:

Text These reports tend to be lengthy and contain a wealth of charts and data.

Distribution The distribution of key elements and key sentences is irregular. This is an obstacle to automated summarization.

Dataset There are currently no training data available for summarizing futures research reports. Therefore, supervised machine learning and deep learning methods are not applicable.

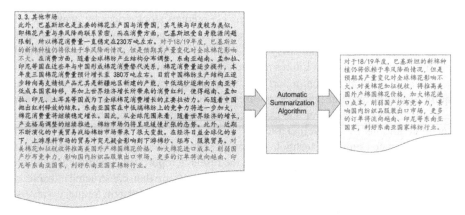

Fig. 1. Description of automatic summarization problem for futures research reports. (Color figure online)

3   Method

In response to the above problems, a method for automatically extracting **summaries** from a futures research report is proposed. The process of the method is illustrated in Fig. 2. First, key sentences are selected from the report using an enhanced domain-specific word list combined with words from lexical chains. Second, Vectors combining Word2Vec [9] and TF-IDF are used to represent these key sentences. Third, based on the vectors of these key sentences, candidate summaries are automatically extracted using the TextRank algorithm. At the same time, for some important but isolated sentences of the report, the supplementary summaries are extracted from the full report by the MMR algorithm. Finally, to obtain the final summary, the supplementary summaries are merged with the candidate summaries.

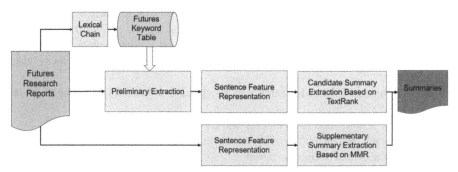

Fig. 2. Method diagram for automatic summarization of futures research reports based on TextRank.

3.1 Preliminary Extraction

Futures research reports have special characteristics, such as a large amount of content, an abundance of information and an irregular distribution of the key sentences. Consequently, the direct application of the TextRank method for summary extraction proves to be insufficient. To solve this problem, we pre-extract key sentences from futures research reports using futures keyword table manually constructed. These key sentences become the basis for accurate summary extraction by the subsequent TextRank algorithm. An example of a futures keyword table is shown in Table 1.

Table 1. A part of the futures keyword table.

Key elements	Keywords
Supply and Demand	Supply, Provision, Demand
Inventory	Inventory, Stockpile, Inflow, Outflow
Industry	Supply Chain, Upstream, Downstream, Raw Materials
Weather and Agriculture	Weather, Cultivation, Cost
Risk Factors	Risk Points, Risk Factors, Risk Elements

The complex and varied key elements in different types of futures reports may not be fully covered by a manually constructed domain-specific keyword list. To solve this constraint, dynamically constructed lexical chains are used to extend the futures keyword table for a research report that needs to be summarized. A group of semantically related words belonging to the same topic are clustered into a lexical chain [10]. Several lexical chains are included in a futures report. The central idea of the report is jointly reflected by these lexical chains, and the lexical chains are different in each research report.

There are several steps involved in building some lexical chains for futures reports. First, the futures report must be segmented, stop words removed, and part-of-speech tagged. Next, nouns, verbs, and gerunds are selected as candidate words. Then, multiple lexical chains are iteratively formed based on word similarity. By scoring the lexical chains, several lexical chains with high scores are selected as robust lexical chains to represent the entire report. Finally, by combining the robust lexical chains and the futures keyword table, an enhanced futures keyword table is formed, which is used to pre-extract key sentences.

The process of constructing a lexical chain is outlined in Algorithm 1.

Algorithm 1. Construction of lexical chain.

Enter: a futures research report.

Output: several robust vocabulary chains.

Start

① Segment the report and delete stop words, then mark the part of speech, select nouns, verbs, and gerunds, and create a candidate word set;

② Pick out the first word in the candidate word set and add it to a newly created lexical chain;

③ Calculate the similarity between each word in the candidate word set and the current lexical chain, and add it to the lexical chain when the similarity exceeds a certain threshold;

④ Form a new candidate word set from words that have not been added to the vocabulary chain;

⑤ Repeat steps ③-④ until all words in the candidate word set are added to the lexical chain;

⑥ Calculate the score of each lexical chain and select several robust lexical chains according to the selection criteria;

End

The function used to calculate the lexical chain score is presented in Formula (1). In this equation, Chain$_i$ represents the i-th lexical chain. The frequency of the j-th word within the lexical chain in the text is indicated by the term wordnum$_j$. Finally, len$_i$ denotes the number of words in the lexical chain.

$$score(chain_i) = \sum_{j=1}^{n} wordnum_j - len_i \tag{1}$$

The criteria for choosing robust lexical chains presented by Zhang et al. [11] are applied here. Lexical chains are considered robust if their score, score(chain), exceeds a * AVG(score) + b * STD(score). AVG(score) and STD(score) denote the average value and standard deviation of the lexical chain scores, respectively, according to Formula (1). The variables a and b are employed as weights.

3.2 Sentence Feature Representation

The set of key sentences that have been pre-extracted undergo sentence feature representation. The objective is to convert unstructured sentences into structured vectors, while minimizing the loss of semantic information.

Given the diversity of futures research reports, sentence vectors computed by a single word vector model may not be effective. To solve this problem, extended word vectors, which combine Word2Vec and TF-IDF, are used to compute sentence vectors. Specifically, for each word in a sentence, Word2Vec maps it to a word vector, and the TF-IDF value of that word represents its frequency in all sentences and is multiplied by the word vector as a weight to form enhanced word vectors. Each enhanced word vector in a sentence is then summed and averaged to produce a sentence vector.

The calculation is represented in Formula (2), where V_i denotes the sentence vector of the i-th sentence. Word$_{ij}$ represents the j-th word in the i-th sentence. Word2Vec(word$_{ij}$)

and TF-IDF(word$_{ij}$) respectively signify the word vector and TF-IDF value of the j-th word in the i-th sentence. M$_i$ stands for the number of words in the i-th sentence.

$$V_i = \frac{\sum_{j=1}^{M_i} Word2Vec(word_{ij}) \times TF-IDF(word_{ij})}{M_i} \tag{2}$$

3.3 Candidate Summary Extraction Based on TextRank

TextRank is a text summarization algorithm that calculates the importance of sentences based on an association graph constructed from an original text. In this sentence association graph, each sentence in the original text is considered as one of its nodes. These nodes are connected by edges, and the similarity between two sentences represents the weight of this edge between the two nodes. In this way, the adjacency matrix of this graph is equivalent to the similarity matrix between sentences of this text. The importance of a sentence is computed iteratively by this algorithm.

In the traditional TextRank algorithm, only the literal information of the text is used, resulting in the loss of most of the semantic information of the text. Therefore, in the field of futures, sentence vectors combining Word2Vec and TF-IDF are used to retain text semantic information. Then the association graph is obtained by calculating the similarity matrix between sentence vectors.

The method for calculating similarity between sentence i and sentence j is presented in Formula (3). Here, W$_{ij}$ is the similarity between two sentence vectors, while V$_{ik}$ and V$_{jk}$ denote the values of the k-th dimension of the sentence vectors V$_i$ and V$_j$, respectively.

$$W_{ij} = \frac{\sum_{k=1}^{n} V_{ik} \times V_{jk}}{\sqrt{\sum_{k=1}^{n}(V_{ik})^2} \times \sqrt{\sum_{k=1}^{n}(V_{jk})^2}} \tag{3}$$

The association graph is used to iteratively compute the importance score of each sentence. The calculation formula is presented in Formula (4). In this equation, S$_i$ and S$_j$ denote sentences i and j, respectively. WS(S$_i$) and WS(S$_j$) represent the weights of sentences i and j respectively, which are updated iteratively during the calculation process. The parameter d stands for damping factor.

$$WS(S_i) = (1-d) + d \times \sum_{j=1}^{n} \frac{W_{ji}}{\sum_{k=1}^{n} W_{jk}} WS(S_j) \tag{4}$$

The description of the candidate summary extraction algorithm based on TextRank is shown in Algorithm 2.

Algorithm 2. Candidate summary extraction based on TextRank.

Input: The candidate key sentences and their sentence vector sets, as well as the number of sentences n required for the summary.

Output: Candidate summaries.

Start:

① Calculate the cosine similarity of the candidate key sentence vectors and obtain the similarity matrix of the candidate key sentences;

② Initialize the scores of candidate key sentences;

③ Use Formula (4) to iteratively calculate the score of the candidate key sentence;

④ Determine whether the score set of candidate key sentences converges. If not, repeat ③;

⑤ Sort the score sets of candidate key sentences;

⑥ Select the n candidate key sentences with the highest scores to form the candidate summary;

End

3.4 Supplementary Summary Extraction Based on MMR

The TextRank algorithm relies on the similarity of sentence vectors for the automatic summarization of futures research reports. Therefore, sentences with high similarity to many other sentences are selected. This results in some important but "isolated" sentences being missed when selecting candidate summaries. The MMR algorithm is used to alleviate this problem.

The process of extracting supplementary summaries based on MMR is as follows. First, each sentence in the report is converted into a sentence vector using the sentence feature representation method mentioned in Sect. 3.2. Then, the similarity between the current sentence and the entire research report is iteratively computed. This process reflects its relevance to the report. Third, calculate the similarity between this sentence and the current summary. This represents its divergence from the current summary. A hyperparameter λ is used to balance relevance and divergence, and a greedy method is used to optimize the sentence score. Finally, all the sentences are ranked and selected according to their scores to form the supplementary summaries.

The objective function for balancing relevance and divergence is shown in Formula (5). Here, Q represents the original text of the futures research report. C denotes a collection of sentences formed after splitting the text of the futures research report. R represents the currently extracted summary; $sim(Q, d_i)$ means the similarity between a certain sentence d_i in the report text and Q, i.e. the relevance of sentence d_i to the report text. And $sim(R, d_i)$ shows the similarity between sentence d_i in the report and R, indicating the divergence of the summary. λ is used to balance the relevance and redundancy of the summary.

$$MMR(Q, C, R) = argmax_{d \in C}^{k} \left[\lambda sim(Q, d_i) - (1 - \lambda)sim(R, d_i) \right] \qquad (5)$$

The following shows the role of the MMR algorithm in maintaining the relevance and conciseness of summary sentences through an example.

原文: 2.1.2.短期库存高位，但现货资源却日偏紧

国内棉花从2016年开始进入去库存周期，棉花产量的大幅缩小，使得近几年产消缺口持续维持在300万吨左右，除了配额限制下的进口，国储棉抛出成为了保障市场棉花供应的主要途径。但是就近两年的抛出数据来看，15/16年国内棉花缺口在167万吨，16/17年度缺口为236万吨，而这两年的国储棉抛出量分别为266万吨，322万吨，轮储量大幅高于市场缺口量也就意味着有相当一部分的国储库存转化以社会库存。另一方面，17/18年度国内棉花丰产，产量的大幅影响也在一定程度上保障了棉花供应。因此，短期棉花供应充足。

Original text of a futures research report(partial): 2.1.2. Short-term domestic cotton stocks are high, but there is still a shortage of cotton spot resources.

The domestic destocking cycle for cotton began in 2016, generating a production-consumption gap of approximately 3 million tons within the last several years. In addition to easing cotton supply through imports under quota restrictions, the rotation of cotton from state reserves has become the main way to ensure the supply of cotton in the market. Nevertheless, according to rotation data from the last two years, there was a shortage of domestic cotton of 1.67 million tons in 2015/16 and 2.36 million tons in 2016/17. During this period, the state reserve released 2.66 and 3.22 million tons of cotton, respectively, leading to a greater cotton output than the market gap. On the other hand, domestic cotton production in the 2017/18 season was abundant, leading to significantly increased output and ensuring a certain cotton supply. Therefore, the domestic supply of cotton is sufficient in the short term.

基于TextRank的候选摘要: 国内棉花从2016年开始进入去库存周期，棉花产量的大幅缩小，使得近几年产消缺口持续维持在300万吨左右，除了配额限制下的进口，国储棉抛出成为了保障市场棉花供应的主要途径。

Candidate summaries based on TextRank: The domestic destocking cycle for cotton began in 2016, generating a production-consumption gap of approximately 3 million tons within the last several years. In addition to easing cotton supply through imports under quota restrictions, the rotation of cotton from state reserves has become the main way to ensure the supply of cotton in the market.

基于MMR的补充摘要: 国内棉花从2016年开始进入去库存周期，棉花产量的大幅缩小，使得近几年产消缺口持续维持在300万吨左右，除了配额限制下的进口，国储棉抛出成为了保障市场棉花供应的主要途径。另一方面，17/18年度国内棉花丰产，产量的大幅影响也在一定程度上保障了棉花供应。

Supplementary summaries based on MMR: The domestic destocking cycle for cotton began in 2016, generating a production-consumption gap of approximately 3 million tons within the last several years. In addition to easing cotton supply through imports under quota restrictions, the rotation of cotton from state reserves has become the main way to ensure the supply of cotton in the market. On the other hand, domestic cotton production in the 2017/18 season was abundant, leading to significantly increased output and ensuring a certain cotton supply.

This example presents a portion of the original text from a futures research report, a candidate summary based on TextRank, and a supplementary summary based on MMR. The red section in the original text serves as the reference summary. It can be seen that the key sentence in the research report - "In addition to easing cotton supply through imports under quota restrictions, the rotation of cotton from state reserves has become the main way to ensure the supply of cotton in the market." - has a low similarity with the above-mentioned "The domestic destocking cycle for cotton began in 2016". Therefore, it is missed by the TextRank-based extraction algorithm. However, this sentence is extracted by the MMR algorithm because of this divergence.

4 Experiment and Result Analysis

Upon investigation, there is no public summary dataset of futures research reports. To remedy this, 15 futures research reports are collected, each of which covers only a single product. These reports are written by different futures analysts and include weekly, monthly, quarterly, semi-annual, and annual reports in terms of time granularity. These reports cover popular futures commodities such as cotton, sugar, peanuts, glass, soda ash, and oils. Four domain experts each manually constructed reference summaries for these reports. These reference summaries are standard answers to evaluate the effectiveness of the proposed method.

4.1 Evaluation Indicators

ROUGE is a commonly used automatic evaluation metric for text summarization. It is an evaluation method that focuses on n-gram recall, which evaluates the quality of automatic summarization based on the number of overlapping basic units of automatic summarization and reference summarization. It includes metrics such as ROUGE-N, ROUGE-L, etc.

ROUGE-N is primarily used to calculate the recall rate on N-gram. Its calculation is presented in Formula (6). In this equation, reference-summaries denote reference summaries. N signifies the length of N-gram (1 and 2 are used in the experiment). $Count_{match}(gram_N)$ is the count of identical N-grams in both the automatic summary and reference summary. $Count(gram_N)$ represents the count of N-grams in the reference summary.

$$ROUGE - N = \frac{\sum_{S \in (reference-summaries)} \sum_{gram_N \in S} Count_{match}(gram_N)}{\sum_{S \in (reference-summaries)} \sum_{gram_N \in S} Count(gram_N)} \tag{6}$$

ROUGE-L computes the overlap rate of the longest common subsequence. The calculation for this is presented in Formula (7). Here, X and Y denote the automatic summary and reference summary, respectively. LCS(X, Y) signifies the count of words in the longest common subsequence of both the automatic summary and reference summary. Lastly, m represents the count of words in the reference summary.

$$ROUGE - L = \frac{LCS(X, Y)}{m} \tag{7}$$

4.2 Experimental Design

In this section, we aim to evaluate the efficacy of the proposed approach through validation experiments involving the pre-extraction module, sentence representation, and overall method. The methods and functional descriptions used in the experiments are shown in Table 2.

Table 2. Method name and function introduction.

Method	Function
TR	TextRank algorithm
W-TR	TextRank candidate abstract extraction algorithm based on word vector sentence representation
WTI-TR	TextRank candidate abstract extraction algorithm based on fusion of word vectors and word frequency inverted document frequency sentence features
WTI-TR-MMR	WTI-TR fusion based supplementary abstract extraction algorithm based on MMR

Table 3. Experimental results with and without pre-extraction modules.

Pre-Extraction	Method	ROUGE-1	ROUGE-2	ROUGE-L
Without	TR	0.69	0.50	0.62
	WTI-TR	0.70	0.55	0.62
With	TR	0.73	0.59	0.67
	WTI-TR	**0.74**	**0.60**	**0.69**

4.3 Experimental Design

To evaluate the effectiveness of the pre-extraction module, we conducted a comparative experiment on the TR and WTI-TR algorithms. The outcomes of these trials are displayed in Table 3.

As evident from Table 3, both TR and WTI-TR, which did not utilize the pre-extraction module, scored low on ROUGE. This finding indicates that the pre-extraction module significantly limits the search range of the summary candidates. This leads to an improved quality of the results in the following stages.

Comparative experiments are conducted on TR, W-TR, and WTI-TR to verify the effectiveness of the sentence representation method. Table 4 displays the results of these experiments.

Table 4. The ablation experiment of automatic summarization based on sentence feature representation fused with Word2Vec and TF-IDF.

Method	ROUGE-1	ROUGE-2	ROUGE-L
TR	0.73	0.59	0.67
W-TR	0.71	0.56	0.65
WTI-TR	**0.74**	**0.60**	**0.69**

According to Table 4, TR obtains a higher ROUGE score than TR. Our hypothesis is that the Word2Vec model used in this paper is general, rather than specific to futures. Moreover, futures research reports exhibit diverse writing styles and encompass a wide range of essential elements. This leads to the conclusion that a singular Word2Vec representation may not accurately depict the original report. Nevertheless, WTI-TR achieves higher ROUGE scores than both TR and W-TR. This suggests that the combination of Word2Vec and TF-IDF is more effective in capturing the semantic features of sentences.

Taking into account the aforementioned comparison experiments, the results of each stage of the proposed method are shown in Table 5.

Table 5. Final experimental results.

Method	ROUGE-1	ROUGE-2	ROUGE-L
TR	0.73	0.59	0.67
WTI-TR	0.74	0.60	0.69
WTI-TR-MMR	**0.77**	**0.64**	**0.72**

As illustrated in Table 5, WTI-TR outperforms TR in terms of ROUGE-1, ROUGE-2, and ROUGE-L. It shows that the TextRank method that combines the sentence feature extraction algorithm of Word2Vec and TF-IDF is more effective in summarizing futures research reports.

Compared to WTI-TR, WTI-TR-MMR exhibits a 3% improvement in ROUGE-1 and ROUGE-L and a 4% improvement in ROUGE-2. These suggest that the results of the WTI-TR method are effectively complemented by the results of the MMR method. This provides further evidence of the success of the final WTI-TR-MMR method for futures research reports.

5   Conclusion

A method for automatically extracting summaries from futures research reports is proposed in this paper. First, a set of key sentences is pre-extracted from the original text of a futures research report using a futures vocabulary integrated with lexical chains. Second, these key sentences are converted into sentence vectors using a method that combines Word2Vec with TF-IDF. Third, candidate summaries are extracted by TextRank algorithm based on key sentence vectors. Fourth, important but "isolated" supplementary summaries are extracted by the MMR algorithm. Finally, supplementary summaries are added to the candidate summaries, which ensure that futures research report summaries are both concise and relevant to the original report. Use ROUGE to evaluate the efficacy of the approach. Experimental results show that this method meets the needs of futures market regulators. This approach increases the effectiveness of futures market regulators in extracting critical information from futures research reports, and thereby reduces the manual workload. The challenge of automatic summarization of futures research reports is solved in a simple and effective manner.

References

1. Baidu Encyclopedia. https://baike.baidu.com/item/%E8%84%B1%E6%B0%B4%E7%A0%94%E6%8A%A5/22673277?fr=aladdin. Accessed 9 May 2023
2. Qiu, Z., Peng, N., Zhu, A.: Exploration and practice of intelligent analysis technology for Huatai asset management research report. Front. Trans. Technol. **48**, 4–7 (2022)
3. Mao, T., Peng, Y., Zhang, Y.: A classification method for Chinese word semantic relations based on TF-IDF and CNN. In: Hong, J.F., Su, Q., Wu, J.S. (eds.) The 20th Chinese Lexical Semantics Workshop. LNCS, vol. 11173, pp. 509–518. Springer, Heidelberg (2018). https://doi.org/10.1007/978-3-030-04015-4_43
4. Mihalcea, R., Tarau, P.: TextRank: bringing order into texts. In: Proceedings of the 2004 Conference on Empirical Methods in Natural Language Processing (EMNLP), pp. 404–411 (2004)
5. Cheng, K., Li, C., Jia, X., Ge, J., Luo, B.: News text extractive summary method based on improved MMR algorithm. J. Appl. Sci. **39**(03), 443–455 (2021)
6. Lin, C.: Rouge: a package for automatic evaluation of summaries. In: Proceedings of the Workshop on Text Summarization Branches Out (WAS 2004), pp. 74–81 (2004)
7. Luhn, H.: The automatic creation of literature abstract. IBM J. **2**(2), 159–165 (1958)
8. Li, J., Zhang, C., Chen, X.: Review of automatic text summary research. Comput. Res. Dev. **39**(1), 1–21 (2021)
9. Mikolov, T., Chen, K., Corrado, G., Dean, J.: Efficient estimation of word representations in vector space. Computer Science (2013)
10. Zhang, M., Xie, Z.: Research on Chinese lexical chain construction algorithm based on China national knowledge infrastructure. Softw. Guide **7**(10), 3 (2008)
11. Zhang, X., Lv, X., Li, Z.: Topic phrase extraction method combined with LDA and lexical chain. J. Small Micro Comput. Syst. **39**(11), 2457–2463 (2018)

Automatic Question Generation for Language Learning Task Based on the Grid-Based Language Structure Parsing Framework

Tian Shao[1,2(✉)], Zhixiong Zhang[1], Yi Liu[1], Gaoqi Rao[2], and Endong Xun[2]

[1] National Science Library, Chinese Academy of Science, Beijing, China
shaotian@mail.las.ac.cn
[2] Beijing Language and Culture University, Beijing, China
edxun@126.com

Abstract. In the field of natural language generation in Chinese, there has been limited attention to question generation tasks, partly due to constraints related to knowledge acquisition. With the increasing popularity of online education, the automatic generation of questions has become a major point in the context of language intelligent education. In this regard, this paper is oriented towards international Chinese language education. This paper constructs a domain knowledge database and utilizes the grid-based language structure parsing framework in conjunction with the domain knowledge database to perform syntactic and semantic analysis on text. In turn, this enables the automatic generation of short-answer questions based on the results of syntactic and semantic analysis, along with predefined question keywords, achieving an accuracy rate as high as 94% . This not only provides a high-accuracy domain-specific research model for automatic question generation but also offers high-quality question-answer pairs for second language learning.

Keywords: Grid-based language structure parsing framework · Syntactic and semantic analysis · International Chinese language education · Domain knowledge database · Automatic question generation

1 Introduction

1.1 Origin of the Research

Automatic question generation is one of the important tasks in natural language generation. Unlike automatic question answering, which primarily focuses on generating answers, automatic question generation places greater emphasis on the generation of questions. Automatic question generation encompasses four sub-tasks: content selection, determination of question type, question construction, and question evaluation. The primary focus of this paper's research is on constructing questions for short-answer. Furthermore, automatic question generation plays a significant role in intelligent tutoring systems and online education. In the domain of international Chinese language education, second language learners typically engage with materials such as dialogues and readings, followed by exercises to reinforce their understanding of relevant knowledge

M. Dong et al. (Eds.): CLSW 2023, LNAI 14515, pp. 192–206, 2024.
https://doi.org/10.1007/978-981-97-0586-3_16

points. In today's increasingly popular online education environment, both teachers and second language learners seek a broader range of exercises based on the course materials to enhance the students' mastery of these important knowledge points. Therefore, taking the perspective of international Chinese language education, this paper constructs a domain knowledge database and employs the Grid-based Language Structure Parsing Framework to conduct syntactic and semantic analyses of text. Based on the analysis results, it automatically generates question-answer pairs to meet the needs of both the teachers and second language learners.

Automatic question generation is closely related to the syntactic and semantic structure of the text. Therefore, to accomplish the task of automatic question generation, it is essential to enable the computer to comprehend natural language and grasp the syntactic and semantic structure of the text. Xun [1] introduced the Grid-based Language Structure Parsing Framework (GPF), which understands natural language from a structural perspective, transforming natural language understanding into a process of language structure analysis. The primary method is to transition from shallow structural analysis to deep structural understanding. It effectively leverages the role of language structure in natural language understanding and provides the added advantage of customizable knowledge analysis. Therefore, this paper uses the GPF as a tool for syntactic and semantic analysis. This paper constructs a knowledge database specific to the field of international Chinese language education and conducts syntactic and semantic analysis of the input text. Based on the analysis results of syntactic and semantic aspects, the task of automatic question generation can be successfully accomplished.

The content of this paper is arranged as follows. Firstly, it introduces the current state and limitations of research in automatic question generation. Secondly, it provides a brief overview of the components of GPF. Thirdly, in response to the knowledge customization feature of the GPF, this paper constructs an international knowledge database for international Chinese language education. Lastly, it elaborates on the framework for automatic question generation based on the GPF and outlines the experimental procedure. This not only offers a paradigm for domain-customized automatic question generation research but also has the potential to alleviate the teaching burden on educators and empower learners for independent knowledge acquisition.

1.2 Related Research

Currently, there are two primary research approaches to automatic question generation: rule-based methods and statistical-based methods.

Rule-based automatic question generation often relies on predefined templates to generate questions. In foreign research, examples include Yllias [2], Mass [3], and others. In domestic research, for instance, Tan [4] utilized the C programming language to design addition and subtraction questions within the range of 10. Li [5] and Tang [6] both used specific textbooks from university-level computer science courses as data sources to construct templates for automatic question generation. Li [5] employed ontology technology in conjunction with the structural elements of common conceptual questions, proposing various question generation patterns through the description of logical reasoning functions. Tang [6] utilized logical expressions to formalize descriptions of concept hierarchy, concept relationships, concept definitions, and concept characteristics. For different knowledge representation systems, they incorporated various question templates to generate question stems. Both of these approaches relied on logical expressions to describe domain-specific ontology knowledge, but they exhibited limited scalability. Constructing the knowledge database required a thorough understanding of domain knowledge and methods for logical semantic representation. Additionally, relying solely on the manual construction of knowledge databases and template libraries may lead to potential incompleteness, which is also a common issue in rule-based methods.

Statistical-based automatic question generation primarily leverages deep learning methods. In foreign research, examples include Mazidi [7], who applies natural language understanding to question generation. Serban [8], who employs recurrent neural networks for question generation, and Kumar [9], who uses deep reinforcement learning to generate questions from text. In domestic research, Wu [10] introduced a topic modeling approach to segment articles and extract sentences for generating question-answer pairs, while Liao [11] proposed an integrated strategy using various transfer learning techniques for automatic question generation. Statistical-based methods are data-driven, offering robustness and scalability within different domains. However, the quality of generated questions depends on the feature learning capabilities of the network structure and the quality of training data. Additionally, these methods require a substantial amount of labeled question-answer pairs, which can be resource-intensive in terms of human labor and effort.

The GPF integrates the advantages of rule-based and statistical-based methods. Furthermore, we can use its knowledge customization feature to construct a knowledge database specific to the field of international Chinese language education. Therefore, we can accomplish the task of the automatic generation of questions for international Chinese language education based on GPF.

2   Grid-Based Language Structure Parsing Framework

GPF is a programmable language structure analysis framework that employs an expert system based on symbolic computation as its central control. It collaboratively handles data and knowledge operations, enhancing the control capabilities of existing deep learning frameworks to address practical problems. Simultaneously, it explores how to formalize knowledge and leverage its significant role in natural language understanding. GPF supports multilingual analysis and can perform syntactic, semantic, and pragmatic structure analysis and processing of various levels of language units, such as words, sentences, and texts. It can be employed to perform shallow NLP structure calculations using a simple framework or to achieve complex, precise, and deep semantic structure analysis using composite methods. This NLP application, primarily driven by symbolic computation, possesses controllability, interpretability, scalability, and customizability.

GPF has designed four functional components to perform language structure analysis, namely the grid, data tables, finite state machine, and data interfaces. Specifically, it utilizes the grid as a computational platform, data tables as the knowledge storage structure, finite state machine as control components, and achieves the exchange of local and cloud-based data through data interfaces.

Firstly, the grid, serving as a computational platform, encapsulates computations for various types of knowledge and language structures. It aligns language units with grid units, focusing structural analysis on the attributes and relationships of grid units. Secondly, language knowledge is encapsulated using data tables, with the data tables containing lists of language units and their attributes. Thirdly, finite state machine is introduced as context-condition control components, enabling corresponding calculations based on context condition evaluations. Lastly, language structure data is exchanged through data interfaces to coordinate symbolic computations within the grid and end-to-end services outside. Additionally, GPF utilizes key-value expressions ($K = V$) to describe attributes and attribute values of language units and grid units, participating in relevant computations.

In this paper, we have chosen GPF as a tool for syntactic and semantic analysis. Leveraging its knowledge customization feature, we construct a knowledge database specific to the field of international Chinese language education. This approach enables us to obtain more accurate attributes of language units, their relationships, and attribute information, laying the foundation of knowledge for automatic question generation.

3 Construction of Knowledge Database in the Field of International Chinese Language Education

Knowledge is a crucial foundation for natural language generation, and within the realm of tasks such as automatic question generation, knowledge holds significant importance. Moreover, conducting syntactic and semantic analysis on text relies on the support of both structural and semantic knowledge. In this study, structural knowledge primarily originates from chunk dependency analysis results, while semantic knowledge is extracted from chunk dependency corpora through human-machine interactive annotation. This knowledge is stored in a knowledge database specific to the field of international Chinese language education, facilitating its accessibility during the syntactic and semantic analysis phase.

3.1 Data

The data for constructing the knowledge database specific to the field of international Chinese language education primarily comes from two sources. Firstly, international Chinese language education textbooks serve as the data source for automatic question generation. Secondly, chunk dependency analysis is performed on the textbook data using the chunk dependency analysis model, which is proposed by Qin [12]. On one hand, the results of chunk dependency analysis provide syntactic and semantic knowledge for syntactic and semantic analysis. On the other hand, these Chunk dependency analysis results serve as the data source for extracting information into the knowledge database specific to the field of international Chinese language education.

The primary sources of international Chinese language education textbooks in this paper are widely used textbooks and their corresponding examination documents, totaling 26 sets of textbooks and approximately 210,000 sentences. These materials cover introductory, intermediate, and advanced levels of education. Additionally, this research employs the chunk dependency analysis model to perform chunk dependency analysis on the 210,000 sentences of international Chinese language education textbook data. Chunk dependency data centers around predicates, indicating the relationships between core predicates and modifying components such as subject and object elements, as well as adverbial complements. The format is as follows:

Eg:

借助这个反馈模型，分析人员就可以了解管理政策和私人商业投资对国民收入的全部影响。

Jièzhù zhège fǎnkuì móxíng, fēnxī rényuán jiù kěyǐ liǎojiě guǎnlǐ zhèngcè hé sīrén shāngyè tóuzī duì guómín shōurù de quánbù yǐngxiǎng.

With the help of this feedback model, analysts can understand the full impact of management policies and private business investment on national income.

借助(*jièzhù*, with the help of):

1: 分析人员(*fēnxī rényuán*, analysts)
3: 这个反馈模型(*zhège fǎnkuì móxíng*, this feedback model)

了解(*liǎojiě*, understand):

1: 分析人员(*fēnxī rényuán*, analysts)
2: 就(*jiù*, a function word); 可以(*kěyǐ*, can)
3: 管理政策和私人商业投资对国民收入的全部影响(*guǎnlǐ zhèngcè hé sīrén shāngyè tóuzī duì guómín shōurù de quánbù yǐngxiǎng*, the full impact of management policies and private business investment on national income).

First is the original sentence, followed by the annotation of the sentence's syntactic relationships and shared relationships. In the example above, "借助(*jièzhù*, with the help of)" and "了解(*liǎojiě*, understand)" are core predicates, position 1 is the subject, position 3 is the object, and position 2 is the modifying component of the core predicate. This modifying component includes adverbials and complements, which are separated by semicolons when there are multiple modifiers. Additionally, the missing subject and object are complemented; for example, the subject of "借助(*jièzhù*, with the help of)" which is "分析人员(*fēnxī rényuán*, analysts)" appears in the subsequent clause. This data is organized into chunks, establishing relationships between different syntactic components, which can further enhance the accuracy of syntactic and semantic analysis.

3.2   Construction of Knowledge Database

In this study, the chunk dependency analysis model was used to perform chunk dependency analysis on 210,000 sentences from international Chinese language education textbooks. Core predicates and their collocations were extracted based on their syntactic and semantic labels. After deduplication, a total of 11,367 core predicates were obtained. Table 1 shows the details of the collocations of core predicates.

Regarding the subject and object, it is necessary to determine whether the components are human or non-human in order to generate appropriate question keywords, such as 'who' or 'what,' when automatically generating questions. This paper offers two methods to address this issue. One approach involves integrating the names of individuals labeled

Table 1. Number and proportion of combinations.

Syntactic category	Number	Proportion
Subject	31876	0.2968
Object	49608	0.4618
Adverbial	20876	0.1943
Complement	5056	0.0471

in *HowNet* [13] and the synonym lexicon into a unified named entity list. This list is then matched with the subject and object components. If there is a match between them, the corresponding component is tagged with 'Cat=people'. Another approach utilizes GPF to call data interfaces for sentence tokenization and part-of-speech tagging. By analyzing the part-of-speech tags of the subject and object components and checking if they correspond to 'nr (personal name)' or 'r (pronoun),' the system determines the appropriate keyword for question generation.

For adverbial phrases and complement phrases, it is necessary to determine the keywords for question generation based on the semantic relationships between these phrases and the core predicates. Since the semantic types expressed by adverbial and complement phrases are relatively complex, separate treatments are required for each. In the case of complement phrases, reference is made to the semantic classification of complements as proposed by Liu [14]. Concerning adverbial phrases, given the absence of a comprehensive semantic classification system for adverbial phrases, this paper references the semantic classifications of adverbial phrases presented by Jiang [15], semantic classifications of adverbial adjectives as outlined by Qin [16], semantic classifications of adverbial verbs by Shao [17], semantic classifications of adverbial nouns, as well as the semantic classification system of adverbial prepositional phrases by Zhai [18], and the semantic classification system of adverbial prepositional phrases by Wang [19]. For each, semantic categories for adverbial phrase combinations and complement phrase combinations are annotated, along with corresponding attributes. This process facilitates the construction of a knowledge database specific to the field of international Chinese language education, enriched with both structural and semantic information, to provide a knowledge foundation for automatic question generation.

After obtaining the domain knowledge database with attribute information, this paper proceeds to establish the correspondence between attributes and question keywords based on the attributes of language units and the semantic information they convey. Table 2 shows the details of the attributes and questioning keywords.

The question keywords in Table 2 not only encompass the traditional "5W1H (who, why, what, when, where, how)" but also include inquiries about tools (with what), degree (how much), and purpose (why), thereby further diversifying the types of questions generated.

After constructing the knowledge database specific to the field of international Chinese language education, we proceeded to convert this database into the data table format

Table 2. Attributes and questioning keywords.

Attribute	Keywords for questioning	Attribute	Keywords for questioning
People	谁(*shuí*, who)	scope	什么范围 (*shénme fànwéi*, what scope)
nr	谁(*shuí*, who)	source	从哪里 (*cóng nǎli*, from where)
r	谁(*shuí*, who)	foundation	依据什么 (*yī jù shénme*, base on what)
ns	哪里(*nǎli*, where)	reason	因为什么 (*yīnwei shénme*, why)
entity	什么(*shénme*, what)	purpose	为了什么 (*wèile shénme*, for what)
time	什么时间 (*shénme shíjiān*, when)	place	在哪里 (*zài nǎli*, where)
manner	怎么样(*zen3meyang4*,how)	neighbor	跟谁 (*gēnshuí*, with whom)
degree	有多(*yǒu duōshǎo*, how much)	tools	用什么 (*yòngshénme*, with what)
number	有多少 (*yǒu duōshǎo*, how many)	......	......

within GPF. GPF's data tables support the creation of knowledge objects related to collocations. Governing components are stored in the main table, while governed components are stored in the sub-table. Different collocations are linked through the names of the main table and sub-table. GPF's data table is as follows.

```
1.Table Tab_Event
2.表演(biǎoyǎn, perform) Cat=Event Role=[A0 A1 Place Neighbor Time]
3.喜欢(xǐhuan, like) Cat=Event Role=[A0 A1 Mod Time]
4.
5. Table A0_表演 (biǎoyǎn, perform)
6.小花(xiǎohuā, name) Cat=people
7.男生(nánshēng, boy) Cat=people
8.我们(wǒmen, we) Cat=people
9.
10.Table A1_表演(biǎoyǎn, perform)
11.歌舞(gēwǔ, song and dance) Cat=Entity
12.太极拳(tàijíquán, Tai Chi) Cat=Entity
13.相声(xiàngsheng, cross talk) Cat=Entity
```

Line 1: In the first line, "Table" is a reserved word indicating the start of a data table. In "Tab_Event", "Tab" is also a reserved word, and it connects the main table's name, "Event" using an underscore "_" ensuring global uniqueness.

Lines 2–3: It indicates that the main table "Tab_Event" stores two words, namely "表演(*biǎoyǎn*, perform)" and "喜欢(*xǐhuan*, like)". The subsequent content represents their respective attribute information. For example, "表演(*biǎoyǎn*, perform)" is defined with two attributes expressed using key-value expressions. The first attribute, "Cat=Event," suggests that the word may be an event word. The second attribute, "Role=[A0 A1 Place Neighbor Time]," indicates that the word may have collocation types listed within the square brackets. These collocation types can also be combined with the word "表演(*biǎoyǎn*, perform)" to construct sub-table names, such as "A0_表演(*biǎoyǎn*, perform)", "A1_表演(*biǎoyǎn*, perform)", and so on, establishing relationships between the main table and sub-tables.

Lines 5–8: "A0_表演(*biǎoyǎn*, perform)" represents a sub-table for the "A0" collocation type of the main word "表演(*biǎoyǎn*, perform)". This sub-table lists words that may form subject collocations with "表演(*biǎoyǎn*, perform)", such as "小花(*xiǎohuā*, name)", "男生(*nánshēng*, boy)", "我们(*wǒmen*, we)", etc. Each word is followed by attribute information in key-value expression format, such as "Cat=People".

Lines 10–13: "A1_表演(*biǎoyǎn*, perform)" represents a sub-table for the "A1" collocation type of the main word "表演(*biǎoyǎn*, perform)". In this sub-table, the collocation's attribute is "Cat=Entity".

After converting the knowledge database specific to the field of international Chinese language education into GPF's data table format, it can be directly accessed during the syntactic and semantic analysis stage, providing a source of knowledge for syntactic and semantic analysis.

4 Experimentation of Automatic Question Based on Grid-Based Language Structure Parsing Framework

After constructing the knowledge database specific to the field of international Chinese language education and converting it into GPF data tables, this paper utilizes the GPF to perform syntactic and semantic analysis on sentences. Based on the results of syntactic and semantic analysis, along with the language unit label attributes and question keywords, it can accomplish the task of automatic question generation.

4.1 Framework

The GPF is a knowledge-customizable language structure analysis tool, which means it can conduct syntactic and semantic analysis on text using customized knowledge. Different tasks can be achieved based on the analysis results. In the task of automatic question generation, the first step is utilizing the GPF to analyze the syntactic and semantic relationships among the internal components of a sentence, along with their attribute information. Subsequently, questions are automatically generated based on the analysis results. Accomplishing the task of automatic question generation using GPF, it can be divided into two parts. The first part is grid computing for conducting syntactic and semantic analysis of the sentences. The second part focuses on question generation, completing the task of automatic question generation. The specific workflow is depicted in the Fig. 1.

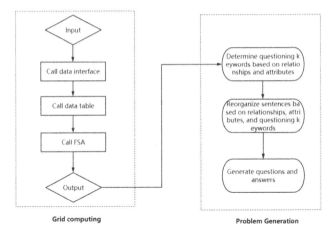

Fig. 1. GPF realizes the process of automatic question setting.

In the first part, the main task is to complete the syntactic and semantic analysis of input text, and output the relationship and attribute information between sentence components. In the second part, the main task is to use the attributes of the language units outputted from the first part of sentence semantic analysis, the relationship between language units, and the information about their attributes, combined with the corresponding relationship between pre-customized attributes and question keywords, to complete the automatic question task.

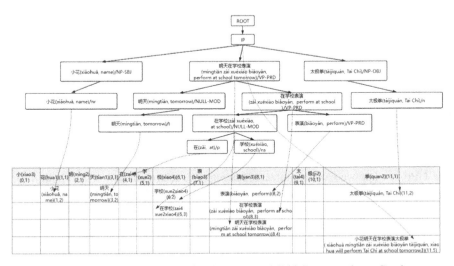

Fig. 2. Chunk Word Segmentation Structure and Grid Correspondence Graph.

4.2 Experimentation

GPF uses a grid as its central control platform, coordinating data tables and finite state machine to perform syntactic and semantic analysis. Therefore, when using the GPF for sentence syntactic and semantic analysis, it requires the collaborative interaction of three parts of code: the main control code, data tables, and finite state machine scripts. GPF's code is based on the Lua language, supplemented with custom APIs. In this paper, we take the example of the code snippet for the sentence "小花明天在学校表演太极拳(xiǎohuā míngtiān zài xuéxiào biǎoyǎn tàijíquán, xiaohua will perform Tai Chi at school tomorrow)" to illustrate the process of performing syntactic and semantic analysis on a sentence and completing the automatic question generation task using GPF. For a detailed explanation of the relevant APIs, please refer to Xun [1]. Main control code is as follows.

```
1.require("module")
2.Sent="小花明天在学校表演太极拳(xiǎohuā míngtiān zài xuéxiào biǎoyǎn
tàijíquán, xiaohua will perform Tai Chi at school tomorrow)"
3.SetText(Sent)
4.DepStruct=CallService(GetText(),"depseg")
5.AddStructure(DepStruct,"depseg")
6.Relate("Tab_Event")
7.RunFSA("Event")
8.module.PrintRelation()
9.GenerateQuestion()
```

The main control code primarily accomplishes two functions, corresponding to the grid computation and question generation parts. Specifically, lines 2–8 perform syntactic and semantic analysis on the input sentence, while line 9 automatically generates questions based on the analysis results.

Grid Computing. The first part is conducting syntactic and semantic analysis on the input text and outputting the attributes of linguistic units and the relationships between them, along with attribute information from the analysis results. This is reflected in the script of lines 1–8 of the main control code.

Line 1 of the main control code: Import the "module" module provided by GPF for future reference.

Line 2–3 of the main control code: Define the input sentence as "小花明天在学校表演太极拳(xiǎohuā míngtiān zài xuéxiào biǎoyǎn tàijíquán, xiaohua will perform Tai Chi at school tomorrow)" and import this sentence into the grid. The result is shown in the Fig. 2.

Lines 4–5 of the main control code: Call the "depseg" data interface accomplishes chunking and part-of-speech tagging analysis of the sentence, and then imports the analysis results into the grid. For instance, grid unit (3,2) corresponds to the linguistic unit "明天(míngtiān, tomorrow)", and it is described with key-value expressions indicating its syntactic attributes, such as "POS=t" and "POS=NULL-MOD," thereby providing syntactic knowledge for grid computations.

Line 6 of the main control code: Call the data table "Tab-Event" to provide semantic knowledge for grid computing.

Line 7 of the main control code: Call the finite state machine "Event". It utilizes the syntactic knowledge provided by the data interface and the semantic knowledge from the data table to conduct context testing and carry out subsequent operations on the input sentence. The script for the finite-state automaton is as follows.

```
1.FSA Event
2.#Entry EntryEvent=[Cat=Event]
3.
4.Word=A0_XB&RHeaddep=sbj&GroupID=UChunk&ClauseID=UChunk Entr
yEvent
5.{
6.Operation
7.}
```

The finite state machine within the GPF serves the purpose of conditional evaluation and execution of operations. In the aforementioned finite state machine script, the specific explanation is as follows.

Line 1 of the finite state machine script: "FSA" is a reserved word, indicating the beginning of a finite-state automaton script, and "Event" is the name of the finite state automaton script, which is globally unique.

Line 2 of the finite state machine script: "# Entry" is a reserved word, indicating the restriction on the entry unit of the finite state machine. This line indicates that the entry unit of the finite state machine has the attribute of "Cat=Event". From the data table listed above, it can be seen that the predicate words defined in this article have the attribute of "Cat=Event", that is, "表演(biǎoyǎn, perform)" has the attribute of "Cat=Event", It can enter the finite state machine as an entry unit.

Line 4 of the finite state machine script: Line 4 is the condition judgment section. Only when the condition judgment is met can subsequent operation steps be executed. In the above example, the condition judgment section has two components separated by spaces, the second component "EntryEvent" represents the entry unit, and the first component is a language unit that has a certain relationship with the entry unit. And further impose conditional restrictions on the first component, multiple conditions are connected by "&". In this finite state machine script, the constraints on the first component are: "Word=A0_XB", "RHeaddep=sbj", "GroupID=UChunk", "ClauseID=UChunk", and are explained in detail as follows.

"Word=A0_XB" restricts the current node from having an "A0" pairing relationship with the entry unit. Among them, "XB" refers to the entry unit "表演(biǎoyǎn, perform)", for example, "小花(xiǎohuā, name)" is an element in the "A0_表演(biǎoyǎn, perform)" table, which meets this restriction. "RHeaddep=sbj" indicates that the current node is the subject of the entry unit (sbj). "GroupID=UChunk" indicates that the current node and the entry unit are a self-sufficient structure (each predicate chunk and its surrounding subordinate components together form a self-sufficient structure); "ClauseID=UChunk" indicates that the current unit and the entry unit belong to the same clause, and this part of information comes from the analysis results of the data interface "depseg".

Line 5–7 of the finite state machine script: Execute the operation "Operation" on the context that meets the conditions. Due to space limitations, the specific internal operation steps are no longer detailed here. Please refer to the website (https://github.com/bien-apprendre/Question). The main function of this part is to add relationships and attribute information to the language unit by obtaining key-value expressions that describe the position information of the language unit in the grid, and also using key-value expressions to describe it, to complete the task of analyzing of syntactic and semantic of the sentence.

Line 8 of the main control code: Call the output function provided by the "module" module in GPF, output all relationships and attribute information after grid calculation, and the running result is as follows.

```
1.=>表演(biǎoyǎn, perform) 小花(xiǎohuā, name)(A0)(sbj) => KV:Cat=People
2.=>表演(biǎoyǎn, perform) 太极拳(tàijíquán, Tai Chi)(A1)(obj) => KV:Cat=Entity
3.=>表演(biǎoyǎn, perform) 明天(míngtiān, tomorrow)(Mod) => KV:Mood=Time
4.=>表演(biǎoyǎn, perform) 学校(xuéxiào, school)(Fram) => KV:Mood=Place
```

Problem Generation. The second part primarily utilizes the attributes of linguistic units and the relationships between these units, as outputted by the first part, to accomplish the task of automatic question generation. Based on the analysis results from the first part, combined with the correspondence between attributes and question keywords in Table 2, the components of the original sentence "小花明天在学校表演太极拳(xiǎohuā míngtiān zài xuéxiào biǎoyǎn tàijíquán, xiaohua will perform Tai Chi at school tomorrow)" correspond to attributes and question keywords as shown in Table 3.

Table 3. Sample sentence attributes and question keywords.

Chunk	Syntactic category	Sematic category	Attribute	Keywords for questioning
小花 (xiǎohuā, name)	subject	subject	people	谁(shuí, who)
明天 (míngtiān, tomorrow)	adverbial	time	time	什么时候 (shénme shíhou, when)
在学校 (zài xuéxiào, at school)	adverbial	place	place	在哪里(zàinǎli, where)
太极拳 (tàijíquán, Tai Chi)	object	object	entity	什么(shénme, what)

This functionality is reflected in the custom function "GenerateQuestion" in line 9 of the main control code, and the specific approach is illustrated in the Fig. 3.

"Event word" refers to words in the data table that have the attribute "Cat=Event," such as "表演(biǎoyǎn, perform)". "Collocation words" are words that have a semantic relationship with event words. For instance, "太极拳 (tàijíquán, Tai Chi)" is the object of the "表演(biǎoyǎn, perform)", and it has a semantic relationship labeled as "A1".

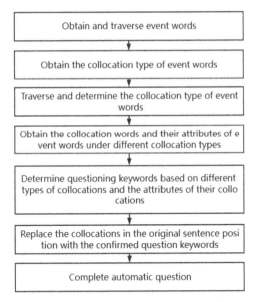

Fig. 3. Automatic Question Setting Flowchart.

Using this, in conjunction with Table 3, questions and answers can be automatically generated. The results of running this function are as follows.

1.question：谁明天在学校表演太极拳？ => answer：小花(*xiǎohuā*, name)
　　Shuí míngtiān zài xuéxiào biǎoyǎn tàijíquán?
　　Who will perform Tai Chi at school tomorrow?
2.question：小花明天在学校表演什么？ => answer：太极拳(*tàijíquán*, Tai Chi)
　　Xiǎohuā míngtiān zài xuéxiào biǎoyǎn shénme?
　　What will Xiaohua perform at school tomorrow?
3.question：小花什么时候在学校表演太极拳？ => answer：明天(*míngtiān*, tomorrow)
　　Xiǎohuā shénme shíhou zài xuéxiào biǎoyǎn tàijíquán?
　　When is Xiaohua performing Tai Chi at school?
4.question：小花明天在哪里表演太极拳？ => answer：学校(*xuéxiào*, school)
　　Xiǎohuā míngtiān zài nǎli biǎoyǎn tàijíquán?
　　Where will Xiaohua perform Tai Chi tomorrow?

Furthermore, this study conducted an accuracy assessment of the method. Specifically, 100 questions were randomly selected from the automatically generated results and manually evaluated. The accuracy rate was as high as 94%, indicating that the approach provided in this research for automatic question generation is feasible.

5   Conclusion

This study accomplished automatic question generation tasks for international Chinese language education based on GPF. Firstly, it built a knowledge database specific to the field of international Chinese language education and transformed this database into GPF's data table format. Different attributes were added to its elements according to existing research, along with customized question keywords corresponding to the attribute types. Secondly, it utilized the GPF in conjunction with the converted knowledge database to conduct syntactic and semantic analysis of the text, thereby producing relationships and attribute information among sentence components. Finally, questions and answers were automatically generated based on the relationship between the analysis results and question keywords, achieving an accuracy rate of 94%. This not only provides an easily extensible and transferrable research model for domain-specific automatic question generation but also has the potential to alleviate the teaching burden on educators and enhance students' grasp of knowledge points.

However, this study still has some limitations. Firstly, the selected international Chinese language education materials are not entirely comprehensive, making it challenging to cover all textbooks adequately. Secondly, concerning the construction of the knowledge database in the field of international Chinese language education, despite referencing existing research achievements, issues remain with regard to incomplete coverage of tags and question keywords. Additionally, semantic labels may lack granularity, leading to a limitation in the diversity of question types. Thirdly, the current method exhibits higher accuracy for simple sentences but requires further experimentation to handle complex sentences effectively. Finally, when using GPF for syntactic and semantic analysis of text, there may be challenges in identifying the main topic sentence in reading materials. Next step in this research is to address these limitations, aiming to provide a more comprehensive, extensible, and transferable domain-specific automatic question generation model for the field of natural language generation.

Acknowledgments. This research achievement is funded by National Key Research and Development Program of China (2022YFF0711900) and National Postdoctoral Research Program (GZC20232930).

References

1. Xun, E.-D.: AI Natural Language Processing - GPF Language Analysis Framework. People's Posts and Telecommunications Press, Beijing (2022). (in Chinese)
2. Yllias, C., Hasan, S.-A.: Towards automatic topical question generation. In: Proceedings of the 24th International Conference on Computational Linguistics, pp. 1–8 (2012)
3. Mass, Y., Carmeli, B., et al.: Unsupervised FAQ retrieval with question generation and BERT. In: Proceedings of the 58th Annual Meeting of the Association for Computational Linguistics, pp. 807–812 (2020)
4. Tan, L.: Implementation of an automatic question generation program for addition and subtraction operations based on VC. Softw. Guide **11**, 81–83 (2010). (in Chinese)
5. Li, H.: Automatic question generation technology based on DL and Domain Ontology. J. Changchun Univ. Technol. (Nat. Sci. Edn.) **4**, 460–464 (2012). (in Chinese)

6. Tang, Q.-F.: Research on Ontology-Based Automatic Question Generation System. Guangxi Normal University (2012). (in Chinese)
7. Mazidi, K., Nielsen, R.-D.: Linguistic considerations in automatic question generation. In: Proceedings of the 52th Annual Meeting of the Association for Computational Linguistics, pp. 321–326 (2014)
8. Serban, I.V., et al.: Generating Factoid questions with recurrent neural networks: The 30M factoid question-answer corpus. arXiv preprint arXiv.1603.06807 (2016)
9. Kumar, V., Ganesh, R., Li, Y.-F.: A framework for automatic question generation from text using deep reinforcement learning. arXiv preprint arXiv.1808.04961 (2018)
10. Wu, Z.-X., Liu, C.-H., Su, P.: Sentence extraction with topic modeling for question–answer pair generation. Soft Comput. **19**(1), 39–46 (2015)
11. Liao, Y.-H., Koh, J.-L.: Question generation through transfer learning. In: Fujita, H., Fournier-Viger, P., Ali, M., Sasaki, J. (eds.) IEA/AIE 2020. LNCS (LNAI), vol. 12144, pp. 3–17. Springer, Cham (2020). https://doi.org/10.1007/978-3-030-55789-8_1
12. Qin, C.: Research on Chinese Chunk Dependency Analysis Based on Pretrained Models. Beijing Language and Culture University, Beijing (2023). (in Chinese)
13. Dong, D.: The Modern Chinese Classification Dictionary. Shanghai Lexicographical Publishing House, Shanghai (1998). (in Chinese)
14. Liu, Y.-H., Pan, W.-Y., Hu, W.: Practical Modern Chinese Grammar, Revised The Commercial Press, Beijing (2017). (in Chinese)
15. Jiang, H.-C., Xu, H.-G.: A Practical Dictionary of Modern Chinese Adverb Classification. Foreign Trade Education Publishing House, Beijing (1989). (in Chinese)
16. Qin, Z., Shao, T., Rao, G.-Q., Xun, E.-D.: Semantic classification of adverbial adjectives based on Chinese Chunkbank. In: Dong, M., Gu, Y., Hong, J.F. (eds.) Chinese Lexical Semantics. CLSW 2021. LNCS, vol. 13250, pp. 194–206. Springer, Cham (2022). https://doi.org/10.1007/978-3-031-06547-7_16
17. Shao, T., Wang, C.-W., Rao, G.-Q., Xun, E.-D.: The semantic change and distribution of adjoining adverbs in modern Chinese. From minimal contrast to meaning construct. Front. Chin. Linguist. **9**, 149–163 (2020)
18. Zhai, S., Shao, T., Rao, G.-Q., Xun, E.-D.: Semantic classification of adverbial nouns based on syntactic treebank and construction of collocation database. In: Su, Q., Xu, G., Yang, X. (eds.) Chinese Lexical Semantics. CLSW 2022. LNCS, vol. 13496, pp. 259–277. Springer, Cham (2023). https://doi.org/10.1007/978-3-031-28956-9_21
19. Wang, C.-W., Qian, Q.-Q., Xun, E.-D., Xing, D., Li, M., Rao, G.-Q.: Construction of a Chinese verb semantic role knowledge base from the perspective of triadic collocations. Chin. J. Inf. Sci. **09**, 19–27 (2020). (in Chinese)

Corpus Linguistics

What Factors Can Facilitate Efficient Propagation of Chinese Neologisms–A Corpus-Driven Study with Internet Usage Data

Menghan Jiang[1]([✉]), Kathleen Ahrens[2], and Chu-Ren Huang[3]

[1] Chinese Language Center, Shenzhen MSU-BIT University, Shenzhen, China
`menghan.jiang@connect.polyu.hk`
[2] Department of English and Communication, The Hong Kong Polytechnic University, Hung Hom, Kowloon, Hong Kong, China
`kathleen.ahrens@polyu.edu.hk`
[3] Department of Chinese and Bilingual Studies, The Hong Kong Polytechnic University, Hung Hom, Kowloon, Hong Kong, China
`churen.huang@polyu.edu.hk`

Abstract. With the development of information technologies, our world currently faces such an overwhelming mass of neologisms. Therefore, the study of neologisms has become an important research topic in recent years [1]. In this research, we investigate the factors that facilitate the efficient propagation of Chinese neologisms, based on Internet usage data extracted from Google Trends. We collected 342 neologisms from the published authoritative lists and annotated them with eight factors that potentially contribute to their popularity. The empirical findings shed light on the predictive potential of specific factors, such as the topic, syntactic type, length, and semantic polarity of the neologisms. Our investigation further assigns weight to each factor, revealing that syntactic type and semantic polarity of the neologisms exert more pronounced effects on their developments.

Keywords: Chinese Neologisms · Internet Usage Data · Corpus-Driven Approach

1 Introduction

With the development of information technologies, our way of life and communication have changed significantly. Instead of traditional face to face communication, people nowadays communicate with others, seek information, and provide opinions online through social media. Ubiquitous and immediate access to information with the potential for real-time responses has provided a strong impetus for creating ideas and has allowed such ideas to be spread more broadly and quickly than ever before. This phenomenon has allowed the emergence and spread of neologisms, particularly those originating from the realm of social media and other online platforms, which are known as Internet neologisms. The neologisms used online have proliferated worldwide.

© The Author(s), under exclusive license to Springer Nature Singapore Pte Ltd. 2024
M. Dong et al. (Eds.): CLSW 2023, LNAI 14515, pp. 209–215, 2024.
https://doi.org/10.1007/978-981-97-0586-3_17

Moreover, due to different sociocultural interests, Internet neologisms that originate from different regions often exhibit distinct characteristics, allow for an examination of social preferences. The investigation of Internet neologisms not only enriches our understanding of various cultures but also provides valuable insights into sociology, human behavior, and especially linguistic trends of novel word usage [2, 3].

Hence, Internet neologisms have attracted the interest of language researchers, especially in investigating the driving factors involved in the development of neologisms, and in predicting the survival chance of neologisms in the language system (e.g., [4–8]). A variety of studies focusing on conditions or factors that could maximally explain lexical establishment, i.e., in determining whether a neologism will disappear or survive (e.g., [9–11]). For example, word frequency is considered to play a very important role in explaining the success story of words, life stages, and the prediction force of whether a word may survive after being coined (e.g., [12, 13]). However, many studies have been conducted under a qualitative paradigm, with only a few exceptions employing statistical methodologies and large-scale data analysis (e.g., [12–15]). The reason for lacking quantitative studies is that it is almost impossible to have reliable documentation for the process of fast changes [16]. Given the observed phenomenon that neologisms nowadays evolve and fade much faster than ever before, traditional linguistic approaches to date have lacked a way to deal with either the scale or the speed of the fast-development neologisms.

To address this problem, Jiang et al. [15, 17] provides a new method to obtain statistical data for neologisms from an Internet statistical tool, Google Trends, to measure the popularity of the fast-changing neologisms. Google Trends is an online search tool that can provide the searched frequency of the selected word within a flexible range of time intervals. They argue that the Internet search frequency is a reasonable approximation of a neologism's popularity and how the word spreads over the Internet. Their study adopts internet-based data from Google Trends to model the life cycle of neologisms, and the results indicate that the propagation of neologisms is similar to the propagation of diseases. However, they have not investigated which factors (such as word length, semantic polarity or syntactic type) might influence the life cycle of neologisms. In this study, we follow the method of Jiang et al. [15, 17] also using Google Trends. Based on the Internet usage data, we aim to examine the factors which can determine the development speed and facilitate the efficient propagation of Chinese neologisms.

2 Method

2.1 Data Source

We collected the neologisms following the published authoritative lists from three platforms: 咬文嚼字 *YaoWen JiaoZi*, National Language Resources Monitoring and Research Center (joint with other platforms), and 上海语言文字周报 *Shanghai Yuyan Wenzi Zhoubao*. These organizations annually release compilations of "neologisms of the year", typically at the end of each year or the commencement of the subsequent year. These selections are based on an evaluation of language development over the preceding year. Although each platform may utilize different criteria for word selection, all adhere to stringent and scientifically grounded identification standards. The results are authoritative and recognized by the public. We have collected the annual neologisms from each year between 2008–2021, for a total of about 342 words. We have not taken the most recent neologisms from the past year to ensure that there is enough longitudinal data for the development of each new word.

2.2 Popularity Measurement

As mentioned in the introduction, we follow Jiang et al. [15, 17] and measure the word's popularity by its internet search frequency to investigate the variation of the rapid change of neologisms. The Internet search frequency is a reasonable approximation of how the words spread over the Internet and the frequency of their use. Fortunately, this data can be easily accessible and downloaded from Google Trends for free. Google Trends is an online tool that provides access to a large sample of actual search requests. The daily search frequency for a given neologism reported on Google Trends is normalized on a scale ranging from zero to one hundred. This normalization serves as a reflection of each word's development, starting from its inception (0) to its peak popularity (100).

In this study, we leveraged Google Trends to generate a data pool of the search frequencies of the 342 selected neologisms as our source data. We calculated the development duration based on the searched frequency, and the duration is defined as how long (how many days) a neologism takes to develop from 0 (or a very low-frequency level) to 100. For example, Fig. 1 illustrates the development of 不差钱 *bu2cha4qian2* 'rich' as observed in Google Trends. The word emerged and started to be popular on Jan 18th 2009, reaching its peak at the normalized value of 100 on Feb 1st 2009.

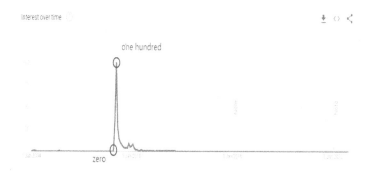

Fig. 1. The popularity of *bu2cha4qian2* 'rich'

2.3 Data Annotation

We manually annotated each neologism with 8 factors which could influence the popularity of the neologisms. These factors were selected based on previous research and our observations (e.g., [18]). The annotation schema is shown below in Table 1. Note there are three topics listed under "Topic", Economic, Social, and Political. We hand coded all the categories in each of the eight factors. The annotator is a trained linguistic expert, and any uncertainties or ambiguities have been discussed with other experts to reach agreement.

Table 1. The annotation schema.

Factors	Explanations	Examples
Length	How many characters a neologism contains	给力 *gei3li4* 'awesome': **2** 挖掘机技术哪家强 *wa1jue2ji1ji4shu4 na3 jia1 qiang2* 'Which company has the best excavator technology': **8**
Time	In which year the neologism was coined	囧 *jiong3* 'embarrassment': **2008** 大 V *da4V* 'social media influencer': **2013**
Platform	On which platform was the neologism published	**National Language Resources Monitoring Center**：脱贫攻坚 *tuo1pin2 gong1jian1* 'poverty alleviation and eradication' （2020） **YaoWenJiaoZi:** 直播带货 *zhi2bo1 dai4huo4* 'livestreaming e-commerce' （2020） **Yuyan Wenzi Zhoubao:** 甩锅 *shuai3guo1* 'shift the blame' （2020）
Topic	The topic the neologism refers to	**Economic:** 口红效应 *kou3hong2 xiao4ying4* 'lipstick effect' **Political:** 反腐 *fan3fu3* 'fight against government corruption' **Social:** 蜗居 *wo1ju1* 'living in a tight space'
POS	The syntactic type of the neologism	**N or NP:** 高铁 *gao1tie3* 'high speed rail' **V or VP:** 打 call *da3call* 'to cheer on' **ADJ or ADJP:** 中国式 *zhong1guo1 shi4* 'Chinese style (ironic)' **Clause:** 我太南了 *wo3 tai4nan2 le* 'I am to difficult'
Polarity	The semantic polarity of the neologism	**Negative:** 坑爹 *keng1die1* 'you (could have) fooled me' **Neutral:** 微电影 *wei1 dian4ying3* 'microfilm' **Positive:** 一带一路 *yi2dai4 yi2lu4* 'belt and road'
Metaphor	Whether the neologism contains conceptual metaphors or not	**Yes:** 油腻 *you2ni4* 'cheesy' **No:** 不差钱 *bu4 cha4 qian2* 'rich'
Coinage	Whether the neologism is a new form or an existing form with new interpretations	**A new word:** 高铁 *gao1tie3* 'high speed rail' **A new meaning is assigned to an existing form:** 山寨 *shan1zhai4* 'reengineered copy'

2.4   Data Analysis

We further utilize a linear regression to examine the relationship between the development duration and the potential factors. The results can be summarized in Table 2. We transfer the results into signs. The " $+$ " can be interpreted as the duration is positively correlated with the factor, while the "$-$" displays that the duration has a significant negative correlation with the factor, and "0" indicates that no statistically significant results have been detected.

Table 2. The results of linear regression.

	Duration		Duration
Time	0	POS-V	+
Platform	0	POS-N	−
Coinage	0	POS-ADJ	0
length	−	Polarity-negative	−
Topic-social	−	Polarity-neutral	+
Topic-economic	+	Polarity-positive	+
Topic-political	−	Metaphor	0

As can be seen from the results, the overall regression is statistically significant ($R2 = 0.73$, $F(2, 17) = 23.46$, $p = < .000$). Particularly, the development duration of neologism is significantly increased by the presence of the economic topic, while it is significantly decreased when associated with the political and social topics. Furthermore, the duration is significantly increased by the verbal neologism, while it is significantly decreased by the nominal neologism. Additionally, the duration is positively correlated with a neutral and positive context, while it is negatively correlated with a negative context. The duration cannot be predicted by factors such as the time being coined, platform, coinage, and metaphorization. In sum, the regression model predicts that a nominal neologism of longer length, with negative semantic polarity, refering to social or political topics, is more likely to spread faster (i.e., it takes a shorter time to reach the peak).

More importantly, instead of investigating the influence of each factor independently, in the subsequent step, we also include the calculation of weight for the significant factors. This is essential since the development of neologisms is influenced by a combination of various factors concurrently. We perform a multivariate regression analysis incorporating these weights, and the results are present in Table 3.. The coefficients in the table illustrate the relative contribution of each factor to the duration of neologism development.

Notably, we find that the "syntactic type–morpheme" factor has the most significant positive effect on the duration, followed by neutral polarity. Additionally, "syntactic type–word" and positive polarity also contribute positively to the duration, while social and political topics have a negative impact. The "Noun" factor, conversely, has the most pronounced negative influence on the duration. In summary, our findings underscore the critical significance of the syntactic type and semantic polarity of neologisms in their dissemination, with these factors playing crucial roles in the duration of their development.

Table 3. The results of linear regression with weight.

features	coef	std err	t	P > |t|	[0.025	0.975]
const	130.0245	24.890	5.224	0.000	81.061	178.988
length	−8.0138	4.955	−1.617	0.107	−17.761	1.733
topic_political	−20.2836	19.793	−1.025	0.306	−59.220	18.652
topic_social	−29.6053	15.912	−1.861	0.064	−60.907	1.697
syntactic type_m	85.9967	51.083	1.683	0.093	−14.494	186.488
syntactic type_p	−0.3953	16.202	−0.024	0.981	−32.268	31.477
syntactic type_w	47.7278	21.982	2.171	0.031	4.484	90.972
POS_ADJP	10.1767	21.119	0.482	0.630	−31.369	51.722
POS_N	−53.5797	31.915	−1.679	0.094	−116.362	9.203
POS_NP	−10.4983	12.367	−0.849	0.397	−34.827	13.831
POS_V	−22.2108	37.363	−0.594	0.553	−95.712	51.290
POS_VP	−0.0737	12.677	−0.006	0.995	−25.012	24.864
POS_clause	v3.3047	29.127	−0.113	0.910	−60.603	53.993
polarity_neutral	69.2954	24.707	2.805	0.005	20.692	117.899
polarity_p	25.1777	12.116	2.078	0.038	1.343	49.012

2.5 Summary

This study examines the potential factors that might contribute to the effective dissemination of neologisms. The results show that the popularity and development speed can be predicted, to some extent, based on specific features, such as the topic, syntactic type, length, and semantic polarity of the neologisms. In future study, more data with more features annotated will be included, to further explore how neologisms are created and developed.

Acknowledgement. This work is supported by 2023 International Chinese Language Education Research Project "Study on Variations in Ditransitive Constructions under the Globalization Perspective (23YH81D), and Guangdong Provincial University Youth Innovation Talent Program "Modeling the Life Cycle of Neologisms based on Internet Usage Data" (2022WQNCX073).

References

1. Jing-Schmidt, Z., Hsieh, S.K.: Chinese neologisms. In: Huang, C.-R., Jing, S.Z., Meisterernst, B. (eds.) The Routledge Handbook of Chinese Applied Linguistics, pp. 514–534. Routledge, Abingdon (2019)
2. Sonnad N.: How brand-new words are spreading across America. Quartz. https://qz.com/465 820/how-brand-new-words-are-spreading-across-america/. (Accessed 6 May 2023)
3. Castellví, M.T.C., Bagot, R.E., Sierra, C.V.: Neology in specialized communication. Terminology - Inter. J. Theoret. Appl. Issues Special. Commun. **18**(1), 1–8 (2012)
4. Schmid, H.-J.: New words in the mind: Concept-formation and entrenchment of neologisms. Anglia **126**(1), 1–36 (2008)
5. Renouf, A.: A finer definition of neology in English: the life-cycle of a word. Corpus Perspect. Patterns Lexis **57**, 177–207 (2013)
6. Hu, X.: A constructional approach to lexical templates in Chinese neologisms. In: Lu, Q., Gao, H. (eds.) CLSW 2015. LNCS, vol. 9332, pp. 320–328. Springer, Cham (2015). https://doi.org/10.1007/978-3-319-27194-1_32
7. Chou, L., Hsieh, S.K.: Qualia modification in Mandarin neologism: a case study on prefix Wéi. In: Liu, P., Su, Q. (eds.) CLSW 2013. LNCS, vol. 8229, pp. 297–305. Springer, Berlin (2013). https://doi.org/10.1007/978-3-642-45185-0_32
8. Teng, S.: Word formation in Chinese dialects: A case study of Hailu Hakka. In: Lu, Q., Gao, H. (eds.) CLSW 2015. LNCS, vol. 9332, pp. 281–293. Springer, Cham (2015). https://doi.org/10.1007/978-3-319-27194-1_29
9. Klosa-Kückelhaus, A., Wolfe, S.: Considerations on the acceptance of German neologisms from the 1990s. Int. J. Lexicogr. **33**(2), 150–167 (2020)
10. Edmonds, B.: Three challenges for the survival of memetics. J. Memetics - Evolut. Models Inform. Trans. **6**(2), 45–50 (2002)
11. Metcalf, A.: Predicting new words: The secrets of their success. Boston, New York: Houghton Mifflin Harcourt (2004)
12. Altmann, E.G., Pierrehumbert, J.B., Motter, A.E.: Niche as a determinant of word fate in online groups. PLoS ONE **6**(5), e19009 (2011)
13. Altmann, E.G., Whichard, Z.L., Motter, A.E.: Identifying trends in word frequency dynamics. J. Stat. Phys. **151**(1–2), 277–288 (2013)
14. Heylighen, F., Chielens, K.: Cultural evolution and memetics. In: Meyers, R.A. (ed.) Encyclopedia of Complexity and Systems Science, pp. 3205–3220. Springer, Berlin (2009). https://doi.org/10.1007/978-0-387-30440-3_189
15. Jiang, M., Shen, X.Y., Ahrens, K., Huang, C.-R.: Neologisms are epidemic: Modeling the life cycle of neologisms in China 2008–2016. PLoS ONE **16**(2), e0245984 (2021)
16. Lei, S., Yang, R., Huang, C.-R.: Emergent neologism: A study of an emerging meaning with competing forms based on the first six months of COVID-19. Lingu **258**, 103095 (2021)
17. Jiang M., Ahrens K., Shen X. Y., Lee, S. Y. M., Huang C.-R.: Do new words propagate like memes? An internet usage based two-stage model of the life cycle of neologisms. Accepted by Journal of Chinese Linguistics
18. Tsur, O., Rappoport, A.: Don't let me be# misunderstood: Linguistically motivated algorithm for predicting the popularity of textual memes. In: Proceedings of the International AAAI Conference on Web and Social Media, pp. 426–435. AAAI Press, Palo Alto, California USA (2015)

COVID-19 Related Expressions and Their Correlation with the Pandemic: An Internet-Based Study

Jia-Fei Hong[✉] and Jia-Ni Chen

National Taiwan Normal University, Taipei, Taiwan
{jiafeihong,jiani}@ntnu.edu.tw

Abstract. At the end of 2019, a new type of coronavirus (coronavirus disease 2019, COVID-19, also known as severe special infectious pneumonia) broke out worldwide. This novel outbreak, with many mutations, was unanticipated and caused panic throughout the global community. Simultaneously, people's lives were flooded with information related to the epidemic; specifically, words highly related to the epidemic were frequently used, such as *"que4zhen3ren2shu4"*, *"qian2fu2qi2"*, *"yi4miao2"*, and other sociological words, such as *"she4jiao1ju4li2"*, *"ge2li2"*. This study focuses on 2020 when COVID-19 caused drastic social changes, and uses the words identified by the World Health Organization to explore collocations that appear frequently due to the epidemic and their relationship with disease names. By collecting the names of COVID-19 diseases commonly used by relevant newspapers and media, the usage frequency over time is analyzed, and possible explanations will be explored. In addition, the high-frequency corpus generated through this research can also be helpful for further research. Furthermore, textbook writers can also refer to the research results to compile themed textbooks to facilitate the further understanding of the use of vocabulary in various countries. Chinese teachers can begin with high-frequency corpus and words, arrange appropriate course content for learners, and enable learners to better understand the impact of COVID-19 on the world through thematic learning.

Keywords: COVID-19 · Correlation · Pandemic · Internet-based study

1 Introduction

According to the World Health Organization (WHO), as of October 11, 2022 there have been over 626 million confirmed cases of COVID-19 worldwide, with a death toll exceeding 6,566 million during the pandemic. While many countries were able to somewhat manage the pandemic, the number of cases and deaths continues to rise. Furthermore, there are still concerns regarding the ongoing development of the pandemic.

M. Dong et al. (Eds.): CLSW 2023, LNAI 14515, pp. 216–233, 2024.
https://doi.org/10.1007/978-981-97-0586-3_18

In late 2019, a novel coronavirus outbreak known as coronavirus disease 2019 (COVID-19), also referred to as severe acute respiratory syndrome coronavirus 2 (SARS-CoV-2), emerged from Wuhan, Hubei Province, China. Despite many countries quickly implementing related policies, conducting research, and developing vaccines, the pandemic still has had a profound impact on society, and the return to normal life has proven to be challenging.

The global impact of the COVID-19 pandemic is evident in multiple areas of life, including the economy and reshaping people's consumption habits. Furthermore, people began to frequently use terms closely associated with the pandemic, such as *"que4zhen3ren2shu4"*, *"qian2fu2qi2"*, *"yi4miao2"*; or other sociological words, such as *"she4jiao1ju4li2"*, *"ge2li2"*. The effects of COVID-19 have been far-reaching, affecting not only the economy but also society as a whole.

2020 is the year that saw the most drastic changes caused by the COVID-19 pandemic; as such, this study uses 2020 as its sample year. Specifically, this study identifies the most frequently used COVID-19 names as the primary search keywords from Taiwanese online news sources to understand and analyze the development of the local pandemic. Additionally, this study compares these terms with the terms designated by WHO. The change in the frequency of usage of these terms will be observed and corresponding reasons will be analyzed throughout this study.

In addition, the high-frequency corpus generated in this study may also be beneficial in teaching research. Textbook writers can refer to the research results to compile themed textbooks so that more people can understand the use of vocabulary in various countries. Chinese teachers can begin with high-frequency corpus and words, arrange appropriate course content for learners to learn, and enable learners to better understand the impact of COVID-19 on the world through thematic learning.

2   Motivation and Purpose

The relationship between language and society is exceedingly intertwined. The transmission of information requires a medium, from traditional newspapers to online media, these real-life language resources reflect the state of society and its responses. Since the outbreak of the pandemic, people's lives have been greatly affected, and it is likely that significant linguistic changes have also occurred.

This study focuses on 2020, when the impact of the pandemic was most severe. Due to the nature of the pandemic, the exchange of most information was through the internet. Therefore, this study has collected online news from Taiwan to analyze the linguistic changes that occurred during the pandemic. By examining the various names of COVID-19 during different time periods, this study aims to analyze the ways in which the pandemic was described in online news and associated collocations. This study also compares these linguistic changes with the progression of the pandemic, investigating the correlation between COVID-19-related vocabularies and pandemic changes. This analysis provides insights into the language habits of individuals and serves as a reference for future analysis of the pandemic and its implications for education.

3   Literature Review

3.1   Corpus-Based Research

A corpus is a large collection of language materials that provide real-world usage contexts and examples for various linguistic needs. [1] conducted semantic and syntactic analyses of the English word 'challenge' used as both a verb and a noun based on a corpus. In addition to its application in academic research, corpora can also be used for teaching purposes. In order to enhance Taiwanese learners' proficiency in Chinese writing, [2] took five Chinese conjunction types from a Chinese Written Corpus (CWC) to analyze semantic features and learners' usage errors.

With the development of internet technology, the sources of corpora have shifted from physical sources like newspapers and books to virtual sources on the internet. [3] and [4] acknowledge that while the internet provides easy access to a wealth of data, there are also several challenges associated with internet-based corpora. First, the development of the internet itself has influenced language, leading to the emergence of graphical characters and symbols, such as emojis, and entirely new writing systems, such as Martian. Second, the dynamic of the internet makes it difficult to find objective and representative data, and various sources can be unreliable. Third, individual habits in utilizing online media vary, and content recommendations by online systems are tailored based on these habits. As such, conducting research based on an internet corpus requires caution and the verification of data quality.

While there are challenges related to internet-based corpora, various researchers have used this type of data. For example, [5] constructed a corpus for minority languages using internet data. They faced challenges such as data redundancy and difficulty verifying the authenticity and correctness of the data. They found that only 2.5% of the data was duplicated, making it challenging to review the authenticity of each piece of data. While this narrowed down the scope and allowed for faster searching, the dataset remained relatively small, enabling quick filtering and validation to create a small-scale corpus based on that specific phrase.

[6] conducted a study comparing the Sinica Corpus and Taiwan Plurk online community corpus created by the research. The aim was to address the challenges associated with large-scale online corpora. However, it was noted that small-scale corpora could have their quality manually confirmed. Still, when analyzing large quantities of data in the online corpus, heavy segmentation errors occurred, especially given that Chinese is a language without clear word boundaries.

This study aims to explore language usage trends and changes during the pandemic. Considering the many changes experienced during the pandemic, this study is internet-based and explicitly limits its scope to news reports with an objective and rational content orientation, ensuring the integrity of data.

3.2   Co-occurrences and Collocations

The word co-occurrence refers to the practice of identifying "keywords" within content that are representative and allow readers to discern the main topic of an article. It involves analyzing the words that occur simultaneously with these keywords, often revealing specific associations between them. [7] and [8] state that the purpose of co-occurrence analysis is to demonstrate the frequency of word usage and co-occurrence relationships, ultimately establishing knowledge links between keywords and their collocates in a specific domain.

[9] compared English (WordNet), traditional Chinese (Chinese WordNet, CWN), and simplified Chinese (Chinese Concept Dictionary, CCD) lexical systems to understand their usage and differences. They also performed a rapid descriptive analysis of Chinese vocabulary usage in both traditional Chinese and simplified Chinese by the Chinese Gigaword Corpus. The result revealed that even though both sides have common Chinese vocabulary, there may be differences in meaning and even mutual influences on language usage.

[7] utilized online resources to collect a substantial amount of business-related information from the internet, establishing the Network Business Chinese Corpus. They then selected 19 nouns related to business as keywords and compared the co-occurrence collocates of these keywords between the Network Business Chinese Corpus and Sinica Corpus.

Through co-occurrence analysis, linguistic features and language usage trends or tendencies can be observed within the associations between keywords and their collocates. These results, collected from natural language environments, not only reflect the social context and attitudes of narrators but also provide a representative and evidence-based auxiliary tool for teaching Chinese.

[10] observed the co-occurrence patterns and syntactic structures to distinguish two set of near-synonyms Chinese words in the Chinese Gigaword Corpus with the Chinese Word Sketch Engine and the Chinese Learner Corpus (of Written Chinese). She compared the different Chinese language usages between native speakers and Chinese learners, and provided approaches to learning Chinese vocabulary.

[11] used the TOCFL Learner Corpus at National Taiwan Normal University as their data source. They analyzed learner errors of directional complement "qi3lai2" and then proposed learning difficulties and teaching suggestions.

Co-occurrence analysis assists researchers in understanding language usage by providing insights into the social context reflected by language. It also offers educators robust examples and reference resources from natural language contexts, which helps learners enhance their language skills while gaining deeper insights into the society and culture of the language. For this reason, this study chose co-occurrence relationships as the entry point to understanding how the pandemic affected language.

4   Corpus Resource

Driven by the pandemic, people have increasingly relied on the internet to access information and communicate with others. Thus, this study is internet-based and uses widely accessed online news media as data.

The United Daily News (UDN) in Taiwan was selected as the study corpus. UDN, established in 1951, officially launched its online platform in 1999. In addition to publishing the United Daily newspaper, the company operates UDN and features columns and social-media platforms dedicated to sharing books and lifestyle content. It even has its own e-commerce platform to sell various lifestyle products and event tickets. Its extensive coverage makes UDN not only a well-known news media outlet in Taiwan but also a platform that reflects the life and thoughts of Taiwanese people.

By using a widely accessed internet media platform like UDN, which is commonly used by the local population in Taiwan, this study ensures the richness and credibility of internet-based data. It also allows for a clear view of the changes in the lives of local people during the year 2020.

5 Analysis

5.1 The Names of COVID-19 During Different Periods

Throughout the COVID-19 pandemic, not only did the frequency of disease names related to COVID-19 increase significantly, but so did medical terminology. Furthermore, the frequency of related co-occurring words increased noticeably, particularly in online news. Online news serves as authentic language data, not only as a medium for people to stay informed about current events but also as an excellent reference for language learners. Therefore, this is an internet-based study that discusses disease names and related collocates by Taiwan online news in 2020.

Upon reviewing all the news data, it was found that there are several official names identical to those designated by WHO, including *"Wu3han4fei4yan2," "Xin1xing2guan4zhuang4bing4du2," "Xin1guan4fei4yan2," "Xin1xing2guan4   zhuang4bing4du2yi4qing2,"   "COVID-19,"*   and *"2019guan4zhuang4bing4du2ji2bing4."* In addition to these six names, another name appeared with extremely high frequency: *"Xin1xing2guan4zhuang4bing4du2bing4."* Therefore, the following discussion will focus on these seven names as core keywords in this study.

Comparing these seven disease names, as shown in Fig. 1, it can be observed that during the initial outbreak of the pandemic, *"Wu3han4fei4yan2"* had the highest usage frequency. Since February 2020, even though the pandemic showed signs of slowing down, *"Xin1guan4fei4yan2"* still remained the most frequently used term.

As shown in Fig. 2, when considering the total usage counts of all these names, the same result can be observed.

Regarding the naming conventions by the WHO in different periods, since the initial outbreak of the pandemic, which originated in the Wuhan region of China, many news outlets used *"COVID-19"* and *"Wu3han4fei4yan2;"* however, *"Wu3han4fei4yan2"* had a higher frequency of use during that period, exceeding 2,000 occurrences. This caused a negative perception of Wuhan, China. To avoid stigmatization, the formal naming adopted the year of occurrence and characteristics of the virus, resulting in names such as "Xin1xing2guan4zhuang4bing4du2bing4," "Xin1xing2guan4zhuang4 *Xin1xing2guan4zhuang4bing4du2yi4qung2*bing4du2," *"Xin1guan4fei4yan2,"* and *"2019guan4zhuang4bing4du2ji2bing4."* Among these names, *"Xin1guan4fei4yan2"* became the primary term used to refer to the disease.

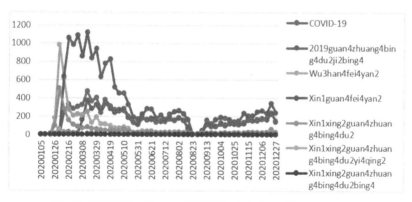

Fig. 1. UDN: The Names of COVID-19 during Different Periods

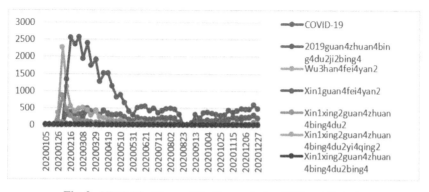

Fig. 2. UDN: The Times of the Names during Different Periods

5.2 Collocations in Different Periods

In accordance with the development of the COVID-19 pandemic in Taiwan, the results presented in Fig. 1 and Fig. 2 show that between January and March, which marked the initial outbreak of the pandemic, there was a very high frequency of COVID-19-related reports. Afterward, there was a slight decrease in frequency.

Following the Qingming Festival holiday in April, there was another noticeable increase in COVID-19-related news. In the same month, however, with the introduction of vaccines, the pandemic began to decline significantly, and related news reports decreased accordingly.

It is worth noting that there was a significant change at the end of August. According to UDN data, this gap was primarily due to the government's decision to gradually reopen physical workplaces and schools in September. This led to an increase in COVID-19 related news.

To effectively understand the connection between the names of COVID-19 and collocations that related to the pandemic, this study took August as division, selected the peak periods from the 11th week to the 17th week and from the 46th week to the 53rd week as analysis range. As for the collocations, the study distinguished the components in the sentence, and used the names of COVID-19 as the basis to determine the distance between the collocations and it. For instance, the collocation word with the first distance is the word right next to the names of COVID-19. This study would take collocations from first distance to third distance as research objects.

Table 1. First distance collocations from the 11th week to the 17th week

	11th	12th	13th	14th	15th	16th	17th
COVID-19	ji2bing4	2019gua n4zhuan g4bing4 du2ji2bi ng4	2019gua n4zhuan g4bing4 du2ji2bi ng4	2019gua n4zhuan g4bing4 du2ji2bi ng4	2019gua n4zhuan g4bing4 du2ji2bi ng4	2019guan 4zhuang4 bing4du2j i2bing4	2019gua n4zhuan g4bing4 du2ji2bi ng4
Wu3han4f ei4yan2	yi4qing2	yi4qing2	yi4qing2	yi4qing2	yi4qing2	yi4qing2	yi4qing2
Xin1guan 4fei4yan2	yi4qing2	yi4qing2	yi4qing2	yi4qing2	yi4qing2	yi4qing2	yi4qing2
2019guan 4zhuang4 bing4du2j i2bing4	COVID-19	COVID-19	COVID-19	COVID-19	COVID-19	COVID-19	COVID-19
Xin1xing2 guan4zhu ang4bing4 du2	gan3ran 3	fei4yan2	fei4yan2	fei4yan2	fei4yan2	fei4yan2	fei4yan2
Xin1xing2 guan4zhu ang4bing4 du2yi4qin g2	chu1xia n4	yin1ying 4	juo4san4	dui4kan g4	jin4zhi3	pu4liu4ch u1	yin1ying 4
Xin1xing2 guan4zhu ang4bing4 du2bing4		Ma3lai2 xi1ya4	COVID-19	Xiang1g ang3			

From Table 1, it can be observed that the collocates closely associated with "*Xin1guan4fei4yan2*" are all related to terms associated with the disease. Both "*Wu3han4fei4yan2*" and "*Xin1guan4fei4yan2*" are collocated with "*yi4qing2.*" "*2019guan4zhuang4bing4du2ji2bing4*" and "*COVID-19*" are collocates of each other. "*fei4yan2*" is a high-frequency collocate used with "*Xin1xing2guan4zhuang4bing4du2.*" Regarding "*Xin1xing2guan4zhuang4bing4du2yi4qing2*" and "*Xin1xing2guan4 zhuang4bing4du2bing4,*" further analysis may be needed to understand their specific collocational patterns and associations.

Similar results were observed in the 46th to the 53rd week. As shown in Table 2, "*2019guan4zhuang4bing4du2ji2bing4*" and "*COVID-19*" are frequently collocated with each other, with both being each other's most commonly used adjacent collocates. "*Wu3han4fei4yan2*" and "*Xin1guan4fei4yan2*" are primarily collocated with "*yi4qing2.*" In addition to "*yi4qing2,*" they can also be collocated with "*yi4miao2*" and "*2019guan4zhuang4bing4du2ji2bing4.*" "Xin1xing2guan4zhuang4bing4du2" is collocated with "fei4yan2," "yi4miao2," and

Table 2. First distance collocations from the 46th week to the 53rd week

	46th	47th	48th	49th	50th	51st	52nd	53rd
COVID-19	2019guan4zhung4bi ng4du2ji2bing4	2019guan4zhuang4b ing4du2ji2bing4	2019guan4zhuang4b ing4du2ji2bing4	2019guan4zhuang4b ing4du2ji2bing4	2019guan4zhuang4b ing4du2ji2bing4	2019guan4zhuang4b ing4du2ji2bing4	2019guan4zhuang4b ing4du2ji2bing4	2019guan4zhuang4b ing4du2ji2bing4
Wu3han4fei4yan2	yi4miao2	yi4qing2	yi4qing2	2019guan4zhuang4bi ng4du2ji2bing4	yi4miao2	yi4qing2	2019guan4zhuang4bi ng4du2ji2bing4	2019guan4zhuang4bi ng4du2ji2bing4
Xin1guan4fei4yan2	yi4qing2	yi4qing2	yi4qing2	yi4qing2	yi4qing2	yi4miao2	yi4qing2	yi4qing2
2019guan4zhuang4bing4du2ji2bing4	COVID-19	COVID-19	COVID-19	COVID-19	COVID-19	COVID-19	COVID-19	COVID-19
Xin1xing2guan4zhuang4bing4du2	fei4yan2	fei4yan2	fei4yan2	fei4yan2	yi4miao2	fei4yan2	bian4zhuo3	yi4miao2
Xin1xing2guan4zhuang4bing4du2yi4qing2	dui4kang4	bao4fa1	e4zhi3	bao4fa1		De2du2o2		
Xin1xing2guan4zhuang4bing4du2bing4	e4zhi3	ren2yin1		gan3ran3				

"bian4zhong3," indicating that the virus remains closely associated with medical-related terms. In the case of *"Xin1xing2guan4zhuang4bing4du2yi4qing2"* and *"Xin1xing2guan4zhuang4bing4du2bing4,"* the discussions mostly revolve around virus variants and measures to control the epidemic, and thus, words like *"dui4kang4,"* *"boa4fa1,"* and *"e4zhi3"* are included.

Comparing these two periods, it can be observed that during the 11th to 17th week, which was shortly after the outbreak, when the pandemic was not yet fully controlled, a significant amount of collocates were related to the epidemic and pneumonia. However, in the 46th to 53rd week, a shift occurred. The disease names that appeared at the beginning of the outbreak remained closely related to the epidemic. *"2019guan4zhuang4bing4du2ji2bing4"* and *"COVID-19"* were significantly collocated with each other regardless of the time period.

Furthermore, although the usage proportions of "*Xin1xing2guan4 zhuang4bing4du2yi4qing2*" and "*Xin1xing2guan4zhuang4bing4du2bing4*" were relatively low, it can still be observed that their adjacent collocates revolved around "*Xin1guan4fei4yan2*." Notably, the concept of "*xin1cing2*" implies virus variants or the introduction of the novel coronavirus into a region where it had not yet appeared, which explains the appearance of country names as adjacent collocates in these categories (Table 4).

Concerning the co-occurrence at the second distance, as shown in Table 3, it compiles the most frequently occurring collocates on a weekly basis. From the 11th to 17th week, the words at the second distance are still closely related to the epidemic. These collocates include "*bing4du2*," "*gan3ran3*," "*zhen3bing4*," "*bing4li4*," "*yi4qing2*," "*Xin1guan4fei4yan2*," as well as others. However, there are differences in the collocates that co-occur with the keywords. "*COVID-19*" has a high proportion of collocates with "*bing4du2*" or "*gan3ran3*." "*Wu3han4fei4yan2*" and "*Xin1guan4fei4yan2*" are often collocated with "*zhen3bing4*" and "*bing4li4*," "*2019guan4zhuang4bing4du2ji2bing4*" has the highest collocation proportion with "*yi4qing2*." "*Xin1xing2guan4zhuang4bing4du2*" co-occurs with "*yi4qing2*" and "*xiang1guan1*."

As for "*Xin1xing2guan4zhuang4bing4du2yi4qing2*," it mainly discusses international developments, so the collocates at a distance of two, apart from "*Xin1guan4fei4yan2*," such as "*kuai4su4*," "*quan2qiu2*," "*yun4song4*," "*lian2shu3*," "*Zhong1guo2*," and "*Ba1xi1*," are not directly related to "*Xin1guan4fei4yan2*." Finally, "*Xin1xing2guan4zhuang4bing4du2bing4*" has relatively fewer mentions in UDN news, with three weeks having no news related to this keyword. However, the collocates used are still mainly related to the epidemic.

From the 46th to the 53rd week, even though the epidemic had eased, another peak emerged towards the end of the year. This study summarizes the most frequent co-occurrences on a weekly basis, which differ from the 11th to the 17th week.

"*COVID-19*" is often collocated with "*lin2chuang2*," "*zhen3bing4*," "*gan3ran3*," "*quan2qiu2*," and "*bing4du2*." Among these, "*gan3ran3*" is most frequently used, indicating discussions primarily related to confirmed infections. "*Wu3han4fei4yan2*" can be collocated with epidemic-related terms, but also has a high proportion of collocation with "*yan2zhong4*," "*qi2jian1*," and "*da4xuan3*." This suggests that Taiwan was facing elections during that time, which diverted public attention.

In the case of "*Xin1guan4fei4yan2*," it is mostly collocated with terms related to vaccine development and the influx of foreigners. "*2019guan4zhuang4bing4du2ji2bing4*" and "*Xin1guan4fei4yan2*" share similar patterns, with the highest collocation proportions related to vaccines and virus variants. For "*Xin1xin2guan4zhuang4bing4du2*" the highest collocation terms are "*xiang1guan1*" and "*Ying1guo2*" reflecting discussions on virus variant spread and related epidemic control policies. UDN's news about "*Xin1xing2guan4zhuang4bing4du2yi4qing2*" and "*Xin1xing2guan4zhuang4bing4du2bing4*" is relatively limited, but it mainly focuses on epidemic development, symptoms, and epidemic control policy measures.

Comparing the 11th to the 17th week with the 46th to the 53rd week, even though the collocates at the second distance are less directly related to the keywords than those at the first distance, the core keyword "*Xin1guan4fei4yan2*" remains dominant in the overall

Table 3. Second distance collocations from the 11th week to the 17th week

	11th	12th	13th	14th	15th	16th	17th
COVID-19	bing4du2	bing4du2	bing4du2	bing4du2	gan3ran3	gan3ran3	gan3ran3
Wu3han4fei4yan2	zhen3bing4	zhen3bing4	zhen3bing4	zhen3bing4	bing4li4	bing4li4	quan2qiu2
Xin1guan4fei4yan2	zhen3bing4	zhen3bing4	zhen3bing4	zhen3bing4	zhen3bing4	zhen3bing4	gan3ran3
2019guan4zhuang4bing4du4ji2bing4	yi4qing2	yi4qing2	Xin1guan4fei4yan2	yi4qing2	yi4qing2	yi4qing2	yi4qing2
Xin1xing2guan4zhuang4huang4bing4du4du2	yi4qing2	yi4qing2	xiang1guan1	xiang1guan1	xiang1guan1	xiang1guan1	xiang1guan1
Xin1xing2guan4zhuang4bing4du4du2yi4qing2	Xin1guan4fei4yan2	quai4su4	quan2qiu2	yun4song4	Zhong1guo2	Ba1xi1	lian2shu3
Xin1xing2guan4zhuang4huang4bing4du4du2bing4		chu1xian4	yi4qing2	yi4qing2			zeng1jia1

Table 4. Second Distance Collocations from the 46th Week to the 53rd Week

	46th	47th	48th	49th	50th	51st	52nd	53rd
COVID-19	lin2chuang2	zhen3bing4	gan3ran3	quan2qiu2	gan3ran3	gan3ran3	bing4du2	gan3ran3
Wu3han4fei4yan2	yan2zhong4	yan2fa1	qi2jian1	can1kao3	zhen3bing4	da4xuan3	bian4zhong3	bing4du2
Xin1guan4fei4yan2	yan2fa1	zhen3bing4	zhen3bing4	yi2ru4	zhen3bing4	bing4li4	bing4li4	bing4du2
2019guan4zhuang4bing4du2ji2bing4	yi4qing2	yi4qing2	yi4qing2	yi4miao2	yi4miao2	yi4miao2	bian4zhong3	yi4miao2
Xin1xing2guan4zhuang4bing4du4du2	xiang1guan1	xiang1guan1	xiang1guan1	xiang1guan1	xiang1guan1	xiang1guan1	Ying1guo2	xiang1guan1
Xin1xing2guan4zhuang4bing4du4du2yi4qing2	zhong4du4	bao4fa1		quan2qiu2		cuo4shi1		
Xin1xing2guan4zhuang4bing4du4du2bing4	Ji1zeng1		zheng4zhuang4	que4ren4				ji1zeng1

use of collocate terms. However, during the 46th to the 53rd week, news unrelated to the epidemic, such as elections, appeared. This suggests that the epidemic's impact on daily life, while still present, became weaker as the association of collocates related to the epidemic became more distant.

Lastly, regarding collocate terms at the third distance, Table 5 provides a weekly breakdown of the most frequently used collocate terms from the 11th to the 17th week. It can be observed that collocates at the third distance tend to discuss changes in the number of cases.

For *"COVID-19,"* the most significant co-occurrence is with *"guan4zhuang4,"* followed by *"xiang1guan1," "Wu3han4fei4yan2"* frequently appears in collocation with *"xin1zeng1," "quan2qiu2," "COVID-19,"* and *"cheng2yuan2."* Collocates of *"Xin1guan4fei4yan2"* include *"quan2qiu2"* and *"xin1zeng1." "2019guan4zhuang4bing4du2ji2bing4"* has a high proportion of co-occurrence with *"su2cheng1"* and *"xin1zeng1." "Xin1xin2guan4zhuang4bing4du2"* can be collocated with *"yi4qing2"* and *"xin1zeng1." "Xin1xing2guan4zhuang4bing4du2yi4qing2"* shows a high proportion of co-occurrence with *""jian3ce4," "kuo4san4," "zhuan1ji1," "bao4fa1," "gong1gong4wei4sheng1"* and *"sheng1ming2."* These terms discuss immigration and emigration-related arrangements, policies, and measures.

Lastly, *"Xin1xing2guan4zhuang4bing4du2bing4"* has fewer news articles, but it can still be deduced, from the terms *"bing4li4," "chi2xu4," "zeng1duo1,"* that the content is related to the cumulative number of cases.

In Table 6, the condition of the 46th to the 53rd week is similar to the condition of the 11th to the 17th week, focusing on the worsening trend of the epidemic, which results in an increase in the cumulative confirmed cases.

The most common collocate terms each week for *"COVID-19"* include *"yan2fa1," "shi4yan4," "Ri4ben3," "guo2jia1," "Ying1guo2,"* and *"bing4du2."* For *"Wu3han4fei4yan2,"* the common collocates are *"ying4dui4," "bing4li4shu4," "zhong1 guo2," "yin1ying4," "zong3tong3," "zhu1wen1,"* and *"bing4du2." "Xin1guan4fei4yan2"* and *"2019guan4zhuang4bing4du2ji2bing4"* mainly collocate with *"xin1 zeng1." "Xin1xin2guan4zhuang4bing4du2"* is primarily associated with *"lei3ji4."* Regarding *"Xin1xing2guan4zhuang4bing4du2yi4qing2"* and *"Xin1xing2guan4 zhuang4bing4du2bing4,"* they appear less frequently in UDN news, so there are several weeks without relevant news data. In these cases, collocates at the third distance show a weaker relationship with the number of cases, with terms such as *"sheng4li4," "da3suan4,"* and *"Ying1guo2"* having no direct relation to the epidemic. Nevertheless, related terms such as *"tong1bao4"* and *"quan2yu4"* still occur.

Comparing the co-occurrence patterns between the 11th week to the 17th week and the 46th week to the 53rd week, both periods show a high proportion of collocates with *"xin1zeng1."* Concerning the number of confirmed cases, this is due to the spread of variant viruses and increased population mobility towards the end of the year, leading to a substantial increase in cases. Terms like *"bing4li4shu4," "lei3ji4," "kuo4san4,"* and *"bao4fa1"* frequently appear in the news content during these periods. It is worth noting that there was more reporting related to the epidemic during the 11th week to the 17th week than the 46th week to the 53rd week. Towards the end of the year, data indicates that Taiwan experienced African swine flu and Russia's military aircraft exercises, among

Table 5. Third Distance Collocations from the 11th week to the 17th week

	11th	12th	13th	14th	15th	16th	17th
COVID-19	guan4zhuang4	guan4zhuang4	guan4zhuang4	guan4zhuang4	guan4zhuang4	guan4zhuang4	ge4an4
Wu3han4fei4yan2	xin1zeng1	quan2qiu2	COVID-19	xin1zeng1	xin1zeng1	quan2qiu2	cheng2yuan2
Xin1guan4fei4yan2	quan2qiu2	xin1zeng1	xin1zeng1	xin1zeng1	xin1zeng1	xin1zeng1	xin1zeng1
2019guan4zhuang4bing4du2ji2bing4	Su2cheng1	xin1zeng1	xin1zeng1	xin1zeng1	xin1zeng1	xin1zeng1	xin1zeng1
Xin1xing2guan4zhuang4bing4du2ji2bing4	yi4qing2	xin1zeng1	xin1zeng1	xin1zeng1	xin1zeng1	xin1zeng1	xin1zeng1
Xin1xing2guan4zhuang4bing4du2yi4qing2	Jian3ce4	kuo4san4		zhuan1ji1	bao4fa1	gong1gong4wei4sheng1	sheng1ming2
Xin1xing2guan4zhuang4bing4du2bing4		bing4li4	chi2xu4	zeng1duo1			

Table 6. Third distance collocations from the 46th week *to* the 53rd week

COVID-19	46th	47th	48th	49th	50th	51st	52nd	53rd
Wu3han4fei4yan2	yan2fa1	shi4yan4	Ri4ben3	guo2jia1	yan2fa1	yan2fa1	Yin1guo2	bing4du2
Xin1guan4fei4yan2	Ying4dui4	Yi4qing2	bing4li4shu4	Chong1guo2	yin1ying4	zong3tong3	bing4du2	Zhu1wen1
2019guan4zhuang4bing4du2ji2bing4	xin1zeng1	xin1zeng1	xin1zeng1	xin1zeng1	xin1zeng1	xin1zeng1	xin1zeng1	xin1zeng1
Xin1xing2guan4zhuang4huang4bing4du2	xin1zeng1	xin1zeng1	xin1zeng1	xin1zeng1	xin1zeng1	xin1zeng1	xin1zeng1	xin1zeng1
Xin1xing2guan4zhuang4huang4bing4du2yi4qing2	lei3ji4	lei3ji4	lei3ji4	lei3ji4	lei3ji4	lei3ji4	chu1xian4	lei3ji4
Xin1xing2guan4zhuang4huang4bing4du2bing4	sheng4li4	quan2yu4	bu2da4	Yin1guo2		xian4zhi4		
	da3suan4	tong1bao4	chu1xian4	shi3de2	xin1zeng1			

other news items. This indicates that the international communities' attitude towards the epidemic was not as focused as at the beginning of the year, and attention started to shift towards international affairs.

5.3 Comprehensive Analysis of Collocations

Overall, there are certain weeks in which "*Xin1xing2guan4zhuang4bing4du2yi4qing2*" and "*Xin1xing2guan4zhuang4bing4du2bing4*" have no collocates in UDN online news. This phenomenon aligns with the trends in Fig. 2 and Fig. 3, where the usage frequency of both keywords is low, resulting in some weeks without news articles related to the keywords.

The collocates at different phases of the pandemic show different patterns during the two peak periods. From the 11th week to the 17th week, the focus was primarily on the epidemic, with content related to topics such as epidemic development, epidemic prevention policies, vaccine development, and confirmed symptoms. In contrast, from the 46th week to the 53rd week, in addition to the epidemic, there were more news articles about the recording of confirmed cases, vaccine administration, variant viruses, and even news unrelated to the epidemic. This phenomenon is particularly evident in the results of collocates at the third distance.

The diversity of collocates reflects various, simultaneous events. To better understand social development, the following chart categorizes collocates at different distances based on their parts of speech and categories.

Regarding the collocates with the highest frequency at different distances in UDN news network data, several observations can be made, as shown in Table 7. First, collocates at the first distance are related to epidemic and epidemic prevention. Only the neutral verb "*chu1xian4*" stands out. Furthermore, the keywords "*2019guan4zhuang4bing4du2ji2bing4*" and "*COVID-19*" frequently appear as collocates, and are often used together.

Second, at the second distance, the phenomenon of "*2019guan4zhuang4bing4du2ji2bing4*" and "*COVID-19*" being collocates continues; however, "*Xin1guan4fei4yan2*" also appears. The collocates at this distance show that epidemic-related content has expanded to different aspects, including "*bing4li4*" and "*zheng4zhuang4*" related to patients, conditions such as "*kuai4su4*" and "*yan2zhong4*" related to epidemic changes, and details related to vaccine trials, such as "*lin2chuang2*" There are also policies related to entry and exit, such as "*yi2ru4*."

Lastly, at the third distance, only "*COVID-19*" remains as a collocate. Discussions about the epidemic mainly focus on the condition of cases. There are different words used for "*bing4li4*," "*ge4an4*," and "*bing4li4shu4*." Additionally, more detailed information, such as testing vaccine results, the number of "*cheng2yuan2*" in cluster infections, and government "*ying4dui4*" measures, is included. However, unrelated to epidemic-related content, there are additional events, such as "*zhuan1ji1*," "*zhu1wen1*," and "*sheng4li4*."

The disease categories used as collocates also change at different distances. At the first two distances, the WHO-named diseases "*2019guan4zhuang4bing4du2ji2bing4*" and "*COVID-19*" are present, with the addition of "*Xin1guan4fei4yan2*" at distance two. At the third distance, the disease categories are reduced to "*COVID-19*" and the virus

Table 7. Classification of the Most Frequent Collocation Words

	part of speech	category	collocation
first distance	noun	disease	*2019guan4zhuang4bing4du2ji2bing4*, COVID-19, *ji2bing4, fei4yan2*
		time	*qi2jian1*
		spot	*Ma3lai2xi1ya4, Xiang1gang3, De2guo2*
		prevention	*yi4miao2, bian4zhong3, ren2yin1*
	verb	prevention	*gan3ran3, yin1ying4, kuo4san4, dui4kang4, jin4zhi3, bao4fa1, e4zhi3, pu4lu4chu1*
		neutral	*chu1xian4*
second distance	noun	disease	*2019guan4zhuang4bing4du2ji2bing4*, COVID-19, *xin1guan4fei4yan2*
		spot	*Zhong1guo2, Ba1xi1*
		prevention	*bing4du2, yi4qing2, yi4miao2, bian4zhong3*
		case	*bing4li4*
		patient	*zheng4zhuang4*
		others	*quan2qiu2, xiang1guan1*
	verb	prevention	*gan3ran3, zhen3bing4, yun4song4, zeng1jia1, lin2chuang2, yan2fa1, yi2ru4*
		state	*kui4su4, yan2zhong4, zhong4da4, ji1zeng1*
		neutral	*lian2shu3, chu1xian4, xiang1guan1*
third distance	noun	disease	*guan4zhuang4*, COVID-19, *ji2bing4*
		figure	*cheng2yuan2, guan1yuan2*
		spot	*Ri4ben3, guo2jia1, Zhong1guo2, Ying1guo2*
		case	*ge4an4, bing4li4, bing4li4shu4*
		disease	*yi4qing2, bing4du2*
		others	*quan2qiu2, zhuan1ji1, gong1gong4wei4sheng1, sheng1ming2, zhu1wen1*
	verb	prevention	*xin1zeng1, jian3ce4, kuo4san4, bao4fa1, chi2xu4, zeng1duo1, yan2fa1,shi4yan4, ying4dui4, yin1ying4, lei3ji4, xian4zhi4*
		patient	*quan2yu4, tong1bao4*
		neutral	*su2cheng1, chu1xian4, sheng4li4, bu2dao4, da3suan4, shi3de2*

feature "*guan4zhuang4*," highlighting a weakened association between disease-related collocates at this distance.

In summary, UDN online news data demonstrates that Taiwan's attention to the epidemic decreased as the epidemic became less severe over time; however, it still maintained a high level of attention. Therefore, collocates at the first distance are predominantly related to the epidemic and exhibit a strong association with it. As the distance increases, the diversity of words increases, which reveals different aspects of the situation under the epidemic and provides insights into various epidemic-related content.

6   Conclusion

This study primarily focuses on UDN news data from Taiwan in 2020, collecting news related to the epidemic, and taking "*Wu3han4fei4yan2*," "*Xin1xing2guan4zhuang4bing4du2*," "*Xin1guan4fei4yan2*," "*Xin1xing2guan4zhuang4bing4du2yi4qing2*," "*COVID-19*," "*2019guan4zhuang 4bing4du2ji2bing4*," and "*Xin1xing2guan4zhuang4bing4du2bing4*" as keywords. The research aims to understand the impact of epidemic development on society and language through the co-occurrence of these keywords over time.

January to March 2020 was the main period of the global outbreak of "*Xin1guan4fei4yan2*." People were highly concerned about the development of the disease and sought to gain an understanding of "*Xin1guan4fei4yan2*." Notably, the key period from the 11th week to the 17th week saw a large number of news reports on the epidemic and epidemic prevention policies. This resulted in the frequent use of related words, such as "*yi4miao2*," policies responding to the epidemic, and restrictions on the "*yi2ru4*" of foreigners. From April, news data showed a decreasing trend as vaccines became available, and it remained nearly zero until August.

After September, there was a resurgence that coincided with an increase in confirmed cases, the emergence of new variants, and events like the reopening of schools, which marked the second peak. It indicates the close relationship between "*Xin1guan4fei4yan2*" and society. It's worth noting that although there was a second peak at the end of the year, it was not as high as the first peak. After nearly a year, people had started to coexist with "*Xin1guan4fei4yan2*," leading to a decreased level of anxiety compared to the 11th to 17th weeks.

In terms of co-occurrence, the closer the distance between collocates and keywords, the higher the association with the epidemic, with content primarily focusing on epidemic development or epidemic prevention policies. If collocates at a greater distance from core keywords are related to the epidemic, then more detailed content is observed. This includes the clinical trial results of vaccines, symptoms, treatments for patients, the challenges to society under the epidemic, events that occurred, and people's attitudes and actions.

Through the analysis of news data, it is evident that the volume of news data and the frequency of core keywords reflect the level of attention that was being paid to the epidemic. People's attitudes and behaviors reflect their response to the epidemic, while the co-occurrence of words portrays a diverse social landscape. The co-occurrence of collocates and keywords, from close to more distant associations, reflects a shift from broad themes to specific details and from a singular focus to the use of diverse words. This confirms the phenomenon of mutual influence and constraint between language change and social change.

Acknowledgements. This study is supported by the National Science and Technology Council, Taiwan, R.O.C., under Grant no. MOST 110-2511-H-003 -034 -MY3. It is also supported by National Taiwan Normal University's Chinese Language and Technology Center. The center is funded by Taiwan's Ministry of Education (MOE), as part of the Featured Areas Research Center Program, under the Higher Education Sprout Project.

References

1. Baker, P.: A Corpus-Based Study on the Semantic Prosody of Challenge. Taiwan Journal of TESOL **13**(2), 99–146 (2006)
2. Hong, J.F.: Chinese Conjunctions in Second Language Learners' Written Texts, vol. 10709. LNCS (LNAI), pp. 510–522. Springer, Cham (2018). https://doi.org/10.1007/978-3-319-73573-3_46
3. Kilgarriff, A., Grefenstette, G.: Introduction to the special issue on the web as corpus. Comput. Linguist. **29**(3), 333–347 (2003)
4. Evert, S., Marco, B.: Testing the extrapolation quality of word frequency models. Corpus Linguistics (2005)
5. Jones, R., Ghani, R.: Automatically Building a Corpus for a Minority Language from the Web (2000)
6. Hsieh, S.K.: Evaluating Chinese web-as-corpus: some methodological considerations. J. Chin. Lingu. Monograph Ser., 16–29 (2015)
7. Wang, C.C., Chen, H.J., Pan, I.T.: The application of web business corpus: a case study on collocation. J. Chin. Lang. Teach. **12**(2), 75–102 (2015). (in Chinese)
8. Chen, L.C., Chang, J.H., Chen, J.H.: the correlation of knowledge management issues based on co-occurrence analysis of keywords-using the co-word and association rule analysis. J. Inf. Manag. **17**(4), 31–60 (2010). (in Chinese)
9. Hong, J.F., Huang, C.R.: Cross-strait lexical differences: a comparative study based on chinese gigaword corpus. Comput. Linguist. Chin. Lang. Process. **18**(2), 19–34 (2013). (in Chinese)
10. Hong, J.F.: The Chinese Near Synonym Study based on Chinese Gigaword Corpus and Chinese Learner Corpus, vol. 8922 LNCS (LNAI), pp. 329–340. Springer-Verlag Berlin Heidelberg (2014). https://doi.org/10.1007/978-3-319-14331-6_33
11. Lin, Y.T., Chen, H.J., Wang, C.C.: A learner corpus-based study on chinese directional complement "*qilai.*" J. Chin. Lang. Teach. **11**(4), 73–109 (2014). (in Chinese)

Chinese Inter-clausal Anaphora in Causal Relation—A Corpus Study

Shunting Chen[(✉)] [iD]

Shanghai International Studies University, Shanghai 201600, China
02351@shisu.edu.cn

Abstract. This research focusing on Chinese inter-clausal subject-subject anaphora in causal relation utilizes a self-constructed corpus to test the validity of five hypotheses proposed in Chen [1]. Results demonstrate support for hypothesis 1, declaring that pronoun and zero coreference and NP and zero coreference are more common than NP and pronoun coreference and hypothesis 3 proposing that NP and zero are more common than pronoun and zero in Subject-Conjunction structure. However, hypothesis 2, which states that pronoun and zero coreference are more common than NP and zero coreference in Conjunction-Subject structure, alongside hypothesis 4, which posits that pronoun and zero would be more in Conjunction-Subject structure than in Subject-Conjunction structure and hypothesis 5, which theorizes that NP and zero would be more in Subject-Conjunction structure than in Conjunction-Subject Structure, currently lack unambiguous substantiation. For instance, *zhisuoyi* and *ji* mainly use fronted structure, while *yinwei* and *youyu* favor unfronted structure.

Keywords: Inter-clausal anaphora · Causal · Corpus Study

1 Introduction

Previous research has extensively examined inter-clausal anaphora across variations in sentence structures and their relation to anaphoric behaviors [1–7]. Specific focus has centered on subordinators such as conditionals. While causal relations have long attracted interest, inter-clausal anaphoric patterns remain unclear due to data limitations. Drawing on topical structure analysis, Huang [8] posited coreference in causal bi-clausal sentences stems primarily from robust semantic ties. However, experiments by [9, 10] targeted subject-object anaphora in causals, excluding subject-subject anaphora. Leveraging a corpus-based approach, the present study tests five original hypotheses from Chen [1] on subject-subject anaphora in causal bi-clausal sentences, elucidating ongoing disputes. The five hypotheses examine if, all else equal, 1) pronoun and zero coreference and NP and zero coreference are more common than NP and pronoun coreference in both Conjunction-Subject structure and Subject-Conjunction structure; 2) pronoun and zero coreference are more common than NP and zero coreference in Conjunction-Subject structure; 3) NP and zero are more common than pronoun and zero

M. Dong et al. (Eds.): CLSW 2023, LNAI 14515, pp. 234–242, 2024.
https://doi.org/10.1007/978-981-97-0586-3_19

in Subject-Conjunction structure; 4) pronoun and zero would be more in Conjunction-Subject structure than in Subject-Conjunction structure; 5) NP and zero would be more in Subject-Conjunction structure than in Conjunction-Subject Structure. Five causal subordinators were selected from Huang and Liao [11]: *yinwei*因为, *youyu*由于, *zhisuoyi* 之所以, *ji*既 and *jiran*既然. This study specifically investigates whether the hypotheses manifest among these causal subordinators.

2 Related Work

In foundational work, Chao [2] first noted a "striking" phenomenon in Chinese bi-clausal sentences utilizing pronoun examples: both "因为你刚吃瓜子, 所以不吃花生 。" and "你因为刚吃瓜子, 所以不吃花生。" meaning 'Since you just ate melon seeds, you don't eat peanuts.' prove possible, yet the second pattern with a pre-subordinator pronoun exhibits higher coreference frequency. Conducting syntactic analysis, Huang [12] characterized this as pro-drop, whereby sentences like (1d) become ungrammatical since the initial subject cannot syntactically control (weakly c-command) the secondary subject:

(1) a. Zhangsan$_i$ suiran meiyou kong,   e$_i$ haishi lai-le.
        though   no   time   still   come-ASP
        'Though Zhangsan$_i$ had no time, [he]$_i$ came nevertheless.'
    b. e$_i$ suiran meiyou kong, Zhangsan$_i$ haishi lai-le.
        though   no   time   still   come-ASP
        'Though [he]$_i$had no time, Zhangsan$_i$ came nevertheless.'
    c. suiran Zhangsan$_i$ meiyou kong, ta$_i$ haishi lai-le.
        though   no   time   still come-ASP
        'Though Zhangsan$_i$ had no time, he$_i$ came nevertheless.'
    d. *suiran Zhangsan$_i$ meiyou kong,   e$_i$ haishi lai-le.
        though   no   time   still   come-ASP
        'Though Zhangsan$_i$ had no time, he$_i$ came nevertheless.'
                                ([12]: 372-374)

Among his examples, NP-zero coreference emerged in (1a), zero-NP coreference in (1b), NP-pronoun coreference in (1c), and an ungrammatical yet extant NP-zero referential pattern in (1d) diverging structurally from (1a), as Zhangsan cannot control the second subject while qualifying as one. Further scrutinizing referentials via corpus methods, Xu [3] determined 1) all patterns manifest including (1d); and 2) despite variability across subordinators, (1a) proves more frequent than (1c). He excluded contextual (1b) requiring textual analysis. Xu designated Zhangsan pre-subordinator as topical [13], generating the coreference per "topic-raising" [13]. Xu also incorporated initial pronoun-subject clauses, providing partial coverage of Chao's [2] intent. Contrastively in pragmatics, Y. Huang [8] argued (2a) and (2b) should demonstrate complementary distribution. However, fronted causals exhibit both due to sturdy semantic ties, especially unanticipated (2b):

(2) a.   Lao Li yinwei   bing le, suoyi   Ø buneng   lai
           Lao Li because   ill CRS   so   not can   come
           'Because Li$_1$ is ill, (he$_1$) cannot come.'

    b.   Lao Li yinwei   bing le, suoyi   ta   buneng lai
           Lao Li because   ill CRS so   3SG   not can come
           'Because Li$_1$ is ill, he$_1$ cannot come.'

                                                    ([8]:323)

While his NP-pronoun and NP-zero examples solely employed fronted structures, limiting understandings of the causal relation's coreference impact, this study leverages corpus methods to contrast three referential patterns across two structures, examining if Huang's [8] claims manifest for non-topical structures while revealing the literature's hypothesized coreferential frequencies. It scrutinizes NP-pronoun, NP-zero, and pronoun-zero coreference when dual subjects surface, per Chen [1], distinguishing when the subordinator precedes versus follows subject-topics.

3 Data Collection

We selected sentences containing these causal subordinators: Sentences were extracted containing the causal subordinators *yinwei*因为, *youyu*由于, *zhisuoyi*之所以, *ji*既 and *jiran*既然, while the accompanying secondary subordinator proved non-compulsory. In fact, most corpus sentences lacked the secondary subordinator. Referential frequencies were subsequently calculated across labeled sentences.

3.1 Corpus Construction

The Center for Chinese Linguistics (CCL) corpus was first queried for each individual subordinator, downloading all occurrences as.txt files. When total sentences exceeded 2,000, the selection randomly sampled 1,000 newspaper and 1,000 literature genre sentences. Otherwise, exhaustive inclusion was conducted.

Among the resultant sentences, annotation only proceeded for those meeting the following criteria:

a) Two clauses present with an independent subject at minimum in clause 1
b) The causal subordinator-initiated clause precedes the matrix clause
c) The causal clause subject accepts nominal types of names, pronouns or noun phrases
d) The second clause contains either an overt subject or null subject
e) Clause 1 can constitute a topical structure while clause 2 offers a comment
f) No additional embedded subordinate clauses surface beyond the causal subordinator.

3.2 Annotation

Annotation followed Xu [3], with coreference marked C and disjoint reference marked D. Fronted subject/topic structures were labeled A, while subordinator-front structures were labeled B. An additional T was incorporated for clausal topics. While several nominal types required differentiation, current annotation prioritized names/nouns, personal pronouns, other pronouns, zero pronouns and wh-words per Table 1 [5].

Table 1. Annotation System

Type of Nouns	Code	Structure and Reference Pattern	Code
Names and nouns	N	CONJ NP1	A
Personal Pronouns	Y	NP1 CONJ	B
Other Pronouns	O	Conjoint Reference	C
Zero Pronoun	Z	Disjoint Reference	D
Wh-words	W	Clausal Topic	T
Coding Patterns	CA/DA/CB/DB(J)(NP1 NP2)(T)		

4 Five Hypotheses

Chen [1] theorizes five predominant bi-clausal coreferential tendencies, inventoried herein using causal sentences via corpus validation. Each hypothesis receives articulation and subsequent evidentiary examination. These proposals centrally scaffold upon two key concepts: topicality and accessibility. Regarding the former, [3] delineates the noun phrase preceding a bi-clausal subordinator as topical, holding primacy over the label of subject, while retaining control over the secondary clausal subject to induce coreference.

Meanwhile, accessibility argues that heightened antecedent salience enables deployment of lesser accessibility markers [15, 16]. Through systematically testing predictions against language data, this investigation clarifies uncertainties around hypothesized patterns.

4.1 Comparisons Within Structures

Hypothesis 1: Other things being equal, NP[1]-zero[2] and pronoun[3]-zero coreference are more common than NP-pronoun coreference in both structure A and structure B.

Table 2 evidence supports hypothesis 1, demonstrating pronoun reference of NP occurs far less than NP or pronoun subjects referred to by zero. Scarcity manifests in structure A for this referential pattern. Please note this calculation basis excludes alternative referential patterns.

All genres in Table 3 indicate corroborative tendencies whereby pronoun-zero combined with NP-zero coreference outstrips pronoun-NP. Newspaper and literature structure A displays the nadir of this phenomenon. In bi-clausals, the heightened accessibility of an antecedent entails that zeros are more frequently employed as lower-accessibility markers, which supports [15, 16].

Hypothesis 2: Pronoun and zero coreference are more common than NP and zero coreference in structure A.

---

[1] NP in this study indexes names and other nominal phrase.

[2] Zero in this study encompasses zero pronouns in the second-clausal subject.

[3] Pronoun in this study subsumes personal pronouns and other pronouns.

Table 2. 3 patterns in Causal: frequency in total occurrences

Name of coreference pattern	Structure A	Structure B
NP and pronoun	32 7.4%	120 16%
Pronoun and zero	215 50.2%	293 39.1%
NP and zero	181 42.3%	336 44.9%

Table 3. 3 patterns in Causal: frequency in different genres

Genre	NEWSPAPER		LITERATURE	
Name of coreference pattern	Structure A	Structure B	Structure A	Structure B
NP and pronoun	23 9.1%	85 14.8%	9 5%	35 20.1%
Pronoun and zero	161 63.6%	257 44.7%	54 30.9%	36 20.7%
NP and zero	69 27.3%	233 40.5%	112 64%	103 59.2%

Table 4. Antecedent of zero anaphor in A

Relation	Subor.	Str. Pat.	Pronoun	NP	Subor.	Str. Pat.	Pronoun	NP
CAUSAL	Yinwei	CA	111 55%	92 45%	Youyu	CA	33 23.4%	108 76.6%
	Zhisuoyi	CA	1 100%	0 0%	Ji	CA	0	0
	Jiran	CA	12 23.5%	39 76.5%				

Hypothesis 2 postulates pronouns in the antecedent role of zeros would outweigh NP antecedents. However, only *yinwei* aligns, per Table 4. Exempting *zhisuoyi* for lack of adoption, *youyu* contravenes predictions via predominant NP references over pronouns. Meanwhile, *jiran* exhibits threefold NP rather than pronoun usage. Additionally, *ji* yields no unfronted coreferential structures.

(1) [由于]人们经过白天敌人围攻微山的炮火, 对这些已感觉不到什么了。

youyu people experience day enemy circle weishan DE cannon fire for these already feel no DAO what LE-ASP

Since people have experienced the threat from enemy's cannon to Weishan in the day, these threats make no sense to them now.

(2) [由于]阿富汗气象局的预报设备均毁于战乱,所以目前不能提供天气预报。

youyu Afganistan weather bureau DE predict equipment all destroy by war chaos suoyi now no able provide weather forcast
Since the prediction devices of Afganistan weather bureau were all destroyed in the war, it cannot provide weather forcast right now.

Not favoring unfronted structure pronoun antecedents, *youyu* Newspaper counter-examples (3)-(4) surface, though *youyu* Literature only furnishes 40 of 108 NP cases. It is plausible newspapers necessitate NPs for reference in previous context when making formal statements. Moreover, this structure predominates bi-clausal coreference rather than fronted counterparts, explaining observed data variance.

(3) [既然]你哥这么坏, 怎么还会有这么多爪牙?

jiran you brother this bad why still will have this many claw teeth
Since your brother is so bad, why does he have so many helpers?

(4) [既然]北京是政治中心, 主要任务是服务, 就不必以经济建设为中心了。

jiran Beijing is politics center main task is service so no must use economy construction as center LE-ASP
Since Beijing is the political center, its main task is serving people, making it unnecessary to focus on economic development.

(5)-(6) exemplify *jiran*'s NP-zero co-reference pattern from clause 1 to 2. Isolating genres uncovers data concentration in Newspaper, potentially reflecting its formal NP antecedents partiality.

Hypothesis 3: NP and zero are more common than pronoun and zero in structure B (Table 5).

Table 5. Antecedent of zero anaphor in B

Relation	Subor.	Str. Pat.	Pronoun	NP	Subor.	Str. Pat.	Pronoun	NP
CAUSAL	Yinwei	CB	17 29%	42 71%	Youyu	CB	7 11%	57 89%
	Zhisuoyi	CB	77 38%	125 62%	Ji	CB	55 25%	166 75%
	Jiran	CB	27 33%	56 67%				

All 5 subordinators support hypothesis 3, aligning with [3]'s topicality concept, as NP antecedents of zeros are less prevalent than pronouns, per *youyu* (7:57), *yinwei* (17:42) and especially *ji* (55:166). Furthermore, *ji* often refers the second subject to the entire first clause, e.g.:

(5) 你[既]不肯说自己姓名,那也罢了。

you ji no will say self name na also BA-LE-ASP
Since you are unwilling to reveal your name, there will be no more enforcement.

4.2 Comparisons Between Structures

Hypothesis 4: Pronoun and zero are more frequently observed in structure A than in structure B (Table 6).

Table 6. Pronoun antecedent of zero anaphor in A and B

Relation	Subor.	Pronoun in CA	Pronoun in CB	Subor.	Pronoun in CA	Pronoun in CB
CAUSAL	Yinwei	111 87%	17 13%	Youyu	33 82.5%	7 17.5%
	Zhisuoyi	1 1.3%	77 98.7%	Ji	0 0%	55 100%
	Jiran	12 30.7%	27 69.2%			

Despite *zhisuoyi* and *ji*'s heavy reliance on fronted subjects, pronoun deployment in structure A exceeds structure B for coreferring in *yinwei* and *youyu*, upholding hypothesis 4. The explanation proffers *zhisuoyi* and *ji* constitute verb-like subordinators mandating succeeding NPs/pronouns - hence structure B predominance. Meanwhile, *jiran*'s structure B pronoun antecedents partiality could be influenced by authorial style factors, which does not contravene hypothesis 4.

Hypothesis 5: NP and zero are more frequently observed in structure B than in structure A (Table 7).

Table 7. NP antecedent of zero anaphor in A and B

Relation	Subor	NP in A	NP in B	Subor	NP in A	NP in B
CAUSAL	Yinwei	92 69%	42 31%	Youyu	108 65%	57 35%
	Zhisuoyi	0 0%	125 100%	Ji	0 0%	166 100%
	Jiran	39 41%	56 59%			

Zhisuoyi and *ji* strongly favor structure B, while *jiran* distributes as predicted, supporting hypothesis 5. However, influential causals *yinwei* and *youyu* elect more NP-zero referential patterns within structure A, indicating that for certain relations, semantic strength trumps structural/topicality effects. Partial affirmation of [8] stems from exclusive concentration on (topic) structure B examples. Current structural comparisons in co-reference showcase structure A's dominance engendered by robust semantic ties, customarily signaling disjoint reference, even over structure B in NP-zero patterns.

5   Conclusion

In summary, robust causal relation subordinators including *yinwei* and *youyu*, drawing upon structure A over B, largely reinforce the hypotheses. Meanwhile, verb-like *zhisuoyi* and *ji* principally adopt fronted, topical structure B. Subordinator *jiran* is frequently associated with journalistic genres and upholds certain hypotheses. Specifically, hypotheses 1 and 3 attain full corroboration, while validity of 2 and 4 remains exclusive to *yinwei*. Currently, homogenously categorizing causal subordinators poses difficulties. Further investigation must determine if and how these entities exhibit differential behavior.

Collectively, while topicality and accessibility influence bi-clausal coreference, the strength of inter-clausal causal semantic ties, alongside particular subordinators' verbal traits, modulate resultant referential patterns. These revelations refine understanding of contributing factors, constructing a framework for forthcoming psycholinguistic experiments and multi-factorial research. The present corpus analysis pioneers future pathways to explicate nuanced inner workings of coreference within the causal relation domain.

Acknowledgements. I extend my sincere thanks to Wang Yixin and reviewers for their advice. This work is supported by the Chinese Ministry of Education Youth Fund for Social Sciences (22YJC740009) and the Chinese National Major Social Science Project (17ZDA027).

References

1. Chen, S.T.: A Corpus Study of Anaphora in Chinese Conditionals. In Dong, M., Gu, Y., Hong, J.F. (eds.) Chinese Lexical Semantics. CLSW 2021. LNCS (LNAI), vol 13250, pp. 365–375. Springer, Cham (2022). https://doi.org/10.1007/978-3-031-06547-7_28
2. Chao, Y.R.: A Grammar of Spoken Chinese. UC Press, Berkeley (1968)
3. Xu, Y.L.: Resolving third-person anaphora in Chinese texts: Towards a functional-pragmatic model. Doctoral Dissertation, The Hong Kong Polytechnic University (1995)
4. Xu, Y.L.: Inter-clausal anaphora in Chinese complex sentences. Contemporary Linguistics **2**, 97–107 (2003)
5. Chen, S.T.: Inter-clausal Anaphora in Chinese: The Case of Conditionals. Doctoral Dissertation, Shanghai International Studies University (2012)
6. Chen, S.T.: Re-approaching Chinese inter-clausal anaphora: the case of conditional sentences. Foreign Stud. **6**, 15–21 (2016)
7. Chen, S.T., Amsili, P., Liang Y.M.: Inter-clausal anaphora in Chinese conditionals: a Multi-factorial analysis. In: Proceedings of the 35th Pacific Asia Conference on Language, Information and Computation (PACLIC 35 (2021)), pp. 140–148 (2021)
8. Huang, Y.: A neo-Gricean pragmatic theory of anaphora. J. Linguist. **27**(2), 301–335 (1991)

9. Xu, X.D., Ni, C.B., Chen, L.J.: The influence of topic structure and verb-based implicit causality on pronoun resolution in Mandarin Chinese: evidence from sentence production and comprehension. Mod. Foreign Lang. **4**, 331–339 (2013)

10. Xu, X.D., Chen, L.J., Ni, C.B.: How is pronoun resolution modulated by topic structures and verb-based implicit causality in Mandarin Chinese? An ERP investigation. Foreign Language Teaching and Research **5**, 323–334 (2017)

11. Huang, B.R., Liao, X.D.: Modern Chinese, vol. II, 3rd edn. High Education Press, Beijing (2002)

12. Huang,C.T.J.: Logical relations in Chinese and the theory of grammar. Doctoral Dissertation, MIT (1982)

13. Tsao, F.F.: Sentence and Clause Structure in Chinese: A Functional Perspective. Student Book Co., Taipei (1990)

14. Center for Chinese Linguistics Corpus online. http://ccl.pku.edu.cn:8080/ccl_corpus/, (Accessed 1 Mar 2011)

15. Ariel, M.: Referring and accessibility. Journal of Linguistics **24**(1), 65–87 (1988)

16. Ariel, M.: Accessing Noun-phrase Antecedents. Routledge, London (1990)

Corpus-Based Study on the Evolution of the Lexical Phonetic Forms from Old Chinese to Middle Chinese

Bing Qiu[✉]

Department of Chinese Language and Literature, Tsinghua University, Beijing 100083, China
qiubing@mail.tsinghua.edu.cn

Abstract. The evolution of lexical syllable forms from Old Chinese to Middle Chinese is an issue of great significance in the study of Chinese lexis. This paper, based on corpus linguistics methodology, selects credible and representative texts from both Old Chinese and Middle Chinese and conducts a quantitative study from multiple perspectives. In terms of word types, polysyllabic words remained the majority in both Old Chinese and Middle Chinese, and those with three or more syllables accounted for an increased proportion in Middle Chinese. In terms of word tokens, the average frequency and total occurrences of monosyllabic words were far higher than that of polysyllabic words, indicating that monosyllabic words occupied a primary position in language use. In terms of high-frequency words, monosyllabic words predominated from Old Chinese to Middle Chinese, but within a certain range of frequency, Middle Chinese translated Buddhist scriptures featured a significantly higher proportion of polysyllabic words than Old Chinese texts as well as Chinese native texts of the same period. In terms of the lexicon of given books, the lexical syllable forms in Chinese native texts displayed a slow and steady development from Old Chinese to Middle Chinese, while Middle Chinese translated Buddhist scriptures demonstrated a much higher degree of polysyllablization than Chinese native texts of the same period. On the whole, the syllable forms of Chinese native words presented a continuous and slow evolution from Old Chinese to Middle Chinese, and language contact accelerated the polysyllablization of Chinese lexis..

Keywords: Corpus linguistics · Middle Chinese · Language contact · Lexical syllable form

1 Introduction

The phonetic form, as the expression of a word, is the material shell on which a word exists; it materializes a word and turns it into something that can be perceived by human beings. Across the different historical periods of Chinese language development, the phonetic forms of its lexis have also evolved. The polysyllablization of Chinese lexis, i.e., the shift from monosyllabic words to polysyllabic words, is the most significant manifestation of the development of the phonetic forms of Chinese lexis, and thus has always been a focus of Chinese lexical research.

© The Author(s), under exclusive license to Springer Nature Singapore Pte Ltd. 2024
M. Dong et al. (Eds.): CLSW 2023, LNAI 14515, pp. 243–256, 2024.
https://doi.org/10.1007/978-981-97-0586-3_20

Old Chinese consisted largely of monosyllabic words, and the development of poly-syllablization was relatively slow before the Wei and Jin Dynasties. In contrast, the rise of Middle Chinese brought about the rapid acceleration of polysyllablization, and resulted in a change in the overall picture of the monosyllabic-word dominated Chinese lexical system in just two or three hundred years. The polysyllablization tendency of the Chinese lexis were qualitatively described in [1–6]. In recent years, scholars have begun to adopt quantitative statistical methods to exhaustively count the polysyllabic words in some representative books, and then make comparative studies in respect of the number and the proportion of polysyllabic words [7–13]. These studies on the evolution of Chinese lexical syllable forms have successively achieved significant progress, exploring the development trend from Old Chinese to Middle Chinese from both qualitative and quantitative perspectives. However, the existing studies still have some ambiguities and deficiencies in terms of the identification criteria, statistical dimensions, data classification and collection of polysyllabic words, which are mainly manifested in the following four aspects:

First of all, the criteria for identifying polysyllabic words are not uniform. As a result, there exist obvious discrepancies in the statistical results of polysyllabic words for the same source of linguistic data, which makes it difficult to draw horizontal comparisons between the quantitative statistics by different scholars. Therefore, a corpus method based on relatively consistent word-segmentation criteria is in urgent need in order to depict the evolution of syllable forms in Old Chinese and Middle Chinese texts.

Secondly, the indicators for the statistical analysis of syllable forms are not uniform. Some studies disregard word frequency and count the types of words only, while some take word frequency into account and count the number of word instances instead. Since studies using different indicators diverge in conclusions and analysis based on a single indicator tends to be one-sided, a muli-dimensional quantitative analysis needs to be carried out.

Thirdly, the distinctive characteristics of texts of different nature in different periods should be taken into full consideration. Middle Chinese witnessed the first large-scale contact between Chinese and external languages in the history of the Chinese language. It was shown that there is a certain correlation between the notable acceleration of poly-syllablization in Middle Chinese and language contact, and that there is a big difference between the lexical features of the Chinese translated Buddhist Scriptures and those of the native texts of the same period [14–17]. Therefore, when studying the evolution of phonetic forms from Old Chinese to Middle Chinese, it is necessary to recognize and differentiate the nature of different texts.

Finally, it is essential to accurately apprehend the relationship between the part and the whole. Quite a few research findings on Chinese lexical polysyllablization are based on the lexical data of given books, but the lexical features of certain books cannot be equated with the overall picture of the whole lexical system. A corpus of representative books of the same period needs to be constructed in order to reflect the lexical features of that period in a more comprehensive and accurate manner.

Therefore, in this paper, based on the methodology of corpus linguistics, we will sort through and select important representative texts of Old Chinese and Middle Chinese, especially Chinese translated Buddhist scriptures, depict the lexical phonetic forms in

Old Chinese, Middle Chinese native texts, and Chinese translated Buddhist scriptures, and present the evolution trend of lexical syllable forms in Old Chinese and Middle Chinese from various perspectives, including word types, word tokens, syllable forms of high-frequency words, and inherent features of the lexicon of given books, in order to provide fundamental data for analyzing and interpreting the motivation of syllable form development.

2 Preliminary

Old Chinese was the initial stage of the Chinese language development, which spanned from the late Shang Dynasty down to the Western Han Dynasty, i.e., from no later than the 11th century B.C. to the 1st century A.D. Middle Chinese marked a transition from Old Chinese to Early Modern Chinese, and its time span is usually believed to have begun in the Eastern Han Dynasty and the Wei and Jin Dynasties, and continued through the Northern and Southern Dynasties till the end of the Sui Dynasty. Middle Chinese was characterized by a multi-faceted social context, with further development of social production, frequent outbreaks of wars and upheavals, intensified mass migration, and increased language exchanges between different regions. It was also during this period that Buddhism was first introduced to China, and the Buddhist scriptures, mostly in Sanskrit, were translated into Chinese in large numbers, creating the first large-scale linguistic contact between Chinese and an external language. The Sanskrit-Chinese language contact, which was mainly mediated by the Chinese translations of Buddhist scriptures, constituted an important external factor in the development of the Chinese language. For purpose of revealing the impact of language contact on the development and evolution of the Chinese lexical syllables, it is necessary to further examine the similarities and differences in lexical phonetic forms between native texts and translations of Buddhist scriptures in the Middle Chinese period.

In order to accurately investigate the evolution of lexical syllable forms from Old Chinese to Middle Chinese, and to take the features of linguistic data from different periods into full account, the corpus constructed in the current study is composed of three parts classified by time and source, i.e., Old Chinese texts, Middle Chinese native texts, and Middle Chinese translated Buddhist scriptures, as shown in Fig. 1.

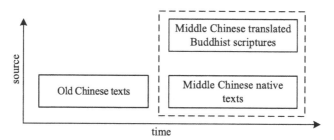

Fig. 1. Composition of the corpus in terms of time and source

The corpus in use is based on the Ancient Chinese Corpus established by Academia Sinica in Taiwan, which consists of two sub-corpora, namely, Tagged Corpus of Old

Chinese and Tagged Corpus of Middle Chinese. It has relatively consistent word-segmentation standards and tagging rules, which makes it easier to carry out a comparative study.

In this paper, we have selected 16 representative texts with accurate dating and authorship from the Tagged Corpus of Old Chinese, labelled with A1-A16, including 诗经 (*Shi jing*), 礼记 (*Li ji*) and so on, which amount to over 1.6 million characters and cover the vast majority of the basic and important linguistic phenomena in Old Chinese, proving to be inclusive and comprehensive in terms of time span, style of writing, and total number of words.

In Middle Chinese there existed two types of literature in terms of source, i.e. native texts and Chinese translated Buddhist scriptures. In this paper, we have selected 5 native texts, labelled with B1-B5, including 抱朴子内篇 (*Baopuzi Neipian*), 世说新语 (*Shishuo Xinyu*) and so on, which add up to around 360,000 characters.

It is quite complicated with the Chinese translations of Buddhist scriptures. All of the Buddhist scriptures included in the Tagged Corpus of Middle Chinese adopt the version in 大正新修大藏经 (*Dazheng Xinxiu Dazangjing*, hereinafter referred to as Dazheng Zang). We have selected 23 credible Chinese translated Buddhist scriptures as the representative text, including 阴持入经 (*Yin Chi Ru Jing*), 道地经 (*Dao Di Jing*) and so on. All the selected translations of scriptures add up to over 1.6 million characters, comparable to the size of the selected Old Chinese texts.

In the statistical survey of the corpus, the identification of words is based on the following principles:

- When two words have the same writing form and the same part of the speech, they are regarded as the same word. Take two instances in 论语(*Lun yu*) for example. In "人(N)不知而不愠" and "为人(N)谋而不忠乎", the two cases of "人(N)" are regarded as the same word, with "N" as a tag for nouns.
- When two words with the same writing form differ in part of speech, they are regarded as different words. For example, "之(T)" and "之(NH)", which are auxiliary and pronoun respectively, are regarded as different words. Here, "T" is the tag for auxiliary words and "NH" for pronouns.

A word identified according to the above principles is called a "word type" in this paper. For example, "之(T)" is one type and "之(NH)" is another type. The same type might have occurred multiple times in the corpus, and each occurrence is called a "word token".

3   Corpus-Based Quantitative Analysis

In this section, we will analyze the trend and characteristics of the evolution of lexical phonetic forms from Old Chinese to Middle Chinese in terms of four indicators: word types, word tokens, syllable forms of high-frequency words, and lexicon of given books.

3.1   Evolution of Syllable Forms Based on Statistics of Word Types

Word types depict the entirety of words present in the lexis, reflecting the richness of the lexical system, yet leaving out the frequency of occurrence of these words in language use. Based on the corpus statistical analysis, there were 54,054 word types in the Old Chinese texts, 23,475 in the Middle Chinese native texts, and 29,193 in the Middle Chinese translated Buddhist scriptures, which are classified according to the number of syllables as monosyllabic, disyllabic, and multi-syllabic (three syllables and above) as shown in Table 1, in which the ratio of polysyllabic types refers to the proportion of polysyllabic types (including disyllabic and multi-syllabic types) in the total of word types.

Table 1. Statistics of word types in the Old Chinese and Middle Chinese texts

Texts Categories	Number of monosyllabic word types	Number of disyllabic word types	Number of multi-syllabic word types	Total of word types	Ratio of polysyllabic word types (%)
Old Chinese texts	9,841	38,690	5,523	54,054	81.8
Middle Chinese native texts	6,230	14,058	3,187	23,475	73.5
Middle Chinese translated Buddhist scriptures	4,991	17,666	6,536	29,193	82.9

It is worth noting that there were 9,841 monosyllabic types in the Old Chinese texts, accounting for only 18.2% of the total of word types, while disyllabic types accounted for 71.6% and multi-syllabic types for 10.2%, which indicates that polysyllabic types made up the majority of word types in the lexical system. The reason for the predominance of polysyllabic types is mainly that there existed a large number of proper nouns in Old Chinese, and those tagged as names of people and places alone added up to over 10,000, the vast majority of which were polysyllabic, such as 孔子 (Kongzi, Confucius), 桓公 (Huangong, Duke Huan), 秦王 (Qinwang, King of Qin) and so on.

Polysyllabic types accounted for 73.5% of the total of word types in the Middle Chinese native texts, retaining predominance and basically inheriting the characteristics of Old Chinese. Among them, the proportion of multi-syllabic types was13.6%, slightly higher than that of 10.2% in the Old Chinese texts, indicating that multi-syllabic words had achieved certain development in the Middle Chinese period.

The ratio of polysyllabic types in the Middle Chinese translated Buddhist scriptures was 82.9%, slightly higher than that of Old Chinese. Among them, multi-syllabic types constituted 22.4%, much higher than that of Old Chinese as well as that of Middle Chinese native texts, showing certain peculiarity. Most of these multi-syllabic types arose from transliteration, which, as the most convenient means in translation, directly adopted Chinese characters to record the pronunciation of the original words and thus produced a large number of multi-syllabic words in the Chinese translations of Buddhist scriptures, indicating certain influence of external language contact on the syllable forms of the Chinese lexis.

3.2 Evolution of Syllable Forms Based on Statistics of Word Tokens

Word tokens take into account the number of occurrences of words in a given text. The numbers of occurrences of words with different syllable forms in texts of different nature across different periods from Old Chinese to Middle Chinese are shown in Table 2, where the ratio of polysyllabic tokens refers to the proportion of polysyllabic tokens (including disyllabic and multi-syllabic tokens) in the total of word tokens.

Table 2. Statistics of word tokens in the Old Chinese and Middle Chinese texts

Texts Categories	Number of monosyllabic word tokens	Number of disyllabic word tokens	Number of multi-syllabic word tokens	Total of word tokens	Ratio of polysyllabic word tokens (%)
Old Chinese texts	1,144,671	216,404	20,110	1,381,185	17.1
Middle Chinese native texts	215,460	34,946	5,325	255,731	15.8
Middle Chinese translated Buddhist scriptures	920,736	270,610	42,135	1,233,481	25.3

A total of 1,381,185 word tokens were found in the Old Chinese texts, among which monosyllabic words appeared 1,144,671 times, accounting for 82.88% of the total, disyllabic words appeared 216,404 times, accounting for 15.67% of the total, and multi-syllabic words appeared 20,110 times, accounting for only 1.45% of the total. In light of word tokens, monosyllabic words occupied the absolute majority in Old Chinese. For this reason, it is generally believed that Old Chinese was dominated by monosyllabic words, which is closely related to the greater number of occurrences of monosyllabic words.

The main reason for the huge number of monosyllabic word tokens in contrast with the small number of monosyllabic word types in Old Chinese is that the frequency of monophonic words was much higher than that of disyllabic words. According to the statistics in Table 1 and Table 2, a total of 54,054 word types appeared 1,381,185 times in the Old Chinese texts, resulting in an average of 25.5 occurrences per word type. However, words with different numbers of syllables varied in their average frequency.

On average, monosyllabic types appeared 1,144,671/9,841 = 116.3 times, disyllabic types appeared 216,404/38,690 = 5.6 times only, and multi-syllabic types had an even lower average number of occurrences, merely 3.6 times. Monosyllabic words, though only making up a relatively small percentage of the word types, enjoyed an extremely high frequency, about 20 times higher than that of disyllabic words.

A total of 255,731 word tokens were found in the Middle Chinese native texts, among which monosyllabic words appeared 215,460 times, accounting for 84.25% of the total, disyllabic words appeared 34,946 times, accounting for 13.67% of the total, and multi-syllabic words appeared 5,325 times, accounting for 2.08% of the total. Therefore, in terms of word tokens, in the Middle Chinese native texts, monosyllabic words remained the majority and polysyllabic words were still in a minor position, with the proportion of each syllabic group inheriting the characteristics of Old Chinese.

However, in the Middle Chinese translated Buddhist scriptures, the proportion of polysyllabic words showed a significant increase. A total of 1,233,481 word tokens were found in the translated scriptures. Among them, disyllabic words appeared 270,610 times, accounting for 21.9% of the total, and multi-syllabic words appeared 42,135 times, accounting for 3.4% of the total; both add up to 25.3% of the total. It can be seen that although monosyllabic tokens still occupied the majority, yet compared with the Old Chinese texts and the Middle Chinese native texts, Chinese translated Buddhist scriptures featured a significantly higher percentage of polysyllabic words.

When we take a further step to consider the average frequency of words in the Middle Chinese translated Buddhist scriptures, it can be calculated that on average, monosyllabic words appeared 184.4 times, disyllabic words 15.3 times, and multi-syllabic words 6.4 times, which indicates that polysyllabic words showed a relatively high frequency in the Middle Chinese translated Buddhist scriptures.

3.3 Evolution of Syllable Forms Among High-Frequency Words

High-frequency words make up an important part of the lexical system. According to corpus statistics, the syllabic composition of high-frequency words varied across texts of different nature in different periods, as shown in Table 3.

In the Old Chinese texts, if we rank the words according to the number of occurrences, 98 of the top 100 high-frequency words were monosyllabic, among which "之(T)" occurred most frequently, reaching 38,551 times, followed by "不(D)", "也(T)", "而(C)", "之(NH)", etc. Among the top 100, there were only two disyllabic words, namely "天下(N)" (ranked 33) and "诸侯(N)" (ranked 67). If we further expand the list, among the top 200 high-frequency words, there were 8 disyllabic words, which included "君子(N)", "天子(N)", "可以(V)" and so on. Likewise, when we expand the list to top 500, 40 of them were polysyllabic; to top 1,000, 138 polysyllabic words were found. Thus, although words with the highest frequency were still dominated by monosyllabic words, polysyllabic words gradually took up a larger share as we extend the frequency range under examination.

In the Middle Chinese native texts, the top 100 high-frequency words were all mono-syllabic. When we expand the list to top 1,000, 75 polysyllabic words were found, among which those with the highest frequency were "可以(V)" (ranked 186), "如此(V)" (ranked 234), "然后(D)" (ranked 303), "以为(V)" (ranked 317) and so on. Compared with Old

Table 3. Statistics of high-frequency words in the Old Chinese and Middle Chinese texts

Texts Categories	Frequency range	Monosyllabic word types	Polysyllabic word types	Ratio of polysyllabic word types (%)
Old Chinese texts	Top 100	98	2	2.0
	Top 200	192	8	4.0
	Top 500	460	40	8.0
	Top 1000	862	138	13.8
Middle Chinese native texts	Top 100	100	0	0
	Top 200	19	1	0.5
	Top 500	482	18	3.6
	Top 1000	917	75	7.5
Middle Chinese translated Buddhist scriptures	Top 100	92	8	8
	Top 200	175	25	12.5
	Top 500	395	105	21.0
	Top 1000	696	304	30.4

Chinese, within the same frequency range, the number of polysyllabic words found in Middle Chinese native texts was slightly lower, which might be accounted for by the fact that fewer Middle Chinese texts were selected and the peculiar features of the high-frequency words in these texts. For instance, 齐民要术 (*Qimin Yaoshu*), a comprehensive agricultural work, presented extensive use of monosyllabic words related to crops, such as "豆" (*dou*, bean), "麦" (*mai*, wheat) and so on.

On the whole, in either Old Chinese texts or Middle Chinese native texts, even when the top 1,000 high-frequency words are examined, the proportion of polysyllabic words did not exceed 15%, which indicates that polysyllabic words were in a minor position among high-frequency words.

In the Middle Chinese translated Buddhist scriptures, 8 out of the top 100 high-frequency words were polysyllabic, and out of the top 1,000, as many as 304 polysyllabic words were found, accounting for 30.4% of the total, more than twice the percentage of polysyllabic words in the same frequency range among the Old Chinese texts. This indicates that an increased number of polysyllabic words had entered the range of high-frequency words in the Chinese translations of Buddhist scriptures.

3.4 Evolution of Syllable Forms from the Perspective of Given Books

The lexicon of a given book mainly presents a picture of the lexical system within a relatively closed collection. Each books carries distinctive characteristics closely related to the language habits of the author, style of writing, contents, etc. Based on the corpus, it is feasible to conduct a comparative analysis of the statistical data of different books, both horizontally and vertically. In this paper, we have carried out a survey on the total

Table 4. Statistics of polysyllabic words in the Old Chinese and Middle Chinese given books

Type of text	Title of book	Label of book	Number of monosyllabic word tokens	Number of polysyllabic word tokens	Ratio of poly-syllabic word tokens (%)
Old Chinese texts	诗经 *Shijing*	A1	20,237	4,709	18.88
	老子 *Laozi*	A2	4,254	515	10.80
	管子 *Guanzi*	A3	92,772	16,569	15.15
	国语 *Guoyu*	A4	51,364	9,095	15.04
	左传 *Zuozhuan*	A5	132,558	29,097	18.00
	论语 *Lunyu*	A6	12,303	1,730	12.33
	墨子 *Mozi*	A7	55,132	9,691	14.95
	商君书 *Shangjun Shu*	A8	16,160	1,956	10.80
	孟子 *Mengzi*	A9	26,077	4,529	14.80
	庄子 *Zhuangzi*	A10	48,224	7,834	13.97
	吕氏春秋 *Lyushi Chunqiu*	A11	73,591	12,692	14.70
	荀子 *Xunzi*	A12	54,746	9,993	15.44
	韩非子 *Hanfeizi*	A13	78,901	13,130	14.27
	战国策 *Zhanguo Ce*	A14	90,750	15,029	14.21
	礼记 *Liji*	A15	70,523	13,455	16.02
	史记 *Shiji*	A16	317,079	86,490	21.43
Middle Chinese native texts	抱朴子内篇 *Baopuzi Neipian*	B1	55,405	8,822	13.74
	世说新语 *Shishuo Xinyu*	B2	40,620	9,339	18.69
	齐民要术 *Qimin Yaoshu*	B3	81,278	11,561	12.45
	洛阳伽蓝记 *Luoyang Qielan Ji*	B4	17,932	5,296	22.80
	颜氏家训 *Yanshi Jiaxun*	B5	20,225	5,253	20.62

(continued)

Table 4. (*continued*)

Type of text	Title of book	Label of book	Number of monosyllabic word tokens	Number of polysyllabic word tokens	Ratio of poly-syllabic word tokens (%)
Middle Chinese Translated Buddhist texts	道地经 *Dao Di Jing*	C1	6,177	1,046	14.48
	阴持入经 *Yin Chi Ru Jing*	C2	6,835	1,200	14.93
	道行般若经 *Dao Xing Bo Re Jing*	C3	40,257	13,240	24.75
	中本起经 *Zhong Ben Qi Jing*	C4	13,182	3,852	22.61
	修行本起经 *Xiu Xing Ben Qi Jing*	C5	8,434	2,871	25.40
	菩萨本业经 *Pu Sa Ben Ye Jing*	C6	3,006	1,084	26.50
	了本生死经 *Liao Ben Sheng Si Jing*	C7	1,587	207	11.54
	义足经 *Yi Zu Jing*	C8	12,804	2,364	15.59
	生经 *Sheng Jing*	C9	27,899	9,462	25.33
	六度集经 *Liu Du Ji Jing*	C10	46,539	9,671	17.21
	正法华经 *Zheng Fa Hua Jing*	C11	43,614	19,560	30.96
	大楼炭经 *Da Lou Tan Jing*	C12	26,022	8,930	25.55
	光赞经 *Guang Zan Jing*	C13	47,281	20,420	30.16
	普曜经 *Pu Yao Jing*	C14	35,076	13,739	28.15
	法句譬喻经 *Fa Ju Pi Yu Jing*	C15	27,212	7,420	21.43
	出曜经 *Chu Yao Jing*	C16	136,949	39,323	22.31
	妙法莲华经 *Miao Fa Lian Hua Jing*	C17	36,917	14,830	28.66

(*continued*)

Table 4. (*continued*)

Type of text	Title of book	Label of book	Number of monosyllabic word tokens	Number of polysyllabic word tokens	Ratio of poly-syllabic word tokens (%)
	维摩诘所说经 *Wei Mo Jie Suo Shuo Jing*	C18	15,148	5,274	25.83
	大庄严论经 *Da Zhuang Yan Lun Jing*	C19	59,039	17,651	23.02
	悲华经 *Bei Hua Jing*	C20	40,882	19,257	32.02
	贤愚经 *Xian Yu Jing*	C21	79,241	23,076	22.55
	百喻经 *Bai Yu Jing*	C22	11,734	2,770	19.10
	佛本行集经 *Fo Ben Xing Ji Jing*	C23	194,901	75,498	27.92

number of word tokens, number of monosyllabic tokens, number of polysyllabic tokens, and ratio of polysyllabic tokens in each of the selected 16 Old Chinese texts, 5 Middle Chinese native texts, and 23 Chinese translated Buddhist scriptures, as shown in Table 4, where the ratio of polysyllabic tokens refers to the proportion of polysyllabic tokens in the total of word tokens in a given book.

In this section, the ratio of polysyllabic word tokens in each of the selected 44 books is plotted in a scatter diagram based on the dating of the text, where the horizontal coordinate indicates the year, and the vertical coordinate depicts the ratio of polysyllabic tokens, with the Old Chinese texts labeled as hollow squares, Middle Chinese native texts as solid triangles, and Middle Chinese translated Buddhist scriptures as solid squares, as shown in Fig. 2.

It can be seen from Table 4 and Fig. 2 that in light of the proportion of polysyllabic tokens, with the advancement of time from Old Chinese to Middle Chinese, polysyllabic words as a whole presented a trend of slow development and growth. Their share remained low across all Old Chinese texts, generally less than 25%.

In the early stage of Middle Chinese, the proportion of polysyllabic words in the native texts such as 抱朴子内篇 (*Baopuzi Neipian*, labelled with B1) was roughly at the same level as that of the Old Chinese texts. However, as time went on, the proportion of polysyllabic words was on a rise, which was quite notable in 洛阳伽蓝记 (*Luoyang Qielan Ji*, labelled with B4) and 颜氏家训 (*Yanshi Jiaxun*, labelled with B5). Chinese translations of Buddhist scriptures on the whole featured a higher proportion of polysyllabic words than the native texts, with 悲华经 (*Bei Hua Jing*, labelled with C20) over 30%; yet exceptions were also found in scriptures like 了本生死经 (*Liao Ben Sheng Si Jing*, labelled with C7), in which polysyllabic words accounted for 11.54% only.

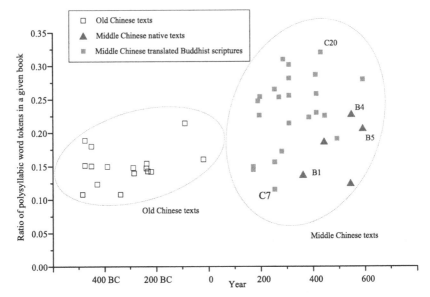

Fig. 2. Ratio of polysyllabic word tokens in books of different nature in different periods

The indicator employed in this section is the proportion of polysyllabic word tokens, and similar conclusions can be attained in light of other indicators such as the proportion of word types and the proportion of polysyllabic forms among high-frequency words. Overall, the evolution of lexical syllable forms in the native texts from Old Chinese to Middle Chinese was gradual and continuous, but translated Buddhist scriptures showed a significant difference, featuring a higher level of polysyllablization than native texts in both Old Chinese and the same period.

4 Conclusion

The evolution of lexical syllable forms from Old Chinese to Middle Chinese is a hot issue of great significance in the study of the history of Chinese lexis. In this paper, in consideration of the existing deficiencies in the identification criteria, statistical dimensions, data classification of polysyllabic words, we have selected representative texts in both Old Chinese and Middle Chinese based on the corpus linguistics methodology for research, and the main conclusions are as follows.

Firstly, in terms of word types, with no consideration of frequency, polysyllabic words remained the majority, even in the Old Chinese lexis, mainly due to the existence of a large number of polysyllabic proper nouns in the lexical system. Meanwhile, the proportion of multi-syllabic words (with three syllables and above) increased in the Middle Chinese period, which was especially evident in the Chinese translations of Buddhist scriptures.

Secondly, in terms of word tokens, the average frequency of each monosyllabic word and the total number of monosyllabic tokens were both far higher in comparison with polysyllabic words, which indicates that monosyllabic words remained in a primary position in language use while polysyllabic words in a secondary position.

Thirdly, in terms of high-frequency words, from Old Chinese through Middle Chinese, monosyllabic words occupied an absolutely dominant position in the top 100 high-frequency words, and remained the majority even in the top 1,000. Within the same frequency range, Middle Chinese translated Buddhist scriptures featured a significantly higher proportion of polysyllabic words than Old Chinese texts as well as native texts of the same period, indicating that polysyllabic words were approaching or gradually entering the lexical core of the translated scriptures.

Finally, in light of the lexicon of given books, lexical syllable forms in the native texts underwent a slow and steady evolution from Old Chinese to Middle Chinese, and the Middle Chinese translated Buddhist scriptures showed a higher level of polysyllablization than native texts of the same period.

In summary, this paper, based on a corpus guided by relatively consistent word-segmentation criteria, presents the evolution of lexical syllable forms from Old Chinese to Middle Chinese from multiple perspectives, further consolidating the fundamental data in the research of lexical polysyllablization. It is pointed out that overall in native texts, from Old Chinese to Middle Chinese, lexical syllable forms underwent a gradual evolution, and polysyllabic words showed a slow increase in general when examined in light of multiple indicators, such as types, tokens, and high-frequency words, which reflects the stability of language development. At the same time, Middle Chinese translations of Buddhist scriptures were higher on all those indicators than native texts of the same period, showing a higher degree of polysyllablization, which not only manifests the peculiar nature of Chinese translated Buddhist scriptures, but also reveals the impact of the external factor of language contact on the evolution of the phonetic forms of the Chinese lexis.

Acknowledgement. This work was supported by the Beijing Social Science Foundation Project (grant No. 17YYC019), the Major Programs of the National Social Science Foundation of China (Grant No.20&ZD304 and 21&ZD310) and The National Youth Talent Support Program.

References

1. Wang, L.: Chinese Language History. Science Press, Beijing (1957). (in Chinese)
2. Zhao, K.-Q.: Summary of Ancient Chinese Lexis. Zhejiang Education Press, Hangzhou (1987). (in Chinese)
3. Jiang, S.-Y.: Outline of Ancient Chinese Lexis. Peking University Press, Beijing (1989). (in Chinese)
4. Shi, C.-Z.: Outline of Chinese Lexis History. Eastern China Normal University Press, Shanghai (1989). (in Chinese)
5. Pan, Y.-Z.: Summary of Chinese Lexis History. Shanghai Guji Press, Shanghai (1989). (in Chinese)
6. Xiang, X.: A Brief History of Chinese Language. Higher Education Press, Beijing (1993). (in Chinese)
7. Cheng, X.-Q.: Research on Polysyllabic Words in Given Books in Chinese Language History. Shangwu Press, Beijing (2003). (in Chinese)

8. Li, S.-C.: Statistics of the Polysyllabic Words in *Shishuo Xinyu*. Doctoral Dissertation of Nanjing University (2007). (in Chinese)
9. Chen, Y.-Z.: Research on the Polysyllabic Vocabulary of *Gao Seng Zhuan*. Doctoral Dissertation of Northeast Normal University (2014). (in Chinese)
10. Qiu, B., Li, J.: Reconstruction of uncertain historical evolution of the polysyllablization of Chinese lexis. J. Appl. Math. **2014** (2014)
11. Dong, S.-Z.: Evolution of Polysyllabic Words from Ancient Chinese to Middle Chinese. Doctoral Dissertation of Nanjing Normal University (2018). (in Chinese)
12. Wu, D.: Research on the Polysyllabic Words in Middle Chinese Taoist Scriptures of Supernatural Arts. Doctoral Dissertation of Northeast Normal University (2019). (in Chinese)
13. Yi, J.-N.: Research on the Polysyllabic Words in *Hanshu*. Doctoral Dissertation of Jilin University (2020). (in Chinese)
14. Liang, X.-H.: Impact of the translated scriptures on the disyllablization of the Chinese lexis in the Han, Wei, and Six Dynasties. J. Nanjing Normal Univ. (Soc. Sci. Edn). **2**, 73–78 (1991). (in Chinese)
15. Zhu, Q.-Z.: Research on Buddhist Scriptures and Middle Chinese Lexis. Wenjin Press, Taipei (1992). (in Chinese)
16. Qiu, B.: A Multi-perspective Study on the Polysyllablization of Middle Chinese Lexis. Nanjing University Press, Nanjing (2012). (in Chinese)
17. Qiu, B., Bian, W.: A quantitative approach to the stylistic assessment of the Middle Chinese Texts. In: 22nd Chinese Lexical Semantics Workshop, LNAI 13250, pp. 163–171, Springer Nature Switzerland AG. (2022). https://doi.org/10.1007/978-3-031-06547-7_13

A Corpus-Based Study of Lexical Chunks in Chinese Academic Discourse: Extraction, Classification, and Application

Qihong Zhou[1]([envelope]) and Li Mou[2,3]

[1] College of Chinese Language and Culture, Sichuan International Studies University,
Chongqing 400031, China
zhouqihong338@hotmail.com
[2] School of Education, Faculty of Social Sciences and Humanities, Universiti Teknologi
Malaysia, 81310 Johor, UTM Johor Bahru, Malaysia
li-20@graduate.utm.my
[3] School of Gerenal Education,
Chongqing City Management College, Chongqing 401331, China

Abstract. This study applies AI technology to build academic Chinese corpora. Python was employed to extract lexical chunks of various lengths, including 3-gram, 4-gram, 5-gram, and 6-gram. The identification of these lexical chunks was performed using the New-MI algorithm and filtered based on semantic relevance completeness. Subsequently, manual intervention was applied to eliminate duplicate entries and identify 1431 continuous word chunks. These lexical chunks were classified into three categories according to their functions: research-oriented, text-oriented, and participation-oriented. It was found that there were some differences in the use of chunks between Korean Chinese learners and native Chinese writers, with research-oriented chunks being used more frequently in both groups than in other categories. Korean Chinese learners used research-oriented, text-oriented, and participant-oriented chunks less frequently than native speakers. This study might provide a reference for academic Chinese writing and academic Chinese textbook development for Chinese language learners.

Keywords: Academic Chinese · Lexical Chunks · N-gram · Lexical Chunks Function · Chinese Learners

1 Introduction

Lexical chunks have garnered increasing attention across diverse academic disciplines, such as linguistics, psycholinguistics, language teaching, and second language acquisition. The concept of a "chunk", initially introduced by Miller and Selfridge [1], plays a fundamental role in memory processing, involving the amalgamation of discrete pieces of information into larger units. Becker [2] further extended this concept within the realm of language research, where he coined the term "lexical chunk". He defined it as a "fixed or semi-fixed patterned plate structure in language use, serving as the smallest unit of human communication, memory, storage, output, and usage."

The pervasive presence of lexical chunks in everyday communication is noteworthy. Empirical studies by various researchers [3, 4] reveal that approximately 50%-70% of human language comprises lexical chunks or formulaic sequences, accounting for about 70%–80% of daily spoken conversations. Additionally, in academic discourse, lexical chunks are extensively utilized, with up to half of academic English texts being composed of these linguistic units [3].

Within the context of second language acquisition, the ability to proficiently employ lexical chunks serves as a pivotal indicator of overall language proficiency. The extent to which second language learners can exhibit native-like selection, fluency, and authentic expressions akin to native speakers largely hinges upon their possession of lexical chunks in their mental lexicons and their ability to rapidly retrieve and apply these chunks during communication [5]. Effectively employing lexical chunks not only enhances the persuasiveness of academic discourse [6] but also mirrors learners' understanding and application of academic language. The adept utilization of lexical chunks not only contributes to high-level academic writing but also plays a role in shaping the learners' disciplinary identity. Given the escalating number of Chinese learners, there is a surging demand for proficient Chinese academic writing skills. Consequently, the mastery of lexical chunks becomes a crucial gauge of Chinese learners' academic expression capabilities. Nevertheless, research on lexical chunks in the context of Chinese academic discourse remains limited, necessitating further investigation. The present study employs computational linguistics methods to extract, classify, and analyze lexical chunks in academic discourse.

Research Questions:

(1) What is the distribution pattern of lexical chunk usage among authors of published journal articles?
(2) How can commonly used lexical chunks in Chinese academic discourse be functionally classified?
(3) How do Chinese learners use lexical chunks in their academic writing?

2 Literature Review

2.1 Definition of Lexical Chunks

The definition of lexical chunks in previous research can be categorized into two approaches: the first approach adopts Wray's [7] perspective from psycholinguistics, which focuses on whether they can be stored and retrieved as whole units. The second approach employs corpus-based methods to extract lexical chunks based on their frequency. In this study, lexical chunks refer to consecutively occurring word sequences known as "n-grams", where "n" represents the number of consecutive words in the sequence, such as trigrams (3-gram), four-grams (4-gram), five-grams (5-gram), and six-grams (6-gram). These lexical chunks consist of two or more consecutive word forms and are commonly found within the same syntactic structure, with their actual co-occurrence probabilities significantly exceeding their theoretically predicted values.

2.2 Classification of N-grams

In the realm of academic English n-gram research, three noteworthy classification schemes have been proposed by Biber et al. [6, 8], Hyland [9], and Salazar [10]. [6] conducted a differential analysis of 3-gram and 4-gram in spoken and written English, utilizing a corpus of 7 million words from English conversations and 5.3 million words from English academic texts. They categorized n-grams into 14 classes based on their structural characteristics. Subsequently, [8] expanded their research by assembling and organizing a corpus of 1.2 million words from classroom teaching and 700,000 words from textbooks, and compared the findings with their previous work on n-gram structures. Additionally, they introduced a functional classification of n-grams, proposing four main categories: Stance Expression, Discourse Organizers, Referential Bundles, and Special Conversational Functions, which are further divided into 11 subcategories. These subcategories encompass Epistemic Stance, Attitudinal/Modality Stance, Topic, Topic Elaboration/Clarification, Identification/Focus, Imprecision, Specification of Attributes, Time/Place/Text Reference, Politeness, Simple Inquiry, and Reporting.

Hyland [9] compiled a corpus of approximately 3.5 million words from four categories of academic journals, including electrical engineering, biology, business studies, and applied linguistics, as well as master's and doctoral theses. The primary focus of their analysis was on 4-gram, and they classified 240 4-g based on their structural and functional characteristics. In terms of functional aspects, Hyland outlined three major categories: Research-oriented, Text-oriented, and Participant-oriented.

2.3 Extraction of N-grams

In the realm of natural language processing, [11] introduced an amalgamation of statistical and rule-based Chinese chunk analysis. Subsequently, [12] proposed a Chinese chunk recognition method based on K-means clustering employing machine learning. More recently, [13] developed a neural network leaning model for Chinese base-chunk identification. Chunk extraction techniques in the domain of computer science primarily serve information retrieval, machine translation, and topic content analysis.

Linguistic researchers predominantly rely on software crafted by computer scientists to conduct their investigations. For instance, software like Wordsmith, AntConc, and PowerConc are utilized for the extraction of n-grams. The "n-gram" analysis method enables the identification of consecutive sequences comprising two or more words. This approach extracts chunks based on the outward physical adjacency of word forms, automatically segmenting them and quantifying their co-occurrence frequency. However, a drawback of this method is its disregard for the internal cohesion of word sequences.

The n-gram extraction software is predominantly designed for English research purposes, and its adaptation and customization for specific Chinese research requirements have progressed at a relatively slower pace. Additionally, tools such as Wordsmith entail usage fees and exhibit constraints when handling extensive Chinese corpora. Furthermore, those software do not possess the inherent capability for direct Chinese word segmentation, thus mandating the supplementary utilization of separate word segmentation tools for the extraction process.

In the domain of academic English research, numerous studies have been conducted on n-grams [14–20]. These studies share a common characteristic of frequency-based extraction, with the minimum frequency threshold in the corpus set between 10 and 40 occurrences. Regarding the extracted lengths, some studies focus on single 3-gram [20], while others extract a range from 3-gram to 8-gram [19]. The most prevalent extractions are 3-gram and 4-gram. Additionally, most of these studies are conducted in English, with sporadic instances in Korean and Spanish.

In the context of academic Chinese research, there remains a paucity of n-gram studies. A noteworthy early large-scale study of n-grams was conducted by Taiwanese scholars [21]. They extracted 195 sets of 3-gram and 105 sets of 4-gram from a 9-million-word academic corpus encompassing 10 major fields in humanities and social sciences. However, this study did not extract 5-gram and 6-gram and encountered several instances of non-contiguous semantic fragments in determining n-grams.

The existing research on n-grams predominantly centers on the domain of computer science, wherein language researchers depend on software developed and tailored by computer scientists to facilitate their investigations. The extraction of n-grams often relies on frequency-based criteria, yet it tends to overlook the internal cohesion of n-grams. Moreover, a clear and definitive standard for the determination and assessment of n-grams is still lacking, resulting in ongoing debates within the academic community.

Addressing these observations, this study integrates methodologies from English academic n-gram research. Initially, relevant academic corpora are collected to construct a Chinese academic corpus. Subsequently, commonly used n-grams are selected based on word frequency and internal cohesion within the corpus. The selected n-grams are then categorized according to their functions, with the overarching objective of offering insights for the teaching of academic Chinese. One advantage of developing such programs lies in their adaptability, enabling modifications based on research design and the incorporation of novel findings from natural language processing, thereby facilitating scientific research. In this study, we endeavor to employ natural language processing techniques and Python programming to extract n-grams (as defined in 3.2).

3   Construction of Corpus and Extraction of N-grams

3.1   Construction of Corpus

The corpora utilized in this study are entirely self-constructed. During the corpus construction process, OCR (Optical Character Recognition) technology was employed, complemented by manual proofreading, to enhance database building efficiency. The corpus underwent standardization, involving the removal of Chinese classification numbers, literature identification codes, article numbers, DOIs, English abstracts, figures, tables, formulas, data, footnotes, endnotes, references, appendices, and author biographies. Two distinct corpora were compiled for this research: the Chinese native speakers' journal articles corpus and the Chinese learners' degree theses corpus.

The Chinese native speakers' journal articles corpus primarily comprises representative papers from four prominent teaching Chinese to Speakers of Other languages journals: *Chinese Teaching in the World, Language Teaching and Linguistics Studies, Applied Linguistics,* and *Chinese Language Learning.* These journals were published during the period from 2016 to 2020.Specifically, papers focusing on second language acquisition, Chinese phonetics research, teaching grammar research, Chinese research, Chinese teaching research, Chinese textbook development, and Chinese as a second language testing research were carefully selected. The corpus consists of 300 journal articles, with a total of 3,537,891 words.

On the other hand, the Chinese learners' degree theses corpus predominantly includes degree theses authored by Korean students learning Chinese. According to the "Statistics of International Students Studying in China in 2018" report issued by the Ministry of Education of the People's Republic of China, South Korea, Thailand, and Pakistan ranked as the top three countries in terms of the number of students studying in China, with South Korea being the foremost contributor. Notably, the total number of South Korean students studying in China in 2018 reached 50,600. Given the substantial proportion and diverse educational backgrounds of South Korean students, it is essential to investigate the language characteristics of academic writing for this demographic. Consequently, the corpus of Korean Chinese learners' degree theses was assembled from 30 undergraduate, 30 master's, and 30 doctoral theses in the field of International Chinese Education and Linguistics at Beijing Language and Culture University from 2010 to 2020. The cumulative word count is as follows: undergraduate theses (317,512 words), master's theses (943,418 words), and doctoral dissertation (3,261,176 words), with a total of 4,522,106 words. Notably, all undergraduate, master's, and doctoral theses within this corpus pertain to linguistics and international Chinese education, aligning with the themes present in the Chinese native speakers' journal articles corpus.

3.2   Operational Definition of N-grams

N-grams are widely applied in natural language processing. The abstract pattern of n-grams segmentation is as follows:

2-gram (w1, w2) --------------------- w1w2;w2w3;w3w4;
3-gram (w1,w2,w3) --------------------- w1w2w3; w2w3w4;
4-gram (w1,w2,w3,w4)------------------- w1w2w3w4;w2w3w4w5;
5-gram (w1,w2,w3,w4,w5) ---------------- w1 w2 w3w4w5;
n-gram (w1,w2,w3,......,wn)--------------- w1w2w3......wn.

The steps for extracting n-grams are as follows:

(1) Sentence Segmentation: The text is divided into sentences based on punctuation marks "。", "?"and "!".
(2) Word Segmentation: The PKUseg toolkit developed by Peking University is utilized for word segmentation. Customized dictionaries are added to correct inaccuracies in word segmentation. For example, the phrase "Jùfǎ xué" (syntax study) may be incorrectly segmented as "Jù fǎxué" (sentence/law study), and this issue can be resolved by constructing a user-defined dictionary [22].
(3) Calculation within a Given Window: Taking 3-gram as an example, a sentence consists of w1, w2, w3, w4, w5,..., wn-2, wn-1, wn. The process starts with forming the first 3-word sequence (Sequence 1) from the first three words (w1, w2, w3) in the text. Then, the second 3-word sequence (Sequence 2) is formed from the second, third, and fourth words (w2, w3, w4). This process continues, and each subsequent

3-word sequence overlaps with the previous one by two words. For instance, the third 3-word sequence (Sequence 3) is formed from the words (w3, w4, w5), and so on, until the last 3-word sequence (Sequence n-2) from the words (wn-2, wn-1, wn) at the end of the text. Due to some physical hard segmentation, numerous interfering and unnatural fragments are generated in the resulting 3-word sequences, requiring removal.

(4) Noise Removal and Frequency Counting of Each Sequence.

After generating the n-gram sequences, noise removal is performed to eliminate any unwanted or irrelevant fragments. Subsequently, the frequency of occurrence is calculated for each retained n-gram sequence. For example, taking the sentence "Wénzhāng zòngshù le wǔ zhǒng fāngfǎ。"(The article provides an overview of five methods) as an example, the first step is to perform word segmentation as follows: "Wénzhāng/ zòngshù/ le/ wǔ/ zhǒng/ fāngfǎ/。" Next, the given window is applied for segmentation, and the results are as follows:

2-gram segmentation results: Wénzhāng zòngshù (w1w2); zòngshù le (w2w3); le wǔ (w3w4); wǔ zhǒng (w4w5); zhǒng fāngfǎ (w5w6).

3-gram segmentation results: Wénzhāng zòngshù le (w1w2w3); zòngshù le wǔ (w2w3w4); le wǔ zhǒng (w3w4w5); wǔ zhǒng fāngfǎ (w4w5w6).

3.3   Calculation of Internal Cohesion

There are various algorithms based on the association and attraction of two words, such as Pointwise Mutual Information (PMI), Log-likelihood ratio, Z-score, T-score, Dice, and SCP (Statistical Co-occurrence Probability). However, these algorithms do not compute cohesion beyond two units (words). The pioneering work in calculating cohesion beyond two words was introduced by Silva & Lopes [23], who proposed a method of using segmentation and recombination to apply the two-word PMI algorithm to measure cohesion within multi-word sequences. Wei & Li [24] adopted the method of Silva & Lopes [23] and made improvements by introducing a probability mean weighting approach to assign weights to all PMI values within the sequence. This method is referred to as New-MI, and the calculation formula is as follows:

$$MI(w_1, w_2, \ldots, w_n) = \log_2 \frac{P(w_1, w_2, \ldots, w_n)}{WAP}$$

$$WAP = \sum_{i=1}^{i=n-1} P_{[p(w_1,w_2,\ldots,w_i).P(w_{i+1},\ldots w_n)]}.[P(W_1, \ldots W_i).P(W_{i+1}, \ldots, W_n)] \tag{1}$$

In this study, we use W to represent an n-word sequence, where W = { $W_1, W_2, W_3, \ldots, W_n$ }. Within the sequence, there are possible discrete points denoted by i. We divide W into two parts, W1, W2,..., Wi, and W(i + 1),..., Wn, where $1 \leq i \leq$ n-1 and n ≥ 2.

The internal cohesion, represented by G, is referred to as the "glue value". The characteristics of internal cohesion (glue value) are expressed as G1 ≠ G2 ≠ G3 [...] ≠ Gn-1.

Using the 3-gram "xuéxí hé yánjiū" (study and research) as an illustrative instance, considering a corpus size of one million, it is assumed that "xuéxí" (study) appears 1000 times, "yánjiū" (research) appears 2000 times, "xuéxí hé" (study and) appears 300 times, "hé yánjiū" (and research) appears 400 times, and "xuéxí hé yánjiū" (study and research) appears 100 times. Now, we will calculate the probabilities as follows:

$$P_{\text{xuéxí}} = \frac{1000}{1000000} = 1 \times 10^{-3}$$

$$P_{\text{yánjiū}} = \frac{2000}{1000000} = 2 \times 10^{-3}$$

$$P_{\text{xuéxí hé}} = \frac{300}{1000000} = 3 \times 10^{-4}$$

$$P_{\text{hé yánjiū}} = \frac{400}{1000000} = 4 \times 10^{-4}$$

$$P_{\text{xuéxí hé yánjiū}} = \frac{100}{1000000} = 1 \times 10^{-4}$$

To calculate the Within-Sequence Adjacent Probability (WAP) for 3-gram, we obtain the expected joint probability E1 of G1 in "xuéxí ⋆ hé yánjiū", and the expected joint probability E2 of G2 in "xuéxí ⋆ hé yánjiū". The specific formulas are as follows:

$$E_1 = E_{\text{xuéxí•hé yánjiū}} = P_{\text{xuéxí}} \times P_{\text{hé yánjiū}} = 0.001 \times 0.0004 \approx 4 \times 10^{-7}$$
$$E_2 = E_{\text{xuéxí hé •yánjiū}} = P_{\text{xuéxí hé}} \times P_{\text{yánjiū}} = 0.0003 \times 0.002 \approx 6 \times 10^{-7}$$

The probability-weighted average is calculated using the formula (1) (New-MI) to obtain probabilities.

$$WAP_{\text{xuéxí hé yánjiū}} = \sum_{i=1}^{i=2} P\left(E_i\right) \cdot E_i = P(E_1) \cdot E_1 + P(E_2) \cdot E_2$$

$$= \frac{E_1}{E_1 + E_2} \times E_1 + \frac{E_2}{E_1 + E_2} \times E_2$$
$$= \frac{4 \times 10^{-7}}{4 \times 10^{-7} + 6 \times 10^{-7}} \times 4 \times 10^{-7} + \frac{6 \times 10^{-7}}{4 \times 10^{-7} + 6 \times 10^{-7}} \times 6 \times 10^{-7}$$
$$= 5.2 \times 10^{-7}$$

$$G_{\text{xuéxí hé yánjiū}} = MI_{\text{xuéxí hé yánjiū}} = log_2(\frac{P(\text{xuéxí hé yánjiū})}{WAP})$$

$$= log_2\left(\frac{1 \times 10^{-4}}{5 \times 10^{-7}}\right) \approx 7.58727$$

4 Results and Discussion

4.1 N-gram Results in Journal Articles

In this section, we present the findings regarding the usage of n-grams by authors in journal articles. Based on our observations, we set the threshold for New-MI to be greater than 3 and the frequency to be greater than 10 for 3-gram in journal articles. The results are summarized in Table 1.

Table 1. Journal Article 3-gram: Top 5

Number	N-gram	New-MI	Frequency
1	shì yī zhǒng to be a kind of	3.26	252
2	zhè liǎng gè these two	3.86	155
3	zhè liǎng zhǒng these two types	4.25	112
4	yīdìng chéngdu shàng to some extent	5.67	103
5	zhījiān de guānxì the relationship between	4.71	97
......	......	......	......
Total	1292		

According to Table 1, there are a total of 1292 3-gram in journal articles that meet the criteria of having New-MI greater than 3 and a frequency greater than 10.

Table 2. Journal Article 4-gram: Top 5

Number	N-gram	New-MI	Frequency
1	zài yīdìng chéngdu shàng to a certain extent	4.62	83
2	zuì cháng míngcí duǎnyǔ the longest noun phrase	7.07	83
3	zài cǐ jīchǔ shàng on this basis	4.87	62
4	zhídé zhùyì de shì it is worth noting that	4.58	53
5	jiāohù zuòyòng bù xiǎnzhù the interaction is not significant	6.98	39
……	……	……	……
Total	339		

As shown in Table 2, there are a total of 339 4-gram in journal articles that meet the criteria of having New-MI greater than 3 and a frequency greater than 10.

Table 3. Journal Article 5-gram: Top 5

Number	N-gram	New-MI	Frequency
1	tígāo yǔkuài yìshí de jiàoxué teaching to enhance collocation awareness	5.67	54
2	mǔyǔzhě hé dìèr yǔyán xuéxízhě native speakers and second language learners	5.92	28
3	zài hěn dà chéngdù shàng to a significant extent	4.54	26
4	guānxì jiěshì hé shǔxìng jiěshì relational explanations and attributive explanations	6.46	26
5	yǔsù yìshí duì yuèdú lǐjiě morphemic awareness on reading comprehension	7.10	22
……	……	……	……
Total	104		

According to Table 3, there are a total of 104 5-gram in journal articles that meet the criteria of having New-MI greater than 3 and a frequency greater than 10.

Table 4. Journal Article 6-gram: Top 5

Number	N-gram	New-MI	Frequency
1	tígāo yǔkuài yìshí de jiàoxué duì teaching to enhance collocation awareness has a	4.51	24
2	shuǐpíng de jiāohù zuòyòng bù xiǎnzhù non-significant level of interaction	5.98	17
3	zài mùdìyǔ huánjìng zhōng yǔyòng nénglì pragmatic competence in the target language context	4.80	17
4	Hànyǔ mǔyǔzhě hé dìèr yǔyán xuéxízhě native Chinese Speakers and Second Language Learners	4.73	17
5	Tèshū yíwènjù de wúbiāojì huíyìng unmarked responses to Wh-Questions	8.20	16
......	......	......	......
Total	36		

As shown in Table 4, there are a total of 36 6-gram in journal articles that meet the criteria of having New-MI greater than 3 and a frequency greater than 10.

4.2 Deletion of Repetitive Segmentation

Upon automatic extraction, instances of repetitive segmentation were identified, such as "zhuǎnbiàn de dòngyīn" (factors of transformation) as a 3-gram, "zhuǎnbiàn de dòngyīn hé" (factors of transformation and) as a 4-gram, and "zhuǎnbiàn de dòngyīn hé jīzhì" (factors of transformation and mechanisms) as a 5-gram. It was necessary to eliminate these word sequences of various lengths generated through repetitive segmentation.

To achieve this, we employed a combination of the threshold and local maximum value methods to determine the boundaries of n-grams. We compared the internal cohesion measure, G-value, of each n-gram, and only when the G-value was greater than or equal to that of the adjacent sequence, it was confirmed as an extracted n-gram.

Additionally, the filtering method involved preserving n-grams with high New-MI values while ensuring their semantic coherence. We compared candidate chunks and eliminated those with low New-MI values while retaining those with higher New-MI values. Although the criteria for n-gram extraction were clear, many extracted units consisted of ambiguous semantic fragments. As pointed out by Simpson-Vlach & Ellis [25], most lexical bundles lack clear and identifiable meanings or functions, which limits their pedagogic utility. To address this, we employed the principles of semantic coherence and local maximum values to select the final n-grams. By comparing the New-MI values, we retained "zhuǎnbiàn de dòngyīn hé jīzhì" (factors of transformation and mechanisms) with a New-MI value of 9.83, while removing "zhuǎnbiàn de dòngyīn hé" (factors of transformation and) with a New-MI value of 4.58. Furthermore, considering that "zhuǎnbiàn de dòngyīn" (factors of transformation) and "zhuǎnbiàn de dòngyīn hé jīzhì" (factors of transformation and mechanisms) expressed relatively complete semantic units, we retained them as shown in Table 5.

Table 5. Examples of Repetitive Segmentation with Varying Lengths of Word Sequences

N-gram	New-MI	Results
zhuǎnbiàn de dòngyīn hé jīzhì factors of transformation and mechanisms	9.83	√
zhuǎnbiàn de dòngyīn hé factors of transformation and	4.58	×
zhuǎnbiàn de dòngyīn factors of transformation	9.27	√

Note: √represents selection, × represents deletion.

Common instances of incomplete semantic units are often associated with stranded conjunctions, such as the 4-gram "zhuǎnbiàn de dòngyīn hé" (factors of transformation and), where the conjunction "hé" (and) creates a stranded condition leading to incomplete semantics, and thus, it is deleted. Similarly, the 6-gram "wàiláiyǔ de fǔyīn xìtǒng duìbǐ jí" (comparison of the consonant systems of loanwords and) exhibits incomplete semantics due to the stranded conjunction "jí" (and), resulting in its exclusion. Another category of incomplete semantics involves stranded prepositions, also leading to their exclusion, as shown in Table 6.

Table 6. Examples of Incomplete Semantic Word Sequences

N-gram	New-MI	Results
zhōng suǒ zhàn de bǐlì wéi The proportion occupied by… is…	4.50	×
zhōng suǒ zhàn de bǐlì The proportion occupied by	4.38	×
zhōng suǒ zhàn occupied by	4.19	×

Note: √ represents selection, × represents deletion

After manual intervention, there are a total of 84 n-grams with New-MI values greater than 3 and a frequency exceeding 40 occurrences in academic journals. Additionally, there are 151 n-grams with New-MI values more than 3 and a frequency exceeding 30 occurrences. Moreover, a total of 351 n-grams have New-MI values higher than 3 and a frequency exceeding 20 occurrences. Furthermore, there are 1431 n-grams with New-MI values greater than 3 and a frequency exceeding 10 occurrences, as shown in Table 7.

Table 7. Results after manual intervention

N-gram Freq	Total
≥ 40	84
≥ 30	151
≥ 20	351
≥ 10	1431

5 N-gram Classification

Following the automated extraction and manual intervention steps, a total of 1431 continuous word chunks were ultimately identified. To categorize these chunks functionally, we adopted the classification method proposed by Hyland [9], which led to their classification into three distinct categories: research-oriented chunks, text-oriented chunks, and participant-oriented chunks.

Research-oriented chunks are closely linked to the content of the paper, encompassing the research scope, procedures, and other relevant aspects. They can be further subdivided into two subcategories: chunks indicating research content and chunks indicating research methods.

Text-oriented chunks primarily pertain to the organizational structure of the paper, adhering to the internal objective writing logic [26]. They can be subdivided into three subcategories: signposting, limiting scope, and transition markers.

Participant-oriented chunks serve to construct the author's stance and engage in interaction with the readers. They can be divided into two subcategories: chunks indicating authorial stance and chunks indicating reader engagement. The classification results are presented in Table 8.

From the perspective of usage frequency, research-oriented chunks have the highest number of occurrences, followed by text-oriented chunks, and then participant-oriented chunks. Research-oriented chunks are closely related to the specific research content of the paper, and different research topics and content show distinct differences. However, it is the text-oriented chunks and participant-oriented chunks that truly embody the common language features of academic papers. Therefore, during teaching, special attention should be paid to text-oriented chunks and participant-oriented chunks.

Among text-oriented chunks, limiting scope chunks have the highest quantity, as they contribute to making the content of academic papers more precise and suitable for specific research scopes. High-frequency limiting scope chunks include phrases like "the highest frequency is". Participant-oriented chunks mainly consist of stance marker chunks, with intervening markers appearing relatively less frequently. Additionally, there are also limiting markers such as "xūyào shuōmíng de shì" ("it needs to be explained") and "xūyào zhǐchū de shì" ("it needs to be pointed out"), which serve as engagement markers to remind readers to pay attention, interact with the readers, and establish a connection between the authors and readers of the academic paper.

Table 8. Functional Classification Results of N-grams

Function	Subcategory	Examples	Number	Total
research-oriented chunks	content focus	yǔkuài yìshi de jiàoxué teaching chunk awareness	570	910
	research methodology orientation	duìbǐ fēnxī xiǎnshì comparative analysis revels	340	
text-oriented chunks	signposting	zài cǐ jīchǔ shàng on this basis	98	334
	limiting scope	shǐyòng pínlǜ zuì gāo de shì the most frequently used is	179	
	transition markers	rúshàng suǒshù as mentioned above	57	
participant-oriented chunks	author's stance	zài yīdìng chéngdu shàng to some extent	132	187
	engagement	zhí dé guānzhù de shì it is worth noting that	55	

6 Application Analysis

Chunks serve as essential indicators for assessing the academic proficiency of second language learners. In order to investigate the utilization of chunks in Chinese language learning, we conducted an analysis of chunk usage in the degree theses of Korean Chinese learners. The findings are presented in Tables 9 and 10.

As shown in Table 9, the top five 3-gram and 4-gram results in Korean Chinese learners' degree theses are closely related to the research content, such as "zài Hànyǔ zhōng"(in Korean) and"Hánguóyǔ hànzì"(Korean words written in Chinese characters).

As shown in Table 10, the top five most frequent chunks are all related to the research content, such as "duìyìng de Hànyǔ yìwén shì" (corresponding Korean translation) and "Hàn-Hán yǔyán jiēchù zài" (Chinese-Korean language contact). We divided the Korean Chinese learners into one group, referred to as the "Korean Chinese learner group", and the Chinese native speakers as another group, referred to as the "Chinese native speaker group", and then compared their results.

Table 9. Results of the Top 5 3-gram and 4-gram in the Degree Theses of Korean Chinese Learners

3-gram				4-gram			
Number	Result	New-MI	Freq.	Number	Result	New-MI	Freq.
1	zài Hànyǔ zhōng In Korean	3.48	268	1	Zhōng-Hán liǎng guó China and South Korea	4.67	141
2	liǎng zhǒng yǔyán Two languages	4.95	262	2	zài Hànyǔ hé Hànyǔ In Chinese and Korean	3.46	88
3	zài Hànyǔ zhōng In Chinese	3.39	227	3	Hànyǔ hé Hànyǔ zhōng In Chinese and Korean	3.56	82
4	Hánguóyǔ hànzì Korean words written in Chinese characters	5.59	209	4	fànchóu hé qí shǔxìng categories and their attributes	6.99	78
5	Zhè liǎng gè These two	3.96	132	5	duìyìng de Hànyǔ yìwén the corresponding Korean translation	7.00	68

The chunks extracted from the degree theses of Korean Chinese learners were categorized based on functionality using the same methods as those applied for the native speakers' chunk selection. The statistical results are presented in Table 11.

Table 11 shows that the differences in research-oriented, text-oriented, and participant-oriented chunks between the two groups of Chinese native speakers and Korean Chinese learners are all statistically significant ($\chi2 = 22.89$, $p < 0.00$; $\chi2 = 104.57$, $p < 0.00$; $\chi2 = 77.95$, $p < 0.00$). This indicates that there are differences in the use of chunks between Chinese native speakers and Korean Chinese learners. In terms of frequency of use, Chinese native speakers use all three types of chunks more frequently than Korean Chinese learners, suggesting that Korean Chinese learners have shortcomings in using chunks and need to strengthen their training in academic teaching and guidance. It is worth noting that the frequency of research-oriented chunks is higher than the other two types in both groups.

Table 10. Results of the Top 5 5-gram and 6-gram in the Degree Theses of Korean Chinese Learners

5-gram				6-gram			
Number	Result	New-MI	Freq	Number	results	New-MI	Freq
1	duìyìng de Hànyǔ yìwén shì the corresponding Korean translation is	4.31	67	1	yǔ Hànyǔ jùjué yányǔ xíngwéi bǐjiào A Comparative Study of Speech Act Refusals in Chinese and Korean	5.56	51
2	Hàn-Hán yǔyán jiēchù zài The language contact between Chinese and Korean	4.33	63	2	zài xiàndài Hànyǔ zhōng shì zhǐ In modern Chinese, it refers to	4.63	43
3	Hànyǔ hé Hànyǔ liǎng zhǒng yǔyán In Chinese and Korean	5.86	56	3	cíyǔ zài xiàndài Hànyǔ zhōng shì In modern Korean language, the term is	4.33	38
4	Hànyǔ jùjué yányǔ xíngwéi bǐjiào A Comparative Study of Refusal Speech Acts in Chines	5.62	51	4	yǔ Hànyǔ bèidòngbiǎoshì fǎ bǐjiào Compared with the passive voice construction in Korean	5.33	36
5	Zài xiàndài Hànyǔ zhōng shì In Modern Korean Language	4.26	44	5	Liǎng gè huò liǎng gè yǐshàng Two or more	6.08	34

Table 11. Comparison Results between Chinese Native Speakers and Korean Chinese Learners

	Chinese native speaker group	Norm.Freq	Korean Chinese learner group	Norm.Freq	χ^2	Sig
research-oriented chunks	910	25.7	930	20.6	22.89	0.00
text-oriented chunks	334	9.4	167	3.7	104.57	0.00
participant-oriented chunks	187	5.3	76	1.7	77.95	0.00

7 Conclusion

This study utilized AI technology to construct Chinese native speakers' journal paper corpus and Korean Chinese learners' degree thesis corpus. By applying natural language processing techniques and calculating the internal cohesion of n-grams, we established thresholds and manually intervened to identify 1431 n-grams in academic texts from the journals. Furthermore, we categorized the functions of n-grams and compared the differences in n-gram usage between Korean learners and native speakers. Learning and employing n-grams in academic texts can facilitate non-native speakers' understanding of academic articles in a more rapid and comprehensive manner. It can also enhance their academic writing, enabling them to express themselves more akin to native speakers' language usage. Additionally, it assists learners in producing more academically-oriented writing, avoiding overly simplistic or repetitive language choices.

However, this study has certain limitations that necessitate addressing in future research. In comparison to English n-gram research, which spans multiple interdisciplinary fields such as humanities, social sciences, and biological sciences, our study is confined to Chinese international education, linguistics, and related domains. Future research should expand the corpus size to enhance the comprehensiveness and richness of the n-gram dataset. Additionally, this research focused on continuous word chunks in academic discourse and has yet to explore frame-based chunk structures. Qualitative methods will be employed in future research to address this aspect.

References

1. Miller, G.A., Selfridge, J.A.: Verbal context and the recall of meaningful material. Am. J. Psychol. **63**(2), 176–185 (1950)
2. Becker, J. D.: The phrasal lexicon. In: Nash-Webber, B., Schank, R. (eds.) Theoretical Issues in Natural Language Processing. Beranek and Newman, Cambridge: Bolt (1975)
3. Erman, B., Warren, B.: The idiom principle and the open choice principle. Text & Talk **20**(1), 29–62 (2000)
4. Oppenheim N.: The importance of recurrent sequences for non-native speaker fluency and cognition. Heidi Riggenbach (2000)

5. Cortes, V.: Lexical bundles in published and student disciplinary writing: examples from history and biology. Engl. Specif. Purp. **23**(4), 397–423 (2004)
6. Biber, D., Johansson, S., Leech, G., et al.: Longman grammar of spoken and written English. Longman, London (1999)
7. Wray, A.: Formulaic sequences in second language teaching: principle and practice. Appl. Linguis.Linguis. **21**(4), 463–489 (2000)
8. Biber, D., Conrad, S., Cortes, V.: If you look at…: lexical bundles in university teaching and textbooks. Appl. Linguis. **25**(3), 371–405 (2004)
9. Hyland, K.: As can be seen: Lexical bundles and disciplinary variation. English Specific Purposes (New York), **27**(1), 4–21 (2008)
10. Salazar, D.J.L.: Lexical bundles in scientific English: A corpus-based study of native and non-native writing, Doctoral dissertation, Universitat de Barcelona (2011)
11. Li, S., Liu, Q., Bai, S.: Chinese chunking parsing using rule-based and statistics-based methods. J. Comput. Res. Developm. **4**, 385–391 (2002). (in Chinese)
12. Liang, Y., Zhao, T., Yu, H., et al.: Chinese text chunking based on improved K-means clustering. J. Harbin Inst. Technol.. **7**, 1106–1109 (2007). (in Chinese)
13. Li, G., Liu, Z., Wang, R., et al.: Chinese base-chunk identification using hidden-layer feature of segmentation. J. Chin. Inform. Process. **2**, 12–17 (2016). (in Chinese)
14. Culpeper J., Kytö M.: Lexical Bundles in Early Modern English Dialogues: A Window into the Speech-related Language of the Past (2002)
15. Cortes, V.: Lexical bundles in freshman composition. In: Reppen, R., Fitzmaurice, S.M., Biber, D. (eds.) Using corpora to explore linguistic variation, pp. 131–145. John Benjamins Publishing Company, Amsterdam (2002)
16. Nesi, H., Basturkmen, H.: Lexical bundles and discourse signaling in academic lectures. Inter. J. Corpus Linguis. **11**(3), 283–304 (2006)
17. Biber, D., Barbieri, F.: Lexical bundles in university spoken and written registers. English Specific Purposes (New York) **26**(3), 263–286 (2007)
18. Cortes, V., Csomay, E.: Positioning lexical bundles in university lectures. In: Campoy, M.C., Luzón, M.J. (eds.) Spoken corpora in applied linguistics (Linguistic Insights 51), pp. 57–76. Peter Lang, Frankfurt am Main (2007)
19. Kopaczyk, J.: Long lexical bundles and standardisation in historical legal texts. Studia Anglica Posnaniensia **47**(2–3), 3–25 (2012)
20. Leńko-Szymańska, A.: The acquisition of formulaic language by EFL learners. Inter. J. Corpus Linguis. **19**(2), 225–251 (2014)
21. Liu, Z., Chen, H., Yang, H.: A study on common phraseological sequences in Chinese humanities and social science papers. J. Chin. Lang. Teach. **14**(1), 119–152 (2017). (in Chinese)
22. Zhou, Q.: The Construction of a Collocation List Based on Academic Papers of Teaching Chinese to Speakers of Other Languages. In: Liu, M., Kit, C., Qi., Su (eds.) CLSW 2020. LNCS (LNAI), vol. 12278, pp. 576–592. Springer, Cham (2021). https://doi.org/10.1007/978-3-030-81197-6_49
23. Silva, J.F., Lopes G.P.: A local maxima method and a fair dispersion normalization for extracting multi-word units from corpora. In: 6th Meeting on the Mathematics of Language, Orlando, FL (1999)
24. Wei, N., Li, J.: A new computing method for extracting contiguous phraseological sequences from academic text corpora. Inter. J. Corpus Linguis. **18**(4), 506–535 (2013)
25. Simpson-Vlach, R., Ellis, N.C.: An academic formulas list: new methods in phraseology research. Appl. Linguis. **31**(4), 487–512 (2010)
26. Snow, C.E., Uccelli, P.: The challenge of academic language. In: Olson, D.R., Torrance, N. (eds.) The Cambridge Handbook of Literacy, pp. 112–133. Cambridge University Press, New York (2009)

Gender Variation in Mix-Gender Conversations in the Semi-institutional Discourse: The Case of Talk Show

Xin Luo$^{(\boxtimes)}$ [iD], Parti Gábor [iD], and Chu-Ren Huang [iD]

Department of Chinese and Bilingual Studies, The Hong Kong Polytechnic
University, Hong Kong, China
{xin-tracy.luo,gabor.parti}@connect.polyu.hk, churen.huang@polyu.edu.hk

Abstract. In this paper, gender-related variations in the semi-institutional discourse are examined. We investigate the cross-gender conversation in the talk show *Behind the Headline with Wentao*, a corpus of around 88,000 words of Mandarin Chinese conversation and identify gender variation between female and male guests. We explore the turn-taking features and characteristic terms that set the gender categories apart. We observe that female speakers tend to produce more and longer turns when discussion topics about people and relationships whereas males have longer turns when discussing leisure activities and issues. Generational differences across binary gender groups show that females use more hedges of various functions than males. The results also suggest that male and female speakers tend to use more gendered terms when the conversational topics involved people and relationships.

Keywords: Gender Difference · Conversation Topic · Hedges · Turn-taking

1 Introduction

Conversation is the primary form of socialized human interaction which is playing a major role in the activities performed in human communities. In this paper, we are going to investigate the gender-related variation of mix-gender conversation in the semi-institutional discourse of the talk show.

When people were asked to evaluate the general perception of 'maleness' and 'femaleness' through the use of adjective pairs, females are evaluated to be less aggressive, less assertive, less dominant, more emotional, and more timid [1,2]. The perception may affect how people evaluate the behaviors of people of different genders. Male managers who are talkative in the meeting may be considered as 'powerful' whereas female managers who are more dominant in the same situation would be considered not feminine or even 'slut'. However, such gendered linguistic practices are socially-constructed behaviors rather than merely based on gender. Therefore, the dominance of female managers is better characterized as 'masculine-stereotyped' than based on their gender [3].

Talkativeness and turn-taking are two common features for investigating substantive gender differences. For talkativeness, Leaper and Ayres [4] observed that males are more talkative in mix-gender conversation than in same-gender conversation. Men's greater talkativeness was more likely to occur during discussion of impersonal topics whereas females are more talkative during socioemotional contexts that involved either interactions with children or self-disclosure topics [5]. In terms of turn-taking which refers to the length of the speaker's conversational turns, it is suggested that men are more likely to dominate in conversation because they are in a high-authority position [6]. However, Leaper and Robnett [7] proposed that gender differences may be mitigated when women and men engage in similar activities or topics.

This study explores the gender variation in cross-gender conversations in the semi-institutional discourse of a talk show. We investigate whether there are gender differences in terms of turn-taking properties and lexical choices in similar conversational topics. We investigate this question using a dataset of the semi-institutional discourse of a talk show in Mandarin Chinese.

2   Literature Review

2.1   Semi-institutional Discourse - Talk Show

Ilie [8] proposed the term semi-institutional discourse to refer to the talk show as a socio-cultural practice marked by a particular component of the participant, i.e. show host, guest speaker, and/or audience and well-established conventions, as well as by spontaneous interventions and unpredictable outcomes. In the talk show, celebrities and/or experts as well as ordinary people can be invited as show guests to discuss a topic on current issues of social and/or personal interests. The asymmetrical role distribution in talk shows determines that the show host has the institutional authority to control the show and monitor most of the conversations by asking questions or giving comments etc. Even the guests or experts whose expertise in a particular field is invaluable to the ongoing discussion have to accommodate their contributions according to the role assigned to them and follow the lead of the show host. Apart from the institutional roles, the participants may also exhibit non-institutional roles when a talk show is meant to provide insights into the participants' real life. Therefore, the talk show becomes the setting for the deconstruction and reconstruction of the participants' complex identities as social individuals [8].

2.2   Gender Difference in Conversational Topics

The systematic study of gender differences in conversation topics started by Bischoping [9]. For investigating the gender difference in the conversational topic, the data of the same-sex and cross-sex conversation were collected from various conversation settings, such as from the audible conversation on the street [9] as well as in a faculty room in a middle school [10]. These conversation topics have been summarized in Bischoping [11]'s quantitative observation study by comparing the gender differences in conversation topics from 1922 to 1990 (Fig. 1). Among the conversation topics in these 5 topic areas, it is observed that the majority of women's conversations are about people and relationship, followed by appearances whereas topics about work and money as well as leisure activities are more popular in men's conversations [9,11]. Issues which include social and political issues were a more popular topic in male conversation [11]. However, Kipers [10] observed in the faculty room in the middle school that the majority of conversations about social issues were discussed by female groups. Politics is the most popular topic in groups comprised of both males and females.

Topic area	Category	Examples
People and relationships	• Persons of same sex	Personalities, biographies
	• Persons of opposite sex	Dating, parents' anniversary
Work and money	• Academic	Studying, professors
	• Career plans	LSAT scores, graduate schools
	• Jobs	Summer jobs, current work
	• Money	Borrowing money, good buys
Leisure activities	• Sports	Football games, working out
	• Other leisure activities	Sorority events, movies
Appearances	• Personal appearance and clothes	Hair style, leather jackets
Issues	• Social and political issues	Abortion, recycling, Iraq

Fig. 1. Categories of conversation topics in Bischoping [11].

Apart from investigating the sex difference, Haas and Sherman [12] suggested that role is a more reliable variable in determining the topic of the conversation. In daily life, it is observed that men and women address different topics when they are in different social roles such as friend, co-worker, sibling, parent, and child in same-sex conversation. For instance, men friends frequently talk about sports whereas family and clothing are popular topics in female co-workers' conversations. In the talk show, participants can be assigned roles as either show host who has the controlling power or invited guest speakers who follow the lead of the host to discuss a topic on current issues of social and/or personal interests. The distribution and sequential occurrence of turn-taking behaviors would reflect the nature of the particular semi-institutional discourse type [8].

2.3   Gender Difference in Turn-Taking and Lexical Use

Two theoretical frameworks are usually used to understand gender differences. One is the subcultural approach which proposes that men and women were brought up differently and they have different communication styles [13]. Another one is the authority approach which emphasizes the power of authority [14]. Time talked, interruption, overlap and hedges are commonly investigated to show gender differences. Under the framework of the subcultural approach, it is generally believed that women's language is marginal, and powerless whereas men's language is important and powerful [6]. Therefore, men will talk more and are more likely to interrupt women in the conversation. However, Liesenfeld et al. [15] observed that females produce significantly more turns than males in British English conversation.

In addition, hedges are the linguistic feature in women's speech to show uncertainty. Since the situational approach believes that authority is more important than gender to understand conversations. Therefore, people who have power, such as managers, regardless of gender, talk more and have a higher rate of interruption. People in the subordinate position talk less and use more hedges [16].

3   Data and Method

3.1   Data Description

The talk show *Behind the Headline with Wentao* enjoys tremendous popularity for several reasons. First, the topics discussed are very challenging, trying to come to the grips with highly problematic and controversial, but widely shared, concerns about current issues in the public and in the private sphere: social and professional conflicts, marginalization, feminism, etc. For this reason, the language usage has attracted attention and represents a typical genre with interesting characteristics. For example, the talk show text *Behind the Headline with Wentao* was used to investigate the gendered-related use of tonal patterns [17]. In the talk show *Behind the Headline with Wentao*, the cross-gender conversation involved one male guest and one female guest whereas another same-gender conversation in which two male guests participated in the conversation can be found.

Following Bischoping [11]'s coding, a total of 95 episodes of same-gender conversation (51) and cross-gender conversations (44) in the talk show were coded. This study focuses on the analysis of 44 cross-gender conversations. Considering the asymmetrical power distribution of show host and guest speaker, only utterances of male and female guests are compared and analyzed. However, the show host's utterances to announce the start of the programme are helpful to determine the conversational topic. Under people and relationship conversational topic, Bischoping categorizes two sub-topics as persons of the same sex and persons of the opposite sex. Considering the nature of the talk show context and the components of the participants, these two sub-topics are changed to celebrities who are known by the public or ordinary people who is the main protagonist in the discussion. I focus on the summary of the episode and/or the topic announced by the show host at the start of the programme to extract the topic area of each episode. For example:

Example 1
本期节目，窦文涛和许子东、马家辉共同讨论环境保护。

ben3qi1 jie2mu4 dou4wen2tao1 he2 xu3zi3dong1 ma3jia1hui1 gong4tong2 tao3lun4 huan2jing4 bao3hu4

In this episode, Wentao Dou, Zidong Xu and Jiahui Ma will discuss environmental protection.

Example 2

他们让我们讲讲一个我们都不太熟的事，马云。

ta1men2 rang4 wo3men0 jiang3jiang3 yi1 ge4 wo3men0 dou1 bu4tai4 shu2 de0 shi1 Ma3Yun2

They asked us to talk about something that we are not familiar with, Jack Ma.

This approach to extract topic area of each episode proved to be reliable. The agreement between my coding and that of a second coder who independently categorized a subsample of 50 conversations into the five broad topic areas and the residual category was 65.44%. 3 topic areas are found in the talk show *Behind the Headline with Wentao* (Table 1).

Table 1. Number of cross-gender conversations in each topic area.

Topics areas	Category	No. of cross-gender conversations
People and relationships	celebrity/ordinary people	8
Leisure activities	sports/other leisure activities	5
Issues	social and political issues	31
Total		44

It is observed that the majority of the cross-gender conversations discussed in the talk show *Behind the Headline with Wentao* are about issues which include social and political issues followed by people and relationship containing celebrity and ordinary people and leisure activities including sports and other leisure activities such as movies.

3.2   Methods

In order to compare the gender variations in language use between male and female guests, 44 cross-gender conversations are selected and each episode contains a male guest and a female guest. It is worth mentioning that the same guest may be re-invited in different episodes. We first examine turn frequency (the number of turns) and length of speakers' conversational turns (words they speak) in each topic area by using HanLP [18] for tokenization. Then we compare the lexical and phrasal differences between male and female guests and use Scattertext [19] to distinguish different categories and visualize the results.

Table 2. Count of turns and words of males and females in each topic area.

Topic areas	Features	Count		Count Total
		Male guests	Female guests	
People and relationships	Turns	268	295	563
	Words	6,519	10,031	16,550
Leisure activities	Turns	125	138	263
	Words	4,740	4,095	8,835
Issues	Turns	819	792	1,611
	Words	33,652	28,915	62,567

4   Results and Discussions

4.1   Gender Difference in Turn-Taking Features

In Table 2, we observe that female guests have more turns and longer turn lengths than male guests in the discussion about people and relationship. Although females have more turns when discussing leisure activities, males produce longer turns. Moreover, males are dominant in the topic of issues. The results may indicate two phenomena. First, since the host has the right to control the question-asking [8], the show host may direct the conversation towards the guest who he thinks is more suitable to speak. For instance, in the below extract from an episode discussing David Beckham, the show host intentionally invited the female speaker to speak because he thought David Beckham and the female guest were both celebrities in the entertainment industry.

H：那小贝你印象怎么样，我觉得他跟你是同行。

na4 xiao3bei4 ni3 yin4xiang4 zen3me0yang4 wo3 jue2de0 ta1 gen1 ni3 shi4 tong2hang2

What's your impression of Beckham? I think he and you are in the same industry.

F：什么意思？

shen2me0 yi4si1

What do you mean?

Another phenomenon is related to the previous analysis where males and females have preferences in discussing different conversational topics [9–11]. It may imply that different gender groups may be more interested in or more familiar with certain topics so they discuss more. In an episode discussing the housing price, the male guest even directed the discussion to focus on the poor people who worked as a security guard in Shenzhen.

M：客观来说中国的房价大概不会超过到纽约或者巴黎这些世界上最大城市。

ke4guan1lai2shuo1   zhong1guo2   de0   fang2jia4   da4gai4   bu4hui4
chao1guo4 niu3yue1 huo4 ba1li2 zhe4xie1 shi4jie4 shang4 zui4da4 cheng2shi4

Objectively speaking, housing prices in China are probably not higher than those in the world's largest cities, such as New York or Paris.

F: 不可能的。

bu4 ke3neng2 de0

Impossible.

M: 你们关心那么伟大的宏图，我最近注意到一件小的事情，就是保安有很多穷人，深圳保安 。

ni3men0 guan1xin1 na4me0 wei3da4 de0 hong2tu2wo3 zui4jin4 zhu4yi4 dao4 yi1 jian4 xiao3 de0 shi4qing2 jiu4shi4 bao3an1 you3 hen3duo1 qiong2ren2 shen1zhen4 bao3an1

You care about such a great plan. I have noticed a small thing recently, that is, there are many poor security guards. Shenzhen security guards.

4.2   Gender Difference in Lexical and Phrasal Choices

In the previous session, we observed that males have longer turn lengths and more turn frequencies in the topic areas of leisure activities and issues whereas females talked more when discussing people and relationship. In this session, we plot gender differences in terms of different topic areas to visualize the cross-gender differences at the n-gram level using Scattertext library [19]. Figure 2 and Fig. 3 show words and phrases that are more characteristic of each gender group as well as presenting their frequencies based on the scaled F-score which is a modified metric of the harmonic mean of precision and recall of F-score.

We observe a range of terms that reflect gender groups in our dataset. For instance, the top 5 characteristic terms that are associated with male guests in leisure activities and issues topics are '中学', '地震', '社会', '不能' and '之间' whereas '真的', '感觉', '之后', '实际上' and '最后' are terms that are more associated with female guests' speech. For people and relationship topics, the 5 characteristic terms that males use most are '嘛', '它', '问题', '一样' and '呢' while that of female groups are '然后', '拍', '我...觉得', '其实' and '应该'.

Although males and females have different characteristic terms in different topic areas, common patterns are observed. It is found that females are more likely than males to use hedges in cross-gender conversations. In the context of Chinese podcast shows, Chai [20] observed similar findings that more hedging behaviors are used in cross-gender conversations. According to Lakoff [6], hedges are words that make things fuzzier or less fuzzy such as 'maybe' and 'perhaps' in English and '我觉得' in Chinese. The function of hedges is more than just to show uncertainty [6]. The four additional functions are the expression of doubt and confidence, sensitivity to others' feelings, researching for the right word, and avoidance of expert status [21]. In our dataset, four functions of hedges can be observed.

(1) Expression of doubt and confidence
F: 其实你刚刚讲到那个消费男色这件事情，其实我觉得我自己属于那种，对于男色比较有抵抗力。

qi2shi2 ni3 gang1gang1 jiang3dao4 na4 ge4 xiao1fei4 nan2se4 zhe4 jian4 shi4qing2 qi2shi2 wo3 jue2de0 wo3 zi4ji3 shu3yu1 na4zhong3 dui4yu1 nan2se4 bi3jiao4 you3 di3kang4li4

Actually, you just talked about consuming male sex. In fact, I think I belong to that kind that is more resistant to male.

(2) Sensitivity to other's feelings

F: 文道 我 感觉 你 不能 这么 太实 的 想 这件 事

Wen2dao4 wo3 gan2jue2 ni3 bu4 neng2 zhe4me0 tai4 shi2 de0 xiang3 zhe4 jian4 shi4

Wen Dao, I feel like you can't think about this matter so seriously.

(3) Researching for the right word

F: 我 觉得 他 已经 把 自己 当成 一个 商品 了

wo3 jue2de0 ta1 yi3jing1 ba3 zi4ji3 dang1 cheng2 yi1 ge0 shang1pin3 le0

I think he has regarded himself as a commodity.

(4) Avoidance of expert status

F: 实际上 要 我们 看 的话 还是 挺 不 道义 的

shi2ji4shang4 yao4 wo3men0 kan4 de0hua4 hai2shi4 ting3 bu4 dao4yi4 de0

In fact, it would be quite unethical for us.

A closer look at the top 10 terms in different topic areas in Fig. 2 and Fig. 3, we observed that gender-neutral terms such as ('学生' and '人') and the gendered terms such as ('男人' and '她') are used in male and female speech. It seems that male and female speakers tend to use more gendered terms when discussing people and relationships.

M: 第一它取悦于男人，不是取悦于女人，高跟鞋和缠足都是这样，她本人 并不舒服

di4yi1 ta1 qu3yue4 yu1 nan2ren2 bu4shi4 qu3yue4 yu1 nv3ren2 gao1gen1xie2 he2 chan2zu2 dou1 shi4 zhe4yang4 ta1 ben3ren2 bing4 bu4 shu1fu2

First, it pleases men, not women. This is true for high heels and foot binding. She herself is not comfortable.

As a genderless language, gender is not grammatically marked in Mandarin. Although Mandarin has 她 and 他 to distinguish female and male, the masculine form of 他们 can be used to refer to both genders. In the above example, male speakers use the gendered term '男人' and '女人' to mark gender in the statement to show that high-heel shoes affect sexes differently. The use of these gender labels in discourse increases the salience of gender stereotyping that females wear high-heel to please male. However, clothing, as a gender performance, can be a way people present themselves [22]. For intersex or transgender people, wearing high-heel shoes may be a way to please themselves or their partners who can be either male or female.

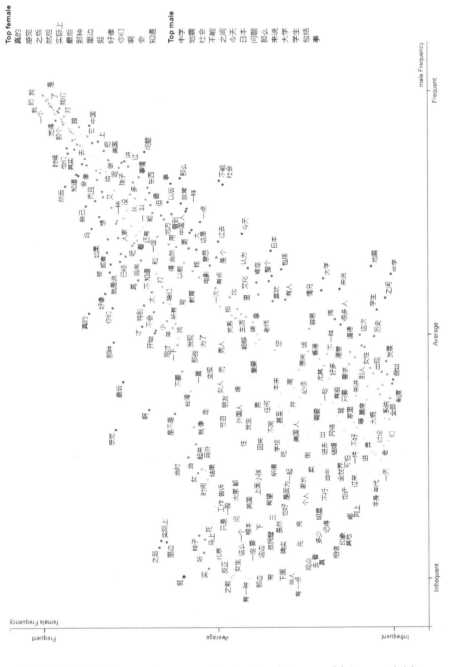

Fig. 2. Lexical difference in conversation topics of issues and leisure activities.

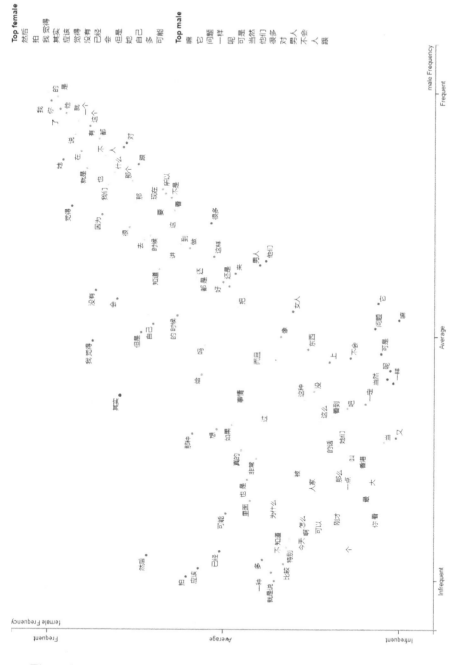

Fig. 3. Lexical difference in conversation topics of people and relationship.

5   Conclusion

In this paper, we investigated the gender-related variations in the semi-institutional discourse in Mandarin Chinese. The results of this pilot study show that gender differences exist when women and men engage in similar topics. Particularly, we are interested in the turn-taking and lexical and phrasal features in cross-gender conversations. We observed that female speakers tend to produce more and longer turns when conversational topics are about people and relationships whereas males are more talkative when discussing leisure activities and social and political issues.

Considering the lexical and phrasal features, we found generational differences across binary gender groups. It is found that females use more hedges of various functions in all three topic areas than males. The result also suggested that male and female speakers tend to use more gendered terms when the conversational topics involved people and relationships. We hope this pilot study can contribute to a deeper understanding of gender-related variation in cross-gender conversation in the semi-institutional discourse.

References

1. Burke, P.J., Tully, J.C.: The measurement of role identity. Soc. Forces **55**(4), 881–897 (1977)
2. Drass, K.A.: The effect of gender identity on conversation. Soc. Psychol. Q. **49**(4), 294–301 (1986)
3. Leaper, C.: Gender similarities and differences in language. In: Holtgraves T.M. (ed.) The Oxford Handbook of Language and Social Psychology, pp. 62–81. Oxford University Press (2014). https://doi.org/10.1093/oxfordhb/9780199838639.013.002
4. Leaper, C., Ayres, M.M.: A meta-analytic review of gender variations in adults' language use: talkativeness, affiliative speech, and assertive speech. Pers. Soc. Psychol. Rev. **11**(4), 328–363 (2007)
5. Newman, M.L., Groom, C.J., Handelman, L.D., Pennebaker, J.W.: Gender differences in language use: an analysis of 14,000 text samples. Discourse Process. **45**(3), 211–236 (2008)
6. Lakoff, R.: Language and woman's place. Lang. Soc. **2**(1), 45–79 (1973)
7. Leaper, C., Robnett, R.D.: Women are more likely than men to use tentative language, aren't they? A meta-analysis testing for gender differences and moderators. Psychol. Women Q. **35**(1), 129–142 (2011)
8. Ilie, C.: Semi-institutional discourse: the case of talk shows. J. Pragmat. **33**(2), 209–254 (2001)
9. Moore, H.T.: Further data concerning sex differences. J. Abnorm. Soc. Psychol. **17**(2), 210–214 (1922)
10. Kipers, P.: Gender and topic. Lang. Soc. **16**(4), 543–557 (1987)
11. Bischoping, K.: Gender differences in conversation topics, 1922–1990. Sex Roles **28**(1), 1–18 (1993)
12. Haas, A., Sherman, M.A.: Conversational topic as a function of role and gender. Psychol. Rep. **51**(2), 453–454 (1982)
13. Tannen, D.: You Just Don't Understand. Virago Press, London (1992)

14. Zimmermann, D.H., West, C.: Sex roles, interruptions and silences in conversation. In: Singh, S. (ed.) Towards a Critical Sociolinguistics. Current Issues in Linguistic Theory, vol. 125, pp. 211–236. John Benjamins BV (1996). https://doi.org/10.1075/cilt.125.12zim

15. Liesenfeld, A., Parti, G., Hsu, Y.Y., Huang, C.R.: Predicting gender and age categories in English conversations using lexical, non-lexical, and turn-taking features. arXiv preprint arXiv:2102.13355 (2021)

16. Johnson, C.: Gender, legitimate authority, and leader-subordinate conversations. Am. Sociol. Rev. **59**(1), 122–135 (1994)

17. Luo, X., Huang, C.R.: Gender-related use of tonal patterns in Mandarin Chinese. In: Su, Q., Xu, G., Yang, X. (eds.) Chinese Lexical Semantics, CLSW 2022. LNCS (LNAI), vol. 13496, pp. 96–107. Springer, Cham (2023). https://doi.org/10.1007/978-3-031-28956-9_8

18. He, H., Choi, J.D.: The stem cell hypothesis: dilemma behind multi-task learning with transformer encoders. In: Moens, M.F., Huang X.J., Lucia, S, Yih, S.W. (eds) EMNLP2021, Online and Punta Cana, Dominican Republic, pp. 5555–5577. Association for Computational Linguistics (2021). https://aclanthology.org/2021.emnlp-main.451

19. Kessler, J.S.: Scattertext: a browser-based tool for visualizing how corpora differ. arXiv preprint arXiv:1703.00565 (2017)

20. Chai, Y.: Gender and hedging behavior: an analysis of functions of hedges employed by women in Chinese conversations. In: Tong, Z., Yan, J. (eds.) ICELA 2021, ASSEHR, vol. 637, pp. 32–38. Atlantis Press (2022). https://doi.org/10.2991/assehr.k.220131.006

21. Coates, J.: 'So i mean i probably ...': hedges and hedging in women's talk. In: Women. Men and Everyday Talk, pp. 31–49. Palgrave Macmillan, London (2013)

22. McConnell-Ginet, S.: Labeling: "what are you, anyway?". In: Word Matters: Meaning and Power, pp. 8–49. Cambridge University Press (2020)

A Comparative Study of Computational Linguistics Terminology in English Papers by Chinese and American Scholars

Yonghui Xie[1,2] , Wei Huang[2], and Erhong Yang[3(✉)]

[1] Faculty of Linguistic Sciences, Beijing Language and Culture University, Beijing, China
202221296009@stu.blcu.edu.cn
[2] Institute of Quantitative Linguistics, Beijing Language and Culture University, Beijing, China
[3] China National Language Monitoring and Research Print Media Center, Beijing Language and Culture University, Beijing, China
1098751719@qq.com

Abstract. This study aims to explore the research hotspots and development trends in computational linguistics through a terminology-based comparison. The specific method involves constructing a corpus of English papers in computational linguistics by Chinese and American scholars from the past decade, then counting the coverage frequency of basic and high-frequency terms in the corpus, and finally conducting a diachronic and synchronic comparative analysis. Our findings are as follows. Over the past decade, there was a decreasing trend in the usage of basic terms among both Chinese and American scholars in computational linguistics. This may be attributed to the continuous production of new terms and the reduction in comprehension difficulty of papers. Nonetheless, certain periods have shown an increase in the usage of specific terms, such as the prevalence of algorithms and models in Chinese scholars' papers from 2012 to 2013, and American scholars' focus on text processing, application systems, and linguistic resources from 2014 to 2015. On the other hand, the high-frequency terms used in the past decade collectively reflect the prevailing research trends in computational linguistics: continuous ascent and evolution of deep learning, consistent research interest and ongoing innovation in machine translation, and significant growth in the study of speech and discourse.

Keywords: Terminology Comparison · Computational Linguistics · Chinese and American Scholars · Research Hotspots

1 Introduction

The rapid development of science and production information has not only brought about the information explosion but has also stimulated the emergence of term explosion. More than 90% of new words in modern language are professional words [1]. As a result, it has triggered a research boom in terminology, encompassing three primary areas: its fundamental principles, its methodologies, and its applications across various disciplines.

Terms act as powerful symbols of advancement within a specific field, and academic papers serve as the means by which these terms are disseminated. By comparing and analyzing the prevalent terms within papers authored by different scholars across distinct timeframes, we can unveil underlying research trends in one field and proactively anticipate future research directions. These insights are pivotal for scientific discoveries and competitive intelligence.

1.1 Related Research

The definition of terms has consistently been a controversial issue within the realm of terminology and linguistics. International standards, national standards, and professional scholars have contributed to the definition and comment of terms [2–4], with little attention to the practical applicability for terms. Building upon the foundation of the national standard *Terminology Work—Computer Application—Data Category (GB/T 16786—2007)*, [5] defined terms as words or phrases with explicit definitions and descriptions within a particular field, designed for the purpose of term recognition.

The comparative study of Chinese and foreign terms usually focuses on two primary aspects. The first aspect involves comparing the translation of Chinese and foreign terms to promote communication and collaboration between China and foreign countries. For example, [6] and [7] conducted comparative analyses of Chinese-English legal terms and Chinese-English scientific and technological terms, respectively. The second aspect entails comparing the lexical features of Chinese and foreign terms to delve into the distinctive features of terms and cultural disparities. For instance, [8] investigated the nomenclature of terms by taking Chinese-English martial arts terms as examples. [9] compared and analyzed the methods of semantic generation and the formation of cognitive models concerning Chinese-Russian engineering terms, so as to explore the similarities and differences of their semantic generation. [10] scrutinized the characteristics of Chinese-Korean medicine terms from the perspective of word formation and etymology. In brief, these previous studies predominantly focused on the synchronic level. The present study, however, intends to undertake a comparative analysis of English terms in computational linguistics, encompassing both synchronic and diachronic perspectives.

Computational linguistics is a burgeoning and interdisciplinary field that employs computer technology to study and process natural language. The development of information technology and globalization has fostered the prosperity of this filed and the proliferation of terms within it. The investigation of terminology in computational linguistics typically includes the exploration of specific terms, such as one term "word embedding" introduced in [11] and a category of terms "indexing and information retrieval" discussed by [12], and the analysis of synonyms in the terminology as examined in [13]. Additionally, efforts have been made in constructing English-Chinese term databases for computational linguistics [14, 15]. However, much research on the development of this field has predominantly relied on the accumulated experiences and subjective comments of scholars [16, 17]. This lacks robust support from quantitative methods and corpora, which are widely utilized in empirical studies, as exemplified in [18]. Therefore, utilizing corpora and statistical techniques for terminology analysis represents a relatively objective research approach.

Recently, the use of literature visualization analysis tools like VOSviewer and CiteSpace has facilitated the exploration of research hotspots from a terminology perspective in various fields, including photosynthesis [19] and eye tracking technology [20]. Notably, [15] extracted high-frequency terms and analyzed research hotspots and trends in computational linguistics based on papers published from 2010 to 2014. However, their focus remained mainly on synchronic research, with little attention given to the diachronic development and changes within computational linguistics. Furthermore, the differences in term usage as a tool for communicating thought and cognition among different groups also warrant further synchronic study.

1.2 Research Design

The research process begins with the construction of a corpus containing papers on computational linguistics authored by both Chinese and American scholars over the past decade. Subsequently, the frequencies of usage for both basic terms and high-frequency terms are calculated, based on corresponding term resources and the self-constructed corpus. At last, an analysis is conducted to explore both the diachronic evolution and synchronic distinctions in the usage of these terms in the two categories of papers. The primary objective of our research is to offer insights and forecast trends for related research endeavors in computational linguistics. The specific research questions are outlined as follows:

1. What is the extent of usage of basic terms in English papers on computational linguistics authored by Chinese and American scholars over the past decade? What trends in research are evident in this field?
2. What is the extent of usage of high-frequency terms in English papers on computational linguistics authored by Chinese and American scholars over the past decade? What trends in research are discernible in this field?

2 Comparison of Basic Terms Used by Chinese and American Scholars

2.1 Corpus

Academic papers hold an increasingly prominent role in natural language processing, leading to the construction of corresponding corpora and datasets. [21] obtained the papers authored by Chinese and American scholars in the field of computational linguistics between 2010 and 2020 using the S2ORC corpus, relying on the commonly used names in China and the United States. The current study specifically targets English papers authored by Chinese and American scholars from 2010 to 2019 based on the forementioned data. The selected data was segmented into five periods, each covering a two-year span. To ensure data balance, approximately 100 papers were chosen for each period. The corpus sizes for each period are presented in Table 1 below.

Table 1. Corpus size of Chinese and American scholars' papers.

Period	Chinese scholar			American scholar		
	Number of papers	Mean number of words	Number of words	Number of papers	Mean number of words	Number of words
2010–2011	100	3584.77	358477	100	3293.73	329373
2012–2013	100	3167.33	316733	100	3154.26	315426
2014–2015	100	3396.25	339625	100	3427.92	342792
2016–2017	100	3696.44	369644	87	2872.46	287246
2018–2019	100	3518.88	351888	94	3300.53	330053
In total	500	3472.734	1736367	481	3209.78	1604890

2.2 Basic Terms

Typically, terms related to computational linguistics are compiled in specialized glossaries, such as *Chinese Terms in Linguistics* [22] and *The Oxford Handbook of Computational Linguistics* [23]. Additionally, they can be found in the appendix glossaries of the relevant books like *Statistical Natural Language Processing* [24] and *Introduction to Computational Linguistics* [25]. For our study, the basic terms used were selected from the *Chinese Terms in Linguistics*, published by the National Committee for Terminology in Science and Technology in 2011. To ensure comparability between the terms found in Chinese and American scholars' papers, we merged the original 11 categories of terms and eliminated those that only appeared in Chinese texts, such as the term "Chinese word segmentation". In the end, 276 basic terms were chosen, and their classification and number are shown in Table 2.

Table 2. Classification and number of basic terms.

Index	Category of terms	Subcategory of terms	Number of terms
1	text processing	word processing sentence processing text processing	39
2	formal method	formal method	52
3	algorithm, theory and model	algorithm, theory and model	91
4	application system	application system machine translation	73
5	language resources	language resources	21

Python scripts were employed to analysis the distribution of five categories of basic terms in Chinese and American papers across five periods. This analysis included calculating the frequency of each category and the frequency of individual terms. The methodology consisted of the following steps:

1. The selected corpus and basic term glossary underwent initial processing, including word tokenization and part-of-speech tagging. We employed the BFSU Stanford POS Tagger software, developed by Beijing Foreign Studies University.
2. Plural nouns marked with "NNS" and "NNPS" in our corpus were lemmatized to ensure accurate counting. It's important to note that terms inherently possess a naming nature; they typically manifest as nouns or noun phrases [1]. Therefore, our focus pays more attention to nouns within our corpus.
3. The frequency of basic terms in our corpus was counted. Besides, we utilized regular expressions for case-insensitive matching to account for terms appearing at the beginning of the sentences.

The statistical results are illustrated in Fig. 1 through Fig. 6. Specifically, Fig. 1 shows the overall usage frequency of all basic terms, while Fig. 2, to Fig. 6 present the usage frequency of each category of terms. In these figures, the blue solid line and the red solid line represent the detailed changes in the term frequency used by American and Chinese scholars, respectively. Meanwhile, the blue dotted line and the red dotted line represent the usage trend lines of terms for American and Chinese scholars, respectively. Due to limitations in text length, the frequency of specific terms within each category is not provided in the form of charts but will be discussed in the subsequent analysis section.

2.3 Comparative Analysis

From Fig. 1, it can be observed that the usage frequency of basic terms in the papers by American or Chinese scholars has consistently decreased year after year, with a slight increase in the usage frequency by American scholars from 2014 to 2015. This suggests an overall downward trend in the usage of these terms in the foreseeable future. In Fig. 2, to Fig. 6, the usage frequency of terms within each category showed a similar declining trend for both Chinese and American scholars, except for the "text processing" category used by Chinese scholars, which presented a slow upward trend. Notably, American scholars experienced a faster decline in the usage of "formal method" and "algorithm, theory and model" categories compared to their Chinese counterparts. Conversely, Chinese scholars showed a steeper decline in "application system" category, while the decline rate was roughly similar for both groups in the "language resources" category.

In summary, the usage frequency, calculated for all categories and each category, displays a consistent downward trend in both types of papers. Several factors could contribute to this trend. Firstly, the field of computational linguistics is rapidly evolving, resulting in the continuous emergence of new terms. Scholars may choose to reduce their reliance on basic terms when these terms no longer adequately represent the cutting-edge research in this field. In addition, the evolving landscape of academic literature dissemination plays a role. Academic papers are now reaching a broader and more diverse readership, extending beyond scientific researchers to include potential investors and government personnel [26]. In response, scholars may opt to reduce the usage of terms that are relatively complex or specialized to enhance the overall readability of their papers and then promote broader dissemination.

Although the majority of trend lines exhibit a consistent downward trend, there are subtle fluctuations in the usage frequency of each category of terms. Furthermore, our study examined the high-frequency basic terms in Chinese and American papers over the past decade and observed that scholars from both countries tended to employ similar choices of high-frequency basic terms. The subsequent section will provide a comprehensive account of the nuanced shifts in usage frequency as well as an overview of the shared high-frequency terms within each category.

According to Fig. 2, within the "text processing" category, the usage frequency by American scholars initially increased, reaching its peak in 2014–2015, and then gradually decreased. However, the variation in the usage frequency by Chinese scholars has remained relatively stable over the past decade. Upon analyzing our corpus, it was discovered that the term "text" had the highest frequency of use by American scholars in 2014–2015, which significantly contributed to the increase in usage frequency for that year. Moreover, the common high-frequency basic terms in "text processing" category for both scholars include "text", "parser", and "disambiguation". These terms indicate that the focus of this field is mainly on tasks related to text parsing and ambiguity resolution.

As for the "formal method" category, Fig. 3 illustrates that the usage frequency among American scholars initially decreased and reached its lowest point in 2014–2015 before rebounding. Thus, the formal method was not highly valued in 2014–2015. On the contrary, the usage frequency among Chinese scholars fluctuated less overall. In addition, our corpus also shows that common high-frequency terms for both scholars include "pattern", "derivation", "child", "slot" and "frame", suggesting the popularity of these basic units.

In Fig. 4, within the "algorithm, theory and model" category, the utilization frequency among American scholars experienced a gradual decline; while the usage frequency among Chinese scholars initially increased and then reached its highest point in 2012–2013, before gradually decreasing. This suggests that the application of algorithms and models by Chinese scholars formed a small surge in 2012–2013. Further examination revealed that the term "matching" had a higher frequency in these two years, which may contribute to that small surge. Additionally, the common high-frequency terms within this category have "clustering", "matching", "feature vector" and "conjunction", implying that clustering and matching methods for processing feature vectors has attracted more attention in this field.

Regarding the "application system" category, Fig. 5 presents that the usage frequency by American scholars initially increased, reaching a small peak in 2014–2015, and then decreased. This reveals that American scholars experienced a minor research boom in various application systems during 2014–2015. Upon closer observation, it was found that the increased usage of terms like "precision" and "query" in these two years might be one of the reasons for this prosperity. Conversely, the usage by Chinese scholars has been declining at a slower pace. Common high-frequency terms within this category include "precision", "recall", "MT", "SMT", "machine translation", "machine learning", and "named entity". This may point to that machine learning is a commonly used method in this field, with a particular focus on machine translation, especially statistical machine translation. Researchers also frequently employ accuracy and recall as performance indicators for testing system performance, and there is substantial attention to named entities, an essential information element.

In the "language resources" category, as depicted in Fig. 6, American scholars' usage initially decreased, then increased, and finally decreased again, while Chinese scholars' usage remained stable initially, followed by an increase and then a decrease. Both countries experienced a minor upsurge from 2014 to 2015. Besides, the common high-frequency terms include "corpus", "test set", "training set", "sampling", and "sampling size", demonstrating that this field places significant emphasis on datasets, particularly test and training datasets, and pays close attention to the sample size of these datasets.

From a synchronic perspective, whether considering all categories or each category, Chinese and American scholars exhibited similar trend in terms of usage changes. Nevertheless, with the exception of the "algorithm, theory and model" category, American scholars tended to have higher usage frequency compared to their Chinese counterparts in each category.

Fig. 1. Frequency of all categories.

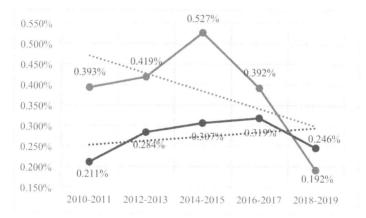

Fig. 2. Frequency of "text processing" category.

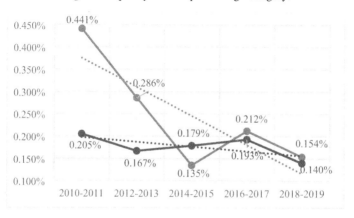

Fig. 3. Frequency of "formal method" category.

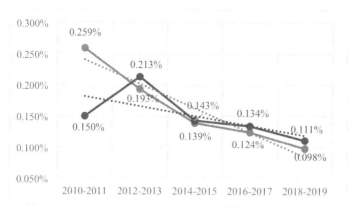

Fig. 4. Frequency of "algorithm, theory and model" category.

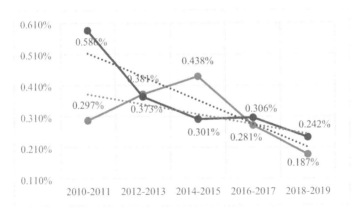

Fig. 5. Frequency of "application system" category.

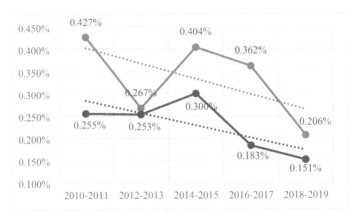

Fig. 6. Frequency of "language resources" category.

3 Comparison of High-Frequency Terms Used by Chinese and American Scholars

Given that computational linguistics is a rapidly evolving and emerging discipline, the ongoing creation and utilization of new terms are a natural consequence. In the previous section, we investigated the development of computational linguistics based on basic terms published in 2011. To gain further insights into the evolution of this field, it is advisable to extract high-frequency terms from the papers used in the last section. This approach allows us to explore the progression of computational linguistics through the lens of high-frequency terms.

3.1 High-Frequency Terms

Term extraction is a fundamental technology in the realm of mining knowledge from academic literature. There are typically three main methods for term extraction, namely rule-based method, statistical-based method and supervised learning-based method. Each of these methods processes its inherent advantages and drawbacks. In this research, we employed a combination of rule and statistical methods, along with the utilization of AntConc corpus software and manual proofreading, to acquire high-frequency computational linguistic terms from the papers by Chinese and American scholars.

The specific operational steps are as follows. First of all, Chinese and American academic papers were taken as the target corpus, and eight literary works such as *Pride and Prejudice*, *Red and Black*, *Jane Eyre* and *Oliver Twist* were taken as the reference corpus. The scale of the reference corpus was set at five times that of the target corpus. Secondly, both the target and reference corpus were input AntConc software, and then about 1,000 highly significant high-frequency keywords were extracted from the target corpus for each time period according to the Keyword List (keyword list) function in AntConc software. Significance was determined based on the maximum likelihood function value (Loglikelihood). Finally, non-noun words within the high-frequency keywords were manually filtered out, resulting in the acquisition of approximately 900 high-frequency terms for each period in Chinese and American papers.

3.2 Comparative Analysis

Through analyzing 900 high-frequency terms across the five periods, it was observed that these terms had relatively stable usage patterns over time. Table 3 provides a snapshot of top 50 high-frequency terms used by American scholars from 2010 to 2011. By classifying these terms, the findings are as follows. Terms such as "word", "lexical", "phrase", "sentence", "grammar", "semantic", and others indicate a comprehensive focus on various aspects of language within computational linguistics. Terms like "model", "algorithm", "training", "parsing", "approach" and "accuracy" underscore that the primary research methods in this field revolve around models and algorithms. "Translation", "dialogue", "classification" and other terms represent diverse research topics within this field. Moreover, "data", "corpus" and "set" suggest that the field places significant emphasis on the processing of large-scale real text.

Additionally, subtle differences and changes were captured by comparing the high-frequency terms used by Chinese and American scholars over the past decade from different aspects, including research objects, models and algorithms, and research themes. Based on these, an analysis of the development trends in research hotspots within the field of computational linguistics were conducted, and the results are presented below.

Continuous Ascent and Evolution of Deep Learning. Table 4 displays the relevant terms associated with deep neural networks and their highest rankings during each period. These abbreviation terms are elaborated as follows: NN (Neural Network), RNN (Recurrent Neural Network), CNN (Convolutional Neural Network), and GNN (Graph Neural Network).

Table 3. Top 50 high-frequency terms.

Index	Significance	Frequency	Term	Index	Significance	Frequency	Term
1	3604.67	1071	**model**	26	1130.82	311	**lexical**
2	3084.56	848	data	27	1101.37	389	**phrase**
3	2798.17	938	**language**	28	1099.49	328	**grammar**
4	2480.75	703	**corpus**	29	1064.1	325	test
5	2015.52	662	**system**	30	1050.81	289	classification
6	1979.84	741	**features**	31	1050.81	289	parsing
7	1881.4	546	**models**	32	1039.9	286	input
8	1808.24	548	results	33	1037.3	303	systems
9	1607.3	442	**semantic**	34	1001.41	371	task
10	1478.11	890	set	35	937.07	277	pairs
11	1468.98	524	example	36	904.48	264	target
12	1454.53	400	**algorithm**	37	899.24	341	source
13	1441.58	534	**sentence**	38	890.8	245	evaluation
14	1436.18	424	languages	39	883.98	290	**phrases**
15	1365.69	408	section	40	872.64	364	**approach**
16	1347.69	528	information	41	856.47	278	rules
17	1333.56	399	structure	42	839.96	244	**accuracy**
18	1265.8	380	training	43	835.53	276	probability
19	1238.55	411	text	44	821.72	268	topic
20	1229.04	920	**word**	45	819.57	762	**words**
21	1196.62	343	context	46	814.8	270	performance
22	1192.43	374	**translation**	47	793.22	231	experiments
23	1186.84	384	**sentences**	48	785.34	216	parser
24	1181.66	539	number	49	776.57	217	linguistic
25	1138.25	363	feature	50	772.94	216	**syntactic**

From a diachronic perspective, high-frequency terms related to neural networks did not appear between 2010 and 2012. However, from 2013–2014 onwards, related high-frequency terms began to emerge, with their rankings gradually increased. Notably, during 2014–2015, the popularity of CNN led to the introduction of terms like TBCNN, which denotes using CNN for learning abstract syntax trees (AST). From 2018 to 2019, GNN gained prominence as a research hotspot within the field of neural networks. This is particularly significant because traditional network models, such as CNN, handle data represented in Euclidean space effectively but struggle with graph data, which can only be represented in non-Euclidean space. Fortunately, GNN offers a solution to this issue.

From a synchronic perspective, the change of terms used by Chinese and American scholars was quite similar. However, there was a distinction in timing: CNN appeared as a high-frequency hot word in Chinese scholars' papers in 2014–2015, while GNN made its debut in American scholars' papers in 2018–2019. In summary, the above two perspectives highlight the continuous ascent and evolution of deep learning.

Table 4. High-frequency terms in deep neural networks.

Period	Chinese scholar		American scholar	
	Term and its highest ranking		Term and its highest ranking	
2010–2012	None	None	None	None
2013–2014	NN	566	RNN	759
2014–2015	RNN, **CNN, TBCNN**, NN	224	RNN	665
2016–2017	RNN, CNN, NN	90	RNN, CNN	222
2018–2019	RNN, CNN, NN	110	RNN, CNN, **GNN**	142

Consistent Research Interest and Ongoing Innovation in Machine Translation. Table 5 shows the relevant terms associated with machine translation for each period, along with their highest rankings. The full names of abbreviation terms are as follows: MT (Machine Translation), SMT (Statistical Machine Translation), NMT (Neural Machine Translation), and WMT (Workshop on Machine Translation).

From a diachronic perspective, terms like "machine", "translation", MT, SMT, and WMT have consistently been high-frequency terms for nearly a decade. Whereas, the high-frequency term NMT emerged between 2016 and 2017. Indeed, computational linguistics originated from the study of machine translation [27]. As a well-established research field, it has maintained its mainstream status. In recent years, the integration of neural network technology has given rise to NMT as a new research trend.

Significant Growth in the Study of Speech and Discourse. In Table 6, the short horizontal line "-" connects the high-frequency rankings of the terms in the left column for each period. A higher ranking indicates a greater research focus and higher research activity in the language aspect represented by the term. Conversely, a lower ranking implies a lower level of research activity.

Comparing term rankings between Chinese and American scholars, it becomes evident that American scholars consistently achieved higher rankings in all language levels than Chinese scholars. This suggests that American scholars engage in more comprehensive and in-depth language research. Furthermore, examining the differences across the seven linguistic levels, it is found that the research in "semantic", "lexical" and "phrase" aspects was more prominent. In contrast, research in "pragmatic", "speech" and "discourse" levels was less prevalent, particularly in the level of "pragmatic". From a diachronic perspective, both countries continued to emphasize research in the "semantic" aspect. Research interest in "discourse" appeared to be on the rise, while research in "lexical" and "phrase" categories was diminishing. However, "pragmatic" research

Table 5. High-frequency terms in machine translation.

Period	Chinese scholar		American scholar	
	Term and its highest ranking		Term and its highest ranking	
2010–2012	MT, SMT, machine, translation	12	MT, SMT, machine, translation	22
2013–2014	MT, SMT, machine, translation	6	MT, SMT, **WMT**, machine, translation	47
2014–2015	MT, SMT, machine, translation	22	MT, SMT, WMT, machine, translation	71
2016–2017	MT, SMT, **WMT, NMT**, machine, translation	37	MT, **NMT**, machine, translation	48
2018–2019	MT, WMT, NMT, machine, translation	30	MT, SMT, WMT, NMT, machine, translation	58

remained undervalued. Notably, American scholars exhibited an increasing inclination toward "phonetic" research.

To sum up, semantics has always been a hot research topic. Lexical and phrase research was popular initially, but there is a tendency for its significance to gradually decrease. Research on speech and discourse has been steadily gaining momentum. The pragmatic research has not received significant attention.

Table 6. Changes in rankings for each language level.

	Chinese scholar	American scholar
Speech	648 – 406 – 462 – None – None	215 – 488 – 256 – 418 – 165
Lexical	159 – 114 – 101 – 173 –345	26 – 54 – 40 – 74 – 67
Phrase	215 – 457 – 167 – 237 –924	27 – 68 – 98 – 346 – 379
Syntax	611 – 681 – 350 – 629 – None	250 – 141 – 155 – 670 – 171
Semantic	21 – 45 – 11 – 28 – 34	9 – 5 – 10 – 7 – 42
Discourse	817 – 303 – 442 – 80 – 257	226 – 34 – 50 – 194 – 216
Pragmatic	None	None – None – None – 285 – None

4 Conclusion

Through investigating the distribution of basic terms and high-frequency terms in computational linguistics based on academic English papers authored by Chinese and American scholars over the past decade, the two research questions in the current study were successfully addressed. Our findings are as follows.

The first finding concerns basic terms. In general, the basic terms used by Chinese and American scholars exhibited a downward trend over the past decade, which may be attributed to the continuous emergence of new terms and an effort to reduce the language difficulty in academic publications. However, there were also periods of increased use, such as the prevalence of algorithms and models in Chinese scholars' papers from 2012 to 2013, and American scholars' focus on text processing, application systems, and linguistic resources from 2014 to 2015. Furthermore, American scholars utilized a greater number of basic terms compared to their Chinese counterparts, suggesting a more comprehensive engagement in fundamental research within this field.

The second finding pertains to high-frequency terms. There was minimal disparity in the utilization of high-frequency terms between Chinese and American scholars' papers in the past decade. Common high-frequency terms reflect the following research trends in this field: continuous ascent and evolution of deep learning, consistent research interest and ongoing innovation in machine translation, and significant growth in the study of speech and discourse.

To conclude, our study offers valuable insights for the future of computational linguistics research and contributes to the field of terminology and bibliometrics. However, it is important to acknowledge some limitations in this study. Firstly, the basic glossary used in this study is relatively outdated. Secondly, the extraction of high-frequency terms relies solely on rule-based and statistical methods, without the integration of the latest technologies. In the future research, we will utilize an updated basic glossary and employ machine learning or deep learning methods for extracting high-frequency terms. This approach may enhance the objectivity and predictive capability of research conclusions, thereby improving the overall quality of the study.

Acknowledgments. I am grateful to the anonymous reviewers of CLSW 2023 for helpful suggestions and comments. This work is supported by the Project commissioned by the National Science and Technology Nominology Committee (No. ZDI135-131), the Beijing Social Science Fund (No. 18YYC016), and the Beijing Language and Culture University Education Foundation "Innovative Practice Project". All errors remain my own.

References

1. Grinev, S.-V.: Terminology. The Commercial Press, Beijing (2011). (in Chinese)
2. Sager, J.-C., David, D., Peter, F.-M.: English Special Languages: Principles and Practice in Science and Technology. Brandstetter, Wiesbaden (1980)
3. ISO/TC 37: Terminology work-Vocabulary-Part1: Theory and application (2000)
4. Feng, Z.-W.: Introduction to Modern Terminology. The Commercial Press, Beijing (2011). (in Chinese)
5. Zhang, R.: Research on term definition based on term identification. China Terminol. **16**(04), 5–8 (2014). (in Chinese)
6. Sheng, C.-L.: Comparative study of English-Chinese legal terms and their translation. Southwest University of Political Science and Law (2011). (in Chinese)
7. Li, H.: A comparative analysis of English and Chinese terms and translation. China Terminol. **20**(03), 5 (2018). (in Chinese)

8. Alimuradov, O.-A., Latu, M.-N.: Features of terminological nomination: a cognitive-semantic approach (based on the material of Chinese and English terminology of martial arts). Philol. Sci. Issues Theor. Pract. **1, Part 2**, 6–13 (2008). (in Russian)

9. Zheng, Y.-T.: A contrastive study on semantic generation cognition of engineering terms between Russian and Chinese. Harbin Normal University (2020). (in Chinese)

10. Han, Y.: A comparative study of Chinese and Korean medical terms. Yanbian University (2014). (in Chinese)

11. Lu, X.-L., Wang, F.-K.: Word embedding: concepts and applications. China Terminol. **22**(03), 24–32 (2020). (in Chinese)

12. Taran, A.: Terminology of computational linguistics in terms of indexing and information retrieval in the system "iSybislaw". In: Proceedings of the 5th International Conference on Computational Linguistics and Intelligent Systems, pp. 225–234. CEUR-WS.org, Lviv (2021)

13. Polshchykova, O.-N., Genkin, Y.-Y.: Synonymy in the terminology of computational linguistics. Res. Result Theoret. Appl. Linguist. **7**(4), 23 (2021)

14. QasemiZadeh, B., Handschuh, S.: The ACL RD-TEC: a dataset for benchmarking terminology extraction and classification in computational linguistics. In: Proceedings of the 4th International Workshop on Computational Terminology (Computerm), pp. 52–63. Association for Computational Linguistics and Dublin City University, Dublin (2014)

15. Sun, M.-T.: Language feature analysis of English abstracts and the construction of a writing assistance knowledge base. Nanjing Normal University (2016)

16. Feng, Z.-W.: Several characteristics of the current development of computational linguistics. Social Sciences in China (A03) (2020). (in Chinese)

17. Feng, Z.-W.: Seventy years of computational linguistics research in our country. Lang. Educ. **7**(04), 19–29+42 (2019). (in Chinese)

18. Xie, Y.-H., Yang, E.-H.: Research on the distribution and characteristics of negative quasi-prefixes in different registers. In: Dong, M.-H., Gu, Y.-H., Hong, J.-F. (eds.) CLSW 2021. LNCS (LNAI), vol. 13250, pp. 376–387. Springer, Cham (2022). https://doi.org/10.1007/978-3-031-06547-7_29

19. Jiang, T., Xu, Z.-P., Chen, X.-J., Lu, Q.-T., Yang, H.-X., Zhu, X.-J.: Frontier and hot researches in the field of photosynthesis: analysis of scientific terms based on WOS highly cited papers. China Terminol. **23**(01), 60–70 (2021). (in Chinese)

20. Sun, X., Zhan, Q.-L.: Visual analysis of the literature on eye tracking technology from the perspective of high frequency terminology. China Terminol. **23**(01), 71–80 (2021). (in Chinese)

21. Xie, Y.-H., Liu, Y., Yang, E.-H., Yang, T.-L.: A comparative study of the features of lexical sophistication in academic English writing by Chinese and American scholars. In: Proceedings of the 20th Chinese National Conference on Computational Linguistics, pp. 454–466. Chinese Information Processing Society of China, Hohhot (2021). (in Chinese)

22. Song, J., Xu, J.-L., Han, Q.-D., et al.: (All members of the sixth Committee of China National Committee for Terminology in Science and Technology): Chinese terms in Linguistics. The Commercial Press, Beijing (2011). (in Chinese)

23. Mitkov, R.: The Oxford Handbook of Computational Linguistics. Foreign Language Teaching and Research Press and Oxford University Press, Beijing (2009). (in Chinese)

24. Zong, C.-Q.: Statistical Natural Language Processing. Tsinghua University Press, Beijing (2013). (in Chinese)

25. Yu, S.-W.: Introduction to Computational Linguistics. The Commercial Press, Beijing (2004). (in Chinese)

26. Jiang, F., Hyland, K.: Interactional metadiscourse: argument and persuasion in changing academic contexts. Foreign Lang. Educ. **41**(02), 23–28 (2020). (in Chinese)

27. Liu, Y.: Computational Linguistics. Tsinghua University Press, Beijing (2014). (in Chinese)

Native Speakers' Judgment of the Epistemic Evidentiality of Synonym Verbs of "Think" in Mandarin: A Corpus-Based Study of Renwei, Yiwei, Juede, Kaolü, and Xiang

Yaoru Ye and Yu-Yin Hsu[✉]

The Department of Chinese and Bilingual Studies, The Hong Kong Polytechnic University, Hung Hom, Kowloon, Hong Kong SAR, China
21058016G@conncet.polyu.hk, yu-yin.hsu@polyu.edu.hk

Abstract. The synonym of epistemic "think" in Chinese is understudied. This study surveys the usage of five synonyms of verbs related to "think" – renwei, juede, yiwei, xiang, and kaolü – by using the Academia Sinica Balanced Corpus of Modern Chinese. By studying the contexts of the target verbs, we report the distributions of three types of nouns and two types of adverbs in relation to the target verbs among three genres, and then we discuss their potential effects on epistemic evidentiality. Next, we conduct a survey study to examine native speakers' judgments of the epistemic evidentiality of sentences that contain the five target verbs with the types of nouns and adverbs extracted from the Sinia corpus. The results show that "renwei" has the highest ratings of evidentiality, followed by "juede," while "yiwei" and "xiang" have the lowest mean ratings. "Kaolü" is often regarded as irrelevant or neutral concerning epistemic evidentiality.

Keywords: Cognitive Verbs · Near-Synonyms · Evidentiality

1 Introduction

"*Renwei, yiwei, juede, kaolü*, and *xiang*" form a group of epistemic verbs that exhibit semantic and pragmatic similarities. Previous research of near-synonyms has analyzed and distinguished them from various perspectives, such as semantics, grammar, and pragmatics. As research has deepened, different scholars have taken a more comprehensive approach to analyzing near-synonyms. In the seventh edition of the Modern Chinese Dictionary,[1] the semantic translations of these words often exhibit overlap and mutual interpretation. However, native speakers choose different words from this group based on the context, and the differences highlighted in the literature often relate to variations in evidentiality. Therefore, this study aims to analyze the differences between "*renwei, yiwei, juede, kaolü*, and *xiang*" based on the degree of evidentiality and the credibility of the information expressed or judged.

---

[1] Institute of Languages, Chinese Academy of Social Sciences: 2021-11-13.

© The Author(s), under exclusive license to Springer Nature Singapore Pte Ltd. 2024
M. Dong et al. (Eds.): CLSW 2023, LNAI 14515, pp. 301–315, 2024.
https://doi.org/10.1007/978-981-97-0586-3_24

"The investigation of the theoretical concept of evidentiality has originated from the analysis of languages like Kwakiutl" [1, 2]. However, recent research in linguistics increasingly asserts that "by marking the source of information and thus the commitment of, or attitude toward, the information, the speaker (or writer) secures a communicative act to the hearer (or reader), or promotes or shares the understanding of a state of affairs" [2]. Currently, there is a paucity of research on the differences between evidentiality in near-synonyms in modern Chinese, with more emphasis on cross-linguistic comparisons. Furthermore, in linguistic research, assertiveness is often confused with concepts such as reliability and trustworthiness. To address this, Li and Huang [3] conducted a corpus-based analysis of the differences among near-synonymous from the perspective of evidentiality. Their motivation stemmed from the idea that the trustworthiness of information in propositions varies depending on the use of 'renwei' or 'yiwei', which relates to the speaker's stances or attitudes. They tested different functions of near-synonyms, including evidential marking, negative forms, and hedging devices.

"Evidentiality is a special kind of grammatical phenomenon" [4], referring primarily to "the information trustworthiness" [3]. Givon [5] argued that evidentiality can be influenced by factors such as stereotypes, biases, and expectations. While reliability expresses established facts regarding events that have occurred or are occurring, evidentiality extends beyond time limitations and may express past, present, future, and potential events. Therefore, it can be hypothesized that evidentiality is not equivalent to the inherent truthfulness of an object but centers on the speaker's or listener's conviction in the conveyed or received information. This certainty can be influenced by factors such as the identity of the speaker, tone of voice, presentation context, and the listener's trust in the source of the information. In the present context, "epistemic evidentiality" refers to the cognitive assessment of the truthfulness and reliability of information by the receiver. That is to say, the receiver makes a cognitive judgment of whether the information is more likely to be true and reliable or not, rather than evaluating the objective truthfulness and reliability of the information itself. Furthermore, the linguistic components within an utterance can contribute to the listener's stereotypes, biases, or expectations regarding the content of the statement, which in turn impact judgments of epistemic evidentiality levels.

This study utilized a corpus to compare and analyze the differences and related influencing factors among "renwei, yiwei, juede, kaolü, and xiang" in terms of epistemic evidentiality. Building on previous research, we have extended the types of evidentiality markers to analyze their distributional differences among cognitive verbs, mainly including the diverse evidentiality markers used in collocations before and after cognitive verbs, as well as their respective positions. This article investigates and examines the judgments of Chinese native speakers on the evidentiality of sentences containing this set of epistemic verbs. Finally, it explores the evidentiality of these epistemic verbs in the cognition of participants and the rationality of their judgments. This paper elucidates the corpus analysis of "renwei, yiwei, juede, kaolü, and xiang" in the second section, presents the questionnaire as well as its outcomes in the third section, and concludes in the fourth section.

2 Investigation of Epistemic Verbs in Corpora Usage

The data used in this study is sourced from the Academia Sinica Balanced Corpus of Modern Chinese version 4.0,[2] comprising eight major categories of word tokens and a total of 46 tags. For our analysis, we selected three major categories of word tokens: "V" representing verbs, including the five epistemic verbs under study, namely "认为 (renwei), 以为 (yiwei), 考虑 (kaolü), 觉得 (juede), 想 (xiang)"; "N" representing nouns, and "D" representing adverbs.

2.1 Data Categorization

In Table 1, we collected ten units[3] of words before and after the epistemic verbs (keywords) from the corpus, filtering words and word tokens with an MI value (mutual information)[4] of ≥1. Sentences related to the near-synonyms "renwei, yiwei, juede, kaolü, and xiang," and those where these words were used as verbs were filtered out. It was observed that "renwei, yiwei, kaolü" function as action accusative verbs (VE) when used as verbs, followed by an action transitive word as the sentence object. "Juede" functions as a state verb (VK) when used as a verb, followed by a state transitive object. "Xiang" is unique, encompassing various lexical categories (VC, VB, VH, VE, VK, V1, and VJ),[5] but when used as VE, it carries the meaning of "believe, consider," which is synonymous with "renwei, yiwei, juede, kaolü." Therefore, for the subsequent data analysis, only data labeled as VE for "xiang" were selected, considering both VE and VK as transitive verbs.

Table 1. Statistics on the total number of sentences related to epistemic verbs

	Renwei	Yiwei	Kaolü	Juede	Xiang
Total relevant sentences	8270	1483	1848	6354	10174
Total number of sentences with verbs	8269	1482	1701	6354	10036
Relevant lexical tokens in the corpus	VE	VE	VE	VK	VE

In the examples (1a, 1b, 1c, 1.d, 1e), when a minor sentence such as "He is also a software engineer" follows the subject "expert" and an epistemic verb, the information receivers may initially perceive these examples as conveying similar information due to the semantic and pragmatic similarities among this group of epistemic verbs. However, depending on the epistemic evidentiality of the "epistemic verb" within the

---

[2] http://asbc.iis.sinica.edu.tw/.

[3] Ten units is the maximum range of queries and data collection allowed in the corpus.

[4] Indicates the relevance of the search content to the keywords. When the relevance is tighter, the mutual information is higher. Here MI ≥ 1 is used to maximize the identification of relevant results and avoid missing important information.

[5] The relevant POS and abbreviations in this study refer to the descriptions of Sinica.

sentence itself, information receivers may discern differences in the epistemic evidentiality of the information conveyed in these five examples. This suggests that the epistemic evidentiality of this group of epistemic verbs is worth investigating.

(1) (a) 专家认为他也是软件工程师。
    (b) 专家以为他也是软件工程师。
    (c) 专家觉得他也是软件工程师。
    (d) 专家考虑他也是软件工程师。
    (e) 专家想他也是软件工程师。
    "The expert thinks he is also a software engineer."

In a study by Li and Huang [3], they demonstrated that words with a certain degree of evidentiality, such as pronouns and proper nouns, influence the evidentiality of the sentence in which an epistemic verb is located. For instance, "Bill Gates" in (2a) is a proper noun, and "I" in (2b) is a pronoun, resulting in inconsistent levels of evidentiality in (2a) and (2b). We found that the corpus of common nouns also includes some nouns[6] related to professionals, professional fields, and professional knowledge, such as "expert" in (2c), which is a professional term with obvious evidentiality and is worth studying.

(2) (a) 比尔盖茨认为个人电脑产业的发展空间还很大。
    "Bill Gates thinks the personal computer industry has a lot of room to grow."
    (b) 我认为个人电脑产业的发展空间还很大。
    "I think the personal computer industry has a lot of room to grow."
    (c) 专家认为个人电脑产业的发展空间还很大。
    "Expert thinks the personal computer industry has a lot of room to grow."

To ensure comprehensive data research on the abovementioned nouns, we conducted data statistics on nouns from the Sinica corpus.

Table 2. Frequency Statistics of Nouns Related to Epistemic Verbs (Percentages Rounded to One Decimal Place)

	Keywords within the top 10				Keywords after the top 10			
	Common nouns	pronouns	Place words	Proper nouns	Common nouns	pronouns	Place words	Proper nouns
Kaolü	51.40%	7.30%	8.80%	3.90%	52.40%	5.50%	10.20%	3.70%
Renwei	50.70%	11.60%	10.10%	9.60%	58.30%	7.10%	0.00%	4.40%
Yiwei	45.30%	19.90%	5.20%	4.90%	43.70%	17.40%	6.20%	4.40%
Juede	35.70%	28.60%	3.70%	3.90%	38.20%	20.60%	4.80%	2.80%
Xiang	38.10%	24.30%	5.10%	4.60%	39.70%	16.90%	5.90%	4.00%

---

[6] Nouns in the corpus include Na, Nb, Nc, Ncd, Nd, Neu, Nes, Nep, Neqa, Neqb, Nf, Ng, Nh, and Nv.

(3) Collocation frequency = (number of collocations/total number of words) * 100%.

To clarify, collocation frequency is calculated as (number of collocations/total number of words) * 100%. For instance, the frequency of *"renwei"* collocating with common nouns within the top 10 range is calculated as (the total number of *"renwei"* collocating with common nouns within the top 10 range/the total number of *"renwei"* collocations within the top 10 range) * 100%.

We have taken data on the nouns through the corpus.[7] Table 2 presents a pairing of common nouns, pronouns, place words, and proper nouns with epistemic verbs, revealing a high frequency of association. However, since place words themselves do not have epistemic evidentiality, they are excluded from the scope of this study. Consequently, we aim to delve deeper into how nouns with different levels of epistemic evidentiality, namely proper nouns, pronouns, and common nouns, can affect the overall epistemic evidentiality of sentences. Table 3 shows that epistemic verbs predominantly collocate with common adverbs, auxiliary words (such as *"de," "zhi," "di"*), and adverbs of degree positioned before verbs within the adverb category.[8] Auxiliary words lacking substantial meaning will not be studied, with our focus primarily on dative adverbs among common adverbs. Post-verbal adverbs of degree in the category of degree adverbs also exhibit distinct epistemic evidentiality. However, due to their rarity in the corpus and the presence of missing cases, they will not be explored in this study.

Table 3. Frequency Statistics of Adverbs Related to Epistemic Verbs (Percentages Rounded to One Decimal Place)

	Keywords within the top 10			Keywords after the top 10		
	Common adverbs	Auxiliary words	Adverbs of degree	Common adverbs	Auxiliary words	Adverbs of degree
Kaolü	70.00%	21.30%	3.80%	48.30%	39.80%	4.50%
Renwei	55.10%	33.60%	5.50%	54.10%	32.20%	8.10%
Yiwei	59.60%	25.80%	4.70%	57.90%	25.40%	5.60%
Juede	60.30%	22.70%	6.90%	53.20%	21.00%	18.90%
Xiang	61.20%	21.60%	6.90%	57.50%	26.10%	5.00%

(4) (a) 一般人可能认为班展十分有趣。
    "The everyman may think that the class show is very interesting."
    (b) 一般人一定认为班展十分有趣。
    "The everyman must think that the class show is very interesting."

---

[7] The maximum statistical range of the database is only 10 units, and the minimum value of MI is 1. When we analyzed the data, we further processed and filtered out the first 10 or last 10 units of the keywords (epistemic verbs), in which MI was ≥1.

[8] In the corpus, DE, Di, Da, Dk, Dh, and Dd are not assertive per se, so they are not taken into account here, and the number of Dd and Dh among them is extremely low and is not informative.

(c) 一般人认为班展一定十分有趣。
"The everyman thinks that the class show must be very interesting."
(d) 一般人一定认为班展有点有趣。
"The everyman must think that the class show is a bit interesting."

Examples (4a) and (4b) show that epistemic evidentiality perceived by the recipient toward "the everyman thinks the class show very interesting" is influenced by the dative adverb (Dba) preceding the epistemic verb. Semantically, the epistemic evidentiality of "must" is higher than that of "may." Consequently, the message "the everyman thinks the class show very interesting" in (4b) is significantly more credible than in (4a). This indicates the impact of dative adverbs on the epistemic evidentiality of a sentence. Similarly, pre-verbal adverbs of degree such as "十分" (very) and "有点" (a bit) in the contrasts (4b) and (4d) significantly affect the perception of the "everyman" regarding the statement "the class show is interesting." In comparison to the modification of "a bit" in (4d), recipients of the message would be more willing to believe the authenticity of the message "the class show is interesting" conveyed in (4b). Consequently, both pre- and post-dative adverbs, as well as pre-verbal adverbs of degree, need to be included in the scope of research. In (2 and 4), when nouns or adverbs are positioned before epistemic verbs, they may impact the epistemic evidentiality of these verbs. Conversely, when placed after epistemic verbs, it cannot be ruled out that they may also affect the overall epistemic evidentiality of the sentence. In order to maximize the comprehensiveness of the research scope, we ultimately decided to count the tagged lexical categories both preceding and following epistemic verbs.

2.2 Data Analysis

The epistemic evidentiality of proper nouns in the corpus is high, while that of pronouns is low. The corpus presents high and low epistemic evidentiality for common adverbs, dative adverbs, and pre-verbal adverbs of degree. Dative adverbs fall under the category of adverbs and require manual screening. Building upon the previously mentioned analysis of the overall combination of epistemic verbs with different tokens within the group "*renwei, yiwei, juede, kaolü*, and *xiang*," we will now further analyze the associations between epistemic verbs and words with epistemic evidentiality tags.

Before conducting data analysis, we conducted a preliminary exploration of the semantics of the epistemic verbs "*renwei, yiwei, juede, kaolü*, and *xiang*." According to the seventh edition of the Modern Chinese Dictionary, "*kaolü*" means to contemplate a problem in order to make a decision, devoid of any speculative or conjectural connotations. Conversely, "*renwei, yiwei, juede*, and *xiang*" all contain the meaning of forming a certain view or judgment regarding a person or thing.

Drawing upon Shen's [6] investigation into pragmatic presupposition, we recognize that when a speaker conveys certain information, they do so with the assumption that the listener already possesses knowledge about it. This assumed knowledge serves as a premise for conveying new information to the listener and constitutes the speaker's presupposition. That is, when the speaker [7] discusses "Y," they presuppose that the previously established condition "X" is a given fact. Hence, we categorize "*kaolü*" as a factual presupposition verb. For instance, in example (5), when the subject conveys the information in the second clause, "the risk of surgical treatment for the condition is relatively high," using the verb "*kaolü*," it is assumed that the information in the first clause "the patient is of advanced age" is an established fact. "*Kaolü*" thus conforms to the concept of a "fact-presupposing verb." Therefore, we hypothesize that "*kaolü*" is mostly followed by established facts. As a result, information receivers are more inclined to perceive the epistemic evidentiality of the clause immediately following "*kaolü*" as high. Similarly, in example (1d) above, the subject, "expert" employs "*kaolü*" to convey the information that "he is also a software engineer." This implies to the information receiver that "he is also a software engineer" is an established fact. Consequently, the information receiver is also inclined to believe that "he is also a software engineer" is true, indicating a higher level of epistemic evidentiality conveyed by the message of "*kaolü*."

(5) 医生考虑这个病人的年纪较大, 通过手术治疗病情的风险会比较大。

"The doctor considers that the patient is of advanced age, and the risk of surgical treatment for the condition is relatively high."

In summary, information receivers tend to regard information following "*kaolü*" as an objective fact with a high level of epistemic evidentiality due to "*kaolü*" functioning as a factual prepositional verb. However, it is important to note that "*kaolü*" itself does not have a high level of epistemic evidentiality. In contrast, "*renwei, yiwei, juede,* and *xiang*" are epistemic verbs characterized by clear deductive information and epistemic evidentiality based on their semantics and pragmatics. In the following analysis, we will use "*kaolü*" as the control group to assess the epistemic evidentiality of sentences containing "*kaolü*" and examine the influence of related nouns and adverbs on its epistemic evidentiality. Additionally, we will compare the data of other epistemic verbs with the data of "*kaolü*" to analyze the degree of difference in epistemic evidentiality among the other four words.

Noun

In their study, Li and Huang [3] showed that in general, information from professionals and professional organizations tends to be more reliable and authentic. Their research considered pronouns as subjects and categorized them as having low epistemic evidentiality. These terms include: *he*, expert, general public, *I*, professional, *they, she*, people, folks, scholar, *we*.

We agree with Li and Huang [3] regarding the high epistemic evidentiality of proper nouns. Speakers use proper nouns in their expressions to enhance the credibility of their statements, resulting in a higher level of epistemic evidentiality in sentences containing proper nouns. Pronouns, on the other hand, exhibit low epistemic evidentiality. When used as subjects, pronouns convey information with a certain degree of subjectivity, resulting in lower epistemic evidentiality in sentences containing pronouns. The epistemic evidentiality of common nouns is more variable, with some common nouns in the corpus including terms related to professionals, specialized fields, and specialized knowledge. Therefore, we classify common nouns associated with higher social status and stronger professionalism as high epistemic evidentiality nouns. There are a total of 631 common nouns in this category, while the proper nouns in the corpus consist of names of celebrities, international organizations, schools of thought, and similar entities, totaling 4,232. Pronouns, on the other hand, comprise the majority 97 instances, including I, they, everyone, and so forth.

Table 4. Frequency and Quantity of Common Nouns Collocated with Epistemic Verbs (Percentage Rounded to One Decimal Place)

	Keywords within the top 10			Keywords after the top 10		
	High-epistemic evidentiality common nouns	Total common nouns	Frequency	High-epistemic evidentiality common nouns	Total common nouns	Frequency
Kaolü	303	3044	10.00%	304	3380	9.00%
Renwei	1950	16006	12.20%	1559	15959	9.80%
Yiwei	142	2280	6.20%	172	2176	7.90%
Juede	381	7817	4.90%	415	7591	5.50%
Xiang	645	12767	5.10%	632	12974	4.90%

Combining the data from Tables 2 and 4, it can be concluded that "*renwei*" is more frequently associated with proper nouns and high epistemic evidentiality common nouns, while it is less frequently paired with pronouns. This indicates that "*renwei*" is often paired with high epistemic evidentiality nouns. The overall data for "*juede, yiwei, xiang*" are quite similar, as all of them tend to pair with pronouns characterized by low epistemic evidentiality. Additionally, they exhibit low frequency associations with high epistemic evidentiality common nouns and proper nouns. In the case of "*kaolü*," it has a low frequency of association with both pronouns and proper nouns, and a high frequency of association with common nouns possessing high epistemic evidentiality. In other words, "*kaolü*" does not exhibit an obvious tendency to collocate with nouns of higher or lower epistemic evidentiality. This implies that information expressed after "*kaolü*" is highly likely to be reliable and can be used in flexible combinations with nouns of varying degrees of epistemic evidentiality.

Adverb

Table 3 from the previous section shows that epistemic verbs are commonly paired with ordinary adverbs and pre-verbal adverbs of degree. However, among ordinary adverbs, only dative adverbs exhibit significant epistemic assertiveness, while adverbs of time and other types do not. Hence, dative adverbs necessitate separate screening.

To categorize dative verbs, we referred to the content and instructions of the Sinica. In total, there are 18 dative verbs, including 也许、大概、大概、或许、一定、可能、似乎、好像、仿佛、可、必须、可以、肯定、必定、必然、定然、必、得. Among them, we categorized "一定、必须、肯定、必定、必然、定然、必" as dative adverbs with high epistemic evidentiality, based on the definition of epistemic evidentiality mentioned earlier. Similarly, we compiled a total of 23 pre-verbal adverbs of degree, including "最、更、甚至、很、超级、太、非常、过于、十分、分外、

异常、极、何其、相当、极、不堪、透、颇、期期、过度、不已、得多." All of these words contribute to enhancing the truthfulness and reliability of the information conveyed in a sentence. Building upon the results of the previous analysis, adverbs with high epistemic evidentiality can modify epistemic verbs to enhance their epistemic evidentiality, consequently elevating the overall epistemic evidentiality of the sentence. This effect is especially noteworthy when a high epistemic evidentiality adverb precedes an epistemic verb, potentially compensating for a lower inherent epistemic evidentiality in the verb itself.

Table 5. Frequency of High epistemic Evidentiality Adverbs Collocated with Epistemic Verbs (Percentage Rounded to One Decimal Place)

	Keywords within the top 10		Keywords after the top 10	
	High-evidentiality dative adverbs	High-evidentiiality pre-verbal adverbs of degree	High-evidentiality dative adverbs	High-evidentiality pre-verbal adverbs of degree
Kaolü	34.00%	45.30%	16.50%	35.60%
Renwei	17.30%	33.50%	32.60%	35.60%
Yiwei	21.50%	29.00%	27.70%	35.90%
Juede	21.40%	25.00%	13.20%	24.60%
Xiang	25.10%	28.80%	35.30%	31.30%

The data in Table 5 exhibit relative similarity and lack pronounced regular pattern as in the case of nouns. This indicates that the main function of high epistemic evidentiality adverbs is to modify the epistemic evidentiality of epistemic verbs. However, their use is not necessary for expression and modification, as epistemic verbs inherently possess a certain degree of epistemic evidentiality. Interestingly, "*kaolü*" ranks very high among the top ten words, primarily due to the fact that the information following "*kaolü*" typically pertains to objective reality. Therefore, "*kaolü*" is often preceded by high epistemic evidentiality adverbs, which tend to be congruent with the epistemic evidentiality of the subsequent clauses.

Summary

Proper nouns inherently possess high epistemic evidentiality, thereby enhancing the overall epistemic evidentiality of a sentence to a certain extent. Conversely, pronouns have the opposite effect. Furthermore, there is a clear distinction between high and low epistemic evidentiality among common nouns, dative adverbs, and pre-verbal adverbs of degree. Based on the total number and frequency of word classes associated with epistemic verbs, we hypothesize that "*renwei*" carries a high level of epistemic evidentiality, while "*yiwei, xiang, juede*" exhibit a lower and similar degree of epistemic evidentiality. It's worth noting that "*kaolü*" is a factual presupposition verb, implying the communication of established facts rather than speculative inferences. Therefore, "*kaolü*" itself does not have a noticeable degree of epistemic assertiveness.

3   Investigation of Native Chinese Speakers' Evidentiality Judgments of Epistemic Verbs

3.1   Questionnaire Design and Experimental Procedure

In the current process of teaching the Chinese language, there is no unified standard for assertiveness. The questionnaire is designed to test the consistency or differences between the conclusions analyzed in the previous section and the perception of native Chinese speakers.

Through this questionnaire survey, we expect to observe whether, for native speakers, the information following "*kaolü*" mostly consists of objective facts. If this holds true, subjects are likely to judge sentences containing "*kaolü*" as having high epistemic evidentiality. Subsequently, "*kaolü*" can be used as a control group to further evaluate the degree of epistemic evidentiality of "*renwei, yiwei, juede, xiang.*" The questionnaire contains both high and low types of common nouns, dative adverbs, and pre-verbal adverbs of degree. In addition, it considers the epistemic evidentiality of proper nouns, which are all high, and pronouns, which are all low. Our analysis will explore whether these five tokens affect the epistemic evidentiality of epistemic verbs and the epistemic evidentiality of the conveyed information by observing the judgments of native speakers of sentences containing them.

A total of 300 sentences related to "*renwei, yiwei, juede, kaolü,* and *xiang*" were selected from the Sinica corpus. The selection criteria include selecting sentences in which five relevant word classes[9] (common nouns, proper nouns, pronouns, dative adverbs, and pre-verbal adverbs of degree) are situated within the themes of humanities, social sciences, and daily life, both before and after the five epistemic verbs. We chose two sentences for each category (one with high epistemic evidentiality and one with low epistemic evidentiality for common nouns, dative adverbs, and pre-verbal adverbs of degree), which is 5 * 3 * 2 * 5 * 2. Finally, the 300 sentences will be randomly shuffled by different epistemic verbs, three major domains, five different lexical properties, and the range of the first and last halves. These sentences will be divided into two questionnaires, each containing 150 sentences. We will distribute 45 copies of each questionnaire, resulting in a total of 90 valid samples. Before administering the questionnaire, we will provide an example (Fig. 1) to prompt participants' understanding of the concept of "epistemic evidentiality." This step is crucial to ensure that participants have fully understood the concept before proceeding with the questionnaire.

In the process of designing the questionnaire, we considered the unfamiliarity of the concept of "epistemic evidentiality" and the lack of a unified standard in current Chinese language teaching. Consequently, it is not advisable to set overly detailed standards that could potentially confuse participants when making judgments during the experiment. Conversely, clear differentiation of high and low epistemic evidentiality

---

[9] There are six major themes in the corpus: philosophy, science, art, literature, society, and life. If all of them are involved, the questionnaire will be too large and exhausting for the participants, and the validity of the questionnaire results cannot be guaranteed. Therefore, we classified them according to the disciplinary composition method [8], and consolidated the humanities into broader categories, specifically "Philosophy, Science, Art, and Literature."

示例

例句：经济学家一致认为，新协定成立之初，必然会有人失业。

（请你站在信息接受者的立场，判断句子内容的信息表述的可靠性、真实性的程度高低，即知识断言性高还是低）

○ 高
○ 低

Example

Example sentence: Economists agree that at the beginning of the new agreement, there were bound to be people out of work.

(Put yourself in the position of the receiver of the information and judge the degree of reliability and truthfulness of the information presentation of the content of the sentence, i.e., whether the epistemic evidentiality is high or low)

○ High
○ Low

Fig. 1. Example of questionnaire content

may actually simplify the judgment process for participants and improve the validity of the experimental results.

Given the relatively esoteric nature of the concept of "epistemic evidentiality," we enlisted native Chinese to take the questionnaire survey. Participants possess diverse academic qualifications, ranging from undergraduate to graduate and doctoral students, representing various fields of study.[10]

Recruitment for the questionnaire survey was conducted through the online platform "Questionnaire Star," with volunteers receiving compensation for their participation. To ensure that participants could confidently judge the epistemic evidentiality of each sentence during the questionnaire filling process, we provided a sample questionnaire that clarified the meaning of epistemic evidentiality. We received a total of 116 responses for the first questionnaire and 103 for the second. We performed background validity checks on the questionnaires and excluded any invalid submissions. Given that epistemic evidentiality is also an unfamiliar concept to native speakers, participants required more than ten minutes on average to complete the questionnaire. After collecting the questionnaires, we initially excluded those with significantly short response times. Then, we conducted randomized interviews (in a 3:1 ratio) with participants to ensure the validity of their responses, continuing until we had collected all the necessary data. The retrieved valid questionnaires were then directly coded and organized in the order of their collection in the backend of the "Questionnaire Star" software.

3.2 Questionnaire Data Compilation and Analysis

Due to the fact that the questionnaire only had two options: "high" and "low," we encoded the options, assigning a value of 2 to "high" and 1 to "low." We then calculated the weighted average[11] (6) for each epistemic verb within the same range and across different

---

[10] Linguistics, Law, Technology, Mathematics, Education, Management, Engineering, Materials Science, Labor Relations, Architecture, Secretarial Science, International Trade, Advertising, Journalism, Environmental Engineering, Comparative Literature, Music, Business Administration, Applied Mathematics, Broadcasting, Nursing.

[11] When the mean is higher than 1.5, it indicates that the majority has chosen the option with high evidentiality. Conversely, when the mean is lower, it shows that the majority has chosen the option with low evidentiality.

tokens. This allowed us to compute the statistics[12] (7) to observe the degree of data fluctuation.

(6) $\overline{X}$ pos = (2 * Total number of selected individuals + 1 * Total number of selected individuals)/Total number of individuals

(7) $S = \sqrt{\frac{1}{90}\left[\left(2 - \overline{X}pos\right)^2 * X1 + \left(1 - \overline{X}pos\right)^2 * X2\right]}$ (X1: The number of individuals who choose "high", X2: The number of individuals who choose "low")

Tables 6, 7, and 8 show that there are no significant differences between the mean and standard deviation, indicating that the epistemic evidentiality of the epistemic verbs among participants is similar.

Table 6. Comprehensive Data of Epistemic Verbs (rounded to two decimal places)

	Keywords within the top 10		Keywords after the top 10		Total	
	Average value	Statistics	Average value	Statistics	Average value	Statistics
Kaolü	1.74	0.44	1.75	0.43	1.75	0.43
Renwei	1.64	0.48	1.71	0.45	1.68	0.47
Yiwei	1.53	0.5	1.55	0.5	1.54	0.5
Juede	1.65	0.48	1.65	0.48	1.65	0.48
Xiang	1.61	0.49	1.57	0.5	1.59	0.49

As predicted earlier, Table 6 affirms that participants generally perceive the information following the verb "*kaolü*" as highly credible. This confirms our initial assumption that "*kaolü*," as a factual presupposition verb, is typically followed by established facts. Consequently, we can use "*kaolü*" as a control group to further examine the epistemic evidentiality of other epistemic verbs. In comparison, most individuals consider the epistemic evidentiality of "*renwei*" to be relatively high, followed by "*juede*," while "*yiwei*" and "*xiang*" are rated lower and very close in value to each other.

The overall results in Tables 7 and 8 are highly consistent with the results of the previous data analysis. Proper nouns consistently receive average values above 1.6, with standard deviations below 0.5, indicating that individuals consistently perceived the epistemic evidentiality of proper nouns as high. Conversely, pronouns receive lower average values, indicating that subjects also judged the epistemic evidentiality of pronouns as relatively low. In sentences containing common nouns, dative adverbs, and pre-verbal adverbs of degree, which exhibit an average distribution of high and low epistemic evidentiality, the data reveals that the judgment of epistemic evidentiality is

---

[12] When the standard deviation is equal to 0.5, it indicates that the same number of people have chosen the high and low options respectively, and that the data are normally distributed. When the standard deviation of the results is greater than the difference of 0.5, it indicates that the subjects have a clear tendency to be consistent in their assertion of the evidentiality of the sentence in which the epistemic verb is located.

Table 7. Top 10 Average Assertion Value and Standard Deviation of Sentences with Epistemic Verb Collocations of Different Parts of POS (rounded to two decimal places)

	Average value (SD)				
	Kaolü	*Renwei*	*Yiwei*	*Juede*	*Xiang*
Common nouns	1.79(0.41)	1.75(0.43)	1.57(0.50)	1.67(0.47)	1.66(0.47)
Proper nouns	1.71(0.45)	1.80(0.40)	1.67(0.47)	1.80(0.40)	1.78(0.42)
Pronouns	1.66(0.48)	1.62(0.49)	1.49(0.50)	1.67(0.47)	1.53(0.50)
Dative adverbs	1.83(0.38)	1.55(0.50)	1.61(0.49)	1.46(0.50)	1.51(0.50)
Pre-verbal adverbs of degree	1.73(0.44)	1.50(0.50)	1.33(0.47)	1.65(0.48)	1.60(0.49)

Table 8. Average Assertion Value and SD of Sentences with Epistemic Verb Collocations of Different Parts of POS (rounded to two decimal places) from after the target verbs.

	Average value (SD)				
	Kaolü	*Renwei*	*Yiwei*	*Juede*	*Xiang*
Common nouns	1.91(0.28)	1.8(0.43)	1.64(0.48)	1.77(0.42)	1.67(0.50)
Proper nouns	1.76(0.43)	1.7(0.44)	1.63(0.48)	1.76(0.43)	1.65(0.50)
Pronouns	1.73(0.45)	1.6(0.49)	1.47(0.50)	1.53(0.50)	1.48(0.50)
Dative adverbs	1.69(0.46)	1.8(0.42)	1.54(0.50)	1.57(0.50)	1.46(0.50)
Pre-verbal adverbs of degree	1.67(0.47)	1.7(0.46)	1.48(0.50)	1.63(0.48)	1.59(0.50)

highest when "*kaolü*" is used in conjunction with these three elements. This implies that the epistemic evidentiality of sentences featuring "*kaolü*" is unlikely to be influenced by the accompanying nouns and adverbs. "*Kaolü*" is perceived by individuals as expressing objective facts, thus maintaining high epistemic evidentiality. Therefore "*kaolü*" remains suitable as the control group for comparison. "*Renwei*" displays a relatively high overall frequency when paired with common nouns, dative adverbs, and pre-verbal adverbs of degree. Although there are fluctuations, the differences between the frequencies of "*yiwei, juede,* and *xiang*" are not significant. Among them, the frequency of "*juede*" is generally higher than that of "*yiwei*" and "*xiang*."

In summary, the high epistemic evidentiality of sentences containing "*kaolü*" results from participants perceiving its expression as more oriented toward established facts, which is consistent with our earlier conclusions. "*Renwei*" generally ranks higher in terms of epistemic evidentiality, while "*juede, yiwei,* and *xiang*" exhibit similar ratings, with "*juede*" typically receiving higher judgments from participants compared to "*yiwei*" and "*xiang*."

3.3 Discussion of Questionnaire Results

Firstly, participants' judgments regarding the epistemic evidentiality of proper nouns, pronouns, common nouns, dative adverbs, and pre-verbal adverbs of degree are consistent with the earlier data analysis. Proper nouns exhibit high epistemic evidentiality, while pronouns demonstrate low epistemic evidentiality. Common nouns, dative adverbs, and pre-verbal adverbs of degree encompass words with both high and low epistemic evidentiality.

Secondly, the majority of participants also judged the epistemic evidentiality of sentences containing "*kaolü*" to be high, consistent with our earlier analysis. This is attributed to "*kaolü*" being a fact-presupposing verb that often follows established facts, thereby maintaining high credibility. "*Renwei*" conveys strong epistemic assertiveness, while "*juede, yiwei, and xiang*" exhibit similar levels of epistemic assertiveness.

Finally, the only notable difference lies in the significantly higher epistemic evidentiality perceived by the participants in their judgment of "*juede*" compared to "*yiwei*" or "*xiang*" based on the questionnaire. This disparity may be related to the following two factors: Firstly, it could be related to the linguistic habits of native speakers in actual use of modern Chinese. For instance, Chinese native speakers often favor more euphemistic expressions, which may lead to the perception that "*juede*" also expresses high epistemic evidentiality. Secondly, the variation in idiomatic usage between the Taiwan corpus, the source of this study's data, and the participants, who are primarily from mainland China.

4   Conclusions and Future Perspectives

The level of epistemic evidentiality varies depending on the type of noun used. Proper nouns exhibit a high level of epistemic evidentiality, while pronouns have a low one. Common nouns, dative adverbs, and pre-verbal adverbs of degree also have varying levels of epistemic evidentiality. "*Renwei*" is associated with a high level of epistemic evidentiality, suggesting that its use indicates the speaker's intention to convey information that is both true and highly reliable. The epistemic evidentiality of "*juede, yiwei, and xiang*" is relatively low, indicating that the speaker's inferences about the statement carry a high degree of subjectivity. This results in skepticism regarding the credibility of the received information. As for "*kaolü*," it operates as a factual presupposition verb, and the subsequent clause is often pertained to established facts. "*Kaolü*" typically serves to describe the thought process without displaying any obvious assertiveness. Interestingly, Chinese native speakers perceive "*juede*" as having higher epistemic evidentiality compared to "*yiwei*" or "*xiang*." This divergence may be influenced by the linguistics habits of native speakers.

It's important to acknowledge certain limitations of this study, particularly in terms of selection of experimental subjects. Future research could involve participants from Taiwan, Hong Kong, and those who speak Chinese as a second language to diversify the sample. Additionally, this study mainly utilized a corpus from Taiwan; therefore, further research could be conducted in conjunction with corpora from the mainland. "Most previous studies focused on a single multifunctional word in a single language" [9], and "due to lack of basic data on syllabic form selection from Ancient Chinese to Middle Chinese" [10], there may remain blanks in research.

References

1. Boas, F.: Introduction. US Government Printing Office, American (1911)
2. Fetzer, A., Oishi, E.: Evidentiality in discourse. J. Intercult. Pragmat. **11**(3), 321–332 (2014)
3. Li, B., Huang, C.R., Chen, S.: Marking trustworthiness with near synonyms: a corpus-based study of "*renwei*" and "*yiwei*" in Chinese. In: Le-Nguyen, M., Chi-Luong, M., Sanghoun, S. (eds.) PACLIC 34, LNCS, vol. 26197782, pp. 453–461. Association for Computational Linguistics, Hanoi (2020)
4. Chafe, W.L., Nichols, J. (eds.): Evidentiality: The Linguistic Coding of Epistemology. Ablex Publishing Corporation, Norwood (1986)
5. Givón, T.: Evidentiality and epistemic space. J. Found. Lang. **6**(1), 23–49 (1982)
6. Ye, F.S., Xu, T.J., Wang, H.J.: Linguistics Outline [*Yuyanxue Gangyao*]. Beijing Book Co. Inc., Beijing (1997). (in Chinese)
7. Jiang, C.L.: The Studies of The Fact-Presupposition Verbs in Modern Chinese. MA Thesis. East China Normal University, Shanghai (2009). (in Chinese)
8. Liu, J.F., et al.: Study on the discipline classification of massive humanities and social science academic literature driven by deep learning. J. Theor. Appl. **2**(46), 71–81 (2023). (in Chinese)
9. Bian, W.: The relationship between the emphatic meaning and the adversative meaning from the perspective of linguistic typology: the cases of Chinese *kě* and *jiùshì*. In: Su, Q., Xu, G., Yang, X. (eds.) CLSW 2022: LNCS, vol. 13495, pp. 169–185. Springer, Cham (2022). https://doi.org/10.1007/978-3-031-28953-8_14
10. Bing, Q., Jia, Y.: A corpus-based study on the syllablic form selection of ancient Chinese high-frequency nouns in the middle ages. In: Su, Q., Xu, G., Yang, X. (eds.) CLSW 2022. LNCS, vol. 13495, pp. 14–24. Springer, Cham (2022). https://doi.org/10.1007/978-3-031-28953-8_2

Investigating Acoustic Cues of Emotional Valence in Mandarin Speech Prosody - A Corpus Approach

Junlin Li[✉][iD] and Chu-Ren Huang[iD]

The Hong Kong Polytechnic University, Kowloon, HKG, Hong Kong S.A.R., China
junlin.li@connect.polyu.hk, churen.huang@polyu.edu.hk

Abstract. The impact of emotion on prosody in the context of speech communication has yielded inconclusive results when it comes to the prosodic patterns associated with high-arousal emotions of different emotional valences, such as "Happy" and "Anger". To clarify the existing ambiguity, this study utilized an emotional speech database to examine prosodic metrics of multi-word verbal speech. The findings suggest that tempo is more of a reliable measure than pitch in conveying emotional valance. The syllables towards the end of a sentence are the most crucial in conveying valence or size projection, while non-final syllables provide a limited indication of valence or size projection.

Keywords: Emotion · Prosody · Emotional Valence · Size-projection

1 Introduction

Following the development of telecommunications, the vocal communication of emotion has received increased attention. The study of vocal patterns of emotion in verbal and nonverbal expressions has gained renewed interest [34]. In the study of emotional prosody as a key aspect of vocal emotion, the acoustic and perceptual discrimination of speech emotion based on prosodic parameters such as tempo, pitch, and loudness has been given numerous studies, with pitch being highlighted as a primary signal of underlying emotion.

Although significant improvements have been made, there is still an unresolved question regarding the acoustic differentiation of high-arousal emotions, specifically Anger and Happiness emotions. In daily communication, high-arousal emotions are easily distinguished by humans in terms of emotional valence, which has been taken into theoretical conceptualization in body-size projection theory and bio-informatic dimension theory. However, few consistent indicators have been identified as potent discriminators, as the empirical studies lead to mixed results concerning the contrast between high arousal emotions with different emotional valence. Against such an inconclusiveness, recent research indicates that specific high-arousal emotions are perceived or encoded at particular positions within the prosodic structure, especially at the beginning or end of utterances [33], which motivates us to test the effect of emotion on prosodic features on special positions within an utterance.

This study aims to enhance our comprehension of how five basic emotions (Angry, Happy, Sad, Surprise) are conveyed through pitch and tempo cues, with a specific focus on emotional valence. The study utilizes a voice corpus and employs text and speech processing algorithms to analyze 190 sentences from 10 participants. By employing word segmentation and forced alignment, this method based on a corpus can detect potential prosodic units, such as word and sentence borders, which enables the modeling of the relationship between emotion and prosodic boundaries. To analyze emotional effect, this work devises a linear mixed model to statistically analyze the variance of multiple prosodic features in different emotions.

The significance of the current research is reflected in (1) broadening our perspective of emotional communication and clarifying the acoustic patterning of valence and size-projection in related work, and (2) investigating boundary prominence by introducing prosodic units in the modeling of emotional prosody.

1.1 Related Work

Dimensional Emotion Model. As a psychological topic, emotion is typically approached through two representative models - the discrete model [9,40] and the dimensional model [35]. Classifying emotions into basic categories with unique vocal patterns, the discrete model [30,31,34] is widely used in vocal emotion research due to its universality and proximity to human communication, though lacking a final set of basic emotions and falling short of explaining emotion effects and similarities in acoustic dimensions [14]. On the other hand, the dimensional model maps emotions onto two major dimensions - valence and arousal/activation, where valence distinguishes between positive and negative emotions, and arousal distinguishes between high-energy emotions (e.g., Happy, Angry) and low-energy emotions (e.g., Sad, Calm) [34]. In terms of vocal effects in dimensional model, it should be noted that the arousal dimension consistently correlates with acoustic parameters, such as F0, intensity level, and intensity variability, while acoustic cues for valence are less consistent, except for spectral slope and intensity variability as indicators of positive emotions [12,22,43].

Emotion Projection in Prosody. The correlation between emotion and speech is conceptualized through body-size projection and bio-informational dimensions (BIDs) theory, building upon Morton's motivational-structural rules. Morton suggests that animals use body-size-associated acoustic cues to express their emotions, with hostility conveyed by harsh and low-frequency sounds, and submission, friendliness, and appeasement conveyed by higher-frequency and more pure-tone-like sounds [25]. Ohala's frequency-coding theory extends Morton's rules to humans, stating that shorter vocal tracts and higher fundamental frequency (F0) encode smallness, non-threatening attitude, and goodwill [28]. Y Xu further extends the size-code hypothesis to distinguish between Angry and Happy emotions, asserting that pitch, formant dispersion, and voice quality are exact size-coding dimensions and that human listeners perceive the lengthening of the vocal tract and lowering of voice pitch as conveying Angry emotion [45]. However, body-size projection alone is insufficient to explain sadness, fear, disgust, and surprise, as their expression, does not extensively involve call center [8,43].

As an extension of body-size projection, BIDs (bio-informational dimensions) theory covers three additional dimensions: Dynamicity, Audibility, and Association [44]. Dynamicity controls vitality vocalization, correlated with faster speech rate, larger range, and higher velocity of F0 change and formant movement [44]. Audibility, which determines the transmission distance of a vocalization, significantly affects intensity and voice quality [37]. Association, which is weak in disgust emotion, leads to F1 raising and devoicing as a consequence of pharynx tightening [37,44]. Perceptual research has demonstrated the effectiveness of BID dimensions by revealing the accuracy of BID-based prediction about people's sensitiveness and response to acoustic manipulation along different BID dimensions [15,27,44] (Table 1).

Table 1. A brief summary of Arousal-Valence Dimensions and Bio-informatic Dimensions

	Dimension	Positive	Negative	Neutral	Related Acoustics
Arousal Valence	Arousal	Happy Angry Surprise	Sad (General)		Higher F0 level Higher intensity level Higher intensity variability
	Valence	Happy	Sad Angry	Surprise	Steeper spectral slope Less intensity variability
Bio-informatic Dimensions	Size Projection	Angry	Happy		Lower F0 level
	Audibility	Happy Angry Sad (grieving)	Sad (Depression)		Higher Intensity Change of Voice Quality
	Dynamicity	Happy Angry	Sad (Depression)		Higher Tempo Larger F0 Variability
	Association		Disgust		Less F1 Raising

Prosodic Features of Basic Emotions. In addition to the ideas on the conveying of emotions through prosody, numerous empirical studies have explored the acoustic indicators that potentially represent vocal emotion. Nonetheless, the discrepancy between Angry and Happy emotions continues to yield conflicting outcomes, underscoring the difficulty of discerning emotional valence in speech data. The following presents an analysis of the significant discoveries related to four fundamental emotions.

Angry and Happy. Angry and Happy are similar in that they are both high-arousal emotions, featuring dynamicity and audibility and are frequently expressed in call center interactions [24]. However, they are at the far end of each other in terms of emotional valence and body size projection. Distinguishing between these two emotions can be challenging [44], as they share similar acoustic features such as high speech rate, short pauses [4,10,17,41], and increased F0 mean and F0 range [11,26,29]. However, some studies suggest that Happy speech may also exhibit slow or normal speech rate [2,11]. The contrast in pitch level between anger and happiness is inconclusive in previous research, with production studies indicating a higher pitch for anger [6,7,22,34], while perceptual studies attribute a higher pitch to happiness [8,44]. Some studies also highlight differences in F0 contour, with anger characterized by steeper F0 fall and longer vocal tract length (VTL) compared to happiness [8,34]. Finally, research based on Bayes classification suggests that anger may be predominantly perceived from the initial portion of utterances [33].

Surprise. In terms of arousal-valence dimensions, Surprise is a typically high-arousal, neutral-valence emotion. Although its position within the BID (body-size projection, intensity, and dynamicity) dimensions are not fully understood, research indicates that Surprise is characterized by high dynamicity and audibility while being neutral with regard to body-size projection and association. This hypothesis is consistent with previous research that has linked astonishment to higher pitch levels, greater pitch variability, and slower timing in speech patterns [13,19,39]. Additionally, it has been pointed out that prosodic cues play a dominant role in identifying surprise in speech, as opposed to segmental cues [3]. Furthermore, features extracted from sentence-final words are more effective in discriminating surprise emotion compared to global features [33].

Sadness. Sadness, a typical negative-valence and low-arousal emotion, can be further categorized into two subtypes: depressed sadness and grieving sadness [18]. These two types of sadness, which are closely located in the valence-arousal space, share features such as reduced F0 variability and speech rate [16,32,38]. However, depressed sadness is often associated with reduced F0, while grieving sadness typically results in raised F0 levels [5]. The mixture of these two types of sadness may explain why the pitch level of sadness, if not specifically categorized, is lower than that of neutral emotion in most studies [13,17,32,36,38], but higher in some recent findings [6]. To accurately describe these two subordinate types of sadness, it has been recommended to treat depressed sadness as a neutral-sized and low-audibility emotion and grieving sadness as a small-sized and high-audibility emotion [44].

2   Research Questions

The primary goal of this study is to broaden our understanding of speech emotion, particularly its manifestation in prosody. Based on the inconclusiveness of past work, we investigate two specific questions.

2.1 Q1: Which Prosodic Cues Encode Emotional Valence or Project Body-Size

Previous research has consistently shown a significant difference between high-arousal emotions (happiness, anger, and surprise) and low-arousal emotions (sadness as instance). This distinction, particularly regarding audibility and dynamicity, aligns with the arousal dimension and has been supported by earlier studies [11,26,29,44]. However, there are limited cues that are consistently reliable in distinguishing high-arousal emotions with different valences, particularly between Angry and Happy emotions. To capture the potential measures reflecting emotional valence or size projection, this research seeks to identify the prosodic cues where Angry and Happy emotions show statistically significant differences.

2.2 Q2: How Sentence Boundary and Word Boundary Interact with Emotional Effect on Speech

Findings from the machine-learning classification of speech emotion have indicated that features extracted from pre-boundary units are more effective in predicting emotion labels [33]. This inspires us to explore how boundaries of prosodic units convey vocal emotion. Based on speech corpus, word segmentation, and force-alignment techniques, this research explores the prominence of two kinds of boundaries, the boundary of a word and the boundary of an utterance. This research introduces boundary levels and their interaction with the emotion category in regression analysis. The significance of the interactions should reflect the boundary prominence of emotional effect.

3 Method

This section introduces the database, data processing procedure, and concrete acoustic measurements.

3.1 Speech Materials

The Mandarin set of Emotional Speech Database (ESD) consists of 350 parallel utterances spoken by 10 native Chinese speakers (5 male speakers and 5 female speakers) and covers 5 emotion categories (neutral, Happy, Angry, Sad and Surprise). All the speech data in ESD database is recorded in a typical indoor environment with a Signal-to-noise ratio of above 20 dB and a sampling frequency of 16 kHz. Each speech data is associated with text content transcribed in Chinese characters [1,46].

3.2 Processing Procedures

Data Filtering. To avoid mixing reported emotion with expressed emotion, this research excludes speech data recorded from text containing emotional content. In this step, "cnsenti" [42] library is introduced to detect emotional words from text transcription. For each speaker, 190 sentences were preserved in each emotion category. (Total data size = 190 sentences × 5 emotions (neutral baseline as one emotion) × 10 speakers)

Forced Alignment and Word Segmentation. This part aims to align speech intervals to their corresponding phoneme, syllable, and syntactic words. We apply Montreal Forced Alignment (MFA) [23] to align speech to syllable and phoneme sequence converted from text transcription. The text-to-syllable and phoneme conversion is completed by the xpinyin toolkit. Following forced alignment, word segmentation information is marked on an additional tier in the output of force alignment. The word segmentation procedure is based on the pkuseg segmenter [20]. The picture below shows the full details of the output of the alignment procedure (Fig. 1).

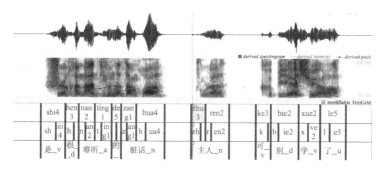

Fig. 1. An illustration of the output of preprocessing procedures. The three interval tiers in the Praat file represent syllable, phoneme, and syntactic words from the top down

3.3 Acoustic Feature Extraction

Based on the contributions of previous work, this research approaches the acoustic measurement of emotional speech from the following dimensions.

- Sentence Level:
    - F0 Level (Average F0), Range F0, F0 Changing Rate (Number of peak and valley points divided by sounding duration), F0 Level of Final Downstep, F0 Slope of Final Downstep and F0 Range of Final Downstep
    - Syllable Number Per Second, Word Number Per Second
- Syllable Level:
    - Duration, F0 Level, F0 range

3.4   Regression Analysis

To robustly estimate the emotional effect, the current research introduces linear mixed regression to resolve the potential gender, social, and linguistic effect from subject variance, sentence content, and lexical tone on the prosodic features. This research implements sentence-level regression and syllable-level regression, the settings of which are listed in Table 2.

Table 2. Settings of Dependent Variable, Fixed Effect and Random Effect for Sentence and Syllable-level Regression

Modeling Level	Dependent Variable	Fixed Effect	Random Slope and Intercept	Random Intercept
Sentence	Sentence-level Measurements	Emotion	Subject ID	Sentence ID
Syllable	Syllable-level Measurements	Emotion Word-Final (Boolean) Sentence-final (Boolean) Word-Final (Boolean) × Emotion Sentence-final (Boolean) × Emotion Syllable Weight	Subject ID Lexical Tone	Sentence ID

To explore the boundary prominence of the emotion effect, we place the interaction between emotion and word-final and between emotion and sentence-final among the fixed effect in the syllable level regression. For the coefficient of interactive fixed effect between emotion and boundary label, the research contends that its estimation and significance represent the boundary prominence of emotion effect.

To interpret the results of regressions, we visualize the coefficients of various emotion categories and their confidence intervals (at the 95% confidence level), from which the pair-wise differences can be determined by determining whether the confidence intervals of a given pair of emotions overlap. We also report the estimates and p-values of the Difference of Least Squares Mean (below referred to as LSM Difference) between the five emotion categories (neutral emotion included) on the relevant acoustic measurements. Using the results of linear mixed regressions, the "difflsmeans" function in R is devised to infer the LSM Differences.

4   Results

This section reports the differences between the five emotion categories in the acoustic measurements, on the sentence and syllable levels respectively.

4.1   Sentence-Level Modeling

Frequency Domain. The F0-related characteristics consist of Average F0, Range F0, F0 Changing Rate, and the average level, range, and slope of the final F0 downstep. (Also see the "Ag-Sd", "Hp-Sd", and "Sd-Sp" columns in

Table 3). However, F0 measurements do not clearly distinguish between Angry, Happy, and Surprise, except for the F0 range (which distinguishes Surprise from the others, see the second figure on row 1 of Fig. 2) and F0 changing rate (which distinguishes Angry, see the third figure on row 2 of Fig. 2). In addition, Table 3 demonstrates that Angry has a steeper F0 slope of the final downstep compared to Happy and Surprise. As for sadness, the results indicate that the F0 level and F0 range are considerably greater than the neutral levels, likely due to the confusion between grief sadness and depression sadness.

Time Domain. As for time domain features, the distribution of estimated levels for each emotion type is identical for the number of syllables per second and the number of words per second (see the third and fourth figures in the second row of Fig. 2). Based on these characteristics, the four emotion categories in question are distinguishable, with surprise consistently matching the level of neutral emotion. Details of the pair-wise contrast between the five emotion categories can be found in Table 3, where it is evident that only the emotion of surprise does not influence tempo.

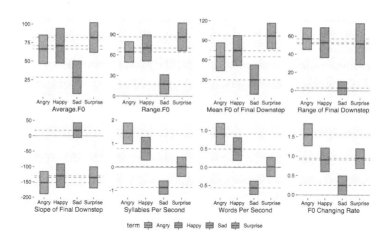

Fig. 2. Estimated level and confidence intervals of the coefficients of emotions (as categorical variables in Fixed Effect) in the regressions against the eight sentence-level acoustic features. Effects from subjects and sentences per se are controlled as Random Effects (See Table 2).

4.2 Syllable-Level Modeling

Frequency Domain From Fig. 3, the main effect of the emotion on the F0 level and F0 range encodes arousal but does not draw a clear line between high-arousal emotions. Similarly, the word boundary is no more effective in discriminating between high-arousal emotions. However, the intermediate effects through sentence boundary (See the right-most subfigures on both rows of Fig. 3) show that

Table 3. Summary of LSM Difference and corresponding p-values (in the parenthesis) between different emotions regarding the acoustic measurements concerned. The asterisks (*) are used to indicate statistical significance.

	Ag - Hp	Ag - Sd	Ag - Sp	Hp - Sd	Hp - Sp	Nt - Ag	Nt - Hp	Nt - Sd	Nt - Sp	Sd - Sp
Average.F0	−4.6 (0.709)	38.1* (0.032)	−16* (0.028)	42.7* (0.011)	−11.4 (0.323)	−66.2*** (0.000)	−70.8*** (0.000)	−28.1* (0.030)	−82.1*** (0.000)	−54.1** (0.007)
F0 Changing Rate	0.6** (0.006)	1.3*** (0.000)	0.6** (0.002)	0.7** (0.010)	0 (0.716)	−1.5*** (0.000)	−0.9*** (0.000)	−0.2. (0.087)	−0.9*** (0.000)	−0.7** (0.009)
Mean F0 of Final Downstep	−9.4 (0.453)	34.7 (0.052.)	−32** (0.001)	44.1** (0.008)	−22.6. (0.051)	−64.8*** (0.000)	−74.3*** (0.000)	−30.1* (0.029)	−96.8*** (0.000)	−66.7*** (0.000)
Range of Final Downstep	4 (0.574)	54*** (0.000)	5.6 (0.501)	50*** (0.000)	1.6 (0.848)	−56.9*** (0.000)	−52.9*** (0.000)	−2.9 (0.429)	−51.3** (0.002)	−48.4** (0.003)
Range.F0	−6 (0.296)	47** (0.002)	−22.5** (0.002)	53** (0.002)	−16.5. (0.069)	−64.6*** (0.000)	−70.6*** (0.000)	−17.7 (0.037)	−87.1*** (0.000)	−69.4*** (0.000)
Slope of Final Downstep	−22.1* (0.032)	−169.4*** (0.000)	−17.1 (0.300)	−147.2*** (0.000)	5.1 (0.759)	151.6*** (0.000)	129.4*** (0.000)	−17.8 (0.178)	134.5*** (0.000)	152.3*** (0.000)
Syllables Per Second	0.6** (0.009)	2.3*** (0.000)	1.4*** (0.000)	1.7*** (0.000)	0.8** (0.005)	−1.4*** (0.000)	−0.8 (0.011)	0.9*** (0.000)	0 (0.889)	−0.9** (0.007)
Words Per Second	0.4** (0.010)	1.5*** (0.000)	0.9*** (0.000)	1.1*** (0.000)	0.5** (0.005)	−0.9*** (0.000)	−0.5* (0.012)	0.6*** (0.000)	0 (0.934)	−0.6** (0.007)

Note: * = p < 0.05; ** = p < 0.01; *** = p < 0.01

the F0 encoding of non-arousal information exhibits notable boundary prominence on the utterance level. Specifically, the lowering tendency of the F0 level (See the negative estimations of sentence-boundary effect on Average F0) in the sentence-final syllable is displayed to be significantly larger in the Angry emotion (as the confidence interval does not overlap with Happy or Surprise), followed by Happy emotion and Surprise. Moreover, the expansion tendency of F0 range in the sentence-final syllable is displayed to be strongest in Happy emotion, followed by Surprise and Angry emotions. This means valence or size projection is intensively predictable from the contrast between sentence-final and non-final syllables rather than from the overall level of the whole sentence or non-final syllables.

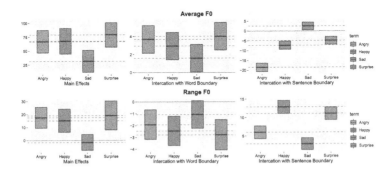

Fig. 3. Estimated levels and confidence intervals of the main effects of 4 emotions (left), and their intermediate effects via word boundary (middle), and via sentence boundary on syllable average F0 (F0 level) and range F0. Neutral emotion is the reference level, visualized as the zero level.

The LSM differences in Table 4 (about F0 level) and Table 5 (about F0 range) display the realization of f0 level and f0 range on different positions. The estimates and significance levels demonstrate that a higher F0 level in sentence-final syllable discriminates surprise from Angry, while a larger F0 range in sentence-final syllable discriminates Surprise from both Angry and Happy. The LME difference between Angry and Happy is not highly significant, but the LME difference of the F0 range in sentence-final syllable shows weak significance (p-value = 0.078), where Happy displays a larger F0 range.

The LSM differences between Angry and Happy in Table 4 and Table 5 are all insignificant on non-boundary, word-final, and sentence-final syllables. However, this does not contradict the findings from the coefficients of intermediate effects on sentence boundary in Fig. 3, since the coefficients in Fig. 3 focus on the contrast between the two emotions on the degree to which the F0 features sentence-boundary syllables are affected by emotional effect so that they are acoustically distinguished from non-boundary syllables. On the other hand, the LMS differences focus on the contrast between sentence-final syllables in Angry emotion and those in Happy emotion on the dimensions of F0 level and F0 range, which means that LMS differences do not reflect the degree of variation between sentence-final and non-final syllables.

Table 4. Pair-wise LSM differences of the pitch levels of non-final syllables, word-final syllables, and sentence-final syllables, with their significance reported by asterisks and P-values reported in the parenthesis

	Ag - Hp	Ag - Sd	Ag - Sp	Hp - Sd	Hp - Sp	Nt - Ag	Nt - Hp	Nt - Sd	Nt - Sp	Sd - Sp
Non-final Syllable	-5.606 (0.629)	26.166 (0.125)	-18.549* (0.024)	31.772. (0.052)	-12.943 (0.27)	-59.521*** (0)	-65.127*** (0)	-33.355** (0.007)	-78.07*** (0)	-44.715* (0.029)
Word-final Syllable	-4.754 (0.681)	27.137 (0.113)	-18.33* (0.026)	31.891. (0.051)	-13.575 (0.249)	-61.936*** (0)	-66.69*** (0)	-34.799** (0.006)	-80.265*** (0)	-45.466* (0.027)
Sentence-final Syllable	-11.905 (0.316)	13.458 (0.412)	-26.795** (0.003)	25.363 (0.11)	-14.889 (0.21)	-48.26*** (0.001)	-60.165*** (0.001)	-34.802** (0.006)	-75.055*** (0)	-40.253* (0.046)

Note: . = p < 0.1; * = p < 0.05; ** = p < 0.01; *** = p < 0.01

Table 5. Estimates and P-values of pair-wise LSM differences of the pitch range of non-final syllables, word-final syllables, and sentence-final syllables, computed from the results of linear mixed model.

	Ag - Hp	Ag - Sd	Ag - Sp	Hp - Sd	Hp - Sp	Nt - Ag	Nt - Hp	Nt - Sd	Nt - Sp	Sd - Sp
Non-final Syllables	-0.111 (0.918)	6.547** (0.007)	-2.409* (0.03)	6.658* (0.019)	-2.298. (0.062)	-8.291** (0.005)	-8.402* (0.011)	-1.744 (0.366)	-10.7** (0.002)	-8.956** (0.005)
Word-final Syllables	0.144 (0.893)	7.13** (0.004)	-1.726 (0.101)	6.986* (0.015)	-1.871 (0.119)	-7.87** (0.007)	-7.725* (0.017)	-0.74 (0.697)	-9.596** (0.004)	-8.856** (0.005)
Sentence-final Syllables	-2.16. (0.078)	6.351** (0.008)	-4.827*** (0)	8.511** (0.005)	-2.667* (0.043)	-9.68** (0.002)	-11.84*** (0.001)	-3.329 (0.105)	-14.507*** (0)	-11.178** (0.001)

Note: . = p < 0.1; * = p < 0.05; ** = p < 0.01; *** = p < 0.01

Time Domain. From the left-most subfigure in Fig. 4, we can see that the main effect of emotion on syllable duration shows the same tendency of sentence-level contrast between the five emotions (Neutral emotion as the zero line), though Angry and Happy are not fully distinguished. From the middle and right-most subfigure in Fig. 4, we can see the general tendency that the existence of emotion shortens word-final syllables (See the middle subfigure of Fig. 4 where all the four levels are below zero), whereas negative emotion exhibits the largest level of word-final shortening. Meanwhile, on the sentence boundary, high-arousal emotions (Ag, Hp, and Sp) generally strengthen the tendency of pre-boundary lengthening. The ranking of their lengthening levels (See the third subfigure of Fig. 4) strictly follows the degree of valence, as is in the rank of "Happy-Surprise-Angry". On the contrary, sadness generally leads to pre-boundary shortening on the utterance level (Table 6).

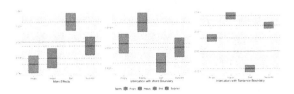

Fig. 4. Estimated levels and confidence intervals of the main effects of 4 emotions on syllable duration (left), and their intermediate effects via word boundary on syllable duration (middle), and their intermediate effects via utterance boundary on syllable duration (right).

Table 6. Estimates and P-values of pair-wise LSM differences of the syllable duration of non-final syllables, word-final syllables, and sentence-final syllables, computed from the results of linear mixed model.

	Ag - Hp	Ag - Sd	Ag - Sp	Hp - Sd	Hp - Sp	Nt - Ag	Nt - Hp	Nt - Sd	Nt - Sp	Sd - Sp
Non-final Syllable	−0.025** (0.002)	−0.063*** (0)	−0.041*** (0)	−0.038** (0.007)	−0.015* (0.027)	0.043*** (0.001)	0.018. (0.097)	−0.02* (0.034)	0.002 (0.786)	0.023. (0.09)
Word-final Syllable	−0.028** (0.001)	−0.061*** (0)	−0.04*** (0)	−0.033* (0.016)	−0.012. (0.066)	0.05*** (0)	0.022* (0.046)	−0.011 (0.218)	0.01 (0.287)	0.021 (0.115)
Sentence-final Syllable	−0.037*** (0)	−0.048** (0.003)	−0.047*** (0)	−0.011 (0.352)	−0.01 (0.115)	0.036** (0.002)	0 (0.97)	−0.012 (0.201)	−0.011 (0.258)	0.001 (0.939)

Note: $*$ = p < 0.05; $**$ = p < 0.01; $***$ = p < 0.01

5 Discussion

According to the significance of pair-wise difference on a certain measurement, the prosodic features can be categorized into three groups, as summarized in Table 7.

The features in the first group exclusively encode emotional arousal. The F0 level of the entire sentence and the principal effect on the F0 level of the syllable are members of this group, which contradicts the body-size projection hypothesis [44].

The two features in the second group, in addition to encoding emotional arousal, also convey Surprise emotion. Both measurements place Surprise at the highest level, followed by Happy and then Angry, which is considerably lower than Surprise. These results may indicate that Surprise should occupy a higher position on the arousal dimension of the dimensional emotion model or the dynamicity dimension of BIDs.

The final group of features in Table 7 equally project emotional arousal and valence (or size-projection), as they invariably distinguish high arousal from low arousal emotion by discriminating at least two pairs of high-arousal emotion. The effect of emotion on the F0 change tendency on sentence-final position shows the cues of size-projection, as the F0 lowering tendency in Angry emotion is tested as larger than in Happy and Surprise emotions (See Fig. 3), while the increase of F0 range on sentence-final position is largest in Happy. These results indicate that the encoding of emotional valence or the projection of body size is intensively reflected in the variation between sentence-final and non-final syllables.

Table 7. Summary of findings from regression analysis. In each column, "+" means the former emotion is significantly higher/stronger than the latter, while "−" means the contrary. Blank denotes insignificance. Ag = Angry, Sd = Sad, Sp = Surprise, Hp = Happy

	Ag-Sd	Hp-Sd	Sp-Sd	Ag-Hp	Ag-Sp	Sp-Hp
F0 Level	+	+	+			
F0 Range of Final Downstep	+	+	+			
Slope of Final Downstep	−	−	−			
Syllable F0 Level (Main Effect)	+	+	+			
Syllable F0 Range (Main Effect)	+	+	+			
F0 Range	+	+	+		−	
F0 Level of Final Downstep	+	+	+		−	
F0 Changing Rate	+	+	+	+	+	
Syllable Duration (Main Effect)	−	−	−		−	+
Syllable Duration Lengthening (Sentence-final)	+	+	+	−	−	−
Syllable Duration Shortening (Word-Final)	+	+	+	−		−
Syllables/Words Per Second	+	+	+	+	+	−
Syllable F0 Level Reduction (Sentence-final)	+	+	+	+	+	−
Syllable F0 Range Augmentation (Sentence-final)	+	+	+	−	−	−

6   Conclusion

Taking the Mandarin speech corpus as the database, our study focuses on the projection of emotional valence in speech prosody. Our results indicate that emotional valence is mostly expressed through tempo, pitch fluctuation rate, sentence-final F0 lowering tendency, the lengthening of final syllables, and the slope of the final downstep. Regarding the differentiation of Angry and Happy emotions, it is noteworthy that Angry exhibits the most pronounced inclination towards sentence-final F0 lowering. On the other hand, Happy exhibits the most pronounced lengthening of the duration, as well as the widening of the F0 range on syllables, to the end of sentences. Furthermore, the Angry emotion exhibits a more observable final downstep compared to other emotions characterized by high arousal. To encapsulate, this study highlights the prominence of sentence-final syllables in projecting emotional valence, where the F0 lowering and F0 range expansion function as the particular cues to express negative and position arousal respectively. Echoing previous research, this result lays emphasis on the investigation of sentence-final units such as sentence-final particles in conveying emotional valence and in improving the recognition of speech emotion [21].

The primary limitation of the present investigation, which focuses on the vocal impact of emotion, is the divergence between the manner in which emotions are acted out during speech data recording in experimental settings, and their authentic manifestation in everyday discourse. To get insights into the encoding of emotions and the projection of body size, it is advisable to record emotional speech during real-time dialogues in the future. Moreover, this study specifically focuses on only five fundamental emotions. It is important to evaluate a wider variety of emotions in the future, including more subtle distinctions in both positive/negative valence and level of arousal.

References

1. Emotional voice conversion: Theory, databases and ESD. Speech Commun. **137**, 1–18 (2022)
2. Abdel-Hamid, L., Shaker, N.H., Emara, I.: Analysis of linguistic and prosodic features of bilingual Arabic-English speakers for speech emotion recognition. IEEE Access **8**, 72957–72970 (2020)
3. Barra, R., Montero, J.M., Macias-Guarasa, J., D'Haro, L., San-Segundo, R., Córdoba, R.: Prosodic and segmental rubrics in emotion identification. In: 2006 IEEE International Conference on Acoustics Speech and Signal Processing Proceedings, vol. 1, pp. I-I. IEEE (2006)
4. Bonvino, E.: Le strutture del linguaggio: un'introduzione alla fonologia. Il suono delle parole. Percezione e conoscenza della lingua nei bambini, p. 157e197 (2000)
5. Burkhardt, F., Sendlmeier, W.F.: Verification of acoustical correlates of emotional speech using formant-synthesis. In: ISCA Tutorial and Research Workshop (ITRW) on Speech and Emotion (2000)
6. Carl, M., Icht, M., Ben-David, B.M.: A cross-linguistic validation of the test for rating emotions in speech: acoustic analyses of emotional sentences in English, German, and Hebrew. Technical report, ASHA (2022)
7. Chong, C.S., Kim, J., Davis, C.: Exploring acoustic differences between Cantonese (tonal) and English (non-tonal) spoken expressions of emotions. In: Sixteenth Annual Conference of the International Speech Communication Association (2015)
8. Chuenwattanapranithi, S., Xu, Y., Thipakorn, B., Maneewongvatana, S.: Encoding emotions in speech with the size code. Phonetica **65**(4), 210–230 (2008)
9. Ekman, P.: An argument for basic emotions. Cogn. Emot. **6**(3–4), 169–200 (1992)
10. Ellgring, H., Scherer, K.R.: Vocal indicators of mood change in depression. J. Nonverbal Behav. **20**(2), 83–110 (1996)
11. Gangamohan, P., Kadiri, S.R., Yegnanarayana, B.: Analysis of emotional speech—a review. In: Esposito, A., Jain, L.C. (eds.) Toward Robotic Socially Believable Behaving Systems - Volume I. ISRL, vol. 105, pp. 205–238. Springer, Cham (2016). https://doi.org/10.1007/978-3-319-31056-5_11

12. Goudbeek, M., Scherer, K.: Beyond arousal: valence and potency/control cues in the vocal expression of emotion. J. Acoust. Soc. Am. **128**(3), 1322–1336 (2010)
13. Hammerschmidt, K., Jürgens, U.: Acoustical correlates of affective prosody. J. Voice **21**(5), 531–540 (2007)
14. Hoffmann, H., et al.: Mapping discrete emotions into the dimensional space: an empirical approach. In: 2012 IEEE International Conference on Systems, Man, and Cybernetics (SMC), pp. 3316–3320. IEEE (2012)
15. Hsu, C., Xu, Y.: Can adolescents with autism perceive emotional prosody? In: Fifteenth Annual Conference of the International Speech Communication Association (2014)
16. Johnstone, T., Scherer, K.R.: Vocal communication of emotion. In: Handbook of Emotions, vol. 2, pp. 220–235 (2000)
17. Juslin, P.N., Laukka, P.: Communication of emotions in vocal expression and music performance: different channels, same code? Psychol. Bull. **129**(5), 770 (2003)
18. Kollias, D., Zafeiriou, S.: A multi-task learning & generation framework: valence-arousal, action units & primary expressions. arXiv preprint arXiv:1811.07771 (2018)
19. Li, A.: Encoding and Decoding of Emotional Speech. PPP, Springer, Heidelberg (2015). https://doi.org/10.1007/978-3-662-47691-8
20. Luo, R., Xu, J., Zhang, Y., Ren, X., Sun, X.: PKUSEG: a toolkit for multi-domain Chinese word segmentation. arXiv preprint arXiv:1906.11455 (2019)
21. Luo, X., Huang, C.R.: Gender-related use of tonal patterns in Mandarin Chinese: the case of sentence-final particle ma. In: Su, Q., Xu, G., Yang, X. (eds.) Workshop on Chinese Lexical Semantics, CLSW 2022. LNCS, vol. 13496, pp. 96–107. Springer, Heidelberg (2022). https://doi.org/10.1007/978-3-031-28956-9_8
22. Mauss, I.B., Robinson, M.D.: Measures of emotion: a review. Cogn. Emot. **23**(2), 209–237 (2009)
23. McAuliffe, M., Socolof, M., Mihuc, S., Wagner, M., Sonderegger, M.: Montreal forced aligner: trainable text-speech alignment using Kaldi. In: Interspeech, vol. 2017, pp. 498–502 (2017)
24. Morrison, D., Wang, R., De Silva, L.C.: Ensemble methods for spoken emotion recognition in call-centres. Speech Commun. **49**(2), 98–112 (2007)
25. Morton, E.S.: On the occurrence and significance of motivation-structural rules in some bird and mammal sounds. Am. Nat. **111**(981), 855–869 (1977)
26. Murray, I.R., Arnott, J.L.: Implementation and testing of a system for producing emotion-by-rule in synthetic speech. Speech Commun. **16**(4), 369–390 (1995)
27. Noble, L., Xu, Y.: Friendly speech and happy speech-are they the same? In: ICPhS, pp. 1502–1505 (2011)
28. Ohala, J.J.: An ethological perspective on common cross-language utilization of f_0 of voice. Phonetica **41**(1), 1–16 (1984)
29. Pereira, C., Watson, C.I.: Some acoustic characteristics of emotion. In: ICSLP (1998)
30. Plutchik, R.: A general psychoevolutionary theory of emotion. In: Theories of Emotion, pp. 3–33. Elsevier (1980)
31. Prinz, J.: Which emotions are basic. In: Emotion, Evolution, and Rationality, vol. 69, p. 88 (2004)
32. Probst, L., Braun, A.: The effects of emotional state on fundamental frequency. In: Proceedings of the 19th International Congress of Phonetic Sciences, Melbourne, Australia, pp. 67–71 (2019)
33. Rao, K.S., Koolagudi, S.G., Vempada, R.R.: Emotion recognition from speech using global and local prosodic features. Int. J. Speech Technol. **16**(2), 143–160 (2013)

34. Scherer, K.R.: Vocal communication of emotion: a review of research paradigms. Speech Commun. **40**(1–2), 227–256 (2003)

35. Scherer, K.R., et al.: Psychological models of emotion. In: The Neuropsychology of Emotion, vol. 137, no. 3, pp. 137–162 (2000)

36. Sobin, C., Alpert, M.: Emotion in speech: the acoustic attributes of fear, anger, sadness, and joy. J. Psycholinguist. Res. **28**(4), 347–365 (1999)

37. Stevens, K.N.: Acoustic Phonetics, vol. 30. MIT Press (2000)

38. Stolarski, L.: Pitch patterns in vocal expression of 'happiness' and 'sadness' in the reading aloud of prose on the basis of selected audiobooks. Res. Lang. **13**(2), 140–161 (2015)

39. Tao, J., Kang, Y., Li, A.: Prosody conversion from neutral speech to emotional speech. IEEE Trans. Audio Speech Lang. Process. **14**(4), 1145–1154 (2006)

40. Tomkins, S.S.: Affect, Imagery, Consciousness: The Positive Affects, vol. 1 (1962)

41. Wang, T., Lee, Y., Ma, Q.: Within and across-language comparison of vocal emotions in Mandarin and English. Appl. Sci. **8**(12), 2629 (2018)

42. Xu, L., Lin, H., Pan, Y., Ren, H., Chen, J.: Constructing the affective lexicon ontology. J. China Soc. Sci. Tech. Inf. **27**(2), 180–185 (2008)

43. Xu, Y.: Prosody, tone, and intonation. In: The Routledge Handbook of Phonetics, pp. 314–356. Routledge (2019)

44. Xu, Y., Kelly, A., Smillie, C.: Emotional expressions as communicative signals. In: Prosody and Iconicity, pp. 33–60 (2013)

45. Xu, Y., Lee, A., Wu, W.L., Liu, X., Birkholz, P.: Human vocal attractiveness as signaled by body size projection. PLoS ONE **8**(4), e62397 (2013)

46. Zhou, K., Sisman, B., Liu, R., Li, H.: Seen and unseen emotional style transfer for voice conversion with a new emotional speech dataset. In: 2021 IEEE International Conference on Acoustics, Speech and Signal Processing (ICASSP), ICASSP 2021, pp. 920–924. IEEE (2021)

Corpus-Based Analysis of Lexical Features of Mongolian Language Policy Text

Annaer[✉] and Dahubaiyila

School of Mongolian Studies, Inner Mongolia University, College Road 235,
Hohhot 010021, China
1286013462@qq.com

Abstract. Like other policy texts, language policy texts also need policy text analysis. Leveraging a corpus of 100 policy documents, this study investigates various linguistic attributes, including the distribution of parts of speech, type-token ratio, and lexical density, through data comparative analysis. Furthermore, the paper categorizes the corpus into twelve distinct types, encompassing instructions, decisions, notices, reports, regulations, ways, rules, methods, summaries, plans, speeches and papers. Employing natural language processing techniques, the study also utilizes frequency statistics and wordclouds to provide both word frequency statistical tables and visual wordcloud representations of the Mongolian language policy text corpus.

Keywords: Mongolian language policy · Policy text analysis · Distribution of parts of speech · Lexical density · Word frequency

1 Introduction

Policy text analysis is a process of combining micro text with macro history contexts, of discovering text's "deep structure" and their inner evolution logic through several methods, of unearthing value allocation and struggle in the policy process, and of text theorization [1] and an essential tool for comprehending, elucidating, and evaluating policies. This analytical approach encompasses a myriad of techniques, including subject word analysis, word frequency analysis, narrative analysis, intertextual analysis, emotional analysis, image perception analysis, metaphor analysis, feature analysis, ideological analysis, and text visualization analysis, among others [2]. As policy documents continue to evolve, they draw inspiration from prior policy measures, aligning themselves with established frameworks and paradigms [2].

One particularly promising avenue within the realm of corpus linguistics is corpus-based word research. This methodology objectively dissects words using authentic language data from corpora, yielding rich insights in recent years. For instance, Ma and Shang, in their research, harnessed reports from China Daily and The Economist pertaining to "The Belt and Road Initiative" as their corpus. Their study identified node words such as China, road, and development, subsequently classifying high-frequency words within their contextual meanings [3]. Wang constructed a corpus of contemporary

M. Dong et al. (Eds.): CLSW 2023, LNAI 14515, pp. 331–341, 2024.
https://doi.org/10.1007/978-981-97-0586-3_26

English reports on China in the major countries along the "Belt and Road," conducting an analysis of high-frequency words, subject words, and index lines to discern media perspectives on China in these regions [4]. Zhang and Su utilized the corpus retrieval software AntConc to extract the top 100 thematic words from New York Times' reports on China and Japan spanning from 1987 to 2006, facilitating classification, statistical analysis, and comparative assessments [5]. It is important to note, however, that most studies have concentrated on the analysis of high-frequency and thematic words in news reports, shedding light on media viewpoints regarding China [6]. Within the context of the Mongolian language, scholars such as Dulaan and Hai employed word frequency formulas to conduct frequency and part-of-speech statistics on D.Nachugdorji's "Old Boy" [7]. Uyutan and Dabhvrbayar employed a complex feature description methodology to process D.Nachugdorj's novel "Old Boy" subsequently examining the linguistic intricacies found within the text [8]. Bao, Dabhvrbayar, and Oyutan conducted a statistical analysis of the lexical features of "Zhanggar" using the Python language, encompassing keywords, vocabulary density, and vocabulary diversity [9]. Annaer and Ajitai utilized AntConc software to analyze the wordcloud of Mongolian poetry, concurrently conducting statistical investigations into the co-occurrence of the word "HIJIG" (epidemic) [10]. These studies, commendably, have undertaken vocabulary statistical research on news or literary texts.

In light of these studies, an important question emerges: what differentiates the vocabulary characteristics of Mongolian language policy texts? What distinctions in lexicon exist among various types of language policies? Therefore, this paper employing natural language processing methods and corpora to provide fresh insights into text analysis and enhance research methodologies. Corpus-based vocabulary statistical research has the potential to unveil intricate linguistic features at the lexical level of language, offering a deeper understanding of the nuances within policy texts.

2   Research Materials and Methods

In this section, we detail the research materials and methods employed in the analysis of Mongolian language policy texts. The study focuses on the extraction, processing, and categorization of a comprehensive corpus sourced from the "Mongolian Language Policy Database". Furthermore, it delineates the methodologies used to explore the lexical characteristics of these texts, encompassing the distribution of part of speech, lexical richness and word frequency distribution.

2.1   Selection and Processing of Corpus

Our corpus consists of 100 text files meticulously extracted from the "Mongolian Language Policy Database". This database aggregates content from multiple reputable sources, including the editorial department of "Mongolian Language", the "Compilation of Ethnic Language Policy Documents" compiled by the Mongolian Language Working Committee of Bayannur League, the Inner Mongolia Ethnic Affairs Committee's website, the Hohhot Mongolian Language Informatization Comprehensive Platform, and the website of the Baotou Ethnic Affairs Committee.

Upon collecting this text corpus, we subjected it to a rigorous processing regimen. The Mongolian Editor for Plain Text system was instrumental in encoding conversion and proofreading. As the website content was encoded internationally, we first converted it to Menksoft code and then conducted meticulous proofreading. This process involved several crucial steps, including Mongolian word form non-word checks, phonetic non-word checks and automatic correction of phonetic non-words. Any words that could not be automatically corrected were manually reviewed and classified based on color-coding: green for mispronounced words, red for unrecognized words, and blue for unrecognized homographs.

2.2 Methods and Steps

Our study is designed to unveil the distinctive lexical characteristics of Mongolian language policy texts from three aspects: the distribution of part of speech, lexical richness and word frequency distribution.

It encompasses the following five key steps:

Participle in Mongolian: We initiated the analysis by segmenting the text using spaces as boundaries.

Stop Words Removal: We eliminated stop words, which comprise words and punctuation marks devoid of independent meaning. Examples include genitive case (-YIN), (-VN/-UN), (-V/-U), dative case (-DV/-DU), (-TV/-TU), accusative case (-YI), (-I), ablative case (-ACA/ECE), instrumental case (-BAR/-BER), (-IYAR/-IYER), comitative case (-TAI/-TEI), and various punctuation marks and Latin letters.

Part of Speech Tagging: The next step involved assigning part-of-speech tags to the text.

Calculation of TTR, Lexical Density, and Part of Speech Distribution: We calculated the Type-Token Ratio (TTR), lexical density, and the distribution of parts of speech.

Word Frequency Statistics and Sorting: We performed word frequency statistics and sorting, and the most frequently occurring words were visualized as wordcloud maps. The programming for these analyses was implemented using the Python language.

2.3 Definition of Text

Language policy, a subject of substantial scholarly interest, has seen varied definitions. Australian linguists Kalpan and Baldauf propose that language policy comprises the language concepts, laws, regulations, rules, and practices formulated and implemented by a society, group or system to achieve planned changes [11]. Chinese scholar Cai, on the other hand, defines language policy as the relevant laws, regulations, measures, and other such guidelines formulated by human social groups during verbal communication, reflecting their stance and viewpoint toward specific languages [12]. Regarding the distinction between explicit and implicit language policies, many academics believe that a distinction must be made between official/explicit and implicit/ambiguous language policies [13]. "Explicit" and "implicit" are the two categories of language policies. Important guidelines and plans explicitly stipulated by the state regarding language constitute explicit language policies; implicit language policy, also known as "language culture," reflects language attitudes, perspectives, and ideologies. Therefore, language policy encompasses both explicit official language policies and implicit unofficial policies that influence the actual use of language [13]. Ignoring either aspect when researching language policy will result in incomplete and biased perspectives [14].

2.4 Categorization of Text

Building upon the distinction between explicit and implicit language policies, we have classified the texts into 12 distinct categories: instructions, decisions, notices, reports, regulations, ways, rules, methods, summaries, plans, speeches and papers. The first ten categories represent explicit language policies, while the last two encapsulate implicit language policies:

Instructions: Official documents assigning work and outlining guiding principles for subordinate organs; includes 2 instructions.
Decisions: Documents for making decisions or arrangements on significant matters; includes 2 decisions.
Notices: Used for approving, forwarding, issuing regulations, and conveying information; includes 21 notices.
Reports: Documents for reporting work, reflecting on situations, responding to inquiries, and providing suggestions; includes 19 reports.
Regulations: Regulatory documents governing organizational activities; includes 5 regulations.
Ways: Documents establishing principles and methods; includes 6 ways.
Rules: Regulatory documents mandating implementation measures within specific scopes; includes 6 rules.
Methods: Documents outlining methods and measures for problem-solving; includes 2 methods. ·
Summary: Documents reviewing, analyzing, and evaluating past work stages to guide future efforts; includes 1 summary.
Planning: Documents planning and arranging future work and activities over specified timeframes; includes 8 plans.
Speeches: Materials related to Mongolian language standardization, application, and development; includes 16 speech materials.
Papers: Documents related to Mongolian language standardization, application, and development; includes 12 papers.

This categorization scheme distinguishes between explicit and implicit language policies, providing a robust framework for the comprehensive analysis of the Mongolian language policy corpus.

3   Research Results

3.1 Distribution of Parts of Speech

Part of speech serves as a crucial classification of the syntactic functions of words. Not only can statistical analysis of the frequency of use of words of various parts of speech in text reveal the characteristics of vocabulary usage, but it can also reveal the grammatical characteristics of the text to a certain extent [15].

To elucidate these aspects within Mongolian language policy texts, this study harnessed the Mglex part-of-speech tagging system, supplemented by manual proofreading. The Mglex software system represents a statistical method-based lexical annotation system, collaboratively developed by the School of Mongolian Studies at Inner Mongolia University and the Institute of Computing Technology at the Chinese Academy of Sciences. Adhering to principles rooted in semantics, morphology, and syntax, Mongolian vocabulary is classified into three categories: content words, function words and exclamation words.

Content words, which possess both lexical and grammatical meanings and can autonomously function as sentence components, encompass nouns, verbs, adjectives, numerals, quantifiers and pronouns.

Function words, on the other hand, cannot independently serve as sentence components and predominantly fulfill grammatical roles. This category includes adverbs, postpositions, modal particles, conjunctions and similar elements.

Interjections, which lack both lexical and grammatical meaning and primarily express emotions or address animals without undergoing morphological changes, are unable to function as independent sentence components.

However, it's noteworthy that image-bearing words, describing the formation of sounds and actions, undergo lexical changes and can serve as sentence components. Hence, they are categorized as substantive words. Modal words, expressing the speaker's affirmation, trust, doubt, emphasis, and the like, undergo only slight lexical changes but cannot serve as sentence components. Consequently, they are classified as function words. This categorization aligns with the "Information Technology - Mongolian Word Markup Set for Information Processing" (GB/T26235-2010), boasting a comprehensive set of part-of-speech markers, totaling 91.

Table 1. Distribution of Parts of Speech.

	Nouns	Adjective	Numerals	Quantifiers
LPP	37.96%	5.67%	1.77%	0.17%
"Old boy" [7]	32.35%	9.11%	3.64%	0.46%
Academic corpus [16]	33.49%	7.22%	1.99%	0.16%
	Tense words	Verbs	Time words	
LPP	1.54%	21.17%	0.18%	
"Old boy" [7]	3.87%	30.30%	2.28%	
Academic corpus [16]	2.85%	23.85%	0.38%	

The data presented in Table 1 highlights the distribution of parts of speech within the Mongolian language policy corpus. Notably, nouns constitute the highest proportion at 37.96%, followed by verbs at 21.17%, and adjectives at 5.67%. Comparative analysis reveals that the "Old Boy" corpus and the academic corpus also exhibit a substantial presence of nouns, accounting for 32.35% and 33.49%, respectively. Additionally, verbs represent 30.30% and 23.85% of these respective corpora, with adjectives constituting 9.11% and 7.22%.

3.2 Lexical Richness

Measuring lexical richness encompasses type-token ratio and lexical density. In corpus research, the Type-Token Ratio (TTR) serves as a metric to gauge vocabulary richness and diversity, calculated as:

$$TTR = V/N \tag{1}$$

where V represents the number of unique words in the text, and N signifies the total word count. A higher TTR value indicates a more diverse vocabulary. Vocabulary density, on the other hand, is computed as [15]:

$$Vocabulary\ density = (number\ of\ content\ words/total\ word\ count) \times 100\% \tag{2}$$

A high lexical density indicates a significant presence of content words, implying a wealth of information within the discourse [15]. Moreover, vocabulary density remains largely unaffected by discourse length, making it particularly valuable for genre distinctions [15]. Mongolian content words span across nouns, adjectives, numerals, quantifiers, tense words, verbs and time words.

Table 2. TTR and Lexical density.

	Token	Type	TTR	Content word	Lexical density
LPP	132254	7227	5.46%	95871	72.49%
Zhanggar [9]	80599	4634	5.75%	68360	84.81%

Table 2 presents a comprehensive overview of the TTR and lexical density within the Mongolian Language Policy Corpus. The dataset comprises a total of 132,254 words, featuring 7,227 unique words and 90,294 content words. Consequently, the TTR value is calculated as (7,227/132,254) × 100% = 5.46%, while the lexical density stands at (95,871/132,254) × 100% = 72.49%. Notably, the TTR value for 'Zhanggar' is computed at 5.75%, accompanied by a lexical density of 84.81%.

3.3 Distribution of Word Frequency

Keywords play a pivotal role in summarizing the core content and essence of a text, serving as a vital tool for quickly comprehending its themes. Keyword extraction methods can be broadly categorized into two approaches: keyword allocation (selecting a few words from a predefined vocabulary) and keyword extraction (extracting words from a new document to serve as keywords). This study adopts the latter approach, specifically utilizing keyword extraction methods grounded in word frequency statistics. Drawing

Table 3. High-frequency Words.

Instructions		Decision		Notice	
(Mongol)	49	(Language)	77	(Govern)	64
(Language)	27	(Absence)	59	(Language)	49
(Need)	27	(Mongol)	52	(Nation)	45
(Word)	15	(Nation)	26	(Big)	42
(Many)	14	(Need)	22	(Oneself)	40
Reports		Regulations		Ways	
(Mongol)	232	(Mongol)	88	(Language)	143
(Language)	175	(Language)	74	(Mongol)	132
(Absence)	111	(Need)	70	(Nation)	76
(Have)	111	(Word)	28	(School)	56
(Correct)	69	(Many)	24	(Word)	50
Rules		Methods		Summaries	
(Mongol)	232	(Absence)	24	(Mongol)	121
(Language)	175	(Language)	24	(Language)	70
(Correct)	69	(Method)	14	(Have)	56
(New)	63	(Word)	13	(Word)	46
(Aspect)	63	(Study)	12	(Need)	45
Plans		Speeches		Papers	
(Mongol)	48	(Mongol)	249	(Mongol)	196
(Language)	33	(Language)	185	(Language)	137
(Word)	31	(Word)	118	(Word)	110
(Have)	24	(Characters)	108	(Have)	91
(Nation)	22	(Have)	87	(Many)	77

from the top 50 high-frequency words, a comparative analysis of the top 5 high-frequency words across the 12 categorized texts is presented in Table 3.

Table 3 reveals that the word " ᠮᠣᠩᠭᠣᠯ"(Mongol) consistently ranks among the top three most frequently occurring words across the corpus, with frequencies of 49, 52, 232, 88, 132, 232, 121, 48, 249, 196. This pattern underscores the text's strong association with the Mongolian language. Furthermore, terms such as " ᠬᠡᠯᠡ"(Language) and " ᠦᠭᠡ"(Word) also exhibit significant occurrence frequency. This robust presence highlights their importance within the text. Additionally, the term " ᠬᠡᠷᠡᠭᠲᠡᠢ"(Need) emerges 27, 22, 70, 45 times in texts such as directives, decisions, regulations, and summaries, underscoring their role in guiding and regulating content. " ᠣᠯᠠᠨ"(Many) appeared 14, 24, and 77 times in instructions, regulations, and papers, and " ᠶᠡᠬᠡ"(Big) appeared 42 times in notices, reflecting their relevance and popularity within these respective texts. Furthermore, " ᠪᠠᠢᠨᠠ"(Have) appears 111 and 56 times in reports and summaries, signifying their association with post-event and summarization aspects of the text.

To enhance the comprehensibility of the core content, this study employs Wordcloud maps, a visually intuitive method that employs font size, color, and shape to convey word frequency and importance. By highlighting frequently occurring "keywords" and "high-frequency words" within the text, Wordcloud maps offer readers a quick grasp of essential information. Notably, the wordcloud method aids in comprehensively understanding the logical structure and characteristics of Mongolian language policy, providing valuable insights for language policy analysis. For the creation of Wordcloud maps, the Wordcloud module was employed, albeit with a few challenges. These challenges included displaying Mongolian characters and addressing Unicode-encoded Mongolian characters that occasionally appeared as nominal characters. These issues were successfully resolved by converting the encoding to Mongolian coding. Ultimately, Wordcloud diagrams for the 12 text categories are presented in Figs. 1, 2, 3, 4, 5, 6, 7, 8, 9, 10, 11 and 12.

Fig. 1. Wordcloud of Instructions   **Fig. 2.** Wordcloud of Decisions

Examining Figs. 1, 2, 3, 4, 5, 6, 7, 8, 9, 10, 11 and 12, it becomes evident that word frequency statistics, while relatively straightforward, are susceptible to various interfering factors, which may affect accuracy. This single keyword extraction method based solely on word frequency statistics may not be exhaustive, emphasizing the need to quantify and calculate additional word features to provide more accurate keyword extraction for complex themes. Additionally, given the wide studies may benefit from setting a

Fig. 3. Wordcloud of Notices

Fig. 4. Wordcloud of Reports

Fig. 5. Wordcloud of Regulations

Fig. 6. Wordcloud of Ways

Fig. 7. Wordcloud of Rules

Fig. 8. Wordcloud of Methods

Fig. 9. Wordcloud of Summaries

Fig. 10. Wordcloud of Plans

Fig. 11. Wordcloud of Speeches

Fig. 12. Wordcloud of Papers

threshold and listing all keywords exceeding this threshold for a more comprehensive analysis, representing a potential area for improvement.

4   Conclusion

In this analysis, we have delved into the richness and characteristics of Mongolian language policy texts, shedding light on key aspects of these documents. We have observed that Mongolian language policy texts exhibit a wealth of vocabulary, boasting a substantial proportion of content words. However, their vocabulary richness appears relatively low, as indicated by their modest Type-Token Ratio (TTR) values. This study represents an innovative approach to the analysis of policy texts, offering a harmonious blend of language policy research and quantitative analysis.

The connection between language and society is intrinsic, and vocabulary is the fastest growing and most direct aspect of the language subsystem that reflects social life [17]. Policy texts serve as condensed expressions of intellectual exchange, and through the employment of corpus analysis tools, we can decode policy concepts through various lenses such as lexical richness, part of speech distribution, and word frequency.

In summary, employing diverse natural language processing methods facilitates systematic and comprehensive research into text content. It enables us to gauge vocabulary application through TTR values and vocabulary density, identify keywords that encapsulate core information via word frequency statistics, and visualize high-frequency words through word clouds, thereby unveiling potential connections and concealed information. By deciphering the structural intricacies of these systems, we can explore internal associations, significantly enhancing our grasp and comprehension of policy texts, both at macro and micro levels. This approach not only deepens our understanding of policy texts but also augments the efficiency of theoretical research in a comprehensive and systematic manner.

Acknowledgments. This paper was sponsored by the Projects of the National Social Science Foundation of China (19AYY018) and (17ZDA316).

References

1. Tu, D.W.: Education policy text analysis and its application. Fudan Edu. Forum **7**(5), 22–27 (2009)

2. Fang, X.B., Zhang, L.P.: Key Terms in Language Policy and Planning, 1st edn. Foreign Language Teaching and Research Press, Beijing (2022)
3. Ma, D.L., Shang, X.N.: Comparative study on the vocabulary "the belt and road initiative" in the news discourse based on the corpus. J. Henan Inst. Educ. **36**(6), 96–101 (2017)
4. Wang, Y.: A discourse analysis on China-related English reports based on corpus- a case of main countries along the "B&R." J. Tongling Vocat. Tech. Coll **19**(1), 49–55 (2020)
5. Zhang, X.Z., Su, K.: A corpus-based comparative study on the agenda setting of China-related and Japan-related reports in New York Times. Contem. Foreign Lang. Stud. **1**(1), 118–125 (2019)
6. Dang, Y.N.: A corpus-based vocabulary comparison of Chinese leader's speeches on the opening ceremony of G20 summit and summer Davos Forum. J. Jilin Inst. Chem. Technol. **37**(12), 91–95 (2020)
7. Dulaan, Hai, Y.H.: A statistical study of type of the words in D.Nachugdorji's novel OLD Boy. Mongolian Stud. China **45**(3), 199–204 (2017)
8. Uyutan, Dabhvrbayar: Analyzing the novel Haguchin Huu based on complex feature description. J. Inner Mongolia Univ. **46**(3), 19–31 (2018)
9. Bao, L.X., Dabhvrbayar, Oyutan: Statistical analysis of lexical features in Zhanggar. Soc. Sci. Inner Mongolia **42**(1), 62–69 (2022)
10. Anar, Ajitai: On the experiment of Mongolian works by Antconc Software. J. Soc. Sci. Inner Mongolia Univ. Nationalities **2**, 83–89 (2020)
11. Kaplan, R.B., Baldauf, R.B.: Language and Language-in-Education Planning in the Pacific Basin. Kluwer Academic (2003)
12. Cai, Y.L.: On the language policy of the United States. Jiangsu Soc. Sci. **36**(5), 194–202 (2002)
13. Schiffman, H.F.: Linguistics Culture and Language Policy. Routledge, London (1998)
14. Li, Y.Z.: Analysis of implicit language policy - taking the United States as an example. Naikai Linguist. **22**(2), 85–93 (2013)
15. Huang, W., Jiang, L.Z.: A comparative study on the vocabulary styles of Jin Yong and Gu Long's martial arts novels. In: Huang, W. (ed.) Quantitative Studies on Vocabulary and Syntax, pp. 69–82. Zhejiang University Press, Hangzhou (2022)
16. Wuyoutan: Quantitative Syntactic Research Based on the Mongolian Academic Corpus, Dissertation, Inner Mongolia University (2022)
17. Li, Z.X., Gao, T.L., Huang, G.J., Rao, G.Q.: Study of Chinese words in diachronic corpus of newspaper. In: Su, Q., Xu, G., Yang, X.Y. (eds.) CLSW 2022. LNAI, vol. 13495, pp. 384–398 (2023). https://doi.org/10.1007/978-3-031-28953-8_29

Offensiveness Analysis of Chinese Group Addressing Terms and Dataset Construction

Shucheng Zhu and Ying Liu[✉]

School of Humanities, Tsinghua University, 30th Shuangqing Road, Haidian District, Beijing 100084, China
zhusc21@mails.tsinghua.edu.cn, yingliu@tsinghua.edu.cn

Abstract. Group addressing terms are a linguistic phenomenon commonly used to reference groups in everyday speech. These terms not only reflect the cultural nuances within a language but also serve as valuable keywords in natural language processing for examining various instances of bias and discrimination against disadvantaged groups in artificial intelligence. This paper presents a comprehensive Chinese group addressing terms dataset, constructed by collecting and annotating 2,483 such terms from diverse sources. The dataset encompasses 10 categories, including gender, race, and religion. Subsequently, the offensiveness of these group addressing terms is annotated through a combination of expert evaluations and crowdsourcing. In general, factors such as gender, age, educational background, and empathy do not exhibit a significant correlation with the perception of offensive group addressing terms. However, there are discernible differences in the perception of offensiveness when individuals evaluate terms that relate to their own respective groups. Offensiveness in group addressing terms shows both commonalities across different categories and distinctive characteristics unique to specific categories. Various linguistic traits can either amplify or diminish the perceived offensiveness. Beyond serving as a means of catharsis, offensive group addressing terms can also play a role in identity construction. When different group addressing terms are used as prompts, the text generated by language models reveals certain biases and stereotypes towards particular groups. In the future, this dataset can be leveraged not only for sociolinguistic research but also for the creation of fairness datasets in the field of natural language processing.

Keywords: Group Addressing Terms · Dataset · Offensiveness

1 Introduction

Addressing terms generally pertain to designations based on the relationships between individuals or other contextual factors, including their identities and occupations [1]. In simpler terms, addressing terms are linguistic expressions that people use in their everyday speech to refer to others. Group addressing terms, on the other hand, are linguistic expressions used to refer to specific groups. As language has evolved, the internet has introduced a plethora of new group addressing terms, which not only expand linguistic choices but also add complexity to the nature of these terms. In this paper, we consider group addressing terms to encompass not only common words and phrases used to refer to groups but also numerous online terms. These online terms may consist of letters or even be entirely composed of letters, as exemplified by 'LGBT'. Additionally, they also include terms formed through homophonic play and word-splitting. For instance, '歪果 仁' (wāiguǒrén), which literally translates to 'crooked nut', phonetically corresponds to ' 外国人' (wàiguórén), meaning foreigners. Similarly, '三折人', literally 'three-fold people', involves word-splitting, with '三折' representing '浙', an abbreviation for Zhejiang province, thereby signifying Zhejiang natives.

Group addressing terms not only serve as reflections of the cultural nuances embedded in a language but also function as pivotal keywords or clues in natural language processing, enabling the exploration of various unjust occurrences pertaining to vulnerable groups in artificial intelligence. In the realm of linguistic research and the practical application of natural language processing techniques on group addressing terms, a crucial consideration is the assessment of whether such terms carry offensive connotations towards the referenced groups. Subsequently, efforts can be made to minimize the utilization of these potentially offensive terms in language strategies or models, fostering a communication environment that is both harmonious and equitable. Linguistically, offensive addressing terms encompass impolite, unfriendly, and even insulting references employed intentionally or unintentionally by the speaker, eliciting emotional reactions from the addressee [2]. In the context of natural language processing, offensive language often equates to hate speech, abusive language, and toxic language. Aligning with definitions from related research in natural language processing [3–5], this paper asserts that offensiveness involves the expression of disrespectful, unpleasant, or toxic content, potentially insulting specific groups. The categorization of group addressing terms as offensive is not a simple binary distinction. Individuals perceive offensiveness of the same group addressing terms differently due to distinct personal experiences and emotions, as well as variations in context and time. Moreover, owing to cultural disparities, Chinese group addressing terms exhibit their own unique characteristics, and their perceived offensiveness may differ from that of other languages. Consequently, a comprehensive examination of the offensiveness of Chinese group addressing terms becomes imperative.

2 Related Works

2.1 Addressing Terms and Offensiveness

In the realm of Chinese addressing terms, the scope of study extends beyond linguistic analyses of individual addressing terms, encompassing both commonplace terms like '先 生' (Mr.), '女士' (Ms.), and '老婆' (wife), as well as the emergence of online addressing terms like '小仙女' (little fairy) [6–9]. Researchers have also delved into the addressing terms used within specific groups, with a particular focus on disadvantaged groups [10]. Within this context, the study of group addressing terms places special emphasis on gender-related terms and the issue of gender discrimination [11–15]. Research methods often involve the examination of a group's identity through relevant sociolinguistic theories [11] or the analysis of extensive group addressing terms using corpora [16]. In the diachronic study of Chinese addressing terms, researchers often center their attention on the identities of minority groups [17]. Furthermore, studies have explored the types, characteristics, functions, and socio-cultural psychology of offensive addressing terms [2]. However, much of the aforementioned research predominantly adopts a sociolinguistic perspective, and the scale and quantity of group addressing terms studied remain limited. This limitation impedes their usefulness in the creation of natural language processing datasets aimed at promoting fairness within diverse groups.

2.2 Offensive Language in Natural Language Processing

In recent years, system fairness has become a prominent topic in the field of natural language processing (NLP). Research related to offensive language and hate speech directed at minority and marginalized groups has seen a steady increase year by year. In addition to standard identification tasks [5, 18–20], there is growing interest in evaluating bias and offensiveness aimed at specific groups within text generation tasks [3, 4]. The fairness of artificial intelligence systems is intrinsically linked to the languages and cultures they operate within. Translation often fails to capture the nuanced offensive and aggressive connotations embedded in cultural contexts. As a result, many of the fairness datasets constructed in English cannot be directly applied to tasks related to the Chinese language. In response to this challenge, offensive language recognition datasets for Chinese have emerged in recent years [5, 19]. However, these datasets often focus on one or two group categories, such as gender, due to the absence of a comprehensive multi-category group addressing terms list. This limitation hinders their applicability to a broader range of contexts. Consequently, there is a pressing need to consider the generalization capability of NLP models. To address these issues, it is essential to develop a comprehensive offensive group addressing terms dataset based on a combination of sociolinguistics and natural language processing. This dataset will play a crucial role in advancing research on the fairness of Chinese artificial intelligence, enabling more inclusive and equitable NLP applications in the future.

3 Construction of Group Addressing Terms Dataset

In our research, we have categorized ten groups that are frequently targeted by offensive group addressing terms based on the experiences of disadvantaged groups in both research and real life. These categories encompass gender, sexuality, body and mind, race, religion, ethnic group, occupation [21], region, nationality, and social class.

According to a diverse range of resources, we aim to compile an extensive dataset of addressing terms. Our goal is to encompass not only commonly used addressing terms in everyday language but also to reflect the evolution and changes in language usage. To achieve this, we have cast a wide net, incorporating both traditional academic sources [2, 10–17, 22] and a substantial selection of online resources.

Finally, we enlisted the assistance of three postgraduate students majoring in linguistics and related fields to annotate the compiled addressing terms. The annotation process primarily involved determining whether an addressing term qualifies as a group addressing term. In the end, we selected the intersection of group addressing terms that all three annotators unanimously agreed upon, designating it as the final dataset of Chinese group

Table 1. Classification and quantity of Chinese group addressing terms dataset.

Category		Amount	Proportion of offensive terms	Category		Amount	Proportion of offensive terms
Gender	Female	443	34.99%	Occupation	Realistic	87	5.75%
	Male	331	25.68%		Enterprising	25	8.00%
	Subtotal	**774**	**31.01%**		Social	49	24.49%
Sexuality	General terms	21	19.05%		Conventional	26	7.69%
	Heterosexuality	2	0.00%		Investigative	21	0.00%
	Gay	31	38.71%		Artistic	50	4.00%
	Lesbian	11	9.09%		**Subtotal**	**258**	**8.91%**
	Subtotal	**65**	**26.15%**	Nationality	Foreign general terms	4	50.00%
Body and mind	Age	129	3.88%		Asia	158	38.61%
	Appearance	27	88.89%		America	70	8.57%
	Disease	67	64.18%		Europe	103	13.59%
	Subtotal	**223**	**32.29%**		Africa	67	0.00%
Race	Yellow	5	20.00%		Oceania	31	0.00%
	White	9	33.33%		**Subtotal**	**433**	**19.17%**
	Black	10	40.00%	Social class	Upper	9	0.00%
	Mixed	5	0.00%		Middle	15	0.00%
	Brown	7	57.14%		Lower	11	9.09%
	General terms	2	50.00%		Other	2	0.00%
	Subtotal	**38**	**34.21%**		**Subtotal**	**37**	**2.70%**
Ethnic group	General terms	19	78.95%	Religion	Buddhism	23	0.00%
	Ethnic groups	414	3.38%		Islam	12	16.67%
	Other	4	0.00%		Christianity	20	10.00%
	Subtotal	**437**	**6.63%**		Other	17	0.00%
Region	Provincial-level administrative region	123	28.46%		Atheism	3	0.00%
	inter-provincial region	18	22.22%		General terms	2	0.00%
	Subtotal	**141**	**27.66%**		**Subtotal**	**77**	**5.19%**
Total		**2483**		**Total proportion of offensive terms**			**20.98%**

addressing terms. These terms were categorized based on the ten main categories and several subcategories established in this paper. The dataset of group addressing terms created in this study has been made publicly available as open source[1], with details of the classification and quantity provided in Table 1. The table encompasses a total of 2,483 Chinese group addressing terms.

---

[1] https://github.com/zhushucheng/Chinese-Group-Addressing-Terms-Dataset.

4 Offensiveness Annotation of Group Addressing Terms

4.1 Types of Offensiveness of Group Addressing Terms

The offensiveness associated with group addressing terms is not a simple binary classifi-cation; it is dynamic and subject to change over time. Some group addressing terms have undergone diachronic shifts, transitioning from non-offensive to offensive. Additionally, the offensiveness of these terms can spread or fade away. In summary, the offensiveness of group addressing terms can change not only over time but also across different regions. Consequently, this paper categorizes the offensiveness of group addressing terms into three synchronic types, as illustrated in Fig. 1.

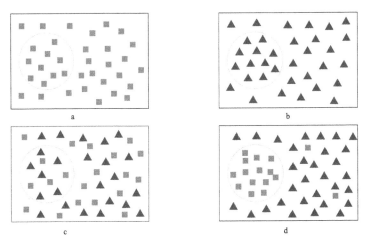

Fig. 1. Three types of offensiveness of group addressing terms. The circle represents a specific community, the yellow square represents individuals who find the group addressing term offensive, and the green triangle represents individuals who do not find the term offensive.

Type 1: As depicted in Fig. 1a and 1b certain group addressing terms are either consid-ered offensive or non-offensive. The rules governing the offensiveness of these terms are widely acknowledged by the public. Even if native speakers are unfamiliar with a par-ticular group addressing term, they can often accurately infer its offensiveness based on their language sensibilities or linguistic habits. For instance, '婊子' (bitch) is universally recognized as an offensive term among native Chinese speakers. However, it's important to note that the consensus on offensiveness also depends on the specific context in which these group addressing terms are employed.

Type 2: As illustrated in Fig. 1c, the offensiveness of certain group addressing terms can elicit varying perceptual sensitivities due to the group characteristics or personal experiences of different individuals. For instance, women may not find the term '假小子' (tomboy) offensive, when used to describe them as having masculine qualities, while men may take offense when referred to as '娘炮' (sissy), likening them to women. The perception of offensiveness may also vary when animals are used to refer to nationals of a particular country, with some individuals finding it offensive while others remain unaffected, often depending on individual sensitivities.

Type 3: As shown in Fig. 1d, the offensiveness of certain group addressing terms may be confined to a specific community, and individuals outside that community may not recognize or perceive the offensiveness. For example, within certain online forums, people from Jiangsu, Zhejiang, and Shanghai may refer to individuals from Anhui as '白完人' ('白完' stemming from '皖', an abbreviation for Anhui Province), which constitutes a derogatory use of group addressing terms for Anhui residents. However, those who are not part of this forum may not view the constructed group addressing terms as offensive expressions.

4.2 Offensiveness Annotation of Group Addressing Terms

In this paper, three doctoral students majoring in linguistics have been tasked with discussing the offensiveness of group addressing terms. Their objectives include defining the group addressing terms (Type 1) that people commonly perceive as offensive or non-offensive. For terms on which the three researchers cannot reach a consensus or for those for which the perceived offensiveness varies based on individual experiences or the affiliations of the group or community to which they belong (Type 2 and Type 3), a questionnaire was employed for further investigation.

The questionnaire was published online through Tencent Questionnaire, resulting in the collection of 376 responses. These responses underwent a thorough cleaning process, with 89 responses excluded for various reasons, such as being completed within 300 s, originating from overseas, lacking occupation information or containing vague responses, and errors in quality control questions. Ultimately, 287 questionnaires remained, resulting in an acceptance rate of 76.33%.

The questionnaire design can be broadly divided into three sections:

Demographic Information: This section includes questions about gender, age, native place, highest education level, and occupation. Statistical results for this section are presented in Fig. 2.

Empathy Scale: In the realm of social psychology, empathy and pain often collaborate to prompt individuals to respond to crises [23]. We posit that individuals with heightened empathy may be more prone to perceiving offensiveness in group addressing terms. Consequently, we have chosen the Chinese version of the IRI-C (Interpersonal Reactivity Index-C) to gauge an individual's empathy capacity. The IRI was originally formulated by Davis, drawing from the multidimensional theory of empathy, to assess empathy levels [24]. Subsequently, it was translated into Chinese [25], and its reliability and validity were established [26, 27]. The scale comprises 22 items, divided into four factors: 5 items for Perspective Taking (PT), 5 items for Personal Distress (PD), 6 items for Fantasy (FS), and 6 items for Empathy Concern (EC).

Offensive Judgment of Group Addressing Terms: There are a total of 199 items in this section. Four quality control questions are included: '婊子' (bitch), '傻缺' (idiot), '放牛的' (cowherd), and '放羊的' (shepherd). The remaining 197 items are questions

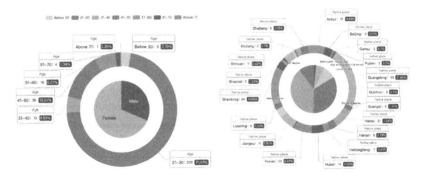

Fig. 2. Demographic information of accepted responses.

related to a participant's judgment (including '放牛的' and '放羊的'). The entire judgment process can be viewed as a form of crowdsourcing, with respondents tasked with determining whether the provided terms are offensive. Prior to commencing the judgment process, participants are instructed to envision themselves as belonging to the specified group and consider whether they would find it offensive to be addressed using these terms, necessitating a degree of empathy. Additionally, to aid comprehension, some terms are explained, such as '腹黑' (black belly), which refers to individuals who appear kind and gentle on the surface but have darker intentions beneath.

5   Offensive Analyses of Group Addressing Terms

5.1   The Relationship Between Group Characteristics and the Offensiveness of Group Addressing Terms

In this study, we calculated the proportion of offensive group addressing terms annotated by each respondent, which we refer to as the offensive score of group addressing terms. This score falls within a range of 0 to 1. A lower score indicates a lower level of awareness regarding the offensiveness of group addressing terms, while a higher score suggests a heightened awareness of their offensiveness.

We examined the relationship between respondents' gender, age, highest education level, and the offensiveness of group addressing terms. To facilitate a more robust statistical comparison, we categorized gender into two groups: male and female, age into two groups: 30 years old and below, and 31 years old and above, and highest education level into two groups: bachelor's degree and below, and master's degree and above. These categories were chosen to ensure a balanced distribution of participants between groups. Subsequently, we conducted independent sample T-tests to evaluate the average offensive scores of each group. Our analysis revealed no statistically significant differences in offensive scores based on gender ($p = 0.602$), age ($p = 0.670$), or highest education level ($p = 0.764$).

Furthermore, we explored the correlation between empathy and the offensive scores of group addressing terms. No statistically significant correlation was found between overall empathy ($p = 0.864$) or its specific components, including PT ($p = 0.614$), PD (p = 0.386), FS (p = 0.540), and EC (p = 0.505), and the offensive scores. However, significant correlations were observed among certain factors within the empathy scale, demonstrating the scale's effectiveness.

In conclusion, it is challenging to make generalizations about which groups are more sensitive to the offensiveness of group addressing terms. This underscores the subtlety of perceiving such offensiveness, which is heavily influenced by individual differences.

5.2 The Impact of Group and Addressing Terms Consensus on the Perception of Offensiveness of Group Addressing Terms

In Type 2 of offensive group addressing terms, individuals may exhibit heightened sensitivity to such terms based on their group affiliations. Therefore, we conducted an investigation into the perceived offensiveness of group addressing terms aligned with three group categories: gender, occupation, and native place.

There were no statistically significant differences in the offensiveness of male terms between males and females (p = 0.351). Similarly, no statistically significant difference was found in the offensiveness of female terms between the two genders (p = 0.699). We also analyzed the variance in offensive perceptions between male and female groups when confronted with group addressing terms opposite to their own gender. Most individuals did not alter their attitudes based on their group membership. For instance, in the case of '女/男盆友' (girlfriend/boyfriend, where '盆友' sounds similar to '朋友', meaning friend), men did not perceive '男盆友' as more offensive simply because they are men, and women did not find '男盆友' offensive due to their gender. In contrast, women tended to find homophonic and family-related terms more offensive, such as '女/男银' (woman/man) and '老婆/爷子' (old biddy/man). On the other hand, compared to women, men considered group addressing terms related to sexual behaviors that deviated from traditional Chinese norms to be more offensive. Interestingly, when comparing '肉食女/男' ('肉食' refers to individuals who actively pursue their interests, expressing their affection passionately upon encountering their favorite object, '女' means woman while '男' means man) and '闷骚女/男' ('闷骚' denotes someone who appears reserved externally but is fervent internally), traditional Chinese culture places a higher emphasis on implication. Consequently, men did not find '闷骚' offensive but found '肉食' offensive. '母1' (sissy top) and '母0' (sissy bottom), which deviate even further from gender norms, were perceived as highly offensive terms by men, while women considered both '公' (virile) and '母' (sissy) to be relatively offensive.

For individuals from various native places, we selected terms such as '老西子' (Shanxi people), '弗兰人' (Hunan people), '川耗子' (Sichuan mouse, pertaining to Sichuan people), '沙东人' (Shandong people), '白完人', '草办人' (Jiangsu people), and '三折人'. Surprisingly, most locals did not find these terms as offensive as foreigners did, especially with regard to the homophonic '弗兰' (pronounced 'fúlán', similar to '湖南' húnán, which means Hunan province) and the somewhat derogatory '川耗子'. Anhui people displayed a heightened sensitivity to the derogatory nature of the term '白完人', which is created through word-splitting, in comparison to foreigners. It's worth noting that if most foreigners are unfamiliar with it, they may not readily recognize that '白完人' constructed through word-splitting is a derogatory label. However, in the BCC corpus[28], it is evident that '白完人' is predominantly used in accusations directed at Anhui people.

For different occupational groups, we selected three distinct professions: programmers, civil servants, and teachers, and examined their corresponding group addressing terms – '程序员' (programmer), '穷教书的' (poor teacher), and '体制内的' (within the system, referring to civil servants) for analysis. Programmers, surprisingly, do not take offense to the term '程序员' at all. The perceived offensiveness of '程序员' primarily stems from individuals outside this group. Concurrently, programmers do not find the term '体制内的' offensive, suggesting that this group of programmers has a generally low perception of offensiveness. Teachers, on the other hand, tend to feel varying degrees of offense when confronted with terms from other occupational groups, such as '程序员'. However, interestingly, when it comes to their own group's term, '穷教书的', they perceive it as less offensive, possibly reflecting a self-deprecating attitude among teachers toward their profession. Civil servants, in contrast, exhibit a notably higher sensitivity to the term '体制内的' when self-referencing compared to other professional groups. This indicates a heightened concern among civil servants regarding their own group addressing terms.

5.3 Analyses of Offensive Group Addressing Terms in Each Category

We computed the average offensive score for each group addressing term, categorizing them as offensive if the score exceeded 0.5, and non-offensive if it fell below 0.5. The statistics regarding the offensiveness of addressing terms in the final dataset are presented in Table 1.

In the gender category, the proportion of offensive terms directed towards women significantly exceeds that for men, indicating prevalent gender bias, discrimination against women, and lower tolerance towards them. Some terms are offensive towards women but not towards men, such as '腹黑女/男' and '闷骚女/男'. Within the sexuality category, a relatively high proportion of offensive terms is directed at homosexual groups, while there are no specific offensive terms targeting heterosexual groups, highlighting the exclusion of minority groups. In the body and mind category, offensiveness primarily revolves around appearance and disease, particularly focusing on physical appearance, accounting for 88.89% of the instances. This underscores that referring to an individual based on their appearance or physical ailments tends to be offensive. Within the race category, offensive language predominantly targets brown and black individuals, while there are fewer offensive terms for yellow-skinned people and more economically developed white populations, underscoring the influence of power dynamics on language. General terms of ethnic group contain the highest proportion of offensive terms, with many of these terms historically incorporating derogatory language such as '蛮', '夷', and '戎'. In the region category, the distribution of offensive terms varies across subcategories. Among occupational groups, social professions encompass a high proportion of offensive terms, largely due to their frequent interactions with people, resulting in a wider range of offensive terms. Regarding nationality, a relatively high proportion of offensive terms target Asian, European, and American countries, which are closely linked to China

---

2 http://bcc.blcu.edu.cn

or possess significant international influence, thus sparking more extensive discussions and subsequently more offensive terms. Conversely, African countries lack offensive terms, indicating their limited influence and absence of distinctive cultural symbols. In the social class category, there are numerous offensive terms directed at lower-class individuals, revealing exclusion and discrimination against this demographic in language use. Within the religion category, offensive terms are primarily concentrated in Islam and Christianity, reflecting recent news reports and real-life events.

In summary, offensive group addressing terms target two levels of groups: they are often employed to satirize and ridicule groups with 'power' and privileges, while simultaneously discriminating against disadvantaged groups.

5.4 The Linguistic Features of Offensive Group Addressing Terms

We have conducted a comprehensive analysis of group addressing terms with distinctive structures to identify the linguistic features that contribute to their offensiveness.

'X佬': Among the group addressing terms featuring the root '佬', there are a total of 18 instances, all of which carry an offensive connotation. Examples include '基佬' (gay guy) and '江西佬' (Jiangxi guy). In its dictionary definition, '佬' denotes an adult man. However, its usage has evolved to encompass women as well. Nonetheless, the underlying sense of contempt associated with '佬' remains intact, making any group addressing term formed by pairing '佬' with other terms inherently offensive.

'X的': There are 43 group addressing terms that incorporate '的' as an auxiliary word to create noun phrases, which tend to be more colloquial and informal in nature. For instance, the formal term for an engineer is '工程师' rather than '跑工程的'. Remarkably, employing this structure does not inherently trigger offense, with only 5 out of the 43 group addressing terms, representing 11.63%, being considered offensive. In these cases, offensiveness is attributed to the preceding words or phrases that accompany '的'. For instance, '穷教书的' conveys offense through the inclusion of '穷' (poor), highlighting the low salary of teachers. This implies that the colloquial and informal structure of 'X的' by itself is not inherently offensive, or perhaps the public exhibits a high level of tolerance towards this specific structural format.

'X子': Among the group addressing terms structured as 'X子', there are a total of 106 instances. Among these, 15 terms have '子' as the root, 90 terms have '子' as a suffix, and one term employs the transliteration of '拆腻子' (Chinese) as an offensive label for Chinese people. Among those with '子' as the root, three terms are deemed offensive, constituting 20% of this subset. These terms include '风尘女子' (coquette), '花花公子' (playboy), and '戏子' (actor). The former two expressions critique specific professions or character traits, while the latter is an offensive reference to actors, stemming from historical disrespect towards the acting profession. In contrast, 58 out of the group addressing terms with '子' as a suffix are considered offensive, accounting for 64.44% of this subset. This prevalence of offensiveness in suffix-based terms is attributed to the diminutive nature of '子', which inherently carries a derogatory connotation during the suffix process [29]. However, offensiveness often correlates with prevailing aesthetic norms. For example, '高个子' (the tall), conforming to mainstream aesthetics, is not offensive, whereas '瘦子' (the thin), '矮子' (the short), and '胖子' (the fat), which do not align with mainstream aesthetics, are considered offensive.

'**老X**': There are a total of 55 group addressing terms structured as '老X', out of which 12 are considered offensive, representing 21.82% of the total. The use of '老' as a prefix in these addressing terms is predominantly in the form of a noun prefix. Originally, '老' carries the connotation of old age or elder [29], and, therefore, it is generally not considered offensive.

'**小X**': Within the group addressing terms incorporating the '小X' structure, there are 54 instances, with 9 of them being offensive, accounting for 16.67%. Most instances of '小' as a prefix in these terms also function as a noun prefix. In this context, '小' has two primary meanings. The '小X' structure that conveys intimacy, such as '小家伙' (little guy), is non-offensive, whereas structures that express contempt, such as '小日本' (small Japan), are considered offensive.

Animals: A total of 70 group addressing terms use animals to refer to specific groups, with 45 of them being offensive, representing 64.29%. This illustrates that using animals to describe people is generally deemed unacceptable by the majority. Animals that are considered acceptable to the public are primarily those that are either cute or dignified. In contrast, animals perceived as unacceptable typically have unattractive appearances or carry negative cultural connotations.

Homophonic Play: There are a total of 87 group addressing terms that employ homophonic play, including some transliterations ('GG') and those that alter the spelling of words based on pronunciation ('歪果仁'). Among these, 25 are considered offensive, making up 28.74% of the total. This suggests that the public generally accepts this playful use of homophones.

5.5 Offensive Group Addressing Terms' Identity Construction Function

Offensive group addressing terms serve expressive functions, allowing individuals to vent their emotions [2]. Simultaneously, these offensive terms also play a role in establishing group identity and confirming one's own identity, a function referred to as identity construction in this paper. For example, terms such as '白完人' and '三折人', formed through the word-splitting method, represent a language usage habit in online forums among netizens. However, individuals outside this forum circle may struggle to comprehend the offensiveness of these terms. In essence, the offensiveness of these terms requires learning. By acquiring knowledge of these offensive terms, one becomes a member of the netizen community within the forum, affirming identities with community members. This process constitutes identity construction.

To explore this phenomenon further, we chose the offensive term '11区人民' (People in District 11, referring to Japanese) and conducted an in-depth interview to investigate the identity construction function of offensive group addressing terms. '11区人民' originates from the Japanese anime series *Code Geass* and has come to refer directly to the Japanese among anime enthusiasts. We interviewed three *Code Geass* fans. They are all males, aged 23 to 29, with occupations including students, civil servants, and teachers.

Each interviewee participated voluntarily and received a reward of 100 yuan after a 30-min online interview conducted via Tencent Conference. Following the interviews, the recordings were transcribed into text, and interviewees were anonymized, resulting in transcribed materials exceeding 20,000 words.

All three interviewees identified themselves as fans of the *Code Geass* series and could articulate the term '11区人民's meaning and its plot origin. They held varying perspectives regarding whether the term '11区人民' was offensive. Overall, the three interviewees exhibited nuanced attitudes towards the offensiveness of '11区人民', generally believing it lacked malicious intent but struggling to empathize with its offensive connotations from another perspective.

Regarding the usage of terms like '11区人民', all three interviewees acknowledged that it serves as a linguistic feature for identity recognition. It provides 'a safer way to find like-minded individuals' and signifies 'a person within the same circle'. In essence, certain offensive terms can serve as linguistic tools for constructing the identity of anime enthusiasts. Drawing from Wenger's concept of the community of practice, these offensive terms constitute a part of the shared repertoire during the process of building a community of practice [30], aligning with Type 3 of offensive group addressing terms. Legitimate peripheral participation offers a model to analyze the learning process, describing individuals' involvement within a community of practice. The degree of participation typically evolves from weak to strong as community members engage in the learning process. All three interviewees believed they had 'passively' learned a significant amount of 'memes' and language usage due to their passion for anime. They noted that these concepts and language usage had become an integral part of their shared repertoire, transitioning from passive to active use, effectively transforming them from novices to experts [31].

5.6 The Impact of Offensiveness of Group Addressing Terms on Text Generation Models

In this paper, we employ the Chinese text generation model GPT2[3]. The model is used with selected group addressing terms, initiating the text generation process with these terms as prompts to create content of approximately 30 characters in length. Each term serves as the basis for generating 100 sentences, with repetition penalty parameters configured to prevent excessive similarity among generated sentences for each term.

We employ two key measurement indicators, namely TTR (Type-Token Ratio) and sentiment, to evaluate the lexical richness and sentiment of each generated sentence. TTR, representing the ratio of unique word types to total words (tokens) in a text, is utilized to assess the lexical diversity of sentences generated for specific group addressing terms. By specifying the length of the generated text, we control for text size variations, making higher TTR values indicative of greater vocabulary richness and reduced stereotyping by the model for that particular group [32]. To analyze sentiment of the generated sentences, we employ the sentiment analysis model from Python's SnowNLP toolkit[4]. The resulting sentiment scores range from 0 to 1, with values closer to 1 indicating a

---

[3] https://github.com/Hansen06/GPT2-Chinese.

[4] https://github.com/isnowfy/snownlp

more positive sentiment and values closer to 0 indicating a more negative sentiment. We selected a total of 36 group addressing terms spanning 10 categories, encompassing both offensive and non-offensive terms. This selection ensured a balanced representation of offensive and non-offensive terms within each category.

Our findings reveal that sentences generated from offensive group addressing terms tend to exhibit lower sentiment scores, reflecting a more negative sentiment. However, they also tend to have higher TTR values, indicating lower stereotyping and greater diversity in expression. Nevertheless, no statistically significant differences were observed between the average sentiment scores (p = 0.299) and TTR values (p = 0.280) of sentences generated by non-offensive group addressing terms.

Additionally, we calculated the average sentiment and TTR values for each category. Religion, nationality, and occupation categories demonstrated high sentiment scores but low TTR values, implying that the generation model consistently produces positive texts for these categories with a high degree of repetition, indicating deep positive stereotypes. In contrast, for the regions and races categories, the model-generated text displayed lower sentiment scores but higher TTR values, suggesting that the text produced by the model consistently exhibits negative sentiments for these categories, yet these negative sentiments are diverse and rich in expression.

6 Conclusion

This paper utilizes a range of resources to gather and annotate 2,483 group addressing terms in Chinese. These terms are then categorized into ten main categories, such as gender and nationality. The ultimate goal is to construct a comprehensive dataset of Chinese group addressing terms. The paper argues that the offensiveness of group addressing terms is both continuous and dynamic. As a result, it categorizes the offensiveness of these terms into three distinct types. Through a combination of expert annotation and crowdsourcing, the offensiveness of the group addressing terms within the dataset is annotated. The study reveals that there is no statistically significant relationship between a group's gender, age, highest education level, empathy, and their perception of offensiveness in these terms. Additionally, the research highlights that the awareness of offensiveness varies among different groups due to their unique characteristics. Furthermore, the paper identifies certain linguistic features that either intensify or mitigate the offensiveness of group addressing terms. It is important to note that offensive terms serve not only as a means to vent emotions but also play a role in identity construction. In the final part of the study, a Chinese text generation model is employed to investigate the impact of using offensive group addressing terms as prompts. The findings indicate that such prompts do not inherently lead to the generation of more rigid or negative text by the model. Looking ahead, the dataset of group addressing terms can find applications in sociolinguistic research and contribute to the development of fair datasets for natural language processing.

Acknowledgments. This work is sponsored by CCF-Baidu Open Fund (CCF-BAIDU 202323) and 2018 National Major Program of Philosophy and Social Science Fund "Analyses and Researches of Classic Texts of Classical Literature Based on Big Data Technology" (18ZDA238).

References

1. Dictionary Editing Office: Institute of Language, Chinese Academy of Social Sciences: Modern Chinese Dictionary (The 6th Edition). The Commercial Press, Beijing (2012)
2. Hu, J.: A study on offensive addressing terms. Shanghai International Studies University Doctor Degree Thesis (2008)
3. Dhamala, J., Sun, T., Kumar, V., et al.: BOLD: dataset and metrics for measuring biases in open-ended language generation. In: Proceedings of the 2021 ACM Conference on Fairness, Accountability, and Transparency, pp. 862–872 (2021). https://doi.org/10.1145/3442188.344 5924
4. Gehman, S., Gururangan, S., Sap, M., et al.: RealToxicityPrompts: evaluating neural toxic degeneration in language models. In: Findings of the Association for Computational Linguistics: EMNLP 2020, pp. 3356–3369 (2020). https://doi.org/10.18653/v1/2020.findings-emn lp.301
5. Deng, J., Zhou, J., Sun, H., et al.: COLD: a benchmark for Chinese offensive language detection. In: Proceedings of the 2022 Conference on Empirical Methods in Natural Language Processing, pp. 11580–11599 (2022). https://doi.org/10.18653/v1/2022.emnlp-main.796
6. Wang, D.: A study on the use evolution of addressing term 'xiansheng' from the pragmatic perspective. J. Tasting Class. **18**, 54–56 (2022)
7. Xing, X.: A study on the semantic generalization of addressing term 'laopo'. Sinogram Cult. (16), 118–120 (2022). https://doi.org/10.14014/j.cnki.cn11-2597/g2.2022.16.054
8. Lu, Q., Li, Y.: A study on the subjectivity of 'xiansheng/nvshi.' Overseas Engl. **11**, 63–65 (2022)
9. Li, L.: Analysis of network addressing term 'xiao xiannv.' Masterpieces Rev. **14**, 151–153 (2022)
10. Wang, D.: Research on disadvantaged groups address terms in contemporary China. Wuhan University Doctor Degree thesis (2013)
11. Zhang, L.: Sociolinguistic research on address gender difference. Minzu University of China Doctor Degree thesis (2007)
12. Yin, X.: A study on sexism in Chinese vocabulary – comparison with English. Heilongjiang University Master Degree thesis (2012)
13. Ai, Z.: Study on Chinese gender appellations in the internet context. Wuhan University Master Degree thesis (2017)
14. Zhou, C., Wu, D.: Study on the title words discriminating against women in Chinese. J. Hubei TV Univ. **29**(07), 111–112 (2009)
15. Ma, L.: On female appellation during the new period. J. Tangshan Normal Univ. **39**(01), 39–44 (2017). https://doi.org/10.3969/j.issn.1009-9115.2017.01.010
16. Jin, Z.: A sociolinguistic study on address terms of social identities – based on the analysis of the corpus of Chinese address terms abstracted by the means of 'keyboard entry'. East China Normal University Doctor Degree thesis (2017)
17. Wei, W.: 'Piaopiao' in the city: the emergence and change of homosexual identities in local Chengdu. Society (01), 67–97+207 (2007). https://doi.org/10.15992/j.cnki.31-1123/c.2007. 01.004
18. Park, J., Shin, J., Fung, P.: Reducing gender bias in abusive language detection. In: Proceedings of the 2018 Conference on Empirical Methods in Natural Language Processing, pp. 2799–2804 (2018). https://doi.org/10.18653/v1/D18-1302
19. Jiang, A., Yang, X., Liu, Y., et al.: SWSR: a Chinese dataset and lexicon for online sexism detection. Online Soc. Netw. Media (27), 100182 (2022). https://doi.org/10.1016/j.osnem. 2021.100182

20. Chiril, P., Moriceau, V., Benamara, F., et al.: An annotated corpus for sexism detection in French tweets. In: Proceedings of the 12th Language Resources and Evaluation Conference, pp. 1397–1403 (2020)
21. Holland, J.: A theory of vocational choice. J. Couns. Psychol. **6**(1), 35–45 (1959). https://doi.org/10.1037/h0040767
22. National Occupational Classification Revision Working Committee: People's Republic of China Occupational Classification. China Labor and Social Security Press, Beijing (2015)
23. Myers, D.: Social Psychology. Posts and Telecom Press, Beijing (2016)
24. Davis, M.H.: A multidimensional approach to individual differences in empathy. JSAS Catal. Sel. Doc. Psychol. **10**, 85–102 (1980)
25. Zan, Z.: The relationship between grade, gender, human orientation and empathy. National Chengchi University Master Degree thesis (1986)
26. Zhang, F., Dong, Y., Wang K., et al.: Reliability and validity of the Chinese version of the interpersonal reactivity index-C. Chin. J. Clin. Psychol. **18**(02), 155–157 (2010). https://doi.org/10.16128/j.cnki.1005-3611.2010.02.019
27. Zheng, J., Yan, S., Lin, Z., et al.: Reliability and validity of IRI-C in medical undergraduates. Chin. J. Health Stat. **38**(05), 721–724+728 (2021)
28. Xun, E., Rao, G., Xiao, X., et al.: The construction of the BCC corpus in the age of big data. Corpus Linguist. **3**(01), 93–109+118 (2016)
29. Wang, L.: History of the Chinese Language. Zhonghua Book Company, Beijing (2004)
30. Wenger, E.: Communities of practice: learning as a social system. Syst. Thinker **9**(5), 2–3 (1998)
31. Dong, J., Zuo, R., He, L., et al.: Sociolinguistic Studies of Communities. Foreign Language Teaching and Research Press, Beijing (2001)
32. Zhu, S., Wang, X., Liu, P.: Who killed Sanmao and Virginia Woolf? A comparative study of writers with suicidal attempt based on a quantitative linguistic method. In: Liu, M., Kit, C., Su, Q. (eds.) CLSW 2020. LNCS (LNAI), vol. 12278, pp. 408–420. Springer, Cham (2021). https://doi.org/10.1007/978-3-030-81197-6_34

Let's Talk About Business: A Corpus-Based Study of 'Business' Related Near-Synonyms and Their Teaching in Chinese as a Second Language

Yin Zhong[(✉)] and Yujing Rao

Center for Language Education, The Hong Kong University of Science and Technology, Clear Water Bay, Kowloon, Hong Kong SAR
`{lcyinzhong,lcemmarao}@ust.hk`

Abstract. The inherent semantic relatedness and closeness of near-synonyms pose difficulties to second language (L2) learners in comprehending and applying lexical knowledge in real situations. Previous studies have shown a sophisticated corpus-based method of distinguishing Chinese near-synonyms from a more 'theoretical-based' approach, the application of corpora in learning near-synonyms in an L2 classroom, however, is underexplored. This study reports both the 'theoretical-based' and 'pedagogical-application' of using corpora in studying 'business' related near-synonyms, and a significant gap between the 'theory' and the 'application' is identified. Our findings not only affirm the 'theoretical-based' method in capturing subtle nuances of near-synonyms but suggest implications of 'pedagogical-application' in teaching and learning near-synonyms with corpora.

Keywords: Near-synonyms · Corpus-based · Blended Learning · Sketch Engine · BCC Corpus · Lexical Semantics · Teaching Chinese as a Second Language

1 Introduction

Near-synonyms are word pairs that share more or less similar meanings [1, 2]; their 'central/core' semantic attributes are mostly identical but may differ in their 'minor/peripheral' aspects [3]. For example, a pair of near-synonyms *create* and *produce* shares a 'core' aspect of 'manufacturing products,' while their semantic distinctions lie in the gradience of 'peripheral' features, such as non-fixed-to-fixed 'property,' low-to-high 'creativity,' few-to-massive 'quantity,' and low-to-high concreteness' [4]. That is, synonymous words can be approached by being placed on a continuum of semantic features; for example, if a product has higher 'concreteness,' is lower in 'creativity,' its 'property' is more naturally fixed, and is more manufactured in massive 'quantity,' there is a higher chance for these products to be selected by the verb *produce* than *create*. Apart from semantic distinctions, near-synonyms can also be differentiated from their stylistic distinctions (e.g., dialect and register), expressive variations (e.g., affective and attitudinal aspects), and structural contrasts (e.g., collocational patterns and syntactic structures) [3].

© The Author(s), under exclusive license to Springer Nature Singapore Pte Ltd. 2024
M. Dong et al. (Eds.): CLSW 2023, LNAI 14515, pp. 357–376, 2024.
https://doi.org/10.1007/978-981-97-0586-3_28

Recent years saw the proliferation of corpus-based studies to sketch and capture the subtle yet significant distinctness of near-synonyms in Chinese [5–10]. Wang and Huang [8] described the current stage as the 'third stage' from the perspective of research methods of synonym discrimination; specifically, succeeding the first stage of introspection of the data and the second stage of examining the KWIC (keyword in context) in the corpus data, the current stage makes use of the functions in the Sketch Engine (https://www.sketchengine.eu/) [11] to automatically generate grammatical and collocational relations of target words, which facilitate researchers in their further analyses. The application and output of the 'third stage' could advance lexicography [8] as well as benefit teaching and learning Chinese as a second language (L2) [12].

Despite the importance of distinguishing near-synonyms in teaching and learning Chinese as an L2, the actual use of corpus data in the L2 classroom has rarely been studied in the past literature. Meanwhile, apart from the Sketch Engine, another widely-used corpus platform in Chinese, BLCU Chinese Corpus (BCC Corpus; http://bcc.blcu.edu.cn/) [13],[1] is suggested as a complementary corpus tool that could be utilized for L2 Chinese learning [14]. In light of the well-developed theoretical construal of near-synonyms using the corpus-based method vis-à-vis the underexplored pedagogical applications of using corpora in teaching and learning near-synonyms, the current paper aims to probe into the 'gap' between the 'theoretical-based' vs. 'pedagogical-application' of using corpora in teaching and learning of Chinese near-synonyms.

The synonymous items we examined here are 'business' related synonyms. The rationale for choosing these words is that in one of the lessons in the teaching material used in an advanced-level Chinese classroom at a university in Hong Kong, *Eyes on China* [15],[2] students need to read a passage talking about 关系、人情、法治 'relationship, favor, and the rule of law;' students were then asked to differentiate a pair of near-synonym appeared in the passage, 买卖 'business' and 交易 'deal; trade.' The sentence contained these two words read: 中国人的许多买卖交易也都是在饭桌上谈成的 'Many Chinese business and deals are also negotiated at the dinner table.' In the textbook, 买卖 is translated as 'buy and sell; business (it is usually commercial),' and 交易 is roughly translated as 'deal and trade (may just be an arrangement for mutual advantage, not necessarily commercial).' Students might simply think their difference is that 买卖 'buy and sell; business' is used for commercial business while 交易 'deal and trade' is not necessarily related to commercial activities. However, in real usage, 买卖 'buy and sell; business' does not limit to 'money-involved' business (in the following sentence, for example); and there is another more frequently used similar word with 买卖 'buy and sell; business'—生意 'business,' was not mentioned in the textbook.

---

[1] Beijing Language and Culture University Corpus Center (BLCU Corpus Center, BCC) is an online corpus with a size of around ten billion words including Chinese and other languages.

[2] *Eyes on China: an intermediate-advanced reader of modern Chinese* is a textbook for intermediate to advanced level students. This book covers a range of timely China-related topics, including the problem of air pollution, corruption, infrastructure development, the development of high-speed rail, the prevalence of knock-off products in the marketplace, new tech trends, the contemporary art scene, and the relationship between mainland China and Taiwan.

(1) 新制度带来的成果，与伴随它而来的问题所引发的代价相比，是不是值得?…
不论从什么角度考虑，这都是一笔赔本的<u>买卖</u>。[3]

    'Are the benefits of the new system worth the costs of the problems accompanying it? …This is a losing business no matter how you look at it.'

For advanced-level learners, it is particularly important for them to learn and practice language usage in real-life situations. In this paper, we will first use the conventions in examining 'business' related near-synonymous words (i.e., 生意 'business', 买卖 'buy and sell; business', and 交易 'deal and trade') with the corpus-based method and then present a case study of applying corpus data in teaching and learning of a pair of near-synonymy (i.e., 买卖 'buy and sell; business' and 交易 'deal and trade') in a university in Hong Kong as an example. After comparing the 'outputs' of the 'theory' and the 'application,' we will identify the 'gap' between the two and suggest improvements that students and teachers could implement in future learning and teaching of Chinese near-synonyms with the corpus-based method.

2 Use Corpora in Teaching and Learning Chinese as an L2

Applying corpora in teaching and learning a second language is usually known as 'data-driven learning' (DDL). DDL applications in an L2 classroom typically involve using the tools (e.g., actual text collections and software packages for corpus access) and methods (e.g., analytic techniques) of corpus linguistics to get learners to work with written or spoken corpus data [16–19]. Learner autonomy and task authenticity are the two main advantages of DDL. On the one hand, as an 'inductive learning process' (i.e., more student-centered), students can observe the language patterns as a "Sherlock Holmes" [20] and formulate their hypotheses about the language use or validate language rules from their textbooks by their own [17]. L2 learners, thus, are more engaged and more autonomous in the learning process, which will be more "empowered" [21] and they will feel more confident and self-esteem in learning a second language [17]. On the other hand, DDL brings authenticity into the classroom, especially learners will be able to expose to a large amount of authentic instances in the target language [17, 22]. Nevertheless, DDL requires certain corpus literacy for teachers and students, which lays out challenges in its implementation. Some problems that teachers and students face include teachers might lack the expertise and/or confidence or finding it too time-consuming to engage with DDL, and students might be barred from formulating any rules or 'seeing anything' from the corpora [17]. In addition, most of the time, corpora data contain 'noise' (e.g., irrelevant hits, non-standard forms, wrongly tagged information) [17], but the learners will not be able to clean the data as a native speaker does because of their insufficient knowledge of the target language.

    Possibly because of the obstacles mentioned, DDL has not been implemented much in the teaching and learning of Chinese as an L2. Past related literature mostly demonstrated how to use corpus tools in designing teaching activities [6, 12, 14, 23]; for example, by making use of the Sketch Differences and Word Sketches functions in the Sketch Engine, Smith [23] proposed several corpus tasks including asking learners to compare a pair of

---

[3] From the Chinese Web 2017 (zhTenTen11) corpus data, accessed in the Sketch Engine.

near-synonyms 后果 'consequence' and 结果 'result' and to classify the objects taken by 吃 'eat' into categories. Wang [14] followed Boulton's [24] 'hands-on' and 'hands-off' approaches and designed teaching plans to demonstrate how to resort to corpus tools and methods in carrying out instructions respectively. For the 'hands-on' approach, after the teacher introduces relevant corpus tools and methods, students need to access the corpus website by themselves, observe the examples, and draw conclusions in order to answer teachers' questions. 'Hands-off' design, by contrast, teachers will take more 'control' of the instruction by selecting and adjusting concordances found in the corpus according to the learners' proficiency levels; students then observe the examples provided by the teacher and answer related questions.

The case study demonstrated in this paper is an attempt of a 'hands-on' approach. However, what departs from other conventional DDL activities, is that we adopted a 'blended-learning' design considering the effectiveness and efficiency of teaching and learning in an L2 classroom. That is, we deliberately design the pre-class instructions (e.g., self-direct learning guides), in-class activities (e.g., presentation of the findings), and after-class reflections (e.g., self-reflection reports), which ensure the cohesive alignment of online corpus tasks and face-to-face teaching activities [25]. The detailed 'hands-on' blended learning design of using corpora in teaching and learning near-synonyms is elaborated in the section below.

3   Method

As mentioned above, this paper comprises two parts, 'theoretical-based' and 'pedagogical-application' of using corpora in teaching and learning Chinese near-synonyms. Therefore, we will first introduce the method for the 'theoretical-based' examination of near-synonyms with the functions of the Sketch Engine (2.1) and then brief the instruction for the 'hands-on blended-learning' of near-synonyms in an L2 classroom in a university in Hong Kong (2.2).

3.1   Method of the 'Theoretical-Based' Near-Synonyms Distinction

To differentiate near-synonyms, we will mainly use the Thesaurus and Word Sketch Difference (WSD) functions in the Sketch Engine. The Thesaurus automatically generates similar words for target words or words belonging to the same semantic category so that we will find the similarity between the words under comparison. Word Sketch portrays the grammatical and collocational behavior of a target word by sorting out its collocates and other words in its surroundings with the logDice score.[4] WSD is thus to compare two words at a time via their collocates according to the grammatical relations for each pair.

All the data and sentence examples presented under the 'theoretical-based' orientation were extracted from a Chinese online corpus, Chinese Web 2017 (zhTenTen11), in the Sketch Engine [11]. This is an annotated web-based corpus consisting of 17 billion Simplified Chinese script texts, and it is the largest and latest tagged corpus in Mandarin Chinese to the best of our knowledge.

---

[4] logDice score indicates how strong the collocation is; the higher the score, the stronger the collocation (for the algorithm of logDice score, see [26]).

3.2   Method of the 'Pedagogical-Applied' Near-Synonyms Distinction

The course offered at this university in Hong Kong is an advanced-level Chinese class for students whose Chinese proficiency reached HSK4 or equivalent last fall semester. Students in this class can be roughly divided into Chinese heritage learners and Chinese second language learners. Their educational background varies; some of them were born in HK and educated in international schools, some were from HK families but received education abroad and returned to HK for higher education, some were from Asian countries like Korea, Indonesia, India, Malaysia, Philippine, Vietnam, and some were from European and American countries.

This learning task required students to watch an instructional video using BCC corpus [13] to explore Chinese near-synonyms from three dimensions: position in sentences, semantic or syntactic collocation, and distribution across genres. The first dimension, that is, position in sentences, the video uses the near-synonyms 面对 'to face' and 面临 'to face' to guide students to observe the subtle differences through BCC concordance. For example, 面对 'to face' can be placed anywhere in a sentence, while 面临 'to face' can only be used at the beginning and the middle of a sentence, but not at the end of a sentence. As for the second dimension, semantic or syntactic collocation, the video uses 恐惧 'fear' and 害怕 'afraid' to demonstrate how students can find the most common as well as dissimilar words paired with these two words. For example, both 恐惧 'fear' and 害怕 'afraid' can be preceded by degree and negative adverbs like 很 'very'; but for the negative adverbs, 恐惧 'fear' can occur with 没有 'not have', but 害怕 'afraid' only occur with 不 'not'. The third dimension, genre distributions in the BCC corpus, provides students with the preferred genre for the words. Taking the synonyms 干扰 'disturb' and 打扰 'disturb' as the example, 干扰 'disturb' is widely used in newspapers and science, followed by literature, and finally social media (Weibo); while 打扰 'disturb' is used frequently in social media (Weibo), followed by literary works, and then newspapers, but relatively less in the field of science and technology.

After students watched the instructional video, they formed a group of 2 or 3, used the basic search functions learned from the video clip, and started an experiential journey with their peers to observe and analyze the semantic or syntactic functions of one pair of near-synonyms assigned by the class teacher. Each group of students will present their findings to the class. After the presentation, each student needs to submit a self-reflection report on this self-directed learning task.

4   Results

4.1   Results of the 'Theoretical-Based' Near-Synonyms Distinction

Before presenting the results generated by the Sketch Engine, we first demonstrate the meanings of the three words in dictionaries in order to show that the definitions given by the dictionaries are not quite possible for learners to tell the nuances of the target words (see Table 1). The dictionaries we consulted include 现代汉语词典第七版 (The Contemporary Chinese Dictionary, 7th edition) [27], Chinese WordNet 2.0 [28],[5] 漢典

---

[5] Chinese WordNet is a platform provides an ontological network of semantic meanings of a word coupled with their semantic relations, including hypernyms, hyponyms, synonyms, among others. Accessed at https://lopentu.github.io/CwnWeb/.

(Zdic),[6] and an online version of 教育部《重編國語辭典修訂本》2021 (https://dict.rev ised.moe.edu.tw/).

Table 1. Word meanings for the 'business' related synonyms defined in the dictionaries.

Word	Definitions	Source
生意 *shēngyi*[7] 'business'	商业经营 'business operation'	《现代汉语词典第七版》
	商買交易、買賣 'merchant trade, buy and sell'	《重編國語辭典修訂本》
	①商业经营; 买卖或往来 'business operation; buy and sell or dealings' ②指经商的店铺 'refers to the shops doing business' ③工作; 活儿, 也泛指职业 'work; tasks, also generally refers to profession'	《漢典》
	①商業買賣的活動 'activities of commercial transactions' ②商業買賣的交易數量 'transaction volume of commercial trades'	Chinese WordNet 2.0
买卖 *mǎimai* 'buy and sell; business'	①生意 'business' ②指商店 'refers to a shop'	《现代汉语词典第七版》
	①商場上買進賣出的交易行為、生意 'buying and selling transactions in the market, business' ②以非法的途徑奪取財物 'seizing wealth through illegal channels'	《重編國語辭典修訂本》
	①生意 'business' ②指商店 'refers to a shop' ③东西;家伙;货色[8] 'things; stuff; goods'	《漢典》
交易 *jiāoyì* 'deal and trade'	①买卖商品 (动词) 'buying and selling goods (verb)' ②生意 (名词) 'business (noun)'	《现代汉语词典第七版》
	①本指交換、互換。後泛指買賣 'originally refers to exchange, swapping. Later generally refers to buying and selling' ②往來、交往 'contact, communication' ③更換、更替[9] 'replacement, substitution'	《重編國語辭典修訂本》
	原指以物易物, 后泛指买卖商品 'originally refers to barter, later generally refers to buying and selling goods'	《漢典》

---

[6] An online Chinese dictionary; accessed at https://www.zdic.net/.

As seen from the above table, 生意 'business', 买卖 'buy and sell; business', and 交易 'deal and trade' are interpreted by referring to each other; for example, 生意 'business' is explained as '交易' 'deal and trade' and '买卖' 'buy and sell; business;' 买卖 'buy and sell; business' is defined as '交易' 'deal and trade' and '生意' 'business'; and 交易 'deal and trade' is described as '买卖' 'buy and sell; business'. Learners thus will not be able to distinguish their meaning differences by checking dictionaries. Although we may infer from the definitions that 生意 'business' and 买卖 'buy and sell; business' can both refer to a shop while 交易 'deal and trade' cannot, 买卖 'buy and sell; business' might contain negative affection due to its specifically referring to 'illegal occupying of property,' and 交易 'deal and trade' may denote exchange and has an additional part-of-speech as a verb, however, their nuances when referring to 'business' are still indistinguishable from dictionary definitions.

After searching the entries 生意 'business', 买卖 'buy and sell; business', and 交易 'deal and trade' one at a time, in the Sketch Engine, we first identified their frequencies (per million), as presented in Table 2.

Table 2. Total frequencies and frequencies by PoS for the 'business' related synonyms.

Word	Parts-of-Speech (PoS)	Frequencies by PoS	Total Frequencies in the Corpus (per million)
生意 *shēngyi* 'business'	Noun	774080 (99.2%)	779961
	Verb	5881 (0.75%)	
买卖 *mǎimai* 'buy and sell; business'	Noun	447614 (69.3%)	646296
	Verb	198682 (30.7%)	
交易 *jiāoyì* 'deal and trade'	Noun	4886672 (92.6%)	5279615
	Verb	392943 (7.4%)	

The main grammatical function for the three words is a noun, especially for 生意 'business' (99.2%) and 交易 'deal and trade' (92.6%). Note that although 生意 'business' is tagged as a verb in the corpus, we do not consider it a correct annotation because the examples treated 生意 'business' as a verb is only a 'modifier' rather than a bona fide verb; for example, 生意头脑 'business minds,' 生意业务 'business,' 生意触角 'business talents,' etc. Conversely, 买卖 'buy and sell; business' can act as a bona-find verb for its considerable percentage of usage as a verb (30.7%). 买卖 'buy and sell; business' can take objects such as 买卖外汇 'buy and sell foreign exchange,' 买卖股票 'buy and sell stocks,' and enter into a prepositional structure indicated by 以

---

[7] 生意 also reads *shēngyì*, which means 'life and vitality' as in 生意盎然. We will not discuss this meaning in this paper.

[8] Note that this meaning is not existed in contemporary Chinese, therefore, we will not discuss this usage here.

[9] This meaning is not used in contemporary Chinese too.

'with' (e.g., 以港币买卖 'buy and sell with Hong Kong dollars'). 交易 'deal and trade' can also collocate with nouns and be selected by the prepositions 对… 'towards', 以… 'with', 于… 'at', although the usage is not very common (7.4%). For example, 交易 货币 'trade currency,' 开展人民币对新加坡元直接交易 'launching of direct trading of RMB against SG dollars,' 全球市场以美元交易的有色金属 'non-ferrous metals traded in US dollars in the global market,' 美元兑日元仍交易于 100 附近 'USD/JPY still trades near 100.' However, some incorrect tagging of 交易 'deal and trade' as a verb in the corpus was also identified.

After comparing the frequencies for these three words in the corpus, we found that 交易 'deal and trade' has the highest frequencies among the three, and 生意 'business' and 买卖 'buy and sell; business' have more or less similar frequencies. In terms of their parts-of-speech, 买卖 'buy and sell; business' can behave as a verb commonly, but 交易 'deal and trade' and 生意 'business' have very limited usage as a verb, especially for 生 意 'business'. It is worth noting that when 买卖 'buy and sell; business' and 交易 'deal and trade' act as a verb in the sentence, their meanings are not equivalent to 'business' (i.e., 买卖 is referring to 'buy and sell' and 交易 is 'to trade,' as shown in the examples above). Therefore, in the subsequent comparison, we will restrict to the use of 买卖 'buy and sell; business', 交易 'deal and trade', and 生意 'business' as nouns in the corpus.

Next, we compare the similar words for the three words with the function of the Thesaurus. The top 10 are shown in Table 3 below. It is observed that 销售 'sales' and 投资 'investment' are shared by all three words; 市场 'market' and 业务 'business' are similar to 生意 'business' and 交易 'deal and trade', while 投资者 'investor' is more akin to 买卖 'buy and sell; business' and 交易 'deal and trade'. 生意 'business' tends to occur in the same semantic field with shop operation items, like 店 'shop,' 老板 'boss,' and 经营 'manage;' 买卖 'buy and sell; business' leans on foreign exchange and the stock market, such as 外汇 'forex,' 股票 'stock,' and 贷款 'loan;' while 交易 'deal and trade' is more inclined to some service platform and/or company, like 平台 'platform,' 公司 'company,' 客户 'client,' and 银行 'bank.'

Lastly, Word Sketch Difference (WSD) is used to compare the target words two at a time. The grammatical relations that 生意 'business', 买卖 'buy and sell; business', and 交易 'deal and trade' co-occur with are identical, including (indirect-/direct-)object of, subject of, (adj-/noun-)modifier, possession-possessor, and/or, and measure words. Due to space limitation, we only present the following four categories most pertinent to the target words as a noun, including object of, subject of, adjective modifier, and measure words. The collocates are ranked according to the logDice score. As shown in Fig. 1, the collocates in green tend to combine with the green word (i.e., 生意 'business'), and the collocates in red tend to combine with the red word (i.e., 买卖 'buy and sell; business'). The white collocates combine with both words. The darker the color is, the stronger the collocations are.

When 生意 'business', 买卖 'buy and sell; business', and 交易 'deal and trade' act as an object (see Table 4), their common predicates are mostly related to 'engage in' and 'do.' For example, 生意 'business' and 买卖 'buy and sell; business', and 生意 'business' and 交易 'deal and trade', both can be taken by 从事 'engage in;' however, 做 'to do' is more collocated to 生意 'business' and 买卖 'buy and sell; business' instead of with 交易 'deal and trade'. Some exclusive patterns for 生意 'business' include 忙于 'busy

Table 3. Top 10 similar words for the 'business' related synonyms (similarity score is indicated in the parentheses).

生意 *shēngyi* 'business'	买卖 *mǎimai* 'buy and sell; business'	交易 *jiāoyì* 'deal and trade'
店 'shop' (0.447)	交易 'deal' (0.473)	投资 'investment' (0.655)
老板 'boss' (0.419)	生意 'business' (0.354)	业务 'business' (0.631)
店铺 'shop' (0.419)	投资 'investment' (0.349)	市场 'market' (0.616)
经营 'manage' (0.416)	外汇 'forex' (0.333)	平台 'platform' (0.584)
市场 'market' (0.414)	投资者 'investor' (0.325)	服务 'service' (0.577)
销售 'sales' (0.413)	合同 'contract' (0.324)	公司 'company' (0.577)
业务 'business' (0.409)	贷款 'loan' (0.323)	银行 'bank' (0.575)
交易 'deal' (0.408)	股票 'stock' (0.322)	销售 'sales' (0.574)
钱 'money' (0.405)	销售 'sales' (0.316)	客户 'client' (0.571)
投资 'investment' (0.402)	收益 'profit' (0.316)	投资者 'investor' (0.570)

生意 774,080× | 6.0 | 4.0 | 2.0 | 0 | -2.0 | -4.0 | -6.0 | 买卖 447,614×

Fig. 1. Color sample of the WSD for 生意 'business' and 买卖 'buy and sell; business' (screenshot from the Sketch Engine).

with,' 招徕 'solicit,' 接手 'take over,' 加盟 'join in,' 照顾 'take care of,' 打理 'manage,' 谈 'negotiate/talk about.' This unique usage reflects 生意 'business' embracing more 'individuals' than 买卖 'buy and sell; business' or 交易 'deal and trade' because the agents of these actions can be individuals rather than organizations or companies, as in the example sentences below:

(2) 入景区如遇村民招揽生意，还请您自行判断是否购买。
'If you encounter <u>villagers</u> **soliciting business** when you enter the scenic spot, please judge whether to buy it yourself.'
(3) 20岁的他正忙着打理网店生意。
'At the age of 20, <u>he</u> is busy **managing** his online store **business**.'

买卖 'buy and sell; business', on the contrary, has few unique usages when acting as an object. It only has stronger collocations with 'suspend/stop,' such as 暂停 'suspend' and 停止 'stop,' and 代理 'act on behalf of' (when compared with 生意 'business'). These predicates, interestingly, are shared between 买卖 'buy and sell; business' and 交易 'deal and trade', although 交易 'deal and trade' tends to be selected by bank, company, and stock market-related lexical items, for example, 挂牌 'listing,' 开户 'account opening,' 进场 'enter the market,' 收购 'acquire,' and 套利 'arbitrage.' It shows that 交易 'deal and trade' is more applied in formal business activities.

Table 5 compares the use of 生意 'business', 买卖 'buy and sell; business', and 交易 'deal and trade' when they represent a subject in a sentence. Gain and loss of the business is a common 'topic' discussed among all three 'subjects,' including 挣钱 'make

Table 4. 生意 'business', 买卖 'buy and sell; business', and 交易 'deal and trade' act as an object.

Object_of								
生意	忙于 'busy with', 招徕 'attract', 接手 'take over', 揽 'take in', 加盟 'join', 祝 'wish', 招揽 'solicit'	照顾 'take care', 打理 'manage', 抢 'snatch', 谈 'talk', 洽谈 'negotiate'	做 'do', 经营 'operate'	从事 'engage in', 赚 'earn', 亏本 'lose money', 促成 'facilitate'	代理 'agent', 停止 'stop'	暂停 'suspend'		买卖
生意	招揽 'solicit', 打理 'manage', 照顾 'take care', 忙于 'busy with', 招徕 'attract', 接手 'take over'	做大 'expand', 做起 'start up', 祝 'wish', 抢 'snatch', 经营 'operate'	谈 'talk', 洽谈 'negotiate', 谈成 'reach an agreement', 做成 'make it', 想做 'want to do', 赚 'make a profit', 做 'do'	从事 'engage in'	促成 'promote', 进场 'enter the market', 收购 'acquisition'	开户 'open an account', 停止 'stop', 撮合 'matchmaking', 参与 'participate', 达成 'reach'	支付 'pay', 暂停 'pause', 完成 'complete', 套利 'arbitrage', 进行 'carry out', 模拟 'simulate', 挂牌 'listing'	交易
买卖		做起 'start up'		代理 'agency', 促成 'promote', 做 'do', 停止 'stop', 暂停 'suspend'	从事 'engage in', 挂牌 'listing', 撮合 'matchmaking', 挂单 'place an order', 参与 'participate', 进行 'carry out', 模拟 'simulate', 构成 'constitute'	进场 'enter the market', 开户 'open an account', 达成 'achieve', 收购 'acquire', 支付 'pay', 完成 'complete', 套利 'arbitrage'		交易

money,' 赚钱 'earn money,' 成交 'conclude a deal,' 亏损 'loss.' Yet, some exclusive patterns can still be observed for each word. 生意 takes some idiomatic expressions like 生意兴隆 'business is booming', (生意)蒸蒸日上 '(business) is prospering', (生意)风生水起 '(business) is booming,' (生意)一落千丈 '(business) is plummeting.' 交易 'deal and trade' tends to be more involved in 'progress,' denoted by words including 产生 'produce,' 结束 'end,' and 完成 'complete'; while 买卖 'buy and sell; business' seems to be more collocated with planning and decision, such as 策划 'planning' and 决断 'decision.'

The results of the 'adjective' modifiers collocated with 生意 'business', 买卖 'buy and sell; business', and 交易 'deal and trade' are along the line of the findings above. Gain and loss-related items can take all three words, but interestingly, when 生意 'business' is compared to 买卖 'buy and sell; business', more 'gain-related' words such as 红火 'prosperous,' 稳赚 'steady profit,' and 源源不断 'continuous' are used to modify 生意 'business', while 'loss-related' items tend to select 买卖 'buy and sell; business',

Table 5. 生意 'business', 买卖 'buy and sell; business', and 交易 'deal and trade' act as a subject.

Subject_of									
生意	惨淡 'dismal', 蒸蒸日上 'prospering', 一落千丈 'plummeting', 风生水起 'booming', 好 'good', 往来 'come and go'	失败 'failure', 兴隆 'prosperous'	上门 'visit', 做 'do', 亏本 'lose money', 赚钱 'make money'	做成 'accomplish', 挣钱 'earn money', 可做 'doable', 成交 'transaction'	赚取 'earn', 划算 'worthwhile'			挂单 'place an order', 策画 'plan', 纷歧 'divergence'	买卖
生意	兴隆 'flourishing', 惨淡 'bleak', 蒸蒸日上 'prospering', 一落千丈 'plummeting', 风生水起 'booming', 好 'good', 往来 'come and go', 亏本 'lose money', 难做 'hard to do', 好做 'easy to do', 做大 'expand', 可做 'doable'	上门 'visit', 挣钱 'make money', 谈成 'come to an agreement'	做成 'accomplish', 做到 'achieve', 做 'do'	赚钱 'make money', 赚 'earn', 失败 'fail', 亏损 'loss', 成交 'transaction'	成功 'success'	产生 'generate', 涉及 'involve', 结束 'end', 交易 'trade', 达成 'reach', 入门 'beginner'		完成 'complete', 减持 'reduce holdings', 撮合 'matchmaking', 活跃 'active'	交易
买卖	纷歧 'divergence', 策画 'plan', 决断 'decision'	好做 'easy to do'	划算 'cost-effective', 挂单 'place an order'	赚取 'earn', 成交 'transaction', 赚钱 'make money', 赚 'earn', 撮合 'matchmaking'	成功 'success', 涉及 'involve', 活跃 'active', 入门 'beginner'	达成 'reach', 结束 'end', 产生 'generate', 构成 'constitute', 失败 'fail'		完成 'complete', 值 'value', 减持 'reduce holdings', 亏损 'loss'	交易

for instances, 亏钱 'lose money', 赔本 'suffer a loss', 蚀本 'erode capital' and 赚吆喝 (an idiom meaning all the efforts were in vain). 交易 'deal and trade' is again more emphasized on its 'progression,' and its potential unprofitable loss is also highlighted when being compared with 生意 'business' and 买卖 'buy and sell; business' (Table 6).

Last but not least, we compare the measure words that co-occur with the target words. As seen from Table 7, 生意 'business', 买卖 'buy and sell; business', and 交易 'deal and trade' share some common measure words like 笔 'classifier used for transactions, deals, or matters', 桩 'classifier used for affairs or matters', 起 'classifier used for cases or types', 宗 'classifier used for cases or types', and these classifiers are mostly used to measure events and activities [29, 30]. Nevertheless, the three words are also selected by their exclusive classifiers. For example, since 生意 'business' can refer to a specific shop so that it can go together with 一摊生意 'a (booth of) business' and 一桌生意 'a (table of) business,' and normally the business being referred is a stall or a restaurant (with dining tables). 生意 'business' can also be broken down into a number of times of activities, such as 跑一趟生意 'do a (round of trip of) business,' indicating this business needs to go out and negotiate with people, etc. In contrast, when 买卖 'buy and sell; business' is compared with 生意 'business', it refers to the business that can be counted in larger quantity, implied by the measure words 重 'layer' and 系列 'series,' while

Table 6. 'Adjective' modifiers of 生意 'business', 买卖 'buy and sell; business', and 交易 'deal and trade'.

Adjective Modifier								
生意	红火 'flourishing',好做 'easy to do', 火爆 'booming',送上门 'delivered to the door',稳赚 'steady earnings',到手 'in hand',火 'flourishing',源源不断 'endless',好赚 'easy to earn',冷清 'desolate'	经营 'operate',做 'do'	上门 'visit',从事 'engage in'	赚钱 'make money',有利可图 'profitable',挣钱 'earn money',成交 'deal',赚 'earn',一本万利 'make a fortune',赔 'lose',稳赚不赔 'sure win',亏 'loss'	亏钱 'lose money',吃亏 'suffer a loss',赔钱 'lose money',赔本 'suffer a loss',划算 'worthwhile',赚吆喝 'all the efforts were in vain',合算 'cost-effective'	进行 'carry out'	蚀本 'erode capital'	买卖
生意	赔本 'suffer a loss',好做 'easy to do',挣钱 'make money',上门 'visit',一本万利 'make a fortune',送上门 'delivered to the door',铺 'shop',稳赚 'sure win',到手 'in hand',火 'flourishing',源源不断 'endless',红火 'booming',亏本 'erode capital'	经营 'operate',稳赚不赔 'sure win',赚钱 'make money',火爆 'booming'	赔 'lose',有利可图 'profitable'	做 'do',赔钱 'lose money',划算 'worthwhile',成交 'deal'	亏 'loss',失败 'fail',成功 'success'	真正 'genuine',达成 'achieve',完成 'completed'	进行 'carry out',真实 'real',无利 'no profit',盲目 'blind',日复一日 'day after day',发生 'occur',亏损 'loss',交割 'delivery',频繁 'frequent',无谓 'meaningless'	交易
买卖	赚吆喝 'all the efforts were in vain',蚀本 'erode capital',一本万利 'make a fortune',挣钱 'make money',吃亏 'suffer a loss',无本万利 'make a fortune without capital',赔本 'suffer a loss',亏本 'erode capital',稳赚不赔 'sure win'	合算 'cost-effective'	赔 'lose',划算 'worthwhile',赔钱 'lose money',亏钱 'lose money',赚钱 'make money'	你情我愿 'mutual consent',亏 'loss'	进行 'carry out',公平 'fair',频繁 'frequent'	亏损 'loss',无谓 'meaningless',真实 'real'	成功 'success',流行 'popular',真正 'genuine',无利 'no profit',盲目 'blind',日复一日 'day after day',失败 'fail'	交易

生意 'business' is counted in smaller quantity, such as (一)点儿 'a little bit' and 一些 'a few.' When 买卖 'buy and sell; business' contrasts with 交易 'deal and trade', 交易 'deal and trade' is happening in larger-scaled activities, such as 一揽子交易 'package deal.' Moreover, 买卖 'buy and sell; business' and 交易 'deal and trade' can also be measured by specific stock and financial market jargon, like 一手(股票)买卖/交易 'lot (stock) trading' and 一口(期货)交易 'lot (futures) trading.'

Table 7. Measure words of 生意 'business', 买卖 'buy and sell; business', and 交易 'deal and trade'.

Measure Words								
生意	季 'season or quarter',摊 'stall or stand',点儿 'a bit',档子 'stall or stand',桩桩 'affairs or matters',桌 'table',样 'kind',门 'categories or types'	盘 'dish or plate'	点 'a bit',些 'some'	趟 'round trip',笔 'transactions or deals',桩 'affairs or matters',种 'type or kind',票 'transactions or deal'',场 'events or games',档 'stall or stand',宗 'kind or type',次 'time or occasion',起 'events or occurrences'			重 'layers or levels',式 'type or style',系列 'series',手 'a batch or a set',一锤子 'a deal or a matter'	买卖
生意	门 'categories or types',季 'season or quarter',摊 'stall or stand',点儿 'a bit',一档子 'stall or stand',票 'transactions or deals',桌 'table'	趟 'round trip'	一桩桩 'affairs or matters',档 'stall or stand'	些 'some',点 'a bit',家 'shop',年 'year',桩 'affairs or matters'	笔 'transactions or deals',宗 'kind or type',场 'events or games',类 'type or kind'	项 'item',次 'time or occasion',起 'events or occurrences'	手 'a batch or a set'	交易
买卖	票 'transactions or deals',门 'categories or types',重 'layers or levels'		趟 'round trip',档 'stall or stand'	式 'type or style',桩 'affairs or matters',些 'some',系列 'series',点 'a bit'	手 'a batch or a set',宗 'kind or type',种 'type or kind',笔 'transactions or deals',场 'events or games',起 'events or occurrences'	次 'time or occasion',类 'type or kind',项 'item'	口 'deals or transactions',一揽子 'a bunch of'	交易

4.2   Results of the 'Pedagogical-Applied' Near-Synonyms Distinction

In class, two students from Southeast Asian countries reported their findings of using the corpora to differentiate a pair of near-synonyms, 买卖 'buy and sell; business' and 交易 'deal and trade'. They first presented a table to show the basic semantic differences, as below (Table 8).

Table 8. The basic semantic differences between 买卖 'buy and sell; business' and 交易 'deal and trade'.

Near-synonyms	Explanation in English	Examples
买卖 'buy and sell; business'	Buy and sell/transaction. Often used in a commercial or business context	1. 你想清楚了吗?这可是连身家性命都押上去的买卖。 Have you thought it through? This is a business deal where even your life and property are at stake 2. 为了去做买卖, 他每年都会去很多不同的国家。 In order to do business, he travels to many different countries every year
交易 'deal and trade'	Deal, trade. Usually used in a formal context but not limited to commercial situations. May just arrange for mutual benefit	1. 不难认为她们两个人之间有秘密交易。 It's not hard to believe that there are secret transactions between the two of them 2. 他不可靠也不值得信赖, 导致没有人愿意跟他进行交易。 He is unreliable and untrustworthy, which makes no one willing to do business with him

Next, they discussed the basic semantic and syntactic functions of 买卖 'buy and sell; business' and 交易 'deal and trade' by giving examples selected from the BCC corpus. They also used BCC to explore frequently collocated words with this pair of near-synonyms respectively (in Table 9) and their distribution in different genres (in Table 10).

Table 9. The commonly collocated words with 买卖 'buy and sell; business' and 交易 'deal and trade' (frequency is indicated in the parentheses).

Near-synonyms	Part of speech	Words for the collocation
买卖 'buy and sell; business'	Noun	合同 'contract' (1391), 双方 'both sides' (1374), 做 'do' (1281), 进行 'carry out' (139)
交易 'deal and trade'	Noun	市场 'market' (4624), 中心 'center' (2839), 成本 'cost' (1309), 行为 'behavior' (1170), 进行 'carry out' (1118)

Students particularly highlighted the verbs collocated to 买卖 'buy and sell; business' and 交易 'deal and trade', i.e., 做买卖 'do business' and 进行交易 'carry out trade', and they mentioned that even though 进行 'carry out' can co-occur with 买卖 'business', it tends to be used more frequently with 交易 'deal and trade'.

Table 10. The distribution of 买卖 'buy and sell; business' and 交易 'deal and trade' in different genres (sorted by frequency).

Near-synonyms	Newspaper	Science	Social media-blog	Literature
买卖 'buy and sell; business'	17518	5237	3939	3014
交易 'deal and trade'	73431	35824	13904	1940

Students lastly reported that 交易 'deal and trade' is more popular than 买卖 'buy and sell; business' in many genres such as newspaper, technology, and blog. One interesting note is that students also found 交易 'deal and trade' is much less frequent than 买卖 'buy and sell; business' in the literature (1940 vs. 3014), but they did not further attempt to explain the reason.

In their after-class reflection report, two students expressed their positive attitude toward using the BCC corpus to differentiate this pair of near-synonyms. One student reported, "I found that using the BCC website to find out how a word is used or where it is most often used based on statistics gives me a deeper understanding of the definition of a word which in turn also allows me to remember the meaning and application of the word better." Another student found that learning with the help of BCC is much more efficient and simpler than using Google and doing some redundant research for definitions and sentence structures. Nevertheless, they also encountered difficulties and faced challenges, as one mentioned in his self-reflection, "in order to utilize BCC perfectly, we need to actually follow the guidelines given by the teacher and individual exploration of the BCC. It took us a while to familiarize ourselves with how to use all the features in the BCC. Another difficulty I found while using the BCC is that sometimes it requires a lot of time to load."

5   Discussion and Conclusion

After presenting the results from the 'theoretical-based' and 'pedagogical-application' of using corpora in researching and learning of 'business' related near-synonyms (i.e., 生意 'business', 买卖 'buy and sell; business', and 交易 'deal and trade'), we have identified some significant gap in-between.

First and foremost, students are 'misled' by the simple definitions and examples given by the textbook. For example, they failed to notice that 交易 'deal and trade' and 买卖 'buy and sell; business' additionally function as a verb apart from a noun, and such a PoS variant is hard to detect by the BCC corpus if no *a prior* knowledge is given. However, with the Sketch Engine and some other corpus platforms (e.g., Sinica Corpus [31]) providing clear and searchable PoS forms for each lexical item, students may have a better sense of all the PoS variants for the target words and can further analyze their syntactic structures in the sentence. Moreover, textbooks did not provide them with other similar and sometimes, more commonly used words. For instance, we have found in the 'theoretical-based' near-synonyms distinction that 买卖 'buy and sell; business' is equally 'similar' and closed to 交易 'deal and trade' and 生意 'business', and 生意 'business' even has a higher frequency in the corpus than 买卖 'buy and sell; business' (779961 vs. 646296 in per million words). With the Thesaurus function in the Sketch Engine, students can thus figure out all the other similar words with the target words and further complete the semantic lexical network in their mind.

Secondly, students are not capable of delving deeper into the collocational patterns for the target words and, thus, are not able to summarize the 'peripheral' aspects of the near-synonyms. From the results of the 'pedagogical-applied' near-synonyms distinction, students acknowledged the most frequent collocations with 买卖 'buy and sell; business' and 交易 'deal and trade', but they only stopped at presenting their frequencies without probing into the possible reasons. For example, teachers can guide students to summarize that 买卖 'buy and sell; business' may emphasize the 'mutual agreement' (denoted by 合同 'contract' and 双方 'two parties') while 交易 'deal and trade' may focus on the market per se (e.g., 市场 'market' and (交易)中心 '(trade) center'). Interestingly, such collocations found by the students echo the results in the Thesaurus function generated by the Sketch Engine. We showed that 买卖 'buy and sell; business' is more similar to contract, sales, and exchange; 交易 'deal and trade' is more inclined to service platform, company, and market; while 生意 'business' tends to be tantamount to shop and business management. Moreover, even though students realized that 做 'do' is more frequently collocated to 买卖 'buy and sell; business' whereas 进行 'carry out' is selected by 交易 'deal and trade', they were not able to come up with a hypothesis that it might because of their register differences—买卖 'buy and sell; business' is more colloquial but 交易 'deal and trade' is more formal. In fact, another verb that selects both 买卖 'buy and sell; business' and 交易 'deal and trade' (and 生意 'business'), which we found in the 'theoretical-based' method, is 从事 'engage in'. These DO verbs are extremely prevalent and unique in Mandarin Chinese, and they fall into a particular group of 'light verbs' [32, 33]. It is suggested that the teacher can further use these examples to showcase the verb-object constructions and explain the distinctions in using these light verbs in Chinese.

With the WSD function in the Sketch Engine, we revealed that 生意 'business' more refers to 'individual' while 买卖 'buy and sell; business' and 交易 'deal and trade' are more related to 'organizational' business activities, and 交易 'deal and trade' is engaged in more formal business setting than 买卖 'buy and sell; business'. The three words also tend to co-occur constantly with gain and loss related items. But interestingly, 生意 'business' is prone to a 'gain' frame while 买卖 'buy and sell; business' is inclined to a 'loss' frame. We ponder the reason is because 买卖 'buy and sell; business' is composed of both the 'gain and loss frame' (i.e., 买 'buy' indicates gain while 卖 'sell' denotes loss [34]), therefore, the possible loss from the business is foregrounded. 交易 'deal and trade', on the contrary, is more engaged in a 'progress' without much of the outcome being disclosed. We last manifested measure words that learners can choose from when they need to talk about 'business,' and these measure words further exhibit the nuances among them. For example, although the three words can all be selected by event classifiers, 生意 'business' can be deconstructed into number of times of activities and counted in small quantity, 买卖 'buy and sell; business' is usually enumerated in larger quantity (compared to 生意 'business'), and 交易 'deal and trade' is mostly happening in a large-scaled business activity.

To sum up, we believe that the functions in the Sketch Engine (e.g., Thesaurus and WSD) are more effective in uncovering the semantic distinctions and collocational contrasts among near-synonyms, while the BCC corpus may present stylistic distinctions in a straightforward way (for example, students were able to summarize the distributions in different genres quickly). Given the corpus data we chose for analysis (i.e., Chinese Web 2017 (zhTenTen11)) is composed of the internet data, students are not possible to distinguish among stylistic variants. Moreover, students may also be hindered by considerable 'noise' in the corpus data, as we mentioned previously. Therefore, when introducing corpus tools and methods in to an L2 classroom, we recommend teachers first need to familiarize themselves with all the possible corpus platforms and functions, then carefully choose one (or two) that could satisfy their teaching needs. The blended-learning design is seen as a good approach for its maximizing of the learners' autonomy, but more specific questions and tasks are suggested to be assigned. For example, apart from only asking students to summarize the semantic and syntactic collocations, teachers can further ask learners to categorize their frequent co-occurred words into detailed semantic domains. After the in-class activities, teachers can also guide students to explore a few more interesting yet important language points that may not necessarily relate to the distinctions per se (for example, the light verb constructions mentioned above). Generally, teachers and students are better to equip themselves with 'more-than-enough' corpora literacy in order to bridge the 'gap' between the 'theoretical-based' and 'pedagogical-application' of corpora in investigating and differentiating near-synonyms in Chinese.

References

1. Lyons, J.: Linguistic Semantics: An Introduction. Cambridge University Press, Cambridge [England] (1995)
2. Taylor, J.R.: Near synonyms as co-extensive categories: 'high' and 'tall' revisited. Lang. Sci. **25**, 263–284 (2003)
3. Cruse, D.A.: Lexical Semantics. Cambridge University Press, Cambridge [Cambridgeshire] (1986)
4. Chung, S.-F.: A corpus-based analysis of "create" and "produce." Chang Gung J. Hum. Soc. Sci. **4**, 399–425 (2011)
5. Chief, L.-C., Huang, C.-R., Chen, K.-J., Tsa, M.-C., Chang, L.-L.: What can near synonyms tell us? Comput. Linguist. Chin. Lang. Process. **5**, 47–60 (2000)
6. Hong, J.-F.: Chinese near-synonym study based on the Chinese Gigaword Corpus and the Chinese Learner Corpus. In: Su, X., He, T. (eds.) CLSW 2014. LNCS (LNAI), vol. 8922, pp. 329–340. Springer, Cham (2014). https://doi.org/10.1007/978-3-319-14331-6_33
7. Hong, J.-F., Huang, C.-R.: "Sheng" yu "yin" de jinyi bianxi: ciyi yu renzhi gainian de guanxi [Near synonym analysis of "sheng" and "yin": the relation between meaning and cognitive concepts]. In: Ho, D.-A., Yiu, Y.M., Chen, Z., Sun, J., Nin, C.H. (eds.) Frontier of Research in

Chinese and Tibetan – a festschrift for Prof. Pang-Hsin Ting on His Eightieth, pp. 256–278. Social Sciences Academic Press (China), Beijing (2018)

8. Wang, S., Huang, C.-R.: Word sketch lexicography: new perspectives on lexicographic studies of Chinese near synonyms. Lingua Sinica **3**, 11 (2017)
9. Li, L., Huang, C.-R., Gao, X.: A SkE-assisted comparison of three "prestige" near synonyms in Chinese. In: Hong, J.-F., Su, Q., Wu, J.-S. (eds.) Chinese Lexical Semantics, pp. 256–266. Springer, Cham (2018). https://doi.org/10.1007/978-3-030-04015-4_22
10. Dong, S., Lo, I., Li, L., Bai, L.: 'Bus' near synonyms in Mandarin Chinese: a corpus-based study. Presented at the 22nd Chinese Lexical Semantics Workshop (CLSW2021), Nanjing (2021)
11. Kilgarriff, A., et al.: The sketch engine: ten years on. Lexicography **1**, 7–36 (2014)
12. Kilgarriff, A., Keng, N., Smith, S.: Learning Chinese with the sketch engine. In: Zou, B., Smith, S., Hoey, M. (eds.) Corpus Linguistics in Chinese Contexts, pp. 63–73. Palgrave Macmillan, London (2015)
13. Xun, E., Rao, G., Xiao, X., Zang, J.: Dashuju Beijing xia BCC yuliaoku de yanzhi [The construction of the BCC corpus in the age of big data]. Yuliaoku Yuyanxue [Corpus Linguist.] **3**, 93–118 (2016)
14. Wang, B.P.-Y., Hsu, C.-C., Long, S., Lilies, X.: Yuliao qudong xuexi rong ru huayu ketang zhi jiaoxue sheji [Designing data-driven learning activities for the Chinese as a second language classroom]. Huayuwen Jiaoxue Yanjiu [J. Chinese Lang. Teach.] **17**, 103–137 (2020)
15. Chou, C.-P., Liu, J., Zou, X.: Eyes on China: An Intermediate-Advanced Reader of Modern Chinese. Princeton University Press, Princeton (2019)
16. Johns, T.: Should you be persuaded: two examples of data-driven learning. In: Johns, T., King, P. (eds.) Classroom Concordancing, vol. 4, pp. 1–16. Centre for English Language Studies, University of Birmingham, Birmingham (1991)
17. Gilquin, G., Granger, S.: How can data-driven learning be used in language teaching? In: O'Keeffe, A., McCarthy, M. (eds.) The Routledge Handbook of Corpus Linguistics, vol. 10, pp. 359–370. Routledge, London (2010)
18. Römer, U.: Corpus research applications in second language teaching. Annu. Rev. Appl. Linguist. **31**, 205–225 (2011)
19. Szudarski, P.: Corpora and teaching vocabulary. In: Szudarski, P. (ed.) Corpus Linguistics for Vocabulary: A Guide for Research, pp. 96–114. Routledge, London (2018)
20. Johns, T.: Contexts: the background, development and trialling of a concordance-based CALL Program. In: Wichmann, A., Fligelstone, S. (eds.) Teaching and Language Corpora, pp. 100–115. Routledge, London (1997)
21. Mair, C.: Empowering non-native speakers: the hidden surplus value of corpora in continental English departments. In: Kettemann, B., Marko, G. (eds.) Teaching and Learning by Doing Corpus Analysis, pp. 119–130. Rodopi, Amsterdam (2002)
22. Gilquin, G.: Using corpora to foster L2 construction learning: a data-driven learning experiment. Int. J. Appl. Linguist. **31**, 229–247 (2021)
23. Smith, S.: Corpus-based tasks for learning Chinese: a data-driven approach. In: The Asian Conference on Technology in the Classroom Official Conference Proceedings, pp. 48–59 (2011)
24. Boulton, A.: Hands-on/hands-off: alternative approaches to data-driven learning. In: Thomas, J., Boulton, A. (eds.) Input, Process and Product: Developments in Teaching and Language Corpora, pp. 152–168. Masaryk University Press, Brno (2012)
25. Boelens, R., De Wever, B., Voet, M.: Four key challenges to the design of blended learning: a systematic literature review. Educ. Res. Rev. **22**, 1–18 (2017)
26. Rychlý, P.: A lexicographer-friendly association score. In: Sojka, P., Horák, A. (eds.) Proceedings of the 2nd Workshop on Recent Advances in Slavonic Natural Languages Processing (RASLAN-2), pp. 6–9. Masaryk University, Czech Republic (2008)

27. Dictionary Editing Office, I.o.L., Chinese Academy of Social Sciences.: Xiandai Hanyu Cidian [The Contemporary Chinese Dictionary]. The Commercial Press, Beijing (2016)

28. Huang, C.-R., et al.: Chinese Wordnet: design, implementation, and application of an infrastructure for cross-lingual knowledge processing. J. Chinese Inf. Process. **24**, 14–23 (2010)

29. Huang, C.-R., Ahrens, K.: Individuals, kinds and events: classifier coercion of nouns. Lang. Sci. **25**, 353–373 (2003)

30. Ahrens, K., Huang, C.-R.: Classifiers. In: Huang, C.-R., Shi, D.X. (eds.) A Reference Grammar of Chinese, pp. 169–198. Cambridge University Press, Cambridge (2016)

31. Chen, K.-J., Huang, C.-R., Chang, L.-P., Hsu, H.-L.: Sinica Corpus: design methodology for balanced corpora. In: Language, Information and Computation (PACLIC-11), pp. 167–176. Kyung Hee University (1996)

32. Jiang, M., Huang, C.-R.: A comparable corpus-based study of three DO verbs in varieties of Mandarin: gao. In: Hong, J.-F., Su, Q., Wu, J.-S. (eds.) CLSW 2018. LNCS (LNAI), vol. 11173, pp. 147–154. Springer, Cham (2018). https://doi.org/10.1007/978-3-030-04015-4_12

33. Xu, H., Jiang, M., Lin, J., Huang, C.-R.: Light verb variations and varieties of Mandarin Chinese: comparable corpus driven approaches to grammatical variations. Corpus Linguist. Linguist. Theory **18**, 145–173 (2022)

34. Luo, X., Huang, C.-R.: Gain-framed buying or loss-framed selling? The analysis of near synonyms in Mandarin in prospect theory. In: The 36th Pacific Asia Conference on Language, Information and Computation (PACLIC 36), De La Salle University, Manila (2022)

Differences in Word Collocations of "*Jǐnzhāng*" in Cross-Strait Chinese

Yi-Jia Lin(✉) ⓘD and Jia-Fei Hong ⓘD

National Taiwan Normal University, Taipei, Taiwan
{61084014i,jiafeihong}@ntnu.edu.tw

Abstract. Based on the "Sinica Corpus" in Taiwan and the "BCC Corpus of Beijing Language and Culture University" in Mainland, this study explores the semantic prosody differences between the word "*jǐnzhāng*" in cross-strait Chinese and uses the method of Colligation to combine the retrieved corpus. After sorting and classifying, the researcher wants to explore the distribution of collocations and semantic prosody of "*jǐnzhāng*" in cross-strait Chinese, then analyze the different semantic prosody of the word "*jǐnzhāng*" under other collocations. Furthermore, the word "*jǐnzhāng*" shows their characteristics and reflects the differences between cross-straits. The results of the study found that although the collocation habits of the word "tension" in the cross-strait regions are somewhat similar, there are still some differences. The collocation words preferred and concentrated in Taiwan are primarily "Emotion" and "Situation", and the meaning items are concentrated in the usage of "Anxiety"; In Mainland, the preferred collocations are "Situation" and "Resource", but the usage of collocations is more scattered than in Taiwan, and the usage of collocations is mostly "Urgent" in terms of meaning. The specific usage is "Resource", which is collocated with the meaning of insufficient supply. The words that are often used in this usage are things that people can obtain, limited resources, or things that people can control. Only collocations with these common points can be matched with "tension" resulting in insufficient supply. In terms of semantic prosody, most of the usages are neutral semantic prosody, except for the use of "form situation", which is negative semantic prosody. In the "Situation + Urgency" usage, the collocation and semantic prosody between cross-strait Chinese are consistent. On the whole, through semantic prosody analysis of the word "*jǐnzhāng*", it is verified that there are actual "similarities but differences" in the development of vocabulary in cross-strait Chinese.

Keywords: Cross-Strait Chinese · "*Jǐnzhāng*" · Collocations · Semantic Prosody · Regional Variation

1 Introduction

1.1 Cross-Strait Chinese Language Usage

The language used on both sides of the Taiwan Strait is Mandarin Chinese. While they share the same Chinese language, their usage has certain differences. Wang Qian [1] suggests that due to historical, political, and cultural factors, both sides of the Strait

© The Author(s), under exclusive license to Springer Nature Singapore Pte Ltd. 2024
M. Dong et al. (Eds.): CLSW 2023, LNAI 14515, pp. 376–391, 2024.
https://doi.org/10.1007/978-981-97-0586-3_29

have developed distinct language types, with the most noticeable differences found in vocabulary usage. Many Chinese words exhibit semantic variations based on geographical, cultural, and temporal factors, leading to differences in expressions and creating ambiguity in communication between the two sides. The same word may carry different semantic expressions in different regions. For example, the term "*jǐnzhāng*", which is the focus of this study, illustrates such variations. Similarly, even though the meaning remains the same, different character forms are used, such as "tomato," which is written as "*xīhóngshì*" (tomato) in Mainland and "*fānqié*" (tomato) in Taiwan. These differences contribute to a sense of estrangement in cross-strait communication [2]. Despite these distinctions, it is essential to recognize that Standard Mandarin and Taiwanese Mandarin are not considered two separate languages but rather variations within the evolution of Chinese.

In recent years, with the development of the internet, the distance between the two sides of the Strait is no longer as vast as it once was. The geographical separation that led to distinct language usages is now bridged by online communication, enabling Chinese speakers from both regions to easily access information from different Chinese-speaking areas. In this era, the differences in Chinese language usage between Mainland and Taiwan have become a topic of interest for researchers. It is hoped that investigations can delve into the evolving usage of vocabulary in both regions within the context of language environments.

1.2 Usage of "*Jǐnzhāng*"

In modern Mandarin Chinese, "*jǐnzhāng*" is a high-frequency term. In Taiwan, the Ministry of Education has categorized "*jǐnzhāng*" and marked it as a core word in the Taiwan Mandarin Language Proficiency Standards. Despite appearing to have a uniform usage, there are differences in its usage between Mainland and Taiwan. According to the definition provided in the revised edition of the Ministry of Education's Mandarin Chinese Dictionary in Taiwan, "*jǐnzhāng*" is explained as follows:

(1) Urgent or intense, causing mental tension.
      E.g. 这场比赛已经进入最后的紧张阶段。
      (This competition has entered the final tense stage.)
(2) Emotionally fearful and uneasy.
      E.g. 每次考试我都感到十分紧张。
      (I feel very fearful every time I take an exam.)
(3) In the Mainland, it refers to insufficient supply and difficulty in coping.
      E.g. 现在火车票很紧张，一般人根本买不到票。
      (Train tickets are very tight now, and ordinary people cannot buy tickets at all.)

According to the revised edition of the Ministry of Education's Mandarin Chinese Dictionary, it can be observed that there are differences in the usage of the term "*jǐnzhāng*" between Mainland and Taiwan. Despite having the same character form, there are variations in its usage, as pointed out by Hong Jiafei and Huang Juren [2]. Researchers are interested in exploring whether these differences can be further distinguished based on usage or components. Therefore, this study attempts to compare the usage of "*jǐnzhāng*" in both regions and identify the types of words commonly collocated with "*jǐnzhāng*".

By comparing whether similarities or convergences occur, the study aims to investigate the semantic and phonetic variations of "*jǐnzhāng*" in Chinese as used in both Mainland and Taiwan.

2   Literature Review

2.1   Cross-Strait Vocabulary Comparison Studies

The differences in vocabulary between Mainland and Taiwan have always been a topic of interest for linguistic scholars and lexicographers from both regions. Boli Wang and Xiaodong Shi [3] mentioned that the Chinese language used in mainland Taiwan has some differences in pronunciation, spelling system, punctuation, script, vocabulary, and grammar. In terms of vocabulary, some words have completely different meanings. Thus, Zhu Jia-ning [4] suggests that the comparison of cross-strait vocabulary can be discussed from the following three levels: 1. Different character forms representing the same meaning, such as "*qíyìguǒ*" (kiwi) used in Taiwan, corresponding to "*míhóutáo*" (kiwi) in Mainland. 2. The same character form with different usages, like "*tǔdòu*" referring to peanuts in Taiwan but meaning potatoes in Mainland. 3. The same character form and meaning, but with different implications. Regarding the case of "the same character form and meaning," Tseng Ping-ping [5] also shares similar views, pointing out that the term "*xiǎojiě*" (lady)is used as a title for women in the Chinese-speaking region. However, in Mainland, it carries a derogatory connotation, referring to women engaged in certain industries. Thus, there is a significant difference in meaning between the two regions. Hóng Jia-fei and Huang Ju-ren [7] utilized Chinese concept dictionaries and the vocabulary from the Chinese WordNet used by Academia Sinica to investigate the usage of the same concept words in both regions. The results revealed that there is a phenomenon of "similar while different" for shared vocabulary between Mainland and Taiwan, with corresponding terms also showing a mutual influence, which aligns with Zhú's [4] proposition.

Diao Yan-bin [6] believes that the differences in Mandarin Chinese usage between Mainland and Taiwan mainly fall into three categories: 1. Different expressions for the same object, for instance, "*diàncízào*" (induction cooker) in Mainland corresponds to "*diànzǐguō*" (induction cooker) in Taiwan. 2. The same word expresses different objects, such as "*jīchē*" (motorcycle) referring to a locomotive in Mainland but denoting a motorcycle in Taiwan. 3. Region-specific usage, like how "*sānbā*" (silly) in Taiwan means foolish, reckless, or improper behavior, while such usage does not exist in Mainland. Furthermore, Diāo [8] also identifies the reasons behind these three differences: First, historical differences; some words in Mainland have adopted more recent meanings, while Taiwan retains the ancient forms. Second, differences between old and new usages; some words in Mainland have discarded old forms and created new usages. Third, transliteration differences; there are numerous transliterated words in both regions, but the abundance of homophones and near-homophones in Mandarin Chinese, as well as variations in syllable selection during translation, contribute to the differences. Fourth, the choice between direct translation and not; in Taiwan, there are far more transliterated words representing the same meaning, while in Mainland, alternative forms are used. Fifth, dialectal differences; Taiwan prefers using dialectal forms, while Mainland uses alternative forms. Sixth, differences in the use of shortened forms; Taiwan's vocabulary tends to have more shortened forms compared to the Mainland, leading to differences in word forms.

In the usage of vocabulary between Taiwan and the Mainland, although there are differences, Tseng Ping-ping [5] believes that with the leadership of advertising media, the increasing cross-strait exchanges, and the intensification of the internet generation, frequent contact between the two sides have led to frequent exchanges in vocabulary usage. Diao Yan-bin [8] also suggests that over time, the phenomenon of mutual penetration and integration of vocabulary between the two sides will become more evident and widespread.

Summarizing recent studies on cross-strait vocabulary comparison, we can roughly categorize the main differences in vocabulary between Taiwan and Mainland into three aspects. First, differences in the adoption of old and new vocabulary. Second, differences in the use of loanwords. Third, the influence of cultural backgrounds on vocabulary usage. Previous research has shown that the differences in cross-strait vocabulary have reasons behind them, and these reasons are diverse and multifaceted.

2.2 Semantic Prosody Research

In this study, the term "*jǐnzhāng*" shows differences in its usage between Taiwan and Mainland, as observed in section "1.2 Usage of '*jǐnzhāng*'." It was found that when "*jǐnzhāng*" is collocated with different words in different sense categories, it conveys different semantic nuances, leading to different emotional associations for language users. Therefore, this study attempts to use Semantic Prosody as an analytical framework to compare the semantic variations of the term "*jǐnzhāng*".

Semantic Prosody is a collocational phenomenon proposed by Louw [9]. Wang Long-yin [10] explains that when a word that originally lacks significant semantic features is frequently collocated with words that possess a certain semantic characteristic, the word becomes "infected" with that particular semantic feature, resulting in the entire collocation having that semantic atmosphere. Cai-Chen [11] defines "Semantic Prosody" as the semantic coloration certain words acquire due to their frequent collocation with specific semantic features in linguistic units. Stubbs, M. [12] classifies Semantic Prosody into three categories: positive, negative, and neutral. Positive Semantic Prosody indicates that the collocates following the target word have positive semantic features. Conversely, negative Semantic Prosody indicates that the collocates have negative semantic features. Neutral Semantic Prosody suggests that the collocates can be associated with positive or negative connotations but maintain a neutral characteristic. Louw [13] emphasizes the evaluative function of Semantic Prosody, as its primary function is to express the speaker's or author's attitude and evaluation. Cai-Chen [11] states that Semantic Prosody reveals the meaningful atmosphere emanating from the context and the semantic tendencies in word selection while exploring the communicative attitude and intention of the discourse.

3   Research Methodology

This study involves two different regional variants of the Chinese language and aims to compare the potential linguistic disparities between Taiwan and Mainland. To achieve this, two corpora were utilized: the "Mandarin Chinese Balanced Corpus[1]" from the Academia Sinica in Taiwan and the "Beijing Language and Culture University (BCC) Corpus[2]" from Mainland. The "Mandarin Chinese Balanced Corpus" developed by the Academia Sinica in Taiwan is currently at version 4.0, containing articles from 1981 to 2007, with a total of 11,245,932 words. On the other hand, the "Beijing Language and Culture University BCC Corpus," established by the Corpus Linguistics Research Center of Peking University, covers Chinese, English, and French. It is a vast and diverse corpus, containing 15 billion words.

The first step of the research involved searching for relevant examples of the term "*jǐnzhāng*" in both corpora. Initially, the term "*jǐnzhāng*" was categorized into three semantic dimensions: "Anxiety," "Urgency," and "Insufficiency Supply." The collocates for each category were classified based on the provided data in the corpora. Subsequently, using the concept of collocational association, the retrieved data were organized and categorized, aiming to explore the semantic prosody types of the term "*jǐnzhāng*" in the corpora from both Taiwan and Mainland. The study further sought to understand how the semantic prosody of "*jǐnzhāng*" varies under different collocational contexts.

4   Research Results and Discussion

4.1   Analysis of Semantic Categories of "*Jǐnzhāng*"

"*jǐnzhāng*" is a high-frequency vocabulary item in contemporary Mandarin Chinese, often used in various contexts. However, there has been limited individual research specifically focusing on the usage of the term "*jǐnzhāng*" Based on the definitions provided by the Xinhua Online Dictionary and the Ministry of Education's Revised Mandarin Chinese Dictionary, the semantic categories of "*jǐnzhāng*" can be primarily classified into three major types, as shown in Table 1:

Table 1. The semantics of "*jǐnzhāng*" in Different Regions

Xinhua Online Dictionary (Mainland)	Revised Mandarin Chinese Dictionary (Taiwan)
The spirit is in a high state of readiness, excited and restless	Emotional Anxiety
Intense or urgent, making people nervous	Urgency
Insufficiency Supply	Insufficiency Supply

---

[1] Mandarin Chinese Balanced Corpus:: http://asbc.iis.sinica.edu.tw/

[2] BCC Corpus: http://bcc.blcu.edu.cn/

From the dictionaries of the two regions mentioned above, it can be observed that there are overlapping semantic categories in the usage of the term "*jǐnzhāng*" in Taiwan and the Mainland, such as the usage related to "Anxiety". For instance, the sentence " 每次考試我都感到十分緊張。" (I feel very nervous every time I take an exam.) would not lead to miscommunication due to differences in vocabulary usage between the two regions.

However, in Mainland, the sense of "jǐngzhāng" related to "Insufficiency Supply" is used more frequently, whereas in Taiwan, such usage is less common. For example, the sentence "現在火車票很緊張，一般人根本買不到票" ("Train tickets are in short supply now, and ordinary people can't buy tickets at all.") might confuse Mandarin speakers in Taiwan, as they might not grasp the intended meaning. This discrepancy also involves the concept of collocational restrictions. Chen [14] suggests that the combination of words is constrained by their different semantic senses, referred to as "collocational restrictions." For instance, in Taiwan, the word "*jiāotōng*" (traffic) can be collocated with words like "*máng*" (busy) or "*yōngjǐ*" (crowded), but not with "*jǐnzhāng*". Conversely, in Mainland, "*jiāotōng*" can be collocated with "*jǐnzhāng*", indicating differences in the usage of collocations and semantic categories. These differences form part of the issues that this study aims to explore.

4.2 Collocations of "*Jǐnzhāng*" in Language Corpora

"Collocations" is a concept within the framework of word combination restrictions, originally proposed by Firth [15]. He defined it as the collocational relationship between syntax and vocabulary within a grammatical category. Collocations are abstract definitions representing specific words, embodying a higher-level abstract grammatical usage. Researchers, based on the concept of "collocations," aim to understand the collocational restrictions of the term "*jǐnzhāng*".

According to different interpretations of "*jǐnzhāng*" found in various dictionaries, it can be inferred that the term often carries a "negative" connotation when considering its surface-level meanings. The definitions provided by Taiwan's Ministry of Education Mandarin Dictionary include emotional anxiety and urgency.

Through the dictionary definition, it's evident that the term "*jǐnzhāng*" in Taiwan usage often carries both "negative" and "neutral" connotations. The researcher hypothesizes that "*jǐnzhāng*" generally carries either a neutral or negative meaning, but is this consistent in both Taiwan and Mainland? What differences exist? The following sections will categorize the collocations of "*jǐnzhāng*" and analyze the collocations and semantic prosody of "*jǐnzhāng*" in both regions. Finally, a comparison will be drawn to identify the distinctive usage characteristics of "*jǐnzhāng*" in both areas.

4.3 Categorization of Collocational Types for "*Jǐnzhāng*"

Based on the definitions of "*jǐnzhāng*" from Taiwan's Ministry of Education Mandarin Dictionary and Mainland's Xinhua Online Dictionary, the researcher categorizes "*jǐnzhāng*" into three semantic dimensions: "Anxiety," "Urgency," and "Insufficiency Supply. "In the following discussion, these three dimensions will be referred to directly for different usages of "*jǐnzhāng*"".

Furthermore, the researcher conducted searches in both the "Chinese Balanced Corpus" and the "BLCU Corpus", yielding 719 Taiwanese Mandarin examples and 99,122 Mainland Putonghua examples. Due to the significant difference in the number of examples between the two regions, 892 representative examples were selected from the Mainland Putonghua corpus, maintaining a proportional distribution. Analyzing the examples from these distinct corpora, the researcher categorized the collocates and contexts containing "*jǐnzhāng*" into six types: "Emotion," "Situation," "Resource," "Illness," "Relation," and "Atmosphere". "Emotion," is related to emotion type; "Situation," is related to politics and situation; "Resource," is related to energy and natural resources; "Illness," is related to disease type. "Relation," refers to the relationship between people; "Atmosphere" refers to the atmosphere.

4.4 Usage of "*Jǐnzhāng*" in Taiwan

Regarding the 719 example sentences from Taiwan, the researcher categorized them based on different collocates:

Table 2. Distribution of Collocate Types in the Use of "*jǐnzhāng*" in Taiwan

Collocation Type	Taiwan	
Emotion	421	58.55%
Situation	108	15.02%
Resource	20	2.78%
Illness	25	3.48%
Relation	54	7.51%
Atmosphere	89	12.38%
Inconsistent	2	0.28%
Total	719	100%

Analyzing Table 2, it can be observed that the usage characteristics of collocate words in Taiwan include a preference for "emotional" collocations, often used to describe human emotions. There are only a few instances where it describes other living things, such as in the example "竹鸡是个紧张大师, 一害怕就大叫不停." (The Bamboo Chicken is a master of nervousness and will scream incessantly when scared.) In this sentence, "*jǐnzhāng*" modifies the preceding "竹鸡" (bamboo chicken), but it still falls within the emotional collocation usage.

Within the corpus, two instances were categorized as "Inconsistent", as they may originate from essays or scripts where the usage lacks collocation. Therefore, these instances were not included in the collocate count. The distribution of the "*jǐnzhāng*" senses in Taiwan can be seen in the following Table 3:

In Taiwan, the primary semantic categories for the term "*jǐnzhāng*" are "Anxiety" and "Urgency". Among these, the most frequently used semantic category is "Anxiety,"

Table 3. Distribution of "*jǐnzhāng*" Senses in Taiwan

Semantic	Taiwan	
Anxiety	411	57.16%
Urgency	294	40.89%
Insufficiency Supply	14	1.95%
Total	719	100%

appearing a total of 411 times. However, there are still a few instances influenced by usage from Mainland, such as the sentence "开香港往澳门前先购备回程船票, 在假日期间, 船票尤其紧张" (Before traveling from Hong Kong to Macau, it is especially challenging to obtain return ferry tickets during holidays). According to the Ministry of Education's revised national language dictionary, this usage reflects the mainland's usage. This indicates that there are occasional instances of mixed usage from the Mainland in Taiwan. Besides the influence from Mainland, in Taiwan's widely used Minnan dialect, similar usage patterns can be observed for the semantic category of "*jǐnzhāng*". For example, "卖紧张啦, 我就还没讲煞哩。" (Don't be nervous, I haven't finished speaking yet.) reflects a usage similar to "*jípò*" in Taiwan's national language. Both convey the sense of "don't rush." These examples indicate that various Chinese language variations in Taiwan are gradually merging and becoming more similar in terms of semantic usage.

Moving forward, let's examine how the term "*jǐnzhāng*" behaves semantically when paired with different types of collocates and different semantic categories:

Based on the data in Table 4, it can be observed that in Taiwan, the most frequent collocation usage for "*jǐnzhāng*" is "Emotion + Anxiousness", totaling 391 instances. The semantic prosody of this collocation leans towards neutrality, with a significant count of 382 instances exhibiting neutral semantic prosody. This suggests that the semantic prosody of "Emotion + Anxiety" tends to be more neutral. Example (4) illustrates the emotional unease of the subject due to being in a new environment. The narrative style is relatively gentle, and it doesn't elicit an excessively negative sentiment.

(4) 刚到一个新环境, 人生地不熟的, 心中非常紧张。

    (Having just arrived in a new environment and unfamiliar with the place, I feel very nervous.)

In the usage of "Situation + Urgency", there are a total of 108 instances. Out of these 108 instances, 105 instances exhibit negative semantic prosody, which contrasts with the prevailing trend. Example (5) illustrates a situation of urgency between South Korea and North Korea, involving a political issue. The narrative style is more sensational, conveying a sense of threat and negativity. Therefore, the semantic prosody presented in this case is negative.

(5) 南北韩冲突再爆紧张情势, 冲击台湾股市, 今天开盘下跌45点。

    (The conflict between North and South Korea escalated tensions again, impacting Taiwan's stock market, which opened down 45 points today.)

Table 4. Semantic Prosody of "*jǐnzhāng*" in Taiwan by Semantic Categories and Collocate Types

Collocation Types with Semantic	Taiwan		
Emotion+ Anxiety	Neutral382	Negative 9	391
Emotion+ Urgency	Neutral 28	Negative 2	30
Situation+ Anxiety			0
Situation+ Urgency	Neutral 3	Negative 105	108
Resource+ Anxiety			0
Resource+ Urgency	Neutral 8		8
Resource+ Insufficiency Supply	Neutral 12		12
Illness+ Anxiety	Neutral 14	Negative 1	15
Illness+ Urgency	Neutral 8	Negative 2	10
Relation + Anxiety			0
Relation + Urgency	Neutral 50	Negative 4	54
Atmosphere + Anxiety	Neutral 81	Negative 3	84
Atmosphere + Urgency	Neutral 5		5
Inconsistent			2
Total			719

From the above analysis, it can be inferred that in Taiwan, the usage of the word "*jǐnzhāng*" is often paired with vocabulary related to emotions, and the predominant sense is that of "Anxiety". Across all instances, except for the "Situation + Urgency" usage, the semantic prosody leans predominantly towards neutrality.

4.5 Usage of "*Jǐnzhāng*" in Mainland

In the context of 892 examples from the Mainland, the researcher categorized them based on different collocates:

According to Table 5, it can be observed that in Mainland, the choice of collocates for "*jǐnzhāng*" mainly revolves around "Situation", often used to describe political situations or differences in stance between two entities. For instance, in the sentence "非洲跨境的水资源争端不断凸显,乍得湖的缩减引起周边国家局势的紧张。" (The ongoing disputes over transboundary water resources in Africa have continuously highlighted tensions in the surrounding countries' situations), the term "*jǐnzhāng*" is used to modify the situation of countries, reflecting its collocation under the category of "Situation". The collocates used in Mainland for the term "*jǐnzhāng*" appear more diverse, without concentrating on any single collocate. The distribution of semantic prosody for different collocate categories is shown in the following figure:

Table 5. Distribution of Collocates for "*jǐnzhāng*" Usage in Mainland

Collocation Type	Mainland	
Emotion	181	20.29%
Situation	215	24.10%
Resource	208	23.32%
Illness	43	4.82%
Relation	62	6.95%
Atmosphere	184	20.52%
Total	893	100%

Table 6. Distribution of Semantic Prosody for "*jǐnzhāng*" in Mainland

Semantic	Mainland	
Anxiety	193	21.64%
Urgency	493	55.16%
Insufficiency Supply	207	23.20%
Total	893	100%

In Table 6, it can be observed that in Mainland, the term "*jǐnzhāng*" is used with three main semantic senses: "Anxiety", "Urgency", and "Insufficient supply". The usage of the first two senses is similar to that in Taiwan, while the usage of "Insufficient supply" is specific to Mainland. For instance, "到了下班高峰期，来往车辆多，车位比较紧张。"(During peak hours after getting off work, there are many vehicles and parking spaces are tight.) Reflects the sense of "Insufficient supply" when describing a shortage of parking spaces during rush hours. From the data, it can be inferred that the most common semantic sense for "*jǐnzhāng*" in Mainland is "Urgency". The researcher attributes this to the influence of the types of collocates the term is paired with. Furthermore, the analysis of the semantic prosody of "*jǐnzhāng*" when paired with different collocate types and semantic senses will be discussed.

Based on the data in Table 7, it can be observed that the most common collocate usage in Mainland is "Situation + Urgency", totaling 210 instances. Out of these 210 instances, 203 instances present negative semantic prosody. For instance, in Example (6), the emergent situation between Japan and Mainland is discussed in a politically related context. The narrative style is intense and often includes explanations for the occurrence, which creates a sense of oppression and negativity in the reader. Therefore, the resulting semantic prosody in this context is negative.

(6) 日中关系正面临严重困难。特别是围绕钓鱼岛问题，两国关系持续紧张。

Table 7. Semantic Prosody of "*jǐnzhāng*" in Mainland by Semantic Categories and Collocate Types

Collocation Types with Semantic	Mainland		
Emotion+ Anxiety	Neutral 167	Negative 3	170
Emotion+ Urgency	Neutral 11		11
Situation+ Anxiety	Neutral 1	Negative 4	5
Situation+ Urgency	Neutral 7	Negative 23	210
Resource+ Anxiety			0
Resource+ Urgency	Neutral 2		2
Resource+ Insufficiency Supply	Neutral 200	Negative 6	206
Illness+ Anxiety	Neutral 10		10
Illness+ Urgency	Neutral 33		33
Relation + Anxiety			0
Relation + Urgency	Neutral 56	Negative 6	62
Atmosphere + Anxiety	Neutral 14	Negative 3	17
Atmosphere + Urgency	Neutral 154	Negative 13	167
Inconsistent			0
Total			893

(Relations between Japan and China are facing serious difficulties. Especially around the Diaoyu Islands issue, relations between the two countries continue to be tense.)

In the context of "Resource + Insufficient supply", it also appears frequently with a total of 206 instances. Among these 206 instances, 200 instances exhibit neutral semantic prosody. For instance, in example sentence (7), the discussion pertains to a shortage of funds, a topic related to resources. The narrative style is relatively straightforward, and although there might be a slightly negative connotation, the sentence lacks strong cues that would significantly shift the semantic prosody toward negativity. Thus, it is classified as having neutral semantic prosody.

The researcher also observed that when degree adverbs like "*fēicháng*"(very) or "*shífēn*" (extremely) are added to the collocation, it intensifies the negative atmosphere and shifts the semantic prosody from neutral to negative. For instance, in example sentence (8), the addition of a degree adverb enhances the negative connotation, resulting in a shift from a neutral to a negative semantic prosody.

(7) 房地产企业的杠杆转向居民; 去杠杆, 意味着部分企业可能出现资金紧张、经营困难。

(The leverage of real estate companies has shifted to residents; deleveraging means that some companies may experience financial constraints and operating difficulties.)

(8) 水利工程蓄水严重不足，一些城镇和乡村供水极度紧张。

(There is a serious shortage of water storage in water conservancy projects, and the water supply in some towns and villages is extremely tight.)

Based on the analysis above, it can be concluded that in Mainland, the term "*jǐnzhāng*" is frequently collocated with terms related to political situations, and the predominant semantic category is "Urgency". The usage of collocations for "*jǐnzhāng*" in the Mainland is more diverse and not concentrated in specific collocations. Notably, the usage of "Resource + Insufficient supply" is a distinct characteristic of Mainland. It is observed that the collocates that can commonly be paired with "*jǐnzhāng*" are things or resources that people can access, limited resources, or things that people can control. These collocates are often used to express a sense of insufficient supply. This type of usage is also quite common in the corpus, and the semantic prosody is generally neutral, but it can change depending on the inclusion of degree adverbs.

4.6　The Comparison of "*Jǐnzhāng*" Between Both Sides

In the previous two sections, we have gained a comprehensive understanding of the usage of the term "*jǐnzhāng*" on both sides (Taiwan and Mainland). Through Table 8, the differences in the usage of "*jǐnzhāng*" between the two sides become evident. In Taiwan, the "Anxiety" sense is more commonly used, while in Mainland, the "Urgency" sense is more prevalent. Additionally, the "Insufficiency supply" usage is specific to Mainland.

Table 8. Distribution of Semantic Senses of "*jǐnzhāng*" in Taiwan and Mainland

Semantic	Taiwan		Mainland	
Anxiety	411	57.16%	193	21.64%
Urgency	294	40.89%	493	55.16%
Insufficiency Supply	14	1.95%	207	23.20%
Total	719	100%	893	100%

In Table 9, it can be observed that in Taiwan, the usage of "*jǐnzhāng*" tends to be paired with vocabulary related to "emotion", while in Mainland, it is more often paired with vocabulary related to "Situation". The choice of collocates in Taiwan appears to be more concentrated, mainly falling within the "emotion" category. On the other hand, in Mainland, the collocates are more diverse, encompassing the "Emotion", "Situation", "Resource," and "Relation" categories, each with a significant number of instances.

Table 9. Distribution of Collocates for "*jǐnzhāng*" in Taiwan and Mainland

Collocation Type	Taiwan		Mainland	
Emotion	421	58.55%	181	20.29%
Situation	108	15.02%	215	24.10%
Resource	20	2.78%	208	23.32%
Illness	25	3.48%	43	4.82%
Relation	54	7.51%	62	6.95%
Atmosphere	89	12.38%	184	20.52%
Inconsistent	2	0.28%	0	
Total	719	100%	893	100%

Table 10 illustrates the semantic nuances of "*jǐnzhāng*" in different collocations and semantic categories between Taiwan and Mainland, highlighting both the similarities and differences in usage between the two regions:

As shown in the table, the most common collocation in Taiwan is "Emotion + Anxiety", with a predominantly neutral semantic tone. In Mainland, the most frequent collocation is "Situation + Urgent", which often carries a negative semantic tone. The similarity in negative semantic tone between the use of "Situation + Urgent" in Taiwan and the Mainland can be attributed to cultural and political factors. This collocation is often associated with political matters, which tend to have a negative connotation and contribute to the negative semantic tone observed. The usage of "*jǐnzhāng*" in the context of "Resource + Insufficient Supply" is unique to Mainland, even though there are a few instances of this usage in Taiwan. This suggests that despite regional differences, there are still similarities in the development of linguistic variations.

In terms of the usage, semantic categories, and collocations of "*jǐnzhāng*", although there are differences in habits and frequency between the two regions, the similarity lies in the expression of semantic tones. The tones are mostly neutral, but the addition of intensifying adverbs can transform the meaning into a more negative one.

Table 10. Semantic Nuances of "*jǐnzhāng*" in Different Semantic Categories and Collocations between Taiwan and Mainland

Collocation Types with Semantic	Taiwan			Mainland		
Emotion+ Anxiety	Neutral382	Negative 9	391	Neutral 167	Negative 3	170
Emotion+ Urgency	Neutral 28	Negative 2	30	Neutral 11		11
Situation+ Anxiety			0	Neutral 1	Negative 4	5
Situation+ Urgency	Neutral 3	Negative 105	108	Neutral 7	Negative 23	210
Resource+ Anxiety			0			0
Resource+ Urgency	Neutral 8		8	Neutral 2		2
Resource+ Insufficiency Supply	Neutral 12		12	Neutral 200	Negative 6	206
Illness+ Anxiety	Neutral 14	Negative 1	15	Neutral 10		10
Illness+ Urgency	Neutral 8	Negative 2	10	Neutral 33		33
Relation + Anxiety			0			0
Relation + Urgency	Neutral 50	Negative 4	54	Neutral 56	Negative 6	62
Atmosphere+ Anxiety	Neutral 81	Negative 3	84	Neutral 14	Negative 3	17
Atmosphere + Urgency	Neutral 5		5	Neutral 154	Negative 13	167
Inconsistent			2			0
Total			719			893

5   The Comparison of "*Jǐnzhāng*" Between Both Sides

This study analyzed the collocation usage and semantic nuances of the word "*jǐnzhāng*" in two different regions by searching corpora. The research found that, In Taiwan, the preferred collocation words were primarily related to "Emotion" and "Situation", with a focus on the sense of "Anxiety". In Mainland, the favored collocation words were "Situation" and "Resource", though the distribution of collocation usage was more even compared to Taiwan. In terms of semantic nuances, except for the "Situation" collocation with a negative semantic tone, most usages exhibited a neutral tone. This similarity was consistent in the "Situation + Urgency" collocation, where both regions shared a similar collocation preference and semantic tone.

In summary, in Taiwan, the term "*jǐnzhāng*" is often related to the atmosphere of events, frequently combined with "Emotion," "Situation," "Atmosphere," and "Relation," to incorporate the sense of tension into sentences. In Mainland, apart from the aforementioned Taiwanese usages, there is also an additional use where the inherent meaning of tension is associated with the event itself, particularly in the context of "Resource."

This study primarily relied on semantic nuances that are closely related to native speakers' language intuition. To further validate the researcher's categorization and classification of "*jǐnzhāng*", future research could involve collecting data from native speakers in both regions through surveys. By combining substantial corpora with native speakers' language intuition, it would be possible to better verify the accuracy of the researcher's categorization and classification in reflecting actual usage patterns.

Acknowledgements. This study is supported by the National Science and Technology Council, Taiwan, R.O.C., under Grant no. MOST 110–2511-H-003 -034 -MY3. It is also supported by National Taiwan Normal University's Chinese Language and Technology Center. The center is funded by Taiwan's Ministry of Education (MOE), as part of the Featured Areas Research Center Program, under the Higher Education Sprout Project.

References

1. Qian, W.: A review of research on vocabulary differences across the Taiwan Strait. Mod. Chin. **36**, 14–16 (2015). (in Chinese)
2. Hong, J., Huang, C.: A corpus-based approach to the discovery of cross-strait lexical contrasts. Lang. Linguist. **9**(2), 221–238 (2008). (in Chinese)
3. Wang, B., Shi, X.: On detection of synonyms between simplified Chinese of Mainland China and traditional Chinese of Taiwan: a semantic similarity method. In: Lu, Q., Gao, H. (eds.) Chinese Lexical Semantics. CLSW 2015. LNCS, vol. 9332, pp. 91–100. Springer, Cham (2015). https://doi.org/10.1007/978-3-319-27194-1_10
4. Zhu, J.: Ci Hui Zhi Lu. Cheng Chung Book Co., Ltd. (2017). (in Chinese)
5. Tseng, P.: Perceiving the evolution and difference of culture between cross-strait from the use of characters and vocabulary of sinology. J. Chin. Lang. Teach. **6**(1), 110–113 (2009). (in Chinese)
6. Diao, Y.: Cha Yi Yu Rong he. Jiangxi Education Publishing House (2000). (in Chinese)
7. Hong, J., Huang, C.: Cross-strait lexical differences: a comparative study based on Chinese Gigaword corpus. Int. J. Comput. Linguist. Chin. Lang. Process. **18**(2), 19–34 (2013). (in Chinese)
8. Diao, Y.: Differences between Mainland and Taiwanese words and their causes. Magdiction **97**, 7–39 (2015). (in Chinese)

9. Louw, W.E.: Irony in the text or insincerity in the writer? — the diagnostic potential of semantic prosodies. In: Text and Technology: In Honour of John Sinclair, pp. 157–176 (1993). https://doi.org/10.1075/z.64.11lou
10. Wang, L.: The application of semantic prosody research in synonym analysis. J. Normal Univ. **23**(3), 84–87 (2008). (in Chinese)
11. Chen, C.: The semantic prosody of pro-verb Gao "do" in cross-strait varieties between modern Chinese. J. Chin. Lang. Teach. **11**(3), 91–110 (2014). (in Chinese)
12. Stubbs, M.: Collocations and semantic profiles. Funct. Lang. **2**(1), 23–55 (1995). https://doi.org/10.1075/fol.2.1.03stu
13. Louw, B.: Contextual prosodic theory: bringing semantic prosodies to life. Words in Context: A Tribute to John Sinclair on His Retirement (2000)
14. Chen, F.J.: Contrastive Analysis & Its Applications in Language Pedagogy. Crane Publishing Co., Ltd., Taipei City (2008). (in Chinese)
15. Firth, J.R.: Papers in Linguistics 1934–1951. Oxford University Press, London (1957)

A Corpus-Based Comparative Study on the Semantics and Collocations of *meili* and *piaoliang*

Ka Hei Szeto and Yike Yang[✉] [iD]

Hong Kong Shue Yan University, Braemar Hill, Hong Kong
{khszeto,yyang}@hksyu.edu

Abstract. This study demonstrates the importance of corpora in the identification of near-synonyms through a comparative analysis of the near-synonyms 美麗 *meili* 'beautiful' and 漂亮 *piaoliang* 'beautiful'. Chinese Word Sketch (CWS) was used to analyse the frequency, common patterns and only patterns of this pair of near-synonyms. Comparison of word meanings, sentence components, and word collocations was carried out. It has been found that when females are the sentence subject, they generally tend to be described as *meili*. Moreover, when used as a modifier, *meili* is more suitable than *piaoliang* in describing nouns that: 1) have broader meanings; 2) have a wider range of local words; and 3) can indicate places.

Keywords: Lexical Semantics · Corpus · Synonyms · Collocations

1 Introduction

Synonyms have been a topic of interest in the academic community. The teachers or writers may not always find the appropriate answers when comparing synonyms as it is impossible for the dictionaries to include all synonyms. Additionally, the lack of sufficient language data makes it difficult for scholars to analyse synonyms. The development of computer science has led to the emergence of large-scale corpora. In addition to their function in retrieving linguistic data, corpora also contain different levels of linguistic information, such as information about parts of speech. More scholars are using corpora to conduct linguistic research of various subfields as corpora provide massive and authentic data for linguistic analysis. Using corpus data, this article compares the synonyms 美麗 *meili* 'beautiful' and 漂亮 *piaoliang* 'beautiful' and demonstrates the importance of corpora in distinguishing synonyms.

1.1 Research on Synonyms

The statement that "near-synonyms are an important part of synonyms" remains controversial because some scholars believe that true synonyms do not exist. Regarding research on the scope of synonyms, Zhou [1] (p. 10) pointed out that "the so-called sameness or similarity of synonyms is usually referred to within a certain range of

M. Dong et al. (Eds.): CLSW 2023, LNAI 14515, pp. 392–404, 2024.
https://doi.org/10.1007/978-981-97-0586-3_30

scope, that is, one or more particular senses within a semantic field." Therefore, the distinction of synonyms often involves comparing the semantic fields, in order to observe the subtle differences between them. As for the nature of synonyms themselves, Zhou [1] showed that it is impossible to have a group of words that are completely identical in terms of word formation, semantics, and pragmatics.

1.2 Corpora in Linguistic Research

Huang and Wang [2] pointed out that corpus-based linguistic research has achieved fruitful results in recent years, with large-scale corpora becoming the premise and main tool for dictionary compilation. Dictionaries compiled based on bilingual corpora make sure that the word senses and syntactic information are verified by authentic language data, ensuring reliability and accuracy. In recent years, an increasing number of scholars have been studying the distinctions between synonymous words using corpus data. For instance, Huang, Qin and Wang [3] conducted research on a pair of synonymous verbs in Chinese, "*ren3*" and "*shou4*", and examined their semantic representations related to the concept of tolerance.

In addition, Fu [4] has analysed the synonymous words "*meili*" and "*piaoliang*" through corpus exploration. He found that there is a close interaction between semantic features, syntactic functions, and lexical collocations, and further concluded that "*meili*" and "*piaoliang*" have different tendencies in four semantic features: [±dynamic], [±abstract], [±essential], and [±distinctive]. On the one hand, this proves the inseparable relationship between semantics, lexical collocations and syntax. On the other hand, it also provides important directions for distinguishing this pair of synonymous words. However, due to the underdevelopment of corpora at that time and the lack of support from large data, the analysis in the article did not cover all situations. For example, this article believes that further discussion and supplementation can be made regarding the [±distinctive] feature.

2 Research Methods

The data reported in this study were collected from the Beijing Language University BCC Corpus (the BCC Corpus) [5], the Peking University CCL Corpus (the CCL Corpus) [6], and the Sinica Balanced Corpus of Modern Chinese (the Sinica Corpus) [7]. The Chinese Word Sketch Engine [8] was then used to analyse the semantic contrast, syntactic function contrast, and collocation contrast of "*meili*" and "*piaoliang*" to demonstrate their differences.

2.1 Introduction to the Corpora

With billions of words, the BCC Corpus is an online system for research on linguistic ontology and language applications. The CCL Corpus is mainly used for analysing linguistic phenomena in Modern Chinese and conducting comparative studies with corpora of other languages. The Sinica Corpus is the world's first balanced corpus of Chinese with complete part-of-speech tagging, which supports selecting target words from different features.

2.2 Data Analysis

This study mainly compares and analyses the synonymous words "*meili*" and "*piaoliang*" with the data obtained from the aforementioned corpora and the "Word Sketch Difference" function of the Chinese Word Sketch Engine. The interface used is shown in Fig. 1.

Word Sketch Differences Entry Form

Corpus:	gigaword2all ∨
First lemma:	美麗
Second lemma:	漂亮
Sort grammatical relations:	☑
Separate blocks:	○ all in one block ◉ common/exclusive blocks
Minimum frequency:	5
Maximum number of items in a grammatical relation of the common block:	100
Maximum number of items in a grammatical relation of the exclusive block:	100
	Show Diff

Fig. 1. User interface of the Word Sketch Differences Entry Form.

By selecting "Show Diff", we can obtain the analysis results as shown in Fig. 2. The greener a word appears, the higher the likelihood of it being paired with "*meili*". Similarly, the redder a word appears, the higher the likelihood of it being paired with "*piaoliang*". Through this comparative analysis system, we can transform the usage of words into data for comparison, thereby exploring the similarities and differences in the semantics and collocations of "*meili*" and "*piaoliang*".

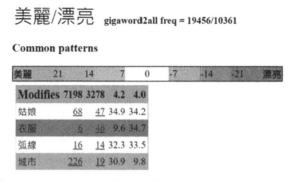

美麗/漂亮 gigaword2all freq = 19456/10361

Common patterns

美麗	21	14	7	0	-7	-14	-21	漂亮
Modifies	7198	3278	4.2	4.0				
姑娘		68		47	34.9	34.2		
衣服		6		16	9.6	34.7		
弧線		16		14	32.3	33.5		
城市		226		19	30.9	9.8		

Fig. 2. Result page of the Chinese Lexical Characteristics Sketch System.

3   Results and Discussion

3.1   Main Findings

From Table 1, the frequency of *"meili"* and *"piaoliang"* in the BCC corpus and CCL corpus is similar, but there is a significant difference in distribution in the Sinica corpus. This is likely due to the size and distribution of the corpus itself. On one hand, compared to the BCC corpus and CCL corpus, the Sinica corpus is smaller in size, so the coverage of the collected data is far less than the former two. For example, the Sinica corpus is mainly divided into four genres in terms of spoken materials (i.e. scripts, conversations, speeches, and meeting records), while the BCC corpus is derived from Weibo[1] and is a better reflection of modern colloquial Chinese in terms of the source material. On the other hand, the Sinica corpus tends to focus on traditional literary works, so it is limited by the smaller range of content sources. As mentioned above, the BCC corpus has a larger amount of data, and it is evident that both words are frequently used by people, so the differences between the two are worth further investigation.

Table 1. Frequency of *"meili"* and *"piaoliang"* in three corpora.

Corpus	*meili*	*piaoliang*	Proportion of *meili/piaoliang*
BCC	106153	109680	0.97
CCL	17694	14461	1.22
Sinica	656	361	1.82
Average	41501	41500.6	1.34

From the analysis of Chinese Word Sketch, we can obtain not only the common patterns of these two words, but also their unique patterns. The words listed all can be paired with both *"meili"* and *"piaoliang"*. It is worth noting that although they can be paired, they have different tendencies. The greener a word appears, the more likely it is to be paired with *"meili"*. Similarly, the redder a word appears, the more likely it is to be paired with *"piaoliang"*. Table 2 lists the shared words that tend to be the sentential subjects of *"meili"* and *"piaoliang"*, namely, *"meili"* and *"piaoliang"* serve as the predicates of the sentences in this case. Table 3 presents the shared words that tend to be the heads of the noun phrases that are modified by *"meili"* and *"piaoliang"*. As shown in Tables 2 and 3, *"meili"* and *"piaoliang"* share many words that can be paired with them, indicating their similarity to each other. However, one should not ignore the fact that there are still many words that can only be paired with each of them separately, which will be demonstrated in the following.

Table 4 lists the unique patterns of the words that can only be paired with *"meili"* or *"piaoliang"*. The listed subjects and head nouns indicate that *"meili"* is used to pair with concrete and identifiable people and things, such as "women", "we", "ourselves", etc., while *"piaoliang"* is used to pair with "people", "balls", or "actions".

---

[1] Weibo a Chinese microblogging website.

Table 2. Common patterns of "*meili*" and "*piaoliang*" (Subject).

meili 21 14 7 0	-7	-14	-21	*piaoliang*
Subject	299	235	1.1	1.8
女人 (Woman)	6	0	19.6	0.0
青春 (Youth)	6	0	19.2	0.0
風景 (Scenery)	6	0	17.4	0.0
球 (Ball)	0	7	0.0	16.0
動作 (Action)	0	6	0.0	15.2
她 (She)	10	0	14.3	0.0
自己 (Oneself)	9	0	12.5	0.0
我 (I)	7	0	12.2	0.0
我們 (We)	7	0	11.6	0.0
建設 (Building)	7	0	7.5	0.0

Table 3. Common patterns of "*meili*" and "*piaoliang*" (Modifier).

meili 21 14 7 0					-7	-14	-21	*piaoliang*			
Modifies	7198	3278	4.2	4.0	**Modifies**	7198	3278	4.2	4.0
姑娘 (Girl)	68	47	34.9	34.2	服裝 (Clothes)	12	23	10.9	20.1
衣服 (Clothes)	6	46	9.6	34.7	小姐 (MIss)	15	16	15.2	19.0
弧線 (Curve)	16	14	32.3	33.5	少女 (Girl)	18	7	17.7	12.0
城市 (City)	226	19	30.9	9.8	句號 (Full stop)	6	6	15.0	17.2
女孩 (Girl)	12	22	17.3	27.4	模特兒 (Model)	9	5	16.9	13.7
圖案 (Pattern)	36	6	27.0	11.8	女性 (Female)	24	6	14.5	7.1
女人 (Woman)	27	16	25.5	22.8	服飾 (Apparel)	8	8	11.9	14.4
建築 (Building)	6	47	3.5	22.8	妻子 (Wife)	6	6	6.8	9.0
公園 (Park)	71	10	22.3	8.4	照片 (Photograph)	8	5	8.0	7.4
地方 (Place)	136	13	22.2	6.0	廣場 (Plaza)	10	7	7.4	7.7
口號 (Slogan)	15	16	17.6	21.4	她 (She)	8	8	2.3	4.8
名字 (Name)	27	7	20.8	11.3	女子 (Woman)	6	5	2.5	3.8

Table 4. Unique patterns of "*meili*" and "*piaoliang*".

Unique patterns of "*meili*"

Modifies	7198	4.2
風 光 (Scenery)	153	49.32
花 朵 (Flowers)	75	49.05
景 色 (View)	67	44.36
寶 島 (Treasure Island (referring to Taiwan))	71	43.46
西 子 湖 (Xizi Lake (a famous lake in Hangzhou, China))	28	41.54
傳 說 (Legend)	60	38.99
風 景 (Landscape)	99	38.66
大 腳 (Bigfoot)	20	38.58
夜 景 (Night view)	37	38.43

Subject	299	1.1
女 人 (Woman)	6	19.6
青 春 (Youth)	6	19.18
風 景 (Landscape)	6	17.4
她 (She)	10	14.31
自 己 (Oneself)	9	12.49
我 (Me)	7	12.22
我們 (We)	7	11.6
建 設 (Building)	7	7.5

Unique patterns of "*piaoliang*"

Modifies	3278	4.0
成 績 單 (transcript)	310	73.17
勝 仗 (Victory)	62	57.78
弧 線 球 (Curveball)	26	48.88
穿 越 球 (Slider)	20	43.52
任 意 球 (Free kick (in sports))	49	43.05
衣 服 (Clothes)	46	34.68
全 壘 打 (Home run (in sports))	36	34.52
姑 娘 (Girl)	47	34.23
球 (Ball)	89	34.12
本 壘 打 (Home run)	12	33.68

Subject	235	1.8
球 (Ball)	7	16.05
動 作 (Action)	6	15.2
人 (Person)	5	4.97

3.2 Similarities Between "*meili*" and "*piaoliang*"

In terms of word collocation, "*meili*" and "*piaoliang*" have similarities when used as attributive modifiers for nouns. When describing females such as "girls", "women", "misses", "young girls", "models", "wives", items like "photos" and places like "squares", they have similar frequencies. This indicates that when they are used as attributive modifiers for these nouns, their functions are very similar. We can refer to the more extensive BCC corpus for richer information. In the BCC corpus, retrieving word collocations can be achieved by using "specific word + part of speech symbol". For example, searching for "打掃n" (cleaning + noun) can retrieve all instances where "打掃" is followed by a noun. The following data was obtained by using the comparative function to search for "美麗的n" (*meili* + *de* + noun) and "漂亮的n" (*piaoliang* + *de* + noun).

Table 5 suggests that "*meili*" and "*piaoliang*" are frequently used as attributive modifiers for the nouns "women", "girls", "eyes" and "faces". Obviously, both are commonly used to express outstanding beauty and appearance, so in terms of word collocation, "*meili*" and "*piaoliang*" are often used as attributive modifiers to describe the beauty of women.

Table 5. Top ten high-frequency words used as adjectives to modify nouns.

Ranking	1	2	3	4	5
美麗的 (meili)	女人 (Woman) 1310	風景 (Landscape) 673	地方 (Place) 599	眼睛 (Eyes) 514	姑娘 (Girl) 485
漂亮的 (piaoliang)	女人 (Woman) 1170	姑娘 (Girl) 497	女孩子 (Girl) 381	女孩 (Girl) 381	人 (Person) 370
Ranking	6	7	8	9	10
美麗的 (meili)	女子 (Women) 475	城市 (City) 466	臉 (Face) 447	花 (Flowers) 377	臉龐 (countenance) 372
漂亮的 (piaoliang)	衣服 (Clothes) 315	眼睛 (Eyes) 303	臉蛋 (Face) 278	小姐 (Woman) 236	臉 (Face) 214

According to the search results from Chinese Wordnet [9], the words "*meili*" and "*piaoliang*" express the same meaning in one of their senses. From Table 6, it can be seen that in one of the semantic features, both words share the same part of speech, definition, semantic relationship, and even English translation. This can be further illustrated by comparing the example sentences provided:

1. 當年, 你媽咪是一流演員, 長得又甜蜜又<u>漂亮</u>。
   Back then, your mom was a top-notch actress, who's sweet and beautiful.
2. 當年, 你媽咪是一流演員, 長得又甜蜜又<u>美麗</u>。
   Back then, your mom was a top-notch actress, who's sweet and beautiful.

From the analysis of Sentences 1 and 2, both words have the semantic meaning of describing a good-looking appearance. There is no semantic difference when interchanging the two words, so it can be concluded that "*meili*" and "*piaoliang*" have no distinction in this aspect of meaning. From a syntactic perspective, both "*meili*" and "*piaoliang*" can be used as attributive modifiers for subjects and objects, as complements, and as

Table 6. Shared Semantic Features of *meiling* and *piaoliang*.

Word	Part of speech	Definition	Semantic relationship	English translation
meili	intransitive verb, VH	To describe the appearance of a person or thing as good-looking, bringing pleasure and admiration to the viewers	Synonyms include "*piaoliang*" and antonyms include '醜' (ugly)	beautiful
piaoliang	intransitive verb, VH	To describe the appearance of a person or thing as good-looking, bringing pleasure and admiration to the viewers	Synonyms include "*meili*" and antonyms include '醜' (ugly)	beautiful

predicates indicating the state of the subject. This can be illustrated by Sentences 3, 4, 5, 6, 7, and 8.

As an attributive modifier:

3. 一匹駿馬、一頭肥牛, 還有一張美麗的毛毯。
   A spirited horse, a fat cow, and a beautiful blanket.
4. 突然覺得怎麼在學校三年卻沒看過這麼漂亮的女孩子。
   Suddenly I felt that I had never seen such a beautiful girl in school for three years.

In Sentences 3 and 4, "*meili*" and "*piaoliang*" are used as attributive modifiers to modify "毛毯" (blanket) and "女孩子" (girl). Referring to Tables 2 and 3, this situation is more common, so they often appear together with the nouns of the subject and object.

As a complement:

5. 説什麼去整容可以使自己更美麗。
   Saying that getting plastic surgery can make oneself more beautiful.
6. 我和城北的徐公比起來, 誰長得漂亮?
   Compared to Mr. Xu from the north of the city, who looks more beautiful?

In Sentences 5 and 6, "*meili*" and "*piaoliang*" are used as predicative complements to complement the result or state of "使" (make) and "長" (look), explaining the characteristics of the action. For example, Sentence 5 supplements how getting plastic surgery can make someone more beautiful.

As a predicate:

7. 有人説女人像春天, 看似溫柔美麗卻又捉摸不定。

Some people say that women are like spring, seemingly gentle and beautiful yet unpredictable.

8. 就如我們現在看天上，白雲飄飄很漂亮。

Just like how we look at the sky now, the floating white clouds are very beautiful.

Sentences 7 and 8 suggest that both "*meili*" and "*piaoliang*" can be used as predicates to describe the state or characteristics of the subject. In Sentence 7, "*meili*" serves as a predicate to describe the appearance or inner qualities of the subject "女人" (women), and in Sentence 8, "*piaoliang*" is used as a predicate to describe the appearance of the subject "白雲" (white clouds).

The above is an analysis and summary of the similarities between "*meili*" and "*piaoliang*".

3.3 Differences Between "*meili*" and "*piaoliang*"

Semantic Contrasts. Referring to the search results from Chinese Wordnet as listed in Table 7, we can see that the word "*meili*" has one more sense than "*piaoliang*". In addition to being an intransitive verb, "*meili*" can also be nominalised and serve as a noun to explain both Senses 1 and 3.

Table 7. Comparison of the Meanings of "*meili*" and "*piaoliang*"

word	definition 1	definition 2	definition 3
meili	intransitive verb, VH; noun, nom To describe the appearance of a person or thing as good-looking, bringing pleasure and admiration to the viewers	Intransitive verb, VH describes metaphorically a kind-hearted nature	Intransitive verb, VH, VH; noun, nom Describes metaphors that can evoke pleasant emotions in others
piaoliang	intransitive verb, VH To describe the appearance of a person or thing as good-looking, bringing pleasure and admiration to the viewers	Intransitive verb, VH describes something being done exceptionally well or with skill	

Although "*piaoliang*" can also express the meaning of Sense 1, it cannot function as a noun. This can be illustrated by sentence 9:

9. 要你放下慣有的武裝和面具，一起來享受春天的美麗。

Let go of your usual armor and masks, and come enjoy the beauty (*meili*) of spring.

From this, "*meili*" can still convey the meaning of something visually appealing and delightful when used as a noun, specifically referring to the unique beauty of spring.

On the other hand, although "*piaoliang*" also has a similar meaning, it cannot replace "*meili*" in both sentences. Interchanging them would result in semantic and syntactic inconsistencies, as "*piaoliang*" lacks the modified subject, such as "景緻" (scenery) or "景色" (view), making the sentences invalid.

When "*meili*" is used as an intransitive verb, it can also be interpreted with the same meaning. This can be exemplified by Sentence 10:

10. 你用棋子創造出美麗的難題，而這種美是用大腦和雙手創造出來的。

You create beautiful (*meili*) puzzles with chess pieces, and this beauty is created with the mind and hands.

Clearly, the "*meili*" here does not describe a visually dazzling appearance, but rather refers to the pleasure and excitement generated by such a chess situation, which can make chess players eager and excited. Although "*piaoliang*" can be substituted in this context, the overall meaning and emphasis would be completely different, shifting towards praising the cleverness of the arrangement, resembling the meaning of Sense 2 of "*piaoliang*". Therefore, "*piaoliang*" cannot replace "*meili*" in expressing the metaphorical meaning of evoking pleasant emotions in others.

As for the second sense of "*piaoliang*", we can illustrate it with Sentence 11:

11. 一個漂亮的棋局是靠棋手與對手相互揣測、積極互動地建構出來。

A beautiful chess game is constructed through players and opponents speculating and actively interacting with each other.

As mentioned above, "*piaoliang*" can also mean praising someone's skill in doing something. Here, it indicates that both players have exceptional chess skills, resulting in a closely contested and exciting game. Clearly, this cannot be replaced by "*meili*".

Syntactic Functions. The previous section has already mentioned the similarities between the two. Here, we mainly discuss their differences in terms of sentence functions. The discussion on semantic differences has already been covered, so we will expand on it here. "*meili*" can function as a noun, while "*piaoliang*" cannot. This means that "*meili*" can be used as a subject or object in a sentence. Let us take Sentences 12 and 13 as examples:

12. 美麗是用錢堆出來的。

Beauty is created with money.

13. 一開始思考心靈的奧祕，發現宇宙蘊含的美麗。

At first, contemplating the mysteries of the soul, I discovered the beauty contained in the universe.

In Sentence 12, "*meili*" functions as the subject and is further defined by the predicate "用錢堆出來的" (created with money). In Sentence 13, "*meili*" functions as the object and is the target of the main verb "發現" (discovered). Apart from being modified by attributive or predicative phrases to modify the subject and object, "*meili*" can also appear in connection with predicates. As a subject, it is often connected with linking verbs to connect the subject and object. As an object, it is more commonly used with sensory verbs expressing visual perception, such as "發現" (discover) or "探索" (explore). This shows the differences between the two in terms of their syntactic functions.

Collocaions. Referring to Table 2, when it comes to the subject, phrases with "女人" (woman), "青春" (youth), "風景" (scenery), and "她" (she) are only paired with "*meili*". On the other hand, sentences with actions or balls as subjects are only paired with "*piaoliang*".

Common collocations with "*meili*":

女人最美麗 (the most beautiful woman)/青春美麗 (youthful and beautiful) /風景美麗 (scenery is beautiful)/她美麗的 (her beautiful).

Common collocations with "*piaoliang*":

動作漂亮 (movements are graceful)/人長的漂亮 (this person is good-looking)/甚為漂亮 (quite beautiful) /比較漂亮 (comparatively beautiful).

Referring to Table 3, in terms of attributive usage, as mentioned earlier, "*meili*" (beautiful) and "*piaoliang*" are more commonly used as attributive descriptions of female beauty, and their frequencies are relatively similar in these contexts. It is worth noting that in the two extremes, the word "衣服" (clothing) is mostly modified by "*piaoliang*", while "城市" (city) is predominantly modified by "*meili*", far exceeding the frequency of "*piaoliang*". This is reflected in language patterns, where "*piaoliang*" is rarely used to describe "城市" (city), and "*meili*" is almost never used to describe "衣服" (clothing). Furthermore, upon further analysis, we can observe an interesting phenomenon where "*piaoliang*" is rarely used to describe "城市" (city), but its frequency is much higher when used to describe "建築" (building), while "*piaoliang*" is still more commonly used to describe "服飾" (clothing). It seems difficult to explain this situation using the [±dynamic], [±abstract], [±essence], [±distinctiveness] framework of [4]. To explore the underlying reasons behind this phenomenon, we can start by examining the semantic interpretations of the words (Tables 8 and 9).

Table 8. Comparison of the Meanings of "City" and "Building"

Word	Definition
城市 (city)	Common noun. A region where population is concentrated, typically serving as the political, economic, cultural, and transportation center of its surrounding area
建築 (building)	Common noun. Man-made structures designed for human activities, commonly known as houses

It is evident that the scale and scope of "城市" (city) in describing places where people engage in activities are much larger than that of "建築" (building), the latter of which is a general term for human-made structures. For the term "城市" (city), its meaning is broad from the description of an area where people gather, and it typically includes the political, economic, cultural, and transportation centres of the surrounding region. Based on this observation, this paper hypothesises that when describing nouns with broader or larger meanings, "*meili*" is more suitable than "*piaoliang*". To verify this hypothesis, we can further analyse other location-related nouns in Table 3 or nouns that represent places, such as "廣場" (square), "地方" (place), and "公園" (park). The frequency of usage for both "廣場" (square) and "地方" (place) is very similar, so they cannot serve as a good basis for comparison.

Table 9. Comparison of the meanings of "城市" (city) and "建築" (building).

Word	Definition
地方 (Place)	Common noun. A regional area described by specific characteristics or with a specific location as a reference point
公園 (Park)	Place words. Public spaces within a city that provide outdoor leisure activities for the general public

The term "地方" (place) has a broader and more abstract meaning, and does not specifically refer to a particular location or area. "公園" (park) usually has a larger scope, generally larger than individual residences or buildings, and is oriented towards the public, serving as a public space that accommodates a large number of people. However, it is difficult to summarise parks in terms of [±abstract] or [±essence]. Based on the similarities between these terms and the term "城市" (city), this further confirms the hypothesis of this paper. For terms related to places or nouns that express a sense of place, those with a larger scope or broader meaning are more commonly described as "*meili*", such as "美麗的藍色星球" (beautiful blue planet), "美麗的都會" (beautiful metropolis), "美麗的島嶼" (beautiful island), etc. Terms with a smaller scope are more frequently described as "*piaoliang*", such as "漂亮的住所" (beautiful residence), "漂亮的房間" (beautiful room), "漂亮的衣帽間" (beautiful dressing room), etc. In addition to the findings from Fu (2009), this paper believes that as an attributive, "*meili*" is more commonly used to describe nouns with a broader meaning or larger scope compared to "*piaoliang*". Common collocations for "*meili*" include "美麗的城市" (beautiful city), "美麗的公園" (beautiful park), "美麗的地方" (beautiful place), "美麗的風光" (beautiful scenery). Common collocations for "*piaoliang*" include "漂亮的成績單" (beautiful report card), "漂亮的勝仗" (beautiful victory), "漂亮的全壘打" (beautiful home run), "漂亮的球" (beautiful ball).

4   Conclusion

This paper analysed the synonyms "*meili*" and "*piaoliang*" from three aspects: the comparison of meanings, their roles as sentence components, and collocation patterns. By examining their similarities and differences, this study demonstrates that even though these two words are closely related, they are not completely identical in terms of word formation, semantics, and pragmatics. It is worth noting that "*meili*" and "*piaoliang*" have the same sentence (beautiful) when they are used as attributive adjectives to describe the appearance of people or things. However, through the analysis of corpus data, this study has two main findings: first, when women are the subject, "*meili*" is commonly used, while "*piaoliang*" is more frequently used to pair with objects and actions; second, as attributive adjectives, the frequency of use for both terms is very close when describing feminine nouns, but "*meili*" is more suitable for describing nouns with broader meanings or larger-scale place nouns.

References

1. Zhou, Y.: Review of research on synonymous words in modern Chinese. J. Ningxia Univ. **5**, 9–13 (2002). (in Chinese)
2. Huang, S., Wang, D.: A review of domestic corpus research. J. Inf. Resour. Manag. **3**, 4–17 (2021). (in Chinese)
3. Huang, C., Qin, P., Wang, X.: Active and passive expressions of tolerance: a semantic analysis of the near-synonyms ren3 and shou4 based on MARVS theory. In: Su, Q., Xu, G., Yang, X. (eds.) CLSW 2022. LNCS, vol 13495, pp. 42–51. Springer, Cham (2023). https://doi.org/10.1007/978-3-031-28953-8_4
4. Fu, K.C.: A Look at "Meili" and "Piaoliang" from the perspective of semantic features and grammatical functions. Teach. Chin. Second Lang. **7**, 33–39 (2009). https://doi.org/10.7083/TCASL.200912.0033(inChinese)
5. Xun, E., Rao, G., Xiao, X., Zang, J.: The development of BCC corpus under the background of big data. Corpus Linguist. **1**, 93–110 (2016). (in Chinese)
6. Zhan, W., Guo, R., Chen, Y.: Beijing University Chinese Linguistics Research Center CCL Corpus (Scale: 700 million words; Time: 11th century BC - contemporary) (2003). http://ccl.pku.edu.cn:8080/ccl_corpus. (in Chinese)
7. Chen, K.J., Huang, C.R., Chang, L.P., Hsu, H.L.: Sinica corpus: design methodology for balanced corpora. In: Park, B.S., Kim, J.B. (eds.) Proceedings of the 11th Pacific Asia Conference on Language, Information and Computation, pp. 167–176 (1996)
8. Huang, C.R., et al.: Chinese Sketch Engine and the extraction of grammatical collocations. In: Proceedings of the Fourth SIGHAN Workshop on Chinese Language Processing, pp. 48–55 (2005)
9. Huang, C.R., et al.: Chinese Wordnet: design, implementation, and application of an infrastructure for cross-lingual knowledge processing. J. Chin. Inf. Process. **24**(2), 14–23 (2010). (in Chinese)

Development of a Chinese Tourism Technical Word List Based on Corpus Analysis

Yue Xu[1], Wei Wei[1], and Zhimin Wang[2(✉)]

[1] Research Institute of International Chinese Language Education, Beijing Language and Culture University, Beijing, China

[2] Faculty of Chinese Language and Culture, Guangdong University of Foreign Studies, Guangzhou, China

wangzm000@qq.com

Abstract. "Chinese + Tourism" is an important subfield of the current research area of "Chinese +" vocational education. This article focuses on the vocational skills training of "Chinese + Tourism", targeting both domestic and foreign tourism practitioners. To accomplish this goal, a Chinese tourism corpus was constructed, and a series of methods including text classification, relevant word frequency theory, vocabulary distribution range, and term frequency-inverse document frequency were employed to design a technical word list construction process. Through human intervention, a sequenced Chinese Tourism Technical Word List (CTTWL) containing 542 words has been developed. This word list is mainly composed of nouns, verbs, and adjectives, with a coverage rate of 11.05% in domain texts. Compared to the HSK (Tourism), although its text coverage rate is 16.59%, it includes 4,674 vocabulary words. In addition, the coverage rate of CTTWL in general texts is less than 1%, indicating that the word list developed in this article covers most professional vocabulary in the text with fewer words. CTTWL can provide vocabulary references for Chinese tour guide training, and tourism Chinese skills teaching and learning.

Keywords: "Chinese+" Vocational Education · "Chinese + Tourism" · Technical Word List · International Chinese Language Education

1 Introduction

"Chinese +" vocational education in the field of "Chinese + Tourism" is currently a prominent area of research. In 2021, the United Nations World Tourism Organization (UNWTO) and the Spanish government officially announced that Chinese has become the official language of the organization, which further promoted the development of "Chinese + Tourism"[1]. In April 2023, the World Tourism Alliance released the "2023 China Outbound Tourism Market Report for the First Half of the Year", pointing out that with the orderly resumption of China's inbound and outbound tourism, China still has

---

[1] The information is sourced from the official website of Center for Language Education and Cooperation: http://www.chinese.cn/page/#/pcpage/article?id=499.

M. Dong et al. (Eds.): CLSW 2023, LNAI 14515, pp. 405–419, 2024.
https://doi.org/10.1007/978-981-97-0586-3_31

huge market potential as the world's largest source of outbound tourists[2]. Relying on China's strong population advantage, the number of Chinese citizens traveling abroad will certainly recover or even exceed pre-COVID-19 level.

Chinese citizens traveling abroad have brought huge economic and social benefits to destination countries and have greatly promoted the development of local tourism industries. Therefore, destination countries must train a group of tourism professionals who are proficient in both local languages and Chinese. In this case, "Chinese + Tourism" as a vocational education has a great practical demand. According to the requirements of vocational application scenarios, Xu [1] pointed out that learning difficulty mainly lies in vocabulary, followed by grammar and discourse. Su [2] proposed that a word list is a list of words that can meet the needs of different learners.

Therefore, developing a Chinese Tourism Technical Word List (CTTWL) with reasonable word selection, appropriate size, based on refined corpora, and selected using scientific methods, can not only cultivate the talent needed for "Chinese + Tourism" vocational education and skills training but also improve the vocational education teaching system and ensure teaching quality.

Currently, there is ample research on word lists for Teaching Chinese as a Second Language, such as business [3], medicine [4], economics and trade [5], applied science and technology majors [6], and so on. However, the development of word lists for the tourism field is relatively lagging. Existing tourism word lists mainly include the HSK (Tourism) Common Word List [7], the Tourism Chinese Topic Word List [8], and the Teaching Chinese as a Foreign Language Tourism Word List [9].

The existing tourism word lists provide useful references for subsequent research, but there are still some problems. First, the service objects and functions of the word lists are not the same, and relevant research focused on vocational skills training is still blank. Second, the methods for compiling the word lists are relatively simple and subjective, lacking systematic analysis and construction. Finally, the scale of the word lists is generally too large, and their professionalism needs to be verified. Therefore, using scientific and systematic methods to develop a Chinese Tourism Technical Word List (CTTWL) has both theoretical and practical significance.

There are many methods for word list compilation. Jin et al. [10] summarized three paradigms: "corpus-driven", "individual textbook-driven", and "specific web-driven". Li [11] and He [12] constructed word lists based on large-scale corpora, adopting certain criteria and methods for word selection. Xie [13] and Guo [14] constructed word lists based on textbook materials or reading texts by calculating their vocabulary coverage. Zhong et al. [15] and Liu [3] constructed word lists based on specific topics, connecting a word with its superordinate words, subordinate words, synonyms, etc. to help learners understand different lexical relationships. The diverse perspectives of the above studies can provide some research ideas for this paper, such as taking the corpus as the drive, using quantitative indicators as the method, emphasizing the semantic association and illustration of vocabulary when constructing the word list, and so on.

This study constructs a word list based on corpus and quantitative methods. The remaining chapters of the article are arranged as follows: Part 2 focuses on introducing

---

[2] The information is sourced from the official website of the World Tourism Alliance: https://www.wta-web.org/chn.

the corpus and methods used in the development of the word list. Part 3 focuses on providing a detailed overview of the specific process involved in developing the word list. Part 4 compares and analyzes the word list coverage, part-of-speech distribution, and lexical level distribution of the word list. The final part concludes the study and offers prospects for future work.

2   Methodology

2.1   Corpus Construction

The corpus consists of 331 introduction texts from 306 AAAAA-level tourist attractions in China. To ensure authenticity and authority, the texts are from the official websites of each attraction and the "Public Tourism Service" platform of the Ministry of Culture and Tourism[3]. On this basis, a Chinese tourism corpus with 267,124 Chinese characters was built. To ensure the professionalism and accuracy of word list construction, the tourism texts were classified by tourist attraction types referring to a Chinese national standard document [16]. Finally, the corpus was divided into 6 sub-corpora, namely geographical attractions, geological attractions, water attractions, biological attractions, cultural attractions, and architectural attractions.

In addition, a general Chinese corpus was constructed for word list construction and effect evaluation. It consists of novels, news, popular science articles, and narrative texts, with a total of 267,198 Chinese characters.

2.2   Main Methods for Word List Construction

In developing an academic word list, Coxhead [17] considered word frequency (beyond the most frequent 2000 words), range, and frequency. Gardner & Davies [18] used frequency ratios, range, dispersion, and specificity to select target words when compiling a new academic word list. Lei & Liu [19] mainly considered minimum frequency, frequency ratio, range ratio, dispersion, and specificity when developing a medical academic word list. Laosrirattanachai & Ruangjaroon [20] proposed 6 methods for constructing word lists for tourism, aviation, and hotel fields: frequency, range, lexical profiling, lexical keyness, expert consultation, and lexical difficulty. Based on previous studies, this paper employs a combination of specific methods to construct CTTWL:

Zipf's Law. Zipf's law describes the frequency distribution of words in a corpus. Zipf [21, 22] proposed that in a word list sorted by frequency, the frequency of a word is inversely proportional to its rank. According to Zipf's law, a small number of words occur very frequently in a language and can maximize text coverage with a limited size, fully conforming to the principle of linguistic economy. Therefore, this study categorizes the words in the tourism text corpus into high-frequency words, medium-frequency words, and low-frequency words based on their frequency. The higher the frequency of a word, the more likely it is to be selected as a candidate word for the CTTWL.

---

[3] "Public Tourism Service Section" platform of the Ministry of Culture and Tourism of the People's Republic of China: https://lyfw.mct.gov.cn/site/special/home.

Frequency Ratio. Frequency ratio is a concept based on the frequency characteristics of technical vocabulary. The basic idea is that the frequency of some words in a specific domain is much higher than that in the general domain. Based on this, the frequency ratios of specific words in domain texts and general texts were calculated and repeatedly considered, and the lower limit of frequency ratio was finally determined. Suppose the frequency ratio of the word i in the domain texts is represented as R_{id}, and the word i in the general text is represented as R_{ig}, the frequency ratio of the word i can be calculated as follows:

$$R_i = \frac{R_{id}}{R_{ig}} \tag{1}$$

R_{id} is calculated by dividing the total occurrences of the word i in the domain texts by the total occurrences of words in domain texts. The calculation of R_{ig} is also the same as R_{id}.

Range. Selecting technical vocabulary should consider not only frequency but also distribution range. A word with high frequency but uneven distribution can hardly be identified as a technical term. The distribution range of words in sub-corpus was counted, and the lower limit of range value was determined based on the actual situation.

Learners' Vocabulary Cognition Level. Most learners receiving Chinese Tourism vocational training have a certain Chinese proficiency and vocabulary cognition level, especially in mastering common words. Therefore, the CTTWL targets intermediate Chinese learners, and Level 1–4 words in the vocabulary level outline in the Chinese Proficiency Grading Standards for International Chinese Language Education are excluded [23].

Part-Of-Speech (POS) Distribution. Chinese vocabulary can be divided into content words and function words. Function words mainly express grammatical meanings and are relatively close in quantity. Therefore, function words have weaker domain features. In compiling CTTWL, content words were mainly considered, with a focus on absorbing nouns, verbs, adjectives, and idioms (also including four-character phrases, and abbreviations).

Term Frequency-Inverse Document Frequency (TF-IDF). TF-IDF is a classic statistical method based on word frequency. TF refers to term frequency while IDF refers to inverse document frequency. Based on the TF-IDF values, keywords can be selected. In other words, the higher the TF-IDF value of a word, the more important it is in the Chinese tourism corpus. Thus, the TF-IDF value can be used to sequence the word list based on the significance of vocabulary. Suppose that the total number of occurrences of a word i in the corpus is represented by n_i, the total number of texts is represented by N, the number of documents containing the word i is represented by m_i, and the total number of words in the corpus is represented by T, the TF-IDF value of a word can be calculated as follows:

$$tf - idf_i = \frac{n_i}{T} \times \frac{N}{m^i + 1} \tag{2}$$

where n_i / T represents the term frequency of the word in the corpus, and $N / (m_i + 1)$ represents the inverse document frequency of the word i. Multiplying these two values together yields the TF-IDF value of word i.

Human Intervention. The introduction text of an 'AAAAA' grade tourist attraction belongs to the category of informational text, which requires rich, complex, and specialized vocabulary. To ensure the accuracy and scientific nature of the CTTWL, manual intervention was conducted on the extracted vocabulary results based on the aforementioned process. The results indicate that the manual intervention has yielded good effects.

3   Compilation Process

3.1   Corpus Preprocessing

To preprocess the tourism texts corpus, including word segmentation and part-of-speech tagging, we utilized the popular Chinese text segmentation library, Jieba. Manual checking was conducted to improve accuracy. Punctuation, numbers, English words, etc. were also removed when extracting category-specific words.

3.2   Construction Process

Frequency Threshold. Word frequency was first considered in word selection. Term frequency represents the distribution level of a word within a corpus and the term frequencies of all words in the corpus exhibit certain interval variations. Thus, the frequency of each word in the corpus was calculated to determine the threshold that can distinguish high-frequency words, medium-frequency words, and low-frequency words. By analyzing the logarithmic values of word frequencies to the base 10 at corresponding ranks, the corpus word frequency distribution intervals were obtained, as shown in Fig. 1.

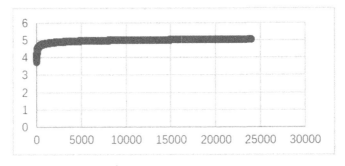

Fig. 1. Distribution of logarithmic frequency values in Chinese travel text

To gain a clearer understanding of the frequency distribution in the travel text corpus, this study calculated the cumulative percentage of word frequency in the corpus and determined the final frequency threshold based on frequency intervals, as shown in Table 1.

Table 1. Word frequency, rank, and cumulative percentage in Tourism Chinese texts

Word Rank	Frequency	Logarithm of word frequency	Cumulative Percentage
7	797	4.054498147	10%
34	268	4.356752262	20%
113	100	4.535002804	30%
284	47	4.659469322	40%
645	22	4.756050062	50%
1367	12	4.835329037	60%
1707	10	4.857471207	63.14%
2477	7	4.892350650	68.41%
2779	6	4.902285798	70%
5688	3	4.960294741	80%
9744–23979	1	5.057209513	100%

From Table 1, it can be observed that when the logarithmic frequency value is less than 4.892350650, which corresponds to a frequency less than 7, the long tail effect of words in the text becomes more pronounced, indicating a lower frequency of word usage. Therefore, this study considers a frequency of 7 as a suitable threshold to distinguish between medium-high frequency words and low-frequency words in the tourism corpus. Based on this, the study initially filtered out 2477 words with a frequency of 7 or higher from a total of 23989 vocabularies.

Frequency Ratio. The calculation of the frequency ratio utilized two corpora constructed in this study. Lei & Liu [19] set the frequency ratio to 1:1.5 when constructing a medical academic word list. Considering the research object, the frequency ratio in this study was initially set to 1:1.5, but some common words like 精彩 (1.590818724, *jingcai,* wonderful), 集中 (1.590818724, *jizhong,* focus), 特点 (1.623284412, *tedian,* distinguishing feature) were found. The ratio was then reset to 1:1.8, but common words like 您 (1.988523405, *nin,* you for polite), 教育 (1.943236122, *jiaoyu,* educate), 中国 (1.954054081, *zhongguo,* China) still occurred. Therefore, the final ratio was determined as 1:2.0, which can better distinguish technical and common words. 1,468 words that did not meet the frequency ratio were removed, leaving 1,009 candidate words.

Range Value. Six sub-corpora which be constructed based on the tourism text corpus and the relevant documents will be utilized in this part. Coxhead [17] argues that a vocabulary item should appear at least 15 times or 10 times in 28 different thematic domains, which means that the term should be present in more than half of the sub-corpora to be selected as a specialized vocabulary. Otherwise, the term is considered to have uneven distribution and therefore cannot be classified as a technical word. Similarly, in this study, the range is defined as a technical word needing to appear in at least half of the sub-corpora. After determining the range, 66 words were removed from the 1,009 candidates, leaving 943 words for the next steps.

Learners' Vocabulary Cognition Level and POS Distribution. In terms of learners' vocabulary cognition level, this article refers to the Chinese Proficiency Grading Standards for International Chinese Language Education to annotate the vocabulary in the corpus with levels. If the word is a "standard" vocabulary, the specific vocabulary level is marked; otherwise, it is marked as "non-standard vocabulary". As mentioned earlier, the target users of CTTWL are intermediate-level Chinese learners in the tourism industry and professional learners, so the vocabulary with levels 1–4 in the corpus was excluded in this study. In the end, a total of 697 vocabulary items were retained for the subsequent POS distribution filtering process.

For POS distribution, CTTWL focuses on absorbing nouns, verbs, adjectives, and idioms, while excluding numerals, classifiers, and other content words. Function words were also excluded from this study. After the POS distribution filtering process, 65 words were removed, leaving 632 for manual intervention.

Manual Intervention. To eliminate omissions and improve accuracy, manual adjustments, and optimizations were made with several considerations:

1. Deleting some monosyllabic words and morphemes with strong classical Chinese style, such as 称 (verb, *cheng*, called), 距 (verb, *ju*, be away from), 至 (verb, *zhi*, reach), 石 (morpheme, *shi*, stone), 园 (morpheme, *yuan*, garden), 筑 (morpheme, *zhu*, construct), etc.
2. Deleting some common words frequently appearing in general domains to improve professionalism and technicality, such as 展示 (*zhanshi*, show), 常年 (*changnian*, perennially), 绿树 (*lvshu*, green trees), etc.
3. Removing some condensed phrase structures appearing in tourism texts, such as 为主 (*weizhu*, give priority to), 地处 (*dichu*, located in), 建有 (*jianyou*, built), 设有 (*sheyou*, set up), 改为 (*gaiwei*, change to), etc.
4. Merging some words, such as combining 唐 (*Tang*, Tang dynasty), 唐朝 (*Tangchao*, Tang dynasty), 唐代 (*Tangdai*, Tang dynasty) into "唐, 唐代, 唐朝".

After manual intervention and proofreading, a 542-word Chinese Tourism Technical Word List (CTTWL) was finally compiled.

TF-IDF Word Ranking. In this part, CTTWL will be sequenced by TF-IDF values. TF-IDF considers both the term frequency (TF) and the inverse document frequency (IDF) of a word, which can effectively measure the importance of a word in a document. Therefore, this study calculated the TF-IDF values of the vocabulary in the Chinese tourism corpus and ranked them in descending order. The smaller the rank value, or in other words, the larger the TF-IDF value, indicates a higher degree of importance for the term. The ranking results are shown in Table 2 as follows:

Table 2. Top 10 words by TF-IDF value in CTTWL

Word	TF-IDF Value
景观 (*jingguan*, landspace)	0.001803246
建筑 (*jianzhu*, building)	0.001630435
旅游景区 (*lvyoujingqu*, tourist attractions)	0.001532759
基地 (*jidi*, base)	0.001292326
风光 (*fengguang*, scenery)	0.001122020
休闲 (*xiuxian*, leisure)	0.001089461
一体 (*yiti*, an integral whole)	0.001036866
景点 (*jingdian*, secenic spot)	0.001036866
火山 (*huoshan*, volcano)	0.001012447
国家级 (*guojiaji*, national-level)	0.000931677

4   Word List Analysis

This section analyzes the text coverage of CTTWL in comparison with the HSK (Tourism) Common Word List. Besides, this study also tries to find the characteristics of CTTWL in POS distribution and lexical level distribution.

4.1   Comparison Between CTTWL and HSK (Tourism)

The Handbook of Tourism Chinese Vocabulary, known as the HSK (Tourism) Common Word List, was compiled by Liu et al. [7]. It contains 4,674 words divided into elementary, intermediate, and advanced levels for common vocabulary used by tourism practitioners. Although developed by experts, it has drawbacks like strong subjectivity and lack of quantitative research. The word selection also lacks professionalism. Therefore, a comparative analysis between CTTWL and HSK (Tourism) was conducted.

Coverage in the General Chinese Corpus. Technical vocabulary frequently appears in professional domains. The lower the percentage of technical words in a general domain, the stronger the professionalism. Thus, the coverage rates of CTTWL and HSK (Tourism) in the general corpus were calculated using the formula (3) and (4).

$$C_1 = \frac{T_{CTTWL}}{T_{GeneralCorpus}} \tag{3}$$

$$C_2 = \frac{T_{HSKTourism}}{T_{GeneralCorpus}} \tag{4}$$

Where T refers to the total number of words, while T_{CTTWL} refers to the total number of occurrences of CTTWL in the general corpus. $T_{general\ corpus}$ refers to the total number of the general corpus. Dividing the two values gives the coverage rate of CTTWL in the general corpus. The calculation method for formulas (4) to (6) is the same as this

Table 3. Coverage rates of CTTWL and HSK (Tourism) in the general corpus

Name	Total Words	Total Frequency	Percentage
General Corpus	25882	129629	—
CTTWL	542	1216	0.94%
HSK (Tourism)	4674	16819	12.97%

and will not be further elaborated in the following text. Table 3 displays the calculation results.

It shows that from the above Table, CTTWL has only 0.94% coverage in the general corpus, while HSK (Tourism) reaches 12.97%, nearly 14 times the former. This indicates HSK (Tourism) contains many common words with inferior professionalism and technicality, while CTTWL has obvious domain attributes and lacks generality.

Coverage in the Chinese Tourism Corpus. Nation [24] divides text vocabulary into high-frequency, academic, technical, and low-frequency words, with technical vocabulary accounting for about 5% of the total. Coverage rates in the tourism corpus were calculated using the formula (5) and (6) to further verify professionalism. The calculation results are shown in Table 4.

$$C_3 = \frac{T_{CTTWL}}{T_{TourismCorpus}} \tag{5}$$

$$C_4 = \frac{T_{HSKTourism}}{T_{TourismCorpus}} \tag{6}$$

Table 4. Coverage rates of CTTWL and HSK (Tourism) in the tourism corpus

Name	Total Words	Total Frequency	Percentage
Tourism Corpus	23978	114080	—
CTTWL	542	12607	11.05%
HSK (Tourism)	4674	18923	16.59%
HSK (Tourism) (excluding Level 1–4 words)	895	8419	7.38%

From Table 4, it can be seen that CTTWL has a total frequency of 12,607 and a coverage rate of 11.05% in the tourism corpus. Despite having 4,674 words, the coverage rate of HSK (Tourism) is only 16.59%. Excluding Level 1–4 words, the 895 remaining HSK (Tourism) words have a coverage rate of just 7.38%. Therefore, although large in scale, HSK (Tourism) does not have a significant increase in coverage in the professional corpus, indicating a lack of professionalism and scientificity in word list compilation. By contrast, CTTWL covers most professional vocabulary with far fewer words, demonstrating better effects that are more suitable for teaching practice.

4.2   POS Distribution of CTTWL

The POS distribution characteristics of CTTWL were further analyzed. The results are shown in Table 5:

Table 5. POS distribution of CTTWL

POS Type	Number	Percentage
Nouns	312	57.56%
Verbs	131	24.17%
Adjectives	78	14.39%
Idioms	21	3.88%

Among the 542 words, nouns account for the largest share with 312 words (57.56%). There are 131 verbs (24.17%), 78 adjectives (14.39%), and 21 idioms (3.88%). The top 10 words of each POS are:

1. Nouns (no proper nouns included): 景观 (*jingguan*, landscape), 建筑 (*jianzhu*, building), 旅游景区 (*lvyoujingqu*, tourist attraction), 基地 (*jidi*, base), 风光 (*fengguang*, scenery), 一体 (*yiti*, an integral whole), 景点 (*jingdian*, scenic spot), 火山 (*huoshan*, volcano), 峡谷 (*xiagu*, valley), 生态 (*shengtai*, ecology).
2. Verbs: 誉为 (*yuwei*, known as) 拥有 (*yongyou*, have), 评为 (*pingwei*, rate as), 占地 (*zhandi*, cover), 示范 (*shifan*, demonstrate), 得名 (*deming*, got the name), 规划 (*guihua*, programme), 打造 (*dazao*, make), 现存 (*xiancun*, existing), 素有 (*suyou*, usually have).
3. Adjectives: 休闲 (*xiuxian*, leisure), 国家级 (*guojiaji*, national-level), 革命 (*geming*, revolutionary), 天然 (*tianran*, natural), 原始 (*yuanshi*, original), 众多 (*zhongduo*, numerous), 悠久 (*youjiu*, long), 罕见 (*hanjian*, rare), 神奇 (*shenqi*, magical), 奇特 (*qite*, peculiar).
4. Idioms: 明清 (*mingqing*, Ming and Qing dynasty), 海内外 (*haineiwai*, home and abroad), 动植物 (*dongzhiwu*, animals and plants), 市政府 (*shizhengfu*, municipal government), 国内外 (*guoneiwai*, home and abroad), 文人墨客 (*wenrenmoke*, ancient scholars and artists), 各具特色 (*gejutese*, each has its characteristics), 自古以来 (*ziguyilai*, since ancient times), 市委 (*shiwei*, Municipal Committee of the CPC), 山海 (*shanhai*, mountains and seas).

Specifically, there are 250 common nouns, 53 proper nouns, and a total of 9 words categorized as time words, directional words, and locational words. It can be observed that CTTWL focuses on the inclusion of proper nouns. This study ranked personal names, place names, and other proper nouns, as shown in Table 6, 7 and 8.

Table 6, 7 and 8 show that CTTWL includes a certain number and diverse types of proper nouns, as travel texts often involve introductions to the cultural and historical aspects of scenic spots. In the context of introducing China's 5A-level tourist attractions, the use of language exhibits distinct characteristics of the Chinese language. For example, listing personal names not only enhances the cultural connotation of the scenic spot but

Table 6. Top 9 ranked words in the categories of personal names in CTTWL

	Personal names	Frequency
1	毛泽东 (*Mao Zedong*)	20
2	李白 (*Libai*)	18
3	邓小平 (*Deng Xiaoping*)	14
4	江泽民 (*Jiang Zemin*)	13
5	胡锦涛 (*Hu Jintao*)	11
6	屈原 (*Quyuan*)	9
7	苏东坡 (*Su Dongpo*)	8
8	苏轼 (*Sushi*)	7
9	周恩来 (*Zhou Enlai*)	7

Table 7. Top 10 ranked words in the categories of place names in CTTWL

	Place names	Frequency
1	西安 (*Xi'an*)	46
2	江南 (*Jiangnan*, the southern of the Yangtze River)	43
3	苏州 (*Suzhou*)	33
4	新疆 (Xinjiang)	31
5	长江 (*Changjiang*, Yangtze River)	30
6	黄山 (*Huangshan*, Huangshan mountains)	29
7	黄河 (*Huanghe*, Yellow River)	28
8	海南 (*Hainan*)	26
9	河南省 (*Henan sheng*)	23
10	中原 (*Zhongyuan*, central plains)	23

also increases its tourism reputation. Listing place names often serves to indicate the geographical location and administrative divisions of the scenic spot. Listing names of dynasties, institutions, and other proper nouns primarily aims to introduce the rich history and scarcity of resources in the scenic spot. Therefore, the concentration of proper nouns in CTTWL reflects the geographical, cultural, and historical characteristics of tourist attractions, and encountering these vocabulary items in teaching or learning can enhance the understanding of professionals in the field about the general situation of China's national conditions.

Table 8. Top 10 ranked words in the categories of other proper nouns in CTTWL

	Other Proper Nouns	Frequency
1	唐, 唐代, 唐朝 (*Tang, Tangdai, Tangchao*, Tang dynasty)	125
2	明, 明代, 明朝 (*Ming, Mingdai, Mingchao*, Ming dynasty)	101
3	清, 清代 (*Qing, Qingdai*, Qing dynasty)	98
4	宋, 宋代 (*Song, Songdai*, Song dynasty)	65
5	国务院 (guowuyuan, the State Council)	32
6	联合国教科文组织 (*Lianheguo Jiaokewen zuzhi*, UNESCO)	22
7	汉、汉代 (*Han, Handai*, Han dynasty)	20
8	春秋 (*Chunqiu*, Spring and Autumn Period)	18
9	三国 (*Sanguo*, Three Kingdoms Period)	17
10	南宋 (*Nansong*, the Southern Song dynasty)	14

4.3　Lexical Level Distribution of CTTWL

The lexical level distribution of words in CTTWL was also analyzed, as shown in Table 9:

Table 9. Lexical level distribution in CTTWL

Lexical level	Number	Percentage
Level 5 Words	56	10.33%
Level 6 Words	50	9.23%
Level 7–9 Words	182	33.58%
Non-standard Words	254	46.86%

According to Table 9, it can be observed that the CTTWL contains a significant number of "non-standard" vocabularies, reaching as high as 254 words, accounting for 46.86% of the total. The vocabulary categorized as levels 7–9 amounts to 182 words, representing 33.58%. The quantity of level 6 vocabulary is 50 words, accounting for 9.23%. Additionally, there are 56 words categorized as level 5, making up 10.33% of the total. It is evident that the vocabulary in CTTWL predominantly consists of "non-standard" words and levels 7–9 vocabulary, with a combined percentage of 80.44%. This indicates that the word list compiled in this study not only considers the inclusion of level-specific vocabulary but also emphasizes the incorporation of "non-standard" vocabulary.

5   Conclusion

This paper takes Chinese AAAAA-level tourist attraction introduction texts as a corpus. Targeting tourism practitioners and "Chinese + Tourism" vocational education, it designs a word list construction process based on corpus classification and method determination. By calculating frequency threshold, frequency ratio, range, POS distribution, lexical level distribution, TF-IDF values, and manual intervention, a sequenced 542-word Chinese Tourism Technical Word List (CTTWL) is compiled.

CTTWL contains mainly nouns, verbs, adjectives, and idioms. It incorporates 53 proper nouns, which can help learners understand the geographical, cultural, and historical connotations of Chinese attractions. For word levels, higher level and beyond-curriculum words account for 80.44%, while also including some intermediate level words, achieving a balance of standardization and professionalism. Regarding coverage, CTTWL reaches 11.05% in the tourism corpus and only 0.94% in the general corpus. In comparison, despite a larger size, HSK (Tourism) does not have greater coverage gains in the professional corpus. This shows that CTTWL covers more professional vocabulary with fewer words.

In summary, CTTWL demonstrates optimization and improvement in the compilation process, scale, and domain vocabulary coverage. It is a scientific and professional domain word list that can provide vocabulary references for "Chinese + Tourism" vocational skill training and teaching. The word list compilation process can also serve as a useful reference for the development of International Chinese Language Education.

In future research, this study aims to further expand the corpus, optimize the process of constructing the word list, and enhance the semantic analysis of the word list. Additionally, in order to construct a richer semantic network of technical vocabulary related to Chinese tourism, this study will endeavor to apply Knowledge Graph technology to construct a technical word list [25, 26]. Furthermore, this study will continually explore the extensive application of the word list in the fields of vocational education for "Chinese+" and International Chinese language education.

Acknowledgments. This article is supported by the Key Project of the National Social Science Foundation of China (18ZDA295), the Research Project of the National Language Commission (ZDI135-139).

References

1. Xu, J.: Compilation of industry English word lists and implementation of "four uses" teaching principles in higher vocational stages. Front. Foreign Lang. Educ. Res. **5**(01), 43–49+90 (2022)
2. Su, X.: Quantitative Linguistics and Its Implementation. The Commercial Press, Beijing (2010)
3. Liu, H.: Reconstruction and level division of business Chinese common word list. Chin. Teach. Res. **69**(01), 35–48 (2018)
4. Liu, H., Li, X.: Construction of a Chinese medicine Chinese thematic word list based on corpus. Chin. Teach. Res. **86**(02), 77–85 (2022)

5. Shen, S.: Analysis of the concept and characteristics of the Undergraduate Teaching Word list for Economics and Trade Chinese. Natl. Educ. Res. **22**(06), 87–91 (2011)
6. Du, X., Shi, S.: Corpus-based vocabulary analysis of specialized Chinese courses for "Chinese + Vocational Skills." J. Tianjin Normal Univ. (Soc. Sci. Edn.) **284**(05), 1–7 (2022)
7. Liu, H., Cai, W., Zhang, S., et al.: Principles of word selection and related issues of HSK (Tourism) common word list. Study Teach. Chin. Foreign Lang. **2005**(00), 151–166 (2005)
8. Deng, L.: Construction of Tourism Chinese Topic Library and Topic Word List Based on Corpus. Jinan University, Jinan (2014)
9. Li, J.: Customization of Teaching Chinese as a Foreign Language Tourism Word List Based on Dynamic Language Updating. Huaqiao University, Quanzhou (2019)
10. Jin, T., Liu, K., Wu, J.: Research paradigms and practical applications of academic English textbook word lists. Foreign Lang. World (05), 21–29 (2019)
11. Li, W.: A corpus-based study of thematic words in English learners. Mod. Foreign Lang. (03), 284–293+283 (2003)
12. He, Q.: Study on the amphibious vocabulary in medical academic English - establishment of word lists and teaching strategies based on the corpus. J. Fujian Med. Univ. (Soc. Sci. Edn.) **23**(01), 65–70+80 (2022)
13. Xie, X.: Updating word lists of Chinese newspapers and magazines teaching materials based on the theory of language homeostasis. In: Proceedings of the 2nd National Seminar on Language in Education Teaching Materials, p. 198. National Language Resources Monitoring and Research Center Education Teaching Materials Language Division, People's Education Press, Beijing (2008)
14. Guo, L.: An investigation and analysis of the compilation method of vocabulary lists in comprehensive Chinese textbooks for foreign learners. In: Proceedings of the 5th Beijing Area Graduate Student Academic Forum on Teaching Chinese as a Foreign Language, pp. 188–193. Beijing University School of Chinese as a Second Language, Beijing (2012)
15. Zhong, Y., Hou, H., Du, H.: Automatic construction of e-government thematic word lists. J. China Soc. Libr. Sci. **175**(03), 97–102 (2008)
16. Planning and Finance Department of the National Tourism Administration, Institute of Geographic Sciences and Natural Resources Research, Chinese Academy of Sciences: Classification, Investigation, and Evaluation of Tourism Resources (GB/T 18972-2017). China Standard Press, Beijing (2017)
17. Coxhead, A.: A new academic word list. TESOL Q. **34**(2), 213–238 (2000)
18. Gardner, D., Davies, M.: A new academic vocabulary list. Appl. Linguis. **35**(3), 305–327 (2013)
19. Lei, L., Liu, D.: A new medical academic word list: a corpus-based study with enhanced methodology. J. Engl. Acad. Purp. **22**, 42–53 (2016)
20. Laosrirattanachai, P., Ruangjaroon, S.: Corpus-based creation of tourism, hotel, and airline business word lists. LEARN J. Lang. Educ. Acquisit. Res. Netw. **14**(1), 50–86 (2021)
21. Zipf, G.K.: The Psycho-Biology of Language. MIT Press, Cambridge (1935)
22. Zipf, G.K.: Human Behavior and the Principle of Least Effort. Addison Wesley Press, Cambridge (1949)
23. Ministry of Education of the People's Republic of China, National Language Commission: Chinese Proficiency Grading Standards for International Chinese Language Education (GF 0025-2021). Beijing Language and Culture University Press, Beijing (2021)
24. Nation, P.: Learning Vocabulary in Another Language, 3rd edn. Cambridge University Press, Cambridge (2022)

25. Yang, X., Jing, S., Chen, X., et al.: Corpus construction for generating knowledge graph of Sichuan cuisine. In: Su, Q., Xu, G., Yang, X. (eds.) CLSW 2022. LNCS, vol. 13496, pp. 34–42. Springer, Cham (2023). https://doi.org/10.1007/978-3-031-28956-9_3
26. Zhang, K., Hu, C., Song, Y., et al.: Construction of Chinese obstetrics knowledge graph based on the multiple sources data. In: Dong, M., Gu, Y., Hong, J.-F. (eds.) CLSW 2021. LNCS, vol. 13250, pp. 399–410. Springer, Cham (2022). https://doi.org/10.1007/978-3-031-06547-7_31

General Linguistics

A Preliminary Study on Japanese CSL Learners' Acquisition of Mandarin Potential Expressions

Anwei Yu🆔 and Huichen S. Hsiao$^{(\boxtimes)}$ 🆔

Department of Chinese as a Second Language, National Taiwan Normal University, Taipei, Taiwan

{yu.anwei,huichen.hsiao}@ntnu.edu.tw

Abstract. This study aims to investigate Japanese Chinese as a Second Language (CSL) learners' acquisition of the Mandarin potential complement 'V *bu* C' (V不C), in hope of shedding light on the effect of language proficiency on the language sense of L2 learners. Based on the results of previous studies [1–3], an acceptability judgment test on a 7-point Likert scale is administered to 58 native Mandarin speakers and 62 Japanese CSL learners, divided into two groups based on Mandarin proficiency, to probe whether there are significant differences between groups for the acceptability of grammatical and ungrammatical sentences containing 'V *bu* C' (V不C) and the negative modal verb '*bu neng*' (不能). The preliminary results indicate a significant difference between the responses of native Mandarin speakers and Japanese CSL learners of all levels for both grammatical and ungrammatical sentences (all $ps < .001$), implying that learners struggle to discern the usages of 'V *bu* C' (V不C) and '*bu neng*' (不能). In addition, a significant difference is also observed between the responses of beginning-intermediate and intermediate-advanced Japanese CSL learners (all $ps < .05$), indicating that the linguistic sense of intermediate-advanced learners is advancing toward that of native speakers, but has not yet reached the near-native level of proficiency.

Keywords: Japanese CSL Learners · Acceptability Judgment Test · Potential Complement · Chinese Modal Verbs

1 Introduction

The acquisition of Mandarin potential expressions is often a challenge for CSL learners. Scholars have pointed out that Mandarin potential expressions, including modal verbs '*neng*' (能), '*hui*' (會) '*keyi*' (可以) and the potential complement 'V *de/bu* C' (V得/不C), differ slightly in meaning [4–6]. '*Neng*' (能) is used to describe that someone has an innate ability or fulfills the conditions to execute an action, whereas '*hui*' (會) describes that someone has an acquired ability to perform an action, and '*keyi*' (可以) expresses that someone has permission to perform an action [4]. However, the potential complement 'V *de/bu* C' (V得/不C) expresses that a certain result is achievable or unachievable by performing an action [5, 6]. Through a comparison of English, Mandarin and Japanese potential expressions, Imaizumi [7] pointed out that the above expressions correspond to only two expressions in Japanese, namely the auxiliary verbs *'eru/rareru'* (える/られ る) and the structure *'koto ga dekiru'* (ことができる). Hence, Japanese CSL learners must have a firm grasp of the meanings and usages of each expression in both languages to communicate effectively in Mandarin without making errors.

In recent years, several scholars have conducted studies on CSL learners' acquisition of Mandarin potential expressions. Although the results showed multiple categories of errors, Wu et al. [1], Yang [2] and Li [3] discovered that the most common error involving potential expressions is misusing modal verb *'neng'* (能) when the potential complement 'V *de/bu* C' (V得/不C) should be used instead. This is because the negative form of modal verb *'neng'* (能), *'bu neng'* (不能), expresses prohibition, which the negative potential complement 'V *bu* C' (V不C) does not express [8, 9]. Based on the Interlanguage Hypothesis put forth by Selinker [10], Wu et al. [1], Yang [2] and Li [3] postulate this type of error may be caused by a combination of interlingual and intralingual transfer due to the similarity in the meanings of Mandarin potential expressions. However, the above scholars did not account for the effect of language proficiency on the ability to use these expressions correctly.

The present study aims to shed light on the abovementioned topics by performing a preliminary investigation on the acquisition of Mandarin potential expressions at different levels of proficiency via an acceptability judgment test administered to Japanese CSL learners with varied Mandarin proficiency and native speakers of Mandarin as a control group. In deciding on an appropriate acceptability judgment test for the present study, we ultimately chose the 7-point Likert test based on Marty et al.'s [11] positive findings on the robustness and sensitivity of such tasks designed for research in syntax. Further details regarding the design of the experimental materials and methods are described in the next section.

2 Materials and Methods

The present study utilizes an acceptability judgment test on a 7-point Likert Scale to test native Mandarin speakers and Japanese CSL learners' abilities to discern grammatical sentences containing potential complement 'V *bu* C' (V不C) and ungrammatical sentences containing the collocation *'bu neng* VC' (不能VC). Detailed information is described as follows.

2.1 Participants

A total of 137 participants were recruited to participate in this study, including 60 native Mandarin speakers from Taiwan and 77 Japanese CSL learners. After eliminating invalid responses[1], there were a total of 120 participants remaining, including 58 native Mandarin speakers and 62 Japanese CSL learners. The Japanese participants were all studying at universities in Taiwan at the time of the study and they were separated into two groups (beginner-intermediate and intermediate-advanced) based on their Chinese language proficiency test scores (i.e., Test of Chinese as a Foreign Language, TOCFL or *Hanyu Shuiping Kaoshi*, HSK). Learners were placed in the beginner-intermediate group if their Mandarin proficiency results were at the CEFR A2-B1 level at the time of the study; participants with CEFR B2-C1 Mandarin proficiency scores were placed in the intermediate-advanced group.

2.2 Experimental Procedure

The acceptability judgment test used in this study was formatted as a multiple-choice survey questionnaire via Google Forms. For each question, participants were shown a single sentence in Chinese and instructed to rate the grammaticality of the underlined part of the sentence presented on a scale from −3 to 3 (−3 being "definitely unacceptable" and 3 as "definitely acceptable") based on their intuition[2]. They were also told to move forward through the questionnaire without stopping and not to return to previous questions in order to prevent participants from changing their responses. In addition, to prevent participants from repeatedly choosing a neutral response, the median value "zero" ('0') was removed from the scale in a similar fashion to a study on the linguistic intuition of native Chinese speakers [12]. This made it so that participants could only choose the responses −3, −2, −1, 1, 2 and 3. The collected responses were then analyzed for validity; i.e., overly similar responses were eliminated before performing data analysis.

2.3 Materials

The experimental materials in this study were designed to compare the linguistic intuition of native Mandarin speakers and Japanese CSL learners of different levels in terms of grammatical and ungrammatical usages of the potential complement and modal verb 'neng' (能). The materials utilized in this study consisted of 23 questions, including

---

[1] Participants responses were eliminated based on two criteria. (1) If responses were overly similar (i.e., over 75% of responses were the identical score '3'), those participants' data were eliminated. (2) If responses to certain filler questions were not in line with basic Mandarin grammar rules, those participants were deemed to have not taken the experiment seriously (i.e., if a participant regarded "*Wǒ hé péngyǒu zuótiān xiě de hěn kāixīn zuòyè*" (我和朋友昨天寫得很開心作業; 'Yesterday, me and my friend wrote very happily homework') as a grammatical sentence, his/her responses were eliminated).

[2] Although there is much debate regarding the sensitivity of various acceptability judgment tests in the study of syntax [13], Marty et al. [11] found that the 7-point Likert scale test is the most effective in tasks asking participants to rate singular items, such as sentences, on a scale. This method is used in various L1 and L2 studies, such as Yuan and Dugarova [14] in their study on English-speaking CSL learners' acceptability of sentences containing *wh*-topicalization and Xue et al. [15] in their investigation on native speakers' acceptability of Mandarin sentences containing complement coercion.

three practice questions, ten target questions and ten filler questions. Instructions were written in both Chinese and Japanese to ensure the participants fully understood how to complete the task; however, stimuli were solely presented in Chinese characters without translation nor romanization. To avoid the sharing of responses between participants, the latter twenty questions were randomly ordered onto two different forms that were administered to participants at random.

The three practice questions were used to teach participants how to complete the experiment correctly, and they consisted of one grammatical sentence (*Wǒ chī bīngqílín* (我吃冰淇淋); 'I eat ice cream'), one ungrammatical sentence (*Wǒ bīngqílín chī* (我冰淇淋吃); 'I ice cream eat') and one controversial sentence that could be acceptable depending on region (*Wǒ yǒu chī bīngqílín* (我有吃冰淇淋); 'I have eaten ice cream'). After answering the practice questions, the participants received feedback in both Chinese and Japanese regarding what their responses imply about their intuition.

The ten target questions used in this study consisted of five grammatical sentences containing the potential complement 'V *bu* C' (V不C) (i.e., *Wǒ zuótiān hěn wǎn cái shuì, suǒyǐ jīntiān zǎoshàng qǐbùlái* (我昨天很晚才睡, 所以今天早上起不來); 'I slept late last night, so I couldn't get up in the morning') and five ungrammatical sentences containing the collocation '*bu neng* VC' (不能VC) (i.e., *Wǒ wǎnshàng jiǔ diǎn hē le kāfēi, xiànzài bù néng shuì zháo* (我晚上九點喝了咖啡, 現在不能睡著); 'I drank at coffee at 9 p.m. and I can't fall sleep now'). The sentences were extracted from the BCC Corpus[3] and modified based on TOCFL's 8000 Vocabulary List[4]. Before distributing the questionnaire, the grammaticality of each sentence was confirmed by five native Mandarin speakers majoring in Teaching Chinese as a Second Language (TCSL) or Chinese linguistics at the graduate level. Grammatical sentences received responses with an average of at least 2.5 and ungrammatical sentences had an average of −2.5 or less on a scale from −3 to 3. Figure 1 below shows an example of a target question; romanization and translation are added for readability but were not included in the original experiment.

The grammatical and ungrammatical sentences were used in this study with the goal of investigating native Mandarin speakers' and Japanese CSL learners' language intuition. If participants answered the questions incorrectly, it implies that their language intuition does not conform with the syntactic rules of Mandarin. In the case of Japanese CSL learners, judging '*bu neng* VC' (不能VC) sentences as "grammatical" implies learners' overgeneralization of the structure [1–3].

As for the ten filler questions used in this study, they consisted of the Mandarin complement of degree 'V *de bu* C' (V得不C). Similar to the target stimuli, they included five grammatically correct sentences (i.e., *Xiànzài shì xiàtiān, tiānqì hěn rè, rè de yǐnliào mài de bù hǎo* (現在是夏天, 天氣很熱, 熱的飲料賣得不好); It is currently summer and the weather is hot; hot drinks are not selling well) and five ungrammatical sentences (i.e., *Wǒ huì shuō yìdiǎn Fǎyǔ, dànshì wǒ shuō de bù hěn hǎo* (我會説一點法語, 但是我説得不很好); I can speak a little bit of French, but I don't speak it very well). The grammatical sentences were designed under the same principles as the grammatical target

---

[3] BBC Corpus, http://bcc.blcu.edu.cn/lang/zh. Last accessed 17 March 2023.

[4] TOCFL 8000 Vocabulary List, https://tocfl.edu.tw/index.php/exam/download. Last accessed 17 March 2023.

Fig. 1. Sample of One Target Question

questions; ungrammatical sentences were formed by adding unnecessary grammatical units, omitting necessary components or changing the word order.

2.4 Data Analysis

After collecting participants' responses, we eliminated items that did not meet presumptions, including two ungrammatical sentences which native Mandarin speakers believed were grammatical[5], and then utilized One-way ANOVA to test the homogeneity of the means of the responses to the target questions within groups (i.e., native Mandarin speakers, beginner-intermediate learners and intermediate-advanced learners) to determine whether participants with the same language backgrounds gave similar responses. The results indicated that participants within the same group gave homogenous responses, i.e., all $ps > .05$, which is exhibited in Table 1 below.

After determining the homogeneity of the responses within each group, we utilized t-test to analyze whether there were significant differences in the responses between three groups. Because the number of participants in each group were not equal, we utilized Welch's t-test, according to Delacre et al. [18], to account for unequal variance. The results are described in further detail below.

---

[5] Two ungrammatical sentences were perceived as grammatical by the native Mandarin speaking group; namely, *Wo wàngjì dài yàoshi le, women bù néng jìnqù* (我忘記帶鑰匙了，我們不能進去) 'I forgot to bring the key. We can't go inside' ($M = 1.897$, $SD = 1.703$) and *Wǒ hěn ài wǒ dì yī ge nánpéngyǒu, dào xiànzài háishì bù néng wàngjì tā.* (我很愛我第一個男朋友，到現在還是不能忘記他) 'I really love my first boyfriend. Even now, I still can't forget about him' ($M = 0.431$, $SD = 2.264$). This may be attributed to the influence of the Southern Min dialect on the Mandarin spoken in Taiwan [16–17]. However, because this topic exceeds the scope of the current paper, the two items are excluded from data analysis and the writers do not conduct further discussion at the present time.

Table 1. Results of Homogeneity Test via One-Way ANOVA

Group	Question Category	M	F-value	p-value
Native	Grammatical	2.789	.814	.517
Native	Ungrammatical	−2.231	1.497	.227
Beginner-Intermediate	Grammatical	1.624	.470	.758
Beginner-Intermediate	Ungrammatical	.517	2.747	.071
Intermediate-Advanced	Grammatical	2.019	2.227	.069
Intermediate-Advanced	Ungrammatical	−.979	1.328	.270

3   Results and Discussion

The first section below presents the preliminary data collected via the acceptability judgment test and shows the average scores (M), including corresponding standard deviation (SD) given by each group of participants. Then, Sect. 3.2 describes the t-test results comparing the responses of native Mandarin speakers, beginner-intermediate Japanese CSL learners and intermediate-advanced learners for the acceptability judgment test. The results are organized in terms of group and question category (grammatical/ungrammatical). Finally, Sect. 3.3 will discuss the results of the present study in relation to those of past studies.

3.1   Preliminary Results

Table 2 below shows the preliminary data collected from the participants for the acceptability judgment test, including average scores and standard deviation.

Table 2. Average Scores and Standard Deviation for All Groups

Group	M (Grammatical)	SD	M (Ungrammatical)	SD
Native	2.789	.595	−2.231	1.346
Beginner-Intermediate	1.624	1.845	.517	2.362
Intermediate-Advanced	2.019	1.432	−.979	1.925

As can be seen in Table 2, the native Mandarin-speaking group's average performance most conformed to the predictions of the study. When presented with grammatical statements, they mostly chose responses from the right side of the Likert scale (1, 2, 3), with an average acceptability level (M) of 2.789. Likewise, when judging ungrammatical statements, native speakers mostly chose responses from the left side of the scale (−1, −2, −3), yielding an average acceptability score (M) of −2.231.

However, the preliminary data indicates that Japanese participants with beginner-intermediate proficiency in Mandarin did not perceive the stimuli the same way the native speakers did. Although their average acceptability score (M) for grammatical statements was in the positive range, an average of 1.624 is much lower than the native Mandarin average of 2.789. As for the beginner-intermediate group's responses to the ungrammatical stimuli, they produced an average acceptability score of .517, indicating that many participants perceived ungrammatical sentences as correct.

Lastly, the intermediate-advanced group's scores were in-between those of the native-speaking group and the beginner-intermediate group, with respective average acceptability scores (M) of 2.019 and −.979 for grammatical and ungrammatical stimuli. These results imply that the linguistic intuition of intermediate-advanced Japanese CSL learners may be closer to that of native Mandarin speakers in comparison to learners with beginner-intermediate proficiency. To further explore the validity of this hypothesis, we conducted inferential statistical testing via Welch's *t*-test, and the results are described in the next section.

3.2 *t*-Test Results

Table 3 below shows the results of native Mandarin speakers vs. beginner-intermediate learners.

Table 3. *t*-Test Results for Native Speakers and Beginner-Intermediate Learners

Category	Group	N	M	SD	*t*-score	*df*	*p*-value
Grammatical	Native	289	2.789	.595	7.485	164	<.001***
	Beginner-Intermediate	149	1.624	1.845			
Ungrammatical	Native	173	−2.231	1.346	−1.111	118	<.001***
	Beginner-Intermediate	89	.517	2.362			

As can be seen in Table 3, native Mandarin speakers were able to correctly identify grammatical usages of 'V *bu* C' (V不C) and ungrammatical usages of '*bu neng* VC' (不能VC), as the means of their responses were 2.789 and −2.231, respectively. As for beginner-intermediate Japanese CSL learners, they were fairly able to identify grammatical usages of 'V *bu* C' (V不C) with a mean of 1.624, but they were not as able to identify ungrammatical usages of '*bu neng* VC' (不能VC), as can be inferred from the mean of .517. After performing Welch's *t*-test, we found strong evidence that the responses of the two groups were significantly different with *p*-values less than .001, implying that beginner-intermediate Japanese CSL learners were not able to complete the task with the same capacity as native speakers. This may also imply that learners at this level do not yet have the proficiency to distinguish between the meanings and usages of the potential complement and modal verb '*neng*' (能), which in this case, the latter contains the meaning of "prohibition;" i.e., *mài bù wán* (賣不完) (cannot sell it all) vs. *bù néng mài wán* (不能賣完) (must not sell it all). Next, we examined the situation of native Mandarin speakers vs. intermediate-advanced learners. Results are recorded in Table 4 below.

Table 4. *t*-Test Results for Native Speakers and Intermediate-Advanced Learners

Category	Group	N	M	SD	*t*-score	*df*	*p*-value
Grammatical	Native	289	2.789	.595	6.471	188	<.001***
	Intermediate-Advanced	149	2.019	1.432			
Ungrammatical	Native	173	−2.231	1.346	−5.605	145	<.001***
	Intermediate-Advanced	89	−.979	1.925			

The results in Table 4 show that intermediate-advanced Japanese CSL learners performed fairly well in both question categories, with a mean of 2.019 for identifying grammatical usages of 'V *bu* C' (V不C) and a mean of −.979 for ungrammatical usages of '*bu neng* VC' (不能VC). However, after performing Welch's *t*-test, we discovered that even intermediate-advanced learners gave significantly different responses compared with native Mandarin speakers (all *p*s < .001). In order to further investigate the effects of language proficiency on the usages of 'V *bu* C' (V不C) and '*bu neng* VC' (不能VC) by CSL learners of differing levels, we continued on to compare the two groups of learners via the same test. Results are shown in Table 5 below.

Table 5. *t*-Test Results for Beginner-Intermediate and Intermediate-Advanced Learners

Category	Group	N	M	SD	*t*-score	*df*	*p*-value
Grammatical	Beginner-Intermediate	149	1.624	1.845	−2.082	279	.038*
	Intermediate-Advanced	149	2.019	1.432			
Ungrammatical	Beginner-Intermediate	89	.517	2.362	4.666	170	<.001***
	Intermediate-Advanced	89	−.979	1.925			

According to Table 5, the responses of beginner-intermediate and intermediate-advanced Japanese CSL learners were also significantly different, with a *p*-value of .038 for identifying grammatical usages of 'V *bu* C' (V不C) and a *p*-value of less than .001 for identifying ungrammatical usages of '*bu neng* VC' (不能VC). These results indicate that although intermediate-advanced learners were unable to complete the task with the same proficiency as native Mandarin speakers, they were still able to perform significantly better than beginner-intermediate learners. The section below discusses the results of the present study in relation to those of previous studies.

3.3 Discussion

According to the data above, our experimental results are in line with those of previous studies [1–3]; these scholars have put forward that CSL learners often have challenges discerning between the different meanings and functions of different potential expressions, especially the potential complement 'V *de/bu* C' (V得/不C). Wu et al. [1], Yang

[2] and Li [3] suggested some possible reasons for this, including interlingual interference; for example, Yang believed this is because the meanings of Japanese potential verbs and the structure 'V *koto ga dekiru*' (Vことができる) correspond to all Mandarin potential expressions, hence it is quite difficult for native Japanese speakers to learn the nuances of different potential expressions in Mandarin. In addition, scholars have also suggested that the similarity of the meanings of the Mandarin modal verbs '*neng*' (能), '*hui*' (會), '*keyi*' (可以) and the potential complement 'V *de/bu* C' (V得/不C) makes it difficult for learners to distinguish which expression should be used in a specific situation [19]. These results indicate that the sequencing of syntactic structures in L2 Mandarin instruction plays an important role in assisting learners differentiate and use similar expressions correctly [20].

The results above not only support the findings of previous studies, but also shed some light on the effect of language proficiency on Japanese CSL learners' acquisition of the Mandarin potential complement 'V *bu* C' (V不C). Although neither of the learner groups performed the experimental task with the same competence as native speakers, we found that participants with higher proficiency in Mandarin could successfully discern grammatical and ungrammatical usages of Mandarin potential expressions more often, indicating that the early stages of L2 acquisition are crucial in the progression toward advanced proficiency. According to the Interlanguage Hypothesis proposed by Selinker [10], the language that second language learners use becomes closer to that of native speakers over time via training and practice in L2; however, learners and instructors must also be careful in avoiding fossilization, which refers to a situation where errors made at the beginning stages of language learning transfer over to the advanced stages due to a lack of proper correction.

4 Conclusion

In sum, the present study utilized an acceptability judgment test administered to native Mandarin speakers and Japanese CSL learners of differing Mandarin language proficiency to investigate the acquisition of the Mandarin potential complement and the modal verb '*neng*' (能). We found that the performance of Japanese CSL learners differed significantly in comparison with native speakers at all levels. However, we also discovered that the performance of intermediate-advanced learners also significantly differed from that of beginner-intermediate learners, indicating that language proficiency should be considered in language acquisition studies. We hope that the results of this study can be further applied pedagogically to help CSL learners of different levels grasp the meanings and usages of complex expressions in Mandarin.

Acknowledgments. This study was presented and discussed at The 24th Chinese Lexical Semantics Workshop (CLSW 2023). We would like to express our gratitude to the anonymous reviewers for their valuable suggestions on this study. All errors are of course our sole responsibility.

Appendix: Target Stimuli

The below presents the target stimuli of the present study, consisting of 5 grammatical sentences containing the negative potential complement 'V *Bu* C' (V不C) and 5 ungrammatical sentences containing the negative modal verb '*bu neng*' (不能) in no particular order. Note that the *Pinyin* romanization and English translation provided in this appendix were not included in the original survey administered to participants.

Grammatical target stimuli (5)

1. 這些漢字我已經練習很久了, 但是我一直寫不好。

Zhè xiē Hànzì wǒ yǐjīng liànxí hěn jiǔ le, dànshì wǒ yìzhí xiě bù hǎo.

I have been practicing these characters for a long time, but I always have trouble writing them nicely.

2. 我昨天很晚才睡, 所以今天早上起不來。

Wǒ zuótiān hěn wǎn cái shuì, suǒyǐ jīntiān zǎoshàng qǐ bù lái.

I slept late last night, so I couldn't get up in the morning.

3. 我覺得這家飯館一點也不好, 菜很貴, 還吃不飽。

Wǒ juéde zhè jiā fànguǎn yìdiǎn yě bù hǎo, cài hěn guì, hái chī bù bǎo.

I think this restaurant is not good at all. The food is expensive and we aren't full after eating.

4. 新來的老師說中文說得很快, 我有點聽不懂。

Xīn lái de lǎoshī shuō Zhōngwén shuō de hěn kuài, wǒ yǒudiǎn tīng bù dǒng.

The new teacher speaks Chinese really quickly. I can't really understand her.

5. 這件事情有點複雜, 我怕我說不清楚。

Zhè jiàn shì yǒudiǎn fùzá, wǒ pà wǒ shuō bù qīngchǔ.

This matter is rather complicated; I'm afraid I can't clearly explain it.

Ungrammatical target stimuli (5)

1. 我的錢包不見了, 已經找了兩個多小時, 但是我不能找到。

Wǒ de qiánbāo bú jiàn le, yǐjīng zhǎo le liǎng ge duō xiǎoshí, dànshì wǒ bù néng zhǎo dào.

My wallet has gone missing. I have been looking for it for over two hours, but I can't find it.

2. 我忘記帶鑰匙了, 我們不能進去。

Wǒ wàngjì dài yàoshi le, wǒmen bù néng jìnqù.

I forgot to bring the key. We can't go inside.

3. 我很愛我第一個男朋友, 到現在還是不能忘記他。

Wǒ hěn ài wǒ dì yī ge nánpéngyǒu, dào xiànzài háishì bù néng wàngjì tā.

I really love my first boyfriend. Even now, I still can't forget about him.

4. 現在沒有什麼客人, 所以我們店的商品都不能賣完。

Xiànzài méiyǒu shénme kèrén, suǒyǐ wǒmen diàn de shāngpǐn dōu bù néng mài wán.

Currently, there aren't many customers, so we can't sell all the products in our store.

5. 我晚上九點喝了咖啡, 現在不能睡著。

Wǒ wǎnshàng jiǔ diǎn hē le kāfēi, xiànzài bù néng shuì zháo.

I drank coffee at 9 p.m. and I can't fall sleep now.

References

1. Wu, L., Lu, D., He, Y., Yang, C.: A Study on Errors in the Acquisition of Chinese by Japanese Students [Riben xuesheng hanyu xide pianwu yanjiu]. China Social Sciences Press, Beijing (2002). (in Chinese)
2. Yang, D.: Dispelling Doubts on Common Grammatical Errors by Japanese People Learning Chinese [Ribenren xue hanyu changjian yufa cuowu shiyi]. Commercial Press, Beijing (2008). (in Chinese)
3. Li, Y.: A study on the acquisition of two types of potential expressions [Liang zhong nengxing jiegou de xide yanjiu]. In: Xiao, X. (ed.) Studies on the Difficulty and Arrangement of Chinese Sentence Structures for Foreign Students [Waiguo xuesheng hanyu jushi xuexi nandu ji fenji paixu yanjiu], pp. 258–278. Higher Education Press, Beijing (2009). (in Chinese)
4. Lü, S. (ed.): 800 Words in Modern Chinese [Xiandai hanyu babai ci]. Commercial Press, Beijing (1980). (in Chinese)
5. Li, C.N., Thompson, S.A.: Mandarin Chinese: A Functional Reference Grammar. University of California Press, Berkeley (1981)
6. Hsiao, H.S., Lin, C.: On Mandarin potential complement constructions. Lang. Linguist. 13(5), 936–998 (2012). (in Chinese)
7. Imaizumi, S.: Typological study on expressions of possibility and their related meanings in English, Chinese and Japanese- How modality and voice intersect. In: Fon, J. (ed.) Dimensions of Diffusion and Diversity, pp. 56–82. De Gruyter Mouton, Berlin (2019)
8. Sugimura, H.: The Mandarin expressions "V de C", "neng VC", "neng V de C" [V de C, neng VC, neng V de C]. Chin. Lang. Learn. [Hanyu xuexi] 6, 23–29 (1982). (in Chinese)
9. Liu, Y.: Studies on the usage of potential complements [Keneng buyu yongfa de yanjiu]. In: Liu, Y. Papers on Chinese Grammar [Hanyu yufa lunji], pp. 1–26. Modern Press, Beijing (1989). (in Chinese)
10. Selinker, L.: Interlanguage. Int. Rev. Appl. Linguist. 10, 209–231 (1972)
11. Marty, P., Chemla, E., Sprouse, J.: The effect of three basic task features on the sensitivity of acceptability judgment tasks. Glossa: J. Gener. Linguist. 5(1), 72 (2020)
12. Wu, S.-C., Hsiao, H.S.: A case study on scalar ordering relations of Chinese adverbs. In: Su, Q., Xu, G., Yang, X. (eds.) Chinese Lexical Semantics. CLSW 2022. LNCS, vol. 13495, pp. 368–383. Springer, Cham (2023). https://doi.org/10.1007/978-3-031-28953-8_28
13. Sprouse, J., Schütze, C.T., Almeida, D.: A comparison of informal and formal acceptability judgments using a random sample from Linguistic Inquiry 2001–2010. Lingua 134, 219–248 (2013)
14. Yuan, B., Dugarova, E.: Wh-topicalization at the syntax-discourse interface in English speakers' L2 Chinese grammars. Stud. Second. Lang. Acquis. 34(4), 533–560 (2012)
15. Xue, W., Liu, M., Politzer-Ahles, S.: A study of complement coercion in Mandarin Chinese: Evidence from an acceptability judgment task. In: Liu, M., Kit, C., Su, Q. (eds.) Chinese Lexical Semantics. CLSW 2020. LNCS, vol. 12278, pp. 775–784. Springer, Cham (2021). https://doi.org/10.1007/978-3-030-81197-6_64
16. Kubler, C.C.: The influence of southern min on the mandarin of Taiwan. Anthropol. Linguist. 27(2), 156–176 (1985)
17. Kuo, W.-J.: Some directional complements in the potential verb-complement construction of Zhuziyulei—compared with Southern Min dialect. Bull. Chin. 49, 107–134 (2011). (in Chinese)
18. Delacre, M., Lakens, D., Leys, C.: Why psychologists should by default use Welch's t-test instead of student's t-test. Int. Rev. Soc. Psychol. 30(1), 92–101 (2017)

19. Wu, P.-H.: Interlanguage Analysis of "Hui": The Case of Japanese Learners. Master's thesis, Taiwan Normal University, Taipei (2009). (in Chinese)
20. Teng, S.-H.: A Pedagogical Grammar of Chinese [Dui wai hanyu jiaoxue yufa]. Crane Publishing, Taipei (2008). (in Chinese)

On the Discourse Functions of *Biede Bushuo* Based on Pragma-Dialectical Theory

Si Chen[1,2] and Lue Huang[3(✉)]

[1] School of Literature, Zhejiang University, Hangzhou, China
[2] School of Humanities, Nanyang Technological University, Singapore, Singapore
[3] Center for the Study of Language and Cognition, School of Philosophy, Zhejiang University, Hangzhou, China
huanglue@zju.edu.cn

Abstract. This study endeavors to elucidate the discourse functions of *biede bushuo* (别的不说) 'leaving aside other aspects' in mandarin Chinese. On the basis of corpus data, we mainly start from the perspective of pragma-dialectical theory, so as to carry out an analysis on occurrences of *biede bushuo* in argumentative discourse. Furthermore, we argue the functions in the four stages of critical discussion in argumentative discourse, and it can draw the conclusions of follows initially. At the confrontation and opening stage, *biede bushuo* can appear in the vicinity of a topic to select and restrict this topic; at the stage of argumentation, the expression can be employed in constructing the argument chaining that follows it; at the concluding stage, it lays emphasis on the authority of the conclusion. This research will help not only to broaden the understanding of the functional aspects of discourse markers but also to deepen philosophical reflections on the intrinsic argumentative nature embedded within language.

Keywords: *Biede Bushuo* · Discourse Functions · Pragma-Dialectical Theory

1 Introduction

The discourse functions of discourse markers involving speech act verbs in different languages have been extensively explored in the literature of esteemed scholars from various perspectives, such as evidential function, topic function, indexical function. Actually, when considering our everyday conversations as instances of argumentative discourse, discourse markers can also serve as indicators of standpoints or arguments. For example:

(1) 他老人家升迁是迟早的事。别的不说, 就凭着他老人家那部神仙胡须, 最次不济也能熬上个巡抚。

'His promotion is just a matter of time. Leaving aside other aspects, just look at his celestial beard; even in the worst-case scenario, he could still rise to become a governor.'

(2) 双双笑着说: "你们打开看看就知道了, 多提意见啊!"一个老汉接着说: "吃李双双做这个饭, 别的不说, 真干净, 挤着眼吃都不要紧。"

M. Dong et al. (Eds.): CLSW 2023, LNAI 14515, pp. 435–446, 2024.
https://doi.org/10.1007/978-981-97-0586-3_33

'Shuangshuang smiled and said, "Just open it and you'll see. Feel free to give your opinions!" An elderly man continued, "Eating the meal Li Shuangshuang made, leaving aside other aspects, it's really clean. You can even eat it with your eyes half-closed."'

As demonstrated in both example (1) and example (2), the discourse marker *biede bushuo* is positioned within a paragraph. In example (1), it is following an assertive sentence containing the copula *shi*, which conveys the author's affirmative assertion regarding a person' promotion. Subsequently, marker *biede bushuo* introduces a piece of evidence, further substantiating the credibility of the preceding statement. In this context, marker *biede bushuo* is commonly considered a conjunction linking the two sentences. Also, if the initial sentence is regarded as an assertion, the subsequent sentence serves as an argument, *biede bushuo* functions concurrently to indicate the evidence, enhance its credibility. While example (2) presents a different scenario, where the marker *biede bushuo* is located within the main clause, providing a comment of the meal in response to the previous speaker's request for opinions. Following this, there is a specific description of why it is considered that. In this case, *biede bushuo* serves as an indicator of the author's viewpoint, emphasizing the objectivity of the author's assertion that they are focusing on a particular aspect.

The examples above highlight that examining the role of discourse markers in real communication from an argumentative perspective can yield new insights, necessitating further exploration. We choose *biede bushuo* as a focus point to explore discourse marker functions. On the one hand, in mandarin Chinese, *biéde bùshuō*, meaning leaving aside other aspects, is characterized by heightened frequency and advantageous argumentative functionality in real communication. Additionally, scholarly discourse on the independent usage of *biede bushuo* is limited, particularly concerning its occurrence and argumentative characteristic within dynamic discourses.

In view of the above, this study applies the pragma-dialectical theory framework to investigate how *biede bushuo* appears in speech acts of argumentation and its discourse functions within dynamic argumentative processes. Adhering to the principles of maximally argumentative interpretation and analysis within this framework, discourse samples are meticulously dissected. The corpus used is drawn from the comprehensive and literary sub-corpus of the BLCU Corpus Center (BCC) and the modern Chinese sub-corpus of the Center for Chinese Linguistics (CCL). Focusing specifically on dialogue samples, 748 instances were meticulously identified, with 631 from the BCC and 117 from the CCL.

2   Occurrences of *Biede Bushuo* in Argumentative Discourse

It is generally recognized that the distributed representations of a syntactic entity in different contexts are closely associated with the functions it serves, therefore we will first delve into how *biede bushuo* appears in argumentative contexts.

In this section, we provide a concise introduction to the pragma-dialectical theory, and elucidate how, under the guidance of pragma-dialectical theory, *biede bushuo* manifests in contexts. This includes its role as an indicator for both standpoints and arguments, as well as its occurrences throughout the four stages of critical discussion.

2.1 Pragma-Dialectical Theory

The pragma-dialectical theory of argumentation, developed by Frans van Eemeren and Rob Grootendorst, integrates pragmatic insights from speech act theory and discourse analysis with dialectical insights from critical rationalism. As van Eemeren (2018: 89) articulates, "The primary goal of the theorizing is to create an adequate basis for improving methodically the analysis and evaluation as well as the oral and written production of argumentative discourse." The theory provides an important theoretical basis for our study in exploring discourse markers functions, as pragmatic factors influencing the communication and interaction process could be taken into account.

Within this framework, researchers like Jansen (2017, 2020) have examined expressions such as 'you think that says a lot, but really it says nothing' and 'not for nothing', exploring their argumentative and rhetorical characteristics and functions by considering these expressions as presentational devices for strategic maneuvering. Similarly, Uzelgun (2015) used the pragma-dialectical perspective to explain the argumentative functions of the concessive construction 'yes, but…'. Drawing on insights from these studies, we ascertain that *biede bushuo* not only facilitates interpersonal interaction but also encapsulates the speaker's strategic argumentative moves.

2.2 *Biede Bushuo* and Argumentative Speech Acts

According to pragma-dialectics, argumentation is defined as "a verbal, social, and rational activity aimed at convincing a reasonable critic of the acceptability of a certain opinion by advancing one or more propositions designed to justify that standpoint" in van Eemeren (2017: 1). This definition, though slightly modified in van Eemeren (2018), emphasizes three key points: firstly, argumentation occurs in everyday life, not just academic contexts; secondly, it deals with differences of opinion, whether explicit or implicit, as long as the standpoint at issue is not fully shared by the discussants; thirdly, it is a dynamic process leading to a reasonable resolution of differences of opinion concerning the acceptability of standpoints, primarily through verbal communication.

Applying this definition to linguistic constructions, we observe that *biede bushuo* frequently emerges in argumentative discourse, aligning with argumentative speech acts.

(3) 徐厂长说："老丁说得对，别人都是狼是虎，只有我是只羊。"老丁有些尴尬说："别的不说，只要你在任上，我保证供销科围着你的指挥棒转。"

'Director Xu said, "Old Ding is right. Everyone else might be wolves and tigers, but I am just a sheep." Old Ding replied awkwardly, "Leaving aside other matters, as long as you are in office, I guarantee that the Supply and Marketing Department will follow your lead."'

Example (3) serves as an illustrative case study of argumentation involving two discussants, director Xu and old Ding. They are in an attempt to convince each other. The difference of opinion at issue is a metaphorical standpoint: "I am the only sheep (that is docile and easy to bully)", which is subsequently resolved through argumentation.

2.3 *Biede Bushuo* as a Part of Standpoints or Arguments

In everyday communication, argumentative speech acts are employed with the objective of defending a standpoint or convincing others of the standpoint in question. As stated by van Eemeren (2017: 41), "In order to determine how a difference of opinion has been resolved, one must first identify what arguments the speaker or writer has advanced in defense of his or her standpoint." This underscores the importance of considering *biede bushuo* as an integral to standpoints or arguments during analysis.

Example (4) further illustrates how *biede bushuo* can be part of standpoints.

(4) 你想, 这件事情否决掉, 我觉得, 我们<u>别的不说</u>, 就从合不合算, 最简单的计较说, 我觉得可口可乐是划算了。

'Think about it, if this matter gets rejected, leaving aside other factors, just considering whether it is cost-effective, I believe the acquisition is a good deal for Coca-Cola.'

In this instance, the standpoint following *biede bushuo* is that 'The acquisition is a good deal for Coca-Cola'. The speaker presents a positive standpoint regarding Coca-Cola's acquisition and proceeds to provide supporting arguments. Through similar instances in the corpus, it can be deduced that when someone adopts a positive standpoint after using *biede bushuo*, their intention is to defend this standpoint by justifying the corresponding proposition.

Additionally, *biede bushuo* can function as a component of arguments, as demonstrated in example (5):

(5) 主持人: "<u>别的不说</u>, 因为一目了然。中国-东盟博览会五周年。最醒目的就是这个。"

'Host: "Leaving aside other factors, it's quite obvious. China-ASEAN Expo Fifth Anniversary. This is the most prominent aspect."'

In example (5), the term *yinwei* (因为) 'because' serves as an argumentative indicator, articulating a reason. Here, *biede beshuo* serves as a segment of the argument supporting the standpoint 'This (logo) represents the 5th Anniversary of the China-ASEAN Expo' which the speaker previously posited.

Differentiating between *biede bushuo* as a component of standpoints and as a part of arguments solely based on its structure can be challenging. Contextual cues and indicators are pivotal in making this distinction within argumentative discourse. Consider example (6):

(6) 关起门来, 说句良心话, 这些情形也是我们造成的, 别的不说, 单讲提税一项, 给国家纳税是工商界天经地义的事吧, 如果我们过去按期如数缴纳, 不拖欠, 就不会搁到现在去补税了。

'Speaking frankly behind closed doors, these situations are also created by us. Leaving aside other factors, just talking about tax payment, it is the legitimate duty of the business community to pay taxes to the country, isn't it? If we had paid on time and in full in the past without any arrears, we wouldn't have to make up for the taxes now.'

Here, *biede bushuo* co-occurs with a comprehensive argument supporting the standpoint 'We are responsible for these situations.' The reasons provided by speaker ('Contributing taxes to the country is a matter of course for the business community' and 'If we had consistently turned over taxes payable on time in the past, we wouldn't have to pay taxes in arrears right now') are well-received because they align with shared background information and are perceived as credible. Factual statements or propositions are commonly used to advance arguments to justify one's standpoint, as people tend to accept information that aligns with their beliefs.

In contrast, considering example (3) mentioned in Sect. 2.2, after uttering *biede bushuo*, old Ding makes an exaggerated commitment unfamiliar to the listener. Consequently, it cannot be readily accepted as true or interpreted as part of the reason-giving process; instead, it should be recognized as a specific standpoint.

In argumentative discourse, applying maximally argumentative interpretation and analysis to *biede bushuo* allows for categorizing co-occurring propositions as either components of standpoints or parts of arguments. This classification relies on argumentative indicators and contextual cues, marking the starting point of our study on *biede bushuo* and its potential functions.

2.4 *Biede Bushuo* in Different Stages of Critical Discussion

Given the observed connections between *biede bushuo* and argumentative speech acts in everyday communication, integrating these findings with the model of a critical discussion is crucial.

According to Van Eemeren's theoretical framework (2017: 19), a critical discussion is defined as 'An ideal argumentative discourse aimed at resolving a difference of opinion in a reasonable way by determining whether the standpoints at issue ought to be accepted or not.' This model comprises four stages: confrontation, opening, argumentation, and concluding stages, although real-life argumentative discourses often align partially with this ideal model and may not necessarily adhere to this order.

Positioning *biede bushuo* within the context of a critical discussion has revealed that it can be reconstructed across various stages, each associated with distinct goals.

Position 1: Confrontation Stage.

In the confrontation stage, the objective is to ascertain the existence or emergence of a difference of opinion and to challenge or critique a standpoint proposed by someone, indicating that it is not universally shared and is met with doubt or criticism. In this context, *biede bushuo* acts as a tool to clearly articulate the discussant's standpoint, as seen in example (7):

(7) 是啊，你。以前胡堂主就老爱在开玩笑的时候说："咱们庄主在武林之中，别的不说，胆子可绝对是一等一的大，只要是他觉得可信用的人，背景来历都不清楚也无所谓。"

'Yeah, you. Old master Hu used to jokingly say during our playful moments: 'Our manor master in the martial arts world, leaving aside other matters, has incredible courage. As long as he finds someone trustworthy, their background and origins don't matter.''

Undoubtedly, in this scenario, the discussants are engaged in the process of identifying the specific standpoint. One of them has put forth the standpoint 'Our master has incredible courage', following *biede bushuo*, which effectively delineates the boundaries of the 'disagreement space', indicating a limited scope for contention.

Position 2: Opening Stage.

In the opening stage, arguments supporting the standpoints are presented, providing the basis for ensuring argumentation. *Biede bushuo* is utilized to introduce information that is widely acceptable to the participants (such as factual propositions mentioned earlier), laying the groundwork for the main arguments to be presented.

Example (4) illustrates this concept. The statement 'If we only consider the cost of the acquisition, taking the simplest way to calculate…' expands 'the zone of agreement' for the discussants.

Position 3: Argumentation Stage.

The argumentation stage is the focal point where discussants present persuasive arguments. Thus, an optimal defense of the standpoint(s) at issue is crucial to convincing those who have yet to agree, employing a reasoned approach. As seen in example (8), it demonstrates a case where *biede bushuo* indicates that the presented argument is compelling and deserving of acceptance.

(8) 这农村的集市是旧风俗，已延续几千年，若完全不让搞，恐怕也不现实。如今的供销社，生产资料供应严重匮乏。别的不说，到了收割的季节，农民要买把镰刀，都难上加难。

'The markets in these rural areas follow ancient traditions, having persisted for thousands of years. It might not be entirely realistic to prohibit them entirely. Nowadays, the supply of production materials in the agricultural cooperatives is severely lacking. Leaving aside other matters, when harvest season comes, even buying a sickle becomes increasingly difficult for the farmers.'

Within the given argumentative discourse, various standpoints and arguments are presented. However, the most compelling argument put forth by the discussant is the one following *biede bushuo*. The standpoint asserted is, 'Nowadays, the supply…' substantiated by the argument 'when harvest…'. In this context, *biede bushuo* unquestionably functions as a component of the argument. The discussant strategically employs *biede bushuo* to underscore the potency of their argument, carefully chosen from the available arguments to align with the discussant's most effective 'line of defense'. This usage enhances the persuasive impact of the argument, emphasizing the critical nature of the issue and highlighting the urgent need for addressing the supply shortages in agricultural cooperatives.

Position 4: Concluding stage.

In the concluding stage, participants evaluate the resolution of the difference of opinion. Here, *biede bushuo* indicates the outcome deemed acceptable by the discussants.

Example (9) illustrates this.

(9) "要是你们将善堂积存移用去办了什么习艺所，别的不说，那一班孤老病穷的可怜人先就不得了呵！"冯梅生知道这位先生的脾气，听这么说，便觉得不好再争，只笑了笑。

'"If you divert the funds Shantang has accumulated to establish some kind of vocational school, leaving aside other matters, those poor and sick elderly individuals would suffer first!" Feng Meisheng understood this gentleman's temperament. Hearing this, he felt it was inappropriate to argue further and just smiled.'

It can be seen from above that *biede bushuo* serves as a significant element, indicating the discussant's prediction about the fate of vulnerable individuals. Moreover, this prediction, emphasized by *biede bushuo*, acts as a conclusive statement, effectively concluding the argumentation and guiding the conversation toward the desired 'scope of conclusiveness'.

Examining the above aspects, *biede bushuo* manifests in different stages of the ideal model of a critical discussion, serving diverse objectives within each stage, either as an integral part of standpoints or as a component of arguments. Consistent with perspectives by Cui (2022), language not only conveys information but also embodies an inherent argumentative dimension intricately linked with its linguistic structure. Generally speaking, linguistic expressions inherently possess argumentative potential, with conveyed information indicating specific directions and intensities of argumentation. It should be noted that discourse functions also operates in contexts alongside these inherent argumentative potential. Therefore, it becomes imperative to ascertain the specific direction it indicates and the degree of argumentative potential it wields when delving into the function.

3 Discourse Functions of *Biede Bushuo*

The function of discourse markers has always been the focus of research in the field of linguistics. Early traditional scholars identified various essential roles for discourse markers, such as organizing discourse, signaling interaction, and marking attitudes. They viewed discourse markers as tools for structuring communication. In the 1980s, Schiffrin (1987), a prominent scholar in the systematic study of discourse markers, emphasized their significant role in shaping patterns of discourse coherence. She proposed a model encompassing five interconnected levels: exchange structure, action structure, ideational structure, participation framework, and information state. Schiffrin (1987) delved into how discourse markers connect adjacent pairs in discourse. Since the 1990s, scholars, including Fraser (1996), approached discourse markers pragmatically, categorizing them into four main types: contrastive markers, elaborative markers, inferential markers, and topic change markers. Fraser (1996) argued that the fundamental significance of discourse markers lies in providing direction for discourse comprehension, guiding listeners in identifying and understanding relationships between preceding and subsequent elements.

The preceding research offers us valuable insights, with an emerging consensus among scholars that discourse markers primarily serve pragmatic functions. They act as guides or signposts for discourse comprehension, aiding listeners in recognizing various pragmatic relationships within discourse and thereby shaping cognitive processes involved in discourse understanding. The exploration of the function of *biede bushuo* is grounded in this viewpoint. We will focus on how it directs the attention of the recipient to subsequent standpoints or arguments, while also examining its role in marking mutual argumentative relationships between adjacent sentences.

A distinctive feature of discourse marker research in Chinese is the emphasis on speech-related markers. Cao (2018) proposed that speech-related discourse markers fundamentally originate from verbal interaction, reflecting linguistic reflexivity. In simple terms, linguistic reflexivity refers to the speaker's intention to guide the listener's understanding of discourse, manifesting intersubjectivity in interaction. Because compared to written language, interactivity has lower controllability, necessitating a one-time, effective guidance for listeners to understand the discourse according to the speaker's expectations. Therefore, speech-related discourse markers exhibit contextual sensitivity, necessitating an examination of their functions within specific contexts. Simultaneously, we should grasp the intersubjectivity and specific connotations of spoken discourse markers.

Building upon this foundation, and integrating the argumentative potential of *biede bushuo* as elucidated in the preceding section, our examination will focus on its guiding and indicative functions within the specific contexts of argumentation where *biede bushuo* appears. Additionally, we will scrutinize how it achieves intersubjectivity.

3.1 Selecting the Topic of Argumentation

Upon examining the corpus, we observe that *biede bushuo* serves the function of selecting the argumentative topic. This refers to the arguer's use of *biede bushuo* in the discourse context to demarcate the scope and subject of the argument, thereby steering the subsequent discourse in a direction favorable to their position.

The topic-selecting function is intricately tied to the nature of *biede bushuo*. It functions as a meta-discourse, meaning linguistic reflexivity as mentioned earlier. It constitutes a self-reflective expression with negotiated interactive significance (Verhagen 2005). Similar expressions like *youyi shuoyi* and *gaishuo bushuo* in mandarin Chinese, all of which indicate the speaker's attitude or cognitive attributes towards the propositional content of the discourse, reflecting the speaker's intersubjectivity in interaction. Subjectivity refers to the speaker's subjective evaluation, attitude, and viewpoints towards things, while intersubjectivity manifests the speaker's acknowledgment and attention to the listener (Verhagen 2005). Through the use of *biede bushuo*, the speaker constructs a mental space (Fauconnier 1997) for the listener, implying that aside from the given topic, there are many other topics left unsaid. This strategy aims to make the listener aware of the uniqueness or significance of the current topic, directing their focus to the given subject. Within the framework of a critical discussion, this function is frequently employed both at the confrontation and opening stages, and can take on two structural forms.

Topic + Biede Bushuo + Comment. The first form involves the structure: *biede bushuo* followed by a comment. Here, *biede bushuo* acts as a linguistic demarcator, subtly guiding the discourse's focus. This nuanced topic selection reflects participants' metapragmatic acumen and strategic maneuvering, aligning the conversation with their objectives.

In example (7) from Sect. 2.4, the discourse narrows down to the lord, and *biede bushuo* is strategically used to articulate the discussant's standpoint, culminating in the proposition 'Our lord is very bold.' This strategic use involves clear articulation of the discussant's stance and exploitation of the available 'disagreement space', shaping the confrontation in line with the discussant's preferences. This demonstrates the intricate interplay of linguistic tactics and argumentative intent within this discourse.

Biede Bushuo + Topic, Comment. The second form, '*biede bushuo* + topic, comment' represents a distinct structure within argumentative discourse. This configuration underscores the strategic use of *biede bushuo* as a meta-discourse marker, delineating the discussant's epistemic stance and guiding the subsequent discourse toward a specific topic. Such deliberate structuring of argumentation showcases the nuanced interplay between linguistic elements, reflecting the metapragmatic awareness of the discussant and shaping the trajectory of the argumentative exchange. *Biede bushuo* becomes the focal point, clearly defining the argumentative topic's boundaries in this form.

Example (4) shows that the subject of *biede bushuo* can be the speaker in its zero form or completed with 'I' or 'we'. The content following *biede bushuo* resembles an introductory structure like *guang/jiu shuo* 'just/only talking about'. This comparative approach, *biede bushuo, jiu shuo*, strategically contrasts with *bushuo* 'not saying' and *shuo* 'saying' emphasizing a common starting point. Subsequent argumentation centers around this shared foundation of *guang/jiu shuo* 'just/only talking about'.

3.2 Constructing the Argument(s) Chaining

In addition, *biede bushuo* plays a crucial role in constructing the argumentative chain. It becomes an indispensable component of the argument, forming a series of interconnected points. In this context, the preceding sentence of *biede bushuo* represents the speaker's presented standpoint, while the immediately following sentence serves as the argument for the preceding standpoint, functioning as evidence. Observing the corpus, it can be discerned that the immediately following sentence often relies on objective facts or conventionalized knowledge. More precisely, it pertains to undisputed facts or fundamental knowledge that the speaker believes to be irrefutable within the listener's cognitive realm.

During this process, even though the speaker may present only one piece of argument, the interactive subjectivity characteristic of *biede bushuo* creates a mental space for the reader regarding the evidence. This triggers a series of implied arguments, implying the persuasiveness of the evidence. Overall, despite these enumerated points possibly being common knowledge or conventional situations, categorized as known old information with low informational value in communication, and seemingly weaker on the surface, they are reinforced by the speaker's imagined, unexpressed, and robust supporting points crafted for the reader. Consequently, they construct a hierarchical defense chain at the reader's psychological level. In this circumstance, *biede bushuo* frequently functions in the argumentation stage, constructing a hierarchical chain of defense, as exemplified below:

Standpoint + Biede bushuo, Argument.

(10) 死去的烈士会不会答应?养育我们的人民能不能答应?!别的不说，单说四三年秋在沂蒙山的那场突围战，我带的那个营是整整四百人哪!可一仗下来，当吴大姐你把我从死尸堆里背出来后，活下来的有多少?

'Doing that, would the martyrs who died agree? Can the people who raised us agree?! Leaving aside other matters, let's talk about the breakout battle in the autumn of 1943 in the Yimeng Mountain. The battalion I led had a full four hundred people! But after that battle, when you, Sister Wu, pulled me out from the pile of corpses, how many survived?'

In this context, *biede bushuo* utilizes 'the grim situation of a certain battle' as evidence, suggesting that even with a high number of combatants, the battle situation was dire, resulting in numerous deaths. Linguistically, 'the autumn of 1943' and 'Yimeng Mountain' serve as temporal and spatial markers, indicating past events and establishing events as credible and reliable. Structurally, it showcases a cascading effect in argumentation, creating an 'argument(s) chaining'. This strategy can be summarized as employing the weakest argument to achieve the most effective reasonableness.

3.3 Making the Conclusions Authority

Moreover, *biede bushuo* can constrain and construct the stance in argumentative discourse, serving to provide a final conclusion. At this juncture, the subsequent sentence of *biede bushuo* is semantically closely connected to the preceding sentence; it represents the author's conclusion derived from the previously discussed phenomenon. In contrast to the previous content, the description concerning the topic concludes at this point. It also embodies the intersubjectivity of *biede bushuo*—while literally maintaining its meaning of 'without saying anything else', it guides the listener to understand the speaker's arrangement of discourse organization, signaling the conclusion of the topic. Simultaneously, *biede bushuo* reflects the speaker's cognition, specifically, the subsequent sentence of *biede bushuo* is a result based on the previously discussed discourse, which is an intra-discourse agreed-upon content after mutual communication. Otherwise, the topic would continue. This kind of basis also indicates the objectivity and fairness of the subsequent sentence of *biede bushuo*. Therefore, it prompts the argumentation to end at a point favorable to the speaker's standpoint.

Argument(s) + Biede Bushuo, Standpoint. In instance (9) from Sect. 2.4, *biede bushuo* is strategically employed to lead to the conclusive statement. The speaker's intent is not a sweeping judgment on all people but a focus on a specific group.

'Epistemic authority' resides with the speaker(s) or listener(s) and can be 'declared' or 'waived', closely tied to their participation and 'discursive authority' over knowledge. In this argumentation stage, the author presents a highly confident proposition or easily accessible information, establishing significant discursive authority over knowledge, leaving no room for further debate and prompting listeners to withdraw their participation.

Table 1 provides an overview of *biede bushuo* forms and functions in the four discussion stages.

Table 1. Forms and functions of *biede bushuo* in the four discussion stages.

Discourse functions	Stage of a critical discussion	Prototypical structure
Selecting the topic of arguing	Confrontation/ Opening stage	Topic + *biede bushuo* + comment *Biede bushuo* + topic, comment
Constructing the argument chaining	Argumentation stage	Standpoint + *biede bushuo*, argument
Making the conclusion authority	Concluding stage	Argument(s) + *biede bushuo*, standpoint

Propositions incorporating *biede bushuo* in different argumentative stages exhibit diverse forms and functions, tailored to specific argumentative goals. These nuanced objectives necessitate corresponding grammatical alterations, leading to a range of discourse meanings. The interplay between grammatical structures and semantic nuances highlights the multifaceted nature of *biede bushuo* in argumentative contexts, contributing to the complexity and richness of the discourse.

4   Conclusion

This study explores the functional analysis of the discourse marker *biede bushuo* based on pragma-dialectical theory. Specifically, the research investigates the patterns of occurrence of *biede bushuo* in argumentation, identifies its positions within arguments, and elucidates its corresponding functions in the realm of argumentative discourse.

The study finds that when transforming everyday discourse into argumentation, *biede bushuo* serves dual functions. On one hand, it functions to indicate the speaker's standpoint or argument, and on the other hand, it embodies intersubjectivity: in the confrontation and opening stages, the use of *biede bushuo* constructs a mental space for the listener, implying that beyond the given topic, there are other aspects not worth mentioning, thus guiding the listener to focus on the given topic; in the argument stage, the speaker creates an evidence chain using *biede bushuo,* presenting the weakest argument to achieve the strongest effect through inference; in the concluding stage, the literal meaning of *biede bushuo* is retained, indicating the authoritative control of the speaker over the conversation, prompting the argumentation to conclude at a point favorable to the speaker's viewpoint.

In fact, these dual functions represent the pragmatic nature of *biede bushuo* in the specific context of argumentation, demonstrating that discourse markers not only organize and connect discourse but also reflect the speaker's subjective attitude and standpoint. This study, grounded in the perspective of pragma-dialectical theory, injects new vitality into discourse marker research, offering a potential new angle for investigation and contributing new examples to the shared understanding of previous research traditions.

Acknowledgments. We would like to mention that this paper is sponsored by the research grant from the National Planning Office of Philosophy and Social Sciences, P. R. China (No. 20CYY05).

References

1. Anka, G.: Characterizing a detached argumentative style: text types as presentational choices. Contemp. Rhetoric **223**(1), 31–43 (2021). (in Chinese)
2. Cui, Y.: An argumentative study on courtroom reported speech. Contemp. Rhetoric **234**(6), 53–67 (2022). (in Chinese)
3. Cao, X., Du, K.: A survey of yanshuo-type discourse markers in Chinese from the perspective of interaction. Chin. Teach. World **2**, 206–216 (2018). (in Chinese)
4. Dong, X.: On the lexicalization of x-shuo. Lang. Sci. **3**(2), 46–57 (2003). (in Chinese)
5. Fauconnier, G.: Mappings in Thought and Language. Cambridge University Press, New York (1997)
6. Fraser, B.: Pragmatic markers. Pragmatics **6**, 167–190 (1996)
7. Li, Z.: Semantic and pragmatic functions of the conjunction bushuo. Chinese Linguist. **27**(3), 2–7 (2009). (in Chinese)

8. van Eemeren, F.: Strategic Maneuvering in Argumentative Discourse: Extending the Pragma-Dialectical Theory of Argumentation. John Benjamins, Amsterdam (2017)

9. van Eemeren, F.: Argumentation Theory: A Pragma-Dialectical Perspective. Springer, Amsterdam (2018)

10. van Eemeren, F., Garssen, B.: Handbook of Argumentation Theories. Springer, Amsterdam (2014)

11. Han, X., Zhan, F.: A study on the semantic change of the Chinese negative adverb bushen. In: Liu, M., Kit, C., Su, Q. (eds.) Chinese Lexical Semantics. CLSW 2020. LNCS, vol. 12278, pp. 100–107. Springer, Cham (2021). https://doi.org/10.1007/978-3-030-81197-6_9

12. Henrike, J.: 'You think that says a lot, but really it says nothing': an argumentative and linguistic account, argumentation of an idiomatic expression functioning as a presentational device. Argumentation **31**, 615–640 (2017)

13. Henrike, J., Francisca, S.: Argumentative use and strategic function of the expression 'not for nothing.' Argumentation **34**, 143–162 (2020)

14. Lin, J.: Grammaticalization of Shuo and Jiang in Singapore mandarin Chinese: A spoken-corpus-based study. In: Hong, J., Su, Q., Wu, J. (eds.) Chinese Lexical Semantics. CLSW 2018. LNCS, vol. 11173, pp. 82–90. Springer, Cham (2018). https://doi.org/10.1007/978-3-030-04015-4_7

15. Östman, J.: You Know: A Discourse Functional Approach. John Benjamins, Amsterdam (1981)

16. Uzelgun, M., Lewiński, M., Castro, P.: Managing disagreement through 'yes, but...' constructions: an argumentative analysis. Discourse Stud. **17**(4), 467–484 (2015)

17. Verhagen, A.: Constructions of Intersubjectivity: Discourse, Syntax, and Cognition. Oxford University Press, Oxford (2005)

18. Schiffrin, D.: Discourse Markers. Cambridge University Press, Cambridge (1987)

X-Copying as Metalinguistic Negation in Chengdu Chinese

Jiajuan Xiong[(✉)]

School of International Studies, Southeastern University of Finance and Economics,
Chengdu, China
jiajuanx@gmail.com

Abstract. In this paper, we investigate the semantics and syntax of the X-copy structure of [X-*təu*-XY] in Chengdu Chinese. The semantics of this structure is rather elusive, as evidenced by the various contexts where it may occur and diversified meanings that it exhibits across contexts. Facing the difficulty in identifying its constructional meaning, we scrutinize the interactions between contexts and implicatures and figure out, for the first time in the literature, the main function of this copy structure as metalinguistic negation. Syntactically, this copy mechanism is proved to be a type of CP negation, as opposed to the propositional negation, such as VP negation and IP negation.

Keywords: The X-copy structure · Metalinguistic negation · CP negation · Chengdu Chinese

1 Introduction

In Chengdu Chinese, a copy structure takes the form of [X-*təu*-XY], in which XY can be a VP, an AP, a NP or a NumP, as exemplified in (1)–(4).

(1) T'oŋ   təu   t'oŋtsʴ   no.   ([V-*təu*-VP])
    notify   DOU   notify   SFP
    'It has been already notified.'

(2) T'aŋ   lən   təu   lən   no.   ([A-*təu*-AP])
    soup   cool   DOU   cool   SFP
    'The soup is cool now.'

(3) Wan   təu   wansaŋ   no.   ([N-*təu*-NP])
    night   DOU   night   SFP
    'It is night already.'

(4) Tɕ'i   təu   tɕ'isʴ   suei   le.   ([Num-*təu*-NumP])
    seven   DOU   seventy   age   SFP
    'S/he is 70 years old already.'

M. Dong et al. (Eds.): CLSW 2023, LNAI 14515, pp. 447–457, 2024.
https://doi.org/10.1007/978-981-97-0586-3_34

The semantics of this copy structure is not immediately clear. As shown in the above free translations, there is no new information to be added in the copy structure. In the literature, this structure is reported to place an emphasis on the completion of an action or the change of a state (Zhang et al. 2001; Hu 2010). Such an emphasis, however, seems not to be derived from the copy structure *per se*, as this emphatic meaning is found to be present in their copy-less counterparts as well, regardless of the presence or absence of an adverbial *yijing* 'already', as illustrated in (5)–(8).

(5) Təu   (jitɕin) tʰoŋtsɿ no.
     DOU   already   notify   SFP
     '(It) has been already notified.'

(6) Tʰaŋ   təu   (jitɕin) lən   no.
     soup   DOU   already   cool   SFP
     'The soup is cool already.'

(7) Təu   (jitɕin) wansaŋ   no.
     DOU   already   night   SFP
     'It is night already.'

(8) Təu   (jitɕin) tɕʰisɿ   suei   no.
     DOU   already   seventy age   SFP
     '(S/he) is 70 years old already.'

Moreover, the copy mechanism does not alter the truth condition of a proposition. For instance, (1)–(4) and (5)–(8) are essentially identical in terms of their propositional meanings. Given the elusive semantics of the copy structure, we intend to figure out its exact constructional meaning in this research. In the literature, in addition to the emphatic meaning, Zhang et al. (2001) identify an implied meaning of concession in the copy structure, on the grounds that this structure can be introduced by the conjunction *tɕizan* 'now that', as exemplified in (9).

(9) Tɕizan   tʰoŋ   təu   tʰoŋtsɿ no,   *(tɕiəu tɕʰy   pa).
    now_that   notify   DOU   notify   SFP   then   go   SFP
    'Now that (I) have been notified, I'd better go.'

The copy structure is semantically compatible with the concession-encoded conjunction *tɕizan* 'now that'. However, one point is note-worthy: semantic concession requires the presence of a continuing clause, without which the sentence at issue is incomplete, as evidenced in (9). By contrast, when *tɕizan* 'now that' is absent, the [X-təu-XY] can stand alone as a complete sentence, without any requirement for a continuing clause, as shown in (1)–(4). In this regard, concession should be a derived but not inherent meaning of [X-təu-XY].

In order to work out the structural meaning of [X-təu-XY], we examine the contexts under which this copy structure occurs, as well as the interactions between the copy structure and the sentence final particles (SFPs).

2 [X-*Dou*-XY]: What It Really Means?

The copy structure [X-*təu*-XY] is pragmatically versatile in the sense that one and the same copy structure may occur in various contexts and give rise to different readings. As presented in Sect. 1, the copy mechanism does not change the propositional meaning, and the exact interpretation depends on contexts. One of the noticeable contexts is the continuing clause, which requires no conjunctions, as exemplified in (10) and (11).

(10)	Wan	təu	wansaŋ	no,	ŋo	pu	nən
	night	DOU	night	SFP	I	NEG	can
	ts'utɕ'iɛ	no.					
	go_out	SFP					

'It is night already. And I cannot go out.'

(11)	Wan	təu	wansaŋ	no,	ŋo	jiau	ts'utɕ'iɛ no.
	night	DOU	night	SFP	I	will	go_out SFP

'It is night already. And I shall go out now.'

It is interesting to note that one and the same [X-*təu*-XY] can be compatible with the continuing clauses of opposite polarities. For instance, the continuing clauses in (10) and (11) are essentially the same other than their polarities, with the former being negative while the latter being positive. Crucially, both (10) and (11) are semantically well-formed.

Similarly, the continuing clauses in (12) and (13) take the form of rhetorical questions and are of opposite polarity as well. Once again, both negative and positive polarity fit well with the same copy sentence.

(12)	Wan	təu	wansaŋ	no,	xai	jiau	ts'utɕ'iɛ a?
	night	DOU	night	SFP	NEG	can	go_out SFP

'It is night already. Why do you still go out?'

(13)	Wan	təu	wansaŋ	no,	xai	pu	ts'utɕ'iɛ a?
	night	DOU	night	SFP	I	will	go_out SFP

'It is night already. Why don't you go out?'

The flexible compatibility between [X-*təu*-XY] and the continuing clauses suggests that their semantic relation is by no means truth conditionally determined as a strict cause-and-effect relation. Rather, we argue that the relation between [X-*təu*-XY] and the continuing clauses is based on a [X-*təu*-XY]-related implicature that can be encyclopedically, culturally and contextually dependent. For example, the same fact, i.e. "it is already night", may be associated with different implicatures, such as "I generally stay at home at night for the sake of safety" or "I usually go out at night for my night shift". These implicatures, albeit being opposite in polarity, make good sense. It is the implicatures that are conducive to the meanings of the continuing sentences. The working mechanism will be elaborated on in Sect. 3.

It is noteworthy that a continuing clause does not necessarily co-occur with the [X-*təu*-XY] structure. Rather, the copy structure can stand alone as a complete sentence in the middle of a conversation, as shown in (14). Suppose that the speaker A is proposing to go out for fun. And the speaker B may respond with an X-copy structure, which functions as a decline to A's proposed invitation, though the decline is not linguistically encoded by negation in this conversation.

(14) A: Women   chuqu ba.
       we   go_out SFP
       'Let us go out.'
   B: Wan dou   wanshang   le.
      night DOU   night   SFP
      'It is already night.'
      (implicature: We cannot go out now.)

In this case, the [X-*təu*-XY]-related encyclopedic knowledge is "we generally do not go out at night (e.g., for the sake of safety)", rather than "we usually go out at night (e.g., for my night shift)". Since an encyclopedic knowledge depends on world knowledge, social convention and contexts, the same situation may be associated with different encyclopedic knowledge. In this connection, a question arises: which encyclopedic knowledge, out of a group of possible encyclopedic knowledge, should be activated for an appropriate interpretation of the X-copy [X-*təu*-XY]? An answer to this question hinges upon the function of [X-*təu*-XY], which will be discussed in Sect. 3.

3 Metalinguistic Negation

Upon examining the data, we find that [X-*təu*-XY] mainly functions as metalinguistic negation (Horn 1972, 1985; Davis 2011; Martins 2020). In what follows in this section, we will analyze (i) what the copy structure negates in Sect. 3.1; (ii) how different interpretations of (implied) conjunctions, apparently in association with aspect, can be unified in Sect. 3.2; (iii) how metalinguistic negation interacts with ordinary negation in Sect. 3.3.

3.1 What Does It Negate?

Metalinguistic negation is particularly evident in (14), in which speaker B declines speaker A's proposed invitation by uttering an X-copy [X-*təu*-XY]. In other words, (14B) is functionally equivalent to a negative reply, such as "*No, we do not go out*". Pragmatically speaking, the utterance of an [X-*təu*-XY] is polite, as it not only declines the invitation but also states the reason for the decline, i.e., the encyclopedic knowledge in relation to the [X-*təu*-XY]. In the case of (14), the encyclopedic knowledge should be "we generally do not go out at night (e.g., for the sake of safety)", instead of "we usually go out at night (e.g., for my night shift)", because only the former one can serve as a reasonable basis for negation (viz. Refusion to one's invitation). Thus, the selection of an appropriate encyclopedic knowledge, out of a group of possible encyclopedic possibilities, is largely determined by the function of metalinguistic negation.

Let us return to (10)–(13), in which [X-*təu*-XY] shows compatibility with the continuing clauses of opposite polarities. All the same, the function of [X-*təu*-XY] is metalinguistic negation. The difference lies in what the speaker negates in a particular context.

For instance, the sentence (10) may function to negate a suggestion, a request or an invitation from another interlocuter, e.g., "let us go out". Alternatively, (10) can also negate the speaker's self-perceived commitment or obligation, such as "I shall go out". In this connection, the encyclopedic knowledge "one does not go out at night (e.g., for the sake of safety)" serves as a befitting reason to negate the aforementioned request or commitment. By contrast, the sentence (11) may negate a request "let us remain at home (not go out)" or a commitment "I shall remain at home", depending on the contexts. In this case, the appropriate encyclopedic knowledge should be "I shall go out at night (e.g., for my night shift)", which constitutes a good reason for negation. This analysis can be extended to (12) and (13), in which the contrast of polarity in the continuing clauses reflects the contrast of polarity in terms of what they negate.

3.2 Apparent Polysemy Derived from Aspect

Having established that the main function of the X-copy structure is metalinguistic negation, we examine the semantic differences in association with aspect, as exemplified in (15) and (16).

(15) ŋo	ŋan	təu	ŋanwei	tʻa	no,	tʻa	xai
I	console	DOU	console	her	SFP	she	still
tsai	kʻu.						
PROG	cry						

'I've consoled her already, but she is still crying.'

Implicature: '**Now that** I consoled her, she should not be crying.'

(16) ni	pu	nən	paŋ	tʻa,	ŋan	təu	jiau
you	NEG	can	help	her	console	DOU	will
ŋanwei	tʻa	i-ɕia.					
console	her	one-bit					

'You cannot help her, but you will at least console her instead.'

Implicature: 'You should help her by consoling her **to the least**.'

The X-copy [X-təu-XY] can be either perfective or imperfective, as exemplified in (15) and (16), respectively. Their meanings are noticeably different. As reported in Zhang et al. (2001), the perfective and imperfective [X-təu-XY] encode two different meanings, viz., tɕisʔ "now that" and tsʔsau "to the least". This contrast is indeed corroborated in the above translations. We wonder, however, why the copy strategy may lead to such semantic differences and whether these meanings can be unified or not.

Firstly, regardless of aspect, [X-*təu*-XY] functions as metalinguistic negation. In (15), it is a complaint (e.g., "she should stop crying!") or a reproach (e.g., "why don't you stop her from crying?") that is negated. In (16), what is negated can be a complaint (e.g., "you won't help her"). As a result of metalinguistic negation, they convey the implicatures of "now that I consoled her, she should not be crying." and "you should help her by consoling her to the least", in (15) and (16), respectively.

Secondly, as analyzed in Sect. 2.2, metalinguistic negation relies on a encyclopedic knowledge, which provides a rationale for negation. In this connection, the aspect of [X-*təu*-XY] plays a role in the composition of the encyclopedic knowledge. Specifically, an event with a perfective aspect usually serves as a reason for the negated proposition, whereas an event with an imperfective aspect tends to be interpreted as a condition for negation. This can be instantiated in (15) and (16), as their encyclopedic knowledge are "since I consoled her, she should stop crying" and "if you console her, you can help her to a certain extent", respectively, as shown in (17) and (18).

(17) Metalinguistic negation of (15):
   Background information: She is crying.
   Complaint: She should stop crying! or
   Reproach: Why don't you stop her from crying?
   Encyclopedic knowledge: Since I consoled her, she should/must stop crying.
   Implicature: **Now that** I consoled her, she should not be crying. (self-defense)

(18) Metalinguistic negation of (16):
   Background information: The listener cannot help her (e.g., lack of time, lack of willingness).
   Complaint: You won't help her.
   Encyclopedic knowledge: If you console her, you can help her to a least extent.
   Implicature: You should help her by consoling her **to the least**. (suggestion)

The above analyses show that the implicatures function as refusal to a contextually-evident complaint or reproach. This is the working mechanism of metalinguistic negation.

Thirdly and importantly, we analyze whether and how aspect correlates with the semantic differences of the X-copy structure (i.e. "now that" in the perfective aspect vs. "at least" in the imperfective aspect). In addition to refusal (metalinguistic negation), there is additional meta-discoursal conjunction encoded in the implicatures, as shown by the highlighted "now that" and "to the least" in (17) and (18), respectively. We argue that the meta-discourse meanings (Cheng 1997) are derived from *təu* 'even' in the structure. Liu (2017) convincingly proves that *dou*, the Mandarin counterpart of Chengdu *təu*, encodes the meaning of "even", which can subsume various interpretations depending on different varieties of alternatives. This analysis applies to *təu* in Chengdu Chinese as well. In the case of perfective [X-*təu*-XY], its encyclopedic knowledge is composed of a reason and a result, which consequently lead to an implicature to negate the background proposition. Crucially, this reason, in comparison with other alternative reasons, must be the least refutable reason. For example, as in (17), "consoling her" should be the least refutable reason for her to stop crying. Put it another way, it should be paraphrased as "at least because I consoled her (in comparison to other alternative reasons, such as ordering her to stop crying or leaving her alone), she should/must stop crying". We argue that, it is the occurrence of *təu* that induces this scalar implicature (see Horn 1972; Chierchia et al. 2012). Now, we turn to the imperfective [X-*təu*-XY], the encyclopedic knowledge of which consists of a condition and a result. In a similar vein, this condition, among a group of alternative conditions, is considered as the least sufficient condition to make the metalinguistic negation. As in (18), "consoling her", in contrast to other alternatives, such as "lending her money" or "assisting her in completing the task", is perceived as the lowest degree of help. Consequently, the complaint "you don't help her" is refuted. This said, the diversified meta-discourse meanings can be unified. Specifically, regardless of aspect, [X-*təu*-XY] encodes the sense of "even" or "least-ness", be it the least refutable reason or the least sufficient condition. Given this, the different conjunctional meanings, i.e. the concessional meaning and the minimum meaning, are not inherent in the structure but contextually constructed, with aspect being a contextual factor. Given the above analysis, we generalize the semantics of the X-copy [X-*təu*-XY] as (i) metalinguistic negation; (ii) "even"-encoding least scalar implicature. In the next section, we discuss how ordinary negative polarity occurs in metalinguistic negation.

3.3 Negation Within Metalinguistic Negation

The X-copy [X-*təu*-XY] encodes metalinguistic negation, which further allows negation within the structure as well. As [X-*təu*-XY] can be either perfective or imperfective, two types of negation, i.e. the perfective negator *mei(jiəu)*[1] and the imperfective negator *pu* (see, e.g., Li 2007), are tested in this structure, as exemplified in (19) and (20). Note that copy may take two forms: either the first syllable X of XY (VP, AP or NP) or the negator can be copied, as shown in the (19a, 20a) and (19b, 20b), respectively, without any noticeable semantic differences.

(19)	a. t'oŋ	təu	mei(jiəu)	t'oŋtsʅ.	
	notify	DOU	NEG	notify	
	'It has not been notified.'				
	b. mei	təu	mei(jiəu)	t'oŋtsʅ.	
	NEG	DOU	NEG		notify
	'It has not been notified.'				
(20)	a. t'oŋ	təu	pu	t'oŋtsʅ	ni.
	notify	DOU	NEG	notify	you
	'I won't notify you.'				
	b. pu	təu	pu	t'oŋtsʅ	ni.
	NEG	DOU	NEG	notify	you
	'It won't notify you.'				

---

[1] According to our consultation with native speakers, the shortened form of perfective negation *mei* is preferred to its full form *meijiəu* in the [X-*təu*-XY] structure.

The presence of negators does not affect the function of metalinguistic negation for the copy structure. As shown in (21) and (22), metalinguistic negation works, irrespective of the value of polarity in the [X-təu-XY]. The negative markers, if present, function to negate the reason or condition in the process of inferencing.

(21) Metalinguistic negation in (19):
Background: You should have attended the meeting, but you did not.
Complaint: Why didn't you attend the meeting?
Encyclopedic knowledge: The fact that you are not notified constitutes a least refutable reason for not attending the meeting.
Implicature: Now that I was not notified, I was entitled to be absent in the conference.

(22) Metalinguistic negation of (20):
Background: After you arrive in Chengdu, come and visit me.
Invitation: Come and visit me when you arrive in Chengdu.
Inference: Notifying me constitutes the least degree of visit.
Implicature: I won't notify you, let alone visiting you in Chengdu.

4 CP-Level Negation

In this section, we study the syntactic nature of metalinguistic negation. Specifically, we examine the interactions between the X-copy structure and various sentence final particles (SFPs) in Sect. 3.1. And in Sect. 3.2, we check whether [X-təu-XY] can be relativized or not.

4.1 (Un)licensing of SFPs

The [X-təu-XY] does not co-occur with the CP-level SFPs, such as such as SFP_{MOD} $t\varepsilon$, SFP_{MOOD} $t\varepsilon ma$, SFP_{INT} wa and SFP_{EXCL} $olio$ (Xiong and Hsieh 2021), as shown in (23a)–(26a). By contrast, the absence of the copy strategy can license the occurrence of the CP-level SFPs, as exemplified in (23b)–(26b).

(23) a. *ŋo   ŋan   təu   ŋanwei t'a   no   **tɛ**.
         I   console DOU   console her   SFP   SFP_MOD
         Intended: 'As against your assumption (that I did not console her), I've indeed consoled her.'
    b. ŋo   təu   ŋanwei t'a   no   **tɛ**.
        I   DOU   console her   SFP   SFP_MOD
        'As against your assumption (that I did not console her), I've indeed consoled her.'

(24) a. *ŋo   ŋan   təu   ŋanwei t'a   no   **tɛma**.
         I   console DOU   console her   SFP   SFP_MOOD
         Intended: 'It is evident that I've indeed consoled her.'
    b. ŋo   təu   ŋanwei t'a   no   **tɛma**.
        I   DOU   console her   SFP   SFP_MOOD
        'It is evident that I've indeed consoled her.'

(25) a. *ɲi   ŋan   təu   ŋanwei t'a   no   **wa**?
         you   console DOU   console her   SFP   SFP_INT
         Intended: 'Did you console her already?'
    b. ɲi   təu   ŋanwei t'a   no   **wa**?
        you   DOU   console her   SFP   SFP_INT
        'Did you console her already?'

(26) a. *ɲi   ŋan   təu   ŋanwei t'a   no   **io**!
         you   console DOU   console her   SFP   SFP_EXCL
         Intended: 'You already consoled her!'
    b. ɲi   təu   ŋanwei t'a   no   **io**!
        you   DOU   console her   SFP   SFP_EXCL
        'You already consoled her!'

Recall that the application of the X-copy strategy does not lead to any change in the propositional meaning (see Sect. 1). Given this, the incompatibility between the copy structure and the CP-level SFPs must be structurally rather than semantically determined. The plausible analysis is that metalinguistic negation lies at the CP level, though it is not overtly expressed, e.g., in the form of a particle.

4.2 Non-relativization

We further find that the [X-*təu*-XY] structure disallows relativization, as illustrated in (27a). Once again, the removal of the copy strategy turns the relativization grammatical, as exemplified in (27b).

(27) a. *ŋo   ŋan   təu   ŋanwei   ko   ni   na   ko
         I   console DOU   console   EXP   DE   that   CL
         ɕosən
         student
         Intended: 'the student whom I already consoled'
     b. ŋo   təu   ŋanwei   ko   ni   na   ko   ɕosən
         I   DOU   console   EXP   DE   that   CL   student
         'the student whom I already consoled'

Given the fact that the relative marker *ni* is base-generated in the C position (Xiong and Hsieh 2021), we argue that the ungrammaticality of (27a) is derived from the clash in the C position, as both metalinguistic negation and relative marker scramble for the C position. Without metalinguistic negation, as in the case of (27b), relativization is well-formed.

5   Concluding Remarks

In this paper, we examine the X-copy structure of [X-*təu*-XY] in Chengdu Chinese and pinpoints its main function as metalinguistic negation. In terms of syntactic distribution, this copy construction can either stand alone as a complete sentence or be in conjunction with a preceding or continuing clause. Pragmatically, the copy construction serves as a response to refute or reject a speech act, such as a complaint, a request, an invitation, a commitment, etc., which is contextually available in conversations. Furthermore, this copy mechanism is analyzed to be a CP negation, which is higher than ordinary negation, such as VP negation or IP negation.

References

1. Xiaoguang, C.: Studies in Metadiscourse. Liaoning Normal University Press, Dalian (1997)
2. Chierchia, G., Fox, D., Spector, B.: The grammatical view of scalar implicatures and the relationship between semantics and pragmatics. In: Maienborn, C., von Heusinger, K., Portner, P. (ed.) Semantics: an International Handbook of Natural Language Meaning, pp. 2297–2332. Mouton de Gruyter, Berlin (2012)
3. Davis, W.: 'Metalinguistic' negations, denial, and idioms. J. Pragmat. **43**, 2548–2577 (2011)
4. Horn, L.R.: On the semantic properties of logical operators in English. PhD thesis, UCLA (1972)
5. Horn, L.R.: Metalinguistic negation and pragmatic ambiguity. Language **61**(1), 121–174 (1985)
6. Hu, G.: Grammar of Zunyi Chinese (Zunyi Fangyan Yufa Yanjiu), Bashu Publishing House (Bashu Shushe) (2010)
7. Li, M.: Negation in Chinese. Shanghai Foreign Language Education Press, Shanghai (2007)
8. Liu, M.: Varieties of Alternatives: Focus Particles and Wh-expressions in Mandarin. Springer and PKU (2017)
9. Martins, A.: Metalinguistic negation. In: Déprez, V., Teresa Espinal M. (eds.), The Oxford Handbook of Negation, Oxford Handbooks (2020)
10. Xiong, J., Hsieh, F.F.: Degree intensification and sentential functions in Chengdu Chinese. In: Liu, M., Kit, C., Su, Q. (eds.) Chinese Lexical Semantics. CLSW 2020. LNCS, vol. 12278, pp. 74–86. Springer, Cham (2021). https://doi.org/10.1007/978-3-030-81197-6_7

11. Xiong, J., Hsieh, F.-F.: Same degree of intensification with different degrees of sentential functions. Lingua Sinica. **7**, 1–22 (2021)
12. Xiong, J.: A deontic modal SFP in chengdu Chinese. In: Dong, M., Gu, Y., Hong, J.F. (eds.) Chinese Lexical Semantics. CLSW 2021. LNCS, vol. 13249, pp. 160–171. Springer, Cham (2022). https://doi.org/10.1007/978-3-031-06703-7_12
13. Zhang, Y., Zhang, Q., Deng, Y.: Grammar of Chengdu Chinese (Chengdu Fangyan Yufa Yanjiu), Bashu Publishing House (Bashu Shushe) (2001)

Duration Phrases as Fake Nominal Quantifiers: A Functional Account with Corpus Evidence

Xiaopei Zhang[1]([✉]) and Meichun Liu[2]

[1] School of Foreign Language Education, Jilin University, Changchun, China
zhangxiaop@jlu.edu.cn
[2] Department of Linguistics and Translation, City University of Hong Kong, Hong Kong,
Republic of China
meichliu@cityu.edu.hk

Abstract. The study reexamines the grammatical status and function of the duration phrase in the V-DurP-*de*-NP structure *wo du le santian de shu* 'I read books for three days.' The DurP, semantically a verbal complement, is taken to be a fake nominal quantifier through a syntactic test. The puzzling form-meaning mismatch in the expression is justified from a functional perspective with corpus evidence. The study proposes that the DurP is incorporated into the object-NP to serve as an event delimiter. It is coerced into a typically nonreferential object to meet the "heavy added information constraint" hypothesized by Chafe [1]. The event-delimiting function is evidenced by the fact that DurPs are mutually exclusive with other event-delimiting measures, which is supported by corpus evidence on the referential properties of the involved NPs. This study provides new insight into the form-function pairing relation of the construction.

Keywords: Fake Nominal Quantifier · Duration Phrase · Form-Meaning Mismatch · Event Delimiter

1 Introduction

The "form-meaning mismatch" issue in sequences like *wo du le santian de shu* 'I read books for three days' has been extensively discussed in the literature [2–4]. In such a structure, the duration phrase (DurP) *san-tian* 'three days' semantically complements the verb *du* 'read' but is syntactically a modifier of the object noun phrase (ObjNP) *shu* 'book' with the presence of *de*, the "marker of explicit modification" [5] or "nominal marker" [6]. The DurP in such a structure is named a "fake nominal quantifier" [2], shorted as FNQ-DurP in this study. It is also well-acknowledged that the sequence Verb + Duration Phrase + *de* + NP (V-DurP-*de*-NP) is structurally ambiguous under certain circumstances [3, 7–9]. For example, the frequently quoted example, *yun le yige yue de liangshi* [9], has three readings: 'delivered grain for a whole month', 'delivered the amount of grain for the consumption of a month' and 'the grain that takes a month to deliver'. Many researchers have noticed that if the particle *de* is deleted, the structure is saved from ambiguity [7, 8]. That is, without the nominal marker *de*, the above example only has the first reading. Then, the question is: Since the marker *de* is optional in the above sequence and its appearance causes structure ambiguity, why bother to involve it in the V-DurP-*de*-NP sequence? From a functional perspective, we believe the appearance of *de* that causes the "form-meaning mismatch" may be functionally motivated for information packaging.

Accounts for the issue have been proposed from different perspectives, for example, the "head movement" account from a generative perspective [2], the "analogical blending" account from a cognitive perspective [4], and the "evaluative construction account" [10]. However, no consensus has been reached on the syntactic status of the DurP, and not much has been mentioned about the function of the FNQ-DurPs. In this study, we account for the function of the FNQ-DurPs and justify the appearance of the particle *de* in the so-called form-meaning mismatch structure with corpus evidence.

We propose that the FNQ-DurPs are event delimiters that are coerced into the object by *de* to form a "measuring object" [11]. The FNQ-DurPs delimits an event and marks it on the time scale. They are incorporated into the objects to meet the "heavy added information constraint" [1] and bear the clause focus. In the following, we first differentiate the DurPs that are "fake nominal quantifiers", from those that are noun modifiers. Then, we account for the function of the FNQ-DurPs in the V-DurP-*de*-NP structure and substantiate our proposal with corpus evidence. In addition to this introduction, this essay consists of another 3 sections. We first review the related proposals in Sect. 2. In Sect. 3, we propose an 'event delimiter' account for the FNQ-DurPs. The functional motivation for the appearance of *de* following the FNQ-DurPs is also addressed. Section 4 recaps the proposal with a concluding discussion.

2   Previous Studies

Previous studies on this issue mainly focus on the structural ambiguity of V-DurP-*de*-NP [3, 7, 9] or the generation of the form oddity in the structure [2, 4, 12–16]. The functional properties of the structure have seldom been investigated. In the following, we first review the literature on the structural ambiguity of V-DurP-*de*-NP and circumscribe the range of FNQ-DurPs. After that, we survey the previous proposals on the FNQ-DurPs.

2.1   Studies on Structural Ambiguity

Huang [3] classified pre-object DurPs into modifiers (1a), quasi-modifiers (1b), and pseudo-modifiers (1c) in relation to the semantic property of the object noun. This classification assumes that if a DurP preceding *de* is semantically compatible with a noun and forms a noun phrase, DurP-*de*-N, the DurP is a modifier. If the noun is a concrete noun or an abstract non-process noun (an abstract noun without time property), the DurP is named a pseudo-modifier because the DurP preceding *de* looks like a modifier but is semantically incompatible with the noun. However, it is observed that the particle *de* is obligatory in (1a) but optional in (1c) [7]. In sentence (1b), the particle *de* is either obligatory or optional with regard to the two different readings of the sentence: 'I watched a movie that is four-hour long' or 'I watched movies for four hours'. In the first reading, *sige xiaoshi* 'four hours' is an attribute of the object, and *de* is obligatory. In the second reading, *de* is optional. The DurPs followed by an obligatory *de* are attributives of the noun.

1a	教务处	安排	了	一年	的	口语课
	Jiaowuchu	*anpai*	*le*	*yinian*	*de*	*kouyu ke*
	The office of the provost	arrange	Asp	one year	de	oral class

'The office of the provost has arranged one-year's oral classes.'

b	他	看	了	四个小时	的	电影
	Ta	*kan*	*le*	*sige xiaoshi*	*de*	*dianying*
	he	watch	Asp	four hours	de	movie

'He watched a movie for four hours.' or 'He spent four hours watching movies.'

c	我	当	了	三年	的	兵
	Wo	*dang*	*le*	*sannian*	*de*	*bing*
	I	serve	Asp	three years	de	soldier

'I have been a soldier for three years.'

While Huang [3] classifies the pre-object DurPs in terms of the properties of the following noun, another researcher [17] notices that in addition to the property of the noun, the meaning of the DurP also determines its compatibility with the noun and further influences the interpretation of the structure. He adds that *yun le yixiu de liangshi* 'delivered grain for a night' is less likely to be ambiguous because there is no such a thing as "a night's grain". In addition, as mentioned by several studies, the aspectual property of the verb also affects the interpretation of the DurP [7, 18]. In a word, the interpretation of the DurP is semantically determined and contextually conditioned.

2.2 Studies on the Syntactic Status of the FNQ-DurP

There are studies from two different approaches, the formal approach and the traditional grammar approach, that consider the FNQ-DurPs as complements. However, 'complement' is defined differently in these two approaches. In the formal approach, particularly the framework of X' theory, a complement is defined as 'an XP that is a sister to a head, and a daughter of a single bar level' [19]. In explaining how to decide whether a phrase is a complement or an adjunct, Carnie [19] also notes that a complement 'seems to complete (or complement) the meaning of' the phrase head. That is, complements are defined in relation to a phrase head and in contrast with adjuncts. The phrase can be a verbal phrase, noun phrase, preposition phrase, or even numeral classifier phrase. The disagreement between formal linguists concerning the FNQ-DurPs is mainly on whether they are complements [13] or adjuncts [20, 21].[1]

---

[1] Example sentences (1a–c) are quoted from Huang [3] and glossed by the authors.

In the studies of the traditional grammar approach, the major dispute over the syntactic status of the FNQ-DurPs is whether they are complements [7] or modifiers [8, 9]. In Chinese pedagogical grammar, complements are defined in relation to objects. All the post-verbal constituents other than objects are called complements [22]. Researchers who argue for complements emphasize the semantic relation between the DurP and the verb. Those who consider the FNQ-DurPs to be modifiers find evidence that the DurP-*de*-N sequence can be topicalized just like other modifier-*de*-N sequences. In this study, we will show that the FNQ-DurPs are different from attributive DurPs by a syntactic test.

2.3 Evaluative Construction Account

The constructional study of Lu and Wang [10] focuses on the function of the V-DurP-*de*-NP and proposes that it pertains to an "evaluative construction". According to their proposal, the default function of the construction is to indicate that "the speaker considers the duration time is too long". It is claimed that the construction either cooccurs with evaluative adverbs like *zhengzheng* 'entirely', *zhishao* 'at least', or a counter-expectation result of the event. It is further argued that besides its default meaning, the construction also displays a marked form, which is indicated by adverbs like *zhi* 'only' and *cai* 'just', implying that the durative time of the event is shorter than expected. Regarding tense and modality features, they propose that this construction can only occur in sentences of realis modality with aspectual markers *guo* or *le* because it is hard to evaluate the duration of a possible event or future event. The particle '*de*' is argued to mark a "mediate focus" following Yuan's [23] distinction of "narrow focus", "broad focus", and "mediate focus".

The authors provide two pieces of evidence to support the claim of an evaluative construction. First, they observe that the construction frequently collocates with "evaluative adverbs" such as *zhishao* 'at least', *zhengzheng* 'entirely'. However, the collocation with evaluative adverbs does not necessarily mean that the construction conveys the meaning of "evaluation". The evaluative meaning may be simply brought out by the evaluative adverbs themselves. On the contrary, they should provide evidence that without collocating with evaluative adverbs or other evaluative measures, the evaluative meaning still remains with the construction. Secondly, they claim that the evaluative meaning of the construction can be inferred from the "counter-expectation" result of the event. Again, this inference is not supported by any evidence that is linguistically observable and is, therefore, considered to be rather subjective.

As most of the previous studies focus on the syntactic status of the FNQ-DurPs, or semantic purpose of the whole structure, the functional motivation for inserting *de* between a verbal complement DurP and the N has not been extensively discussed. Therefore, in this study, we investigate the function of the FNQ-DurPs and justify the appearance of the marker *de* following the FNQ-DurPs from the perspective of information packaging.

3 FNQ-DurPs as Event Delimiter

As mentioned in the previous section, DurPs have different readings in the V-DurP-*de*-NP structure. With a "fake nominal quantifier", the structure is said to constitute a form-meaning mismatch. In this section, we propose that an FNQ-DurP can be viewed as an event delimiter disregarding the semantic property of the following noun. That is, no matter whether the object noun has inherent time property or not, the FNQ-DurP in this structure serves as an event delimiter in the disguise of a modifier preceding the object noun. According to Tenny [11], "delimitedness refers to the property of an event's having a distinct, definite and inherent endpoint in time"; just as a spatially delimited object has some fixed extent in space, a temporally delimited event has a fixed duration. Since the FNQ-DurPs semantically mark the duration of events, we propose that they serve as event delimiters[2]. We provide three pieces of evidence to support this proposal. First, we show the syntactic differences between modifier DurPs and FNQ-DurPs. Secondly, we show that FNQ-DurPs are not compatible with other event delimiting measures, such as "specific or count noun objects," because they lead to "delimited readings" of an event [11]. Thirdly, we provide corpus evidence to show that the DurPs preceding *de* almost exclusively collocate with bare NPs.

3.1 Distinctions Between Modifier DurPs and FNQ-DurPs

Different from previous classifications of DurPs regarding the time property of the N [3], we argue that the DurP in the structure is not purely a modifier of the N, but an event delimiter, disregarding the time property of the noun. The distinction between a prenominal modifier and an event-delimiting DurP can be seen from example (1b) of different readings, copied here as (2a) and (3a).

The DurP plays different roles in the two different readings. In (2a) 'he watched a four-hour-long movie', the DurP *si-ge xiaoshi* 'four-hour' is a durative modifier of the noun *dianying* 'movie'. In this reading, the marker *de* can be stranded when the noun is topicalized as in (2b) or elided as in (2c) in a contrastive context. Whereas, in (3a), the reading is 'He watched movies for four hours', the DurP 'four-hour' delimits the event *kan-dianying* 'watch-movies'. A stranded *de* is not allowed in this reading in cases of noun topicalization, as in (3b) or noun elision (3c). Therefore, we conclude that the different grammatical behaviors under different readings indicate different grammatical statuses of the DurP: either as a nominal modifier or an event delimiter. It is shown that the FNQ-DurPs need to be distinguished from a pure modifier.

---

[2] We thank one of the anonymous reviewers for the suggestion on clarifying the concept of "event delimiter".

2a   他   看   了   四个小时   的   电影

Ta	*kan*	*le*	*sige xiaoshi*	*de*	*dianying*
he	watch	asp	four hour	de	movie

'He watched a four-hour movie.'

b   电影,   他   看   了   四个小时   的

Dianying	*ta*	*kan*	*le*	*sige xiaoshi*	*de*
movie	he	watch	asp	four hour	de

'The movie he watched is four-hour long.'

c   他   看   了   四个小时   的   电影,

Ta	*kan*	*le*	*sige xiaoshi*	*de*	*dianying*
he	watch	asp	four hour	de	Movie

     我   看   了   三个小时   的

wo	*kan*	*le*	*sange xiaoshi*	*de*
I	watch	asp	three hour	de

'He watched a four-hour movie while I watched a three-hour one.'

3a   他   看   了   四个小时   的   电影

Ta	*kan*	*le*	*sige xiaoshi*	*de*	*dianying*
he	watch	asp	four hour	de	movie

'He watched movies for four hours.'

b   电影,   他   看   了   四个小时

Dianying	*ta*	*kan*	*le*	*sige xiaoshi*
movie	he	watch	asp	four hour

'He watched movies for four hours.'

c   他   看   了   四个小时   的   电影,

Ta	*kan*	*le*	*sige xiaoshi*	*de*	*dianying*
he	watch	asp	four hour	de	movie

     我   看   了   三个小时

wo	*kan*	*le*	*sange xiaoshi*
I	watch	asp	three hour

'He watched movies for four hours while I watched for three hours.'

In the next section, we provide further proof to show that the DurP is an event delimiter[3].

3.2 Incompatibility Between FNQ-DurPs and Other Event-Delimiting Measures

We propose that FNQ-DurPs are event delimiters incorporated with the object N to help "measure out" and delimit the event [11]. It is generally agreed that achievement verbs and accomplishment verbs imply a natural endpoint of an event [24]. Therefore, we will first show that the FNQ-DurPs are incompatible with these verbs. According to Tenny [11], and other scholars [25], the aspectual character of a sentence is affected by the mass or count properties of the noun phrase in object position and "mass nouns or bare plural objects lead to non-delimited readings," while "specific or count noun objects lead to delimited readings". We will test the compatibility between FNQ-DurPs and the "specific or count noun objects". A corpus survey of the object types is provided below as independent evidence.

In his seminal work on the relationship of verbs and time, Vendler [24] differentiates verbs into four categories, activity, accomplishment, achievement, and state. Accomplishment and achievement verbs are considered telic verbs entailing a natural end of an event. Based on Vendler's categorization, the English accomplishment verbs "necessarily imply an attainment of the goal" when they are used in past or perfect tenses. However, Tai [26] observes that "Chinese resorts to resultative verb compounds" to "ensure the attainment of the goal". That is, Chinese uses verb-result (V-R) compounds, such as *hua-wan* 'paint-finish', to express accomplishment instead of the single verb *hua* 'paint'. Given that V-R compounds are by definition bounded, they should not be allowed with an FNQ-DurP since V-R compounds entail the attainment of the goal, forming a telic event, which is incompatible with an event-delimiting DurP. Take *hua-wan* 'paint-finish' as an example, the appearance of the resultative *wan* makes sentence (4) infelicitous. Similarly, achievement verbs like *dasui* 'beat-broken' is also not compatible with the FNQ-DurPs, which has been observed in Gu [27].[4]

4	他	画(*完)	了	四个	小时	的	画。
	ta	*hua-wan*	*le*	*si-ge*	*xiao-shi*	*de*	*hua*
	He	paint-finish	Asp	four	hour	de	painting

*He finished painting for four hours.

---

[3] Our hearty thanks go to one of the anonymous reviewers who raised questions that whether this analysis can be extended to other fake nominal modifiers and if a unified account for them is possible. Fake nominal modifiers in Chinese are of diverse nature. For example, six types of them have been mentioned in Shen [4]. Considering their different positions in the clause and their different collocational behaviors, we do not attempt to address them all with one unified account and reserve this analysis only for the fake nominal quantifiers at the present stage. A unified analysis will surely be a significant contribution to the field. Hopefully, this research gap can be bridged by future studies.

[4] The sentence becomes felicitous if the particle de is deleted. However, without de, the DurP is an adverbial of the sentence instead of a fake nominal modifier, which is out of the scope of the present study. Although example (5) is good under a relative clause reading, it is not the concern of the study.

In addition, the DurP is incompatible with nouns of specificity. Chinese nouns occurring with demonstratives, such as *zhebenshu*, 'this book', are considered to be specific-referring [28]. As shown in (5), specific referring objects are incompatible with the FNQ-DurPs. Similarly, a count noun, such as *liangfu hua* 'two-volume painting', is also incompatible with FNQ-DurPs, as shown in (6).

5	*他	读	了	一个	小时	的	那本书[4]。
	ta	*du*	*le*	*yi-ge*	*xiao-shi*	*de*	*naben shu*
	He	read	Asp	one	hour	de	that book

*He read that book for an hour.

6	*他	画	了	一个	小时	的	两幅画。
	ta	*hua*	*le*	*yi-ge*	*xiao-shi*	*de*	*liangfu hua*
	He	paint	Asp	one	hour	de	two pictures

*He painted two pictures for two hours.

With the above evidence, we argue that it is because the FNQ-DurP functionally serves as an event delimiter that it is incompatible with delimited events, of which an endpoint is either implied by a telic V-R compound or by an event-delimiting object. In this sense, we suggest that the FNQ-DurP provides an event delimiter, incorporated into the object noun to form a "measuring object" [11].

To verify our arguments, we build a PoS-tagged corpus of 15 million words and retrieve all the instances of V-DurP-*de*-NP with an FNQ-DurP to examine the possible types of object NPs. After retrieving the instances with the Corpus Query Language powered by Sketch Engine, we manually sift the hits to identify all the FNQ-DurPs based on the *de*-elision test discussed above. The 395 instances of V-DurP-*de*-NP with FNQ-DurPs are then coded in terms of the referential properties of the NP. The NPs are differentiated into three categories: objects with specific referents, quantified objects, and generic referring objects. Based on Chen's [28] theory on referential properties of Chinese NPs, pronouns, proper nouns, and nouns modified by demonstratives, possessors, or other restrictive modifiers that make the referent specific are coded as "Specific referring". Quantified objects are identified by the mark of numeral classifiers since Chinese is a classifier language. Generic referring objects are generally bare NPs. The relative frequencies of these three types of NPs in the V-DurP-*de*-NP structure are shown in Table 1.

Table 1. Distribution of different types of ObjNPs following FNQ-DurPs

ObjNP types	Specific referring	Quantified	Generic referring	Total
Count	1	0	394	395
Percentage	0.25%	0	99.75%	100%

From Table 1, we can see that more than 99% of the NPs following an FNQ-DurP are generic referring, which means that they are low in individuality. As Chinese bare NPs in object position are in line with mass nouns and bare plurals in English [28], they generally "lead to non-delimited readings" [11]. Therefore, adding a DurP to the bare object noun helps to add a measure to the noun. That is why we see the prevalence of an FNQ-DurP in the V-DurP-*de*-NP structure, which is reasonable and predictable.

3.3 Functional Motivations for DurPs as Fake Nominal Quantifiers

In this section, we discuss why the DurPs are packed as fake nominal quantifiers on the surface structure. As reviewed in Sect. 2, several studies have posited the generative mechanism behind the form-meaning mismatch in V-DurP-*de*-NP. Huang argues that in the deep structure, the DurP is a modifier of gerundive and the formal oddity is the result of a "head movement" [2]. Shen suggests that this form-meaning mismatch is a result of "analogical blending" [4]. While the head movement is said to be structurally motivated, the functional motivation for making a DurP a fake nominal modifier has not been resolved in the literature. Based on the information structure theory of Chafe [1], we argue that DurPs are added to the sentence to meet the "heavy added information constraint", which specifies that "added information typically contains one new concept, though it may also contain some accessible concepts or even some given concepts".

As shown in Table 1, almost all the ObjNPs following FNQ-DurPs are bare NPs that have no specific referent. Therefore, these ObjNPs generally do not bear new information. Given that new information tends to come after old information and that Chinese is a "head-final" language, the object at the end of the clause generally bears the focal new information [29]. Therefore, we argue that the DurP is coerced into the object as a fake modifier marked by *de* to meet the "heavy added information constraint" toward the end of the clause.

Another piece of evidence comes from the frequent occurrence of separable V-O combination [12, 14] in the V-DurP-*de*-N. Chafe [1] notes that there are cases "where a single new concept was expressed with a verb object combination," such as "makes a difference" and "gives a lecture". In such cases, the verb-object combination is usually a lexicalized whole. This observation also applied to the Chinese V-DurP-*de*-N structure. In this structure, some lexicalized V-O combinations, such as *xi-zao* 'wash bathe', can be split with the insertion of a DurP in between. Some of these separable words are intransitive compound verbs. When inserted with a DurP to form the V-DurP-*de*-N structure, the originally bare O-morpheme of the compound is packed with a specifier and is no longer a dummy object that bears empty information. Thus, the DurP is incorporated into the bare object to meet the "heavy added information constraint".

In the same vein, Shang [30] compares the DurPs with numeral classifiers and notes that the noun in a V-DurP-*de*-N structure can be topicalized, leaving the DurP in the position of a predicate, but V-NumCl-N structures cannot. This observation echoes our argument that the incorporation of a DurP makes the originally nonreferential object more informative as the new-information-bearing predicate of a clause. In sum, since a DurP is a temporal measure of time, which "has a natural scale" [11], adding it to the object as a modifier help meet the requirement for a measuring object.

4   Conclusion

In this paper, we propose a functional account for the FNQ-DurP incorporated into an object NP in the puzzling structure V-DurP-*de*-NP, which is commonly taken to be a form-meaning mismatch. Through a syntactic test, we first differentiate an FNQ-DurP from a pure nominal modifier with the occurrence of *de* in the sequence. Then, we argue that the FNQ-DurP serves as an event delimiter, which helps to form a measuring object NP in the structure. The marker *de* coerces the DurP into a 'measuring out' object to meet the "heavy added information constraint" in discourse. We also show that FNQ-DurPs are mutually exclusive with other event delimiting measures, including telic verbs, specific referring objects, and quantified objects. Corpus evidence is provided to show that the NPs following an FNQ-DurP are exclusively bare NPs without specific referents. These bare NPs normally lead to non-delimiting readings of events. Therefore, incorporating the DurP to a bare object noun adds a temporal measure to the noun as an event delimiter. Since bare NPs are low in individuality and informativeness, they need the DurP to form a measuring object to delimit the event as added information.

Acknowledgments. The first author is supported by the Fundamental Research Funds for the Central Universities. Project number: 2019QY010.

References

1. Chafe, W.: Cognitive constraints on information flow. In: Tomlin, R.S. (eds.): Coherence and grounding in discourse, pp. 21–51. John Benjamins Publishing Company, Amsterdam Philadelphia (1987)
2. Huang, C.-T.J.: On ta de laoshi dang-de hao and related problems. Linguist. Sci. **3**, 225–241 (2008)
3. Huang, G.: Pseudo-attributive and quasi-attributive (in Chinese). Lang. Teach. Linguist. Stud. **4**, 38–44 (1981)
4. Shen, J.: On ta de laoshi dang de hao and the related constructions. Contemp. Res. Mod. Chin. **9**, 1–12 (2007)
5. Chao, Y.R.: A Grammar of Spoken Chinese. The Commercial Press, Beijing (2011)
6. Liu, J.: Nominal marker "de" in modern Chinese and its role of marking presupposition. In: Liu, M., Kit, C., Su. Q. (eds.): Chinese Lexical Semantics, pp. 34–40. Springer, Cham Switzerland (2021). https://doi.org/10.1007/978-3-030-81197-6_3
7. Lü, W.: On the synonymous structures with duration phrases (in Chinese). Stud. Explor. Grammar. **7**, 280–291 (1995)
8. Ma, Q.: On the order between post-verbal duration phrases and nouns (in Chinese). Essays Linguist. **13**, 40–56 (1984)
9. Zhu, D.: Lecture Notes on Grammar. The Commercial Press, Beijing (1982). (in Chinese)
10. Lu, J., Wang, G.: Exploring Chinese TP para-attributive sentences from the perspective of evaluative construction. Foreign Lang. Literat. Stud. **1**, 19–32 (2020)
11. Tenny, C.: Aspectual Roles and the Syntax-Semantics Interface. Kluwer, Dordrecht (1994)
12. Guo, R.: The mechanism for the formation of separable words and incompleted words: and the mechanism for the formation of pseudo-attributives. Linguist. Sci. **3**, 225–249 (2017)
13. Liao, W.-W.R.: Process-related durative phrases as numeral-classifier phrases in Chinese. Taiwan J. Linguist. **2**, 59–80 (2014)

14. Ye, K., Pan, H.: Revisiting the syntax of separable words: a reply to Yuan (2018) and others. Contemp. Linguist. **4**, 605–615 (2018)
15. Yuan, Y.: Syntactic features of separable words used in separation: from a perspective of formal metonymy. Contemp. Linguist. **4**, 587–604 (2018)
16. Zhuang, H., Zhang, P.: On fake nominal quantifiers in Chinese. Lingua **198**, 73–88 (2017)
17. Yu, J.: An analysis of the ambiguous "V+ le + T + de + N" structure. Linguist. Sci. **4**, 50–55 (2006)
18. Ma, Q.: Time quantifier as an object in relation to verb types. Stud. Chin. Lang. **2**, 86–90 (1981). (in Chinese)
19. Carnie, A.: Syntax: A Generative Introduction, 3rd edn. Wiley, West Sussex (2013)
20. Huang, C.-T.J.: On lexical structure and syntactic projection. Chin. Lang. Linguist. **3**, 45–89 (1997)
21. Huang, C.-T.J., Li, Y.-H.A., Li, Y.: The Syntax of Chinese. Cambridge University Press, Cambridge (2009)
22. Jin, L.: A possoble analysis of Chinese buyu (in Chinese). Stud. Chin. Lang. **5**, 387–398 (2009)
23. Yuan, Y.: The syntactic-semantic functions of non-referential pronoun "ta." Grammatical Res. Explor. **12**, 44–64 (2002)
24. Vendler, Z.: Verbs and times. Philos. Rev. **2**, 143–160 (1957)
25. Zhang, X., Luo, Y., Hu, J.: Accomplishment predicates in Mandarin and their lexical semantics. In: Liu, M., Kit, C., Su. Q. (eds.): Chinese Lexical Semantics, pp. 303–319. Springer, Cham Switzerland, (2021). https://doi.org/10.1007/978-3-030-81197-6_26
26. Tai, J.H.-Y.: Verbs and Times in Chinese: Vendler's Four Categories. Papers from the parasession on lexical semantics. Chicago Linguistic Society, Chicago (1984)
27. Gu, Y.: On the postverbal duration phrases in Mandarin Chinese. In: Xu, L. (eds): The Referential Properties of Chinese Noun Phrases, pp. 117–140. Ecole des hautes études en Sciences sociales, Centre de recherches linguistiques sur l'Asie orientale (1997)
28. Chen, P.: On the four pairs of definitions related to Chinese NP (in Chinese). Stud. Chin. Lang. **2**, 81–92 (1987)
29. Lambrecht, K.: Information Structure and Sentence form: Topic, Focus, and the Mental Representations of Discourse Referents. Cambridge University Press, New York (1994)
30. Shang, X.: A survey on the information structure of temporal verb-object construction "V + T(de) + N": Theory and empirical evidence. J. Foreign Lang. **5**, 46–60 (2020)

A Study on the Position of Preposition-Objects Structures in Kongzijiayu

Yonghong Ke[1,2(✉)]

[1] Research Center for Folklore, Classics and Chinese Characters, Beijing Normal University, Beijing 100875, China
yh8555@126.com

[2] Research Center for Collation and Standardization of Chinese Characters, Beijing, China

Abstract. The position of preposition-object structures has changed significantly from ancient to modern Chinese. A comprehensive description and analysis of the positional relationship between preposition-object structures and the predicate components in Kongzijiayu (hereinafter, Jiayu) and comparisons with the *Zuozhuan, Mozi, and Shiji* can provide more proof in support of the key question of when the completion of *Jiayu* occurred and contribute to the accurate and in-depth interpretation of its text. We analyzed 15 prepositions in 1634 sentences in *Jiayu*, and the preposition-object structures in *Jiayu* occur mainly after the predicate components, accounting for 58.02%, which is very close to the prevalence in *Mozi*. The prepositions that can appear only before predicate components are Cong (从), Yin (因), Dang (当), Yong (用), Zhi (至), Hou (后) Dui (对) and Jiang (将), the prepositions that can appear only after predicate components are Hu (乎) and Zhu (诸), and the prepositions that can appear both before and after predicate components are Yu (于), Yi (以), Zi (自), Wei (为) and Zai (在). When prepositional-object structures introduce time, tools/methods/conditions/basis/etc., cause/purpose and indirect objects, these are usually located before the predicate components. When prepositional-object structures introduce objects, location or the content of instruction or speech, these structures usually come after the predicate components. Only when the predicate component is monosyllabic are the preposition-object structures usually after the predicate components, accounting for 77.52% of instances. When the predicate component is polysyllabic, the preposition-object structure usually occurs before the predicate component. The proportion of preposition-object structures before the predicate components in *Jiayu* is between that of the *Mozi* and the *Shiji* and very close to that of *Mozi*, which may be related to the time when it was written.

Keywords: *Kongzijiayu* · preposition-object structures · predicate components · position

1 Introduction

In modern Chinese, preposition-object structures usually occur before the predicate components, but this is not the case in ancient Chinese. Zhao Yuanren [1] and Wang Li [2] suggested that the position of the preposition-object structures in the contemporary age has changed significantly from their position in ancient times. He Leshi found that the predominant placement of preposition-object structures before the predicate components was just beginning to take shape in the *Zuozhuan* and had basically become naturalized by the writing of the *Shiji* [3]. From this, he speculated that the grammatical features of the *Shiji* changed remarkably from the *Zuozhuan*. Wang Hongbin (2003) [4], Liu Xiaojing (2012) [5] and Yang Jiqing (2021) [6] performed a special analysis of the positions of preposition-object structures in the *Zuozhuan*, *Mengzi* and *Mozi*, respectively. Jiang Shaoyu [7] believes that the structure "Yu (于) + L" in pre-Qin Chinese is always after the verb, which reflects that Chinese is not completely dominated by the "iconic principle" and that the "abstract principle" also plays a role. Zhang Cheng [8] believes that the rise and disappearance of prepositions, the semantics of preposition-object structures, and the development of the VP structure are all reasons for the change in preposition-object structure positions. The positional relationship between preposition-object structures and predicate components can reflect changes in language, so it is an important part of Chinese word order research.

Jiayu is an early Confucian classic that records the deeds and words of Confucius and his disciples, and it is valuable material for studying Confucius and early Confucianism. Influenced by the theory of forgery, research on *Jiayu* in successive dynasties has focused on its version and filiation, while most scholars have ignored the document value and linguistic value. A comprehensive description and analysis of the positional relationship between preposition-object structures and predicate components in *Jiayu* is significant on two levels: (1) studies into the vocabulary and grammar of *Jiayu* are still very few, and a small amount of research has been published, such as Song Yanxia [9], Liu Weiyan [10], Miao Chuanmei [11], Jiang Rumeng [12], Lu Qin [13], Chen Jing [14], etc., which focus on special parts of speech and semantic meanings. Research on the prepositions in *Jiayu* is occasionally seen in special research on prepositions. For example, Lin Qi [15] and Deng Tongxiang [16] cited and analyzed the examples in *Jiayu*. We have not seen any special research on the positions of preposition-object structures in *Jiayu*. A special study of the prepositions in *Jiayu* can fully show the relationship between the preposition-object structure and the predicate components in *Jiayu*, which is helpful in advancing the accurate and in-depth interpretation of the text. The study of prepositions in special books is also an important part of the research into the history of Chinese word order and vocabulary development. (2) Although the moment of completion of *Jiayu* is controversial, its existence as an ancient book is an indisputable fact. The positional relationship between the prepositional-object structures and the predicate components has obvious characteristics of the era in which it was composed, and a comprehensive investigation of the positional relationship between prepositional-object structures and predicate components in *Jiayu* can provide more proof for the key issue of when the book was completed. Today, as the importance of *Jiayu* is gradually recognized, studies of its language are undoubtedly increasingly important.

2   The Position of Preposition-Object Structures in *Jiayu*

The term "preposition-object structures" refers to the preposition and its object. The term "predicate components" include not only predicate verbs or adjectives but also words or phrases with the functions of statement and predication. Wang Li believed that the original meaning of "Yu (于)" could be expressed by both "Yu (于)" and "Yu (於)", while the new meaning and usage of the preposition "Yu (於)" could only be expressed with "Yu (於)" [2]. This paper does not distinguish between "Yu (于)" and "Yu (於)" in the statistics of prepositions, "Yu (于)" in the following is the same as "Yu (于)" and "Yu (於)".

We analyzed 15 prepositions including Yu (于), Yi (以), Zai (在), Zi (自), Wei (为), Zhi (至), Yin (因), Cong (从), Dang (当), Hu (乎), Yong (用), Hou (后), Dui (对), Jiang (将) and Zhu (诸). According to the position of the preposition-object structures, we can classify the prepositions in *Jiayu* into three types: those that can only appear before the predicate components, those that can only appear after the predicate components, and those that appear both before and after the predicate components.

2.1 Before the Predicate Components

There are eight prepositions in *Jiayu* that appear only before the predicate components: Cong (从), Yin (因), Dang (当), Yong (用), Hou (后), Dui (对), Jiang (将) and Zhi (至).

(1) Cong (从)

The preposition "Cong (从)" has 14 cases in *Jiayu*, all of which are used before the predicate components. For example:

Eg. 1 尝从孔子适卫。《七十二弟子解》

cháng cóng kǒng zǐ shì wèi。

[He] once followed Confucius to Wei State.

(2) Yin (因)

The preposition "Yin (因)" has 8 instances in *Jiayu*, all of which are used before the predicate components. For example:

Eg. 2 使大夫因孟懿子问礼于孔子。《冠颂》

shǐ dà fū yīn mèng yì zǐ wèn lǐ yú kǒng zǐ。

[He] sent the official Meng Yi Zi to ask Confucius about the etiquette of coronation.

(3) Dang (当)

The preposition "Dang (当)" has 5 instances in *Jiayu*, all of which are used before the predicate components. For example:

Eg. 3 当今之君，孰为最贤?《贤君》

dāng jīn zhī jūn, shú wéi zuì xián?

Who is the wisest monarch today?

(4) Yong (用)

The preposition "Yong (用)" has 2 instances in *Jiayu*, all of which are used before the predicate components.

Eg. 4 用水火财物以生民。《五帝德》

yòng shuǐ huǒ cái wù yǐ shēng mín。

Use water, fire and property to raise people.

Eg. 5 齐氏用戈击公孟。《子夏问》

qí shì yòng gē jī gōng mèng。

Qi struck Gongmeng with a dagger-axe.

(5) Zhi (至)
The preposition "Zhi (至)" has 2 instances in *Jiayu*, all of which are used before the predicate components.

Eg. 6 至十九, 娶于宋之上官氏。《本姓解》

zhì shí jiǔ, qǔ yú sòng zhī shàng guān shì。

At the age of nineteen, he took the daughter of Shangguan in Song State as his wife.

Eg. 7 及至大王亶甫, 敦以德让, 其树根置本, 备豫远矣。《好生》

jí zhì dà wáng dǎn fǔ, dūn yǐ dé ràng, qí shù gēn zhì běn, bèi yù yuǎn yǐ。

When the time came for the Great King Dan Fu, he exerted benevolence and humility, cultivated the foundation [of virtue], and prepared for the future in advance.

(6) Hou (后)
The preposition "Hou (后)" has 1 instance in *Jiayu*, which is used before the predicate component.

Eg. 8 后三日, 牧来诉之曰……《颜回》

hòu sān rì, mù lái sù zhī yuē……

After three days, the horse breeder came to tell him……

(7) Dui (对)
The preposition "Dui (对)" has 1 instance in *Jiayu*, which is used before the predicate component.

Eg. 9 子服景伯对使者曰……《辩物》

zǐ fú jǐng bó duì shǐ zhě yuē……

Zifu Jing Bo tells the messenger……

(8) Jiang (将)
The preposition "Jiang (将)" has 1 instance in *Jiayu*, which is used before the predicate component.

Eg. 10 天下百姓皆君之民, 将谁攻之?《五仪解》

tiān xià bǎi xìng jiē jūn zhī mín, jiāng shuí gōng zhī?

People all over the world have become your people. Who will attack you?

2.2 Only After the Predicate Components

In *Jiayu*, there are two prepositions that appear only after the predicate components: Hu (乎/虖) and Zhu (诸). We have counted "Zhu (诸)" because its function in *Jiayu* is equivalent to the usage of the pronoun "Zhi (之)" + the preposition "Yu (于)".

(9) Hu (乎)

The preposition "Hu (乎)" has 49 instances in *Jiayu*, all of which are used after the predicate components. For example:

Eg. 11好学近乎智, 力行近乎仁, 知耻近乎勇。《哀公问政》

hǎo xué jìn hū zhì, lì xíng jìn hū rén, zhī chǐ jìn hū yǒng。

Those who like learning are close to wisdom, those who strive to achieve virtue are close to benevolence, and those who understand shame are close to courage.

(10) Zhu (诸)

The function of "Zhu (诸)" is the same as the pronoun "Zhi (之)" plus the preposition "Yu (于)". There are 35 instances in total, all of which are used after predicate components. For example:

Eg. 12子游以问诸孔子。《公西赤问》

zǐ yóu yǐ wèn zhū kǒng zǐ。

Zi You asked Confucius about it.

2.3 Before and After the Predicate Components

Prepositions that can appear before and after the predicate components are Yu (于), Yi (以), Zi (自), Wei (为) and Zai (在).

(11) Yu (于)

There are 788 instances of the preposition "Yu (于)" in *Jiayu*, of which 78 instances are used before the predicate components and 710 instances are used after the predicate components.

An example of usages before the predicate components:

Eg. 13吾穿井于费, 而于井中得一狗, 何也?《辩物》

wú chuān jǐng yú fèi, ér yú jǐng zhōng dé yī gǒu, hé yě?

I was digging a well in Fei and found a dog in the well. What is the matter?

An example of usages after the predicate components:

Eg. 14定公与齐侯会于夹谷。《相鲁》

dìng gōng yǔ qí hóu huì yú jiá gǔ。

Duke Ding and Marquis Qi held a league meeting in Jiagu Mountain.

(12) Yi (以)

The preposition "Yi (以)" has 647 instances in *Jiayu*, of which 514 instances are used before the predicate components and 133 instances are used after the predicate components.

An example of usages before the predicate components:
Eg. 15 以贵下贱, 无不得也。《贤君》

yǐ guì xià jiàn, wú bú dé yě。

Noble people show modesty to humble people, and nothing can be denied.

An example of usages after the predicate components:
Eg. 16 吾闻富贵者送人以财。《观周》

wú wén fù guì zhě sòng rén yǐ cái。

I heard that rich people give money to people.

(13) Zi (自)

The preposition "Zi (自)" has 45 instances in *Jiayu*, of which 35 instances are used before the predicate components and 10 instances are used after the predicate components.

An example of usages before the predicate components:
Eg. 17 自南宫敬叔之乘我车也, 而道加行。《致思》

zì nán gōng jìng shū zhī chéng wǒ chē yě, ér dào jiā xíng。

Since Nangong Jing Shu provided me with carriages and horses, my Tao has become more popular.

An example of usages after the predicate components:
Eg. 18 众之服自此, 故听且速焉。《哀公问政》

zhòng zhī fú zì cǐ, gù tīng qiě sù yān。

Since then, the people have submitted to indoctrination, so they have obeyed orders and implemented them quickly.

(14) Wei(为)

The preposition "Wei (为)" has 28 instances in *Jiayu*, of which 20 instances are used before the predicate components and 8 instances are used after the predicate components.

An example of usages before the predicate components:
Eg. 19 子贡曰: "止, 吾将为子问之。"《子贡问》

zǐ gòng yuē: "zhǐ, wú jiāng wèi zǐ wèn zhī。"

Zi Gong said, "Wait a minute. I will ask for you."

An example of usages after the predicate components:
Eg. 20 古者不祔葬, 为不忍先死者之复见也。《公西赤问》

gǔ zhě bú fù zàng, wèi bù rěn xiān sǐ zhě zhī fù jiàn yě。

In ancient times, people did not bury their relatives together because they could not bear to see the relatives who died first.

(15) Zai (在)

The preposition "Zai (在)" has 8 instances in *Jiayu*, of which 6 instances are used before the predicate components and 2 instances are used after the predicate components.

An example of usages before the predicate components:
Eg. 21 在下位不获于上, 民弗可得而治矣。《哀公问政》

zài xià wèi bú huò yú shàng, mín fú kě dé ér zhì yǐ。

It is impossible to govern the people well when people in lower positions cannot be trusted by people in higher positions.

An example of usages after the predicate components:
Eg. 22 孔子曰: "汝所问苞在五者中矣。"《子路初见》

kǒng zǐ yuē: "rǔ suǒ wèn bāo zài wǔ zhě zhōng yǐ。"

Confucius said, "All the questions you asked are covered in the five aspects I have mentioned."

The positional relationship between the preposition-object structures and predicate components in *Jiayu* is as follows:

Table 1. The distribution of prepositions in *Jiayu*.

Preposition	Before the predicate components	Proportion	After the predicate components	Proportion	Summation
Cong (从)	14	0.86%	0	0.00%	14
Yin (因)	8	0.49%	0	0.00%	8
Yong (用)	2	0.12%	0	0.00%	2
Zhi (至)	2	0.12%	0	0.00%	2
Hou (后)	1	0.06%	0	0.00%	1
Dui (对)	1	0.06%	0	0.00%	1
Jiang (将)	1	0.06%	0	0.00%	1
Zhu (诸)	0	0.00%	35	2.14%	35
Hu (乎)	0	0.00%	49	3.00%	49
Yu (于)	78	4.77%	710	43.45%	788
Yi (以)	514	31.46%	133	8.14%	647
Zi (自)	35	2.14%	10	0.61%	45
Wei (为)	20	1.22%	8	0.49%	28
Zai (在)	6	0.37%	2	0.12%	8
Dang (当)	4	0.24%	1	0.06%	5
Total	686	41.98%	948	58.02%	1634

It can be seen from Table 1 that (1) the use of prepositions is uneven. Of the 1634 instances, "Yu (于)" and "Yi (以)" were the most frequently used, with 788 and 647 instances, accounting for 48.23% and 39.60% of the total, respectively. Other prepositions appear less frequently. (2) There are eight prepositions in *Jiayu* that appear only before the predicate components: Cong (从), Yin (因), Dang (当), Yong (用), Hou (后), Dui (对), Jiang (将) and Zhi (至). The prepositions Hu (乎) and Zhu (诸) can only appear after the predicate components. (3) The prepositions that can appear before and after the predicate components are Yu (于), Yi (以), Zi (自), Wei (为) and Zai (在). The prepositions with a more obvious tendency to appear before the predicate components are Yi (以), Zi (自), Wei (为), and Zai (在), and the prepositions with a more obvious tendency to appear after the predicate components are Yu (于).

The following table shows the use of prepositions in the four books (Table 2).

Table 2. The distribution of prepositions in *Jiayu*, *Zuozhuan*, *Mozi* and *Shiji*.

Book	Prepositions before the predicate components	Prepositions after the predicate components	Prepositions before and after the predicate components
Mozi	Wei (为), Cong (从), Yin (因), You (由), Yong (用), Yu (与) Dang (当)	Hu (乎), Zhu (诸)	Yu (於), Yi (以), Zi (自), Yu (于), Zhi (至)
Zuozhuan and *Shiji*	Yu (与), Wei (为), Cong (从), Yin (因), You (由), Yong (用), Dang (当), Dai (代), Dao (道), Xian (先), Xun (循), Jiang (将), Dai (逮), Xiang (乡/向)	Yu (于), Hu (乎)	Yu (於), Yi (以), Ji (及) Zi (自), Zai (在), Di (抵)
Jiayu	Cong (从), Yin (因), Dang (当), Yong (用), Hou (后), Dui (对), Jiang (将), Zhi (至)	Hu (乎), Zhu (诸)	Yu (于), Yi (以), Zi (自), Wei (为), Zai (在)

Among the prepositions we analyzed, Cong (从), Yin (因), Dang (当), Yong (用), Jiang (将), Yi (以), Zi (自), and Zai (在) appear in the same position in *Zuozhuan*, *Shiji* and *Mozi*, while Zhi (至) and Wei (为) are different in the *Mozi*. Hou (后) and Dui (对) have no statistical significance in the *Zuozhuan*, *Shiji and Mozi*.

In *Jiayu*, the prepositional-object structures are mainly after the predicate components. We counted 1634 instances of preposition-object structures, with 686 instances before the predicate components and 948 instances after the predicate components. The proportion of prepositional structures occurring before the predicate components was 41.93%, and the proportion occurring after the predicate components was 58.02%. We compared *Jiayu* with *Zuozhuan*, *Mozi* and *Shiji* (Table 3):

It can be seen from the above table that in *Zuozhuan*, *Mozi* and *Jiayu*, preposition-object structures mainly occur after the predicate components, and in *Shiji*, the

Table 3. Comparison of *Jiayu* with *Zuozhuan*, *Mozi* and *Shiji*.

Book	Proportion of Before	Proportion of After
Zuozhuan	40.22%	59.78%
Mozi	41.30%	58.70%
Jiayu	**41.93%**	**58.02%**
Shiji	75.29%	24.71%

preposition-object structures occur mainly before the predicate components. The proportion in *Jiayu* is between that in *Mozi* and *Shiji* and very close to *Mozi*.

3 The Relationship Between the Semantic Features of Preposition-Object Structures and Their Position

Referring to Yang Bojun's research [17], we divide the semantics represented by the prepositional object structure into the following categories (Table 4):

Table 4. Categories of preposition-object structures modifying predicate components.

No	Category
1	Introducing time
2	Introducing objects
3	Introducing locations
4	Introducing tools, methods, conditions, basis, etc
5	Introducing cause or purpose
6	Introducing the content of instruction or speech
7	Introducing indirect objects

(1) Introducing time

Eg. 1 <u>自吾有由</u>, 而恶言不入于耳。《七十二弟子解》

zì wú yǒu yóu, ér è yán bù rù yú ěr。

Since I had You, those malicious words can no longer reach my ears.

Eg. 2 <u>后三日</u>, 牧来诉之曰……《颜回》

hòu sān rì, mù lái sù zhī yuē……

After three days, the horse breeder came to tell him……

(2) Introducing objects

Eg. 3 孔子侍<u>坐于哀公</u>。《大昏解》

kǒng zǐ shì zuò yú āi gōng。

Confucius sat beside Duke Ai of Lu State.

Eg. 4 子服景伯对使者曰……《辩物》

zǐ fú jǐng bó duì shǐ zhě yuē……

Zifu Jing Bo tells the messenger…

(3) Introducing locations
Eg. 5 先时, 季氏葬昭公于墓道之南。《相鲁》

xiān shí, jì shì zàng zhāo gōng yú mù dào zhī nán。

Earlier, Ji buried Duke Zhao in the southern tomb passage of the former Duke of Lu State.

Eg. 6 三揖至于阶。《观乡射》

sān yī zhì yú jiē。

After bowing down three times, walk to the steps in the front of the hall.

(4) Introducing tools, methods, conditions, basis, etc.
Eg. 7 因颜克而问礼于孔子。《曲礼子贡问》

yīn yán kè ér wèn lǐ yú kǒng zǐ。

Ask Confucius for etiquette through Yan Ke.

Eg. 8 齐氏用戈击公孟。《子贡问》

qí shì yòng gē jī gōng mèng。

Qi struck Gongmeng with a dagger-axe.

(5) Introducing cause or purpose
Eg. 9 大夫以罪免卒。《公西赤问》

dà fū yǐ zuì miǎn zú。

Officials were dismissed for a crime.

Eg. 10 凡渔者为得, 何以得鱼即舍之?《屈节解》

fán yú zhě wèi dé, hé yǐ dé yú jí shè zhī?

All fishermen want to get fish. Why did you release the fish you caught?

(6) Introducing the content of instruction or speech
Eg. 11 公曰: "前日寡人问吾子以东野毕之御。"《颜回》

gōng yuē: "qián rì guǎ rén wèn wú zǐ yǐ dōng yě bì zhī yù。"

Gong said, "The day before yesterday, I asked you about Dongye Bi's driving. "

Eg. 12 子游以问诸孔子。《公西赤问》

zǐ yóu yǐ wèn zhū kǒng zǐ。

Zi You asked Confucius about it.

(7) Introducing indirect objects
Eg. 13 孔子曰: "古之君子, 忠以为质, 仁以为卫。"《好生》

kǒng zǐ yuē: "gǔ zhī jūn zǐ, zhōng yǐ wéi zhì, rén yǐ wéi wèi。"

Confucius said, "The ancient gentleman took loyalty as the essence and benevolence as protection."

Eg. 14 穆子反鲁, 以牛为内竖, 相家。《正论解》

mù zǐ fǎn lǔ, yǐ niú wéi nèi shù, xiāng jiā。

Mu later returned to Lu State. He made Niu a small official and made him a family minister when he grew up.

We counted the semantic categories of the prepositional-object structures of the 1634 sentences, and the specific distribution of the semantic position is shown in the following table (Table 5):

Table 5. Categories of preposition-object structures modifying predicate components.

Semantic category	Before the predicate components	After the predicate components	Proportion of Before: After	Total	Proportion of Total
Introducing time	45	14	2.75%: 0.86%	59	3.61%
Introducing objects	75	478	4.59%: 29.25%	553	33.84%
Introducing locations	26	311	1.59%: 19.03%	337	20.62%
Introducing tools, methods, conditions, basis, etc	381	127	23.32%:7.77%	508	31.09%
Introducing cause or purpose	89	12	5.45%: 0.73%	101	6.18%
Introducing the content of instruction or speech	3	4	0.18%: 0.24%	7	0.43%
Introducing indirect objects	67	2	4.10%: 0.12%	69	4.22%

From the above table, the following can be seen: (1) The most common types of prepositions are those that introduce objects, tools/methods/conditions/basis/etc. and places, accounting for 33.84%, 31.09% and 20.62% of the total, respectively; (2) When prepositional-object structures introduce time, tools/methods/conditions/basis/etc., cause/purpose and indirect objects, they usually occur before the predicate components. (3) When prepositional-object structures introduce objects, locations and the content of instruction or speech, they usually occur after the predicate components.

The semantic category of the prepositional-object structure has an impact on its position. Taking the prepositions that introduce locations as an example, the ratio of the quantities before and after the predicate components is 26:311, which has obvious connections with "Yu (于)", which is often used to introduce location. Xie Xinyi (1991) [18] proposed two kinds of principles for the combination and arrangement of language symbols—iconic principles and abstract principles. Jiang Shaoyu [19] noted that using abstract principles to organize sentences generally depends on morphological signs. In ancient Chinese (especially pre-Qin Chinese), the preposition "Yu (于)" is an obvious mark, and "Yu (于) + location" is always placed behind the verb.

4 The Relationship Between the Characteristics of Predicate Components and the Position of Preposition-Object Structures

4.1 Relationship Between Grammatical Features of Predicate Components and the Position of Preposition-Object Structures

The predicate components modified by the prepositional-object structures in *Jiayu* include words and phrases; words include monosyllabic and polysyllabic words, and phrases include verb-object phrases, subordinate phrases, parallel structures, and serial verb constructions, etc.

(1) Words
Eg. 1 定公与齐侯会于夹谷。《相鲁》

dìng gōng yǔ qí hóu huì yú jiá gǔ。

Duke Ding and Marquis Qi held a league meeting in Jia Gu Mountain.

Eg. 2 逍遥于门而歌曰……《终记解》

xiāo yáo yú mén ér gē yuē……

Confucius strolled at the gate, singing……

(2) Verb-object phrases
Eg. 3 邻敌构兵于郊。《贤君》

lín dí gòu bīng yú jiāo。

The troops of the neighboring countries gathered in the suburbs.

Eg. 4 先时, 季氏葬昭公于墓道之南。《相鲁》

xiān shí, jì shì zàng zhāo gōng yú mù dào zhī nán。

Earlier, Ji buried Duke Zhao in the southern tomb passage of the former Duke of Lu State.

(3) Subordinate phrases
Eg. 5 今使祝嘏辞说徒藏于宗祝巫史, 非礼也。《礼运》

jīn shǐ zhù gǔ cí shuō tú cáng yú zōng zhù wū shǐ, fēi lǐ yě。

It is against etiquette to keep the words of prayers and blessings only for the lord's sacrificial officials and diviners.

Eg. 6 夫江始出于岷山, 其源可以滥觞。《三恕》

fū jiāng shǐ chū yú mín shān, qí yuán kě yǐ làn shāng。

When the Changjiang River has just exited Min Mountain, its current is very small.

(4) Parallel structure
Eg. 7 以养生送死, 以事鬼神。《礼运》

yǐ yǎng shēng sòng sǐ, yǐ shì guǐ shén。

It is used for people to wear in life and when managing funerals, as well as to worship ghosts and gods.

Eg. 8 天子常以季冬考德正法。《执辔》

tiān zǐ cháng yǐ jì dōng kǎo dé zhèng fǎ。

In ancient times, the emperors often inspected political achievements and adjusted decrees at the end of winter.

(5) Serial verb construction
Eg. 9 下止于殿前, 舒翅而跳。《辩政》

xià zhǐ yú diàn qián, shū chì ér tiào。

(The bird) flew down and landed in front of the palace, stretching its wings and jumping.

Eg. 10 每孺子之执笔记事于夫子。《七十二弟子解》

měi rú zǐ zhī zhí bǐ jì shì yú fū zǐ。

Every time when schoolboys were writing beside Confucius...

(6) Verb-complement phrase
Eg. 11 季孙于是乎可谓悦人之有能矣。《正论解》

jì sūn yú shì hū kě wèi yuè rén zhī yǒu néng yǐ。

Through this affair, Ji can be called akin to those with talent.

Eg. 12 孔子以公与季孙、仲孙、叔孙, 入于费氏之宫。《相鲁》

kǒng zǐ yǐ gōng yǔ jì sūn、zhòng sūn、shū sūn, rù yú fèi shì zhī gōng。

Confucius led Duke Ding, Ji, Zhong, and Shu into Fei's palace.

(7) Omission of the predicate

In ancient Chinese, predicates are sometimes omitted, such as:

Eg. 13 昔黄帝以云纪官, 故为云师而云名, 炎帝以火, 共工以水, 太昊以龙。《辩物》

xī huáng dì yǐ yún jì guān, gù wèi yún shī ér yún míng, yán dì yǐ huǒ, gòng gōng yǐ shuǐ, tài hào yǐ lóng。

Once upon a time, Emperor Huang named his official positions after clouds, so all the officials were named after clouds. Emperor Yan named his official positions fire, Gong Gong named his official positions water, and Tai Hao named his official positions dragon.

Eg. 14 子曰: "赠汝以车乎?赠汝以言乎?"子路曰: "请以言。"《子路初见》

zǐ yuē: "zèng rǔ yǐ chē hū?zèng rǔ yǐ yán hū?" zǐ lù yuē: "qǐng yǐ yán。"

Confucius said, "Shall I give you a chariot or some advice?" Zi Lu said, "Please give me some advice."

In the above examples, "yán dì yǐ huǒ (炎帝以火)", "gòng gōng yǐ shuǐ (共工以水)", and "tài hào yǐ lóng (太昊以龙)" both omit "jì guān (纪官)". The word "zèng (赠)" is omitted after "qǐng yǐ yán (请以言)".

We have calculated the statistics on the ways grammatical structure of predicate components and the preposition-object structures relate positionally, as shown in the following table (Table 6):

It can be seen from the above table that (1) the most common predicate components are monosyllabic words and verb-object structures, accounting for 50.73% and 43.02% of the total, respectively. (2) When the predicate components are monosyllabic words, polysyllabic words, serial verb constructions and verb-complement phrases, the preposition-object structures mainly occur behind the predicate components, with monosyllabic predicate components accounting for 68.04% of the total; and (3) the instances of parallel structures and subordinate phrases in the predicate components are rare and have no significant statistical significance. When the predicate is omitted, the preposition-object structure is usually before the predicate components.

In the above statistics, the largest number of predicate components are monosyllabic words, polysyllabic words and verb-object structures, and the relationships of the preposition-object structures to these three types of predicant components are similar to the statistics for the *Mozi* [6].

4.2 Relationship Between the Number of Syllables in the Predicate Components and the Positions of Preposition-Object Structures

We analyzed the number of syllables in the predicate components and the corresponding position of the preposition-object structures, and the statistical results are as follows (Table 7):

Table 6. Position of the predicate components and preposition-object structures.

No	Grammatical Structure of Predicate Components	Preposition-object Structures Before	Preposition-object Structures After	Proportion of Before: After
1	Monosyllabic words	190	646	22.73%: 77.27%
	Polysyllabic words	18	28	39.13%: 60.87%
2	Verb-object phrases	456	251	64.50%: 35.50%
3	Serial verb construction	7	11	38.89%: 61.11%
4	Verb-complement phrase	13	5	72.22%: 27.78%
5	Parallel structure	5	2	71.43%: 28.57%
6	Subordinate phrases	0	7	0.00%: 100.00%
7	Omission of predicate	5	2	71.43%: 28.57%

Table 7. Number of syllables in the predicate components and the corresponding position of the preposition-object structures.

Syllable number	Preposition-object structures before	Proportion	Preposition-object structures after	Proportion
1	187	22.48%	645	77.52%
2	335	58.77%	235	41.23%
3	112	70.44%	47	29.56%
4	24	72.73%	9	27.27%
5	16	61.54%	10	38.46%
6	6	60.00%	4	40.00%
7	7	100.00%	0	0.00%
9	1	100.00%	0	0.00%
13	1	100.00%	0	0.00%

It can be seen from the above table that (1) the most common predicate components are monosyllabic, or 2 and 3 syllables, and the proportions of preposition-object structures that occur before the predicate components are 22.48%, 58.77% and 70.44% for each of those predicate types. (2) Only when the predicate components are monosyllabic are the preposition-object structures mainly positioned after, accounting for 77.52% of instances. (3) When the number of syllables in the predicate components is greater than 1, the preposition-object structures usually occur before the predicate components.

In general, the statistics for the positional relationship between the number of syllables in predicate components and the preposition-object structures in *Jiayu* is similar to the statistics in *Mozi*. Why do the preposition-object structures tend to follow the predicate components only in instances of monosyllables? There may be two reasons: (1) Chinese is often composed of two syllables to form a relatively close rhythm unit. When the predicate component is one syllable, the monosyllabic predicate components can be combined with the preposition to form a metric foot. (2) The combination frequency of the preposition "Yu (于)" and monosyllabic predicate components is very high; while "Yu (于)" was used 788 times in *Jiayu*, 710 instances were behind the predicate components. The use characteristics of the preposition "Yu (于)" affect the statistical results.

5 Conclusion

We counted 15 prepositions and 1646 sample sentences in *Jiayu*. Prepositions in *Jiayu* that appear only before the predicate components are Cong (从), Yin (因), Dang (当), Yong (用), Hou (后), Dui (对), Jiang (将) and Zhi (至); prepositions that appear only after the predicate components are Hu (乎) and Zhu (诸), and prepositions that can appear before and after the predicate component are Yu (于), Yi (以), Zi (自), Wei (为) and Zai (在). Among the prepositions we analyzed, Cong (从), Yin (因), Dang (当), Yong (用), Jiang (将), Yi (以), Zi (自), Zai (在) tend to appear in the same position in the *Zuozhuan, Shiji and Mozi*. Zhi (至) and Wei (为) differ in the *Jiayu* from the *Mozi*, while Hou (后) and Dui (对) are not statistically significant in the *Zuozhuan, Shiji and Mozi*. We also compare the use of these prepositions with the *Mozi, Zuozhuan* and *Shiji* from various angles.

Overall, the ratio of prepositions before and after the predicate components in the *Jiayu* is 686: 948, in the *Zuozhuan* (2228: 3312), in the *Shiji* (1447: 175) and in the *Mozi* (481: 674). This indicates that the ratio in *Jiayu* is less than that of the *Zuozhuan* and *Mozi* and larger than that of the *Shiji*, which may reflect the grammatical features of the times when the *Jiayu* was composed.

Acknowledgments. This research is sponsored by the National Social Science Fund of China (No. 20BYY137).

References

1. Zhao, Y.R.: A Grammar of Spoken Chinese. Commercial Press (1979). (in Chinese)
2. Wang, L.: Chinese History Manuscript. Zhonghua Book Company, Beijing (1980). (in Chinese)
3. He, L.S.: A comparison of the positions of preposition-object structures in Zuozhuan and Shiji. Stud. Lang. Linguist. **1**, 57–65 (1985). (in Chinese)
4. Wang, H.B.: A Study on Prepositions in Zuozhuan. Fudan University, Doctor (2003). (in Chinese)
5. Liu, X.J.: Study on Prepositions in Mozi. Heilongjiang University, Master (2012). (in Chinese)

6. Yang, J.Q., Ke, Y.H.: A study on the positional relationship between preposition-object structures and predicate components in mozi based on corpus. In; Chinese Lexical Semantics: 23rd
   Workshop, CLSW 2022, Virtual Event, 14–15 May 2022, Revised Selected Papers, Part I.
   Springer-Verlag, Berlin, Heidelberg, pp. 414–431. https://doi.org/10.1007/978-3-031-28953-
   8_31
7. Jiang, S.Y.: Chouxiang Yuanze he Linmo Yuanze Zai Hanyu Yufa Shi Zhong De Titian. Res.
   Ancient Chin. Lang. **4**, 2–5 (1999). (in Chinese)
8. Zhang, C.: Historical Evolution of the Word-Order of Prepositional Phrases in Chinese.
   Beijing Language and Culture University Press, Beijing (2002). (in Chinese)
9. Song, Y.X.: Study on the Lexicon in Kongzijiayu. Shandong Normal University, Master
   (2021). (in Chinese)
10. Liu, W.Y.: Study on the complex tone words in Kongzijiayu. Master, Northeast Normal
   University (2009). (in Chinese)
11. Miao, C.M.: Study on Antonyms in Kongzijiayu. Master, Shandong Normal University
   (2017). (in Chinese)
12. Jiang, R.M.: Research on antonyms in Kongzijiayu. Cult. Educ. Mater. **04**, 33–36 (2018). (in
   Chinese)
13. Lu, Q.: A study of adverbs in Kongzijiayu. Master, Shandong Normal University (2017). (in
   Chinese)
14. Chen, J.: Analysis of Pronouns in Kongzijiayu. Qufu Normal University, Master (2011). (in
   Chinese)
15. Lin, Q.: The Historical Evolution and Part of Speech of "Zai." Bohai University, Master
   (2013). (in Chinese)
16. Deng, T.X.: Constructionalization and Development of Common Frame Construction in
   Ancient Chinese. Hunan Normal University, Doctor (2016). (in Chinese)
17. Yang, B.J., He, L.S.: Ancient Chinese Grammar and its Development. Language and Culture
   Press, Beijing (2001). (in Chinese)
18. Xie, X.Y.: Time and Imagery in Chinese (I). Foreign Linguist. **4**, 27–32 (1991). (in Chinese)
19. Jiang, S.Y.: The embodiment of iconic principles and abstract principles in the history of
   Chinese grammar. Res. Ancient Chin. Lang. **4**, 2–5 (1999). (in Chinese)

A Structural Priming Study of the Information Function of the Chinese *Ba* Construction

Bingxian Chen and Yu-Yin Hsu[✉]

The Department of Chinese and Bilingual Studies, The Hong Kong Polytechnic University, Hung Hom, Kowloon, Hong Kong, China
yu-yin.hsu@polyu.edu.hk

Abstract. Much research on the function of the *ba* construction in Mandarin Chinese has been conducted. However, there is a controversy about the *ba* NP regarding whether it expresses a topic denotation, a focus denotation, or neither. To study its information function, the present study has adopted a structural priming paradigm in a self-paced reading experiment to investigate whether Mandarin native speakers' reaction times (RTs) when reading *ba* sentences can be influenced after reading a priming sentence of the following three types: topic, focus, and subject-verb-object (SVO). The results revealed that the information conditions had a significant effect on the RT of processing the *ba* sentence ($p < .001$), while the RT for the *ba* NP in the condition of the priming focus sentences was significantly faster than the others. As priming effects occurred in the condition of priming focus sentences, processing the *ba* NP may be more similar to processing focus than to topic and canonical sentences in language comprehension.

Keywords: The *Ba* Construction · Structural Priming · Information Function

1 Introduction

The *ba* construction is a structure that is peculiar to Chinese and can be regarded as an object preposing construction representing a subject-object-verb (SOV) word order sentence with the particle *ba*. The *ba* construction can be summarized as [Subject + *Ba* + Object + Verb (+ Other Elements)]. The preposed object NP in the *ba* construction is often referred to as the *ba* NP. Although many previous studies have focused on the syntactic and semantic functions of the *ba* NP, there is still no consensus regarding whether it expresses the topic, the focus, or neither. Several researchers [1–3] have argued that the *ba* NP is a type of topic, while others [4–6] have considered it to be a focus. Nonetheless, these points of view do not accord with those of LaPolla [7], who stated that the *ba* NP was neither the topic nor the focus.

Most discussions about the function of the *ba* NP have been from the perspectives of grammatical form and grammatical meaning. Unlike previous research, the present study adopted a structural priming paradigm in a self-paced reading experiment to explore the information function of the *ba* NP. We investigated whether 60 native Mandarin speakers' reaction times (RTs) when reading *ba* sentences could be influenced after reading three different types of sentences, namely topic sentences, focus sentences, and the canonical active SVO sentences (baseline).

M. Dong et al. (Eds.): CLSW 2023, LNAI 14515, pp. 486–497, 2024.
https://doi.org/10.1007/978-981-97-0586-3_37

2   Literature Review

2.1   Views on the Information Function of the *Ba* NP

Deciding whether the message conveyed by a sentence in a discourse expresses a topic or a focus role is an important issue in grammar and in language comprehension [8–10]. Following Li & Thompson [11], many scholars have assumed that Chinese is a topic-prominent language, and the notion topic is generally expressed by a definite noun phrase occupying the sentence-initial position [11–13]. Although the *ba* NP is often referential, its position is not at the beginning of the sentence, which appears to be inconsistent with the definition of the topic. However, some researchers have maintained that Chinese allows for a topic that appears in the middle domain of a sentence [1, 14, 15]. Meng [2] also pointed out that whether the topic appeared in the sentence-initial position depended on its nature, and the secondary topic may be allowed depending on the verb's property, suggesting that the *ba* NP can belong to the latter.

The focus often expresses the key message that the speaker intends to convey [8]. In Chinese, the focus is generally expressed via intonation emphasis and syntactic structure (for a review, see [16]). Unlike the topic, which is usually located at the beginning of a sentence, the position of the focus is not fixed. As a sign of new information, it strengthens the semantics of the relevant components [17]. Focus can be divided into two categories according to the type, namely unmarked focus (also called natural focus) and marked focus [18]. The unmarked focus in Chinese is usually on the sentence-final position, while the position of the marked focus is more flexible and can appear at the beginning, middle, or end of a sentence, and is often realized via the focus marker [18]. For example, many researchers [19–21] have identified the focus marker "*lian* (even)……*dou* (also)". Similar to the preposed object in the *ba* construction, the object focus sentence marked by the focus marker "*lian* (even)……*dou* (also)" also requires the object to be marked in a preverbal position, as shown by the contrast shown between (1) and (2).

(1)	Zhexie	ren	lian	**yi dian**	**xiaoshi**	dou	bu	yuanyi	zuo.
	these	people	LIAN	a little	thing	DOU	not	want	do.

'These people don't even want to do the little things.'

(2)*Zhexie	ren	lian	dou	bu yuanyi	zuo **yi dian**	**xiaoshi**.
these	people	LIAN	DOU	not want	do a little	thing.

'These people don't even want to do the little things.'

Several scholars have studied the *ba* construction from the perspective of

Several scholars have studied the *ba* construction from the perspective of language information structure. Tsao [1] proposed that the function of the *ba* was to mark the object NP as a secondary topic. By comparing the characteristics of the regular topic NP and the *ba* NP, Tsao [1] found that the *ba* NP shared most of the properties of the regular topic NP and proposed four aspects in his topic theory. First, He claimed that the referential constraint of the *ba* NP resembled that of the sentence-initial topic. As is the case for the topic NP, the *ba* NP is specific, definite, or generic. Second, Tsao [1] revealed that the *ba* NP could be separated from the rest of the sentence by the pause particle *a/ya*, which is the same as for the regular topic. Third, Tsao [1] stated that the property of the *ba* NP occupying the sentence-initial position in the first sentence in a topic chain was the same as that of the topic. An example is presented below:

(3) Ta	ba	shu	zhang-le	jia	zai	mai	gei	women.
She	BA	book	raise-ASP	price	then	sell	to	us.

'She raised the price of the book before selling it to us.'

Tsao argued that in Example (3), the *ba* topic chain contains two clauses, both of which pertain to the same topic—*shu* "book". In this sentence, *shu* "book" is the *ba* NP, and occurs at the head of the chain. In other words, the *ba* NP can head a topic chain that is embedded in a larger topic chain that is headed by a typical topic. Finally, as with the typical topic, Tsao [1] pointed out that the *ba* NP was also in control of all the pronominalization and coreferential NP omitted in a topic chain. Concerning Example (4), Tsao [1] claimed that the first *ba* NP was the controller and the second *ba* NP was the victim in the coreferential processes of pronominalization and deletion.

(4) Ta	ba	shu	zhang-le	jia	zai	ba	ta	mai	gei	women.
She	BA	book	raise-ASP	price	then	BA	it	sell	to	us.

'She raised the price of the book before selling it to us.'

In summary, Tsao [1] concluded that the *ba* NP was a special kind of topic because it had most of the characteristics of the regular topic NP. Slightly different from Tsao's [1] view, Xue [3] argued that the *ba* NP was the main topic, and the subject served as the secondary topic. Xue [3] claimed that the verb phrase in the *ba* construction was a descriptive statement about the *ba* NP's condition as a result of a certain action and that the *ba* NP was the topic of this descriptive statement. Second, he argued that the verb phrase in the *ba* construction was related more closely to the *ba* NP than it was to the subject. That is, in the *ba* construction, the sentence is still grammatical if the subject is omitted (5b), but the sentence becomes ungrammatical if the NP after *ba* is omitted (5c).

(5) a. Zaogao,	wo	ba	zhe jian	shi	wang-le.
oops,	I	BA	this classifier	thing	forget-ASP.

'Oops, I forget this thing.'

b. Zaogao,	ba	zhe jian	shi	wang le.
oops,	BA	this classifier	thing	forget-ASP.

'Oops, (I) forget this thing.'

c.*Zaogao,	wo	ba	wang le.
oops,	I	BA	forget-ASP.

'Oops, I forget.'

Nonetheless, still some researchers believed that the *ba* NP was not the topic, but the focus. Li et al. [4] proposed that the Chinese *ba* construction was a common grammatical means of attracting the listener's attention to a specific object or problem through a certain activity or object and argued that the *ba* NP was the prominent part of the *ba* sentence; therefore, it was the focus. Similarly, Zhang [5] proposed that the *ba* NP could be treated as a secondary focus. Unlike Tsao [1], who stated that the character of the *ba* NP, which is definite, was the same as that of the regular topic, Zhang [5] argued that the *ba* NP did not need to be definite as long as it was an actual or referential entity, such as "a big tree" or "two sheets of paper." Furthermore, he claimed that, although the *ba* NP preceded the main verb, it differed from the topic structure. The topic structure only concerns two dimensions, "who (what) - what result/extent" [5], while the *ba* structure has three: "who (what) - manipulates (disposes, causes) what (who) - to what result/extent" [5]. To differentiate it from the primary focus in the *ba* construction, Zhang [5] suggested that the *ba* NP could be considered to be a secondary focus, because in the *ba* construction, as *ba* can be seen as part of the entire action process, the *ba* NP can never be separated from its ensuing verbal complement; it can only be regarded as part of the rheme or comment, rather than being part of the theme or topic. Shao and Zhao [6] also proposed that, instead of stating that the *ba* NP was a topic, it could be considered as a focus. They believed that the object after *ba* was the stress, and that the *ba* not only introduced a general semantic role, but also a pragmatic marker, namely a focus marker showing the speaker's emphasis. In conclusion, these researchers believed that the *ba* NP was either a focus to emphasize the point that the speaker wanted to highlight or became a secondary focus as an integral part of the primary focus at the end of the *ba* sentence.

LaPolla [7] proposed a different view that the *ba* NP was neither a topic nor a focus and illustrated his points according to two dimensions. First, LaPolla [7] stated that *ba* could allow for new referents to be treated as a portion of the presupposition. The function of the *ba* construction was to allow part of the presupposition to be treated as being within the scope of the assertion that contained the *ba* NP and everything that followed it. Therefore, the *ba* NP could be regarded as a new referent. However, this only occurred when the *ba* NP was not treated as salient new information because it was not placed in the neutral focal position; that is, the sentence-final position. According to LaPolla [7], the *ba* NP was not a typical focus (correlated with new information) or a topic (correlated with old information). In addition, LaPolla [7] argued that many *ba* NPs were neither topics nor second topics. He confirmed that the *ba* NP did not have the same distribution characteristics as the regular topic. The examples he gave are as follows.

(6) Ta   ba   xiezi   tuo-le,   cai   jin-lai.
    He   BA   shoes   Take-off-ASP,   then   enter come.
    'He took off his shoes, then came in.'

(7)*Ta   xiezi   tuo-le,   cai   jin-lai.
    He   shoes   Take-off-ASP,   then   enter come.
    'He took off his shoes, then came in.'

(8)*Xiezi   ta   tuo-le,   cai   jin-lai.
    Shoes   he   Take-off-ASP,   then   enter come.
    'He took off his shoes, then came in.'

(9) Ta   tuo-le   xiezi,   cai   jin-lai.
    He   Take-off-ASP   shoes   then   enter come.
    'He took off his shoes, then came in.'

Lapolla [7] explained that if removing *ba* from (6), as in (7), or place *xiezi* "shoes" in the initial position, as in (8), making the *ba* NP *xiezi* "shoes" as a topic, and these sentences became ungrammatical (or at least more marked). According to LaPolla [7], if moving *xiezi* "shoes" to the post-verbal position, the sentence is acceptable, as in (9). We noticed that the acceptability of these example sentences may vary by context. LaPolla's views began with the pragmatic function and structural characteristics of the *ba* construction. He argued that the *ba* NP could be used as a new referent (when it is not treated as salient new information), and it has no common characteristics with the typical topic. Unlike other studies, LaPolla [7] rejected the view that the *ba* NP is a topic or focus; this provided other theoretical sources for the examination of the function of the *ba* NP.

2.2   The Structural Priming Paradigm

Structural priming refers to facilitating the processing of the present syntactic structure through exposure to the same or similar structures. For example, people read a reduced relative clause sentence more quickly if they have previously read a sentence with a similar structure [22]. It has been acknowledged that structural priming exists in the production and comprehension of adult monolinguals and bilinguals [23]. Many studies have used structural priming to study language production, language comprehension to production, or priming within comprehension. One of the most popular methods is self-paced reading, in which participants read words in a sentence one by one in order by pressing keys on a keyboard and controlling the reading time for each sentence region according to their speed. Self-paced reading experiments approximate normal reading and can reflect the comprehension process of natural language. Hsieh [24] reported on a self-paced reading experiment to investigate the influence of Chinese passive relative clauses on the interpretation of English sentences that were temporarily ambiguous between an active main clause and a passive reduced relative structure.

In the present study, the *ba* NP is a preposed object, which is in the medial domain (below TP and above VP) in the *ba* construction [14]. As object preposed to the medial domain can be interpreted either as topic or as focus [14], by setting mini-discourses of topic, focus, and general declarative (baseline) as priming sentences, this study adopted a self-paced reading experiment to assess whether the information function of the *ba* NP was more similar to the focus denotation or to the topic denotation in language comprehension.

2.3 Research Questions

As a unique syntactic structure in Chinese, the *ba* construction has been studied by many linguists from various perspectives. However, as mentioned above, their opinions diverge regarding whether the information function of the *ba* NP is the topic, the focus, or both diverge. The dominant research direction on this topic has focused on analyzing the grammatical form and grammatical meaning of the *ba* construction.

However, we believe that the study should not be limited to the grammatical level, as the psycholinguistic perspective is also worth exploring. Specifically, we can investigate native Mandarin speakers' comprehension of the *ba* construction after reading topic sentences, focus sentences, and SVO sentences by adopting a structural priming paradigm. Two specific research questions that this study intended to answer are: (a) Do the different information conditions (topic versus focus) expressed by a preposed object influence native speakers' reading of the *ba* construction? (b) What is the information function of the *ba* NP? Is the *ba* NP's function more similar to focus, to topic, or to neither? We hypothesized that, if the *ba* NP functioned more similarly to the focus, the RTs of the *ba* sentences following the focus condition should be shorter than those in the other two conditions; however, if the *ba* NP functioned more like a topic phrase, the *ba* sentences should be read more quickly after the topic condition than after focus and SVO conditions.

3 Materials and Methods

3.1 Participants

66 native speakers of Mandarin (aged 20–29 with an average age of 24; 32 males) participated in the study. None of them had linguistic backgrounds. The participants' language proficiency and backgrounds were confirmed via a questionnaire on which they rated their proficiency in Mandarin/Cantonese/English/Min dialect/Hakka using a seven-point scale (1 = do not know the language, 7 = native). The mean proficiency of our participants was 6.48 in Mandarin, 1.7 in Cantonese, 4 in English, 1.05 in Min dialects, and 1.28 in Hakka.

3.2 Materials

To guarantee that the created materials were sufficiently natural, we adopted Su's [25] finding about speakers' choice-making of the *ba* construction that, when speakers marked a transitive event as being highly consequential, highly challenging, or highly important, or when explicitly blamed or praised the causer, they tended to use a *ba* construction rather than the other constructions. Based on this view, the target sentence in this experiment was designed to contain a context sentence and a *ba* sentence that was derived from this context. Similarly, to maintain consistency with the target sentence, the priming trials also contained a context sentence, followed by a topic/focus/SVO sentence. An example of primes and target sets is shown below. After reading a pair of sentences of one type of the prime (9), a target pair of a simple context and a *ba* sentence was presented (10). In each target pair, RTs in the regions 8 to 13 of each condition were used for analyses.

(9) Prime pair
Context Sentence 珊妮打扫卫生认真又细致。
                             'Sunny is conscientious and meticulous in cleaning.'
a. Focus Sentence 她$_{-8}$/连屋顶$_{-9}$/的$_{-10}$/灰尘$_{-11}$/都$_{-12}$/清理了$_{-13}$。
                             'She cleaned even the dust on the roof.'
b. Topic Sentence 屋顶$_{-8}$/的$_{-9}$/灰尘$_{-10}$/她$_{-11}$/都$_{-12}$/清理了$_{-13}$。
                             'She cleaned up the dust on the roof.'
c. SVO Sentence 她$_{-8}$/清理$_{-9}$/干净了$_{-10}$/屋顶$_{-11}$/的$_{-12}$/灰尘$_{-13}$。
                             'She cleaned up the dust on the roof.'

(10) Target pair
Context Sentence 珊妮打扫卫生认真又细致。
                             'Sunny is conscientious and meticulous in cleaning.'
Ba Sentence 她$_{-8}$/把屋顶$_{-9}$/的$_{-10}$/灰尘$_{-11}$/清理$_{-12}$/干净了$_{-13}$。
                             'She cleaned up the dust on the roof.'

The priming topic sentence in this experiment was designed based on the two salient properties of the topic, that is, the topic is in the sentence-initial position and is definite. The priming focus sentence was designed as an object focus sentence marked with "*lian* (even)……*dou* (also)", and the SVO sentence was a general declarative sentence with SVO word order. All experimental sentences were subject to an acceptance check using a seven-point scale by 117 Mandarin native speakers who did not participate in the formal experiment. Only sentences with a mean acceptance rating greater than 5.5 points were selected as the experimental items.

This study included 36 prime-target pairs of experimental items and 108 filler items. The experimental sentences included 12 pairs of Prime Topic - Target *Ba* (henceforth, topic-*ba*) discourse, 12 pairs of Prime Focus - Target *Ba* (henceforth, focus-*ba*) discourse, and 12 pairs of Prime SVO - Target *Ba* (henceforth, SVO-*ba*) discourse. The 36 pairs of experimental materials were divided into three lists, and we used the Latin square design to ensure that each pair of experimental materials appeared only once in each list. Each list contained four pairs of topic-*ba* discourses, four pairs of focus-*ba* discourses, four pairs of SVO-*ba* discourses, and 36 filler items. The experimental materials were divided into 14 regions, in which the *ba* NP appeared in Regions 9, 10, and 11. Each *ba* sentence contained six regions.

3.3 Procedure

The experiment was conducted using PCIbex (https://farm.pcibex.net/). The participants were tested individually and were assigned randomly to one of the three lists. Each participant was instructed to complete six practice trials prior to beginning the formal experiment. Each trial began with a fixation cross (1,500 ms), and the sentences were then presented on the screen one word at a time in a moving window display; the participants could press the space bar to read the next word. Each sentence was followed by a comprehension question, and no feedback about the participants' responses was given during the formal test. The participants' RTs and answers were recorded digitally, and the entire experiment lasted for approximately 40 min.

4   Results and Discussion

The priming effect estimates were based on measuring the participants' RTs for the *ba* sentences. Prior to the analysis, data from four participants were excluded because the accuracy was lower than 80%. In addition, the results for the two participants were not recorded by PCIbex successfully, thus they were excluded as well. Furthermore, RT results lower than 100 ms and exceeding three standard deviations, accounting for about 2% of all the data, were removed from the analysis.

The average accuracy on comprehension questions of remaining 60 participants was 96.5%. The accuracy results of the reading comprehension questions for the three conditions are in Table 1. We can see that the differences in the answers among the three conditions are minuscule, and all have high accuracy.

Table 1. Accuracy results of comprehension questions for the three conditions

Three Conditions	Standard Deviation	Standard Error
Prime Focus	.190	.123
Prime Topic	.180	.116
Prime SVO	.180	.116

We then used lme4 in R to perform a linear mixed-effects analysis of the relationship among the RTs for the ba construction and the three conditions. We included participants, items, and lists as random effects. Then, we used two fixed effects, priming condition (the topic condition, the focus condition, and the SVO condition) and sentence regions, and their interaction in the model. The results revealed that the model comparison was significant ($\chi^2 (17) = 47872, p < .001$), thus indicating that the three conditions and the six regions had a significant impact on the RTs. In addition, the results of the pair-wised comparison of the conditions (see Table 2) illustrated that the.

RTs of focus condition were significantly faster than that of the topic condition ($p = .009$), the focus condition was significantly faster than the SVO condition ($p = .025$), and the topic and the SVO conditions were not significantly different ($p = .945$). Therefore, we identified that there was priming tendency in the focus condition.

Based on the above analysis, we examined the mean RT for each region in the *ba* construction (see Fig. 1). As shown in the figure, except for Region 8 (where the subject was located) in the *ba* constructions that shared similar log RTs, the remaining regions'

Table 2. Pair-wise comparisons results for the three conditions on the RTs of the *ba* sentences

Pair-wise comparison	Estimated Standard	Standard Error	Z Value	P Value
Prime Focus vs. Prime SVO	−.168	.064	−2.612	**.025**
Prime Topic vs. Prime SVO	.021	.065	.320	.945
Prime Topic vs. Prime Focus	.189	.064	2.933	**.009**

RTs in the focus condition were the lowest. The RT for the *ba* NP (Regions 9–11) in the focus condition was significantly less than it was in the other two conditions. Thus, the participants read the *ba* sentence more quickly after reading the priming focus discourse than they did after reading the priming topic discourse or the priming SVO discourse; some priming effects were more obvious in the focus condition.

Furthermore, we continued to use a linear mixed-effects model to examine the relationships of the RT for each region and the three conditions (see Table 3).We entered three priming conditions as fixed effects into the model, namely the topic condition, the focus condition, and the SVO condition. We still used intercepts for.

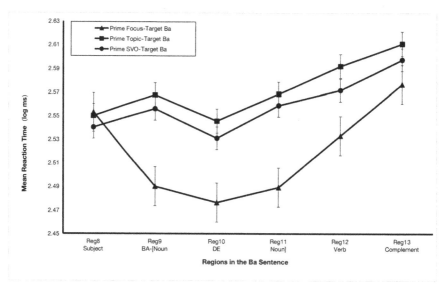

Fig. 1. Log RTs for the region in the *ba* sentence according to the three conditions

the participants and the items as random effects. Following the analysis, we found that the model comparison results were significant (Reg 9: χ^2 (2) = 8.737, p = .013; Reg 10: χ^2 (2) = 9.706, p = .008; Reg 11: χ^2 (2) = 7.315, p = .026) in the region of the *ba* NP (Regions 9–11), as the three conditions were the main effect. In addition, we observed a spillover effect in Reg 12 (χ^2 (2) = 4.992, p = .082). This indicated that these three conditions also had an impact on the verb's RT in the *ba* construction.

Table 3. Relationship among the RTs for each region and the three conditions

Regions in the *ba* construction	Chi square	P Value
Reg 8 Subject	.322	.851
Reg 9 BA -Noun	8.737	**.013**
Reg 10 DE	9.706	**.008**
Reg 11 Noun	7.315	**.026**
Reg 12 Verb	4.992	.082
Reg 13 Complement	1.230	.541

Besides, the results of the comparisons of the conditions (see Table 4) showed that, in the *ba* NP region, the focus and the topic condition had a significant effect (Reg 9: $p = .010$; Reg 10: $p = .005$; Reg 11: $p = .024$), as did the focus and the SVO condition (Reg 9: $p = .036$; Reg 10: $p = .027$; Reg 11: $p = .057$). However, there was no significant difference between the topic and the SVO condition (Reg 9: $p = .891$; Reg 10: $p = .849$; Reg 11: $p = .944$), which was consistent with the results that were observed in Fig. 1. It was noteworthy that the difference between the topic and the focus condition was more obvious in Region 12 ($p = .057$), but there were no significant differences in the comparisons of the other two conditions. Based on the above analysis of all the regions, we determined that there were indeed priming effects in the *ba* NP region. This meant that the *ba* NP function was more similar to the focus denotation than it was to the topic.

Table 4. Pair-wise comparisons results for the three conditions on the RTs of Regs 9–12

		Estimated	S.E	Z Value	P
Reg 9	Prime Focus vs. Prime SVO	53.680	21.732	2.470	**.036**
	Prime Topic vs. Prime SVO	−9.972	21.768	.458	.891
	Prime Topic vs. Prime Focus	−63.651	21.740	−2.928	**.010**
Reg 10	Prime Focus vs. Prime SVO	44.706	17.329	2.580	**.027**
	Prime Topic vs. Prime SVO	−9.453	17.353	− .545	.849
	Prime Topic vs. Prime Focus	−54.159	17.316	−3.128	**.005**
Reg 11	Prime Focus vs. Prime SVO	56.038	24.468	2.290	.057
	Prime Topic vs. Prime SVO	−7.924	24.483	− .324	.944
	Prime Topic vs. Prime Focus	−63.962	24.462	−2.615	**.024**
Reg 12	Prime Focus vs. Prime SVO	31.06	21.64	1.435	.323
	Prime Topic vs. Prime SVO	−18.53	21.65	− .856	.668
	Prime Topic vs. Prime Focus	−49.59	21.65	−2.291	.057

5 Concluding Remarks

This study revisited the debate about the information function of the *ba* construction. Whether the *ba* NP expresses a topic denotation, a focus denotation, or neither, remains controversial. The present study's findings, which were based on a structural priming paradigm in a self-paced reading experiment, revealed that different information conditions (topic versus focus) expressed by a preposed object may influence native speakers' reading of the *ba* construction. Sixty native Mandarin speakers read the *ba* NP more quickly when they had previously read the focus discourse rather than the topic discourse, and priming effects occurred in the focus condition. The *ba* NP in the.

ba construction may be processed in a way that is more similar to the focus than it is to the topic in language comprehension. In terms of the theoretical and methodological implications of the present study, it serves as a contribution to the current controversy.

on the information function of the *ba* NP in Mandarin Chinese, which remains an under- investigated field in prior research. Besides, the use of the well-established methodology, a structural priming paradigm in a self-paced reading experiment, is a novel approach that adds to the existing literature on the *ba* construction.

However, the current experiment also had several limitations. The *ba* NP in this study was divided into three regions (*ba* Noun + *de* + Noun), which may have influenced.

the RTs for the *ba* NPs in the three conditions. In future research, we suggest simplifying the *ba* NP and allowing it to be present in one region. Moreover, we selected the "*lian* (even)...*dou* (also)" construction for our priming focus sentences, even though it is widely acknowledged that "*lian* (even)...*dou* (also)" is a typical focus marker [17, 19, 20, 26]. In future research, other focus makers, such as *zhiyou* 'only', could be used to test whether the results will differ from those in the present study. Finally, the present experiment could be repeated with L2 Chinese learners, and then the data of the L2 Chinese learners could be compared with the data collected under the current study to further explore whether there is any different performance between L2 and native speakers in the information function of the *ba* NP.

References

1. Tsao, F.: A topic-comment approach to *ba* construction. J. Chin. Linguist. **15**, 1–54 (1987)
2. Meng, Y.: On the topic and focus of *ba*-sentences. J. PLA Univ. Foreign Lang. **23**, 44–46 (2000). (in Chinese)
3. Xue, F.: On the semantic characteristics of the ba sentence. Lang. Teach. Linguist. Stud. **1**, 4–22 (1987)
4. Li, Y., Zheng, L., et al.: Practical Chinese Reference Grammar. Beijing Language and Culture University Press, Beijing (1990). (in Chinese)
5. Zhang, P.N.: Word order variation and end focus in Chinese: pragmatic functions. Ed.D. Thesis, Teachers College, Columbia University (1994)
6. Shao, J., Zhao, C.: Cognitive interpretation of *ba*-construction and *bei*-construction. Chin. Lang. Learn. **4**, 11–18 (2005). (in Chinese)
7. Lapolla, R.J.: Grammatical Relations in Chinese: Synchronic and Diachronic Considerations. University of California, Berkeley (1990)
8. Chafe, W.: Givenness, contrastiveness, definiteness, subjects, topics, and point of view. In: Li, C.N. (ed.) Subject and Topic, pp. 25–56. Academic Press, New York (1976)

9. Krifka, M.: Basic notions of information structure. Acta Linguistica Hung. **55**, 243–276 (2008)

10. Hsu, Y.-Y.: Associations between focus constructions and levels of exhaustivity: an experimental investigation of Chinese. PLoS ONE **14**(10), e0223502 (2019)

11. Li, C.N., Thompson, S.A.: Subject and topic: a new typology of languages. In: Charles N. Li (ed.): Subject and Topic, pp. 457–489. Academic Press, New York (1976)

12. Tsao, F.: A functional study of topic in Chinese: The first step towards discourse analysis. Unpublished Ph.D. Dissertation, University of Southern California (1977)

13. Shi, D.: The nature of Chinese topics. Mod. Foreign Lang. **2**, 40–57 (1998). (in Chinese)

14. Hsu, Y.-Y.: Two functional projections in the medial domain in Chinese. Concentric Stud. Linguist. **38**, 93–136 (2012)

15. Paul, W.: Sentence-internal topics in Mandarin Chinese: the case of object preposing. Lang. Linguist. Compass **3**, 695–714 (2002)

16. Hsu, Y.-Y.: Information structure in Chinese discourse. In: Chris, S., (ed.): Routledge Handbook of Chinese Discourse Analysis, pp. 130–144. Taylor & Francis/Routledge, London (2019a)

17. He, Y.: On the syntactic structures of focus constructions in Mandarin Chinese. Chin. Linguist. **2**, 53–68 (2010). (in Chinese)

18. Liu, X.: Focus, distribution of focus and focusing. J. Ningxia Univ. (Humanities & Social Sciences Edition). **17**, 79–84 (1995). (in Chinese)

19. Fang, M.: The syntactic expression of Chinese contrastive focus. Stud. Chin. Lang. **4**, 279–288 (1995). (in Chinese)

20. Liu, D., Xu, L.: Focus, background, topic and *lian* construction in Chinese. Stud. Chin. Lang. **4**, 5–14 (1998). (in Chinese)

21. Tsao, F.: Topic and *lian...dou*/ye construction revisited. Functionalism in Chinese Syntax. Chinese Language Teachers Association Monograph **1**, 245–278(1989)

22. Wei, H., Boland, J.E., Cai, Z., Yuan, F., Wang, M.: Persistent structural priming during online second-language comprehension. J. Exp. Psychol. Learn. Mem. Cogn. **45**, 349–359 (2019)

23. Pickering, M.J., Ferreira, V.S.: Structural priming: a critical review. Psychol. Bull. **134**, 427–459 (2008)

24. Hsien, Y.: Structural priming during sentence comprehension in Chinese-English bilinguals. Appl. Psycholinguist. **38**, 657–678 (2017)

25. Su, D.: Significance as a lens: Understanding the mandarin *ba* construction through discourse adjacent alternation. J. Pragmat. **117**, 204–230 (2017)

26. Ma, T.-M., Hsu, Y.-Y., Han, T., Tack, D. Activation of alternatives by mandarin sentence-initial and sentence-internal foci: a semantic priming study. In: Dong, M., et al. (eds.) Chinese Lexical Semantics, CLSW 2021. LNAI, vol. 13249, pp. 263–270. Springer International Publishing Cham (2021). https://doi.org/10.1007/978-3-031-06703-7_20

A Case Study of a Preschool Child's Compliment Expression Based on Schema Theory

Siqi Xie[1,2](✉)

[1] Research Center for Languages and Language Education, Central China Normal University,
152 Luoyu Road, Wuhan, China
sqxie@mails.ccnu.edu.cn

[2] Surveillance and Research Center for National Language Resources (Internet Media),
Central China Normal University, 152 Luoyu Road, Wuhan, China

Abstract. Compliments, as an essential type of evaluation expression, are also considered an important factor in assessing pragmatic competence. This paper analyzes how children organize their compliment expressions under the framework of schema theory. It describes the characteristics and developmental trajectory of children's compliment expression based on the four parts of language schema and 16 types of high-frequency expression. The analysis also reveals a continuity of sentiment strength, indicating that schema patterns differ significantly across various degrees of compliments. This novel approach can not only shed light on the realization of children's compliment expression but also provide a new avenue for research of speech acts and enhance the accuracy of sentiment analysis in natural language processing.

Keywords: Child language · Compliment · Expressive speech acts · Schema theory

1 Introduction

Children's language abilities develop significantly through pragmatic use. In disciplines ranging from child psychology to developmental pragmatics, considerable focus has been placed on children's language and social competencies. A crucial aspect of these competencies is the mastery of using language appropriately to encode and decode communicative intents or speech acts [1]. Many scholars [2, 3] have posited that core human speech acts encompass various forms, including inquiry, imperative, narration, and evaluation. Evaluation, in particular, involves expressing positive or negative value judgments about specific individuals, objects, or events [4]. This form of expression is integral to assessing children's pragmatic competence.

Compliments, as a form of evaluative expressions, are considered essential in demonstrating pragmatic competence. For example, an individual with pragmatic competence should not only have the knowledge of how to employ linguistic resources effectively to deliver compliments but also be able to discern appropriate contexts and recipients for such expressions [5]. This ability reflects a nuanced understanding of social and

M. Dong et al. (Eds.): CLSW 2023, LNAI 14515, pp. 498–513, 2024.
https://doi.org/10.1007/978-981-97-0586-3_38

linguistic norms, underlining the importance of complimenting as a key component of language development and interpersonal communication skills.

While there has been extensive research on compliments and praises, the majority of these studies have focused on adults. Research specifically addressing children's expressive speech acts related to praise remains comparatively sparse. The process of children's language acquisition, particularly how they develop pragmatic competence and acquire the skills to select appropriate linguistic tools for effectively offering compliments, continues to intrigue scholars. Empirical research in this area, especially on children's compliment speech acts, is still limited.

Ninio et al. developed the Inventory of Communicative Acts-Abridged (INCA-A) system to study children's speech acts and pragmatic abilities [6]. However, INCA-A falls short in explaining how children organize the sequence of vocabulary or phrases to express their communicative intent and the illocutionary force of an utterance. Most scholarly focus in children's speech acts has been on the function of word choice and sentence patterns, with less attention paid to the development of sequential discourse and pragmatic competence. Additionally, there has been inadequate exploration of the differences between the sequences in children's simple and complex utterances of specific speech acts, and the developmental trajectory of their communicative competence remains insufficiently detailed.

Schema theory presents itself as a promising framework for a "constructive" or "sequential" study of this nature. However, it has been seldom applied in examining children's pragmatic competence. Therefore, this study aims to investigate how children construct compliment speech acts through the lens of schema theory. To achieve this objective, the study employs a self-constructed children's corpus and a newly developed analytical framework to examine the schema of compliments. This approach involves summarizing core words and common sentences and establishing a continuum of compliment degrees. The ultimate goal is to uncover the developmental path of children's compliment speech skills and enhance tasks such as automatic sentiment analysis.

2   Theoretical Basis and Related Work

2.1   Schema Theory and Its Application in Language Acquisition

In recent decades, schema theory has emerged as a significant approach in modeling language acquisition patterns. The concept of "schema" was first introduced by philosopher Immanuel Kant in 1781. Kant posited that schemas are products of a purely transcendental imagination or represent structures of knowledge that learners have previously acquired. Subsequently, scholars from various disciplines have presented diverse perspectives on the concept of "schema." Some view a schema as "the structure of previous knowledge (i.e., background knowledge) acquired by learners". Psychologists like Piaget and Bartlett conceptualize a schema as a mental network and classification system of information and experience, comprising several variables that represent and conceptualize elements [7, 8]. Linguist Carroll, on the other hand, defines schema as a structure within semantic memory [9]. Despite variations in definitions across different fields, a consensus exists that a schema is a structure focusing on organized key information.

This aspect of schema has led to its widespread application in fields such as psychology, linguistics, and artificial intelligence.

In the context of child language learning, schema theory has been instrumental in understanding how children acquire and organize new vocabulary and grammar. A fundamental principle of schema theory is that new information is assimilated into existing cognitive structures or schemas. This implies that in language acquisition, children utilize their pre-existing knowledge and experiences to understand new linguistic inputs. As Anderson and Freebody [10] indicate, research shows that children who have a schema for story structure demonstrate better comprehension and recall abilities than those without such schemas. Additionally, parents play a crucial role in nurturing their children's textual frameworks (encompassing both written and spoken language), aiding various communicative purposes such as expressing compliments, offering congratulations, or making requests. These texts possess a unique organizational structure that requires specific connections and sequencing, often referred to as language text schema.

2.2 Children's Compliment Expression in Natural Interaction

Compliment expression. Compliments are categorized as a type of expressive speech act, following Searle's classification [11]. Widely recognized as the "lubricant of society," Holmes describes a compliment as a speech act that explicitly or implicitly attributes credit to someone other than the speaker, usually the person addressed, for some 'good' (such as a possession, characteristic, skill, etc.) that is positively valued by both the speaker and the hearer [12]. Research on the speech acts of compliments is predominantly situated within the field of sociolinguistics. Válková [13] suggests that a compliment can be seen as the outcome of an exchange between the speaker's intended message and the recipient's understanding of it, which also includes a response from the recipient. In other words, she views the compliment as exhibiting behavioral characteristics of "negotiation." Wu [14] conducted a comprehensive study examining various aspects, such as the nature of compliment behavior, forms of compliment discourse, and responses adjacent to compliments. His work has essentially addressed the 'Why, What, and How' of compliment speech acts. However, his research did not include a quantitative analysis of the sentiment strength of compliments.

Children's compliment expression. Multiple research studies have delved into children's speech acts, with a particular focus on expressive speech acts in some cases. For example, Luo [15] carried out a comprehensive study on verbal communication among 5-year-old children in her doctoral dissertation. However, her research did not extensively cover the realization mechanisms of compliment speech acts. Similarly, Burdelski et al. [16] investigated the use of the word "kawaii" in kindergarten interactions between teachers and children. Their study centered on identifying the types of objects children compliment, and examining how gender and interpersonal relationships influence the execution of compliment speech acts. Despite these insights, there remains a gap in understanding the structural embodiment and developmental trajectory of children's compliment speech acts in actual dialogues.

To date, no article has specifically analyzed the detailed manifestation and structural framework of children's compliment speech acts within natural interactions. Children's verbal expressions are indicative of their intellectual and cognitive development, and the process of schema construction is mirrored in their natural conversations. This raises several questions: Can children's compliment speech acts reflect the construction of schema? When do children develop the verbal skills necessary for structuring compliment expressions? How are the structural elements of these expressions arranged and combined? What does the acquisition process of children's compliments reveal? In the preschool stage, there is a notable evolution in children's pragmatic environment, with the influence of adult evaluations, peer assessments, and self-evaluation becoming increasingly significant [4]. Is there a specific point at which children's compliment speech undergoes a marked change? What factors contribute to this transition? These are among the many questions that remain to be explored.

3   Case Study of a Child's Pattern of Compliment Schema

3.1   Data Collection and Annotation

The data for this study is derived from the interactions of a child in ages from 0;0 to 6;5. Considering that corpora can significantly contribute to the acquisition and restructuring of the schematic knowledge underpinning communicative competence [17], a specialized child corpus was established based on the book 人生初年 (*The Early Years of Life: a Chinese Girl's Language Diary*) [18–20]. This book chronicles the language development of a Chinese girl named Dongdong, whose parents are both linguistics scholars. It encompasses over 800,000 words, documenting Dongdong's natural conversations from birth to the age of six.

The analysis of compliment expressions in this paper is based on 96 items extracted from this corpus. To identify these expressions, we employed a methodology that involved retrieving positive keywords and utilizing language models for automatic text sentiment analysis. Each item was meticulously screened from texts labeled as positive. The study employed a labeling system with six major parameters: characters (complimenter and hearer), object (complimentee), scenes, content (vocabulary and syntactic schema), strategies, and motivations. Characters and objects form the core of the compliment speech acts. Strategies are primarily categorized as either upgrading or downgrading, while motivations are broadly classified into four groups: compliance with self-face, alignment with positive emotions, fulfillment of self-needs, and adherence to power or closeness relationships.

3.2   Compliment Schema

In this article, a schema is defined as a constructive pattern manifesting in children's utterances during social interactions. The findings related to the expressions of compliments are categorized into four parts: A. Attention utterance; B. Lead-out utterance; C. Core utterance; D. Auxiliary utterance.

The attention utterance consists of words or phrases that generate interest or attention towards specific topics or issues.

The lead-out utterance is an expression that paves the way for the core compliment. It sets the stage for subsequent compliments and guides listeners or readers to anticipate what will be expressed next.

The core utterance is the central compliment expression, usually involving positive evaluations of an object's form or characteristics, or a person's qualities, abilities, achievements, or behaviors.

The auxiliary language includes speech elements that support and elaborate on the core compliment. These elements provide additional details, examples, or evidence to reinforce the rationality of the evaluation.

The ABCD structure constitutes the overall schema for compliment expression. The most frequently occurring part or combination is termed the 'commonly used schema'. The 'variant schema' emerges from the commonly used schema through repeated superposition or mixed combinations. 错误!书签自引用无效。 illustrates the eight patterns of the commonly used schema, and Fig. 1 displays its distribution across different ages (Table 1).

Table 1. Patterns of Context Schema

Patterns	Examples	Percent
A	谢谢你，我的好妈妈。	3.37%
	Thank you, my dear mother.	
AC	我看看(A)，好漂亮啊！(C)	**22.47%**
	Let me see, how beautiful!	
ACD	你们的席子(A)，比我的好得多得多！(CD)	3.37%
	Your mat is much better than mine!	
BC	我知道妈妈很棒的!	3.37%
	I know Mom is great!	
BCD	这比我想像的好吃多了，榨菜蛮好吃的。	2.25%
	This is much more delicious than I thought. The pickles are delicious.	
C	好甜哪!	**48.31%**
	How sweet!	
CD	姐姐买的好喝，爸爸买的更好喝。	**14.61%**
	My sister bought a good drink, while my father bought a better one.	
D	活要活得痛快，死要死得干净!	2.25%
	Live happily and die cleanly!	

From the table above, we can divide 8 patterns into two kinds of schema. The commonly used schema encompasses patterns C, AC, and CD; and the other patterns consist of the variant schema. Among the commonly used schema patterns, AC and CD are particularly noteworthy.

The analysis reveals a clear and notable observation: Dong-dong's ability to give compliments showed significant growth between the ages of 2 and 3, expanding in

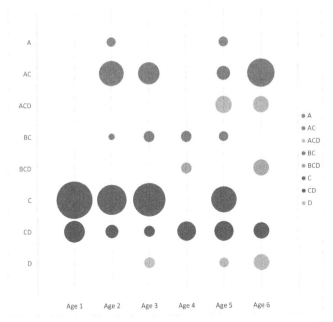

Fig. 1. The distribution of the compliment expression schema of different ages of Dongdong. The bigger the bubble, the higher the frequency of use.

both quantity and diversity. Furthermore, at ages 5–6, Dongdong's compliment schema became increasingly complex. An interesting finding is that the schema patterns of C and CD are the most frequently used in the entire corpus, while patterns of ACD, BCD, and D are predominantly used at ages 4–6. This suggests that the use of schema type D is associated with children's advanced compliment-giving skills.

The observed variance could potentially be linked to the development of children's awareness and cognition. As children have their own rules for evaluation, their unique cognitive perspectives and modes of thinking can be quite remarkable. As they mature through socialization, their methods of expressing evaluations gradually become more similar to those of adults. The language used by children directly reflects their experiences, with many of their expressions demonstrating compliments and affirmation drawn from everyday life, including interpersonal interactions, narrative activities, and media exposure. A prime example is the statement "Live happily and die cleanly!" which Dongdong made after watching a television drama. Through socialization, children gradually shift from the intimate world of fairy tales to the complexities of the real world. Fairy tales are characterized by simple themes and binary evaluations, whereas the real world offers a more diverse evaluation system and a perspective of relative morality [4].

3.3 High-Frequency Utterance

High-frequency words and sentences of compliment expression are concluded. From Table 2, we can see that there are 16 micro types of compliment schema.

Table 2. Taxonomy of Context Schema

Macro Types	Micro types	Words and structures	Examples
A: Attention utterances	A1 appellation	好+称谓（亲属/职位）	好爸爸
		Dear + appellation/position	Dear father
	A2 exclamation	啊！哇！哎哟！太+adj+了！	太好看了！
			So beautiful!
		a, wa, eiyo, so+adj!	
	A3 attention	听，看，瞧	快来看看！
		Listen, see, watch	Come and have a look!
	A4 confirmation	当然是+名词了！	当然是三套好了！
		Of course, is + noun!	
B: Lead out	B1 agreement	我知道	我知道妈妈最棒了！
		I know that……	I know that mom is the greatest!
		不愧是	
		Indeed	
	B2 likeness	我喜欢	我最喜欢吃无花果了。
		I like	I like to eat figs the most.
	B3 assume	要是，如果，肯定，本来	要是奶奶在就好了！
		If, for sure	If only grandma were here!
	B4 Amendment	想不到，没想到	真没想到，这比我想象中的好吃多了！
		Unexpected, can't believe it	I Can't believe it! This is much more delicious than I expected!
C: Core utterances	C1 Commendatory words	真+adj，好+adj,挺+adj的，可+adj，蛮+adj，adj+得很，adj+极了	好厉害呀！
			How awesome!
		very+ adj, extremely + adj	XXX 长得最漂亮。
			XXX is the most beautiful.
			幼儿园里好玩极了。
			The kindergarten is very interesting.
	C2 Identify utterance	称谓（亲属/职位）+好/真好/最好	爸爸好。
			Dad is good!
		appellation/position + is good!	
	C3 sensory words	好+adj,挺+adj的,可+adj	好香啊！
			It smells good!
D: Auxiliary utterances	D1 Truth explanation	记得，忘不了	她们给了我很多知识，我永远也忘不了她们。
		Can't forget	They have given me so much knowledge that I will never forget them.

(continued)

Table 2. (*continued*)

D2 Ask for agreement	这不是……吗? Isn't this ...?	这不是两全其美吗? Isn't this the best of both worlds?
D3 Homogeneous analogy	和……一样 Be same as 也…… also	你别说我画得好，你写字也写得好呀! Don't tell me that I draw well, you write well too!
D4 Comparative judgement	不像…… don't like...... ……好，……坏 ......is good, ...is bad	爸爸好，姐姐坏 Dad is good, sister is bad.
D5 Suggestion	……也行 ...... is fine. ……（就）要…… ......should be	她长得好看，选她做妻子也行啊! She is good-looking, so you can choose her as your wife!

From the table above, it is evident that the "language resource bank" for children's compliments is becoming increasingly rich.

First, C1 words are often used in conjunction with degree adverbs such as "最、蛮、太、可、多、挺、特别、非常、极、好" [*most, quite, too, so, quite, especially, very, extremely*] (most, very). In addition, positive words can also be used with degree complements such as "死了、极了、得很" [*extremely*] and advanced modifiers "这么，那么" [*so*]..

Secondly, compliment expressions have changed from direct external expression to indirect and covert ones. Generally, children's emotional expressions are relatively overt and easily excitable, and their ability to control and regulate emotions is comparatively weak. In early stages, children often use A1, A2, and A3 forms to emphasize their emotions. As they grow older, they learn to use more abstract and narrative expressions of compliments, such as D1, D2, and D5 types, which are closer to the strategies adults use in social interactions.

Thirdly, Dongdong uses upgrading strategies to pay compliments. For example, in B1 type recognition language such as "I know" can be used to enhance the cognitive position and strengthen the power of speech.

Thirdly, Dongdong employs upgrading strategies to deliver compliments. For example, in B1 type recognition language, phrases like "I know" can be used to enhance the cognitive position and strengthen the power of speech.

Finally, Dongdong's use of D3 type and D4 type indicates that preschool children are developing comparison and classification abilities. The standard for expressing compliments is also based on personal subjective judgment. By the age of 5–6 years, the number of compliment speech acts based on objective judgment begins to increase.

Although children's expressions of compliments are not as rich and diverse as adults', the four characteristics outlined above demonstrate children's sensitivity to schema structure design and discourse organization. They also effectively reflect the psychological characteristics of children.

3.4 Sentiment Strength

This paper divides the sentiment strength of compliment expression into 5 grades: very slight, slight, normal, strong, and very strong, as Table 3 shows:

Table 3. Continuum of Sentiment Strength

Compliment pattern	Example	Score
Use adverbs of the highest degree.	他骑车是天下第一好的。	very strong/5
Core utterance reuse	He's the best rider in the world	
	刘伟哥骑车厉害的，他好厉害呀，他可厉害了！	
	Brother Liu Wei is great, he is so amazing, he is so awesome!'	
Use adverbs with a high degree of expression.	太好了！太棒了！	strong/4
	So great! Awesome!	
Use agreement like "I know that".	他骑车好厉害呀！	
	He rides so great!	
	我知道妈妈很棒的。	
	I know that mom is great!	
Normal commendatory terms	爸爸是有用的人	normal/3
The principle of politeness complies with each other's emotional needs.	Dads are useful people.	
	好, 好听, 好吃	
	Good, nice, delicious	
Indirect praise such as "I like…"	我喜欢吃无花果	
	I like figs	
Separate B4 modifier	比我想象中的好	slight/2
D4 comparative judgement	It's better than I thought.	
Separate A1 appellation	虽然人长得丑，但是心很善良	
B3 hypothesis	Although the person looks ugly, the heart is very kind.	
	我的好姐姐	
	My dear sister	
	要是奶奶在就好了！	
	If only grandma was here!	
Separate D Auxiliary utterances.	活要活得痛快, 死要死得干净！	Very slight/1
	Live happily and die cleanly!	
Use questioning or asking for approval.	这不是两全其美吗？	
	Isn't this the best of both worlds?	
Form a concessionary transition relationship with the next clause.	舒服是舒服, 但我又不是毛毛	
	It's comfortable, but I'm not a baby.	

Based on the above table, the nonparametric test was used to study the different relationship between schema and compliment degree, and the results are shown in Table 4 and Fig. 2:

Table 4. Compliment Schema and Nonparametric Test of Sentiment Strength

Schema patterns (median)	Sentiment strength
A($n = 3$)	2.000
AC($n = 23$)	4.000
ACD($n = 4$)	3.500
BC($n = 3$)	4.000
BCD($n = 2$)	3.500
C($n = 42$)	4.000
CD($n = 15$)	3.000
D($n = 4$)	1.000
Kruskal-Wallis Test H-value	20.820
p	0.004**

* $p < 0.05$ ** $p < 0.01$

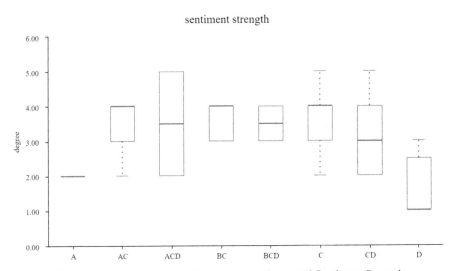

Fig. 2. Box-Line Diagram of Compliment Schema and Sentiment Strength

As evident from the table and diagram above, there is a significant difference between the schema patterns used by children and the associated sentiment strength. Different schema patterns exhibited a 0.01 level of significance for sentiment strength ($p = 0.004 < 0.01$). Generally, the sentiment strength of compliment schemas with pattern C tends to be in a higher range, whereas those with pattern D tend to be in a lower range. For example, the median sentiment strength for AC is greater than A, ACD is greater than A, and CD is greater than D. Additionally, the sentiment strength of schema patterns that include D is usually lower than those that do not, such as ACD is lower than AC, BCD is lower than BC, and CD is lower than C.

4 Discussion

4.1 Findings

The main findings of this article are:

(1) Children aged 0 to 4 often express their gratitude in a straightforward and explicit manner, while children aged 5 to 6 tend to use more advanced levels of abstract and implicit expressions of compliments. This observation aligns with previous conventional wisdom and research findings. As children grow older, they increasingly employ auxiliary language schemas such as analogy and contrast judgment to articulate compliments. This intellectual and psychological maturation, influenced by socialization, leads to evolving standards in expressing gratitude. The world of expression is no longer unitary but pluralistic, consistent with Rao's conclusions about children's evaluation and expression [4]. The forms of discourse used to express compliments become more diversified, with the age range of 5–6 years showing the greatest proficiency in compliment schema.

(2) There are notable distinctions in children's degrees of compliment for different schema patterns, particularly in patterns C and D. Schemas incorporating pattern C correlate with higher levels of compliments, often being the focal point. Conversely, schemas with pattern D are less complimented, especially when used alone. When combined with other schemas, the D-type schema can affect the overall level of compliment, resulting in a decrease compared to ACD. This is largely because the D-type schema, focusing on non-marked expressions like requests for consent and suggestions, lacks a marked core of compliments, thereby lowering the level of compliments compared to other schemas.

(3) The parameters governing children's compliment schema include crucial aspects like subject, content, motivation, and strategy. These parameters coexist and interact, influencing both the implementation and the level of compliment speech acts. The identity of the subject is particularly significant, as it is influenced by social, discourse, and emotional relations. The relationship between subjects profoundly impacts the motivation behind the expression of compliments and shapes the strategy used. Children are increasingly aware of using compliment expressions to navigate power dynamics within social relationships, recognizing that complimenting others can fulfill emotional needs and meet aspirations.

The subject, motive, and context are structural elements of compliment speech acts and are important parameters affecting the degree of compliment expression. For instance, when children aim to fulfill their own needs, they often use upgrading strategies, as demonstrated in the following example:

  ♀妈妈："拿过来，我看看。"

  冬冬马上高兴了："这有什么难的呢？"

  妈妈："真的很难，不好画。"

  冬冬："我知道妈妈很棒的，画一下吧，妈妈？"

  [*Mother: "Bring it over, let me see."*
  Dongdong immediately became happy: "What's so difficult about this?"
  Mother: "It's really difficult, not easy to draw."
  Dongdong: "I know mom is great, can you draw it for me, mom?"]

In this conversation, Dongdong's motivation for complimenting was to align with the positive emotions of the other party. In other words, her intention in expressing compliments was to persuade the person being appreciated to fulfill her wishes. The context here is to encourage her mother to paint, so she adopts a positive tone and an upgrading strategy to emphasize and express her compliments.

However, when there is a power dynamic between the complimenter and the complimentee, children's emotional expressions tend to conform to this power relationship, often using more neutral expressions of compliment. Example 2 illustrates this:

②早上醒来，冬冬说："妈妈好，爸爸坏。"

爸爸说："爸爸坏？爸爸不扶你上椅子了！"

冬冬赶快改口，说："爸爸好。"

[*Upon waking up in the morning, Dongdong says, "Mom is good, Dad is bad."*
Dad responds, "Dad is bad? Didn't dad help you up onto the chair?"
Dongdong quickly changes her words, saying, "Dad is good."]

In this context, the relationship between the complimenter and the complimentee is a familial one, with the parent holding a position of greater power. Children understand that they need to express their compliance through praise to satisfy their needs.

Notably, in Example 1 and Example 2, when Dongdong praises her mother and father, we observe that her compliment expressions are intended to satisfy the emotional needs of the other person to achieve her desired outcome. Therefore, she employs the BC pattern schema to emphasize her willingness. Under these circumstances, children typically use more articulated strategies to express their compliments.

4.2 Limitations

Firstly, regarding the data source: The original text was recorded in the form of a diary, not as directly transcribed dialogue. Due to the limitations of the text recording medium, without live or video recording, much real dialogue information such as actions, expressions, tones, pauses, laughter, and other non-verbal cues is difficult to capture in the text.

Secondly, although the corpus data encompasses over 800,000 words, it exhibits a limited variety of children's expressions of compliments. The sample size is constrained, and the distribution of text lacks balance. For instance, the corpus for 5 and 6-year-olds is significantly smaller than that for 4-year-olds in terms of text volume, thus it may not fully represent Dongdong's actual language expression. As a case study, this article centers on a research subject from a family with a highly intellectual background, which suggests that the results may be incidental.

4.3 Future Work

On the one hand, one potential approach this study may adopt is to expand the database of young children to effectively monitor the development of their ability to express compliments. Considering Dongdong's upbringing in an intellectually advanced family, her acquisition of compliment proficiency might be unique compared to children from typical households. This distinction can lead to broader insights, offering greater discernment and laying the groundwork for more comprehensive conclusions.

On the other hand, the findings of this study hold significant implications for sentiment analysis and intent classification. Despite recent notable advancements in pre-trained language models, such progress is less evident in emotional recognition tasks involving children's language data. For example, the ERNIE 3.0 model, a leading pre-trained language model in the field of Chinese Natural Language Processing [21], has demonstrated suboptimal accuracy. For instance, the sentence "活要活得痛快，死要 死得干净" [*Live happily and die cleanly*], while deemed negative in sentiment analysis, is actually an expression of compliment that embodies the attitude of living happily and dying cleanly. Previous studies have indicated that integrating linguistic knowledge into deep neural networks can improve sentiment analysis accuracy [22]. By identifying more non-marked expressions of compliments and their diverse variations under schema theory, we could significantly enhance the performance of language models and the accuracy of sentiment analysis.

5 Conclusion

This study examines the expression of compliments during the growth process of a 6-year-old child and analyzes their development and changes based on the schema theory. The study summarized eight common schema combinations derived from the overall schema and further subdivided the four main parts into 16 subcategories. This was done to identify high-frequency expressions in children's compliments and to describe their characteristics and developmental trajectory. The study found that children under the age of 4 typically use more explicit, specific, and marked compliment expressions. In contrast, at ages 5–6, they tend to use more abstract, unmarked, and advanced compliment schemas. Additionally, this article established a continuum of five levels of sentiment strength and identified a certain correlation between these levels and the schemas used. The findings of this research offer valuable insights for the study of children's compliment expression and provide enlightenment for sentiment analysis.

Language serves as a window into society and is not merely an isolated system. As children develop their language skills, they concurrently exhibit growth in both cognitive and psychosocial domains. Moreover, the manner in which children incorporate compliments into their language schema offers insights into their assimilation of adult concepts and knowledge systems. To gain a deeper understanding of children's language, it is crucial to pay close attention to their pragmatic competence, extracting internal schemas and mechanisms from the interactive conversations in which they engage.

Acknowledgement. This research is sponsored by the National Social Science Foundation of China "A study on the construction and operation of Chinese preschool children corpus" (19AYY010).

References

1. Bloom, L., Lahey, M.: Language development and language disorders. Wiley (1978)
2. Couper-Kuhlen, E., Selting, M.: Interactional Linguistics: Studying Language in Social Interaction. Cambridge University Press, Cambridge (2018)
3. Thompson, S.A., Fox, B.A., Couper-Kuhlen, E.: Grammar in Everyday Talk: Building Responsive Actions. Cambridge University Press, Cambridge (2015)
4. Rao, H.Q., Li, Y.M.: Evaluation Expressions and Knowledge Building in Children's Interaction. Appl. Linguist. 37–50 (2021)
5. Taguchi, N.: Advanced Second Language Pragmatic Competence. In: Malovrh, P.A., Benati, A.G. (eds.) The Handbook of Advanced Proficiency in Second Language Acquisition, pp. 505–526. Wiley, Ltd (2018)
6. Ninio, A., Snow, C.E., Pan, B.A., Rollins, P.R.: Classifying communicative acts in children's interactions. J. Commun. Disord. **27**, 157–187 (1994)
7. Bartlett, F.C.: Remembering: a study in experimental and social psychology. Cambridge University Press, Cambridge, England (1932)
8. Piaget, J.: The Child's Conception of the World. Routledge, New York (1929)
9. Carroll, D.W.: Psychology of language. Thomson Wadsworth, Toronto, CA (2007)
10. Anderson, R.C., Freebody, P.: Vocabulary Knowledge and Reading. International Reading Association, Newark, DE (1981)
11. Searle, J.R.: Expression and Meaning: Studies in the Theory of Speech Acts. Cambridge University Press, Cambridge (1979)
12. Holmes, J.: Paying compliments: a sex-preferential politeness strategy. J. Pragmat. **12**, 445–465 (1988)
13. Válková, S.: Speech acts or speech act sets: apologies and compliments. Linguistica Pragensia. **2**, 44–57 (2013)
14. Wu, X.B.: The Research on Praise Speech Act in Modern Chinese. Jilin University (2022)
15. Luo, L.L.: On Communication of Chinese Five-year-old Children. Jinan University (2012)
16. Burdelski, M., Morita, E.: Young Children's Initial Assessments in Japanese. In: Bateman, A., Church, A. (eds.) Children's Knowledge-in-Interaction: Studies in Conversation Analysis, pp. 231–255. Springer, Singapore (2017)
17. Aston, G.: Enriching the Learning Environment: Corpora in ELT. In: Wichmann, A. and Fligelstone, S. (eds.) Teaching and Language Corpora, pp. 51–64. Addison Wesley Longman Limited, England (1997)
18. Li, Y.M.: The early years of life: a Chinese girl's language diary 1st 1985.1.16–1987.1.15. The Commercial Press, Beijing (2009)
19. Li, Y.M.: The early years of life: a Chinese girl's language diary 2nd 1987.1.16–1989.1.15. The Commercial Press, Beijing (2009)
20. Li, Y.M.: The early years of life: a Chinese girl's language diary 3rd 1989.1.16–1991.7.29. The Commercial Press, Beijing (2009)

21. Liu, W., et al.: ERNIE 3.0 Tiny: Frustratingly Simple Method to Improve Task-Agnostic Distillation Generalization. arXiv preprint arXiv: 2301.03416 (2023)
22. Du, C., Liu, P.: Linguistic Knowledge Based on Attention Neural Network for Targeted Sentiment Classification. In: Hong, J.F., Zhang, Y., Liu, P. (eds.) Chinese Lexical Semantics. CLSW 2019. Lecture Notes in Computer Science (LNAI), vol 11831, pp. 486–495. Springer, Cham (2020)

Author Index

Printed in the United States
by Baker & Taylor Publisher Services